MAGILL'S
LITERARY ANNUAL

1985

MAGILL'S
LITERARY ANNUAL
1985

*Essay-Reviews of 200 Outstanding Books
Published in the United States during 1984*

With an Annotated Categories Index

Volume Two

Ki-Z

Edited by
FRANK N. MAGILL

SALEM PRESS
Englewood Cliffs

LIBRARY OF CONGRESS CATALOG CARD No. 77-99209
ISBN 0-89356-285-8

FIRST PRINTING

PRINTED IN THE UNITED STATES OF AMERICA

MAGILL'S
LITERARY ANNUAL

1985

THE KING'S WAY

Author: Françoise Chandernagor (1946-   )
Translated from the French by Barbara Bray
Publisher: Harcourt Brace Jovanovich (San Diego, California). 497 pp. $15.95
Type of work: Novel
Time: 1635-1719
Locale: France

Madame de Maintenon relates the remarkable circumstances which, combined with her wit and beauty, raised her from poverty to the heights of power as the second (and unacknowledged) wife of Louis XIV

Principal characters:
> FRANÇOISE D'AUBIGNÉ (MADAME DE MAINTENON), Louis XIV's second wife
> MADAME DE VILLETTE, the beloved Huguenot aunt of Françoise who reared her
> PAUL SCARRON, a poet, satirist, and wit who was Françoise's first husband
> NINON DE LENCLOS, a famous courtesan and wit
> MADAME DE MONTESPAN, the most enduring of Louis XIV's mistresses who brings Françoise to court as governess to the royal bastards
> LOUIS XIV, King of France

As a legal adviser for the French Council of State, Françoise Chandernagor is familiar with historical research and documents. As a result, her re-creation of the life of Madame de Maintenon, the second wife of Louis XIV, has an aura of authority. Chandernagor's task of assembling Madame de Maintenon's correspondence, which included almost eighty volumes; the memoirs of her secretary and niece, Madame de Caylus; and the records of such royal memorists as Madame de Sévigné and Saint Simon, is monumental. In her first novel, Chandernagor succeeds masterfully in re-creating seventeenth century France in its glory and squalor. She draws a vivid portrait of court and court politics and introduces her readers to the luminaries of their day through the eyes of Madame de Maintenon, who knew everyone of importance. Consequently, as history *The King's Way* (published in France in 1981 as *L'Allée du roi*) both informs and fascinates. As a novel, unfortunately, it fails to create a sufficiently vivid sense of its central figure and narrator, Françoise d'Aubigné, Madame de Maintenon, celebrated for her wit as well as her beauty. Chandernagor's creation lacks the brilliance which her original must have possessed in order to have become the most powerful woman in France. Perhaps the author's ambitious research overwhelmed her creative imagination; the narrative character never entirely captures the reader's sympathetic imagination, although there is no question that the story of Madame de Maintenon and her times is thoroughly fascinating.

From its beginning, Françoise d'Aubigné's life was improbable. She was born in 1635 in Noirt prison, where her father was an inmate. Though a member of the minor nobility, he was wildly profligate—a murderer, thief, traitor, and con artist who never troubled very much about his children. Françoise's mother thrust her daughter upon the charity of her aunt and uncle, the Villettes, frugal Huguenots, with whom the child remained until she was nine. Early in her life, Françoise was taught her precarious social position. She was a Catholic in a Huguenot family, a girl without dowry or prospects who must make the best of her situation. By the time she was twelve, Françoise was schooled in close observation, patience, poverty, deception, and humility. Out of this was born a fierce ambition. Given the choice of entering a convent or marrying, sixteen-year-old Françoise wed Paul Scarron, a crippled, middle-aged satirist and wit. Then her second education began, for Scarron not only encouraged her reading but also introduced her to politics and Parisian society. As Madame Scarron, Françoise cultivated the social skills and contacts which later brought her to court as the governess to the royal bastards and culminated in her marriage to Louis XIV, the Sun King.

Throughout *The King's Way*, politics are Machiavellian and inescapable, as parties align themselves for or against Cardinal Mazarin, the king's favorite mistress, and much later his possible successor. Everyone and everything falls under political influence, from gaining a license to manufacture gold to having a religious preference and marrying. Emerging from Chandernagor's novel are rationales for such momentous decisions as Louis XIV's revocation of the Edict of Nantes, which again outlawed Protestantism in France, and his justification for continuing the War of Spanish Succession.

Important as it is, the political scene does not dominate the foreground of this novel; it remains masked by the surface monotony of daily activities: card games, chitchat, desultory gossip. Nevertheless, there is a restless sense of networks, scheming, and backbiting to attain position—all conducted in the open. There are few secrets at court. Indeed, there are few secrets in society. When rumors of her growing influence begin, Madame de Maintenon issues disclaimers of political interest. She pleads reluctance—at times ineptitude—while all along she sways the king's judgment. A perceptive analyst and astute judge of politics, she quickly adopts a background role, giving the king credit for decisions. (Thus, she exercised power in the only way a woman could during that era.)

Instead of secular politics, the politics of religion is brought to the foreground, for its influence is pervasive. Politically powerful and corrupt, the Church exercises its authority on a broad scale under Cardinal Mazarin and then assumes a lesser role once Louis XIV comes to full authority as king. Unfortunately, religion is not directly related to morality, though some gestures are made. Too often the spiritual advisers of the powerful—including

Madame de Maintenon's—fear the wrath of their patrons more than they fear the wrath of God. Consequently, moral corruption spreads from the very highest echelons of religious and political power. Nor is religion directly related to political and social reform, except in a conviction that there is room for only one religion in France: Roman Catholicism. The retribution against stubborn Huguenots who refuse conversion leads to persecution and social upheaval. The Church's conservative attitudes toward women ("ignorant in the eyes of the world; perfect in the eyes of God") do not encourage education, let alone women's participation in society.

Still, the Church and religion come to play important roles in Madame de Maintenon's life. Knowing of her essentially moral character, the Church encourages the king to marry her, and Madame de Maintenon, discovering the spiritual emptiness of wealth and power, ardently seeks God. Her modesty, charity, and concern for the poor indicate the depth of her nature and stand out in bold relief against the prevailing social approval of extravagance and disdain for the lowborn.

The King's Way reveals to its readers a wealth of social customs. Many are surprising, such as the requirement that a widow not attend her husband's funeral; others remind the reader of some human improvements in the past three hundred years—specifically in the areas of child rearing and education. These two subjects arouse Madame de Maintenon's passion, as expressed in some of the book's finest passages. The entire era gave little thought to practices of child rearing. Indeed, most of its children (including the young Louis XIV) were sadly neglected and shabbily educated. Madame de Maintenon was particularly interested in the most humane and effective means of training children and used kindness, logic, praise, and love in her role as royal governess. Her early support of women's education through her founding of the girls' school at Saint-Cyr set a precedent for French culture.

Sadly, the main social focus of the time was dictated by the nobility's extravagances. Versailles, Marly, Fontainebleau, Trianon—these architectural wonders remain as monuments to Louis XIV's greatness. In *The King's Way*, however, architecture is one mask among many. Whatever the flaws of this novel, its focus on the interplay of masks during the seventeenth century is admirable. Chandernagor brings her reader to understand the prominent role of deception in its various guises, from the great buildings, designed for the eye but with no regard for human comfort, to the role of costume. Libertines appear in modest gowns; lavish balls fool creditors and enemies. The French love of gilding the ordinary reveals a refusal to look honestly at human conditions. Having adapted to these methods, Madame de Maintenon reports them without moralizing.

Indeed, for all the words devoted to her search for God, her religious exercises, her attempts to become pious, there is little in the tone of *The King's Way* to convince its readers that the narrator ever felt anything other than a cold detachment. Tone, motive, and the narrator's reliability all present certain problems. There is in this long, rich narrative a surprising lack of tonal variety. Part of this flaw results from the fact that the work is presented as a memoir written at the end of the writer's life. An eighty-four-year-old woman could hardly be expected to recall her love affairs or her great disappointments with the immediacy of the present. Consequently, this novel lacks the intensity of passion. Another reason for this deficiency might lie in the narrator's motivation. *The King's Way* is addressed to Madame de Maintenon's seven-year-old niece, Marie de La Tour, to be read when she is twenty. Because the novel is to a large extent written as a cautionary tale, there might be a need for emotional restraint in order to seem credible. Cautionary tales, however, by their very nature, include extremes, especially those written expressly for women (as many have been). After reading this memoir, one suspects that Marie would not take seriously her aunt's advice to enter a convent. Why should Marie abandon her life to God when her aunt readily admits that she found satisfaction neither in worldly success nor in God? Indeed, at the beginning of the memoir, she feels "abandoned" by God.

Doubtless this sense is contradictory, as are many of Madame de Maintenon's words and actions. Thus, one comes to the problem of the narrator's reliability. Although understanding the necessity of a certain degree of duplicity, what is one ultimately to believe? Was Françoise an innocent victim who, through luck and God's will, rose to power? Or was Françoise a brilliantly perceptive manipulator who, with luck, used her wits to achieve her ends? Both characters are presented simultaneously. In presenting her narrator thus, the author fails to create emotional contact between reader and character. In the end, Françoise appears to be merely a crotchety old woman. Too late, she rebukes the king for never caring for her comfort, for never asking if she were happy, and too late she appeals to her reader's sympathies. So careful has this narrator been to protect herself from blame that she generates a gap which cannot be bridged. Chandernagor's Madame de Maintenon is too modest to reveal her genius, too cautious to reveal her passion. Most of all, she is too opaque to reveal her wit. Though she expresses her admiration for scintillating conversation and verbal play, she expresses herself in a very ordinary way.

The King's Way had the potential to be a good—possibly great—biography. As fiction, however, its pretense is far too apparent. Chandernagor's work lacks the texture of a novel; in the end, one must conclude that she has the skills of a historian, not the imagination of a novelist.

Karen Carmean

self-portrait, for it traces Miłosz's intellectual and spiritual pilgrimage. Still, here as in *Native Realm*, Miłosz's emphasis is not on his experience for its own sake but rather on its exemplary character. If in *Native Realm* he bore witness as a child of the "corner of Europe" that shaped him, here he speaks as one who has dwelled in Ulro.

What—or where—is Ulro? The book's epigraph, taken from William Blake's *Jerusalem*—"They rage like wild beasts in the forests of affliction/ In the dreams of Ulro they repent of their human kindness"—gives the reader a clue, and Miłosz soon provides a fuller answer:

> The name Ulro is from Blake. It denotes that realm of spiritual pain such as is borne and must be borne by the crippled man. Blake himself was not one of its inhabitants, unlike the scientists, those proponents of Newtonian physics, the philosophers, and most other poets and artists of his day. And that goes for their descendants in the nineteenth and twentieth centuries, up to and including the present.

What has crippled human beings in the period demarked by Miłosz is the ever-growing "dichotomy between the world of scientific laws—cold, indifferent to human values—and man's inner world." This dichotomy produces what Erich Heller has termed "the disinherited mind," defined by Miłosz as "a mind torn between the certainty of man's insignificance in the immensity of a hostile universe, and an urge, born of wounded pride, to endow man with preeminence."

At this point, the reader may become impatient, asking: Is the Land of Ulro merely another name for "the Waste Land"? Is Miłosz's book, then, an all-too-familiar account of the modern malaise? The answer to the first question is a qualified yes. Not only T. S. Eliot but also countless other writers, both famous and obscure, have shared Miłosz's conviction "that since the eighteenth century something, call it by whatever name one will, has been gaining ground, gathering force." Miłosz's diagnosis of this malign condition must of necessity resemble other testimony concerning the same reality. To the second question, however, the answer is an unequivocal no: There is nothing overly familiar in Miłosz's wrestling with the demons of the twentieth century. Indeed, it is the freshness of his perspective—the freedom from all the intellectual fads and orthodoxies of the day, each with its own predictable language—that gives *The Land of Ulro* such authority.

When Saul Bellow wants to commend a book, he says that it is "essential" or "necessary": "We are always looking for the book it is *necessary* to read next." *The Land of Ulro*, although not written with English-speaking readers in mind, is necessary reading for them precisely because it brings news from the "peripheries," not from the American-Western European axis. One of the strangest features of the contemporary intellectual scene is the radical overvaluation of books written in "major" languages, particularly English and French, simply because of sociopolitical factors such as the international hegemony of the English language and the accompanying indifferences to and ignorance of "minor" literatures. Art has nothing to do with numbers, nor does the quality of a philosopher's thought depend on the language in which, by historical circumstance, he happens to write. Language barriers pose formidable obstacles, but Swedish or Catalan should prove no more or less resistant to translation than the Greek of Homer or the Italian of Dante.

Against such condescension, Miłosz has suggested, in his preface to *Emperor of the Earth: Modes of Eccentric Vision* (1977), that "in the new context of this last quarter of the twentieth century, the possibility of a shift from the center to the peripheries cannot be dismissed lightly." From his "marginal" vantage point, then, Lithuanian-born, educated in Poland, resident of France for almost a decade in the 1950's, writing in Polish in the mid-1970's on the California coast, Miłosz constructs an eccentric tradition of thinkers who have struggled in or sought exit from the Land of Ulro. They include, in addition to Blake, the Swedish mystic Emanuel Swedenborg; the national poet of Poland, Adam Mickiewicz; Fyodor Dostoevski; Miłosz's older cousin, Oscar Milosz, a poet and seer who, although reared in Polish-speaking Byelorussia, spent most of his adult life in Paris and wrote in French; the French philosopher and religious writer Simone Weil; and Miłosz's contemporary and compatriot, the novelist, playwright, and diarist Witold Gombrowicz.

Blake, whom Miłosz first read under unusual conditions ("I acquired my English in wartime Warsaw—self-taught, but enough to read the poets"), is of particular importance in this tradition because he *consciously* resisted the dichotomy between the scientific (or scientistic) worldview and the human scale of values, according to which each individual man or woman is more than a particle in a mechanistic universe. Blake saw that his contemporaries were willing to compartmentalize their experience, at terrible psychic cost, giving "science" its due in one realm while paying tribute to "the spirit" in another. Thus, as Miłosz writes, when Blake said that "Earth is flat, circumscribed by the horizon and the celestial dome," he was not propounding "scientific fact"; rather, "he treated both images"—that is, both the scientific description of the Earth as a sphere and the image of the Earth as flat— "as constructively antithetical, in the sense of issuing from the power of the intellect, whereas man's spiritual needs are better satisfied by the 'naïve' imagination."

To those who would say that Blake's visions are indeed poetic and can be appreciated as such but have nothing to do with the real world, Miłosz would reply that they are under the spell of a materialistic dogma which forces them to deny their deepest longings, their very humanity—a denial the extent of which can often be gauged by an explosion of repressed spirituality, as in the nineteenth century fad for spiritualism and psychic research in Great Britain and the contemporary vogue for the occult.

All the thinkers in Miłosz's ad hoc tradition experienced this conflict; all share an anthropocentric vision and a resistance to Nature (that is, the purely material world). Miłosz takes seriously the "bizarre tangle" of their thought, well aware that in doing so he is opening himself to condescension if not outright ridicule: "To speak of Swedenborg is to violate a Polish taboo that prohibits writers from taking a serious interest in religion. The penalty is already preordained in the form of the parroted cliché: 'He succumbed to mysticism.' " As he explicates the writings of Oscar Milosz, Mickiewicz, and the others, Miłosz does not hesitate to criticize their flights of messianic delusion, their wild excesses, yet his criticism is sympathetic, for he suggests that such is the price that one pays for resistance to Ulro:

> Here I must touch on a painful dilemma. That which is most crucial to the human imagination, indeed, that which Blake took to be its very essence, namely, a rebellious attitude toward Nature in the name of an august hope, is also fraught with peril because it verges constantly on folly, on a mania for self-destruction, on mental illness.

In tracing the growth of his own hard-won and unorthodox faith, then, Miłosz does not announce an imminent millennium. Rather, suggesting that "we are too apt to think of the 'final things' in solemn and august terms, as the province of gray-bearded sages and prophets," he notes as a corrective "how much of millenaristic yearning betrays a childish instinct." He would not renounce that instinct, for the boy who dreamed in Lithuania of "an idyllic earth" and the "old professor in Berkeley" who has written this book "are the same man." Thus, he concludes with a request: "Reader, be tolerant of me. And of yourself. And of the singular aspirations of our human race."

John Dugdale Wilson

Sources for Further Study

America. CLI, December 15, 1984, p. 409.
Book World. XIV, September 2, 1984, p. 14.
Booklist. LXXXI, September 1, 1984, p. 18.
Kirkus Reviews. LII, June 15, 1984, p. 571.
Library Journal. CIX, September 1, 1984, p. 1675.
Los Angeles Times. August 24, 1984, V, p. 22.
New Leader. LXVII, October 15, 1984, p. 13.
The New York Times Book Review. LXXXIX, September 2, 1984, p. 1.
The New Yorker. LX, September 17, 1984, p. 142.
Publishers Weekly. CCXXVI, July 6, 1984, p. 56.

LAST DAYS

Author: Joyce Carol Oates (1938-   )
Publisher: E. P. Dutton (New York). 241 pp. $15.95
Type of work: Short stories

A powerful collection of stories that center on the dislocations of modern consciousness

Last Days is a collection of short stories by Joyce Carol Oates, all of which have been previously published between 1981 and 1984. Characteristic products of her frenzied and prolific imagination, the stories are uneven in quality, though at least two of them—"Last Days" and "My Warszawa: 1980"—are first-rate.

The collection is divided into two sections: "Last Days" and "Our Wall." The first explores familiar terrain—the fictive world that Oates excels in representing—a melodramatic world which is disturbingly analogous to the so-called real one mirrored in the daily papers, the television news, the soap operas, the talk shows, and the popular magazines. This is a world of senseless violence, fanatic religiosity, neurotic anxiety, spiritual despair, truncated love, and pervasive guilt. Unsurprisingly, a number of Oates's characters undergo mental breakdowns, sometimes resorting to murder or suicide as a way of coping with their desperation. In each of the stories in the first section, at least one of the characters is on the way to, on the way back from, or currently incarcerated in a mental institution.

"The Witness" is written from the first-person point of view of an incipiently psychotic young girl who may or may not have witnessed a brutal murder. Since the reader is confined to her unreliable narration, fantasy and fact blur and merge. It would seem that insanity runs in the family, for the girl's father is a former mental patient who now devotes his time exclusively to smoking Camels, drinking whiskey, and waxing mystical about the ubiquity of God and His unconditional love. God's love may be unconditional and His presence ubiquitous, but redemption is no certainty. In this story, only suffering and despair enjoy that status.

If, as the female narrator in "The Man Whom Women Adored" maintains, artists do not explain but survive and suggest pathways, then the only redemptive pathway in this first section is offered by "Funland." (In "Night. Sleep. Death. The Stars.", a former mental patient who lost custody of her child born out of wedlock is abandoned by her academic husband and left with his three daughters; in "Last Days," the protagonist assassinates his rabbi in the midst of a religious service and then takes his own life; there are no pathways out of the abyss in these stories.)

In "Funland," a father and his young daughter embark on what proves to be an abortive pilgrimage to visit her mother, who resides in a mental institution. They end up instead in a dilapidated amusement park and experience a kind of communion, the father rediscovering the power to bless. Nevertheless, Mel's Funland offers minimalist redemption at best, providing but a momentary stay against confusion, a temporary respite from despair.

The stories in the first section are bleak and pessimistic. Although they are deftly constructed and packed full of realistic detail, they are in general somewhat predictable. An exception is the title story, "Last Days," which, though equally bleak and pessimistic, is an excellent piece of fiction.

The principal character of this story, Saul Morgenstern, agonizes over the fact that he was born too late, using the recurrent image of suffocation. As he puts it:

> The real thing is, God's curse on me is, *I was born too late. All the suffering is over—all the memoirs have been written. Every breath of Saul's has been breathed by someone else.*

That he is Jewish is symbolically appropriate, for it means that he grievously feels the pain and anguish of the slaughter bench of recent history and that he has inherited the guilt that accompanies survival. For Saul, the crushing weight of tradition—with its myriad works of genius, acts of heroism, and moments of suffering—produces an overriding sense of belatedness, an anxiety of influence: "The unflushed toilet in the hall. Waste, foul and sickening and *not his own*. His fear is of being unoriginal, accused of plagiarism, exposed, ridiculed, cast aside as ordinary."

A figure of the alienated artist, Saul gives utterance to the postmodernist dilemma, for the burdensome omnipresence of the past tends not only to undercut the chances of "making it new" but also to create that special postmodernist alienation called "literary autonomy," the last refuge of individual subjectivity from the historical forces that threaten to annihilate it. As Harold Bloom suggests in *The Anxiety of Influence* (1973), strong writers make literary history by misreading and misinterpreting one another so as to clear imaginative space for themselves. Saul is no person of capable imagination; he cannot expropriate the past for himself. He trades his creative freedom for the deadly determinism of murder and suicide, becoming in the process an integer of statistical reality, an item in a news report, an image on a television, and, ironically, an object about which others write. He chooses the fixity of death over the fluidity of freedom: "Better to die, Saul instructs Saul, than to crawl like a dog into someone else's sheets. . . . " He ultimately decides that he has been born too late, that all the words have been used, and that all the oxygen has been breathed; the past asphyxiates him.

The reference in the text to Jean-Paul Sartre's famous "Portrait of the Anti-Semite" is apt and telling; like the anti-Semite, Saul "is a man who is afraid . . . of himself, of his conscience, of his freedom, of his instincts, of his responsibilities, of solitude, of change, of society and the world." His decision to become a murderer and a suicide is an attempt to render himself into an object, a fixed essence, just as a person's decision to become an anti-Semite gives that person a sense of unchangeable identity and a world knowable in advance. Both acts are escapes from freedom and abdications of humanity.

Oates implies that the murderer or suicide is a species of the artist manqué in that such a person yearns to convert the contingency of life into the necessity of art by imposing order on the chaos of history. Saul envisages his success: *"He cannot fail, he has entered History. . . .* He belongs to history now. Every syllable will be taped and preserved." Saul, however, may be mistaken, for history today has an obscenely short memory and moves at an accelerated pace. Murder and suicide are invidiously commonplace. His event will no doubt be forgotten.

Saul is an image of the postmodernist artist who with his ideal of aesthetic privilege and his experience of social alienation and fragmentation forgets that all intellectual activity is a kind of praxis, a way of being in the world. Such an artist views his work as a self-enclosed universe of discourse and retreats from history to his sphere of alienated subjectivity, seeing his art as a courageous refusal of everyday life and forgetting, as Rabbi Reuben Engelman is always telling Saul, "that it is the *routine* of life, the 'happy dailiness' in which Faith and Practice are 'wed,' that constitutes the real challenge." No doubt aesthetic isolationism has its compensations, but the art it produces does not suggest pathways; such art loses itself in the verbal labyrinth of its own construction and deconstruction. The reader is lost in a funhouse of signs and symbols, and there is no exit, no outside the text. Art becomes a totalitarian system that walls in the reader. Such art, Oates suggests in the second half of her book, is a bourgeois privilege: The Western writer has the luxury of misinterpreting his predecessors to make room for himself because nothing is really at stake save his own narcissistic satisfaction. Misremembering is his way of carving out his own literary identity, but the situation alters drastically when the state itself is a monolithic instrument of organized forgetting. Because most of the stories in the second half of her book are either set in Eastern Europe or involve the cultural clash between East and West, Oates is able to penetrate the guilt of Western writers in confrontation with their Eastern counterparts, political activists who are victimized by repressive regimes and who risk their lives for the sake of freedom of expression.

In *The Book of Laughter and Forgetting* (1980), the Czechoslovakian author Milan Kundera, who saw his country invaded by the Soviet Union in 1968, notes that "the struggle of man against power is the struggle of memory against forgetting." He goes on to say that "in times when history still moved slowly, events were few and far between and easily committed to memory." Nowadays, however, "history moves at a brisk clip," and "we can no longer assume any single historical event, no matter how recent, to be common knowledge." When the state's control over its citizens burgeons to Orwellian proportions, the state becomes the destroyer of memory and of history. As Kundera puts it:

> The first step in liquidating a people . . . is to erase its memory. Destroy its books, its culture, its history. Then have somebody write new books, manufacture a new culture, invent a new history. Before long the nation will begin to forget what it is and what it was. The world around it will forget even faster.

Such systematic forgetting is no creative attempt to clear out imaginative space for the artist; it is an attempt to obliterate all imaginative space, an attempt to make the imagination itself an occupied territory. This is one version of the wall, a trope that Oates deploys several times.

In "Our Wall," for example, the forbidden zone is beyond the wall, a zone wherein reside traitors, criminals, subversives, degenerates, and enemies of the people, all those who challenge the forces of normalcy and power. In "Ich Bin Ein Berliner," a story written from the point of view of "the younger brother . . . of a 'notorious' deceased" who challenged the Berlin Wall and was shot down by the East Berlin guards, the narrator seeks to exhume the motives behind his older brother's death. Was his brother a suicide—a representative of "the triumph of the will over biology"—or was he an existential hero for whom ' "*freedom' (though also Death) exerted its ineluctable attraction over imprisonment (though also Life)?*" Ambiguously symbolizing both finitude and freedom, the wall is at once a limit and a challenge.

"Détente" depicts the cultural clash of East and West by chronicling the events of a Russian-American literary conference that takes place in the United States. Antonia Haas, a successful American woman of letters, is the central consciousness, and the story documents her deepening disillusionment with the rhetoric of détente, a disillusionment which parallels the failure of her attempt at romance with Vassily Zurov, her Russian counterpart. Détente, it would seem, works neither on the personal nor the political level.

At the beginning of the conference, high-sounding language predominates. As Antonia reflects, "There were the usual promising words, she liked them well enough to half-believe in them, *unity, cooperation, universal understanding, East and West, friendship, sympathy, common plight, peace, hope for the future.*" Soon enough, however, the words become "elegant static," "the ballet of détente," a verbal ritual devoid of significance.

Antonia finds herself echoing the Western platitude that

> in its essence art isn't political, it's above politics, it refers only to itself. . . . Politics necessitates choosing sides, it excludes too much of life, life's nuances and subtleties; art can't be subservient to any dogma, it insists upon its own freedom.

She expatiates on the virtues of the " 'post-modern' novel and its movement inward toward lyricism and poetry, away from the statistical world, the objectively historical or political world." Eventually, however, she comes to realize that art "is always political. It seeks to alter human consciousness, hence it is a political act." "Political" is not necessarily a synonym for "didactic," even though the Soviet dogma of Socialist Realism makes such an equation. Her revelation, however, has come too late to be of any consequence. "When the conference officially ended, Antonia's romance with Vassily Zurov ended as well." She is left with a gnawing sense of guilt, spawned by the recognition "of how little she and her fellow Americans risked in publishing whatever they chose."

"My Warszawa: 1980" and "Old Budapest" continue the theme of Western guilt. The former revolves around an international conference on American culture taking place in Warsaw. Judith Horne, "clearly the most important member of the American delegation," comes to realize that "Americans 'of literary distinction . . . can *never* get themselves into trouble . . . for anything they might say or write. Their defiance of their government might be published in foot-high headlines, or engraved in stone, and they will never be arrested or imprisoned or executed or even interrogated." She asks the ultimate question: "Does anything we say or write or publish *matter* . . . when we risk nothing?—we who are free." She is forced to ponder the meaning of time and history, for her journey into Poland—land of bigotry, racism, and pogroms—is a journey into the Jewish heritage she has heretofore repressed. This is a masterful story to which analytic summary does no justice.

Excluding "Lamb of Abyssalia," a quasi-allegorical dreamscape, the stories in the second section constitute a profound exploration into the nature and meaning of time, history, freedom, responsibility, and guilt; they expose the poverty of the postmodernist ideal of literary autonomy. According to Oates, art is not a self-enclosed universe of discourse—it is a mode of activity in the world and a natural enemy of any totalitarian scheme of living. The aesthetic retreat to the sphere of alienated subjectivity is an escape from freedom and a denial of history.

Last Days is a powerful collection of short fiction. Although the first section is weaker than the second (the exception being the title story), the book as a whole does what Oates suggests art ought to do: It seeks to alter human consciousness and to suggest redemptive pathways.

Greig E. Henderson

Sources for Further Study

Book World. XIV, September 30, 1984, p. 6.

Booklist. LXXX, June 1, 1984, p. 1361.
Chatelaine. LVII, November, 1984, p. 4.
Kirkus Reviews. LII, June 15, 1984, p. 544.
Library Journal. CIX, August, 1984, p. 1468.
Los Angeles Times Book Review. September 30, 1984, p. 10.
The New York Times Book Review. LXXXIX, August 5, 1984, p. 7.
Publishers Weekly. CCXXV, June 8, 1984, p. 55.
Vogue. CLXXIV, August, 1984, p. 212.

A LATE DIVORCE

Author: A. B. Yehoshua (1936-   )
Translated from the Hebrew by Hillel Halkin
Publisher: Doubleday & Company (Garden City, New York). 354 pp. $16.95
Type of work: Novel
Time: The 1980's
Locale: Israel

A novel that recounts the psychological strains on an already disturbed Israeli family—the aging husband and wife, the grown children and their spouses, and the grandchildren—when the husband and wife divorce

> *Principal characters:*
> YEHUDA KAMINKA, the father, visiting from America
> NAOMI KAMINKA, the mother, who resides in an insane asylum
> YA'EL "YA'ELI" KAMINKA KEDMI, their daughter, the oldest child
> YISRA'EL KEDMI, her husband, a lawyer
> GADDI KEDMI, the grandson, a fat second grader
> RAKEFET KEDMI, the infant granddaughter
> TSVI KAMINKA, the older son, a homosexual
> REFA'EL CALDERON, his lover, a banker
> ASA "ASI" KAMINKA, the younger son, a university history teacher
> DINA KAMINKA, his wife, an aspiring writer
> CONNIE, Yehuda's pregnant mistress in America

The Kaminkas are not a family one would care to get close to, for fear their plagues might rub off. Merely reading about them in *A Late Divorce* (published in Israel in 1982 as *Gerushim me'uharim*) is a painful experience at times, despite a leavening of humor ranging from farcical to dark, since even the humor concerns a series of human disasters ranging from minor to major. Overall, *A Late Divorce* is no laughing matter. On a primary level, the novel is a close psychological study of a disintegrating Israeli family. On a secondary level, the novel has profound social implications, suggesting the growing secularization of Israel, a state founded by Zionists and closely identified with Judaism. Both of these levels of meaning also have universal significance: *A Late Divorce* pictures the kind of troubled modern family to be found almost everywhere, and on a societal level it develops the familiar theme of desacralized life, life without a spiritual basis. In *A Late Divorce*, the Waste Land, or the Secular City, has come to Israel.

The novel is told through nine interior monologues, one for each day of the action. Each of the monologues reveals the character speaking and helps piece together the family's story with bits of timely and shocking information. Each of the monologues is loaded with symbols; in addition, the total structure of the novel is symbolic, like a tragicomic journey through the Israeli inferno, with each sin (or failure) depicted becoming progressively more serious and complex until the father is reached at the center.

For example, the novel begins with the simplest monologue, spoken by

Gaddi, the fat second grader, whose stage of development represents a kind of limbo but who already shows marked tendencies toward gluttony and violence: He eats any food within reach and beats up a smaller third grader who taunts him with the innocuous nickname of "Boxer." During the course of the first section, Gaddi is left to care for his infant sister, Rakefet, who messes her diaper and sets up a howl. Donning raincoat, leather gloves, and a kerchief over nose and mouth, Gaddi climbs into the crib and extricates Rakefet from her full diaper with a pair of sugar tongs. Unhappily, he then goes off and leaves the diaper in the crib; Rakefet rolls around in it, smears it all over, and possibly even samples its flavor. This scene seems to symbolize the nasty mess into which the Kaminka family has gotten itself generally.

Also placed in the outer circles of the hierarchy of the damned is the son-in-law, Kedmi, who narrates the second section. With his physical bulk and uncomplicated animal nature, Kedmi illustrates the sins of the flesh: He shows where Gaddi's gluttony came from. Kedmi enjoys wallowing in the bed with Ya'el, even when his father-in-law can hear their grunts and cries through a thin wall. (Significantly, Kedmi and Ya'el have produced the only grandchildren so far, with little hope for progeny from other quarters; sterility in the Waste Land is rampant.) In keeping with his simple, direct nature, Kedmi says whatever crosses his mind, which means that he is sometimes witty and sometimes vulgar and tactless. As a lawyer, he shows little promise of distinction, but he does display the right instincts: Sweating and puffing, he goes chasing all over town after a big check.

The cowlike Ya'el seems a proper spouse for Kedmi, though her monologue does not come until much later in the novel (hers is seventh). The position of her monologue is perhaps determined by the plot—speaking three years later, she ties up loose ends—but it could also indicate her status in the hierarchy. A more complex personality than Kedmi, Ya'el on the one hand is mother to the whole crowd, and her tendency to empathize with and accept but not judge people shows a spirit of love needed in the family, perhaps even qualifying her as a spokesperson for the author. On the other hand, her passivity prevents her from doing enough to try to redeem her parents and brothers. Despite her Earth Mother fertility, Ya'el communicates the same ineffectual quality as all the Kaminkas.

Much easier to figure are Asa and Dina Kaminka, exemplars of young pride. Both are vain about their physical appearance: Dina is struck by how her beauty collects and slays admirers, while Asa thinks that he cuts a dramatic figure as a lecturer. Their pride also leads to intellectual pretensions. Asa confidently plans to construct a theory of history whereby the pattern of the past can be used to predict the future, while Dina's shallowness induces her to believe that she can be a creative writer. Neglecting her job and household, Dina roams about all day collecting phrases in her little notebook or running them through her head; significantly, she does her best writing when she pulls off her clothes and jumps into bed (her best story is about a woman who steals a baby in the supermarket). When these two great ones actually get into bed together, however, nothing happens.

Tsvi, the older brother, also has sexual problems. He is not the good, clean, homosexual type but a degenerate one who preys on older men, seducing them and then extorting money from them. His latest victim is Refa'el Calderon, a middle-aged banking executive—otherwise the most sensible person in the book—who gives Tsvi not only "loans" but also privileged investment information, including the exchange rate of the Israeli pound for the forthcoming business day. Whether Tsvi gets up early enough to capitalize on this information is uncertain, since he seems to sleep for half the day. In fact, it is not clear whether Tsvi, despite all of his wheeling and dealing, is making any money at all—another case perhaps of Kaminka impotence. Still, his criminal mentality knows no bounds: He hopes to get his hands on the family-owned apartment so that he can sell it out from under his mother and thus raise capital for investment. He even cheats on his psychoanalyst by evading questions.

Apparently, the sickness in the Kaminka family began with the parents, whose monologues are saved for last. Naomi, the mother, is an inmate of an insane asylum, though scheduled to get out soon. At first, she seems the calmest one around (the result, perhaps, of years of shock treatment and other therapy), but she was originally institutionalized for trying to kill Yehuda, the father, with a kitchen knife one morning after he had fixed his own breakfast. Naomi says that she did it because he "disappointed" her— perhaps as good a reason as any to kill someone, especially a spouse. Then she says that she was merely trying to "cut him loose," for which a kitchen knife seems an effective instrument. Her chilling thoughts have their source in her witchlike double, who flies through the air, inhabits a fundamentalist rabbi, and is finally transformed into the desert goddess Godina.

If Naomi cuts people loose literally, Yehuda cuts them loose in his heart. In his early sixties, he returns to Israel from America, where he has made a fresh start in Minneapolis with another woman. He arrives in Israel already dressed for the new life, American style, in youngish clothes, long locks, and eau de cologne, and with a new baby on the way. His children hardly know him, and he hardly knows them or wants to, though he is willing to tolerate a little inconvenience to conduct his business. (He does, however, take a swift liking to his new daughter-in-law, Dina, and to his grandchildren.) Naomi considers Yehuda "a handsome but weak, degenerate intellectual," though she probably exaggerates his good looks. True to the Kaminka spirit, Yehuda snatches defeat out of the jaws of victory: His mission accomplished, he dies with a pitchfork through his heart in one of the most bizarre endings on record.

Besides exemplifying the Kaminka spirit, Yehuda represents the contemporary spirit, the secular spirit, and finally the American spirit: His heart was freeze-dried in cold Minneapolis. The symbols connecting these themes in *A Late Divorce* are stacked even higher than the Minneapolis snow. Such dense symbology defies detailed explication, but the general drift seems to be that Israel has become infected by the spirit of the age. God was always divorcing David and the old Hebrews; now it is the other way around— Yehuda and the Israelis are divorcing God. With a well-placed donation to a school, Yehuda bribes four rabbis to conduct the divorce proceedings on the day of the Seder, the ceremonial feast celebrated on Passover eve. A similar corruption has taken root in the State of Israel: The streets are crowded and filthy, pimps and prostitutes cruise the bus stations, and a degenerate homosexual has his sticky hands on Israel's inflationary pound. The corruption, its source, and its consequences are humorously symbolized in the Seder ceremony when a pretty but ignorant American woman mistakenly drinks from the bowl of plagues as though she is taking Communion.

There are, however, other ways to read *A Late Divorce*, since Yehoshua leaves a certain amount of ambiguity. One can hardly blame Yehuda for wanting to divorce Naomi and to start a new life, and, in his fumbling way, he tries to stay within the legalistic bounds of Judaism. On a social level, too, not all the signs are bad: Israel is "out of control," not yet a "homeland," but it is also "full of strange mutations different people odd permutations new sources of unexpected energy." A modest revival of religion is even taking place, and Yehuda himself attends an informal gathering of awkward, self-conscious new worshipers. Unfortunately, the return to religion is dredging up some fundamentalist, primitive elements which might better be left to barbaric prehistory. Just as the fundamentalist rabbi tries to obstruct the divorce proceedings, so one of Naomi's minions, a pitchfork-wielding giant straight out of folklore, cuts down Yehuda on the first day of Passover. He is not passed over. The message seems to be that people who do not answer to God must answer to Godina.

The ultimate shaggy-dog story, with a straying family dog and a contrived ending, *A Late Divorce* is an ambitious novel but also somewhat pretentious, derivative, and clumsy. Yehoshua ostentatiously lays on the symbolism and varieties of interior monologue to show off what he can do, but most of his tricks come from William Faulkner, who did them better. Yehoshua even makes the mistake of giving an interior monologue to a character who dies. Formerly a short-story writer, Yehoshua is currently experiencing the difficulties of writing in a language without much tradition in the novel. These difficulties are balanced in Yehoshua's work by his ability to draw on the strong mythological, poetic, and ethical traditions of Hebrew.

Harold Branam

Sources for Further Study

America. CL, May 26, 1984, p. 405.
Christian Science Monitor. LXXVI, February 1, 1984, p. 22.
Library Journal. CIX, March 15, 1984, p. 598.
The New Republic. CXC, March 12, 1984, p. 38.
The New York Review of Books. XXXI, June 14, 1984, p. 11.
The New York Times Book Review. LXXXIX, February 19, 1984, p. 1.
The New Yorker. LX, March 19, 1984, p. 147.
Publishers Weekly. CCXXIV, December 23, 1983, p. 50.
The Wall Street Journal. CCIII, February 1, 1984, p. 22.
West Coast Review of Books. X, May, 1984, p. 27.

LEAVING THE LAND

Author: Douglas Unger (1952-   )
Publisher: Harper & Row, Publishers (New York). 277 pp. $13.95
Type of work: Novel
Time: The years immediately following World War II; the 1980's
Locale: The farm lands of South Dakota

The destruction of a farming community through the incursion of big business is reflected in the struggles of one family to maintain its heritage

Principal characters:
>MARGE HOGAN, the protagonist, who fights to hold her land against the encroachment of the Nowell-Safebuy conglomerate
>JIM VOGEL, a lawyer for Nowell-Safebuy and the man Marge marries
>KURT VOGEL, their son, from whose point of view part of the story is told
>BEN HOGAN, Marge's father, a Dakota farmer
>VERA HOGAN, Marge's mother
>DAN GOOCH, a part-Sioux former rodeo star who for a time becomes Marge's lover

Inspired in part by the recession of the late 1970's and early 1980's, the United States is renewing its romance with the land. It gives shape to America's national myth; it serves as emblem of its past achievements. In his poem "Hamatreya," Ralph Waldo Emerson observed that man can never truly own the land, that it inevitably outlasts its momentary possessors and passes from one hand to the next. Still, there is pride in ownership of land, and more: trust and identity and responsibility. Thus, when Ike McCaslin voluntarily repudiates his ownership of land in *Go Down, Moses* (1942), William Faulkner presents the act as an abdication of duty. Even more tragic is to have the land taken away, to be stripped of the past, to lose the generational investment of blood. The archetypal novel (and film) of such loss is *The Grapes of Wrath* (1939); it is a theme recently rediscovered by Hollywood in such 1984 films as *Country*, *The River*, and *Places in the Heart*. It is further reflected in the writings of such regional writers as Bobbie Ann Mason and Lee Smith, and it is the central theme of Douglas Unger's *Leaving the Land*, a novel which, as the title's twofold thrust suggests, tells of a rural community's gradual loss of economic and social identity, and of one family's attempt to maintain its property as inheritance for another generation.

Unger's novel is divided into two sections. Part 1 is told in the third person and concentrates on Marge Hogan and her family in the years immediately following World War II, a time of violent and disturbing change. Marge's father, Ben, raises turkeys for the Nowell-Safebuy turkey processing plant, as do most of the farmers in this region of South Dakota. Like the other farmers, Ben began to raise turkeys in response to pressure from the

government, which argued that the diversified farming practices these
ranchers had long followed no longer met the war needs. Because Ben's two
sons are killed in battle, he finds it impossible to return to his former crops
when the war ends; such farming demands full family participation. He, his
daughter, Marge, and his wife, Vera, are able to manage a turkey farm,
although it is a backbreaking and uncommonly demeaning occupation, for
turkeys are incredibly stupid and troublesome creatures, as Unger makes
clear. Thus, even before Marge's story begins, the pattern is set for the
series of incursions by which the government and big business, working
hand-in-hand, bring radical change to a traditional way of life.

The Unger focuses his attention both on Marge's personal story and the larger
story of the community of Nowell, which is transformed into a company
town by the Nowell-Safebuy plant. The town and the neighboring farmers at
first prosper in their cooperation with the company, although their financial
gain comes at the expense of self-respect. When Ben, for example, tries to
break with the company and sell his turkeys at his own price, his truck is
hijacked and set afire by hired thugs, and Ben resigns himself to doing company business. Marge, meanwhile, dreams of escape from the farm: from
turkeys and awkward, crude suitors and limited opportunities. When former
soldier Jim Vogel, a Safebuy company lawyer, comes into town, Marge is
ready for whatever he has to offer. They embark on a scandalous affair, and
the first section of the book ends with their marriage and Marge's first in-
timations that their future may not match her romantic expectations.

The second section of the novel is narrated by Marge and Jim's grown
son, Kurt, and is set in the 1980's, years after the marriage has failed.
Nowell is dying as a community, having been used and discarded by the
Safebuy company. Jim Vogel played an important role in the takeover, writing unfair contracts and representing the company in its questionable legal
maneuvers. His guilt and Marge's outrage have combined to destroy their
relationship. When Kurt returns at Christmas after a stint in the navy and a
time of wandering, his mother is still living in the pretentious home her husband built for her in celebration of their marriage, a house that she cannot
now sell. In the intervening years, she has watched her marriage self-
destruct, taken jobs as an Elks Club hostess and a waitress at the Cove Cafe
(one of the few remaining businesses in town), gone through a tumultuous
affair with Dan Gooch, a wild, part-Indian rancher, cared for and buried
her parents, and tried to raise her son in a dying land. Despite her dreams,
she never left Nowell, and now she has nowhere to go.

For all the hardships and disappointments she has suffered, Marge is not
seen by her son as a defeated character. Indeed, he tends to romanticize her.
On his return, he realizes to his discomfort that she has plans in which he
will figure. The plans center on the land—in this case, the family farm which
Marge has held on to and now intends to pass on to Kurt. She tells him:

"You may be right there's only one chance in this world, and thank God for that. Well, now I've done all I had to do with mine. I'm free of it. I've left you with an opportunity and you can do anything you want with it now. But for me there's something after. I know it. I know it and I can feel it. . . . Human souls never die. They just trade places."

The book ends with Kurt's contemplation of his inheritance and of the past, which he thinks of as "an all-but-unobtainable secret once a wisdom strong enough to move whole tribes across mountains, whole nations across oceans, my own grandfather across half a continent in a Model T Ford. . . ." He concludes, *"There must be other secrets now and I don't know them."*

Leaving the Land is an impressive first novel. It is very traditional in both subject and style and, unlike many first works, rarely sacrifices story to rhetorical flourish (although Unger can write powerful descriptive scenes). A few critics have attempted to link Unger with such Naturalist writers as Theodore Dreiser and Frank Norris, but although his characters are often subject to economic and social forces beyond their control, his is basically a romantic view. Marge is a survivor. Not only does she stay in Nowell, but also she holds onto the farm and has at least the hope that Kurt will discover the same sense of responsibility within himself. She is a healer as well, who looks after the other remaining members of the community. Unger may draw a picture of despair—the ramshackled houses, the acrid wind, the blistered and abandoned land—but he clearly finds strength in the world he describes.

The novel is distinguished by individual scenes of great power, ones in which Unger's control and command are extremely effective. Among these are the housewarming episode, when Marge and Jim show off their expensive and somewhat ostentatious new home to their envious and disapproving neighbors; the stripping of the Hogan family farm by these neighbors immediately after Ben Hogan's funeral; the final dissolving of the marriage, when Jim Vogel attempts suicide before his son; Kurt's summer living alone on the abandoned farm, working as a sheepherder for Dan Gooch.

Other episodes, however, point up a weakness of the novel, which is that Unger finally tries to do too much, to cover too large a subject. Attempting to describe both the death of a community and the destruction of a family, Unger must jump back and forth between the two stories. At times, the two lines merge naturally, as in the aforementioned description of Ben Hogan's funeral. Here, the personal grief and outrage Marge feels is balanced by her acceptance of social custom. As she tells an angry and horrified Kurt,

"If your grandpa were here today, he'd probably join them. . . . He was always one for looting funerals. He was the kind who made a party out of the occasion. . . . When the neighbors see a place that's going to be sold after a funeral, or one that's bound to sit idle, they come for things. That's the way they do it. And it's better this way. It's better than letting all this stuff sit around and rot. It's better the neighbors, your Grandpa's friends, end up with something."

More often, however, the episodes of community life seem extraneous. The description of Buster Hill's death and the story of Beatrice Ott's knitting machine, for example, work as individual scenes, but they lie outside the basic movement of the novel. There is the sense of a writer's bringing in his best bits whether they fit or not.

There is, moreover, a problem with the overall structure of the novel. The first section, told by the omniscient narrator and concentrated on the young Marge, is, in general, stronger than that section told by Kurt. In fact, there seems little reason for the shift. Kurt sometimes takes on the omniscient role as he recounts past experiences he has heard about rather than witnessed himself. Kurt is not as strong or convincing a character as Marge, and the older Marge, seen through her son's eyes, is not as effective or compelling or real as she appears in the first part of the book. Indeed, too many characters come and go throughout the novel, and one might wish for greater continuity and cohesion.

Still, if the individual scenes are stronger than the whole of the novel, and if the specific characters are sometimes lost in the scope of the telling, there is no denying the emotional investment Unger has placed in his work. According to a note in *The New York Times Book Review* (February 5, 1984), Unger and his wife have been trying to keep possession of a farm in Washington State which has belonged to her family since 1886 but which has been threatened with government takeover. Unger has also worked on a sheep ranch and observed at firsthand the hardships of such a life. A graduate of the University of Iowa's Writers' Workshop, he has been teaching in the writing program at Syracuse University. He is a writer of both promise and substantial accomplishment.

Edwin T. Arnold

Sources for Further Study

The Atlantic. CCLIII, March, 1984, p. 133.
Christian Science Monitor. LXXVI, June 20, 1984, p. 21.
Kirkus Reviews. LI, November 1, 1984, p. 1144.
Library Journal. CVIII, December 1, 1983, p. 2263.
Los Angeles Times. February 15, 1984, V, p. 6.
The New York Review of Books. XXXI, May 31, 1984, p. 35.
The New York Times Book Review. LXXXIX, February 5, 1984, p. 7.
The New Yorker. LX, April 2, 1984, p. 133.
Publishers Weekly. CCXXIV, December 9, 1983, p. 42.
Time. CXXIII, February 20, 1984, p. 78.

THE LEDGE BETWEEN THE STREAMS

Author: Ved Mehta (1934-   )
Publisher: W. W. Norton and Company (New York). Illustrated. 525 pp. $17.50
Type of work: Autobiography
Time: 1942-1949
Locale: Northwestern India

Ved Mehta, blind since age four, writes about his difficult boyhood quest for an education and the experiences of his well-to-do Hindu family through various moves and the traumatic partition of India and Pakistan

Principal personages:
  VED PARKASH "VEDI" MEHTA, the author
  AMOLAK RAM "DADDYJI" MEHTA, his father, a public-health official
  SHANTI DEVI "MAMAJI" MEHTA, his mother
  PROMILA "POM" MEHTA, his oldest sister
  NIRMILA "NIMI" MEHTA, his next oldest sister
  URMILA "UMI" MEHTA, his third oldest sister
  OM PARKASH MEHTA, his older brother
  USHA MEHTA, his younger sister
  ASHOK KUMAR MEHTA, his younger brother

The Ledge Between the Streams is the fourth volume in Ved Mehta's large, continuing family history and autobiography, the saga of a middle-class Indian family and its blind son who comes to the United States. Previous volumes include *Daddyji* (1972), *Mamaji* (1979), and *Vedi* (1982). The first two of these briefly explore the nineteenth century roots of the Mehta and Mehra families, then relate the biographies of Mehta's father (Amolak Ram Mehta) and mother (Shanti Devi Mehra Mehta) up to the time of Mehta's blindness (from cerebrospinal meningitis around his fourth birthday) and departure to the Dadar School for the Blind in Bombay. *Vedi* treats Mehta's intermittent stay, from the age of five to the age of nine, at Dadar, a Dickensesque school for blind orphans and street urchins located in the Bombay slums. *The Ledge Between the Streams* covers the period from about the age of nine, when Mehta returns home permanently from Dadar School, until the age of fifteen, when he leaves India to attend the Arkansas School for the Blind, the only school in Great Britain or the United States that will have him.

Like *Vedi*, *The Ledge Between the Streams* enlarges on material already covered in a youthful autobiography, *Face to Face* (1957), the first of Mehta's many books. Repetition or overlapping here of the early work is, however, of little consequence, except as an important measure of Mehta's growth. In a foreword to *The Ledge Between the Streams*, Mehta calls *Face to Face* only "a sort of outline" for his larger autobiography, which he hopes will continue "for many years." He dictated the sketchy *Face to Face* during his early twenties, when he was a college student; reading it is like going back and reading one's own college compositions. Since writing *Face to Face*, Mehta has not merely lived longer but has also developed, matured, and—so the preface to *Vedi* states—learned "that memory expands by some kind of associative process." As life lengthens and understanding grows, the past expands exponentially, becomes richer, fuller of memories and meaning. (Perhaps some such explanation will also pacify skeptics who marvel at autobiographers' powers of recall and consider autobiography the premier revisionist art.)

Mehta's style has developed with his memory and understanding, but his mastery of the English language merits attention for additional reasons. Like Joseph Conrad and Vladimir Nabokov, Mehta is a consummate stylist whose original language was not English; he first spoke Punjabi, then Marathi. He began learning English along with Braille at Dadar School (no Braille texts were available in Indian languages); after one year, he had accomplished the remarkable feat of learning more than two hundred English words. Later, his progress improved, as he eagerly read every Braille book or magazine he could find (*Reader's Digest* was a staple), but his typed letter of application to the Arkansas School for the Blind was filled with funny misspellings, quaint constructions, and other mistakes. *Face to Face* is passable, but, in the preface to *Vedi*, Mehta admits that he wrote *Face to Face* before he had "quite found" his "voice as a writer" or "acquired even the rougher implements of the craft." Mehta's style soon developed beyond the passable: Since 1959, when he was twenty-five, Mehta has been a regular contributor to *The New Yorker*, a magazine that prides itself on good writing. Indeed, all of Mehta's volumes of family history and autobiography first appeared in installments in *The New Yorker*.

Mehta's style, as demonstrated in *The Ledge Between the Streams*, is a variety of *The New Yorker* style with a bit of Ernest Hemingway thrown in. It is easy, understated, and factual—the basis of good reporting. It is a pure style, free of localisms, slang, jargon, mannerisms, and posturing: It sets a standard for English in the global village. As the reader might expect, visual elements, so predominant in most writing, are downgraded, while the other senses get ample play. Mehta's world is delineated by sound and touch (which sometimes escalates to bumps and hard knocks), and he also runs across his share of pungent Indian breaths at fairs and markets. At Saint Dunstan's, a school for blinded soldiers where the young Mehta is a student, he is shocked to shake hands with a hooked prosthesis, and he is repelled by sweaty soldiers putting their arms around him and breathing on him.

Mehta generally stays away from interpretation, except as implied by his choice of details and vocabulary. In any case, his tone is well controlled and understated. For example, when his father collides with office politics right after the family has settled in Lahore, Daddyji walks into the house and says, "Dr. Harnath Singh has done his dirty work. I have been transferred again. I have been posted to Rawalpindi." Mehta's sense of humor is sometimes reminiscent of James Thurber (Thurber also inhabited the pages of *The New Yorker* and himself was going blind): With a note of gentle sadness, it thrives on ironic situations and eccentric characters, including a whole gallery of teachers and servants, such as the young maidservant Raj Kumari, who maintains that she is actually a princess only temporarily working for the Mehtas until the right prince comes along. The humor rises to a high point in the servants' description of sister Pom's traditional wedding, which calls for the bridegroom's entourage of fifty male relatives and friends: "Only healthy men came, because the bride had to be protected and guarded—the world was full of bride thieves.... Police? They were good in their way, but they couldn't take the place of blood relatives."

Sometimes the humor becomes stronger, fiercer, ranging into caricature or black humor, especially when Mehta describes the folly of Hindu-Muslim antagonism. One of Mehta's more colorful teachers, the blind Muslim Mr. Baqir, issues a steady stream of insults against Hindus, which he reinforces on the Hindu boys with blows from his cane. Mr. Baqir's insults forebode the confrontation's rhetorical phase, which combines intensity with banality. The nightly chants of the Muslim mobs ("Death to Hindustan!" "Death to the infidels!") are matched by the exhortations of a Hindu extremist group: "Rise, Hindus, rise! Guard your supply of milk and yogurt. Guard your supply of dung and fuel. Guard your mother cow, whose look is love." Sohan, a member of the Hindu extremist group, slips his young friend Mehta a knife, an enormous switchblade with a clublike wooden handle and foot-long, curved blade guaranteed to twist lethally in the belly of any Muslim. Soon all the Hindus are carrying weapons; even the women pack pistols, knives, and vials of poison (for themselves, in case they fall into the hands of Muslim men).

Eventually, even the black humor dissipates, as the hostile buildup leads inevitably to the horror of atrocities during the Partition, an event on a scale with the Holocaust. Before Lahore is assigned to Pakistan, most of the seven Mehta children are sent to relatives in the new India, but the parents, with the youngest child, Ashok, have to wait until the last minute to flee. At the border they are stopped by Muslim guards brandishing weapons. The road and roadside are littered with writhing, mutilated bodies and with severed heads and limbs. The canal at the border runs red. Somehow the Mehtas are allowed to pass through safely.

Although the Partition dominates the last half of *The Ledge Between the Streams*, history here is conveyed novelistically—that is, the focus remains on the experiences of young Mehta and his family. Before the Partition, the Mehtas are shown going about their daily life, and a rather good life it is, supported by Daddyji's position as a high-ranking public-health official and by a staff of servants. There is an emphasis on education in the household, and the family members carry on discussions about such topics as the British, the status of women, and the Hindu-Muslim rift. Though tightly knit as a family, they have diverse personalities and opinions. The children are pulled in different directions by the Westernized Daddyji and by Mamaji, a traditional Hindu, though Mamaji is probably correct in thinking that Daddyji's influence is stronger.

During one of the family's many travels, a holiday outing to the Vale of Kashmir, they stop overnight at a mountain bungalow. In the gorge below run two streams, one clear, one muddy: One is the turbulent, icy Jhelum River flowing out of the Himalayas, the other a sluggish, tepid local river. Separating the two streams is a narrow ledge, and the family climbs down onto the ledge to investigate. They are delighted to squat on the ledge and feel the tepid water with one hand and the icy water with the other, but in the process they narrowly escape being swept away by a wall of water rushing down the Jhelum from a cloudburst upstream. In *The Ledge Between the Streams*, this incident reverberates with numerous symbolic possibilities: The two rivers are suggestive of the streams of influence (Mamaji, Daddyji; East, West; traditional, liberal) which converge on the Mehta children, who can dip their fingers into either of the streams, but only at some risk to their identity.

Facing the most danger is young Ved, who must reconcile not only the other influences but also bridge the gulf between the blind and the sighted. Much of his early life is devoted to proving that the blind can do anything the sighted can do. In hair-raising episodes, he clambers about the rooftops with other children flying kites, rides his bicycle and roller skates down the road, shins up and down the moving cables inside an elevator shaft, and hangs by his fingers over Himalayan precipices (apparently, not seeing is not fearing). His greatest challenge, however, is getting an education. In India, the blind are (or were at the time of the book) considered fit only for caning chairs, singing, or begging, so young Ved must look elsewhere for education beyond the rudimentary level. At the end, he is really going out on the ledge—leaving for the United States. Pandit Nehru salutes him as the first blind Indian boy to study in the United States; Ved's extended family gathers to see him off at the airport; young Ved eagerly anticipates reaching the land of opportunity.

Mehta has continued his narrative at the Arkansas School for the Blind (in "Sound-Shadows of the New World," *The New Yorker*, February 11 and 18, 1985), and presumably future volumes will continue to trace young Ved's stay in the West. Possibly Mehta at the same time will keep readers posted on family members back in India. In any event, Mehta's combination family history-autobiography has already grown into a significant work about Indian society and about blindness. It is also a valuable existential document:

Ved Mehta has gone to a hard school, and what he has learned should be of interest to everyone.

Harold Branam

Sources for Further Study

Booklist. LXXX, March 15, 1984, p. 1016.
The Economist. CCXCII, July 28, 1984, p. 77.
Kirkus Reviews. LII, March 1, 1984, p. 246.
Library Journal. CIX, March 15, 1984, p. 580.
Los Angeles Times. April 16, 1984, V, p. 6.
New Statesman. CVIII, August 10, 1984, p. 25.
The New York Times Book Review. LXXXIX, May 6, 1984, p. 14.
The Observer. July 8, 1984, p. 21.
Publishers Weekly. CCXXV, March 2, 1984, p. 78.
Smithsonian. XV, August, 1984, p. 128.

LETTERS FROM THE FLOATING WORLD
Selected and New Poems

Author: Siv Cedering (1939-   )
Publisher: University of Pittsburgh Press (Pittsburgh, Pennsylvania). 183 pp. $14.95;
   paperback $6.95
Type of work: Poetry

At times, Cedering's poems project a sexually defined universe, as many of D. H. Lawrence's works do

Siv Cedering is a prolific writer of diverse aims. She has published two novels in her native Swedish, eight collections of poetry in English, and one children's book in each language. She has also translated two volumes of contemporary Swedish poetry into English and a volume of Native American poetry into Swedish. Accomplished in many fields, Cedering's work has been acknowledged by numerous awards and fellowships. Unfortunately, her work is still unknown to the general public, and many of her peers have yet to discover Cedering's rich and varied achievement.

The appearance of this generous volume in a prestigious poetry series could make a difference: There is a chance now for a wider readership to discover Cedering's striking sensibility. Her work probes deeply into mythic strains of human experience, though experience itself is most often rendered in vibrant physicality. She writes of the human body, of the senses, and of sexuality with a cleansing frankness. Attentive to craft, Cedering fashions poems of precision and grace. Her imagination darts in unexpected, tantalizing directions. It is both unsettling and satisfying to come upon this imagination at work. *Letters from the Floating World* should bring Cedering the larger audience and the greater recognition that she deserves.

The "selected" sections of this book provide two poems (one a six-part sequence) from *Letters from the Island* (1973), eleven from *Cup of Cold Water* (1973), twenty from *Mother Is* (1975), and eleven from *The Juggler* (1977). The remaining "new" poems constitute half of this collection and clearly were meant to appear as a separate publication. Entitled *Ukiyo-E: From the Floating World*, this ninety-page gathering is in itself a fascinating, significant achievement. The decision to incorporate a whole book concept into the "selected and new" format is probably to be explained by the strange exigencies of poetry publication in the United States. Rather than being subordinated in this way, *Ukiyo-E* deserves its own separate publication. Nevertheless, why complain? The University of Pittsburgh Press has given readers two books for the price of one.

Cedering's special talent is to press mysterious evocations out of everyday diction and ordinary syntax. Her imagination makes juxtapositions that resonate. For example, in the middle of a short poem called "Figure Eights," the following passage occurs: "The moon is trapped/ in the ice. My body flows// across it." In this poem about human balance and grace, the interpenetration of various planes of action, experience, thought, and feeling is suddenly caught in this vision of the body flowing across the reflected moon. For a moment, cutting perfect figure eights becomes a kind of conjuring which lifts the speaker-skater to another level of apprehension. The speaker is, in a sense, flying beyond the moon:

> I lean into the cutting edge: two circles
> interlock, number eight drawn
>
> by a child, a mathematician's
> infinity.

Conjuring, magic, transformation—these are concerns that link Cedering's poems together. A sense of the marvelous is never long absent, and at the center of marvel is the human body, itself a transforming instrument as the senses receive and interpret the world. At times, Cedering's poems project a sexually defined universe, as many of D. H. Lawrence's works do. The human body becomes a reciprocating agent in an erogenous environment. Many of these poems, which often pulse with the rhythms of charms or riddles, suggest that all mystery and all truth have a sexual dimension. While this is not a unique theme, Cedering's treatment is especially effective. She hones a purity of line and image that depersonalizes and universalizes without becoming overly abstract. Cedering's work is not for prudes, but neither is it aggressively shocking. She creates a world that is inviting in spite of its risks; a healthy disorientation is offered from which, with the help of this caring poet, the reader can recover. Frequently, the lifeline of wit is provided as a means of escape from dangerous whirlpools of feeling and sensation. Unlike many poets of mythic, sensual, subterranean impulse, Cedering has a sense of humor. Laughter, too, is transforming.

Cedering's wit is but one manifestation of a lively intelligence. For a poet of feeling and of the body's knowledge, she is unusually careful about craft. Her poems, upon analysis, reveal reasoned construction, functional line and stanza breaks, and many other aspects of prosodic concern. These are intelligent shapes. Cedering knows about readers and how to manipulate them, yet she is not a poet whose craft is on display—she is not showy. Cedering's intelligence also reveals itself through the many special areas of knowledge that she has learned well enough to share. She is, by turns, naturalist, anthropologist, psychologist, and astronomer. Beyond knowledge, there is wisdom. Cedering's poems provide that, too.

Cedering has challenged herself in various ways, insisting that her art broaden and mature. The excerpts from her earlier collections show a poet at home working with the short line and writing almost exclusively out of her own direct experience. The poems in *Mother Is* take this technique and this stance to its limit. Because of its astonishingly evocative exploration of female roles and female consciousness, *Mother Is* could well be the centerpiece of any survey of contemporary women's literature. In *The Juggler*, Cedering inhabits less intimate personae and forces a change of compositional habit by casting many of the poems in prose paragraphs. There has been a continuity of interest in her use of dramatic and epistolary modes throughout her career. In the *Ukiyo-E* poems, Cedering is even more adventurous. The range of tones and voices is expanded, as is the range of poetic shapes and ways of handling the line. Though an affinity with Oriental aesthetics is observable in her earlier work, in these newer poems it is far more than a casual factor.

As Cedering explains to the reader in a headnote to this section, "Ukiyo-E is the Japanese term for a genre of painting and woodblock-printing, presenting scenes of everyday life in Japan, by artists who lived between 1600 and 1900." The five subdivisions of this section are based on five translations of "Ukiyo-E": "Pictures of the Floating World," "Pictures of the Fleeting World," "Images from the World of the Senses," "Images from This World of Sorrow," and "Pictures of the Ordinary World." There is a certain arbitrariness in this arrangement, but Cedering does manage five distinct moods that nevertheless blend, with dreamlike reverberations, into a coherent whole. Myth, folklore, astrology, astronomy, alchemy, natural history, sexuality, and feminine identity remain Cedering's primary concerns and the sources for her figures of speech. At this point in time, however, her work seems even deeper and more polished than before. Informed by Eastern sensibility, her internationalist and sometimes exotic imagination is more fully realized than ever.

In these poems, Cedering breaks down the boundaries between science and art, theory and dream, algebra and language. The human imagination is what she celebrates in all of its manifestations. A sequence called "Letters from the Astronomers" presents the voices of Nicolaus Copernicus, Johannes Kepler, Galileo Galilei, Caroline Herschel, and Albert Einstein as they wrestle with their human limits and their boundless visions and aspirations. Finally, they are all poets. In "Almagest, Last Letter to Zakarias," Cedering's focus is plain:

> And as the homing pigeon knows
> by the slant of sunlight, the rotation
> of stars, the magnetism of the earth,
> how to find its way home,
> the word sings through my bones,
> as if they too were hollow.

Probably the best assurance the general reader can be given about Cedering's work is that it is never boring. Intelligent, profoundly moving, dramatic, sensual, and carefully made, these poems will reach a wide variety of readers on many different levels. For a collection of this magnitude, it is startling to discover such a consistently high level of performance. Every poem in *Letters from the Floating World* has freshness. Going her own way, Siv Cedering has created a body of work that stands tall.

Philip K. Jason

Source for Further Study

Library Journal. CIX, December, 1984, p. 2284.

LETTERS OF DELMORE SCHWARTZ

Author: Delmore Schwartz (1913-1966)
Edited, with an introduction, by Robert Phillips, and a foreword by Karl Shapiro
Publisher: Ontario Review Press (Princeton, New Jersey). Illustrated. 384 pp. $24.95
Type of work: Letters
Time: The 1930's to the 1960's
Locale: The Eastern United States

A selection from the correspondence of an important American poet and critic, spanning thirty-four years of literary history

Principal personages:
DELMORE SCHWARTZ, a prominent author of poetry, fiction, and literary criticism
GERTRUDE BUCKMAN, his first wife
JOHN BERRYMAN, a noted poet and friend of Schwartz
RICHARD P. BLACKMUR, a prominent literary critic and theorist
JAMES "JAY" LAUGHLIN, the founder of New Directions Press
ROBERT "CAL" LOWELL, a noted poet and friend of Schwartz
DWIGHT MACDONALD, an editor and critic with the *Partisan Review*
JOHN CROWE RANSOM, a noted poet, critic, and former editor of *The Kenyon Review*

That Delmore Schwartz's letters should be so full of eloquent descriptions of events and places, of impassioned analyses of himself and others, and of concise and carefully reasoned literary criticism may be a surprise to those who know only the stereotyped clichés about this epitome of America's "lost generation," which included his friends and associates John Berryman, Robert Lowell, and Randall Jarrell. Although Schwartz published before any of them (*In Dreams Begin Responsibilities*; 1938), he lived long enough to believe himself to be the greatest failure of that group. Nevertheless, he left behind a body of creative poetry and prose, of critical essays, and a voluminous correspondence which is of importance in understanding not only Schwartz and his works but also his associates and his era.

Letters were important to Schwartz. In 1937, when he wrote, "I have the feeling that letter writing aspires to conversation," he was beginning to fulfill his early promise. By 1951, toward the end of his most productive period, he wondered about his correspondence being read in "international salons and boudoirs of the future.... Will they recognize my prime feelings as a correspondent ... seeking to secure some word from the real world?" He was excessively worried that some readers would see only his negative characteristics and was almost unwilling to believe that others might see his good traits. By 1959, he noted: "Letter writing is an inferior form of friendship, at least for me." In these comments regarding his letters, the reader can trace what Schwartz himself saw as an irreversible downward curve of his life and career. Speaking in his own voices (authoritarian, pleading, angry,

humorous) Schwartz's living presence stands before the reader of Robert
Phillips' edition of the *Letters of Delmore Schwartz* in a manner that biography can only weakly imitate.

Indeed, Schwartz's letters do reveal much of himself: his famous sense of
humor; his ideals and standards for creative and critical writing; his problematic relationships with wives, other writers, publishers, and academia.
Comments on his era range beyond literature—from World War II, the
Ezra Pound treason trial, and Adlai Stevenson's campaign for president to
prejudice against Jews and the New York Yankees baseball team. His angry
denunciations of others are balanced by his often comically Machiavellian
schemes to advance himself and his friends in jobs and in publishing. Out-
bursts of destructive anger are balanced by spontaneous enthusiasm and almost vaudevillian humor. Certainly, no reader of his letters will find
Schwartz a one-sided man. He emerges as complex as the political and literary era in which he lived. Politically, he rejected the optimistic Marxism of
most of his elders at the end of the Depression, rejected the patriotic fervor
of World War II, and rejected the optimistic complacency of the Eisenhower
years. He enthusiastically embraced literary politics, from his ingenuous
cultivation of heroes to his elaborate schemes against those whom he perceived as enemies bent on persecuting him.

James Atlas, in his biography entitled *Delmore Schwartz* (1977), analyzes
Schwartz's paranoid, manic-depressive behavior as essentially caused by
drug and alcohol abuse. Unless Phillips' selection is biased, and there is no
evidence that it is, Schwartz was quite candid about discussing alcohol abuse
but never mentioned sleeping pills or Dexedrine dependence, even when
discussing his psychiatric treatments. From these letters, it would appear
that Schwartz was largely unaware of the dangers of mixing drugs and alcohol. In an effort to cure his mental illness, he analyzed seasonal cycles of his
psyche, took injections for a glandular condition diagnosed by one doctor,
read Sigmund Freud's works, and underwent Freudian psychoanalysis—all
to no avail. Schwartz's inner conflicts and uncontrolled psyche affected almost every facet of his life. "The demon of the absolute has me in thrall,"
he reported early in life, with none of the sense of foreboding that the
reader feels.

Dedicating his life to poetry, Schwartz found himself famous at the age of
twenty-three for a short story. Desiring not to be merely an influential poet
but a great one, such as T. S. Eliot and William Butler Yeats, he immersed
himself in a translation of Arthur Rimbaud, for which his French was inadequate, and a long narrative poem, *Genesis* (1943), of which only book 1 was
published. Craving recognition as an outstanding critic, he postponed finishing contracted reviews and essays, unsatisfied or "ill" again; his thrice-
reworked book on Eliot was never published. Searching, often frantically,
for teaching jobs, he would suddenly flee from them with no notice, as he

did at Harvard University in 1947 and at Syracuse University in 1966. Desperate for marriage and family, he pursued the one woman who always disclaimed interest in both; finally wedding her, he immediately began to distance himself emotionally from her. When was he divorced, he felt so guilty and ashamed that he did not want his Harvard colleagues, his mother, or his draft board to know of his failure. His second marriage followed the same pattern, ending in a paranoid-aggressive situation that finally led his wife to have Schwartz forcibly taken to Bellevue Hospital, a detention that embroiled him in an alienating series of legal suits against his wife, James Laughlin, Saul Bellow, William Styron, Perry Miller, and Harry Levin.

From the letters, the reader learns that Schwartz was often aware of what was happening to him and, to some extent, why. His psychological cycles became clear to him. When he experienced a manic high of hyperactivity, he was optimistic and uncritically productive; he overextended himself, agreeing to teach, to edit or write reviews, criticism, poetry, and prose. Then he would find himself moving into depression, exhausted and trapped, his hopes shattered, wallowing in guilt and emptiness: "Each time, as I look back," he wrote, "I see the growth of anxiety, the outbreaks of anger and accusation, and then the helplessness of mind." He was often so painfully honest with friends that he alienated them. To Gertrude Buckman, his first wife, he confessed that it was "my gross need for affection which makes me cut off one by one those who come near me and violate it." Recognition, however, was no cure, as the end of his life shows. After his attack on Allen Tate, whose criticism he had earlier endorsed enthusiastically, he reassured R. P. Blackmur that no such rupture could separate them, promising monthly letters to cement their bond. After sending Dwight MacDonald several highly critical letters, Schwartz wrote two semiapologies. In the second one he said, "If I must choose between friendship and saying what I think (rightly or not), I choose friendship. (I hope this does not seem immoral.)" He did manage to keep at least these two men as friends longer than most. To John Berryman, a lonely Schwartz fantasized a birthday party for himself and "for friends absent, dead, misunderstood, offended (but this list will take too long)." The letter ends: "Here I go down the roller coaster." His delight and comfort in the male fellowship of literature made him wish it never to end; he assured both Laughlin and Blackmur that they would talk of such matters through eternity in Purgatory.

With female relations—especially marriage—it was a different matter. Even though there are hardly any significant letters to Elizabeth Pollet, Schwartz's second wife, the ones to Gertrude Buckman after their separation were honest and sympathetic. He said that he had underestimated her lack of sexual desire and tried to force her to love him "as in a deadly sin." At one point, he commented ironically that "marriages not made in heaven ought to be made in the id, and not the ego, ought they not?" There are multiple suggestions that Schwartz himself had some difficulty reconciling his own ideals of love and marriage with his sexual urges. He indulged in fantasies, suggesting, for example, that Blackmur be the "better man" at a triad marriage between himself, Tessa Horton, and Helen Blackmur, but only if R. P. Blackmur would propose to Helen for Schwartz. Altogether, Schwartz seemed more comfortable loving and sleeping with his cat, Oranges, than with a woman. To Blackmur and Lowell, he chronicled her sexual adventures. Lowell, in turn, honored Oranges in his poem "To Delmore Schwartz" in *Life Studies* (1959).

Within the confidential format of the letters, without the pressures of facing critical reviewers, Schwartz was fluent, insightful, witty, and full of response to the life and literature around him. Here he could lightly, if unkindly, refer to John Middleton Murry as a possible "one-man plague," since his wives kept dying. Eliot's "East Coker," which Schwartz did not like, became "East Coca-Cola"; wildly fantastic ideas for plays concerning Henry James evolved. During a visit to a bookstore, Schwartz discovered that "I have a sensibility that can be violated by *any* idea; which puts me at the North Pole from H. James." He mixed odes to American popular culture— from his beloved Giants (he marked his first divorce by not listening to the World Series) to films—with comments such as, "am very pleased to be a classic, which I should have suspected for some time, in view of the fact that a classic is what no one reads." He suggested that television's main benefit was in its depiction of the banality and vulgarity of life, because it would make the viewer wish to escape into "actual existence." In the midst of a deep depression, Schwartz, after a first sentence of fifty-one words, told Berryman: "This long sentence, just written, gives me much pleasure, since it is the most extended composition of my 30th year." Such comments are the authentic voices of Schwartz, a side alluded to by friends but never heard by the public until this volume.

There are also many comments in the letters that clarify or reinforce concepts developed in Schwartz's critical and creative writings. Many of his ideas endured throughout his lifetime. His concern for the moral implications of a work is seen in his earliest critical quarrel (1937), with Phillip Horton, about his biography of Hart Crane. Later, Schwartz's negative comments on Eliot and James, as well as his affirmation of James Joyce's works, resulted from this same moral sensibility. Schwartz was equally concerned with the essential interrelationship between form and content. His instinctive eye and ear led him to the best (and worst) of any poet's work—except his own. Of W. H. Auden, Schwartz, in 1938, observed, "a very sensitive mind which lifts up images of the greatest import and shows them in rugged, crabbed, hard language with the kind of 'implicatory' power which is always a sign of poetic mastery." He told Ezra Pound, Mark Van Doren, and the Modern Language Association audience in 1940 that narrative poetry was needed to recapture an audience. In his own long, autobiographical poem, *Genesis*, he tried to practice what he preached. Of contemporary poets, Wallace Stevens received Schwartz's highest praise for *The Auroras of Autumn* (1950): "The feeling as one looks up from the page, that everything has been made very interesting and new and strange and exciting all over again. . . . One's sense of language was awakened and intensified." This is exactly the same prescription for great poetry that he gave to Julian Sawyer in 1931. Schwartz's critical concerns and attitudes carried over into his teaching of freshman composition. As he told William Carlos Williams: "I try to explain that they have misunderstood some words and might do better with other words. . . . Words have idiomatic and metaphorical qualities which require careful handling." Throughout his career, Schwartz was at war with lifeless, hackneyed prose.

Although this necessary and welcome collection of letters gives one a clearer picture of the agonized and complex writer, clarifying, in the process, important literary relationships in the 1940's, the editor's selection and format pose some serious problems. He has included a fact sheet on Schwartz's life and has tried, in footnotes, to identify minor characters as well as the relevant events of Schwartz's life. Nevertheless, the casual or selective reader is likely to be baffled by the many references left unexplained. Who, for example, is William? Why did Schwartz request his father's ledgers? What should be made of Schwartz's casual comments to his estranged wife, Gertrude Buckman, about committing adultery in New York with her help? To read the letters correctly, one also should read the Atlas biography, or one will miss implications and connections. Phillips expects of his readers a high degree of prior knowledge.

There is another problem which will only worsen with the passage of time. Phillips assumes that the once well-known recipients of the Schwartz letters are still familiar, but how many younger scholars will know who Paul Goodman was? Van Wyck Brooks, Mark Van Doren, Dwight MacDonald, Philip Rahv, James Laughlin, Conrad Aiken, Alfred Kazin, Harry Levin, Allen Tate, R. P. Blackmur, and John Crowe Ransom—the publishers and critics of the postwar literary scene—all require, if not a short biographical appendix, then at least extensive footnotes. One needs to be reminded of the importance of *The Southern Review* and the *Kenyon Review* now that the reader is a generation past the heyday of those publications.

On the plus side, Phillips provides an admirable index, listing each of Schwartz's works. As the acknowledgments show, the editor has meticulously tracked down letters from sometimes obscure sources. His selection, arranged by decades, is well balanced, allotting the most pages to the 1940's, when Schwartz's literary reputation was at its peak. In spite of some deletions, the letters indicate the breadth and depth of Schwartz's concerns and correspondents. Problems with the editorial apparatus are balanced by the pleasure of having Schwartz tell his own story. For Robert Phillips, this collection of letters is a difficult job well done.

Ann E. Reynolds

Sources for Further Study

Book World. XV, January 13, 1985, p. 6.
Library Journal. CIX, December, 1984, p. 2273.
The New York Times Book Review. LXXXIX, December 30, 1984, p. 1.
Publishers Weekly. CCXXVI, November 9, 1984, p. 54.

THE LETTERS OF JEAN RHYS

Author: Jean Rhys (1890-1979)
Selected and edited by Francis Wyndham and Diana Melly
Publisher: The Viking Press (New York). 301 pp. $22.50
Type of work: Letters
Time: 1931-1966
Locale: England

Selected letters from a modernist fiction writer to her editors, friends, and daughter

The charming and pleading voice Jean Rhys employed with marvelous wit, tact, and power in her letters should send readers to her fiction, where her ironic and playful verbal creativity and her meticulous critical and editorial judgment produced some of the greatest prose of the modernist period. Like many collections of authors' correspondence, *The Letters of Jean Rhys* teases readers who wish to know more about the process of literary creation. The glimpses onto Rhys's desk, the references to her eclectic and enthusiastic reading of other authors and to her extensive cutting and revising of her own manuscripts, only begin to reveal the secrets of her art.

It is misleading to suggest, as Francis Wyndham, her literary executor, asserts in his introduction to this volume of letters, that Rhys's correspondence can convey her personality or her life story. This selection of letters begins only in 1931, excluding her experiences in London and Paris in the 1920's. It continues in another form the narrative begun in Rhys's autobiography, *Smile, Please* (1979), which covers her early life but gives less information about the 1920's and stops at 1930. Even within the years covered by this selection, 1931 to 1966, there are chronological gaps imposed by missing or excluded letters, and these omissions certainly disqualify any claim to a comprehensive life. There are no letters to Jean Lenglet, her first husband. Excluded are those written before 1931, to Ford Madox Ford, to Edward Garnett, to the admirers and critics of her first published work. Missing are any letters written between spring, 1941, and fall, 1945, during World War II. Omitted are the letters written after 1966, after the publication and successful reception of her best novel, *Wide Sargasso Sea* (1966). The editors have various good reasons for these omissions: Some of the letters are lost, some will not be released by their owners for publication, some are boring or incoherent; nevertheless, the resulting book of letters cannot be read as an artist's biography.

Through spontaneous as well as calculated notes to reviewers, publishers, editors, patrons, and friends, Rhys projects her complaints, her thanks, and her apologies with the skill of a performer and a creator. She creates brilliantly entertaining comic sketches in which poor Jean Rhys is the victimized heroine. Her cold and damp England, hostile to artist and outsider, is only partially real, yet the reader willingly suspends disbelief. It is possible that the walls of Rhys's various dwellings always dripped, wet from leaking pipes or from the rain. It is verifiable that two of her husbands were white-collar criminals, convicted of violating laws regulating the flow of paper money (illegal currency exchange and fraudulent check writing). It is certain that Rhys won the admiration and loyalty of many literary lions, including the two editors of this book: Francis Wyndham and Diana Athill (Diana Melly). An intentionally farcical and sometimes revealing portrait of the artist does emerge.

What was Jean Rhys like, as a friend? She was difficult. Her long memory cherished acts of kindness as well as betrayals. Her short memory glossed over her alcoholism and her self-destructive choices—though perhaps this revision of her character is aided by the editors' selection of letters. One suspects that she lost friends not simply because they suddenly turned against her, but because they could not forgive or forget her insults. In this selection of her letters, Rhys usually absolves herself of responsibility for the consequences of her own difficult behavior. One suspects that for months at a time she was desperately lonely. She lived isolated from the literary culture that had once lionized her. One suspects that she managed money with no calculation and little skill. She lived on advances, small allowances, loans, and credit. From the selection of letters included in this volume, it is impossible to weigh the effects on her of alcohol, of amphetamines, of hallucinogenic drugs, and of recurrent attacks of flu, all mentioned by Rhys as valid reasons for her tiredness and for her repeated failure to meet her writing deadlines.

Reading these letters as a partial self-portrait of the artist, one must be careful not to accept the made-up face as reality. Anne Tyler, in *The New Republic* review of the letters, assumes that she now can sum up Jean Rhys: "Whining, raging, rationalizing, self-deprecating, she emerges from these pages as a charter member of the 'Of course it rained' school." Even though Tyler's response may easily be supported by ample evidence drawn from the letters, it obviously simplifies the voice of the artist. One can hardly imagine a similarly dismissive appraisal of another alcoholic, self-excusing, nontyping, complaining, and, at times, paranoid letter writer, who also happened to be a great modernist fiction writer: James Joyce. Neither Joyce nor Rhys would have been an ideal spouse or a reliably loyal friend, but those criteria are irrelevant to their literary achievements.

Two mistaken impressions can now be corrected: that Jean Rhys abandoned fiction writing during her middle years, or that she wrote spontaneously, almost unconsciously. During the thirty-five years covered by these letters, Rhys completed three major novels: *Voyage in the Dark* (1934), *Good Morning, Midnight* (1939), and the novel generally acknowledged as a masterpiece, *Wide Sargasso Sea*. She also completed several short stories published in the collection *Tigers Are Better-Looking* (1968), and she wrote radio plays for BBC productions of her fiction. She was not unproductive, despite her own repeated apologies for unfinished work. Even though she did not publish between 1939 and 1966, Rhys did not suspend her writing for any period longer than a year, judging from evidence in this collection of letters. When her personal relationships failed or dissolved, her writing did not cease; indeed, her writing was, in otherwise unbearable times, her lifeline.

The war years in Great Britain silenced many writers; from this collection of letters, one cannot judge what Jean Rhys the writer did during those years. The brief allusions Rhys makes to contemporary politics—a Jewish friend who was forced to flee Berlin, the terrible war in Spain—indicate that she kept herself informed and that she responded emotionally to the horrors of Fascism and violence. She certainly knew that her former husband and her beloved daughter remained in Holland during the Nazi occupation; she discovered that they were active in the Resistance; she learned that her first husband was imprisoned in a concentration camp. The effects of this on her character or her writing are impossible to evaluate without consulting letters omitted from this volume.

In a letter of October, 1945, as Rhys writes to a friend of the sudden death of her second husband, she also mentions her work in progress on a novel and her recently completed collection of short stories. She connects her work to her struggle against grief. On March 9, 1949, she first defines her idea for that same novel-in-progress, which she eventually completed and published as *Wide Sargasso Sea*. From the scanty evidence supplied in this volume, it appears likely that Rhys continued to write, in isolation, during the 1940's. For a writer such as Rhys, who had been celebrated and congratulated by the leading literary critics of the modern period, it must have been disheartening to endure the silence and the inattention of the war years and the postwar slump. When she read, in the November 5, 1949, issue of the *New Statesman and Nation* an inquiry requesting information about the author of *Good Morning, Midnight*, she responded. That inquiry initiated her friendship with Selma Vaz Dias, who, by performing adaptations of Rhys's fiction in BBC dramatic readings, resurrected a reputation that had died. In 1949, the discovery that she had readers who were enthusiastic and sympathetic about her work certainly helped her resume regular composition.

Like most modernistic writers, Rhys wrote self-consciously. She substantially and compulsively revised her work before publication, making major structural changes, experimenting with various narrators, and cutting to improve the style. She wrote alternative endings for her novels. She used poetry writing as a technique, which enabled her to solve some knotty problems of characterization in her fiction. She rewrote some fiction as drama; she drafted plays which she later revised into novels. All literary modes were open to her. She polished her prose so extensively that the process of writing seemed, at times, interminable to her and to her editors.

Critics interested in new literary analysis of her work may glean valuable information about the writing process from Rhys's comments on *Wide Sargasso Sea*. She began her novel to correct Charlotte Brontë's unsympathetic portrait, in *Jane Eyre* (1847), of the first Mrs. Rochester. Rhys set her novel in her native West Indies, in 1840, and she investigated the historical details for her novel as carefully as some of the nineteenth century realist fiction writers had. Beginning with her resistance to Brontë's characterization, Rhys explores the behavior of a West Indian girl and her English husband, invents a plausible psychology for each, places them in the cultural and historical contexts that shape their characters, and wrestles with fair treatment of protagonist and antagonist. In the letters on the composition of *Wide Sargasso Sea*, her professional craftsmanship and her artistic dedication are compelling.

Given the evidence in these letters, it is not possible to regard Rhys as a marginal, isolated British West Indian writer who, under the patronage of Ford Madox Ford, managed to get a few novels published. Her literary contacts, both personal and intellectual, were extensive and wide-ranging. For much of her life, she lived in poverty that was not genteel; she did, however, enrich her life by reading. When her finances fell so dismally low that she was forced to sell her library to pay for food and lodging, she grieved over the loss. She treasured the few excellent booksellers and lending libraries that she found outside London, in the various locations where she lived. Her favorite gifts to her daughter and her granddaughter were books. As she writes about her daily life in her letters, she mentions names and titles: Guy de Maupassant's *Fort comme la mort* (1889), George Moore's *Esther Waters* (1894), Franz Kafka's *The Castle* (1930), Jean-Paul Sartre's plays and novels, Henry Miller's *Tropic of Cancer* (1934), Georges Bernanos' *Journal d'un curé de campagne* (1936), F. Scott Fitzgerald's *Tender Is the Night* (1934), J. D. Salinger's *Catcher in the Rye* (1951), James Joyce's *Finnegans Wake* (1939). She read more widely than most members of the lost generation, and she understood what she read, to judge from her brief but perceptive comments in her letters. Her own fiction deserves reassessment within the modern European literary tradition.

A woman who could call herself attractive to an albatross commands attention. A reader who could recognize that James Joyce's prose voice in Anna Livia Plurabelle (*Finnegans Wake*) imitated grand opera provokes intelligent discourse. A writer as self-aware, as perceptive of other writers, and as inventive as Jean Rhys the novelist invites critical admiration.

Judith L. Johnston

Sources for Further Study

The Atlantic. CCLIV, August, 1984, p. 109.
Booklist. LXXX, May 15, 1984, p. 1288.
Book World. XIV, October 7, 1984, p. 7.
Horizon. XXVII, July, 1984, p. 58.
House and Garden. CLVI, July, 1984, p. 18.
Kirkus Reviews. LII, June 15, 1984, p. 573.
Library Journal. CIX, June 1, 1984, p. 1126.
Los Angeles Times Book Review. November 4, 1984, p. 4.
The New Republic. CXCI, September 10, 1984, p. 29.
The New York Times Book Review. LXXXIX, September 30, 1984, p. 3.
Publishers Weekly. CCXXV, June 1, 1984, p. 55.
Vogue. CLXXIV, August, 1984, p. 222.

THE LETTERS OF MARGARET FULLER
Volume III: 1842-1844

Author: Margaret Fuller (1810-1850)
Edited, with notes, by Robert N. Hudspeth
Publisher: Cornell University Press (Ithaca, New York). 269 pp. $25.00
Type of work: Letters
Time: 1842-1844

The third volume of Margaret Fuller's letters covers the crucial professional years in which she gave up editorship of the Dial, *traveled in the Midwest, left the New England of Transcendentalism (and her family circle) to become book-review editor for Horace Greeley's* New-York Daily Tribune, *and wrote* Woman in the Nineteenth Century

The first two volumes of Robert N. Hudspeth's meticulous edition of Margaret Fuller's letters, which appeared in 1983, made it possible to trace the formation of a remarkable American intellectual and her engagement with the persons and minds central to the "flowering of New England" in the years before the middle of the nineteenth century. In this volume's letters—covering the years 1842 to 1844—Fuller's correspondents include Ralph Waldo Emerson, Sophia Peabody, Nathaniel Hawthorne, Henry Wadsworth Longfellow, Henry David Thoreau, Lydia Francis Child, and William Henry Channing. The accurate and fully annotated texts would be, on any grounds, an important resource for examining the period's intellectual currents, but the nature of Fuller's own development over these years— during which she shifted her interest from literary to social criticism, disengaged herself both physically and intellectually from the Transcendentalists, and produced one of the central documents of American feminist thought—also accounts for her problematic placement in the literary canon. Insights derived from the letters in this volume bear directly on current efforts to reconstruct and reinterpret the literary history of the United States.

Fuller is one of the few women who seems to fit neatly into a slot in the standard outline of American literature: the Puritans, the Age of Reason, Nationalism, Transcendentalism, and so on. Therefore she is sometimes included in conventional textbooks; after all, she did occupy a central position in the Concord circle and edited (which often meant writing up to half the contents of an issue) the journal which Transcendentalists established to circulate their literary and philosophical ideas. Fuller's most famous book, however, is violently at odds with many features of the category in which she "fits." Critical and biographical studies of her life and work make an illuminating case study of the shifting cultural pressures that determine what literature is valued.

These cultural pressures are also, in part, what have made Hudspeth's task in editing the letters so difficult—and so crucial. Fuller's family and friends censored and recopied to eliminate improprieties and passages on possibly sensitive subjects. (This is the case with virtually all nineteenth century editions of letters, whether the writer is female or male, but the cultural idealization of women intensifies the problem since it drastically limits the range of acceptable thought.) *The Memoirs of Margaret Fuller Ossoli*, edited by Emerson, Channing, and James F. Clarke (2 vols., 1852), was a deliberate attempt to produce a "monument"; Emerson excised, connected, and reshaped Fuller's letters and journals to create a woman in his own image, despite the fact that she had written to him, in a letter of July 13, 1844, "You are intellect, I am life." The "unattractive" assurance and passion which Transcendentalists left out of their official monument surfaced in Hawthorne's *The Blithedale Romance* (1852)—a distorted fictional treatment which remains the source of many people's impression of Fuller as woman.

After the generation of her close associates had passed away, romantic interest in the person (rather than the intellect) led to a quite different published collection of correspondence: *Love-Letters of Margaret Fuller, 1845-1846* (1903). In the twentieth century, Fuller continues to occupy a situation just beneath the main current of literary studies. She has been regularly rediscovered, each time with a focus that reflects the era's own concerns. The first modern biography, written in 1920 by Katherine Anderson, is entitled *Margaret Fuller, a Psychological Biography*; a 1930 biography by Margaret Bell featured an introduction by Eleanor Roosevelt; one published in 1957 is called *In Quest of Love* and rearranges the materials to produce a highly romantic heroine; and much of the most recent work has dwelt almost exclusively on feminist materials.

It is for these reasons that Hudspeth's meticulous care (the labor of many years) in examining the manuscripts, comparing versions, and tracking references is so impressive and so essential. Textual variations and interpolations are rigorously identified without using devices that mar the book's readability. The footnotes are a study in themselves: The substantive notes fill in social and intellectual history, and the biographical notes—which are often able to identify mutual friends referred to by only a single initial—depend on an incredibly full knowledge of the people and families in Fuller's circle.

The Fuller revealed in these letters is a woman supporting herself by writing and teaching, intellectually confident enough to criticize both the ideas and the attitudes of the men who were identified as the country's intellectual and literary elite, fully involved in the practical life of her family and friends, and learning to see that practical life and intellectual life should not be separate and mutually exclusive. When Sophia Peabody became engaged to Nathaniel Hawthorne, Fuller wrote to her:

> And for daily life, as well as in the long account, I think there will be great happiness, for if ever I saw a man who combined delicate tenderness to understand the heart of a woman, with quiet depth and manliness enough to satisfy her, it is Mr. Hawthorne. How

simple and rational, too, seems your plan of life. You will be separated only by your several pursuits and just enough daily to freshen the founts of thought and feeling; to one who cannot think of love merely in the heart, or even in the common destiny of two souls, but as necessarily comprehending intellectual friendship, too, it seems the happiest lot imaginable that lies before you.

The manuscript of *Woman in the Nineteenth Century* (1845) was produced at the end of the period covered by this volume of Fuller's letters. Her correspondence provides little direct commentary on the book's substance, though it does take up some associated practical matters: the need to have time and solitude for writing, the discovery that it was turning into something much longer than the essay with which she began, the arrangements for publication and distribution, the justification of style growing out of her decisions about the work's purpose and the audience she hoped to reach. Read in chronological sequence, however, the letters help to explain (particularly with the benefit of hindsight) how Margaret Fuller, four years before American women first organized to seek legal and political rights, came to occupy her unique position as the woman at the center of New England's philosophical and literary tradition who used the methods and premises of that tradition to question its assumptions about women in society.

In the spring of 1842, Fuller gave up her editorship of the *Dial*. The work was exhausting and demanding—and unpaid. The letters covering the journal's transfer to Emerson reveal her close grasp of practical details. She is also reluctantly aware of the changes which will occur once Emerson takes control. "You have always had in view to make a good periodical and represent your own tastes," she writes on April 9, 1842, "while I have had in view to let all kinds of people have freedom to say their say, for better, for worse." Though she remained personally close to the Emerson circle, she also saw grounds for criticism. A letter to William Henry Channing calls him to task for the narrow parochialisms of a sermon: "I was surprized to hear you speak . . . as if the extent of the Christian triumph proved its superiority; that of other faiths is numerically greater. . . . You spoke, too, as others do as if Europe was the world, merely because civilization is more active there." Learning of Emerson's reaction to the birth of a friend's child ("Though no son, yet a sacred event"), she responded with a deceptively genial scolding: "Why is not the advent of a daughter as 'sacred' a fact as that of a son. I do believe, O Waldo, most unteachable of men, that you are at heart a sinner on this point. I entreat you to seek light in prayer upon it."

During the same period, Fuller was conducting the "conversations" on literary and philosophical subjects which she held (for pay) for small groups of women. The quality of the sessions varied with the group; some people let social engagements come first. Others, however, were the self-taught scholars who flourished in the years before any adequate secondary education was available to women. They had sampled the literature on various subjects, learned languages by translating, absorbed their brothers' college classes secondhand but with double value because they did the background and collateral reading themselves instead of deriving it from classroom lectures. In the "conversations" at their best, Fuller tapped the enormous energy generated by a group of women discussing significant ideas on their own, without the voice of an intervening masculine authority. The arguments and structure of *Woman in the Nineteenth Century* were nourished in this ground, and Fuller's intellectual activities in the years between 1842 and 1844 account for the bafflement of modern readers who begin her key work expecting to find horror tales about women's social and legal wrongs and are disappointed to find themselves sinking beneath the weight of Greek references.

The letters, however, also make clear how much of Fuller's energy was poured into the practical concerns and emotional housekeeping that make up the other portion of women's lives. She writes to the brother at college about his reading and about making contacts that will further his career; she provides comfort when his grades are disappointing, nags gently about his clothing, arranges to have money sent. She makes several unsuccessful attempts to find a niche for another brother who seems to have been mildly retarded. She is annoyed by the pliability and indecisiveness of Frances Fuller, her brother William Henry's wife—but she is also sympathetic to the situation of any woman married to a man with that brother's difficult nature. A sister marries Ellery Channing, who seemed uninterested in taking up any line of work. Her mother's health requires decisions about living arrangements and finances.

Finally, the important third strand of Fuller's life developed in the period covered by this volume. For the first time, she began turning her attention to social issues in addition to intellectual and personal concerns. Traveling to the Midwest in 1843, she was impressed by the enterprise that had already built businesses and schools and thriving institutions in Milwaukee, Wisconsin, which had been Indian territory five years earlier—and looking at the site and the land, she also suddenly appreciated the blood which Native Americans had spent struggling to retain control of such glorious country. Another significant series of letters was written to Georgiana Bruce, an English friend employed by the women's prison at Sing Sing. Fuller encourages her to remain and observe, urges her also to write, finally makes a visit and appreciates how protected her own life of the mind has been. She makes an effort to look at the world through other eyes:

> You say few of these women have any feeling about chastity. Do you know how they
> regard that part of the sex, who are reputed chaste? Do they see any reality in it; or
> look on it merely as a circumstance of condition, like the possession of fine clothes? You
> know novelists are fond of representing them as if they looked up to their more pro-
> tected sisters as saints and angels!

Fuller wrote in another letter to Bruce that "these women in their degradation express most powerfully the present wants of the sex at large. What blasphemes in them must fret and murmur in the perfumed boudoir, for a society beats with one great heart."

By the end of 1844, Fuller had moved from Boston to New York, traded the rarefied intellectual atmosphere of the *Dial* for Horace Greeley and daily journalism, and produced a book whose reputation made her welcome in the revolutionary capitals of Europe. The decisions which can be traced in the letters of this volume thus had the ultimate effect of moving Fuller's work out of the categories neatly covered by the literary canon. One can only be grateful that her letters are now appearing in a sound and authoritative edition instead of a hurried selection which would have appealed only to the "feminist market." It is materials of this sort that scholars need to reconceptualize the history of American literature.

Sally H. Mitchell

Source for Further Study

Choice. XXII, April, 1985, p. 1157.

THE LIFE OF JANE AUSTEN

Author: John Halperin (1941-   )
Publisher: The Johns Hopkins University Press (Baltimore, Maryland). Illustrated.
   399 pp. $25.00
Type of work: Literary biography
Time: 1775-1817
Locale: Southern England

A lucid scholarly biography examining Jane Austen's complex character and showing how her personal circumstances colored her novels

> *Principal personages:*
> JANE AUSTEN, a novelist
> GEORGE AUSTEN, her father, a clergyman
> CASSANDRA LEIGH AUSTEN, her mother
> CASSANDRA AUSTEN, her sister
> JAMES AUSTEN, her brother, a clergyman
> EDWARD AUSTEN KNIGHT, her brother, adopted heir of a wealthy
>   landowner
> HENRY AUSTEN, her brother, a banker and later clergyman
> FRANCIS AUSTEN, her brother, a naval officer
> CHARLES AUSTEN, her brother, a naval officer

"He has become his admirers." This phrase formulated by W. H. Auden refers to the poet William Butler Yeats, but it holds true for artists in general and Jane Austen in particular. At the time of her death in July, 1817, Austen had published four of the finest novels in the English language. For these works she had earned a few hundred pounds, one serious and appreciative literary assessment (Walter Scott's praise of *Emma* in the *Quarterly Review*), and almost no personal acclaim. On her death, Jane Austen became her admirers quite literally. Her family constructed memoirs, ignored certain qualities and achievements, destroyed certain letters—in short, did what they could to turn the woman and writer into a paragon of all the Christian virtues. Sharp-eyed readers, Virginia Woolf and D. H. Lawrence among them, have reacted and sometimes overreacted to the eulogy; for the most part, however, the legend of the saintly spinster serenely but incisively producing brilliant novels in a Hampshire country house has endured. With the publication of John Halperin's *The Life of Jane Austen*, sentimentalizing and image making—both of which are ultimately acts of condescension—became impossible. By presenting Austen as a real person with problems and peculiarities as well as virtues and talents, Halperin allows her the dignity that readers, even modern ones, have more freely accorded to male writers—Lord Byron, Mark Twain, Marcel Proust. Some specialists may quarrel with specific points of Halperin's biographical interpretation, but everyone must respect his method of proceeding. Halperin draws usefully and critically on what primary sources there are and comments on the significance of the gaps; he examines the novels in a subtle, never reductive way for links between the life and the work. He makes appropriate use of what has been written and said of Austen and incorporates fresh findings from peripheral studies. For example, a close look at the family tree yields a surprising number of the names used in the novels and demonstrates Jane Austen's wide connection to nobles, society people, and politicians, as well as clerics; exploring the streets and monuments of Bookham in Surrey yields various details from *Emma*. Now that Halperin's biography has been written, Austen's audience will have the chance to come to terms with the woman and then grant her genius a respect profounder for taking account of her weaknesses.

Halperin's study begins at "The End." He presents Jane Austen dying in Winchester, her survivors creating through their tributes to her character (praises which tend to ignore her novels) a flawless fiction, and critics reacting to this concocted sweetness and light. From this narrow beginning, Halperin widens his focus to treat Jane Austen's age in all of its Georgian and Napoleonic ambiguities and her family in its sociological complexity. Austen was, by birth and education, a conservative person in a conservative class in a country where conservative policies prevailed. Through his careful account of Austen's background, Halperin permits the reader to see her nature in its context. In her parents' social positions (George Austen toward the lower range of gentility, his wife, Cassandra, whose family retained a barony near the top) and the details of their family's life at the Steventon rectory and beyond (readings, theatricals, the education of Jane Austen, her sister, Cassandra, and her brothers), one finds material later encountered in the novels. In Jane Austen's juvenile works, one sees evidence of both the talent and the temperament that were to distinguish the mature woman.

Writing as a biographer first and a critic second, Halperin takes Austen's juvenilia more seriously than most of his predecessors, B. C. Southam excepted, have done. In these works completed by her twentieth year, Austen shows herself a parodist, cynic, and critical reader. Halperin argues that the juvenilia shed light on her novels—for example, the sibling rivalry in "The Three Sisters" foreshadows what one sees in *Sense and Sensibility* (1811), *Pride and Prejudice* (1813), *Mansfield Park* (1814), *Northanger Abbey* (1818), and *Persuasion* (1818)—and her character as well. Austen's penchant for mockery, detachment, and ridicule came to full flower early, as the juvenile pieces suggest, and Halperin agrees with Marvin Mudrick in seeing Austen's preferred mode, irony, as a defense against other people and against her own feelings. He suggests that toward the end of this phase of her life, Austen, unmarried and twenty, must have been seriously concerned to marry, whether for love or for comfort and security. She would not have expected or wished to remain a spinster, but, given her clear-eyed detachment, she must have seen that finding a husband who would be equal to her would not be an easy thing to do.

In welcome contrast to those who have studied Austen's novels in linear fashion, as they were published, Halperin sees them as developing in clusters, during two bursts of creativity. He refers to the first such period (1796 to 1799), which saw the Austen family's last years of stability at Steventon and their move to Bath, as "the years of the first trilogy." During this time, Austen wrote "First Impressions," "Elinor and Marianne," and "Catherine," which were revised as *Pride and Prejudice*, *Sense and Sensibility*, and *Northanger Abbey*, respectively. Halperin's account of these years draws acutely on Austen's chatty letters to her sister, Cassandra. These letters are often cited by hostile readers bent on proving Austen's triviality or malice: How can she talk of a hat "on which you know my principal hopes of happiness depend" when Napoleon is rampaging across the Channel? One answer to such charges is that kind hearts and sharp tongues are not mutually preclusive, that minds capable of deep thoughts can also entertain bagatelles, but Halperin does Austen justice by reminding his readers about the matter of audience and instructing them on the rules of the Georgian post. In those days, when recipients rather than senders paid postage, Jane Austen would have sent her absent sister what she wanted—information amusingly conveyed. There was no need for Austen to spell out the serious views with which Cassandra would have been quite familiar, nor would she describe events that anyone could find in the newspapers. One major occurrence of this period in Austen's life, flippantly described though it may be in the letters, is her brief romance with Thomas Lefroy, later to be the chief justice of Ireland. Austen's disappointment in this first love may have contributed to her habitual detachment and was very likely the source of her characteristic point, most centrally made in *Persuasion*, that women's attachments are more lasting than are men's.

Halperin makes a detailed and convincing case for "First Impressions"/*Pride and Prejudice*, which he sees as Austen's finest novel, as also her first one—the "natural spiritual heir" of the juvenilia. Halperin presents the novel as showing much about Austen's family and her personal circumstances. There are two lively sisters as well as an ineffectual, unloving mother—not for the last time in the Austen world. The author's own temperamental reserve and the qualities that she would welcome in a suitor are projected on Darcy, as her wit and philosophical detachment are on Elizabeth and, in a darker case, on Mr. Bennet, whose character Halperin sees as Austen's indictment of her own detachment. "Elinor and Marianne"/*Sense and Sensibility* coincides with a less happy period in Austen's letters, and the novel as Halperin sees it is "bleak and black and nasty," where its predecessor is "light and bright and sparkling." This rather misanthropic novel articulates Austen's attitudes at twenty-two toward men and money. Emphasizing the difficulties that an intelligent, undowered woman encounters in finding a husband, it comes to endorse the middle course

between sense and sensibility—the purely sensible. All that was sensible in
Jane Austen must have then been making her face the possibility, though by
no means the certainty, of spinsterhood. "Catherine"/*Northanger Abbey*,
written after the Austens' move to Bath, differs in many ways from the
other novels. Unlike the previous two, it was but lightly revised. Wholly
satirical, it mocks Gothic literature as much as real life. It is set chiefly in
Bath and an isolated country house rather than in a village. It offers a heroine with whom Austen is out of sympathy and a hero who shares her ironic
viewpoint to the extent that he is virtually the central consciousness. In his
discussion of *Northanger Abbey*, like those of the two earlier books,
Halperin comments on the rushed and bungled ending, where Austen's superbly effective dramatic presentation gives way to hurried reportage. A
compelling reason for this recurrent flaw, he argues, may be Austen's personal resentment of the literary event—the happy ending she as a writer
was obliged to supply for her heroines but could not see as likely for herself.

The fifth and sixth chapters of Halperin's *The Life of Jane Austen* treat
the fallow decade between the two periods of fertility. These years of
rootlessness that began with her father's retirement were hard on Austen,
who valued comfort, security, and privacy but instead found herself shifting
about to various lodgings in Bath with Cassandra and her parents or to
brothers' houses, where one or the other of the sisters would go to assist as
maiden aunt to growing families. On the death of George Austen in 1805,
the Austen women, whose income was greatly reduced, moved to Southampton and set up housekeeping with Frank Austen, one of the seagoing
brothers, and his wife.

No letters exist for part of this period (May, 1801, to September, 1804)—
an indication, according to Halperin, that Cassandra destroyed evidence
which she thought would darken posterity's view of her sister. Although
Northanger Abbey, then under the title "Susan," was purchased by the publisher Crosby in 1803, Austen apparently wrote only one fragment during
these years. This piece, "The Watsons," voices the loneliness and obsessions—fears of being old, poor, and scorned—that haunted Austen's middle years. Halperin's account shows Austen placed under the worst conditions: She lived as a dependent in close quarters with aging parents and
then with her uncongenial mother, enduring frequent separations from the
beloved Cassandra and frequent sojourns in her brothers' increasingly
crowded and noisy houses. Not surprisingly, a number of her less admirable
qualities surfaced or became aggravated. Neurasthenic, anxious for comforts, and unsympathetic though she may have been, Austen, in the face of
great personal and professional discouragement, bravely cherished her
determination to write. "She was thirty-one and unpublished," Halperin says
of Austen during the Southampton residence. The last word of this description signals Halperin's sense that Austen had moved, though her commit-

ment had yet borne no fruit, away from the nineteenth century woman's conventional means of gaining identity and toward a renewed sense of vocation.

That literary rebirth became possible when Edward Austen Knight, who had inherited substantial property from the family whose surname he took, offered his mother and sisters Chawton Cottage, near one of his manor houses in Hampshire. With the return of security and stability, Austen found herself able to write again. The work she first began revising was *Sense and Sensibility*, the early version of *Pride and Prejudice* having been "tainted" by a publisher's rejection and *Northanger Abbey* languishing unpublished with Crosby. When *Sense and Sensibility*, published at her own risk, earned her money (£140 on the first edition), she went on to sell the copyright of *Pride and Prejudice* for £110. These two successful revisions established momentum for the years of the "second trilogy" (1811-1816).

Halperin sees the first new novel of this period, *Mansfield Park*, as less difficult to explain than it is generally acknowledged to be. *Mansfield Park* offers Austen's personal preferences (in Fanny's fondness for peace and quiet, dancing, and clerical life, and dislike of selfishness, noise, and being neglected) and her moral perspective, along with numerous details from the Austen family (among others, the sailor brother, the unsympathetic mother, and the bossy, thieving aunt). Halperin sees this sober book as not at all "uncharacteristic," as it has often seemed when set beside *Pride and Prejudice*, which immediately preceded it into print. He usefully reminds the reader that the woman who wrote *Mansfield Park* was very different from the one who had drafted "First Impressions" years earlier. Halperin's treatment of *Emma* pays homage to its deserved popularity among modern readers and brings out many biographical connections—the Surrey details that Austen must have observed, her parents' role reversal in becoming Emma's admirable dead mother and foolish, hypochondriacal, surviving father. Again, Halperin stresses the defective, rushed ending—an accepted proposal and marriage being something that she could not faithfully portray, not having experienced them. His account of *Persuasion* highlights the book's comparison of true and false ways of perceiving, its argument for intelligence and insight, and its harsh swipes at romanticism and fuzzy sentimentality of all sorts (even the uncritical love of a parent for a child) and masculine fickleness.

If Austen's middle years evoked her frailties, her painful final illness, miliary tuberculosis of the adrenal cortex, they also called forth her greatness of character. Halperin's account of Austen's last months shows her courage, generosity, faith, and unfailing humor. Halperin rates her last unfinished piece, *Sanditon* (1975), high in the canon. As satire, it proves powerful in its indictments of hypochondria and the nineteenth century spa spirit; as character study, it breaks new ground in the portrayal of Sir Edward Denham, a theoretical rake instructed in vice by literature. The value and cogency of Halperin's comments on this fragment given cursory attention by most Austen critics epitomize the excellence of his biography. His own work is, like his subject's self-described "bits of ivory," sane, keen, and careful in minute particulars. A reader comes away from *The Life of Jane Austen* with many answers—and better yet, with fresh and fascinating questions.

Peter W. Graham

Sources for Further Study

Book World. XV, January 13, 1985, p. 4.
Kirkus Reviews. LII, August 1, 1984, p. 730.
Library Journal. CIX, September 15, 1984, p. 1752.
Los Angeles Times Book Review. November 4, 1984, p. 6.
The New York Times Book Review. XC, February 24, 1985, p. 25.
Publishers Weekly. CCXXVI, July 27, 1984, p. 134.
The Wall Street Journal. CCIV, December 26, 1984, p. 9.

LINCOLN
A Novel

Author: Gore Vidal (1925-   )
Publisher: Random House (New York). 659 pp. $19.95
Type of work: Novel
Time: 1861-1865; 1867
Locale: Washington, D.C., Virginia, and Paris

A historical novel about Abraham Lincoln's White House years that portrays him as a masterfully shrewd politician who succeeded in his paramount goal, to preserve the Union

> *Principal characters:*
> ABRAHAM LINCOLN, sixteenth President of the United States, 1861-1865
> MARY TODD LINCOLN, his adoring, neurotic wife
> JOHN HAY, his youthful presidential secretary
> SALMON P. CHASE, an Abolitionist, Secretary of the Treasury, 1861-1864, Chief Justice of the United States Supreme Court, 1864-1873
> KATE CHASE, his selflessly devoted daughter
> WILLIAM SPRAGUE, a pompous millionaire governor of Rhode Island, Kate's husband
> WILLIAM H. SEWARD, Secretary of State, 1861-1869
> EDWIN M. STANTON, Secretary of War, 1862-1868
> DAVID HEROLD, a young pharmacy assistant and Southern spy
> ULYSSES S. GRANT, the foremost commander of Union forces
> JOHN WILKES BOOTH, a popular actor, fanatical Confederate, and presidential assassin

Like Babe Ruth, Abraham Lincoln was a powerfully talented Yankee who inspired genuine affection even in opponents. Like Samuel Gompers, his dominant passion was Union, and he would do anything—even condone slavery—to prevent the United States of America from disintegrating. The author of more than thirty books, Gore Vidal has, as a congressional candidate from New York and a senatorial candidate from California, also been a politically active Democrat. His historical novel about the first Republican president, the sixteenth president of the United States, came just as the sixteenth Republican president was seeking reelection. *Lincoln* joins *Burr* (1973), *1876* (1976), and *Washington, D.C.* (1967) in Vidal's American chronicle sequence. It is an enthralling narrative about The Great Emancipator—a gangling man who achieved greatness by cunning indirection and emancipation by inadvertence.

Lincoln begins at dawn on February 23, 1861, as the disguised president-elect, elevated from the obscurity of his Illinois law practice by a mere plurality of the vote, slips into Washington to avoid assassination. There is a brief epilogue set in a Paris drawing room on January 1, 1867, but the body of the work concludes on April 15, 1865, with Lincoln's death at the hands of a vainglorious young actor. The novel is set during an era of fratricidal strife and in a revolting Southern city of sewage canals and stinking swamps. The White House, infested with rats, termites, and flies and devoid of plumbing, is referred to by one of its inhabitants as "the miasmic mansion." Office seekers besiege it more persistently than do Confederate troops. A cow grazes on its lawn, and an abattoir operates nearby. The Washington Monument remains unfinished.

Lincoln is no hagiography, no pious monument to "Honest Abe." Vidal had, in *The Second American Revolution* (1982), earlier written that "the actual Lincoln was cold and deliberate, reflective and brilliant." This novel focuses on the wily tactician who took office without an overwhelming popular mandate and despite the Southern view that his inauguration represented a *casus belli*, yet who eventually managed to rout his political and military opposition. Lincoln's reverence for the Constitution did not prevent him from taking considerable liberties with its legal guarantees; he suspended habeas corpus, jailed hostile newspaper editors and political adversaries, and had the Secret Service inspect private letters and telegrams. This is not exactly the sentimental saint of Carl Sandburg and civics texts. Vidal's Lincoln is a genial manipulator of his own myth of frontier bumpkin, one adept at deflecting anger with a rustic anecdote.

Lincoln appoints his principal political rivals, William H. Seward and Salmon P. Chase, to the Cabinet, where they neutralize each other and sabotage their own ardent ambitions for the presidency. Seward dreams of an imperial republic which will encompass the entire continent and is impatient with intersectional rivalries that stand in the way of that goal. Aside from the advancement of his own career, Chase is devoted to nothing so much as the total and unconditional abolition of slavery. Each is convinced that their Chief Executive is a mediocrity who will, in any case, never be reelected. By 1863, however, Seward has relinquished his own personal aspirations and has been converted to an admiration for Lincoln's ability "to make himself absolute dictator without ever letting anyone suspect that he was anything more than a joking, timid backwoods lawyer, given to fits of humility in the presence of all the strutting military and political peacocks that flocked about him."

Chase's ambitions are so intense that, merely in order to acquire more capital to finance his campaigns, he sacrifices his complaisant daughter Kate to a loveless marriage with a wealthy fool, William Sprague. Lincoln slyly traps Chase in some unethical transactions and forces him to resign from his position as secretary of the treasury, administering the *coup de grâce* to Chase's bid to become president when he appoints him to the Supreme Court.

The supporting cast includes politicians and generals who are either venal or inept and who serve as a foil to Lincoln's genius. Lincoln's achievement is also measured against the sorrows of his domestic life. He dotes on his wife, Mary, an aging Southern belle whose compulsive spending almost causes a major scandal and whose fits of insanity become progressively more prolonged and intense, particularly after the death of their son Willie. Lincoln himself is presented as a brooding giant, plagued by headaches, melancholy, and premonitions of his own death.

Vidal enlarges upon the meager historical evidence to interweave the story of David Herold, a spirited young man who works as a druggist's assistant in a shop near the White House. Herold's background and sympathies are with the South, but what propels him into espionage and into conspiracy to assassinate the President is not so much his dedication to the rebel cause as his longing to do something important. *Lincoln* is a meditation on ambition, its uses and perversions, and Herold, like Seward, Chase, and Lincoln himself, is one of its embodiments. He is a pointed analogue to John Hay, Lincoln's youthful secretary who was to go on to a very distinguished diplomatic career.

Vidal has been a flamboyant presence for three decades—erudite, witty, and abrasive in his novels, plays, and essays, and in his two bids for elective office. Not the least remarkable feature of *Lincoln* is the self-effacement of its idiosyncratic author. The novel is constructed around the crisp conversations of its major characters, and there is far more dialogue—dramatic and pungent—than narration. It gracefully assimilates reams of historical scholarship, particularly that of David Herbert Donald, into a text that, for all of its 659 pages, seems as plaintively brief as the life of its subject. Though some critics have faulted this book for a failure of imagination, for being impersonal transcription rather than fiction, it represents a remarkable feat of narrative organization and self-restraint. Still, and especially, when he creates explicit entertainments, such as *Myra Breckinridge* (1968), or retrospective nonfiction novels, such as the present one, Vidal is exercising the moral imagination.

In *The Executioner's Song* (1979), Norman Mailer, Vidal's persistent nemesis, performed a similar act of literary ventriloquism, extinguishing his own proud, distinctive voice for that of Gary Gilmore, a wretched psychopath. Mailer's accomplishment was to magnify the ordinary into the bizarre. Vidal's achievement, transforming the familiar (surely more has been written about Lincoln than any other American, and part of the pleasure in reading *Lincoln* is in experiencing how effectively Vidal manages to pull off such set pieces as the Gettysburg Address and the final visit to Ford's Theatre) into the enigmatic, is of lesser magnitude. Nevertheless, Vidal's novel is Shakespearean not simply in Lincoln's ultimately fatal fondness for theatergoing, his melancholy, or his mad queen. A bloody stage for conflicting ideals and aspirations, the Lincoln years, more than any other American era, recall the great English history plays. Vidal suggests that it was during the period 1861 to 1865 that the United States was created, and by Abraham Lincoln more than anyone else.

Close to the end, Lincoln confides to Seward, who has now become his very devoted servant: "I may once have wanted—even lusted—for power, but all that has been burned away. There is nothing left of me. But there is still the President." Lincoln is Henry IV being cauterized of personal appetite, even Gore Vidal abjuring the eccentricities of his own famous style. Lincoln transcends the egotistic preoccupation with power through the pursuit of an elusive quality that can only be, awkwardly, termed "greatness." The reader witnesses Lincoln's education not through clumsy soliloquies or authorial intrusions but through his conversations and actions and through the words and deeds of those surrounding him.

Of particular importance is the perspective of Lincoln's young acolyte John Hay, who is permitted the novel's final words. Hay's traumatic four years in the White House during the Lincoln Administration have been a coming-of-age for him, and *Lincoln* is to some extent his *Bildungsroman*. Hay's final assessment of his master's achievement and sacrifice is "that Lincoln, in some mysterious fashion, had willed his own murder as a form of atonement for the great and terrible thing that he had done by giving so bloody and absolute a rebirth to his nation."

Steven G. Kellman

Sources for Further Study

American Heritage. XXXV, August, 1984, p. 18.
Christian Science Monitor. LXXVI, July 25, 1984, p. 19.
Library Journal. CIX, June 1, 1984, p. 1146.
Los Angeles Times Book Review. June 24, 1984, p. 1.
The Nation. CCXXXVIII. June 16, 1984, p. 744.
The New Republic. CXCI, July 2, 1984, p. 32.
The New York Review of Books. XXXI, 12, July 19, 1984, p. 5.
The New York Times Book Review. LXXXIX, June 3, 1984, p. 1.
Newsweek. CIII, June 11, 1984, p. 74.
Publishers Weekly. CCXXV, May 4, 1984, p. 49.
Time. CXXIII, May 21, 1984, p. 87.
The Wall Street Journal. CCIII, June 27, 1984, p. 32.

LIVES OF THE POETS

Author: E. L. Doctorow (1931-   )
Publisher: Random House (New York). 145 pp. $14.95
Type of work: A novel in the form of a collection of short fictions
Time: Primarily 1955 to the 1980's
Locale: Primarily New York City

Six stories and a novella that explore the increasingly difficult and necessary process of making or imaginatively improvising lives as well as poems and stories in the contemporary age

> Principal characters:
> JONATHAN, the author of the six stories as well as the journal that forms Doctorow's novella
> JACK, his father, a Willy Loman figure whose death precipitates Jonathan's earliest fiction writing
> THE BLACK-BEARDED CAPTAIN, one of several fictional versions of members of Jonathan's family
> THE LEATHER MAN, the archetype of the estranged, migratory figure that appears throughout *Lives of the Poets*
> WILLI, one of Jonathan's several semiautobiographical narrators
> ANGEL, Jonathan's wife

Readers do not expect to find in a collection of short fictions—in this case, "six stories and a novella"—the same degree of narrative continuity one finds in a novel, but readers do expect some continuity: similar character types, settings, plots, at the very least "style." Consequently, what will especially disconcert readers of *Lives of the Poets* is the absence of any continuity whatsoever until partway through the closing work, at which point the reader slowly begins to realize that *Lives of the Poets* is not an author's more or less random gathering of short fictions and not even the kind of unified collection exemplified by James Joyce's *Dubliners*, Sherwood Anderson's *Winesburg, Ohio*, and John Cheever's *The Housebreaker of Shady Hill*. Rather, it is a disguised novel, E. L. Doctorow's most artfully ambiguous and most subtly crafted work to date, a brilliantly conceived and subtly unified meditation on the individual's search for self, on the increasingly difficult and necessary process of making lives, as well as poems and stories, in the contemporary age. *Lives of the Poets* is itself in process; its meaning unfolds not in any one of its parts but in the evolving relationship that exists in the writing and reading of those parts. Only in the title novella does the reader discover that the confused narrator, Jonathan, is (or, more ambiguously, appears to be) the author of the six preceding stories, which are autobiographical in a double sense. Not only do they derive from materials drawn from Jonathan's "real life," as that life is described in the novella, but also, and more important, they evidence, by their variety as much as their content, Jonathan's search for a distinctive authorial voice, the literary equivalent of the search for one's own self.

Jonathan appears directly only in the closing novella and the opening story. "The Writer in the Family" is Jonathan's backward glance at two related events: his father's death in 1955 and, shortly after, his metaphorical birth as a writer—the three letters he wrote at his aunt's request and in his father's voice. Written to protect Jonathan's ailing grandmother from the news of her son Jack's death, the letters soon raise old family hostilities, of which the writer was apparently unaware. The letters also "implicate" him in his father's life in two quite different ways. They enable the son to know his father imaginatively and in this way to understand more clearly both the man's failings and his dreams, especially his dream of a sailor's life on the free and open sea. The letter writing also forces Jonathan to become his father, to adopt Jack's voice, and that entails his losing his already tenuous hold on his own life, his own voice. Thus the irony of Doctorow's title: The family is at once the wellspring of the writer's art and the prison that limits his personal and artistic freedom. The relationship between art and life and between the writer and his world, the son and the father, remains problematic.

However disconcerting it may be for Doctorow's readers, it is entirely appropriate that in the next story Jonathan should in his quest for authenticity adopt a new narrative voice and a style so entirely different from the realism of "The Writer in the Family" that the reader may very well lose sight of the important connections between the two works. Also told in the first person, "The Water Works" is cast in the form of nineteenth century Gothicism, to which Jonathan-Doctorow adds a dash of Franz Kafka. The detective-narrator follows a mysterious "black-bearded captain" into the labyrinthine waterworks building, where, to their horror, they discover

> a small human body. . . pressed against the machinery of one of the sluicegates, its clothing caught as in some hinge, and the child, for it was a miniature like the [toy] ship in the reservoir, went slamming about, first one way and then the next, as if in mute protest, trembling and shaking and animating by its revulsion the death that had already overtaken it.

Instead of pursuing the captain, who carries the body off to the city, the narrator remains at the waterworks to ponder this new and more troubling mystery of human limitation, as imaged in the body of the drowned child struggling futilely against the sluicegates and against death, and to feel "the oppression of a universe of water"—the same water which in the previous story is associated with the father's dream of freedom.

The sense of human limitation becomes still more acute in "Willi," told by yet another first-person narrator whose distinctive style reflects his own particular and evolving sensibility. As the story begins, the thirteen-year-old Willi feels a transcendental oneness with his world; gradually, however, as the harmonious song of the universe modulates into "a woman's pulsating

song in the act of love," the Emersonian vision gives way to the sight of his
mother (a "headless corpse") and tutor copulating in the barn. "I was given
double vision, the kind that comes with a terrible blow." No longer a child
but not yet a man, Willi feels both betrayed and aroused. His mother's sin
becomes his guilt over his sexual fantasies. Fearing that he will be caught,
he goes to his father "for absolution," confessing not his own dreams but his
mother's adultery. His confession implicates him both in his father's brutal
revenge and in the eventual destruction of the godlike father who had lived
"in the pride of the self-constructed self." Willi's final words—"This was in
Galicia in the year 1910. All of it was to be destroyed anyway, even without
me"—suggest more than the narrator's weary indifference, for like Edgar
Allan Poe's "The Cask of Amontillado," Willi's story is less an account than
a confession told some fifty years after the fact by a narrator who continues
to struggle with his own obsessive guilt and apparent insignificance.

The same struggle of the human heart in conflict with itself (as William
Faulkner called it) reappears in the next two stories, which are narrated in
the bleakly objective, third-person style of contemporary "minimalist" writers such as Raymond Carver, Leonard Michaels, and Bette Pesetsky. "The
Hunter" is set in winter in a small, economically and emotionally depressed
town. The young schoolteacher, apparently an outsider, would save the children in her class (as well as herself) if she could, but what she and the
reader feel most intensely is not hope but instead the constricting power of
the wintry world inexorably closing in, as it did on Willi's father, narrowing
the possibilities, forcing the self to retreat into numb despair and slow
death. Wanting to stop time and to ward off the encroaching emptiness, she
hires a photographer to take the class picture. "Take it," she says in a fierce
whisper. "Take it as we are. We are looking at you. Take it." Morgan in
"The Foreign Legation" is equally fierce, equally desperate, now that his
wife has left him. "Homes," he contends, "were for people's lives to explode
in like those steel-mesh hutches used by police bomb-disposal squads." Like
Doctorow's other emotionally displaced persons, he is an observer, a voyeur,
biding his time, waiting for the carnage to begin. When a bomb explodes at
a nearby foreign legation—personal terror exploding into an act of political
terrorism—Morgan feels both pleasure and guilt, responsible yet helpless,
terrorist and victim.

A similar ambiguity characterizes "The Leather Man," a story in which
even the point of view is deceptive. The story appears to be a monologue
delivered by an unidentified speaker, perhaps an FBI or CIA expert in
surveillance and social control, to a group of people engaged in the same
kind of work. As it turns out, the monologue, or report, makes up nearly
the whole of the slightly larger story, narrated in the third person, which encloses it: a story within a story, a voice within a voice. In his report, the
speaker makes an effort to explain—actually to understand—the recent

increase in the number of estranged people, from bag ladies to exemplary husbands, suddenly turned Peeping Toms and to astronauts turned criminals. "They're nothing new," he declares, "you can read about the Leather Man, for instance, a hundred years ago making his circuit through Westchester, Connecticut, into the Berkshires in the summer. . . ." The speaker's desire to understand the phenomenon and not merely to control it distinguishes him from his kind and, as a result, estranges him. Like a cornered Leather Man, he seems engaged (as is Jonathan) in "the sincere struggle for words." It is appropriate then that in discussing the Leather Man phenomenon, he should recall a girl he had observed at Woodstock, whose strange pantomine, when photographed, diagrammed, and analyzed, proved to be about "someone in a straitjacket, it was the classic terror enacted of someone straitjacketed and trying to break free."

The young woman's pantomine, her desperate art, aptly sums up the struggles of all the characters in *Lives of the Poets*, especially Jonathan. If "The Writer in the Family" is a portrait of the writer as a young man, then the title novella is a portrait of the artist as a leather man, a frayed, uncertain creature beset by all the various medical, marital, and professional problems that comprise the human condition in its most contemporary manifestation: a tragicomic Everyman whose salvation lies not in finding his elusive self but in stubbornly continuing to search it out, to inquire into its nature, which is, of course, his being. It is Jonathan's wife Angel's "primeval urge to siamate, to speak with my voice, to think my thoughts, to use my gestures, to mingle our souls" that has caused him to flee alone to a writer's garret in New York's Greenwich Village, where "whatever can be tried to stem disaster is tried here." Like his own characters—Willi, Morgan, and the others—Jonathan is troubled by feelings of guilt and doubt: "Between the artist and simple dereliction there is a very thin line. I know that." This knowledge results in emotional and professional paralysis, ambivalence. Wanting both stability and freedom, he finds that he can neither make nor break commitments; he is, to use his own apt phrase, one "of the neither married nor divorced but no longer entirely together." His life as a writer is in even worse shape. He attends a showy publication party in order to "remember what it is we do" only to discover that the guests include Boy George. There, another writer, more brilliant than Jonathan but less financially successful, asks him, "Is there a writer here who really believes in what he's doing? Does any one of us have a true conviction for what he's writing? Do I? Do you?" Jonathan's answer, which is imagined but not spoken, is indicative of both the extent of his paralysis and of the depth of his need: "Oh Leo, I wanted to say, each book has taken me further and further out so that the occasion itself is extenuated, no more than a weak distant signal from the home station, and even that may be fading." In a world of ceaseless migrations (a favorite metaphor in this book), the home signal must inevitably fade and the individual must forlornly ask himself, "What has happened to my life?"

Doctorow has, however, always been interested less in despair than in the transformational possibilities of the human spirit, in its struggles and migrations rather than in its defeats. "Poor Father," Doctorow writes in *Ragtime* (1975) of a character who went down with the *Lusitania* in 1915. "I see his final exploration. He arrives at the new place, his hair rises in astonishment, his mouth and eyes dumb. His toe scuffs a soft storm of sand, he kneels and his arms spread in pantomimic celebration, the immigrant, as in every moment of his life, arriving eternally on the shore of his Self." Jonathan undergoes a similar transformation at the end of the novella, "Lives of the Poets." Having fled from his own family, he now finds himself distracted and displaced by a family of Latin American refugees for whom he has turned his writer's apartment into an illegal hideaway. Stranger still, having come to think of writing as a dread task that he must complete each day, he finds himself sitting at his typewriter, in his lap a Salvadoran child for whom writing is play. "Hey, who's writing this?" he asks in words that the child has typed: a question that the reader has probably been asking himself for the past hundred pages or so. Is Jonathan worried or pleased by this new turn of events? Does he feel his voice becoming nothing more than "a weak distant signal" or is it growing younger, stronger, and more resonant as it merges with the voice of the child? Both, one suspects, with the emphasis decidedly on the latter, for what the plurals in Doctorow's title and the Whitmanesque omission of any punctuation following the last sentence strongly suggest is that the lives of poets, which are the lives of all men, are, like the forms of fiction, not static and closed but various and open-ended, not complete but in process—a process made up of a bewildering but nevertheless redemptive succession of migrations and transformations that will last until, as Jonathan well understands, death makes *a* story of all men.

Robert A. Morace

Sources for Further Study

Book World. XIV, November 11, 1984, p. 3.
Library Journal. CIX, November 15, 1984, p. 2161.
Los Angeles Times Book Review. November 25, 1984, p. 1.
The Nation. CCXXXIX, November 17, 1984, p. 515.
The New Republic. CXCI, December 3, 1984, p. 31.
The New York Review of Books. XXXI, December 6, 1984, p. 33.
The New York Times Book Review. LXXXIX, November 11, 1984, p. 1.
Newsweek. CIV, November 19, 1984, p. 107.
Publishers Weekly. CCXXVI, September 28, 1984, p. 99.
Time. CXXIV, December 24, 1984, p. 69.

THE LOST FLYING BOAT

Author: Alan Sillitoe (1928-   )
Publisher: Little, Brown and Company (Boston). 287 pp. $15.95
Type of work: Novel
Time: Several years after the end of World War II
Locale: South Africa, the Kerguelen Islands, and the Indian Ocean

An adventure story of a postwar quest for Nazi gold by a group of former Royal Air Force fliers in a Sunderland flying boat which becomes as well a vehicle for complex moral and metaphysical exploration

> Principal characters:
> CAPTAIN BENNETT, the pilot of the *Aldebaran*
> ROSE, the navigator and chief mate
> WILCOX, the flight engineer
> NASH, the chief gunner
> BULL,
> ARMATAGE, and
> APPLEYARD, the gunners
> ADCOCK, the radio operator and narrator

The Lost Flying Boat is the latest novel in Alan Sillitoe's continuing literary search for some sort of moral and metaphysical order in the chaos of postwar (World War II) existence—a search which began less in his celebrated first novel, *Saturday Night and Sunday Morning* (1958), than in its immediate successors, *The General* (1960) and *Key to the Door* (1961). Like *The General*, *The Lost Flying Boat* is a philosophical thriller to an almost parabolic nature, and, like *Key to the Door*, it draws on Sillitoe's experience as a radio operator in the Royal Air Force (1946-1949) to create a central character who has "been trained to create order from a multiplicity of signals" but who finds it immensely difficult to solve the confusion in himself.

The novel's dust jacket compares it to B. Traven's *Treasure of the Sierra Madre* (1935), and certainly it is the story of an "odyssey. . . in which men become desperate and dangerous . . . from which few will return," but it has even more striking connections with other mythic journeys, such as those of Odysseus and Jason and most especially with Ishmael's metaphysical whaling voyage in Herman Melville's *Moby Dick* (1851). Like Ishmael, the narrator of Sillitoe's novel, Adcock, has signed on for a dangerous sea voyage "when life on land looked too bleak for comfort." His marriage has broken up in great part because he could not abide an earthbound life which did not offer him any possibility of answers to the substantial questions concerning life and death:

> Instead of being a shop assistant, I preferred listening to the traffic of the spheres. . . . My spirit wanted to reach space where noises multiplied, in the hope that they would provide me with an answer as to why I was alive. I would stave off death by listening for the last message from ship or aircraft, or even while sending one of my own, and forget that I did not know what life was all about.

His spiritual lassitude is appropriate to that of the rest of the crew of the flying boat *Aldebaran*, all of them flattened and drained of meaning by life in Great Britain after a war that did not end in genuine peace and which saw the departure of the captains and the kings and, with them, the larger worldview of the British public. (Or, as Nash, the chief gunner, puts it, "There's eff-all in Blighty, these days.") Yet where they find solace in alcohol or gambling or simply in action, Adcock seeks his solace and his answers in alphabets and anagrams, in codes and signs; like a medieval Cabalist, he seeks to interpret everything he sees and hears. "Of all the things dead and living," he says, "only God has no name, but the newly discovered is immediately delineated on becoming known." Throughout the novel, he seeks God through the names of known things, only to give in finally to bare action and impulse, stripped of language, of thought, and of easily interpretable meaning.

In Malaya, Adcock and his fellow military operators called anyone sending Morse whom they could not identify as OOJERKERPIV, a nonsense word of their invention signifying unknown, as though by naming the unknown, even nonsensically, they had somehow solved its mystery. Nevertheless, the unknowns in the great journey in the novel remain, like God, unnamed and unnameable.

Adcock does try to read signs and portents before the voyage begins. Captain Bennett smokes Partagas cigars, and Adcock notices that the word spelled backwards is SAGA TRAP. He starts to mention his discovery, but, as with most of his later discoveries, he keeps it to himself. He labels the crew "Alpha Rats" after Alpheratz, a star in the constellation Pegasus, an appropriate name for the crew of a great flying craft (for, after all, Pegasus was a great flying horse) and also for a crew blindly risking their lives like rats aboard a sinking ship. He listens intently to the messages and fragments of messages on his radio, interpreting them as best he can. The inner voice, however, does not speak to him and interpret the events he witnesses until twenty-five years later, when he tells the tale. Like Ishmael, he participates in great events and alone survives to report and interpret them. Yet even in his rendering and reading of the events, the unknown, the OOJERKER-PIV, remains at the vital center.

Bennett, the Captain Ahab of this novel, is driven by an obsessive desire for freedom, a freedom he cannot find at home in Great Britain nor even in the freedom of flight (for what goes up must come down). He despises the loss of spirit and enterprise in the postwar world and yearns to be free of all political and social restraints:

> The twentieth century has been poisoned by two bestial systems that have tainted everyone whether they embraced them or fought against them. For myself, I want to push this expedition through so that I can be independent of all systems. To become rich is the only defence against being without hope.

Bennett knows the location of a large cache of buried Nazi gold in the French Kerguelen Islands near Antarctica. He gathers his wartime flying crew with one exception (the radio operator, who is replaced by Adcock), finds a financial backer, and outfits a war surplus Sunderland flying boat to fly to the islands, unearth the gold, and fly it on to Perth, Australia. They will be refueled by a ship, the *Difda*, which is scheduled to meet them at the islands. The elaborate plan and the flying boat are necessitated by the discovery of the gold's location by another group, an unknown group who will be looking for another ship and not a plane. Bennett's crew are drawn into the plan by their own greed but even more by their faith in Bennett and by their need, too, to be free of the malaise of "Blighty" and the modern world. Like Ahab, Bennett is remarkably competent and has the power to bind others to him and to his obsessive dream.

Even Adcock, the outsider and newcomer to the crew, is drawn in by Bennett and converted to the cause. The reasons for his conversion are complex, but they revolve around both his alienation from ordinary life, his sense of honor and loyalty to a cause to which he has pledged himself, and his own need to identify and decode his own nature. He believes that the captain can depend on him not so much from loyalty as from his own strong urge to get into the unknown, his "acceptance being composed of pride, tradition, greed, honour and a desire to explore my nature to the utmost." As the journey progresses, Adcock feels himself splitting, as though two selves were contending within him, as though he were whirling about himself like a double star, like Aldebaran its double self. He acts and watches himself act; he doubts those around him and himself; he feels guilt but continues to act wrongfully. His journey into his own nature does not lead him to a calm insular Tahiti as Ishmael's did but rather to the crashing seas of conflicting thought and motive; when he finally does act beyond that confusion, the only wholeness he finds is that of loss—the lost flying boat and all that it contained and meant.

The whale of Sillitoe's novel is the *Aldebaran* itself: a Short Sunderland flying boat, a four-engined behemoth, eighty-five feet long, thirty-two feet high, weighing 50,100 pounds loaded, arguably the finest (and certainly one of the finest) military aircraft of the war. It comes to mean many things to the members of its crew: To Bennett, it is both the pathway to freedom and freedom itself; to Rose, the war-scarred navigator and star reader, it is proof of human free will and also an awesome absence of walls and limits; to Adcock, it seems like a cathedral, a human construct of great beauty, one of man's "most graceful endeavours, a spiritual extension with a practical purpose." To lose it, then, would be to lose the emblem of freedom and choice, of the human capacity for beauty and the idea of a union of spirituality and practicality. "No great and enduring volume," Melville said, "can ever be written on the flea," and the *Aldebaran* is certainly no flea.

Adcock's metaphoric identification of the flying boat with a cathedral is certainly appropriate to the metaphysical quality of all of his musings. Adcock and Rose help the captain steer the *Aldebaran* by sounds and by the stars, but all three of them are also concerned with God's presence (or absence). The captain believes that God is with those who seek to be free of anyone but Him, but Adcock knows that freedom is always at the expense of somebody else. When Rose gives in to despair and decides that God is no longer with them, Adcock wonders how long it has been since God has been with anyone, but then he adds that "you had to be with Him, not Him with you." As Adcock sends out his radio dots and dashes to vanish in the void, he compares them with thoughts, also fading into the vastness of space unless they are noted by God and ricocheted back into the heart as God's explanation for that person's life. The quest for gold and the quest for God are inextricably involved in the flying boat's journey as Sillitoe probes the essence of human experience with his cryptographer's eye and ear. The complex irony of his discoveries is expressed at its clearest and simplest in the concluding stanza of a ballad that the crew compose and sing:

> God will help us, God will help us,
> God will help us, don't you know?
> For we're lost and gone forever
> To the land of ice and snow. . . .

The flying boat's journey to the land of ice and snow is as ill-fated and as symbolically rich as the journey to the mythic South in another of this novel's great predecessors, Edgar Allan Poe's *The Narrative of Arthur Gordon Pym* (1838). The journey to the Kerguelen Islands takes the plane and its crew deep into a barren wasteland where even in the Antarctic summer of January the land itself is dangerous and cruel. As in Poe's novel, it is an alien land where rationality and even moral thought cease to function, a place of savage birds and an unfamiliar sky (one in which neither Alpheratz nor Aldebaran ever appears). Poe's Pym must depend on the primitive strength of Dirk Peters to survive; Sillitoe's Adcock must finally depend on his own instinctive behavior beyond thought in order to save himself.

In the terrible land where the crew are decimated by accident and harsh choice, the flying boat is tracked by an unknown armed force also seeking the gold. They are also stalked by their own fears and suspicions, and they betray one another and themselves. The quest becomes a moral nightmare as double cross and freedom entangle themselves beyond definition. The journey into the self arrives at a moral quagmire in which all choices are suspect and inner and outer confusion becomes perfectly matched. Adcock himself, conscience stricken at his own infractions of the code of the radio operator, cannot resist the need of the radio man to send as well as receive. Brian Seaton, in *Key to the Door*, rebelliously taps out the whole of "Kubla

Khan" on his radio in Malaya, and in this novel Adcock sends out a love poem to his lost wife after the initial break in discipline of sending a single letter (one dot, an E), and then a HAPPY BIRTHDAY to anyone who might be listening, only to sink under the weight of his guilt as the wrong people, the unknown enemy, do hear.

As the quest collapses into chaos after the captain's decision to run for Ceylon (another double cross) rather than Perth, Adcock moves irrevocably away from listening and interpreting into instinctive action, "as if the ultimate word came back and told me what to do, taking thought out of responsibility and leaving me only with action." The flying boat and the dream are both lost, casting Adcock, the sole survivor, adrift on a heavy sea and in a sea of confused dreams, knowing that communication, the purpose of his life, has gotten him nowhere and to nowhere.

He is rescued, and some twenty-five years later he comes to some understanding of his story and himself. He tells that story to the reader, omitting the years after the journey, knowing that in some real sense he went down with the lost flying boat. The ultimate mystery remains, the OOJERKERPIV, its only possible interpretation the very act of attempting to solve it, the telling of the tale.

The Lost Flying Boat may not be the massive work that *Moby Dick* is, but it is a more than worthy addition to that long line of books which tells of the great journey into the mythic South of the self. Alan Sillitoe's risks are real ones; his losses and gains are real as well. He has built his book with all of the practical purpose and meaningful beauty of a cathedral or a great flying boat.

R. H. W. Dillard

Sources for Further Study

Best Sellers. XLIV, November, 1984, p. 290.
Kirkus Reviews. LII, July 1, 1984, p. 598.
Library Journal. CIX, September 15, 1984, p. 1774.
Listener. CX, December 15, 1983, p. 30.
London Review of Books. V, November 17, 1983, p. 12.
The New York Times Book Review. LXXXIX, October 14, 1984, p. 26.
The Observer. November 6, 1983, p. 31.

LOVE MEDICINE

Author: Louise Erdrich (1955-   )
Publisher: Holt, Rinehart and Winston (New York). 275 pp. $13.95
Type of work: Novel
Time: 1934-1984
Locale: A North Dakota Indian reservation and nearby towns

Stories from several narrators weave a remarkable novel exploring the ties of blood, knowledge, love, and mystery that link the people of a Chippewa family

Principal characters:
> NECTOR KASHPAW, the grandfather, a former tribal chairman
> MARIE LAZARRE KASHPAW, Nector's wife, who once wanted to be a nun
> LULU LAMARTINE, a loving woman who has eight sons by Kashpaw, Nanapush, and other men
> GERRY NANAPUSH, Lulu's son, a hero of the American Indian Movement
> ALBERTINE JOHNSON, a nursing student and member of the youngest generation
> JUNE MORRISSEY KASHPAW, a troubled woman
> LIPSHA MORRISSEY, June's unacknowledged son

Winner of the National Book Critics Circle Award for Fiction for 1984, *Love Medicine* is a truly impressive first novel. Author Louise Erdrich is a member of the Turtle Mountain band of Chippewa, was one of the first women students admitted to Dartmouth in 1972, and has published a collection of poetry. In *Love Medicine*, she not only opens up a new territory of contemporary Native American life and demonstrates a compassionate yet uncompromising attitude toward its people but also crafts a fascinating piece of fiction whose technique amplifies its theme.

Love Medicine is a series of stories. Many of them are quite independent; they have been published in *Atlantic Monthly*, *Kenyon Review*, *Ms.*, *North American Review*, and in various prize-story collections. As independent stories, they have many virtues. One is the creation of language that reflects the age, education, attitude, and experience of each narrator. The images, phrasing, and vocabulary of the urbanized characters such as Beverly Lamartine differ from the language of those whose lives still center on the reservation; the expressions used by some people in the older generation (particularly Marie Lazarre) subtly suggest translation from thoughts that come in another language. Even in the youngest generation, Albertine Johnson, who has left the reservation to go to college, uses words quite differently from her cousin Lipsha, who has stayed behind.

As independent stories, also, each has a sharp focus, a clear narrative line reaching some resolution, and images that expose the event without intervening explanation. Nevertheless, impressive as the stories are, the novel created by weaving them together is stronger than any of its parts. The first story takes place in 1981, the second in 1934—and midway in the second story, the reader begins to understand that the young girl Marie Lazarre, who tells about fighting devils in the convent, is the same person as Grandma Kashpaw, who was fetched from the senior citizens home in the first story. As one tale follows another in a sequence that skips back and forth through the years, the reader has the pleasure of fitting together the jigsaw puzzle, teasing out the identities hidden in the various names that result from marriages, unwed parenthood, and children fostered by neighbors or relatives, and realizing, with sudden delight, that one is getting a second viewpoint on an incident already known from an earlier story. The layers of understanding created by the linked-story technique ensure that many readers will finish the last page, turn the book over, and start once more from the beginning in order to read each story with the added insight that grows from enlarged knowledge.

More significantly, in doing the work to trace relationships, keep track of the characters, and understand how they are tied together, the reader becomes a part of the linking and weaving that is the novel's theme. The pleasure of solving puzzles is subordinate to this revelation of the bonds of love and mystery and anger, the desires and strengths and weaknesses that keep these people together, even though some are reservation bound, others thoroughly urbanized, and a few only fractionally Chippewa.

The physical center of the stories is a piece of land originally allotted to Nector Kashpaw's mother, Rushes Bear. Most of her children were assigned to parcels in Montana, but she managed to get a piece of North Dakota wheatland and live on it with her young twins, Nector and Eli. Nector went to boarding school, learned white reading and writing, and grew up to be tribal chairman and a man of importance; Eli, hidden by his mother in a root cellar, lived in the woods and kept some of the old skills. These two men, who became adults in the 1930's, represent the oldest generation in the novel; the women with whom their lives become entangled include Marie Lazarre and Lulu Lamartine. Marie goes into a convent intending to become a saint; after marrying Nector, she compulsively takes in unwanted children. Lulu, with what seems equal compulsion, makes her own babies— eight boys, each by a different father, who grow up supporting, fighting, and caring for one another. Both Marie and Lulu know how to use power; Marie pushes Nector into becoming tribal chairman, and Lulu, in a truly wonderful scene, forces the council not to sell her land by threatening to reveal publicly—right then in the meeting—who fathered each of her children. Both remain vivid into their old age, strong and salty women using very different tactics to win what they desire.

The middle generation is not quite so compelling—perhaps its members are seen less clearly (none is actually a narrator for any extended story) or perhaps they are the generation that suffers most from the dislocation between reservation ways and the modern world. June Morrissey dies in the first story, virtually whoring for her busfare back to the reservation. Her discarded husband, Gordon Kashpaw, is the viewpoint character (though not the narrator) of the story "Crown of Thorns," which is a careful, vivid, underplayed, and thoroughly convincing portrait of delirium tremens. Lulu Lamartine's son Gerry Nanapush spends half his adult life in prison after a three-year sentence for assault (he keeps escaping and being recaptured and doing additional time for escape) before he makes the mistake of hiding out on the Pine Ridge Reservation, where he inevitably kills a state trooper.

Albertine Johnson and Lipsha Morrissey, from the youngest generation, are, to a certain extent, consciously searching for their roots and for a way to understand their ties to the past. Most of their generation have disappeared to Minneapolis or Chicago or somewhere even farther beyond the pull of the house and land that form the gravitational center of the Kashpaw constellation. Both Lipsha and Albertine are still in the process of becoming. Albertine, in particular, can change quite dramatically from one story to the next, but despite her relatively small share of Chippewa genes and her sustained drive for education—she is studying medicine by the end of the book—she knows her own need for the bonds of blood and tradition. She tries to talk to her grandfather about tribal politics and how he got things done in the old days. Lipsha, who seems virtually impervious to any kind of teaching (he manages to mangle and misunderstand both the traditional skills he learns from Eli Kashpaw and the education he suffers in white schools), is a wonderfully naïve narrator in the Huck Finn tradition. At the end of the book, however, he turns to home instead of lighting out for an individual destiny.

Because the stories are presented through their narrators, with no outside viewpoint to provide explanations, the evocation of Native American life is clean and subtle, without pandering to the picturesque or the sentimental. Here again, the book's structure is used to alter the reader's consciousness from within. For example, although June Morrissey Kashpaw dies in the first tale, her character is one of the threads that provides links among the people and the stories—various characters talk about her; there are questions about her own parentage and about the husband she left and the baby she never acknowledged; Gordon takes to drink after her death; Albertine's mother and aunt tell their version of an incident from June's childhood. In other words, Erdrich, beginning the novel within the literary conventions of a white cultural tradition, demonstrates that a person who is dead can remain an important presence for the living. From that point, it is only half a step to the other stories, the ones in which a dead person's spirit actually appears.

Even though traditional ways are not glamorized, there is a sense of loss as they diminish. The family pattern that gives a woman a considerable amount of choice about who will father her children and how long her liaison with any particular man will last has a joyous (if semicomic) treatment in the case of Lulu Lamartine. In the next generation, however, June Morrissey seems more of a slut than an Earth Mother. The army, which in traditional sentiment and in the eyes of reservation boys, is a heroic experience that brings the Indian into his own, has a devastating effect on the Vietnam generation. Significantly, American Indian Movement hero Gerry Nanapush gives Lipsha Morrissey the gift of a blood tie that will free him from his decision to join the military.

The sense of place is also strong, though the setting is seldom described. The Kashpaw land is nearly off the edge of the map, in that part of North Dakota where the nearest city (the place to which Lipsha hitchhikes when he has an irresistible urge to play Space Invaders) is Winnipeg. The setting, like the story, reflects a jumble of old and new; the bare box cabins and the modern "Senior Citizens"; the Kashpaw house that no one really owns, but where everyone gathers.

There is a considerable amount of humor in the book. Some of it is raucous slapstick (the rest of the American public is slowly realizing that the wooden-faced Indian is a myth as well as a stereotype). More impressive are the flashes of wit that crystallize bits of Native American viewpoint. Eli sings "hunting songs used to attract deer or women." Marie Lazarre says that as a girl she had "the mail-order Catholic soul you get in a girl raised out in the bush, whose only thought is getting into town." Lipsha Morrissey discovers that Grandpa Kashpaw always shouts in church because God will not hear him otherwise:

> I sweat. I broke right into a little cold sweat at my hairline because I knew this was perfectly right and for years not one damn other person had noticed it. God's been going deaf. Since the Old Testament, God's been deafening up on us. I read, see. Besides the dictionary, which I'm constantly in use of, I had this Bible once. I read it. I found there was discrepancies between then and now. It struck me. Here God used to raineth bread from clouds, smite the Phillipines [sic], sling fire down on red-light districts where people got stabbed. He even appeared in person every once in a while. God used to pay attention, is what I'm saying.

The Chippewa gods, Lipsha continues, would still do favors if one knew the right way to ask—but the problem is that "to ask proper was an art that was lost to the Chippewa once the Catholics gained ground. Even now, I have to wonder if Higher Power turned it back, if we got to yell, or if we just don't speak its language."

The Chippewa viewpoint here, as elsewhere, sees many disadvantages of white ways; the Chippewa also (like humans almost everywhere) crave the material goods that seem to rain on hardworking white Americans. The only character who really romanticizes the Indian past is Lynette Kashpaw, the wholly white wife of one of the younger men. After several generations of interracial marriage and sexual encounter, blood in the strictest sense is not very important. To be Indian is, to a certain extent, a state of mind. The urbanized Cree Beverly Lamartine had parents who "always called themselves French or Black Irish and considered those who thought of themselves as Indians quite backward." Albertine, however, though she describes herself as "light, clearly a breed," always thinks of herself as Indian. "I raised her an Indian," says her mother, "and that's what she is."

Love Medicine helps to decode that mystery along with the others. Like Lipsha Morrissey's meditation on God, the book begins in high humor and grows steadily more somber and serious. It introduces a new voice and a new fictional territory; both are extraordinarily impressive. Despite aspects of sadness and bitter pain in the situation and despite the pettiness and brutality of some of the characters, Louise Erdrich has created a world of life, survival, love, and great power.

Sally H. Mitchell

Sources for Further Study

Booklist. LXXXI, September 1, 1984, p. 24.
Christian Science Monitor. LXXVI, November 27, 1984, p. 33.
Glamour. LXXXII, December, 1984, p. 190.
Los Angeles Times. December 20, 1984, V, p. 34.
The New York Times. December 20, 1984, p. 25.
The New York Times Book Review. LXXXIX, December 23, 1984, p. 6.
The New Yorker. LX, January 7, 1985, p. 76.
Newsweek. CV, February 11, 1985, p. 70.
Publishers Weekly. CCXXVI, August 10, 1984, p. 73.
Saturday Review. X, November, 1984, p. 83.
Washington Post. November 14, 1984, p. D2.

MACHINE DREAMS

Author: Jayne Anne Phillips (1952-   )
Publisher: E. P. Dutton (New York). 331 pp. $16.95
Type of work: Novel
Time: The 1940's through the 1970's
Locale: A small town in West Virginia

The experiences, told from several points of view, of an American middle-class family from the Great Depression and World War II through the Vietnam War and the civil rights movement

> *Principal characters:*
> JEAN, the daughter of a spouse-abusing father who marries a potentially violent man but finally breaks away
> MITCH, Jean's husband, an initially gentle man altered by his World War II experiences and his growing sense of rootlessness
> DANNER, Jean and Mitch's sensitive daughter
> BILLY, Jean and Mitch's son
> BESS, Mitch's aunt
> CLAYTON, Mitch's uncle
> KATIE, Bess and Clayton's sickly daughter
> GLADYS, Jean's tough-minded, independent aunt

Jayne Anne Phillips' *Machine Dreams* follows her highly successful and critically acclaimed collection of short stories *Black Tickets* (1979). The novel, for all its occasional beauty, seems to be an example of a major talent gone wrong in satisfaction of what the late Katherine Anne Porter called "a perfectly artificial demand . . . to do the conventional thing"—produce a novel. Porter expressed her warning of the "trap lying just ahead" of "every short story writer of any gifts at all" in her 1941 introduction to Eudora Welty's first collection of stories, *A Curtain of Green* (1941). From great success in the short story, which Porter recognized as "a special and difficult medium," Jayne Anne Phillips has done the "conventional thing," and the resulting novel is an essentially conventional achievement. *Machine Dreams* is neither remarkable for its story nor memorable for its characters. Such a seemingly important figure as Dr. Reb, for example, a friend of all the principal characters, never assumes real importance, though Phillips inexplicably reveals much about his early love life and hints even more about his unsatisfactory marriage. Other characters, the sickly Katie, for example, take on real importance early in the book and then drop out of sight until much later, when they reappear in altered circumstances as almost incidental characters.

Phillips has divided *Machine Dreams* into seventeen sections varying in length from better than thirty pages to a single page. A few sections are written in the first person, and all focus upon the experience of an individual character. The table of contents identifies the focus of each section. The book achieves apparent structural unity through recurrence of titles and content. Two chapters, for example, focus on Jean and are titled "Reminiscence to a Daughter: Jean." Section 3 provides the letters Mitch wrote during World War II (1942-1945), and section 15 provides his son Billy's war letters (1970). Two chapters are entitled "Machine Dreams," and one "Machine Dream," and each focuses on a different character: Mitch (1946), his son, Billy (1957), and his daughter, Danner, in the book's final, undated, page-long section.

Jean's "Reminiscence to a Daughter," with which the book opens, and Mitch's first-person narrative "The Secret Country: Mitch," both undated, provide the retrospective structure to be filled in by subsequent chapters, for both sections are written in knowledge of what is to follow. "Reminiscence to a Daughter: Jean, 1962" looks more narrowly at the events leading to Jean's decision to divorce Mitch.

Repetition of section titles, of war letters, and of characters' individual machine dreams suggests recurrence of basic experience despite the external differences between the 1940's and the 1970's. Jean, the daughter of an older man married to a younger wife, attaches herself increasingly closely to her mother, particularly when her father, a failure in business, takes to alcohol and becomes a physical threat to her mother. Later, when her mother lies dying of cancer, Jean also marries an older man, and the cycle repeats itself. The initially gentle Mitch is obliged to sell his concrete business and become a salesman, while Jean, who has earned her college degree, provides more of the family's support than he and eventually divorces him before his pent-up anger turns against her.

The first nine sections of *Machine Dreams* suggest that Jean is to be the book's central consciousness, for her voice is heard in two first-person reminiscences to a daughter, and a third section (written in the third person) focuses on her ("Anniversary Song: Jean, 1948"). The focus of the remaining eight chapters, however, clearly shifts to Jean and Mitch's daughter, Danner, though her brother, Billy, is also prominent: His death in Vietnam, or rather its effect on his family, climaxes the book. The last eight chapters are divided between Billy (three chapters) and Danner (five chapters). The shift to Danner's perspective fulfills Jean's final statement in the opening chapter, where she writes, "Still, you and I will go on." In recalling the difficulties of Danner's birth, Jean writes that at first she thought she had a boy, for "no girl would cause such trouble." She concludes the section with her thankfulness that she had a daughter—"like my own mother had come back to me."

Machine Dreams, like many another novel, chronicles a family and suggests that each generation somehow perpetuates the legacy which it receives from the previous generation. Mitch, abandoned by his mother and rejected by his father, is unflaggingly loyal to his aunt Bess and her husband, the almost-alcoholic Clayton. Mitch lavishes on Bess and Clayton's sickly daughter the affection he can never give his own children. After Clayton's death, resulting from a stroke witnessed by Billy, Mitch must sell the concrete business he and Clayton had run. Loss of his own business begins Mitch's decline. Jean, who shared with her mother the shame of her father's deterioration and fear of his violence, marries Mitch during her mother's final illness. She nurses her grief for her mother, and, increasingly, she sees her father's failings in her husband. Nevertheless, she waits until she is able to support her almost-grown children before breaking away from Mitch and his incipient violence.

Jean and Mitch's children grow up in a tense household, but Danner responds to her parents' conflict more intensely than does Billy. From the start, Billy is fascinated by machines—his father's concrete trucks, airplanes, and trains. Phillips suggests that machines dominate the male's life in twentieth century America, for Billy, faced with the likelihood of military service in the Vietnam War, places his trust in machines—he hopes to get into planes and thus into the air where he can spot and avoid danger. Billy refuses Danner's offer of money she has borrowed to allow him to escape the draft. The year is 1969, and the lottery has recently been initiated; Billy has decided to "go with the numbers," for, as he reasons, "bad things can happen anywhere." He dies in Vietnam on a helicopter mission.

One of the most effective images in *Machine Dreams* is the lottery machine as Billy imagines its tumbling balls with his and other men's dates of birth written on them—"hundreds of days of white balls tumbling in a black sphere, silent and very slow, moving as though in accordance with physical laws. A galaxy of identical white planets." Billy's evocation continues with his imagining the universe stopping and a hand drawing out one of the balls; then the imagery shifts from planetary to biological: color slides of "microorganisms, bacteria, swimming shapes." Billy's "crazy dream," as he calls it, is like an earlier dream of looking into the turning cylinder of the concrete mixer and seeing his uncle Clayton spinning inside it. Later the same day, Clayton suffered his fatal stroke. The link between these dreams serves to foreshadow Billy's death.

The next to last chapter of *Machine Dreams* dramatizes, from Danner's point of view, her family's anguish while trying to learn whether Billy is dead or missing in action, as was first reported. This chapter recapitulates some of the earlier action and Danner's perceptions, but it concentrates on Danner's relationship with her brother, the facts of his induction into the military, and his death; it also details the slow process of Danner's coming to terms with the fact of Billy's death.

Two of the final sections of *Machine Dreams* demonstrate Mitch's inability to understand, much less deal with, the changing realities of his children's lives. In "November and December: Billy, 1969," Billy tells his father, now living with Aunt Bess, that Danner has been arrested on a drug charge in

Florida. At first, Mitch cannot comprehend: "Possession of what? What are you talking about?" When Billy tries to cheer him, telling him that the charge will be a light one, Mitch bursts out again: "Grams? What the hell do you mean? What do you know about grams?" Throughout, he tries to blame his former wife. "I hope your mother is satisfied now." And later, "This would never have happened." At length, scowling, he demands Danner's telephone number. "I want to talk to Danner," he says. Poor Mitch continues to think masculine bluster the answer to his children's needs and believes, pathetically, that he can make a difference in their lives.

Similarly, Danner confronts her father with the suggestion that Billy resist the draft and go to Canada. All Mitch can think of is that if Billy flees, he will never be able to "come back here." "Well, *hell yes* it matters," he says when Danner asks if it matters where Billy lives. He tells her that in Billy's place, he would go to war, and he reminds Danner that "lots of boys went to Korea. Lots of boys from around here." Mitch is reduced to senseless profanity; all he can say is "Godammit to hell." Phillips, with economy, dramatizes the two issues most divisive of families and generations in the 1960's and 1970's: drugs and war.

Early in the book, Mitch is a sympathetic character. He recalls for years his regret for punishing Katie by switching her. He tells of visiting the deserted family farm a final time before going into the army, and he worries about his aunt Bess and her husband. "Machine Dreams: Mitch, 1946," narrated in the third person, combines an account of his war experiences with his love and concern for the chronically ill Katie. He suffers from a terrible dream about the war, but he also suffers from an equally terrible dream in which he has unwittingly been responsible for Katie's death. Phillips underlines the cyclical nature of her story when Mitch dreams of dancing with Katie against the backdrop of the Gulf of Papua, and then, suddenly, Katie becomes Jean dancing with him, and he wakes to the reality of his marriage and the news that Jean is pregnant a second time.

After section 6 ("Coral Sea: Mitch, 1950"), Mitch becomes a character in other people's lives; his thoughts and feelings are never again reported. Katie also drops out of prominence and appears again only toward the end of the book as she is perceived by Danner. Katie is linked subtly with Danner, for the flying horse (the Mobilgas emblem), which was important to Katie when Mitch used to take her for drives, recurs as an element in Danner's "Machine Dream," with which the book ends.

In Danner's one-paragraph "Machine Dream," she and Billy walk in the forest, he making airplane sounds and she "stalking the magic horse." Billy has followed Danner into the forest "almost accidentally." She loses sight of him but can hear him behind her, "imitating with a careful and private energy the engine sounds of a plane that is going down." The book ends with "war-movie sounds":

Eeee-yoww, ach-ack-ack. So gentle it sounds like a song, and the song goes on softly as the plane falls, year after year, to earth.

The book's poetic ending links the Mobilgas flying horse (so important to Katie) to the magic horse, the mare with large and certain eyes, which Danner stalks. Those images take the reader back to the book's opening page of epigraphs, a series of quotations dealing with flying and with the flying horse Pegasus. The second of the epigraphs, taken from *Pegasus: The Art of the Legend* by Nikolas Yalouris, tells that the Greeks "believed that their heroic dead appeared before the living in the form of a horse." Phillips implicitly denies that the horse Danner stalks could be her brother's spirit, for she specifies that the horse is a mare and that Billy is in the forest "almost accidentally." Billy's "war-movie sounds" of a plane falling "year after year, to earth" seem to link him irrevocably to the perennial fact of war and destruction. The fourth of the epigraphs suggests the commercialization and debasement of the ancient dream of flying:

> Here come the planes
> So you better get ready. Ready to go. You can come
>   as you are, but pay as you go . . .
> They're American planes. Made in America.
> Smoking or non-smoking?

Phillips apparently intends her images and metaphors to unify *Machine Dreams*, but the reader lacks sufficient information about what to make of the metaphors, particularly the one of the flying horse. All of the book's three "machine dreams" include death or images of death, and only one of them (the last) introduces the horse. Earlier in the book, Phillips links an allusion to flying horses with Danner's awareness of her parents' lovemaking and of her own sexuality. At the end of "The House at Night: Danner, 1956," Danner hears "the brief mechanical squeak of springs" and her "father's breath, harsh, held back." Then she hears her mother sigh and say to no one, *"Oh, it's hot."* Danner sinks into the dream Phillips says she will have all of her life; it is initiated by "the loneliness of her mother's voice." Flying horses, "dark like blood," appear in the dream, and "in the dream it is the horse pressed against her."

According to legend, the Greek flying horse Pegasus is able, with a stroke of its hoof, to cause Hippocrene, the fountain of the Muses, to well forth—the inspiration of poetry. Perhaps Phillips intends nothing more than to suggest that Danner, who shares her father's and brother's machine dreams, has metamorphosized incipient violence into art. Danner stalks the magic horse at the end of a book in which women have provided the only stability and order, and the reader is left wondering if planes falling to earth year after year are in fact the product of one gender. *Machine Dreams* provides a series of fine studies of the several members of a family perhaps typical of

American life during the mid-twentieth century, but the several parts do not come together in a way likely to explain or mitigate a nation's suffering. The once-gentle father lapses into bitter ineffectuality, and his son, a boy able to love but not to commit himself, goes to his death. Billy seems to deserve better than to be typified as mindlessly crooning the century's sounds of death and destruction. *Machine Dreams* disturbs because of its power and because of its facile reduction of complex causes to an easy answer, apparently tied to gender.

Leon V. Driskell

Sources for Further Study

Boston Review. IX, August, 1984, p. 27.
Kirkus Reviews. LII, May 1, 1984, p. 424.
Library Journal. CIX, July, 1984, p. 1348.
Los Angeles Herald Examiner. June 17, 1984, p. F6.
Los Angeles Times. July 9, 1984, V, p. 1.
Ms. XII, June, 1984, p. 33.
The New York Times Book Review. LXXXIX, July 1, 1984, p. 3.
The New Yorker. LX, July 30, 1984, p. 87.
Newsweek. CIV, July 16, 1984, p. 78.
Publishers Weekly. CCXXV, April 27, 1984, p. 73.
Time. CXXIV, July 16, 1984, p. 69.
Working Woman. IX, October, 1984, p. 174.

MADAME DE SÉVIGNÉ
A Life and Letters

Author: Frances Mossiker (1906-   )
Publisher: Alfred A. Knopf (New York). Illustrated. 538 pp. $22.95
Type of work: Historical biography
Time: The seventeenth century
Locale: France

A biography which traces the life of Madame de Sévigné through contemporary documents and her own letters to family and friends, all translated by Mossiker

> *Principal personages:*
> MARIE DE RABUTIN CHANTAL, Marquise de Sévigné, a French noblewoman and literary figure whose letters to family and friends became famous for their charm and the descriptions they give of seventeenth century French life and the court of Louis XIV
> FRANÇOISE-MARGUERITE DE GRIGNAN, her daughter, Countess of Grignan and Vicereine de Provence, the recipient of the largest surviving body of letters from Madame de Sévigné

Marie de Rabutin Chantal, Marquise de Sévigné, flourished during the acknowledged classic period of French art and literature. She has long been recognized (and anthologized) as a premier star among the literary lights of her time and is the prime example of sparkling epistolary style, wherever such examples are given. Her letters occupy a place next to the drama of Pierre Corneille, the tragedy of Jean Racine, La Rochefoucauld's *Maximes*, La Fontaine's *Fables*, and the fiction of Madame de La Fayette. The edition of her letters (1862-1868) by Nicolas Monmerqué inaugurated the "Grands Écrivains de France" (Great Writers of France) series of definitive editions, a signal honor for a writer of personal letters. Subsequent discoveries of copies of letters written to family and friends, in particular the massive manuscript discovered by chance by Charles Capmas in 1872, led to reevaluation of the Monmerqué edition and more complete editions of the letters under Émile Gérard-Gailly (*Madame de Sévigné: Lettres*, 1953-1957) and Roger Duchêne (*Madame de Sévigné: Correspondance*, 1972-1978). Frances Mossiker, in *Madame de Sévigné: A Life and Letters*, uses the Duchêne edition as the basis for her translations of Sévigné's letters.

The wit and style of the "divine marquise" have won for her admiration from major literary figures on both sides of the Atlantic, ranging from Horace Walpole in the eighteenth century to Marcel Proust, Virginia Woolf, and Thornton Wilder in the twentieth. Her letters, however, although widely read and circulated in the French-speaking world and among cultivated readers of other lands, have remained essentially inaccessible to the greater English-speaking public, for whom there is no major translation available. This lack is particularly severe in the American reading public, where

French is not as widespread a study as in Great Britain and Canada. Even among American scholars, Sévigné's work, although acknowledged a classic in its genre, remains essentially unstudied, and it was not until the late 1970's that the first American doctoral theses were devoted to her letters.

How can a figure so long recognized as a major writer be at once so revered and so neglected? One answer lies in the genre that she embraced. Sévigné was an *épistolière*, a writer of letters to friends, family, and business contacts, most particularly to her daughter, Madame de Grignan. While the formal constraints of the novel and the public intentions of drama or pulpit oratory are easily recognized, those of the familiar letter are popularly ignored. The letter is defined as the antithesis of literature, and this woman who became unwittingly famous for her correspondence is rather an unclassed member of literary society. Madame de Sévigné was a personal friend of many major figures of the seventeenth century French literary and social world. Madame de La Fayette and the Duke de la Rochefoucauld were particular intimates, but she maintained friendly ties with Madame de Rambouillet, Mademoiselle de Scudéry, and Madame Scarron, who later became Madame de Maintenon, morganatic wife of the Sun King Louis XIV. Sévigné chronicled the intellectual and social life of Paris in letters renowned for their verve, wit, and natural style. These letters have served nobly as primary documents in histories of the period. Frances Mossiker herself refers often and at length to Madame de Sévigné in her history of *The Affair of the Poisons: Louis XIV, Madame de Montespan, and One of History's Great Unsolved Mysteries* (1969). These vignettes of court life sparkle—they are the ultimate in quotable quotes—but is their merit a literary one, or are the letters a written form of conversation, a mirror of the vivacious writer in her roles as friend and mother? The common use of letter passages as historical documentation focuses on their factual content while profiting from their grace: Their place within the larger context of the correspondence is disregarded. If the letters have charmed readers, it is the *épistolière's* biography that has chiefly attracted scholars, and studies have made much of the attachment of Madame de Sévigné to her daughter, much also of their reputed beauty, their personalities, and the possible romantic liaisons enjoyed by Sévigné in her early widowhood.

Mossiker's *Madame de Sévigné: A Life and Letters* is the most recent and by far the most readable in the long line of Sévigné biographies. For every student of high school French who has labored, dictionary in hand, through Sévigné's account of the suicide of Vatel, the betrothal of the "Grande Mademoiselle," or another famous piece from a textbook anthology, there must be dozens more potential readers who will welcome this biography and the generous selection of letters translated by Mossiker from Sévigné's own correspondence and that of her contemporaries. Mossiker, the author of several popular French histories, has produced a work of great charm. A bilingual child, Mossiker was herself well acquainted with the Sévigné of the anthologies, then became closer acquainted while researching and writing *The Affair of the Poisons*. This examination of corruption and Satanic worship in the court of Louis XIV contains more than fifty quotations from Sévigné's letters, translated by Mossiker from "the best French of a century renowned for the best French ever spoken." Mossiker also confesses a personal affinity with Sévigné in the preface to her biography, an early identification and sympathy not only with Madame de Sévigné, who reminded her of her own brilliant and beautiful mother, but also with Madame de Grignan, the destined reader of the bulk of Sévigné's surviving correspondence.

Mossiker's stated intention as biographer is "to turn over the story of her life—insofar as possible—to Madame de Sévigné herself; to allow her to tell it in her own glowing words." The biographer must and does choose, snip, edit, and chisel out her own view of the "divine marquise" from the text of the voluminous correspondence, and that portrait is a dazzling one. Mossiker's thesis is that Sévigné, by virtue of her beauty, charm, intelligence, and graceful wit so shone in her circle of friends and acquaintances that her daughter, the beautiful and intelligent Françoise-Marguerite, grew up in a shadow, incurably shy, stiff, and hypersensitive to her mother's influence. Françoise-Marguerite's marriage as the third wife to the Viceroy of Provence, the Comte de Grignan, and the necessary separation that occasioned the great correspondence also led to her metamorphosis into an independent woman, a painful transition in the mother-daughter relationship. The passionate attachment of Madame de Sévigné to her daughter appears in these years of turmoil and conflict, scandalizing their friends and preoccupying Madame de Sévigné's thoughts for years. As Mossiker follows the marquise into old age, she presents the *épistolière* in contemplation of her mortality. The biographer confesses a new identification with Sévigné herself as the letters speak of her confrontation with death, her acceptance also of her daughter as a separate person.

Although the letters to Madame de Grignan (those from the daughter are lost, destroyed in circumstances recounted by Mossiker) are not the only point of reference for Mossiker's biography, they are the major source for information on the marquise's mature and declining years. For the many years of Sévigné's life before her daughter's removal to Provence and during their periods of reunion, Mossiker refers to other correspondences and contemporary references to "fill in the gaps." Mossiker's documentation is impressive, and if she does completely ignore prominent German scholars such as Fritz Nies (author of the valuable *Gattungspoetik und Publikumstruktur: Zur Geschichte der Sevignebriefe*, 1972), she is well-grounded in the most prominent French *sévignistes* and makes proper reference to Gérard-Gailly and Duchêne.

The letters to Madame de Grignan were written with a faithful regularity predicated on the departure of mail packets for Provence. Madame de Sévigné often speaks of how and when she writes and how carefully she attends to her epistolary schedule, recognizing and appreciating a similar care in her daughter's replies. Mossiker profits from the chronological arrangement and even rhythm of the correspondence, using this skeleton to shape the main body of her biography. She points out the gaps left by letters gone astray and keeps her readers marginally conscious of the epistolary rhythm that otherwise tends to disappear in the marshaling of phrase after phrase, paragraph after paragraph, snipped from so many of the long letters. Unlike Madame de Grignan, the modern-day reader, if fluent in French, can fly through a year of Madame de Sévigné's letters in a day; the selection of key passages for translation and placement in a biography further mutilates the discreet character of the individual letter written within the context of a continuing chain of response. Sévigné biographer-analysts often show much less respect than does Mossiker for the chronology and rhythm of the correspondence. Many biographies are instead structured around a thematic development. Harriet Ray Allentuch's *Madame de Sévigné: A Portrait in Letters* (1963) is an example of such an analysis. Letter passages are studied as examples of certain character traits, producing the portrait of a primary, spontaneous Sévigné, transformed by time, circumstance, and study to a secondary, reflective character similar to her daughter, Madame de Grignan. Allentuch's study is a classic in the Sévigné bibliography; the portrait it produces is similar in many respects to that which Mossiker provides, yet the more recent book gives the reader a better feeling for the correspondence itself. Mossiker's adoption of the framework of the correspondence allows her to present her conception of Sévigné's development while preserving the illusion of natural change in the marquise's outlook on life.

Although *Madame de Sévigné: A Life and Letters* is outwardly shaped by its chronological arrangement, its inward arrangement progresses through three movements: the exposition of Madame de Sévigné's family and personal past, with the development of an initial physical and psychological profile, the middle years of her conflicts with Françoise-Marguerite de Grignan as gleaned from the pages of the correspondence and contemporary commentary (here also developing an understanding of Madame de Grignan in her roles as daughter and wife), and the final years when Sévigné deals with mortality, both in the deaths of her friends and the ill-defined specter of her own confrontation with eternity. Along the way, Mossiker deals with many old war-horses of the Sévigné biographies: Was her childhood a happy one? Was she pretty? Did she love her husband? Did she take any lovers? Why did she favor her daughter over her son? Many of these questions are unresolvable, many of them are really not pertinent to an understanding of the correspondence, but Mossiker tries to give a balanced attention to them all.

Perhaps the most interesting question, as measured within the context of the developing themes of this particular biography, is the reputed absence of Madame de Grignan from her mother's deathbed. Because Madame de Sévigné fell ill and died while in residence with her daughter, why does history report no tearful farewell, no dramatic scene of filial affliction at the death of this most loving parent? Mossiker carefully documents the little that was written in contemporary sources about Madame de Sévigné's illness and the condition and whereabouts of her family. There is little doubt that the Comte de Grignan spoke with his mother-in-law during her last illness, for example, but one finds no direct reference to the countess. Mossiker speculates on these known and unknown factors, then posits an interpretation that intriguingly combines the twin elements highlighted in her portrait of the marquise: her passionate maternal love and her stern, Jansenist-tinged faith. Did the "real" Madame de Sévigné refuse her daughter the last words of affection for fear of imperiling her own immortal soul by excessive devotion to the creature of God in neglect of the Creator? It is certainly plausible within the framework that Mossiker has painstakingly constructed, and the process of reaching this unprovable conclusion is intriguing—the exercise of the informed imagination as it reaches back through the centuries to try and answer these questions so temptingly posed and unresolved in the letters.

Although Mossiker's biography is remarkable mainly for its charm and for the balanced and thorough manner in which the various points of Sévigné's life are covered rather than for any startling revelations or reinterpretations of fact, it is unique in offering so many and such lengthy translations from the letters. This is a constant facet of Mossiker's work: Her *Affair of the Poisons* and *Napoleon and Josephine* (1964) both quote heavily from contemporary sources, and Mossiker supplies her own translation for these works. (The first pages of *Napoleon and Josephine* are almost wholly composed of Napoleon's letters to his bride.) The Sévigné biography is based on the newest and most complete of the Sévigné editions, that of Roger Duchêne in the Bibliothèque de la Pléiade, and Mossiker faithfully renders, in most cases, both the content and the familiar style of the individual passages. Certain translations are always arguable; the vigor of Madame de Sévigné's French makes it difficult to render into an English that sounds natural in context and yet remains faithful to the original. Such objections, however, are not only trivial but also remarkably infrequent in this text.

A more comprehensive objection is that in giving so much, Mossiker does not give enough. The reader who is already well acquainted with Madame de Sévigné will miss certain scenes and wish that many fleeting quotes could be expanded by the addition of the voluminous fore- and background of the entire letters. In the discussion of Madame de Sévigné's relationship with her difficult cousin Roger, Comte de Bussy-Rabutin, Mossiker must synop-

size a sparkling and most revealing series of letters in which Madame de
Sévigné duels with Bussy-Rabutin in a most aggressive style, turning her pen
into a sword, in a battle that nearly ends one of her major correspondences.
Can this be our maternal turtledove? Certainly the depth of her portrait,
the health of her self-esteem, would both be served by a broader sampling
from these Rabutin letters. It may well be that a first-time reader too will
feel the absences that the biographer's chosen length, her editing, and
choice of material made inevitable.

The extremely dramatic, highly flavored paragraphs included in this and
all biographies are drawn from an original position deep in pages of less
emotional material. The interpretation of these passages and their impact
on the reader is necessarily changed by their removal from context. The passionate love passages addressed to Madame de Grignan, to which so much
commentary has been addressed, are a particularly good example of this
removal from context. Isolated from the round dozen of other concerns
treated in a given letter, they may well lend themselves to analysis as evidence of personal pathology. Weighed within their letter context, they seem
more natural. The wonder is rather that Madame de Sévigné could fill page
after page with gossip, reflections on her reading, news of her handwork
projects, and her many other concerns, knowing her daughter to be of delicate health, the third wife of a man whose two previous wives had died in
childbirth and herself perpetually pregnant and often suffering a miscar-
riage, premature birth, or stillbirth. Madame de Sévigné was scrupulous in
her letter-writing schedule, even knowing as she did that in a day of common sudden, premature death, her daughter or grandchildren might be
dead as she wrote, since the process of communications was so very slow as
to admit almost any possibility to an active imagination. Many twentieth
century readers, safe in the ease of modern-day travel, might well be a bit
more dramatic under seventeenth century conditions.

Mossiker's study of Madame de Sévigné follows the tradition of Sévigné
studies in that she praises her subject's virtuosity as a writer without examining it, using the epistolary text as a more or less transparent means of access
to the writer. Naomi Bliven, in a review of *Madame de Sévigné* in *The New
Yorker*, remarks: "The only test of a great writer which Madame de Sévigné
has not passed is that of form or construction, but then, of course, she never
took it." Certainly Sévigné's letters, like all good correspondence, were not
formed on the linear logic of essays, history, or even memoirs, but their very
success as letters enmeshed in long, satisfying correspondences argues
another kind of form. Letters establish contact between their absent writers.
Sévigné's letters in their extraordinary attention to all aspects of the process
of writing and transmission, their scrupulous reply to letters received and
eager solicitation of response are sturdy links in a chain binding the separate
poles of correspondence. Far from formless and unexamined, the letters

were written in a context demanding the highest degree of control, where even repetition (and the very formulae deprecating that repetition) serves to knit closer the epistolary fabric.

Mossiker's interest in the letters is essentially confined to their content, although she respects their style in her translation and their chronology in her structure. The letters are not often considered as written texts, although such consideration might deepen the reader's understanding of the complexity of access to their factual and emotional/psychological content.

One stated purpose of Mossiker's portrait of Madame de Sévigné is to popularize her subject and, by making a selection of passages from the letters accessible to the English-speaking world, encourage the translation of the entire correspondence. Why does Mossiker so modestly decline the task herself? Perhaps, after having juiced the most remarkable pages and blended them into her story, the biographer was understandably too weary to attack the hundreds of letters diffuse in form, repetitious and often elusive in their reference to letters and events lost in the depths of the seventeenth century. As an essentially popularizing work, Mossiker's study may well attract the necessary notice to entice a competent translator, even among academics, for Mossiker is an expert in clear exposition of the sometimes murky points where scholars have differed. Her explanation of Sévigné's early life, or the steps by which the letters appeared before the public and in what condition, are particularly illuminating. Sévigné studies have sometimes seemed a private club. There are relatively few specialists in the field, and Mossiker's passing references to them are adequate to direct interested readers to secondary sources with a more strictly scholarly orientation. *Madame de Sévigné: A Life and Letters* supplies the reader with a chronological table of dates relevant to the marquise's life, a history of the letters after her death, and a bibliography which, while not exhaustive and certainly not adequate for a Sévigné specialist, is more than sufficient to respond to the desire of readers to explore further in Sévigné studies.

Indeed, there certainly will be such readers, for the greatest praise and criticism of Mossiker's work is that, like the best novels, it makes one wish for more. In all the Sévigné bibliography, there is not another book so charmingly and lucidly written, so illuminating on so many points, except the correspondence itself.

Anne W. Sienkewicz

Sources for Further Study

The Atlantic. CCLII, November, 1983, p. 148.
Choice. XXI, February, 1984, p. 826.

Christian Science Monitor. LXXVI, December 2, 1983, p. B14.
Library Journal. CVIII, September 15, 1983, p. 1791.
The New York Times Book Review. LXXXIX, January 8, 1984, p. 25.
The New Yorker. LIX, January 16, 1984, p. 102.
Publishers Weekly. CCXXIV, August 12, 1983, p. 61.
Time. CXXII, October 10, 1983, p. 74.
The Wall Street Journal. CCIII, February 7, 1984, p. 30.
Wilson Quarterly. VIII, Spring, 1984, p. 148.

MAKING CERTAIN IT GOES ON
The Collected Poems of Richard Hugo

Author: Richard Hugo (1923-1982)
Publisher: W. W. Norton and Company (New York). 456 pp. $25.00
Type of work: Poetry

A superbly realized collection, testifying to the power of a poet of the American Northwest whose vision of dispossession and community have earned for him the status of a major voice of his generation

Any accurate descriptions of Richard Hugo's poetry risks sounding sentimental. Words such as "courage," "compassion," "love," and, most frequently, "humanity" recur in commentary on Hugo, who died unexpectedly in 1982. Nevertheless, such words and such risk seem appropriate acknowledgment of Hugo's willingness to affirm "simple" values in contexts, both social and aesthetic, in which they appeared unfashionable or archaic. Although Hugo received some recognition during the last decade of his life—he was named editor of the Yale Series of Younger Poets in 1977—he remained a somewhat anomalous figure in American poetry: a working-class Western populist in a world defined largely by Eastern academics. The difference in sensibility and voice becomes clear when one attempts to imagine the concluding lines of Hugo's aptly titled "What Thou Lovest Well Remains American" in a poem by John Ashbery, Marvin Bell, or Charles Simic:

> You loved them well and they remain, still with nothing to do, no money and no will.
> Loved them, and the gray that was their disease you carry for extra food in case you're
> stranded in some odd empty town and need hungry lovers for friends, and need feel you
> are welcome in the secret club they have formed.

Rarely engaging in the ironic deconstructions of the academic mainstream, Hugo identifies deeply with the members of the "secret club" that exists more in psychological than in social terms. *Making Certain It Goes On* testifies to his ongoing attempt to forge a social reality out of the psychological situation, to articulate the dispossession—social, psychological, sexual, economic—and to envision a community in which suffering elicits compassion rather than withdrawal.

This superbly assembled collection offers a comprehensive overview of Hugo's development from a Northwestern regionalist fascinated by what Michael Allen, Hugo's most sensitive critic, calls the "poetics of sound" to a major American poet basing his work on what Allen calls the "poetics of need." Including all but two poems from the out-of-print collections *A Run of Jacks* (1961), *Death of the Kapowsin Tavern* (1965), and *Good Luck in Cracked Italian* (1969), *Making Certain It Goes On* suggests the centrality of two early influences on Hugo's development: Theodore Roethke, his mentor at the University of Washington, whose sense of verbal music had a profound impact on Hugo's technique; and William Wordsworth, whose sense of the interaction of psyche and landscape helped provide a base for Hugo's later, more Whitmanesque, explorations of community. While these volumes include several excellent poems ("At the Stilli's Mouth," "Road Ends at Tahola," "Death of the Kapowsin Tavern," "G.I. Graves in Tuscany"), they only intermittently intimate the power of the mature voice Hugo discovered in *The Lady in Kicking Horse Reservoir* (1973), *What Thou Lovest Well, Remains American* (1975), and *31 Letters and 13 Dreams* (1977). Together these three volumes mark one of the most intensely creative periods of a single artist's career in American literature; among the poems of lasting significance published during a five-year span are "A Map of Montana in Italy," "To Die in Milltown," "Helena, Where Homes Go Mad," "Three Stops to Ten Sleep," "Letter to Levertov from Butte," "In Your Bad Dream," and "Degrees of Gray in Philipsburg," a poem deserving recognition as one of the handful of truly great American lyrics. Supplemented by twenty-two new poems, several of which rank with Hugo's best, *White Center* (1980) and *The Right Madness on Skye* (1980), which together extend Hugo's vision beyond the Western American landscape without betraying its roots, make it clear that Hugo remained in full possession of his poetic power during his final years.

In addition to charting Hugo's career, *Making Certain It Goes On* clarifies the concerns linking the stages of his development. The emphasis on specific landscapes—especially those around Seattle and Missoula where Hugo directed the University of Montana's creative writing program—reflects both his love for his native region and the belief articulated in "A Snapshot of Uig in Montana" that "all cause is local, all effect." Perceiving the feeling of dispossession, whatever its local roots, as a pervasive aspect of contemporary consciousness, Hugo consistently returned to the problem of how that shared experience of alienation could be transformed into the base for a true community. The resulting focus on the necessity for breaking through the silence separating individuals dictated Hugo's choice of a voice accessible not only to academic readers but also to the lovers, bartenders, softball players, fishermen, writers, and waitresses populating his poems. Reflecting his rigorous commitment to exploration and ultimate acceptance of the full complexity of the self—which he sees as the necessary concomitant of meaningful participation in a community—Hugo frequently addressed the reader directly. His use of the second-person pronoun and definite articles contributes to the rhetorical specificity that combined with Hugo's mastery of the spoken word to make him a brilliant public reader of his own work. If one problem emerges from rereading Hugo's poetry, it is that some poems in print fail to establish the nuances of voice, particularly of the delicately sympathetic humor, so clear in his performances. Fortunately, Hugo's best poems avoid this difficulty almost entirely. The bittersweet juxtapositions of "Three Stops to Ten Sleep" retain comic bite on the page as does the mock heroism of "Kilmuir Cemetery: The Knight in Blue-Green Relief." The gentle satire of "A Snapshot of the Auxilary," which concludes with a deadpan description of "our annual picnic. We are having fun," intimates, both in written and spoken form, the affinity between Hugo's humor and that of Garrison Keillor of "A Prairie Home Companion." Similarly, Hugo establishes convincingly the nuances of tone in more somber poems such as "Death of the Kapowsin Tavern," a meditation on the limits of imagination as a compensation for external disaster, and "Degrees of Gray in Philipsburg," which portrays a more successful struggle against despair.

Close examination of "The Lady in Kicking Horse Reservoir," a powerful lyric shaped by a complex combination of nostalgia and rage, reveals both Hugo's control of voice and his intense confrontation with the psychic responses—particularly those derived from the Western American macho sensibility—which implicated him in the social violence described in "Letter to Levertov from Butte": "hate takes over, hippie, nigger, Indian, anyone you can lump/ like garbage in a pit, including women." Structured in part as a murder mystery, "The Lady in Kicking Horse Reservoir" opens with the male persona imagining a former lover submerged beneath "Summer slime" and "Four months of ice." Mingled with his memories of making love in the foam on an ocean beach, these images express a sexual rage and incipient violence that identify the persona as a suspect in the murder/rape. Abruptly, however, the tone of the poem shifts in the fourth stanza: "All girls should be nicer." Macho aggression gives way to its subtext: whining insecurity. Gazing at black water associated with the distant mountains and with the cries of "dying Indians," the persona senses his own dispossession which in turn suggests to him the futility of remorse for dispossessing others, whether the Indians or his lover.

Subsequently the persona traces his ambivalence to his memory of a childhood humiliation that links him explicitly with the drowned lover. Slapped by another boy, a part of the persona—his "dignity"—disappears beneath the surface of a "company pond," an image recalling the "cold music" of the exiled Indians and suggesting the socioeconomic dimension of the persona's humiliation. The resolution of the "mystery," then, involves not only the discovery of the murderer but also of an additional victim. Confronting the connection between self-hatred and sexual rage, the persona abandons his "landlocked" feeling and imagines a revitalization of his relationships with self and with women, both imaged in a return to the ocean beach.

From a feminist perspective, Hugo's focus on the male reality and the hint of a stereotypical plea for female forgiveness for all past failings and violence appear as disquieting elements in this process. Nevertheless, Hugo clearly refuses to gloss over any aspect, however difficult or shameful, of the male imagination which he believes must be substantially reconstructed if there is to be any real diminishment of the (dis)possession of women by masculine physical violence. As he underscores in "To Women," Hugo expects no special approval from women for engaging in this process: "That is release you never expected/ from a past you never knew you had." Acknowledging his own failures, Hugo provides a model for American males more interested in confronting the roots of their largely self-imposed sexual dispossession and their violence against women than in retreating to politically acceptable but ultimately shallow rhetorical feminism.

In addition to encouraging renewed understanding of compelling individual poems, *Making Certain It Goes On* suggests the need for reassessment of *31 Letters and 13 Dreams*, which has been viewed both as Hugo's strongest and as his weakest volume. Written during a period of extreme personal depression, *31 Letters and 13 Dreams* concentrates on the process of reestablishing contact with psychological resources and with an outside community. Because the significance of individual poems in the book derives largely from their place in this process, Hugo's decision to excise more than half the book from *Selected Poems* distorted their reputation, encouraging the perception, aimed primarily at the Letters, of an unmusical slackness in Hugo's language. Nevertheless, reading the poems in context suggests that the "prosaice" openings and conclusions of the Letters, like the equally prosaic catalogs of Walt Whitman's "Song of Myself," contribute directly to the rhetorical effectiveness and psychological power of the sequence. Montaged with the Dream expressions of internal intensities, the Letters focus on the tension between mundane and intensified vision in everyday experience. Emphasizing the intricate interrelationship of seemingly disparate states, Hugo demonstrates the emergence of highly charged poetic passages from flat descriptions of seemingly insignificant, frequently annoying events. "Letter to Scanlon from Whitehall," which loses much of its effectiveness when taken out of context, exemplifies this process. The second of three crucial transitional Letters placed between the feverish anxiety of "In Your Racing Dream" and the tentative release of "In Your Wild Dream," "Letter to Scanlon from Whitehall" opens with a distinctly prosaic complaint against the "rotten winter" in which Hugo's car has broken down. A meditation on isolation gradually builds to a passage comparable with the finest lyrics in *The Lady in Kicking Horse Reservoir* or *What Thou Lovest Well, Remains American*. Thinking of the dispossessed whose final joke is that the country must pay for their burial, Hugo suddenly leaps into poetry:

                                                                                    And dear
         Dennice, bring their laughing bones no flowers. Pay them the honor
         of ignoring their graves, the standard bird authorities
         chip on stones, a magpie designed by the same man

> you always see in towns like this, sitting in the station,
> knowing the trains don't run.

In addition to implying a profound connection between Hugo, the impoverished dead and the man in the station, this "vision" turns the poem toward
affirmation of community, which will be fulfilled only later in the sequence.
Significantly, Hugo expresses the beginning of the affirmation in prosaic
terms—his soup is good, the car is fixed at no charge by a friendly me-
chanic. The transformation of anxiety into a feeling of community, wrested
from unpromising quotidian events, creates the necessary conditions for the
transformation of the dream life which in turn alters the perception and
experience of quotidian events. A similar dynamic directs most of the
dream-letter sequences, applying the principle to a range of psychological
states ranging from depression ("In Your War Dream," "Letter to Simic
from Boulder") to quiet celebration ("In Your Dream After Falling in
Love," "Letter to Oberg from Pony"). If for no other reason, *Making Certain It Goes On* is important because it makes it possible for new readers to
engage the full complexity of *31 Letters and 13 Dreams* and reach their
judgments on the basis of the full original text.

The tension between individual psyche and social context continued to
inform Hugo's later poetry, though the torment visible in *31 Letters and 13
Dreams* gradually receded after his second marriage. Like *The Right Madness on Skye*, a fitting recapitulation of Hugo's major themes stressing the
need for the transformation of the wrong madness of alienation into the
right madness of community, the new poems in *Making Certain It Goes On*
intimate the possibility of a deeply felt peace at the end of the process of
psychological reconstruction. The humorously Stevensesque "Stone Poems,"
the memorial poems to Hugo's father, who abandoned his family, and to
James Wright, the contemporary with whom Hugo felt the deepest affinity,
and the concluding "Making Certain It Goes On" all sound notes of affirmation derived from experiences of negation. Hugo never escaped the
sense of dispossession as a reality capable of disrupting the texture of life at
any moment. He did, however, develop a profound faith in the ability of the
individual and the community to imagine and maintain the strength needed
to survive and go on.

Craig Werner

Sources for Further Study

Booklist. LXXX, March 15, 1984, p. 1023.
Choice. XXI, May, 1984, p. 1305.

Christian Science Monitor. LXXVI, August 3, 1984, p. B3.
Hudson Review. XXXVII, Summer, 1984, p. 337.
Los Angeles Times. July 13, 1984, V, p. 20.
The Nation. CCXXXVIII, March 17, 1984, p. 324.
The New York Times Book Review. LXXXIX, February 26, 1984, p. 12.
Virginia Quarterly Review. LX, Summer, 1984, p. 91.
Western Humanities Review. XXXVIII, Autumn, 1984, p. 261.
World Literature Today. LVIII, Autumn, 1984, p. 608.

MIDSUMMER

Author: Derek Walcott (1930-   )
Publisher: Farrar, Straus and Giroux (New York). $12.50; paperback $7.95
Type of work: Poetry

In poems characterized by strength and subtlety, the author continues to plumb the meaning of his double identity and to map the reality of a colonial with allegiance to both the periphery and the center of empire

In this gathering of fifty-four numbered poems (corresponding to the author's age), his seventh collection published in the United States, Derek Walcott continues to be concerned with problems that have preoccupied him for more than two decades: his relationship as a Caribbean colonial to European culture and literary traditions; to the United States; to the English language; and the resulting doubleness of his identity. Of mixed blood and cultural heritage, he is unself-consciously at home neither in his native West Indies, nor in the United States, nor in the Europe that colonized his homeland, bastardizing and compromising the native culture. As a poet of two worlds, an exile wandering between cultures and traditions, he risks being regarded as a colonial in the mother country while seeming, in the Caribbean, to pay too much deference to Europe and the United States. Despite demonstrated virtuosity, he is not entirely at home in either British or American English and risks becoming a "mulatto of style."

Walcott renders his divided self in mirror images and other versions of doubleness. Returning from the United States to Port of Spain, he looks into his "first local mirror" and thinks of "The child who died in me." Gazing at the alleys and shacks of the town, he notes evidence of American influence and remembers "that phrase in/ Traherne" (III). Later, "My double, tired of morning, closes the door/ of the motel bathroom; then, wiping the steamed mirror,/ refuses to acknowledge me" (XI). Remembering a local storyteller and acknowledging her literary influence ("Her leaves were the libraries of the Caribbean./ . . . her voice travels my shelves"), he employs the fact that he is a twin in an image of his double identity: "She was the lamplight in the stare of two mesmerized boys/ still joined in one shadow, indivisible twins" (XIV). Elsewhere the northern and southern hemispheres suggest his divided self: "The hemispheres lie sweating, flesh to flesh" (V).

The felt lack of a literary tradition in the Caribbean accounts for the many images in which the natural and cultural landscape are seen as parts of a text. Returning to the West Indies on a plane, he notes "the sharp exclamations of whitewashed minarets" and "pages of earth, the canefields set in stanzas" (I). A tadpole wriggles "like an eager comma," a snake coils "in an ampersand" (XXIV). He observes "the ideograms of buzzards/ over the Chinese groceries" (VI); "lightning's shorthand"; "the sea repeatedly tearing up paper"; "the stones crawling toward language every night." He is dissatisfied because "Language never fits geography/ except when the earth and summer lightning rhyme" (IX).

Traveling somewhere in the Caribbean, he is, typically, at home yet not at home. "This is my ocean, but it is speaking/ another language, since its accent changes around/ different islands." Here too the tendency is to impose a literary tradition on a place that has none: "The boulevards open like novels/ waiting to be written. Clouds like the beginnings of stories" (XLIII, Tropic Zone/i). Here he sees language employed ideologically, not for artistic purposes. He writes of "opposing alphabets" in city squares where "children lie torn on rubble for a noun" (XXII).

At home, he finds little to sustain or guide him. Poverty and death are ominously near: "Our houses are one step from the gutter.../ and the doors themselves, usually no wider than coffins." Walking about his city, he recalls "a childhood whose vines fasten your foot." He wanders with the knowledge that "exiles must make their own maps" (VII), aware of the imposition of empire, noting it is but one step from the schooner basin in Port of Spain to "the plate-glass fronts/ of the Holiday Inn . . . and from need to greed . . ./ a few steps more." He considers the swiftness of change from one way of life to another: "The world had no time to change/ to a doorman's braid from the loincloths of Africa." He sees nature thrusting up beneath the veneer of Western influence: "It is not hard to see the past's/ vision of lampposts branching over streets of bush,/ the plazas cracked by the jungle's furious seed" (IV). Writing to a friend in Rome, he contrasts his Caribbean world with the culture and traditions of Europe: "you are crouched in some ancient pensione/ where the only new thing is paper, like young St. Jerome/ with his rock vault." Instead of sacred domes, Walcott has "Corals up to their windows in sand"; instead of St. Mark's, "gulls circling a seine" (II).

This felt lack of history and literary tradition accounts for the many references and allusions to European, British, and American writers. Anxious and uncertain about his literary ability, Walcott feels both a part of the lush, organic Caribbean world of light and sea, foliage and teeming life— and at the same time alienated from it: "leaves . . . keep trying to summarize my life./ Under the brain's white coral is a seething anthill./ You had such a deep faith in that water, once." His deference to writers secure in a tradition causes him to envy even their fatal illnesses: "Perhaps if I'd nurtured some divine disease,/ like Keats in eternal Rome, or Chekhov at Yalta . . ./ my gift would increase." Still, he knows that "to curse your birthplace is the final evil" (XXIX).

In the United States, Walcott longs for the sea in which he realized he had lost faith while he was home. "Going to the Eastern shuttle at La-Guardia,/ I mistook a swash of green-painted roof for the sea" (XXXIV). In Boston, where blocks are "long as paragraphs," he is acutely aware of literary traditions and reputations—"the shade of Henry James" (XXX).

Teaching, he is aware of the achievement of Robert Lowell: "Cal's bulk haunts my classes" (XXXII). He feels self-consciously black in New England and observes "white harbors/ white spires, white filling stations" (XXXI). In Boston, pedestrians "move in schools, erect, pale fishes in streets;/ transparent, fish-eyed, they skitter when I divide,/ like a black porpoise heading for the straits" (XXXII).

Such are the outlines of Walcott's dilemma. He is at home nowhere, with an ambivalent relation to literary tradition, and acutely aware, in his midfifties, of the passage of time: "before you look, a year's gone/ with your shadow. The temperate homilies can't take root in sand" (XXVI); "O Christ, my craft, and the long time it is taking!" (XIII).

The nature of the dilemma, however, is not as important as Walcott's manner of dealing with it, which he often does brilliantly, heroically. He keeps a faith in the power of art to salvage life from time. Since he is not a direct heir to a single, well-defined literary tradition, he accepts his wandering as a perpetual exile, accepts the necessity to construct his own map. Walcott has the grace and wit to parody his situation. Well aware that he defers to European history and traditions, he also knows that "No language is neutral" (LII), that "a raceless critic is a primate's dream." If he has been ambivalent toward the land of his birth, he cannot deny who he is and where he comes from: "you shall not find peace/ till you and your origins reconcile; your jaw must droop/ and your knuckles scrape the ground of your native place." He imagines in poem LI the reception of his work and its continuing influence on a posterity consisting of a mongoose, mandrills, elephants, lizards, and chimpanzees:

> . . . a dew-lapped lizard discourses on "Lives
> of the Black Poets," gripping a branch like a lectern for better
> delivery. Already, up in that simian Academe,
> a chimp in bifocals, his lower lip a jut,
> tears misting the lenses, is turning your *Oeuvres Complètes.*

Walcott does not resolve his dilemma; he endures it, sometimes thoughtfully, humorously, painfully. Often imagery suggests that his past holds him prisoner in the present. In a hotel room, he observes how afternoon sunlight falling through window bars stripes a sleeper like a prisoner. In a motel in England, he feels "like a drummer selling colored poetry," like a primitive among the cultured, his métier labor on a chain gang. Staring at the "charred cave of the television," its image flickering on his brow, he imagines himself "the first Neanderthal/ to spend a whole life lifting nouns like rocks" (XL).

Walcott's task is not to resolve his dilemma but to give expression to it, to see and say, thereby illuminating his own experience and the experience of others. This he does well. He is particularly adept at recording the imposition of empire upon local culture. In a kind of hyperbole, he sees this imposition even in details of nature: In the Caribbean, even the "jellyfish trails its purple, imperial fringe" (XXIV).

Nowhere is he more successful in expressing the felt presence of empire than in his rendering of American influence on the landscape, culture, and people of his native place. In poem XXVII, Walcott blends statement, detail, and image in a subtle and brilliant poem. Noting that "Certain things here are quietly American," he enumerates details: a chain-link fence that separates a beach from a baseball park; an airstrip with white Cessnas; the "brown, functional hangar" which resembles those of the World War II military occupation; bulldozers gouging out a hill. The American presence is so pervasive that a pelican coasts "with its engine off," like the Cessnas. The sea is corrugated like "sheets of zinc"; even the rain that falls is "American rain." Walcott knows that while he is an observer, he also is a participant in the increasing Americanization of his island: "My own corpuscles/ are changing . . . fast." He senses "fealty changing under my foot."

Midsummer has stylistic and structural faults that have been noted in Walcott's earlier work. Sometimes there is a discrepancy between the high tone of his diction and the ordinariness of his subject. Occasionally his images and figures, dense and rich, nevertheless have a centrifugal tendency, flying away from any center into incoherence. His personification of aspects of nature is too frequent and easy.

Walcott's rhymes are not always successful or even functional. Full rhymes in *abcb* patterns alternate with slant rhymes ("breaks"/"bricks," XXXVIII) and occasional couplets. There is no sense of stanza construction, however, and rhymes are sometimes internal ("fish-eyed" and "divide" in the same line in poem XXXII). At other times, rhymes fall at such distances from one another that it becomes questionable whether they function as rhymes at all. Where distance combines with slant rhymes, where the angle of the slant is great or even synthetic ("accept the"/"scepter" in poem XLVIII), the rhyme achieves nothing. Macaronic rhymes, which consist of foreign words rhymed with English words or phrases, such as "*lederhosen*"/"cause in" from poem XLI or "*la muerte*"/"shirt A" from poem XLIII, Tropic Zone/i, might be theoretically justified as part of Walcott's subject or theme—the dilemma of living in two worlds. In practice, however, the result is questionable.

Walcott is at his best when his language is adequate to his observations and insights but not rhetorically in excess of them, as in poem XXVII, "Certain things here are quietly American" and poem XLIV, "I drag, as on a chain behind me." If he is sometimes derivative of William Butler Yeats or some other admired poet (as in "the sodden red rag of the heart"), he is also capable of arresting images of his own making: "those hopping buzzards/ trailing their torn umbrellas in a silvery drizzle" (XLIX). He is capable too of making the reader feel, through revealing detail, the reality of social, political, and economic situations, as when, writing of life after a revolution in the Caribbean, he notes "that the smallest pamphlet is stamped with a single star./ The days feel longer, people resemble their cars/ that are gray as their uniforms" (XLIII, Tropic Zone/vii). He can also take his own situation, that of a colonial under the influence of foreign empire, and raise it to a metaphysical level: "my own prayer is to write/ lines as mindless as the ocean's of linear time,/ since time is the first province of Caesar's jurisdiction" (XLIII, Tropic Zone,ii).

Despite the faults and blemishes of individual poems, *Midsummer* slowly gathers power. Much of this power derives from the genuineness of Walcott's predicament. He is not to be confused with the alienated, isolated sensibility whose work is foredoomed to solipsism. The isolation of this wandering exile has the power, paradoxically, to draw together people with experiences that parallel his own. In a world where cultural and economic imperialism has resulted in an increasingly global civilization of a certain kind, which uproots, unsettles, or overwhelms local cultures, Walcott gives expression to experience that is both personal and universal. The map which he makes of his personal exile also maps the reality of millions of people.

Jim W. Miller

Sources for Further Study

Booklist. LXXX, February 15, 1984, p. 841.
Christian Science Monitor. LXXVI, April 6, 1984, p. B9.
Georgia Review. XXXVIII, Summer, 1984, p. 402.
Hudson Review. XXXVII, Summer, 1984, p. 331.
Library Journal. CIX, January, 1984, p. 97.
The New Republic. CXC, January 23, 1984, p. 31.
The New York Times Book Review. LXXXIX, April 8, 1984, p. 14.
Poetry. CXLV, December, 1984, p. 171.
Publishers Weekly. CCXXIV, December 9, 1983, p. 42.
Virginia Quarterly Review. LX, Summer, 1984, p. 90.

MIKHAIL BAKHTIN
The Dialogical Principle

Author: Tzvetan Todorov (1939-   )
Translated from the French by Wlad Godzich
Publisher: University of Minnesota Press (Minneapolis). 132 pp. $29.50; paperback
$10.95
Type of work: Literary history and literary criticism
Time: 1895-1975
Locale: Orel, Russia; Vilnius, Russia; Odessa, Russia; Nevel', Russia; Vitebsk,
U.S.S.R.; Kazakhstan, U.S.S.R.; Kustanaj, U.S.S.R.; Klimovsk, U.S.S.R.

An analysis of the thought and literary criticism of a major Russian theoretician of literature in the twentieth century

> *Principal personages:*
> MIKHAIL MIKHAILOVICH BAKHTIN, a twentieth century Russian philosopher, literary critic, and semiotician
> FYODOR DOSTOEVSKI, a nineteenth century Russian novelist
> SIGMUND FREUD, the originator of psychoanalysis
> V. V. IVANOV, a Soviet semiotician and admirer of Bakhtin
> ROMAN JAKOBSON, a Russian Formalist critic
> P. N. MEDVEDEV, a twentieth century Russian literary critic and theoretician, an associate of Bakhtin
> FRANÇOIS RABELAIS, a sixteenth century French prose writer
> V. N. VOLOSHINOV, a twentieth century Russian literary critic and theoretician, an associate of Bakhtin

Unknown in the West until fairly recently, the great Russian humanist and theoretician of literature Mikhail Mikhailovich Bakhtin is finally coming to be recognized as one of the most significant thinkers of the twentieth century. He is the subject of two excellent new works, *Mikhail Bakhtin* (1985), by Katerina Clark and Michael Holquist, and the present study, *Mikhail Bakhtin: The Dialogical Principle*, by Tzvetan Todorov. Todorov's book is not intended to be exhaustive, being rather an introduction to Bakhtin's thought. It serves as a corrective to critics in the West, particularly Structuralists, who have incorporated undigested segments of Bakhtin's thought into their own systems and appropriated him as one of their own. Todorov segments Bakhtin's work into linguistic, literary, philosophical, and anthropological categories, demonstrating how these seemingly disparate groupings are actually mutually dependent and interrelated. While Bakhtin's writing cannot be narrowed to one single field of study, it nevertheless provides a methodological bridge across the gaps which unnecessarily and arbitrarily divide human knowledge and thought.

The intricacies and difficulties of the Soviet system of censorship, coupled with Bakhtin's own idiosyncracies, have burdened scholars with additional problems, for work written during the 1920's was often hidden away for years. He published his famous book on Fyodor Dostoevski in 1929, yet it was only with the second edition, in 1963, that Western scholars became aware of its existence. Similarly, his book on François Rabelais was finished in the 1940's but published only in 1965. Bakhtin was in part reluctant to publish because the very concept of a finalized, completed text was antithetical to his conception of dialogue in flux as the basis for human expression. The above difficulties are compounded still further by the probability that several of his theoretical works were published under the names of his associates, P. N. Medvedev and V. N. Voloshinov. It is only now that scholars are beginning to sort out the writings of Bakhtin himself from those of his colleagues.

Bakhtin was born in Orel in 1895, the son of an impoverished aristocratic family. While teaching elementary school in Nevel', he was part of a circle including Valerian Voloshinov, the literary scholar Lev Pumpian'ski, the musician M. Yudina, the poet B. Zubakin, and the philosopher Matvei Kagan. Because Kagan had been a student of the philosopher Hermann Cohen (the mentor of Boris Pasternak as well), the group met to discuss philosophy and give lectures. In time, the circle regrouped in the town of Vitebsk, where they were joined by the literary critic Pavel Medvedev and the musicologist I. I. Sollertinsky. After Bakhtin's move to Petrograd in 1924, the third circle included Voloshinov, Pumpian'ski, Medvedev, as well as the novelist K. Vaginov and the poet N. Klinev.

It was at this time that Bakhtin brought out the first edition of *Problems of Dostoevsky's Poetics* (the revised version of which is reviewed in this volume). Bakhtin was arrested in 1929, because of his links with Orthodox Christianity. Because of his poor health, his prison sentence was commuted to exile in Kazakhstan. He moved to the town of Kimr, near Moscow, in 1937. Bakhtin's absence from Moscow and Leningrad during the period of the great purges undoubtedly saved him from arrest and internment, since he was removed from the immediate notice of the political apparatus. His final years were enhanced by the appearance of the second edition of the book on Dostoevski and by the long-awaited publication of his work on Rabelais, *Rabelais and His World*.

Over the course of his career, Bakhtin tended to return repeatedly to those questions that had intrigued him in his youth. He developed a consistent system for analyzing literature, approaching a work from the perspective of those linguistic principles that he deemed central to all communication. Literature represented one sort of communication for Bakhtin, and communication was itself based on the utterance. Utterance is the primary component of dialogue, in turn the basis for the novel. Bakhtin insisted that utterance could not exist in a vacuum, for it is always determined by the interlocutor to whom it is addressed and has, of necessity, always to be addressed to someone. Utterance adapts itself to circumstances; it is a social phenomenon, displayed not only in literature but also in other so-called "human sciences," history, anthropology, and sociology.

Human utterances, be they oral or written, take the form of discourse; in the human sciences, utterances taken together comprise texts transmitted from author to interlocutor. It is in this very use of the text that the human sciences are differentiated from the mathematical and natural sciences, for the latter rely upon data rather than discourse. Every discourse, every text, has an author, a subject, who is its transmitter. The very notion of a discrete text is inconceivable without the assumed existence of its author. The presence of the author drives yet another wedge between the human and natural or mathematical sciences. Instead of striving to know an object, as in the latter fields, the reader instead strives to know the subject who produced the text. The final object is not the accumulation of bits of data but the increase in the penetration of understanding, of insight.

It is at this point that the split between the Formalists and Bakhtin becomes clear. The Formalists divorced the text from its author and dissected it according to its formal components. It is not possible, Bakhtin believed, to separate the author from the text in this manner, since the text is primarily the expression of a particular subject, not object. He condemned Structuralism for the same sin, that of "shutting oneself away in the text" and, as a result, depersonalizing it. Todorov notes that Bakhtin's injunction against Formalism and Structuralism is but part of a larger argument between objectivism and subjectivism; Bakhtin supports the subjectivity of the "thing" to be known as itself the product of a particular subject.

Because each author is an individual, the text that he produces in a unique experience, never to be duplicated. This being the case, how can a text be comprehended by the interlocutor? More significantly, how can unique utterances be examined scientifically? This leads back to Bakhtin's argument that no text, no discourse, is produced without the awareness of an audience; it is the existence of this audience that is central, even vital, to the utterance which constitutes the basis of a text. The individual utterance is one discrete particle of the larger entity that is the language itself. Although the particular utterances may vary, they still must, of necessity, function within a system to be intelligible. Speech, says Bakhtin, belongs to the social order, not merely to the individual, and just as it is expressed through that order, so, too, is it apprehended in the same manner. Both speaker and listener are members of society, a group bonded by a system of communication that all of its members use.

Society is a crucial concept for Bakhtin. He views human existence as social, for each individual is from birth an integral part of a group, interacting with another. Human existence reduced to biology is no longer human, Bakhtin maintains. Even the name received at birth is bestowed by another. It is here that Bakhtin takes issue with Sigmund Freud, holding that Freud reduces the psyche to a biological concept in regarding the unconscious as outside of language, although language is the only medium by which the analyst can penetrate into that unconscious. Additionally, writes Bakhtin, the session between analyst and patient is a form of discourse which can itself shape the perceptions of the patient and can alter them to fit a given situation, much in the way a photon alters the position of a particle. It is to Dostoevski, with his concept and use of dialogue, not to Freud, that Bakhtin looks for his formulations of psychological concepts.

Bakhtin regarded Dostoevski as the greatest of novelists. Given that the novel was, for Bakhtin, the most highly developed form of dialogical expression in literature, Dostoevski has emerged as its most ingenious practitioner. Only Dostoevski was aware of the crucial importance of the voice of each character in the fabric of his work. More significantly, Dostoevski respected the voices of his characters sufficiently to grant them equal status with his own author's voice, producing thereby a system of discourse analogous to that found in actual social exchanges.

Although Bakhtin is known in the West principally for his books on Dostoevski and Rabelais, he has produced illuminating work on literary theory as well. Todorov informs the reader that Bakhtin did not subscribe to the dichotomy between form and content but linked the two instead. He sought to surmount both the narrow formalism of concentrating exclusively on form and simultaneously the pitfalls attendant upon examining ideology alone at the expense of form. Bakhtin makes this point in *Problems of Dostoevsky's Poetics*, reiterating it also in his preamble to "Discourse in the Novel." As with other critical constructs developed over the course of years, Bakhtin returned to this synthesis of form and content again.

Similarly, he preferred to examine a literary character within the context of the work and the work in the context of the whole of literature, not neglecting those historical and social factors that would also have been influential. It is precisely those factors which Bakhtin considered in his study of Rabelais, *Rabelais and His World*. In the works of Rabelais, writes Bakhtin, one finds those elements of popular and comic culture running counter to so-called "high culture" all through the Middle Ages and the Renaissance. The most highly developed medium for popular culture was carnival, which, writes Todorov, "concentrates and reveals all the features of popular comic culture." Carnival means change, "death-rebirth," "destructive-creative time." The ambivalence of carnival underscores its roots in popular culture, which undermines and parodies high culture. Its ancestors are found in the dialogues of Socrates and in Menippean satire, with its highest polyphonic voice that of Dostoevski. Given the development of the *annales* school of history, with its emphasis on popular culture to provide entrée into the social structure of, particularly, the early modern period, it is easy to see why Bakhtin's work on Rabelais should have been so popular in the West. He has once again anticipated a major Western intellectual current.

Bakhtin's conception of the significance of the utterance and his emphasis on literature, especially the novel, as the arena in which the utterance achieves its fullest development was related to his interest in philosophical anthropology. According to Bakhtin, the author does "not get involved in the event." He is not a participant, but an outside viewer who knows what is happening. The author is the external force making it possible for the character to achieve wholeness. Is this not directly related to the position of the anthropologist observing a group toward which he is the outsider, a scholar who assesses a culture without himself being involved in it, but nevertheless knowing what is happening?

Ironically, this places the author outside his own culture, an observer who never really belongs. His only satisfying relationships may be those in which he exchanges utterances with his characters, engaging in dialogue with them. Todorov extends this authorial loneliness to Bakhtin himself, lamenting that the theoretician of dialogue was condemned to suffer the absence of response to his work. His works were often published under another's name (Voloshinov's or Medvedev's), or else they were filed away without publication for years, suffering the common fate of many Soviet writers and scholars, if not necessarily for the same reasons. Bakhtin's ultimate loneliness must have stemmed from the fact that only a small audience was able to appreciate his work—an audience which generally was obliged to read him in translation, not in the original. The thinker who stressed the importance of utterance within a cultural framework was eventually to have his writing wrenched from that milieu and transplanted to a foreign environment, achieving thereby an indirect response. Only through the efforts of such scholars as Todorov can the dialogue so essential to Bakhtin begin.

Janet Tucker

Sources for Further Study

Journal of Modern History. LVI, June, 1984, p. 301.
The New York Times Book Review. XC, February 10, 1985, p. 32.

MR NOON

Author: D. H. Lawrence (1885-1930)
Edited by Lindeth Vasey
Publisher: Cambridge University Press (New York). 370 pp. $24.95
Type of work: Two novellas
Time: c. 1912
Locale: The English Midlands, Germany, Italy, and Switzerland

Two novellas with the same title, published for the first time in a single volume; the second Mr Noon, *unfinished, has never before been published*

> Principal characters:
> Part I:
> GILBERT NOON, a spoony youth with several girlfriends
> EMMA GRACE ("EMMIE") BOSTOCK, a spooning partner of Gilbert and girlfriend of Walter George Wiffen
> WALTER GEORGE WIFFEN, a suitor of Emmie Bostock
> MR. AND MRS. LEWIE GODDARD, friends of Gilbert Noon
>
> Part II:
> GILBERT NOON, a person very much like D. H. Lawrence in 1912
> JOHANNA KEIGHLEY, the lover of Gilbert Noon; modeled after Frieda von Richthofen Weekley Lawrence
> DR. EVERARD KEIGHLEY, her husband
> WILHELM FREIHERR VON HEBENITZ, her father
> BARONESS VON HEBENITZ, her mother
> FRAU PROFESSOR LOUISE KRAMER, the elder sister of Johanna (also called her "school-sister")

The discovery and issue of a previously unpublished novel by D. H. Lawrence is an event. Lawrence's position among the giants of twentieth century English literature has long been secure, but fully to appreciate the significance of this publication, now meticulously edited by Lindeth Vasey in a volume of the definitive Cambridge Edition of the *Works*, it is necessary to qualify some terms. *Mr Noon* (note that Lawrence left out the period to signal an abbreviation of "Mr.") has, at least in part, already been known to readers since 1934, when a story of the same title was originally published in the collection *A Modern Lover*, then included in the volume of miscellany titled *Phoenix II* (1968). That story, altered very slightly from the 1934/1968 version on the basis of editorial collation of the texts from an autograph manuscript and typescript copies revised by Lawrence, remains part 1 of this book.

The existence of a second part of *Mr Noon* has also been known to a much smaller group of Lawrence scholars through the writer's mention of his progress on the manuscript. In letters to his American publisher Thomas Seltzer, for example, as well as to his literary agent Curtis Brown and to his typist Ruth Wheelock, Lawrence left a tantalizing series of tracks for specialists to hunt down—but where was the manuscript itself? Had it disappeared? By October 6, 1922, approximately two years after he had begun the project, Lawrence stopped referring to *Mr Noon*. Thereafter, as Vasey puts it, the traces for part 2 had "effectively disappeared for fifty years." Not until October 31, 1972, was the manuscript of *Mr Noon*, together with a typescript copy and a carbon copy of part 2, auctioned by Sotheby Parke Bernet and purchased by the Humanities Research Center of the University of Texas (Austin). At that point, scholars could assemble parts of the present volume.

Two questions remain: Is *Mr Noon* indeed a novel? And is this indeed the book that Lawrence had intended to publish? Certainly the volume has the length and structural complexity of a novel—or rather of two distinct novellas. Although the central character, Gilbert Noon, appears in both parts, he is clearly a different personality in each. In part 1, Noon is a feck-less lover, a character resembling such weak, self-conscious, sexually un-assertive types as Cyril Mersham in "A Modern Lover," Edward Severn in "The Old Adam," or Bernard Coutts in "The Witch *à la mode*"—all stories from the 1934 collection. Like these deficient males, the first Gilbert Noon is attracted to a "fatal" woman who teases him, ignites his passion, but who cannot bring him to the point of asserting his virility. More vigorously than these typically weak types, the first Mr Noon pursues several acquiescent young women who submit to his spooning and caresses but who deny him sexual release. To be sure, he is quite satisfied with the coquettish liberties that they offer—chief of which is the prolonged kissing-and-cuddling rite of courtship that Lawrence describes (in chapter 2) as spooning. By the end of part 1, the tepid Mr Noon almost falls into his own amorous trap by winning the heart of Emma Grace ("Emmie") Bostock, but he is saved at the end from a committed relationship when Emmie's faithful but equally doltish ad-mirer, Walter George Wiffen, proposes marriage to the girl. Lawrence con-cludes this trivial tale of flirtation and its consequences with a comic-ironic postscript: "Gentle reader, this is the end of Mr Noon and Emmie. If you really must know, Emmie married Walter George, who reared prize cauli-flowers, whilst she reared dear little Georgian children, and all went happy ever after."

Lawrence's novel (or pair of novellas), however, does not truly end at page 93 of the text. The author warns the reader: "As for Mr Noon! Ah, Mr Noon! There is a second volume in store for you, dear reader. Pray heaven there may not be a third." In part 2, one continues to learn about the adventures of Gilbert Noon, but he is not at all the personality whom the reader remembers from the first section. This Mr Noon merges very quickly with chapter 13 into the persona of D. H. Lawrence, and the novella itself becomes a slightly fictionalized autobiography that might be under-stood as a Portrait of the Artist as a Young Lover. After Noon awakens the next morning in Munich, Germany, he resembles the Lawrence of May,

1912, a former teacher from Croyden who had recently met Mrs. Frieda
Weekley, the wife of his French professor a few months earlier, in March.
Also in March, he had attended the wedding of George Henry Neville, the
model for the first Mr Noon (just as Emmie is probably modeled after
Sarah Ethel Giddens, and Mr. and Mrs. Lewie Goddard are modeled after
William Edward Hopkins and his wife, Sarah Anne, friends of Lawrence's
youth). Indeed, the two parts of Mr Noon—based upon different life situations from the author's background—have altogether different characters
(or, as in the case of the hero, a person whose nature is altogether different
in the second part). The Lawrence-Noon relates to events and persons from
the author's relationship with Frieda. Thinly disguised, or not at all disguised except for the different names, are most of the characters in part 2:
Professor Alfred Kramer is a re-creation of Edgar Jaffe; Frau Professor
Louise Kramer is based upon Elisabeth Frieda Amalie Sophie ("Else") von
Richthofen, Frieda's sister; Professor Ludwig Sartorius upon Alfred Weber;
Dr. Everard Keighley upon Ernest Weekley, Frieda's first husband;
"Eberhard" upon Dr. Otto Gross, one of her lovers; and so on. Mrs. Jo-
hanna Keighley is Frieda herself—born Emma Maria Frieda Johanna von
Richthofen.

The parts of *Mr Noon* are dissimilar with not only respect to the characters and the ways that they relate to two different sets of experience in
Lawrence's life but also in structure and tone. Part 1 has a unified structure,
leading to a resolution of conflict. The conflict involves the rivalry between
two men for the affection of a woman—a customary Lawrentian three-
some—but with unusual twists. Gilbert Noon and Walter George Wiffen
are unequal suitors for Emmie. Noon is a philanderer (indeed, not even a
serious one), who enjoys recreational spooning with complaisant young
women but has no stomach for a deeper commitment to any of them. Walter George, on the other hand, is serious; he loves Emmie and, incited by
jealousy toward Noon (and concern for "poor" Emmie's health and well-
being), takes the plunge to marriage. Thus the triangle conflict is somewhat
contrived. Lawrence scorns all three lovers. Emmie is the clever flirt, a variation on the witch-women types in his stories; Walter is the loyal but
unimaginative persistent suitor, a feeble variation on the virile types; and
Gilbert, "a first-rate spoon" but sexually timorous lover, resembles other ef-
fete types that Lawrence usually satirizes as mechanical and overcivilized.
Appropriate to this simple structure in part 1, the tone is comic-satiric with
little variation. Lawrence's diction resembles that of such light moralistic satires as "Two Blue Birds": arch, detached, playful.

Part 2, on the other hand, lacks the unified structure typical of the writer's short stories and novellas, and its tone similarly lacks focus. The second
Mr Noon is an episodic romance, one following rather directly the actual
events in Lawrence's life. To be sure, part 2 has several patterns of conflict,

but they are not connected: Gilbert and Johanna quarrel and reconcile; Johanna quarrels with her parents and her sister over the wisdom of eloping with a young, unpromising artist, for whose sake she abandons home, husband, and children; and Gilbert quarrels with almost everybody, yet is a likeable sort after all. In place of a unified structure, the second part of the volume follows the loose organization of travel literature; indeed, Lawrence covers the same general ground that he had earlier in *Twilight in Italy* (1916) and in a number of the poems from *Look! We Have Come Through!* (1917), especially the love poems and descriptive verses on landscapes of Germany and Northern Italy. The difference is that *Mr Noon* places a Lawrence-like hero directly in the action of the tale. Gilbert's feelings are Lawrence's; so are his philosophical maunderings. Because of this close identification between writer and subject, the tone of part 2 is quite different from that of the first. Still generally ironic, the tone is much less facetious, less unified. A reader can easily detect two separate (and sometimes contradictory) tones: one of genial satire, especially toward the amorous fumblings of Gilbert and Johanna as they attempt to establish a secure relationship, and the other of mystical-passionate rhapsody, directed usually toward the "dark gods" of intuition and blood knowledge. For by 1920-1922, when Lawrence was working on the two parts of *Mr Noon*, he had already worked out his philosophy of vitalism. The second, more nearly intense tone gradually replaces the jaunty satire early in part 2; beginning, one night say, with chapter 16, Lawrence writes in a style familiar to his general readers—not that of his greatest prose, perhaps, but solid enough and perfectly distinctive. It is the tone of genuine Lawrence, not hackwork.

If readers must settle for only so much, one still owes a debt to the editorial staff of the Cambridge *Works*, and especially to Lindeth Vasey. The volume that they have offered is not vintage quality; nevertheless, it is more than a curiosity for specialists. In part 2, one has a finely observed record of the early period of Lawrence's relationship with Frieda. At first hesitant and ironically detached, Lawrence in time warms to his subject. He tells the reader little that scholars had not already known, at least in general terms, but here he describes with marvelous touches his feelings, images that are fixed sharply in his recollection, above all sensory details that still are plangent. Far less sentimental than Frieda's account of their courtship and flight to the Continent (*Not I, but the Wind . . .*, 1934), Lawrence's version of the story is tinged with a certain retrospective sadness. After all, by 1920-1922, the passion of their first weeks and months together had cooled, to be replaced by affection and habit. Looking backward to his love for Frieda (Johanna) in a damp haystack or at a tawdry inn; his memories of estrangements and reconciliations; his recollection of meals eaten with savory gusto or of scanty repasts and hunger also; of tender moments shared—all of these scenes are presented with vividness. For what Lawrence has saved, the reader must be grateful.

Yet the publication of *Mr Noon* is a mixed blessing. Readers who expect too much from this posthumous volume are certain to be disappointed. The work is not a true novel but two novellas, the second one incomplete. Part 2 comes to a sudden end at chapter 23, without a resolution even to the line of narrative. Lawrence must have realized that his work-in-progress was deficient, so he neglected to complete (or round off) the fragmentary edges. Certainly Lawrence had reason to feel qualms about the two *Mr Noon* stories. As an artist, he must have been aware that the parts did not cohere; as a husband, he must have questioned whether the publication of certain frank descriptions of Frieda's family, of her previous love affairs, or of his own rather censorious opinions about their early months together might have injured her—although she generally accepted with good grace her husband's freedom as a writer to be honest with his life experiences. Fortunately, in the case of *Mr Noon*, her tolerance was never put to the test— and fortunately for admirers of Lawrence, one more legacy of his genius has been made accessible.

Leslie B. Mittleman

Sources for Further Study

Listener. CXII, September 13, 1984, p. 24.
Los Angeles Times Book Review. November 4, 1984, p. 3.
The New Republic. CXCI, December 10, 1984, p. 96.
New Statesman. CVIII, September 14, 1984, p. 32.
The New York Review of Books. XXXI, October 25, 1984, p. 18.
The New York Times Book Review. LXXXIX, December 16, 1984, p. 3.
The New Yorker. LX, January 28, 1985, p. 97.
Publishers Weekly. CCXXVI, September 21, 1984, p. 89.
Time. CXXIV, October 15, 1984, p. 101.

MODERN GREEK POETRY
Voice and Myth

Author: Edmund Keeley (1928-   )
Publisher: Princeton University Press (Princeton, New Jersey). 232 pp. $22.50
Type of work: Literary criticism, literary history

A collection of essays analyzing the work of the most important Greek poets of modern times

The extraordinary renaissance of poetry in modern Greek has been acknowledged by eminent poets as diverse as T. S. Eliot and Czesław Miłosz, and many young American poets have indicated their debt to figures such as Constantine Cavafy, Odysseus Elýtis, Yánnis Rítsos, and George Seferis. Even such major voices in modern Greek poetry, however, are not as well-known as their French or German or Italian counterparts. Edmund Keeley (in collaboration with Philip Sherrard, whose book *The Marble Threshing Floor*, 1956, was a pioneering study of modern Greek poetry) is one of the preeminent translators of modern Greek poetry into English. In this critical study, he continues the work begun in his translations, making a rich poetic tradition more accessible to the English-speaking reader and perhaps inspiring a few readers to study these great poets in the original.

Modern Greek Poetry: Voice and Myth consists of nine essays written during a seventeen-year period; in addition, there is an interview with Seferis. This work should be regarded as a collection of discrete, separate pieces rather than as a single coherent whole, yet Keeley's obvious mastery of his subject and his sensitivity to the values of the writers under consideration serve the purpose of a unifying theme. Keeley has himself bestowed a central thesis on his work, stating in his preface that the essays "illustrate how the best of the contemporary Greek poets succeeded in solving the problem of expressing themselves in the particular language and literary tradition they inherited." They have combined this adaptation of the contemporary language and cultural heritage with a sense of man's fragile position in life, an awareness that has been part of Greek civilization since classical times. One of the problems faced by the modern Greek poet has been, according to Keeley, that of accommodating the multivalent structure of the past to his own individual expression. Each essay focuses on the individual writer's solution to this challenge.

The first poet whom Keeley considers (the subject of one of the two longer essays) is Constantine Cavafy. Cavafy was a member of the Greek community in Alexandria, Egypt, one of the "Greek diaspora." In his poems, he reminds the reader that Greek ethnicity and culture became increasingly complex from the Hellenistic period and that this "foreign" strain has set the Greeks of the diaspora apart from those of the mainland.

Cavafy's principal theme is history, for he writes about and judges figures and events of the past, his exile from the mainland furnishing him with a unique perspective. This perspective, coupled with the often puzzling relationship between the poet himself and his persona, complicates the tone of his work. The opposition between persona and poet duplicates in microcosm the tensions and complexities of the situation or personality with which Cavafy is dealing, providing an entrée into history at a particular time, in a particular place. Cavafy's apparent obsession with history is not merely a game, for knowledge of history is knowledge of self. It enables him to define himself as a Greek and, by extension, all Greeks. It is vital, therefore, as both Seferis and Keeley maintain, to examine all of Cavafy's work as a unit, seeing the expansion of his perspective during his career as a poet.

Keeley devotes two essays to Angelos Sikelianos, who was instrumental, along with Cavafy, in establishing demotic as the language of modern Greek poetry. Sikelianos is not nearly as well-known in the West as are his compatriots Cavafy, Seferis, Elýtis, and Rítsos, yet he is considered a fine poet; Keeley informs the reader that Seferis regarded Sikelianos as being as important to Greek poetry as William Butler Yeats was to modern British letters. Sikelianos' best poems are his later ones, but because of his unfamiliarity in the West, Keeley has provided a discussion of the early Sikelianos and his background.

His work, centered on the pre-Socratic tradition, Orphism, the cult of Dionysus, the teachings of Pythagoras, the Mysteries of Eleusis, and the mantic center at Delphi, differs both from Cavafy's Hellenism and Seferis' Homeric and Platonic settings. The scholar Philip Sherrard has noted that Sikelianos considered man the means of communication between upper and lower states of existence, the visible and invisible. The poet is not, as is Cavafy, a recorder of history, functioning instead as a seer, a prophet, an interlocutor between the apparent and the hidden. It is through myth that the poet exercises his divine gift, myth as a revelation, a rift in the curtain between the seen and the unseen, the temporal and the timeless. His gods are not fabrications or rationalizations of the mysteries of nature; instead, they move in the modern Greek landscape as its original landlords. As a result, nature is synonymous with Greece. Sikelianos' persona communicates with the gods and speaks in unison with a voice from the beyond, a bard more than a versifier. It is a voice lost, Keeley laments, in translation, perhaps even in being read silently. Sikelianos' persona hails from the Dionysian world, not the Apollonian, a world misunderstood and only grudgingly accepted by Western readers.

Personal crisis before World War II was coupled with an ominous sense of the larger catastrophe through which Greece suffered early in the war to produce a changed, tragic note in Sikelianos' verse. The bardic persona recedes from the center of the poem, and the myth is narrated without an interlocutor. Keeley discusses two poems, "The Sacred Way," with its poignant story of the suffering mother bear, and "Agraphon," containing the parable of Christ viewing the body of the carrion dog, symbol of decay and the tragedy of the time. There has been a rupture between the earlier Sikelianos, part of a sheltering larger world emblematized by the gods, and this poet, sharply aware of the disjointedness of existence. Coupled with his expanded use of myth, this awareness is testimony to his greatness as a mature poet.

The Nobel Prize-winning poet George Seferis, subject of three essays and an interview with Keeley, resembles Sikelianos in his incorporation of myth into the contemporary Greek landscape. So subtle is Seferis at splicing the ancient world with the contemporary that the reader is caught off guard, initially unaware that the men with the broken oars in poem number 12 of *Mythistorima* (1935) are actually Odysseus and his crew on their way back from Troy. Seferis focuses on two men, Odysseus and Elpenor, the youngest member of the crew, frustrator of his captain's attempts to return home. The insignificant Elpenor of the *Odyssey* is shoved into the center of the stage in Seferis' lyric, reminding the reader of the sudden importance of Rosencrantz and Guildenstern, minor characters in William Shakespeare's *Hamlet*, who acquire tragic significance in Tom Stoppard's *Rosencrantz and Guildenstern Are Dead* (1967). This is the frustrated minor figure, incapable of greatness, yet capable of suffering, who populates such works as T. S. Eliot's "The Love Song of J. Alfred Prufrock." Elpenor's uniqueness lies in his awareness of his limitations, his resigned acceptance of his narrowness. He symbolizes the diminution of the hero in modern literature.

Like all the modern Greek poets, Seferis suffers from the language barrier. Few readers in Europe or the United States—or indeed anywhere outside Greece—can read modern Greek poetry in the original. Moreover, poems are often selected for translation less on the basis of merit than because they fit the preconceptions of the target culture. Thus, Anglo-American interest in Seferis can in part be attributed to the parallels that have been seen between his attitudes toward myth and those of Eliot, particularly in *The Waste Land* (1922). A more thorough examination of Seferis' work, however, suggests that these parallels are of limited value, for Seferis' mythological personages spring directly from his cultural background, from a cultural subconscious, while Eliot's are deliberate, part of a complex of demonstrated learning on the surface of his own heritage. There is an immediacy in Seferis, writes Keeley, in striking contrast to the remoteness of Eliot, the intricacy of James Joyce. As with Cavafy, Seferis defines the essence of Greekness in the modern world, and this essence is organically bound up with a past that is only superficially remote.

Like their Russian counterparts, Greek poets have a multifaceted importance extending beyond cultural life into politics, perhaps a natural occurrence in countries where writers have established and defined the essence of nationalism. Seferis, therefore, has been considered a political figure, a role thrust upon him more by heritage and events than by inclination. While out of the country, he remained silent about the excesses of the colonels' dictatorship, his indignation over the regime's excesses against freedom finally culminating in a statement broadcast over the BBC on August 28, 1969. As with the great poets of Russian literature in the Soviet period, his protest was torn from him, testimony to the poet's acknowledgment that freedom and independence are vital for artistic expression. He came to be regarded as a counterweight to the regime, and his funeral was attended by an enormous crowd of mourners, a state funeral for a Greek poet.

Odysseus Elýtis was not widely known outside Greece when he won the Nobel Prize for Literature in 1979, yet his work has long been esteemed by fellow poets. Elýtis' poem *To áxion estí* (*The Axion Esti*, 1974) elicited ambivalent and confused response upon its appearance in Greece in 1959, with a similar reaction in the English-speaking world following the translation of the work into English several years later. Those readers, whose familiarity with the restrained style of Cavafy and Seferis caused them to find Elýtis' rhetorical generosity difficult to understand or accept, should turn for comparison, says Keeley, to the bardic, uninhibited, first-person verse of Walt Whitman and Dylan Thomas, poets writing in a similar mode in English. For both Thomas in "Fern Hill" and Elýtis in *The Axion Esti*, the first-person narrator is an innocent observer at one with his surroundings; the nearness of the ancient gods to Elýtis' world underscores his persona's position as an infant at the bosom of nature, with nature an extension of himself. There is a fall from grace for Thomas in his discovery of death and for Elýtis in his sudden awareness of evil existing in paradise. Still, the bond with the earth, reinforced by the identification of nature with the myths informing Greek civilization, is never severed. The reader enters into Elýtis' "This Small World the Great," the world of an individual symbolizing his people, with the sense of a temporal interruption that is at the same time part of a great continuum.

As with his great predecessors, Cavafy and Seferis, Elýtis' Greece is not synonymous with the Greece familiar to Western readers. Classical culture is only a segment of Greece, a nation whose later history separates it from the West rather than linking them together. Ancient Greek culture became part of the Renaissance in the West, but the Renaissance was never successfully incorporated into Greek culture. Far more important were Byzantine civilization, the influx of the folk tradition, and the impact of the demotic which began with the Cretan Renaissance and continued through the eighteenth and nineteenth centuries. These elements are part of Elýtis' verse, which spans the entire range of Greece from the earliest cultural developments to the present. From this amalgam, he has fashioned a new, current

Greece. It is this Greece that forms the subject of his poetry.

If Elýtis' voice is encompassing and loud, that of Yánnis Rítsos is delicate, understated, and subtle. Rítsos, a committed leftist who himself has often been mentioned as a candidate for the Nobel Prize, writes about the gulf between individuals, between the poet and his readers, men and women. Two of his early volumes of verse are aptly entitled *Parentheses* (1946-1947; 1950-1961), two signs that enclose a world in miniature, forming an unbridgeable gap between them. Life within the parentheses is mysterious, like the houses with smoking chimneys that seem to be confessing a secret to the sky. The landscapes of his poems are stripped down, bare, seemingly barren and poor, but actually concealing hidden mysteries, like the bundles of the political prisoners of "Change of Habits." There is a mirror in "Privilege," providing an entry into a world normally closed, an escape from the everyday. The glass eye in "Completeness Almost" encloses a personal, secret, impenetrable world, symbol of the gap between people, even those joined in an intimate relationship. Rítsos' verses are strewn with safety valves into secret worlds; in "In the Ruins of an Ancient Temple," the statue and veil of the goddess Hera are not only incorporated into the ordinary world but also simultaneously provide an exit from it. The exuberance of Elýtis is curtailed in Rítsos; it is approachable only indirectly through the medium of his images.

Keeley's book closes with a conversation with Seferis which took place at the Institute for Advanced Study at Princeton University. Among other points discussed during the interview, Seferis stressed that "ancient Greece" is not a calcified entity in Greece but is part of a continuing tradition in language and culture. It is as continuators of this tradition that all the poets of Keeley's fine study must be regarded, even as they regard themselves.

Janet Tucker

Sources for Further Study

Book Review Digest. LXXX, January, 1985, p. 61.
Choice. XXI, May, 1984, p. 1313.
Library Journal. CIX, March 1, 1984, p. 490.
Times Literary Supplement. August 24, 1984, p. 938.
World Literature Today. LVIII, Summer, 1984, p. 452.

MONTGOMERY'S CHILDREN

Author: Richard Perry (1944-   )
Publisher: Harcourt Brace Jovanovich (San Diego, California). 282 pp. $12.95
Type of work: Novel
Time: 1948-1980.
Locale: Montgomery, New York

Focusing on the experience of the black community in a small upstate New York community, Montgomery's Children *portrays an unsuccessful struggle to realize an African-based vision of transcendence in a social context increasingly characterized by failures of communication*

> *Principal characters:*
> GERALD FLETCHER, a member of the younger generation
> ALEXANDER FLETCHER, his father
> ABIGAL FLETCHER, his mother
> MARGARET FLETCHER, his wife
> JOSEPHINE "Josey" MOORE, his young girlfriend, an incest victim
> PERCY MOORE, Josephine's stepfather
> GERTRUDE MOORE, Josephine's mother
> ZACHARIAS "ICEMAN" POOLE, Gerald's closest friend
> NORMAN FILLIS, a visionary and/or madman
> CLAIRE FILLIS, Norman's wife
> HOSEA MALONE, a dope dealer and a murder victim
> MEREDITH MALONE, Hosea's abandoned wife
> RACHEL MALONE, Hosea's daughter
> HOSEA MALONE, JR., Hosea's deformed son
> ALICE SIMINESKI, Hosea's partner who is white

Richard Perry's second novel, *Montgomery's Children*, a multifaceted exploration of black experience in a small upstate New York community, addresses a complex of issues central to the developing dialogue among contemporary Afro-American novelists. Like Ralph Ellison, Toni Morrison, Alice Walker, and David Bradley, Perry perceives a serious threat to the integrity of the Afro-American tradition and attempts to recover or rediscover modes of perception capable of resisting the social and psychological failures of the American mainstream. Where most of his contemporaries offer at least tentative hope that such resistance may succeed, however, Perry remains profoundly doubtful that any transformed vision can be brought to bear on the problems of the community once it has been transplanted to the North from its Southern origins. Although myths rooted in Southern experience and the African continuum may provide momentary respite for individuals, the encompassing failure of personal communication, especially between men and women, leads Perry to question not only the celebratory vision of Walker's *The Color Purple* (1982) but also the ambivalent optimism of Morrison's *Song of Solomon* (1977), Ellison's *Invisible Man* (1952), and Bradley's *The Chaneysville Incident* (1980).

Set in a predominantly white community which undergoes the transition from rural town to small city between 1948 and 1980, *Montgomery's Children* focuses on a group of Afro-Americans who, disillusioned by their experiences in Philadelphia, New York City, and Newark after leaving the South, settle in Montgomery because it fulfills their three primary requirements: "that it be rural, that it be northern, and that it have jobs." To begin with, Montgomery provides an idyllic setting; prior to 1948, no black resident, for reasons partly practical and partly theological, has died. By 1980, however, all sense of community cohesion, both within and between races, has collapsed. A large number of blacks die violent and/or accident-related deaths; the younger generation has turned to drugs; interracial dating disturbs both black and white parents; older blacks feel as distant from their children and grandchildren as from whites. Against this historical backdrop, Perry sets in motion a large group of characters, including Norman Fillis, who recaptures aspects of the African tradition but, unable to accept family responsibility and viewed as insane by the community, cannot pass his knowledge on to the younger generation; Gerald Fletcher, a member of the younger generation ultimately incapable of fulfilling his potential for personal and cultural development; Hosea and Meredith Malone, whose alienation typifies male-female relationships in Montgomery and contributes to an accelerating cycle of violence; and Josey Moore, who as an incest victim and convicted murderer provides an emblem of the meaning of physical and social deformity. In addition, Perry sketches at least a dozen other characters, most of them members of the Fletcher, Moore, and Malone families. Intended to add scope to Perry's historical meditation, this large cast in fact constitutes the central problem of *Montgomery's Children*. Able to grant only limited attention to each of his conceptually significant characters, Perry glosses over complex psychological dilemmas and transformations, such as those associated with Gerald's marriage and Meredith's repression of the knowledge that she has murdered her infant son. Without the fully rounded individual characterizations provided by Bradley and Morrison, Perry's explorations of alternative perspectives on similar issues seem somewhat abstract and unconvincing, effectively subverting his implicit challenge to the reader to assume responsibility for interpretation of the novel's events.

Whatever the limitations of its realization, Perry's treatment of the tension between the decaying community and Norman's alternative vision provides an intriguing center of attention. Viewed by most of the community as a harmless madman who is periodically in need of institutionalization, Norman preaches of "the miracle of flight and the properties of fire," hoping to pass his knowledge on to Gerald, who has a mole in his eye which, Norman believes, marks him as Norman's spiritual heir. For Norman, fire represents the heritage of black suffering, especially at the hands of lynch mobs, a heritage increasingly alien to a younger generation immersed in white society's version of normalcy. Alongside this suffering, Norman envisions a heritage of flight, drawing on the mythological image of the Flying African—also invoked by Morrison and Bradley—whose refusal to accept Euro-American reality enables him to transcend the fire without denying its reality. Refusing to accept technological or economic progress as normal or desirable, Norman immerses himself in nature to warn the forest animals that their habitat will be destroyed to make way for a racetrack, and ultimately he learns to fly himself, providing a powerful image of potential transformation. Presenting Norman's flight as an actual event, Perry seems momentarily to endorse the African tradition as a potential source of release from the forces that limit the individual sense of personal and social possibility. Nevertheless, the potential remains unfulfilled. Norman cannot communicate his vision to the community. Living materially comfortable lives but unable to understand or allay their feelings of alienation, the members of the Afro-American community dismiss Norman as a curiosity. His attempt to convince Gerald to attempt flight, ironically interrupted by a fire alarm, fails in part because Gerald, like the majority of his elders, associates "magic" with Christian demons rather than African heroes. Even Gerald's friend Iceman, himself deeply interested in alternative modes of perception derived from Asian philosophy, warns him to stay away from Norman. Nowhere in Montgomery does Gerald find any support for the notion that black experience can or should differ from that of the white mainstream. Ultimately a tragic figure, Gerald finally declares his acceptance of "normalcy" by deciding to have his distinguishing mole surgically removed. Ironically, the absence of the mole leads Norman to perceive Gerald as a kind of demon, an incomplete simulacrum, when the two meet near the end of the novel in a final scene suggesting the possibility of flight above the fire. Discouraged, exhausted, and alone after this confrontation, Norman attempts one final flight, only to crash to his death. Contrasting sharply with the transcendent deaths of Moses and C. K. in Bradley's *The Chaneysville Incident* and the potentially liberating surrender to the air at the end of Morrison's *Song of Solomon*, this concluding crash emphasizes Perry's pessimism.

The removal of Gerald's identifying mole seems particularly significant in relation to Perry's treatment of physical and psychological deformity as a major motif. Most of the important characters in *Montgomery's Children* suffer from some deformity, real or imagined, which makes them feel grotesque. Josey loses her hand in an "accident" at an early age; her mother suffers a debilitating stroke; Hosea's son is born blind and misshapen; his drug-selling partner Alice Simineski is extremely overweight. Equally significant are the grotesque events which demonstrate the community's inability to live the normal life it seeks. Iceman, who kills a kitten when he is young in a scene recalling Richard Wright's *Black Boy* (1945), dies when he falls onto a power line while attempting to rescue a white woman's pet cat. Meredith Malone kills her deformed son and constructs an elaborate compensatory fantasy after Hosea leaves her; Josey becomes a member of a rich white man's sexual freak show after her release from prison; later, she forces Gerald to share her deformity by binding his hand and blindfolding him while he plays the role of erotic slave. Perry occasionally hints that this shared experience of the grotesque may provide the basis for a breakthrough into some higher level of understanding concerning the position of the individual in a homogenized society. Recalling Norman's belief that Gerald's mole signifies power rather than deformity, Josey claims that the orgies among the deformed helped her to self-acceptance and self-discovery. Her actual contact with Gerald, however, generates little sense that this self-realization will be of more avail than Norman's vision of flight, in part because of the failure of self-acceptance represented by Gerald's surgery and in part because of the profound collapse of communication between men and women.

Alienation and violence characterize practically every male-female relationship in *Montgomery's Children*. Following the archetypal American masculine pattern identified by Leslie Fiedler in *Love and Death in the American Novel* (1966), the black fathers in Montgomery react to what they feel as the stultifying pressure of responsibility by abandoning their families, frequently physically but almost always emotionally. Hosea undergoes a spiritual crisis and leaves Meredith, an action that precipitates the death of their son; Gerald's father beats him mercilessly; Percy Moore repeatedly rapes his stepdaughter. Even Norman's vision of transcendence reflects in part an inability to communicate with his family. When Norman's wife, Claire, justifiably accuses him of ignoring his responsibilities after he begins to have visions of fire and flight, he feels an urge to "disappear, fly away," linking even the "miracle of flight" with the decay of social cohesion. Faced with the absence of husbands and fathers, the women and children of Montgomery withdraw into alienated silence or strike out violently. Gertrude Moore refuses to acknowledge the stepfather-daughter incest, thereby consigning both herself and Josey to silence. The only alternative, however, seems to lie in the reciprocation of brutality by women driven to extremes by abandonment and unable to endure further silence. Meredith's infanticide, Rachel Malone's attempted patricide, and Josey's killing of her stepfather when he attempts to rape her yet again all attest to the deep undercurrent of violence inherent in the breakdown of sexual communication.

This emphasis on sexual alienation, specifically on its origins in the masculine psyche, aligns Perry's work with that of Bradley and Morrison, each of whom also underlines the connections among sexism, racism, and the general spiritual malaise of Northern Afro-American society. Unfortunately, Perry provides neither fully individualized portraits of women comparable to Morrison's Sula, Pilate, and Jadine, nor detailed exploration of a masculine psyche such as that of Bradley's John Washington. As a result, *Montgomery's Children* in some ways perpetuates the very problems it identifies. Throughout the novel, women are identified primarily in terms of their relationships to men. Even when abandoned, they continue to view their experience almost entirely in terms established by sexual and/or romantic relationships. With the possible exception of Josey, following her enslavement of Gerald, none seems capable of even conceiving of an alternative vision such as Norman's. Even while delineating the realities of sexual alienation, then, Perry falters when he attempts to imagine modes of interaction or being not grounded in those realities.

On some levels, Perry strains against the limits of normalcy both in style and in theme. He intersperses historical digressions in his text, underlining the importance of a contextual approach to his observations. Simultaneously, he merges fantasy and reality without establishing hierarchical superiority, signifying the arbitrariness of such distinctions. Pioneered by Gabriel García Márquez and introduced into contemporary Afro-American fiction by William Melvin Kelley, Morrison, and others, these stylistic devices seem considerably less revolutionary than Perry's seems to have intended. His closing paragraphs draw attention to the significance of the intermixture of fantasy and reality, implying that reality, whether that of Montgomery society or of Perry's text, is primarily a creation of individual perception and choice. The closing paragraphs in fact challenge the reader to reperceive the events of the novel on a plane beyond that suggested by Norman's crash to earth:

> In the country of their imagination, into which we are seldom permitted, madmen fly. One man's sleight of hand is another's magic. According to those given to such inquiry, a vast range of experience lies just beyond ordinary vision. What you see is what you get.

To the end, what Perry sees, or wishes his readers to see, remains unclear. Even the final challenge suggests that Norman's flight occurs within his imagination, yet it continues to assert the reality of experiences lying beyond the range of vision. Again, the absence of fully detailed character studies makes it nearly impossible to determine the direction or degree of irony in Perry's own vision. Although he suggests the desirability of a mode of perception in which Norman's flight functions as magic rather than madness, Perry sees little realistic hope for such transformation. As a result, what the reader is likely to get from *Montgomery's Children* is a bleakly ironic vision that subverts even the hopes of its own concluding lines.

Craig Werner

Sources for Further Study

Black Scholar. XLIV, April, 1984, p. 8.
Booklist. LXXX, November 15, 1983, p. 470.
Kirkus Reviews. LI, October 15, 1983, p. 1106.
Library Journal. CVIII, December 1, 1983, p. 2262.
Los Angeles Times Book Review. February 19, 1984, p. 7.
The New York Times Book Review. LXXXIX, August 5, 1984, p. 18.
The New Yorker. LIX, February 6, 1984, p. 124.
Publishers Weekly. CCXXIV, October 28, 1983, p. 60.
Village Voice. LIX, February 6, 1984, p. 124.
West Coast Review of Books. X, May, 1984, p. 30.

THE MORTAL HERO
An Introduction to Homer's *Iliad*

Author: Seth L. Schein
With a preface by the author
Publisher: University of California Press (Berkeley). 223 pp. $22.00
Type of work: Literary criticism

Schein's wide-ranging study of the Iliad *attempts to sum up the research findings of modern classical scholars pertaining to this epic poem, including those of his own, for the benefit of both the neophyte and the professional Hellenist*

Seth L. Schein's *The Mortal Hero: An Introduction to Homer's "Iliad"* is a work that endeavors to accommodate the needs of two diverse groups. Although its primary audience is the body of nonspecialists who are obliged to read the Homeric epics in translation, the work also aims at providing classical scholars with a comprehensive survey of contemporary research on the *Iliad*. Anyone who hopes to succeed in writing concurrently on both levels needs to possess expository skills of a high order, and Schein more than measures up to the task. All passages from the *Iliad* that are used to support his analysis were, moreover, translated into English by the author himself for the sake of providing the reader with a more literal, and hence more accurate, rendition of Homer's lines than is available in other sources. The opening chapters focus on the technique of oral composition, the function of the gods in the *Iliad*, and the concept of heroism among the ancient Greeks. These sections are followed by an extensive analysis of Achilles' character, and the concluding chapter is devoted to a discussion of Hector and the Trojans. Schein not only synthesizes the views of many other classical scholars on each of these topics with great expertise but also supplements their findings with numerous perceptive insights of his own in the process.

Although the *Iliad* and the *Odyssey* were widely recognized as the products of an oral tradition as early as the first half of the eighteenth century, the technical procedures used in oral composition as such were never adequately understood prior to the field research that was conducted among illiterate Yugoslav bards by the American philologist Milman Parry between 1933 and 1935. It was his analysis of the formulaic character of oral poetry which first connected the extensive repetition of groups of words in Homeric verse with the metrical requirements of lines composed in dactylic hexameter. Perhaps the most accessible account of these findings and their implications for the study of folk epics is contained in a work written by Parry's colleague Albert B. Lord, *The Singer of Tales* (1960). Schein himself, in the process of explaining the manner in which the system of formulas operates in Homeric verse for his own readers, underscores the modifications and extentions of Parry's analysis that have been set forth by a new generation of classical scholars. It is, for example, argued that Parry overemphasized the mere metrical utility of such epithets as the phrase "of the shining helm," which Homer repeatedly attaches to Hector's name, at the expense of their associative value. Schein thus appears to suggest that Homeric epithets may actually serve the same function as do leitmotifs in the music of Richard Wagner or in the writings of Thomas Mann. By the same token, in his view, the originality of Homer is in no way diminished by the fact that he was constrained to work within the formulaic system of oral poetry.

Parry's discovery of the formula had an enormous impact on the Homeric Question and was largely responsible for the sudden demise of the view that both the *Iliad* and the *Odyssey*, in their present forms, are essentially collections of shorter poems by different poets which first came into being as the result of a process of editing that took place sometime during the sixth century B.C. Those who held this view are known as Analysts, and it was this school of thought that prevailed among classical scholars in the opening decades of the twentieth century. A serious shortcoming in Schein's discussion of the Analysts lies in his failure to explain precisely why this viewpoint proved to be so persuasive once it was promulgated in Friedrich August Wolf's *Prolegomena ad Homerum* (1795). Although Schein makes a passing reference to this treatise, he never discloses the set of assumptions that led this renowned German philologist to his conclusion. In essence, Wolf held that the original versions of the Homeric poems were composed orally during the tenth century B.C. and that the use of alphabetic writing among the Greeks did not take root until the sixth century B.C. Since the memorization of poems the length of the *Iliad* and *Odyssey* seemed to be beyond the powers of the human mind, he concluded that both epics must have originally consisted of a number of shorter poetic narratives which were later unified by editors living in literate times. Once having come to this conclusion, Wolf was able to find much additional evidence to corroborate his thesis. Parry, for his part, decisively discredited the notion that poets operating within an oral tradition need to memorize the songs which they perform before the public. Once a poet has committed the requisite traditional formulae to memory, moreover, he is able to compose poems of almost any length at will.

Two further developments also contributed to undermining the viability of the position espoused by the Analysts. First, textural analysis of the Homeric epics themselves has yielded convincing evidence that they may actually have been composed during the eighth century B.C. Second, inscriptions employing the Greek alphabet that were found on the island of Thera (also called Santorini) have been estimated to date from the first half of the eighth century B.C. or even earlier. Hence, it is entirely possible for both the *Iliad* and the *Odyssey* to have been put into written form at the time of their composition. The solution to the problem of the origin of the *Iliad* favored by Schein is basically the same as that proposed by Cedric H. Whitman in *Homer and the Heroic Tradition* (1958). Whitman, after demonstrating that the very complexity of the structure of the *Iliad* precludes the possibility of its oral transmission, postulates that an oral poet dictated the entire epic to a scribe in essentially the same form that has been handed down to today's readers. As sensible as Whitman's solution appears to be, it has not gone unchallenged. The foremost dissenter to Whitman's thesis is G. S. Kirk, a distinguished British classicist whose counterarguments are set forth in *The Songs of Homer* (1962). Although Kirk concurs with the view that the Homeric epics were most likely composed in the eighth century B.C., he maintains that they were first committed to writing in the sixth century B.C. and that rhapsodies transmitted these compositions over a period of nearly two centuries with an extraordinary degree of accuracy. It should be noted that *The Songs of Homer* has also been issued in a shortened version under the title *Homer and the Epic* (1965). Unaccountably, neither of these works is listed in Schein's rather extensive bibliography.

Another issue upon which classical scholars are still divided pertains to the question of whether the same poet is responsible for both the *Iliad* and the *Odyssey*. Those who hold that these two epics are the work of a single poetic genius are called Unitarians, while those who assign responsibility for each to a different poet are designated Separatists. Since the *Odyssey* never repeats any of the incidents relating to the Trojan War which are dealt with in the *Iliad*, it is reasonable to assume that the two poems were designed to complement each other. Whether such coordination constitutes proof that a single poet composed both epics is obviously debatable. In spite of his acknowledgment of the inconclusive nature of the available evidence, Schein unequivocally identifies himself as a Unitarian. His reasons are, in the final analysis, intuitive. In this context, it is highly instructive to consider the case of Richmond Lattimore. In the introduction to his widely acclaimed translation of the *Iliad* that was published in 1951, Lattimore expressed a preference for the position of the Unitarians. When his translation of the *Odyssey* appeared fourteen years later, however, Lattimore confessed in the introduction to this work that he had changed his mind and had come to favor the theory of separate authorship. More recently, Julian Jaynes has proposed a far more radical separation of the two epics than anything remotely contemplated by Lattimore. In *The Origin of Consciousness in the Breakdown of the Bicameral Mind* (1977), Jaynes argues that the *Odyssey* was composed at least one hundred years later than the *Iliad* itself. Jaynes, a research psychologist at Princeton University, bases his conclusion on the controversial premise that consciousness in Greek culture first came into being around 800 B.C. Because the behavior of characters in the *Iliad*, in contrast to that of those in the *Odyssey*, is controlled by voices from the gods at moments of crisis, there is considerable merit to his contention that the two poems belong to different epochs in the development of human consciousness. Schein, like most classical scholars, chooses to ignore Jaynes's provocative thesis entirely.

One aspect of Schein's analysis of the *Iliad* that is likely to perplex many readers pertains to his interpretation of the word "fate" (*moira*). At the close of a chapter on the gods, one finds a special appendix entitled "On Fate" where the author denies that the concept of fate denotes a predetermined course of events or that it is incompatible with freedom of choice. Students of Homer who have perused the writings of such eminent classical scholars as C. M. Bowra and Hermann Fränkel, however, have been exposed to a different viewpoint. Both of these men regard the destinies of mortals to be predetermined in the theology of the *Iliad* but at the same time underscore Homer's inconsistency in ascribing the source of fate's inexorable decrees. On the one hand, Homer seems to view fate as one of the primeval offspring of Night (Nyx), and on the other hand, he sometimes equates the decrees of fate with the will of Zeus. The same inconsistency appears in Hesiod's *Theogony* (c. 700 B.C.), where fate is described as the offspring of Night at the outset of the poem and then at the end comes to be personified as the three daughters of Zeus and the Titaness Themis. Both Homer and Hesiod are thus transitional figures in the evolution of Greek religion, and each man's work still retains elements of a theology in which fate is independent of the will of Zeus and not yet subordinate to his subsequent supreme power. Schein, for his part, must surely have specific reasons for not subscribing to this more traditional account of the manner in which fate functions in the *Iliad*, but he simply sets forth his own hypothesis without challenging the opposing viewpoint directly.

At the heart of *The Mortal Hero* are two chapters devoted to Achilles, the first of which deals with both his character and his role in the epic prior to the death of Patroclus and the second with the way that each of these elements is subsequently altered by this tragic event. Since Schein holds that warfare and death are indispensable conditions for the exercise of heroic virtue among the ancient Greeks, the slaying of Patroclus obviously provides Achilles with a legitimate motive to return to the field of battle where he is destined to die in glory. Not only does Achilles know full well that he will die at Troy, but also he is privy to the knowledge that his own death will shortly follow the demise of Hector. In an endnote to a passage where he underscores the vulnerability of Achilles, Schein takes the occasion to disabuse his readers of the notion that the myth of the Achilles' heel is an implicit part of the narrative background against which the plot of the *Iliad* unfolds. In his view, if Homer were ever aware of such a tradition of near-invulnerability on the part of Achilles, he chose to ignore it in view of its incompatibility with the theme of mortality that pervades the *Iliad*. Schein further indicates that the earliest literary account of Achilles' being immersed in the protective waters of the river Styx by his mother, Thetis, occurs in the Roman poet Statius' *Achilleid* (c. A.D. 95-96), but even in this work there is no reference to the Achilles' heel as such. The only other mention of his immersion in the river Styx which dates from antiquity is to be found in Servius' fourth century commentary to Vergil's *Aeneid*. It would be interesting to know whether it was Servius who first recorded the myth of the Achilles' heel in written form, but Schein never refers to the Roman grammarian or his commentary at all. The author more than makes up for this minor oversight, however, by his astute demonstration that the theme of the *Iliad* is by no means restricted to Achilles' *mēnis* (wrath) but also encompasses his *philotēs* (love and friendship) for Patroclus and many others.

In his preface, Schein mentions that he has been teaching the *Iliad* since 1968, both in the original and in translation, and *The Mortal Hero* obviously represents the intellectual distillation of this experience. Teachers of classical or world literature are, in fact, his true audience, and it is safe to say that those who have been charged with these duties will never teach the *Iliad* in exactly the same fashion once having perused this stimulating and informative treatise. At the same time, it may also be highly recommended to anyone having an abiding affection for the Homeric epics. Above all else, it is Schein's own love for the *Iliad* that manifests itself on every page of *The Mortal Hero*.

Victor Anthony Rudowski

Sources for Further Study

Choice. XXII, October, 1984, p. 264.
Library Journal. CIX, July, 1984, p. 1328.

MYSTERIES OF WINTERTHURN

Author: Joyce Carol Oates (1938-   )
Publisher: E. P. Dutton (New York). 482 pp. $16.95
Type of work: Novel
Time: The late 1800's and early 1900's
Locale: Winterthurn City, a fictional town in Upstate New York

An intricately plotted novel that adapts for modern purposes many of the conventions of nineteenth century popular fiction

> *Principal characters:*
> XAVIER KILGARVAN, the youngest son of Lucas Kilgarvan (disinherited half brother of Erasmus Kilgarvan)
> PERDITA KILGARVAN, his half cousin and the youngest daughter of Erasmus Kilgarvan
> GEORGINA KILGARVAN, his half cousin, about twenty-five years his senior, and the oldest daughter of Erasmus Kilgarvan

Mysteries of Winterthurn is Joyce Carol Oates's fifteenth novel. This fact becomes startling only with a consideration of Oates's preceding accomplishments, for the forty-six-year-old Oates, a faculty member in Princeton University's English department, has so far produced an oeuvre of such proportions as to beggar the strength and imagination of ordinary mortals. Her first novel, *With Shuddering Fall* (1964), was published but twenty years ago. In the interim, in addition to the other fourteen novels, Oates has also published nearly a dozen volumes of short stories (the first in 1963) as well as volumes of poems and essays. Also she has published a play and edited anthologies of literature. At the same time, Oates has taught English at the University of Detroit, Michigan; the University of Windsor, Ontario, Canada; and Princeton. So prolific an output in so short a time might suggest to the casual observer a certain dilettantism, but Joyce Carol Oates is no dilettante; she is a serious writer of fiction and an important figure in the contemporary American literary scene.

Oates has won many awards and honors: a Guggenheim Fellowship, the Rosenthal Foundation Award, the Lotos Club Award of Merit, the National Book Award (for the novel *them*, 1969), among others. She won a first prize in the O. Henry Awards for short stories and has had many of her short stories published in the annual volumes of *The Prize Stories: The O. Henry Awards*. Further, her novels have been offered as main selections or as alternates by the Book of the Month Club and by the Literary Guild of America. She is a member of the American Academy and Institute of Arts and Letters as well as the Modern Language Association. In fact, one critic cogently wondered when Oates found time to eat or sleep or teach or carry on other normal activities. Certainly, Oates's energy is daunting.

During the last few years, Oates has, in her novels—according to her own admission—been experimenting with form. *Bellefleur* (1980) was designated "a gothic family saga"; *A Bloodsmoor Romance* (1982) was a romance; and *Mysteries of Winterthurn* deals with mystery and murder. All of these novels focus on late nineteenth century and early twentieth century experiences in the American Northeast—a locale with which Oates is very familiar. Although this series of novels presents slightly different perspectives on similar situations, the basic literary approach remains constant: Oates takes her point of departure from the conventional eighteenth and nineteenth century Gothic novel.

This genre, which is still popular in the late twentieth century in the form of paperback gothic romances, can be traced to such works as Horace Walpole's *The Castle of Otranto* (1764) and Mary Shelley's *Frankenstein* (1818). Apparitions, supernatural occurrences, and unfathomable terror are the stock-in-trade of the Gothic novel; Oates updates the genre and shifts the locale, while retaining many of the conventions of the classic Gothic. Thus, in *Mysteries of Winterthurn*, a figure in a mural sheds not a tear but a drop of blood; grotesque deaths occur; the protagonist is inexplicably shut in a dungeon; mysterious evidence and so-called clues appear and disappear; murder suspects are and are not verified; and the innocent are punished while the guilty go free. Oates treats the Gothic novel ironically by exposing transparent inconsistencies.

In *Mysteries of Winterthurn*, Oates also mimics various practices of nineteenth century popular fiction not exclusively associated with the Gothic. She makes liberal use of dashes, preceded or followed by other marks of punctuation; a comma, for example, consistently precedes a dash and sometimes follows the paired dash; often, a dash will be followed by an exclamation point. In personal correspondence, reproduced to create the aura of verisimilitude, the ampersand replaces the word "and." Words within a sentence are capitalized for emphasis: "believing in the Unknown"; "wreak Justice upon his head." Likewise, words, phrases, and even entire sentences are, contrary to contemporary typographical practices, italicized for emphasis, for the same reason that some words and phrases are put in quotation marks. Diction, too, mirrors earlier conventions: Someone sends a "missive," not a note or a letter; "naught" is used for nothing; "albeit" functions mostly for although and occasionally for however. Chapter titles are reminiscent of those of Victorian novels, and the narrator—for the most part following the objective, third-person point of view—deviates periodically according to Victorian usage, to address the reader directly and to comment freely on the events taking place. These devices contribute to the ambiance of a period piece; in a 482-page novel, however, the overall effect of such devices on modern readers, accustomed to a somewhat more spare style, is rather like being force-fed a double portion of chocolate-mousse cake after a ten-course dinner: It is simply too rich, too elaborate.

Structurally, *Mysteries of Winterthurn* is a trilogy, each of the three novellas covering a separate group of murders. Each novella is introduced by an "Editor's Note" and concluded with an "Epilogue," in the fashion of many classic mysteries; further evoking the mystery genre, the endpapers of the novel feature a map of Winterthurn City. The first novella deals with a series of vicious murders in and around Glen Mawr Manor, ancestral home of the Kilgarvan family, sparking the interest of the then sixteen-year-old protagonist, Xavier Kilgarvan (from the disinherited side of the family), and inspiring him to become a detective. The action of the second novella takes place twelve years later, when Xavier is twenty-eight and an established detective in New York City. Recently returned from a trip abroad to study foreign crime-detecting techniques, Xavier visits his family in Winterthurn, by chance only four days after the discovery of the fifth victim in a series of grisly homicides involving factory girls. The last novella, set another twelve years later, as Xavier approaches his fortieth birthday, begins with an urgent anonymous telegraphed summons for Xavier to return from New York City to his hometown of Winterthurn. Again a charnel house of brutal murders awaits Xavier upon his return to Winterthurn. The investigation so strains his already overextended intellect and ingenuity that at its conclusion, Xavier decides to retire from his career as a detective. The plot intertwines all three of these murder cases so that they are not, in fact, separate. Such intricacies—Oates meticulously commands incredible quantities of detail with no apparent anomalies—will delight murder-mystery buffs as well as aficionados of Victorian novels.

The novel's love interest begins in the first part when Xavier becomes infatuated with his twelve-year-old half cousin Perdita—whose name, interestingly, has severely pejorative connotations when traced etymologically to its Latin roots: ruined, morally lost, profligate, hopeless, past recovery. In the second part, Xavier despairs of ever winning Perdita, since she announces her intention to marry the Reverend Henry Bunting and carries out that intention. In the third part, however, Perdita, by then a widow, consents to marry Xavier—a typical Victorian-novel "happy ending."

Further interrelated complexities of plot arise from Xavier's investigations of the three murder cases. In the first case, Xavier tentatively concludes that Perdita's older half sister Georgina—then about forty-two—was the perpetrator of the four bizarre murders, with strong implications that Georgina also garroted and mummified five infants (probably later disposed of in quicklime) resulting from an incestuous relationship with her father. Before a definitive resolution can be reached, Xavier is felled by "brain fever," and Georgina commits suicide by ingesting arsenic. Significantly, the family name, Kilgarvan—traced to its Gaelic roots—can be broken down into kil (cill), meaning burying ground, and garvan (garbh), meaning rough, coarse, harsh, thus suggesting burial in a rough place, which is quite in keeping with events narrated in this portion of the novel.

In the second case, Xavier confronts five ritualistic murders of factory girls and suspects the murderer of two additional murders of other women. In the meantime, the anti-Semitic sentiments of Winterthurn's citizens focus on Isaac Rosenwald, a Jewish office manager in Shaw's textile mills, as the likely suspect. Rosenwald is lynched by the Brothers of Jericho (a local version of the Ku Klux Klan) before Xavier gathers evidence suggesting the guilt of Valentine Westergaard, scion of a prominent Winterthurn family. Westergaard, however, claims that he was possessed by the malevolent spirit of an eighteenth century maniac who is buried on the outskirts of Winterthurn. Westergaard is acquitted, while Xavier's older brother, the ne'er-do-well Colin, is sent to prison as an accessory to the crimes.

In the final case, Xavier arrives in Winterthurn to find the Reverend Henry Bunting (Perdita's husband); a parishioner, Amanda Poindexter; and Bunting's mother, Letitia Bunting, savagely hacked to death by an axe murderer, and Perdita, clothed in her wedding gown, raped in her bedroom. Again, an innocent suspect, Jabez Dovekie, is killed, this time in police custody, which fires Xavier's zeal to find the real murderer. Despite discouragement, depression, and alcohol, Xavier ultimately identifies the murderer as Ellery Poindexter, husband of the murdered Amanda Poindexter, pinpointing the motive as jealousy, although Poindexter is discovered to have an illegitimate mulatto family in the suburbs. Evidence further indicates that the Reverend Henry Bunting was in the habit of sending anonymous obscene letters to women parishioners; thus, Ellery Poindexter's motive had some foundation. Before Xavier can bring him to justice, however, Poindexter dies of an apparent heart attack.

These meager details can but hint at the convolutions of plot and character which connect the three murder cases in the three novellas, but connected they are, in such tightly woven patterns that the cloth is whole. Nevertheless, the critical reader will be troubled by questions of credibility. Some specifics fit into the time frame—most of the characters, for example, behave and react in a manner appropriate to their time and place—but among the important characters, inconsistencies are noticeable. Perdita is portrayed as a mid-Victorian woman subject to various hysterias, instead of being depicted as a turn-of-the-century woman in a more assertive role suited to her social status. Conversely, Xavier is much ahead of his time in sensitivity and sensibility, not to mention technological awareness. As a consequence, the closely meshed plot and character development is slightly flawed, if historical consistency is a gauge.

Despite the trappings of a period piece, then, Oates has produced an existential novel in which Xavier Kilgarvan comes to terms with his life, his heritage, his time, and his place. Subtleties shade into significance as suspense builds. Minute details call attention to nuances of human behavior that otherwise might escape unnoticed. Xavier grows and learns through a tangled skein of experiences and ultimately—in a *Bildungsroman* tradition—accepts his own human fallibility, if not the fallibility of others.

Oates is a master of the novel form: She handles a complex plot with finesse; she develops characters in appropriate depth; she chooses significant themes. For these reasons, she has earned a deserved position of respect in American letters.

Periodically, however, as in *Mysteries of Winterthurn*, Oates becomes her own victim. Her experimentation with form and style, as in this novel, overwhelms her own best instincts as a novelist. The result is not a flaw in craft, for the craft of the novel will carry Oates through any difficult situation. Rather, the accretion of details in obeisance to genre opens floodgates of trivia and irrelevance; the minutiae clog the novel and try the patience of the reader. An intriguing story, well told, will captivate an audience. Oates has proved, in past novels, that she is capable of such a feat. In *Mysteries of Winterthurn*, however, Oates falls a little short of her mark because she tries too obviously hard to replicate Victorian fiction in a relatively modern setting with a protagonist who thinks too much like a modern man.

Joanne G. Kashdan

Sources for Further Study

Christian Science Monitor. LXXVI, February 1, 1984, p. 19.
Kirkus Reviews. LI, December 1, 1983, p. 1221.
Library Journal. CIX, January, 1984, p. 111.
Los Angeles Times Book Review. January 8, 1984, p. 1.
Macleans. XCVII, February 20, 1984, p. 60.
The New York Times Book Review. LXXXIX, February 12, 1984, p. 7.
The New Yorker. LX, February 27, 1984, p. 133.
Newsweek. CIII, February 6, 1984, p. 79.
Publishers Weekly. CCXXIV, December 23, 1983, p. 49.
Times Literary Supplement. July 20, 1984, p. 801.

THE NIGHTMARE OF REASON
A Life of Franz Kafka

Author: Ernst Pawel (1920-   )
Publisher: Farrar, Straus and Giroux (New York). 466 pp. Illustrated. $25.50
Type of work: Literary biography
Time: 1883-1924
Locale: Primarily Czechoslovakia; briefly, Germany and Austria

The most comprehensive English-language biography yet published of one of the twentieth century's greatest prose writers

> *Principal personages:*
> FRANZ KAFKA, the noted Prague-born author of fiction and parables
> HERRMANN KAFKA, his father
> JULIE KAFKA, his mother
> OTTLA KAFKA, his favorite sister
> MAX BROD, his best friend and literary executor
> FELICE BAUER, his fiancée for five years
> MILENA JESENSKÁ, his deepest love
> DORA DIAMANT, his last love
> OSKAR POLLAK,
> HUGO BERGMANN,
> FELIX WELTSCH,
> OSKAR BAUM, and
> FRANZ WERFEL, Kafka's lifelong friends
> ROBERT KLOPSTOCK, Kafka's friend during the final years of his illness

No modern reader needs persuasion that Franz Kafka (1883-1924) is one of the "sacred untouchables" of contemporary literature; that along with Thomas Mann, James Joyce, Marcel Proust, and possibly William Faulkner he ranks among the greatest prose masters of the century. His conversions of his private fantasies of guilt, shame, solitude, and dread into the materials of universally applicable art have succeeded both admirably and appallingly: The world has behaved as mindlessly and madly, cruelly and bafflingly as any image dramatized in his nightmarish fiction. Our time provides a continual exegesis of his work, which in turn has become an inner echo in our lives.

Kafka's posthumous reputation has been both enhanced and confused by a labyrinthine interpretive literature comprising, by Ernst Pawel's count, fifteen thousand titles. Some of the critical studies have been incisive, even profound: Walter Sokel's (1964), Heinz Politzer's (1966), Wilhelm Emrich's (1968), Walter Benjamin's (1968), and Erich Heller's (1974) come prominently to mind. Others, best unnamed, distort Kafka's work in pursuit of special pleas. The list of biographies is comparatively modest, headed by Max Brod's critical biographical text of 1937. Brod deserves acclaim for his honorable disloyalty to Kafka's last will, which instructed him to destroy all

Kafka's unpublished writings. Brod's interpretation of his best friend's work, however, as religious prophecy and a proto-Zionist affirmation of life reveals much about Brod's temperament but very little about Kafka's art. More recently two German researchers have published scholarly, detailed monographs on Kafka's life: Klaus Wagenbach (1958, 1964) and Hartmut Binder (1976, 1979); these have not yet been translated into English. In 1982, the British biographer Ronald Hayman published a detailed but sometimes softly defined life. Pawel's work is clearly the most comprehensive and best-contoured account available in English.

Ernst Pawel was born in 1920 in Berlin, moved to Yugoslavia when thirteen, to the United States when eighteen. His career provides several parallels to his subject's: From 1946 to 1982, he worked for a life-insurance company, like Kafka; like Kafka, he wrote at night after a full day at the office, turning out three novels and numerous book reviews; like Kafka, he composed his firm's annual reports. The idea of a Kafka life was inspired by a visit to Prague made in 1980 with his wife, who is a native of the city.

Pawel takes great pains to rescue Kafka's Jewishness from critics who regard him as a crypto-Christian saint or member of a German—let alone pan-European—pantheon of classic writers:

> . . . to read him as a latter-day Kleist, to trace his inspiration back to primordial *Angst* or Kierkegaard, and to invoke Goethe, Dickens, and Dostoevsky is to confuse form and substance, is to miss the essence of who he was and what he was struggling to discover within himself. Kafka's true ancestors, the substance of his flesh and spirit, were an unruly crowd of Talmudists, Cabalists, medieval mystics resting uneasy beneath the jumble of heaving, weatherbeaten tombstones in Prague's Old Cemetery, seekers in search of reason for their faith. He was their child, last in a long line of disbelieving believers, wild visionaries with split vision who found two answers to every question and four new questions to every answer in seeking to probe the ultimate riddle of God.

Kafka, Pawel insists repeatedly, "was, for better and for worse: a Jew from Prague." Such a statement will appear stubbornly reductive to interpreters aware of Kafka's affinities with Frederick Buechner, Heinrich von Kleist, Fyodor Dostoevski, Charles Dickens, Søren Kierkegaard, Martin Heidegger and others, and Pawel at least has the good sense to limit his critical reading of Kafka's work to an occasional paragraph or two. On the other hand, the statement points to this life's leading strength: Pawel's solid immersion of his protagonist in Prague's streets, schools, coffeehouses, parks, and—rarely—synagogues. He provides for the reader the specific, thickly textured circumstances of Kafka's daily life, particularly of Prague's German-Czech cultural tangles within the sprawling tentacles of the anachronistic Austro-Hungarian Empire. He flavors his biography with vivid accounts of the city's gymnasiums, universities, newspapers, periodicals, literary salons, brothels, theaters, spiritualist and dietary cults, history and politics, and he gives the reader superbly realized portraits of Kafka's family, friends, and women. The book's command of social density is splendid.

As a German-speaking Jew in a Czech-dominated milieu, Kafka suffered from multiple alienations. The city's population averaged ninety percent Czech to ten percent German during his lifetime. To the traditionally anti-Semitic Czech majority, Prague's Jews were doubly dislikable for being Jewish and German; to the increasingly anti-Semitic Germans in Prague, the Jews who shared their language were emphatically *not* Germans but a separate, detested race; and within the feudal Habsburg Monarchy at large, pools of bigotry widened and deepened against both Jews and Czechs. In the year of Kafka's birth, 1883, Czech, German, and Hungarian extremists organized an Empire-wide anti-Semitic movement. At about the same time, a theology professor at the University of Prague wrote a book accusing Jews of all sorts of immoral behavior; it became one of the bibles of Austrian Nazism. In 1899, a nineteen-year-old Czech girl's murder was attributed to a Jew allegedly intent upon draining her blood for ritualistic purposes. The accused was sentenced to death; his prosecutor became the virulently anti-Semitic lord mayor of Prague, holding office contemporaneously with Vienna's even more volubly anti-Semitic lord mayor. Anti-Jewish riots flared up throughout the Austro-Hungarian Monarchy from time to time, fueled by the siege mentality endemic among both the middle and working classes.

Kafka's parents considered themselves nonobservant Jews assimilated to Prague's mixed Gentile culture, "Austrian citizens of the Mosaic faith." Pawel sardonically notes that "what the assimilated Jew assimilates . . . is the anti-Semitism of his role models—one source of the corrosive self-hatred so widespread among Western Jews in the pre-Holocaust era." (The contemporary Israeli author Aharon Appelfeld has made Jewish anti-Semitism the dominant theme of his fiction.) When Franz received his appointment in 1908 as an attorney in the quasi-governmental Workmen's Accident Insurance Institute for the Kingdom of Bohemia, he was indebted for it to the father of a schoolmate, Otto Příbram, who had formally resigned from the Jewish community of Prague. Without such action, Příbram could never have become chairman of the Institute's board of directors. During the fourteen years in which Kafka worked for the Institute, he and Příbram were the only Jews among 250 employees. It is sad to learn that when asked to sponsor the job application thereto by an Orthodox Jewish friend, Kafka felt himself forced to refuse: "The Institute is off limits for Jews." When the Institute became nationalized as an agency of the newly created Czech Republic in 1918, all German-speaking executives were replaced by Czech managers. Kafka, who had performed valuable enough services in his position to be exempted from conscription during World War I, was kept in it, ironically, as a Jew who, unlike ethnic Germans, would support the integrity of Tomáš Masaryk's new state.

As a good biographer must, Pawel devotes much attention to Franz's antiromance with his parents. Herrmann Kafka (in 1917, with the Habsburg Monarchy crumbling and Czech nationalism rapidly rising, he dropped the second "r" from his first name to become less conspicuously Teutonic) was a butcher's son. With enormous energy and self-confident single-mindedness, Herrmann expanded a small haberdashery into a flourishing wholesale dry-goods business. During Franz's infancy, he seldom got to see his narrowly materialistic sire; the dominant impression Herrmann left upon his young and only son was of his raucous voice at mealtimes. "The booming parade-ground voice of that distant divinity," Pawel writes, "its ear-splitting vulgarity and thunderous threats, helped to stoke fantasies that never quite yielded to the prosaic image of the real-life father. It also left Franz with a lifelong morbid sensitivity to noise."

The mother, born Julie Löwy, was socially superior to her husband, descended from a line of middle-class rabbis and visionaries whose unworld-liness clearly stamped Franz's nature. Julie was a meek and passive twenty-six when the thirty-year-old Herrmann, hard-driving and irrepressibly robust, sought her hand in marriage. The match was not made in heaven: "You did not marry the man you loved," writes Pawel in a self-consciously sententious tone, "but loved the man you married. Marriages endured, because women endured marriage. Julie endured."

All Kafka students know that at the age of thirty-six he wrote his father a forty-five page letter that sought—but failed—to reduce the son's image of an omnipotent father-God and father-judge to the tangible dimensions of a flawed, capricious, often irrational human being. Franz wrote it as a plea for mutual understanding between them in their lifelong Oedipal struggle, but the purported love offering is, understandably, pervaded by his fear and envy of and rage against this man whom he regarded as a petty yet awesome despot, grossly crude, vicious toward his employees, selfish toward his family, smugly successful in the business world but contemptuous of his son's artistic genius.

Critics have hailed the *Letter* (which Herrmann never read) as Kafka's literary testament, outlining the underground foundation upon which he built his art. Pawel, recognizing his interpretive limitations, is shrewd enough not to explore its aesthetic import. Instead, he sensibly states that blindness of insight and failures of sympathy are inescapable in the Freudian triad of father-mother-son. He wonders that Franz should have expected the intellectually primitive Herrmann to follow the tortuous, Talmudic reasoning of this sophisticated brief, and he takes pains to point out that the father must have been dumbfounded by his brilliant, neurotic offspring's behavior:

> The man whom he in effect accused of having ruled and ruined his life, and of still dominating all but one single aspect of it—his writing, sole sanctuary and means of escape—was, as Kafka must have been well aware, scared of him, a bumbling clod helpless against the icy contempt of the certified intellectual. In the opening sentence of the

letter, Kafka quotes his father as having "recently asked why I maintain that I am afraid of you." Herrmann's real question, which remains unanswered along with the rhetorical one, was "How can you be afraid of me, when I am afraid of you?"

What is most significant about Kafka's family dynamics is that he was to feel throughout his life that they crippled him psychically, rendered him unfit to be "a healthy animal in a happy herd," left him locked in guilt feelings beyond his control. Self-disdain to the point of self-hatred and despair marked his view of himself in many *Diary* entries and letters. His strategy of dying in life became an obsession estranging him from close relationships with almost all women, let alone marrying and founding his own family. Pawel is illuminating in drawing the atmosphere of *fin-de-siècle* European sexual manners, which swung between extremes of license and repression, with women treated as either whores or madonnas. Kafka himself was characteristically ambivalent about women: He despised his frail body, dreaded physical intimacy, often regarded sex as the quintessence of filth and antithesis of love. His sexual initiation occurred at the age of twenty with a shopgirl freelancing as a prostitute; the experience repelled and depressed him. While occasionally indulging in inconsequential sexual connections with working-class women, he devoted most of his social energy during his twenties to friendships with men.

Pawel provides excellent character studies of them. The reader meets Oskar Pollak, of Kafka's age but far more self-assured and eclectic in his interests, passionate about art history and downhill skiing, dying a soldier's death in Italy in 1915; Hugo Bergmann, a classmate from preschool to the university, a brilliant student with whom Kafka discussed problems of Jewish identity and Zionism, who later became rector of the Hebrew University in Palestine; Felix Weltsch, whom Kafka met during his first year in law school, and who obtained degrees in both law and philosophy, became a librarian and wrote a book on *Religion and Humor in the Work of Franz Kafka*; and Oskar Baum, a handsome blind man, who became one of Prague's outstanding music critics. The basic foursome during Kafka's university years consisted of Weltsch, Baum, Kafka, and Max Brod.

Brod deserves and receives treatment in depth. Pawel informs the reader that by 1924, when Kafka died in relative obscurity, Brod had already published thirty-seven volumes of fiction, poetry, essays, and drama. He was a man of extraordinary vigor, critical acumen, and generosity of spirit. Not only did he promote Kafka's literary career, but also, working as a music critic and feature writer, Brod propelled to worldwide recognition Leoš Janáček's operas and Jaroslav Hašek's great comic novel, *The Good Soldier Svejk* (1930). Early in his association with Kafka, Brod came to the conviction that Kafka would become Europe's most important contemporary prose writer. He therefore became Kafka's unofficial publicist and impresario, only to discover his own authorial reputation eclipsed by his friend's posthumous fame: Brod's biography of Kafka is presently the only one of his works available in English.

After Brod, Kafka's closest companion was the youngest of his three sisters, Ottla, born in 1892. She proved the family's rebel, defying her parents by marrying a Gentile. Her passion for the outdoors encouraged her brother occasionally to garden, hike, and swim; her devotion to his welfare was boundless, and in a letter he called her "the kind of mother I would have liked to have." Ottla's spirited temperament enabled her—unlike Franz—to best Herrmann Kafka in head-on disputes. When Kafka found his parents' apartment too noisy for his writing, she put her little, medieval cottage at his disposal. During his last years of illness, she did her best to nurse him. Pawel tells the reader of the three Kafka sisters' tragic deaths: In October, 1941, the two older siblings, Elli and Valli, were deported to the Lodz ghetto, to perish there. Ottla, married to an "Aryan," was exempt from such a roundup. She thereupon deliberately divorced her husband, voluntarily registered as a Jew, and was deported to the Terezin ghetto, then to the Auschwitz concentration camp, where she was killed. Her husband and two daughters survived the war.

Outside his family, Kafka was able to relate with near-total intimacy to three women: Felice Bauer, Milena Jesenská, and Dora Diamant. His five-year courtship of Felice is documented in more than five hundred of his letters, which she was prevailed upon in 1955 to release for publication; a scholarly edition of them was issued in 1973. No letter from her to him has survived. Kafka was twenty-nine and Felice twenty-four when they met on August 13, 1912, in Max Brod's apartment. On September 20, he wrote Felice his first letter; two days later, he sat up all night to write his first great story, "The Judgment," dedicating it to her and giving the fiancée in the story her initials, F. B. (the same for Fraulein Bürstner in *The Trial*, Frieda in *The Castle*). Patently, life and literature intersect here for Kafka; tragically, they are at odds. Pawel calls Kafka's correspondence with Felice "his longest novel, the only one he ever completed." Felice grew up in Berlin as one of five children in an unhappy household; her parents were separated from 1904 to 1910; at age twenty-one she started working for a recording-equipment firm; by the time she and Kafka met she had become its executive officer, a testimony to her remarkable, lifelong efficiency and practicality—qualities which he lacked, admired, and feared.

This correspondence constitutes one of modern literature's most soul-withering texts, as Kafka pours out, sometimes three times a day, a monumental case history of his melancholic despair of self, his obsessive divination of life as his merciless enemy. A note of macabre *angst*, of nervous self-derision is present from the beginning: "I am just barely healthy enough for myself, but not healthy enough for marriage, let alone fatherhood." His only magnificent passion proves to be for his writing. The nerves of this patently ordinary woman are understandably shaken, as Kafka's self-lacerating letters inundate her from the dark labyrinth of his morbid pathology. During their infelicitous courtship, they meet half-a-dozen times, usually avoiding sex. After one such encounter, Kafka writes: " . . . all the time there is a tension as though someone were continuously slicing the air between us with a sword." He finds himself increasingly disabled by frequent headaches and insomnia. They become engaged in April, 1913, disengaged that July, reengaged in July, 1917, and finally disengaged that fall, after Kafka suffers a pulmonary hemorrhage on August 9 and is diagnosed as having tuberculosis in the apexes of both lungs. In his next-to-last letter to Felice, he writes, " . . . secretly, . . . I don't believe this illness to be tuberculosis, or at least not primarily tuberculosis, but my all-around bankruptcy. . . . I shall never get well again."

In the last, increasingly illness-wracked years of his life, Kafka did experience real love and brief happiness with two other women. The first was Milena Jesenská, daughter of a gifted Gentile Prague surgeon who hated Jews rabidly. The rebellious Milena defied her father by mixing with German-Jewish intellectuals in their coffeehouses. When Milena began an affair with Ernst Polak, a Jewish litterateur and seedy sexual athlete, Dr. Jesenska had her committed to a lunatic asylum for nine months. Upon her release, she married Polak and moved with him to Vienna. From there she corresponded with Kafka in the winter of 1919-1920, requesting permission to translate some of his work into Czech. Their letters soon turned intimate, with Milena relating to him her husband's neglect and abuse: He refused to support her, so she had to work as a baggage porter at the railroad station. Unlike the prim, composed Felice, Milena was vital, fiery, intellectually attuned to Kafka's art, impatient of the barriers that he erected to their meeting. In the summer of 1920, they spent four blissful days together in Vienna, avoiding sexual intercourse, after which he wrote her, "Since I love you, I love the world." Alas, the tempestuous Milena was still in sexual thrall to her husband and unwilling to leave him for Kafka, who urged her to do so. By December, 1920, they agreed to cease their correspondence, yet they remained friends. In 1921, he gave her his cherished diaries to read, with instructions to forward them to Brod after his death. Shortly after Kafka's death, she found the strength to separate from her husband. Pawel tells the reader that she made her Prague apartment a center for the underground rescues of Jews after the German invasion of Czechoslovakia in 1939. She was soon arrested by the Gestapo and died in the Ravensbrück concentration camp in 1944.

Kafka's last love was Dora Diamant, nineteen to his forty when they met on a Berlin beach. She had already left her ultra-Orthodox Hasidic family in Galicia, was preparing herself to become a Hebrew scholar, was idealistic, passionate, and lonely, and immediately fell under his spell. She gave him the courage finally to escape from his family in Prague and settle with her in Berlin. Pawel notes the irony of Kafka's finding serene happiness, in the final year of his life, in the least peaceful of European cities during the 1920's, wracked as it was by stratospheric inflation and nightly rioting by rightist and leftist extremists. In the last months of his life, Dora became his empathic companion, nurse, mistress, and daughter figure. Kafka's disease was rapidly gaining on him: On April 7, 1924, his larynx was found to have tubercular lesions, making eating and drinking terrifyingly painful. Dora took him to sanatoriums in and near Vienna, to no avail. When Max Brod visited Kafka on May 11, he found him literally dying of starvation while correcting the galley proofs of his great allegory, *A Hunger Artist*—whose protagonist fasts to death because the public has become indifferent to his talent. "Fate," writes Pawel, "lacked the subtle touch of Kafka's art." When death arrived on June 3, 1924, it released Kafka from excruciating pain.

Milena Jesenská's obituary article, published two days later, said in part:

> He wrote the most significant works of modern German literature; their stark truth makes them seem naturalistic even where they speak in symbols. They reflect the irony and prophetic vision of a man condemned to see the world with such blinding clarity that he found it unbearable and went to his death.

Gerhard Brand

Sources for Further Study

America. CLI, November 3, 1984, p. 282.
The Atlantic. CCLIV, August, 1984, p. 112.
Commentary. LXXVIII, November, 1984, p. 62.
Library Journal. CIX, June 1, 1984, p. 1125.
Los Angeles Times Book Review. June 17, 1984, p. 1.
The Nation. CCXXXIX, August 4, 1984, p. 90.
The New York Times Book Review. LXXXIX, June 10, 1984, p. 1.
The New Yorker. LX, June 18, 1984, p. 108.
Newsweek. CIII, June 18, 1984, p. 94.
Publishers Weekly. CCXXV, March 30, 1984, p. 50.

NOTEBOOKS
1960-1977

Author: Athol Fugard (1932-   )
Edited by Mary Benson
Publisher: Alfred A. Knopf (New York). 238 pp. $14.95
Type of work: Notebooks
Time: 1960-1977

This volume of Athol Fugard's Notebooks *is a record of his responses to the people, events, and country around him and reflects the concerns of a man working in the
theater as a playwright and director*

In December of 1960, at the end of a year in Europe, Athol and Sheila
Fugard prepared to return to South Africa. The overseas visit had been, at
best, a mixed success. Unable to secure a position in any of the British theaters, not even as a stagehand at the Royal Court, Fugard had been forced
to take a job cleaning houses and scrubbing floors. He had, however, been
exposed to the burst of theatrical activity around him, especially the work of
the so-called angry young men. He had also written one play, *A Kakamas
Greek*, for a company called New Africa Group that he helped found. It
went unproduced because a better play was written by another company
member. Fugard acted in this production on the Continent, which led to a
directing job in the Netherlands for another play.

The sojourn overseas might have been an even greater creative disappointment if Fugard had not begun what he considers one of the most
important writing exercises of his life, his notebooks: "It became a daily ritual to record anything that happened to me which seemed of significance—
sensual fragments, incidents, quotations, speculations. Writing now, I find
in them the content of all I can possibly say about my work." Excerpts from
these notebooks were first published in a South African newspaper in 1966.
Other brief selections have previously appeared in literary and theatrical
journals and, especially, in the introductions to Fugard's plays.

Fugard states, "Though I never consciously used the notebooks as a playwright, everything is reflected there—my plays come from life and from
encounters with actual people. But I found that as soon as I got deeply
involved with writing a play, I either forgot the notebooks completely or had
no need of them." Fugard may not use the notebooks "consciously" as a
playwright, but the record of past impressions and incidents has often
served as a catalyst to his imagination or as a reminder of dramatic
possibilities.

Although Fugard is never an impersonal writer—his last three plays, *A
Lesson from Aloes* (1978), *"MASTER HAROLD" . . . and the Boys* (1982),
and *The Road to Mecca* (1984), are especially autobiographical—the
notebooks reveal aspects of his life and personality that can only be inferred

from his plays. From the notebooks, one also gets glimpses of Fugard's relationship with his wife Sheila, and with their daughter, Lisa, born in 1961. The description of Sheila's labor, for example, is an extraordinary set piece which deserves a permanent place in any collection on the experience of birth; it is especially remarkable in that it antedates by a decade the explosion of interest in natural childbirth and the father's role.

Sometimes, the notebooks reveal Fugard through what they omit. There is, for example, no reference to the revocation of his passport and the fact that he could not leave South Africa from 1967 to 1971. Similarly, there are no complaints about money or hardship, except by implication. Fugard says nothing about the circumstances that forced him, Sheila, and Lisa to live with his mother for several years, but he does note: "Life in this flat has always been marked by a fight for privacy—a feeling that it is too small for the four of us."

Most of all, the notebooks reveal the openness of Fugard's senses to the life and the world around him and his ability to capture the essence of an observed character or overheard conversation with only a few strokes of his pen. He quotes his mother about his father: "His common knowledge was very wide. He had encyclopedes." The malaprop suggests the difficulty she, as an Afrikaner, may have had with English, but it is also a hint at the roots of Fugard's own relish of language. He tells another story about his mother and her advice that conditioning pills sold for dogs can also be helpful to humans: "But you must remember to order for the 'medium' dog. You get them for small dogs, medium dogs, and big dogs—you know. Great Danes. Well, the medium dogs is the one for human beings." When the anecdote was originally published, the big dogs were "Grey" Danes, perhaps another delicious malaprop rather than a typo to be fixed.

A dramatist is very much at work throughout the notebooks, but the dialogue here is with himself rather than the public. Fugard's musings on the boycott against South Africa's segregated theaters by British Equity reveals an aesthetic and moral debate within himself:

> The supposition seems to be that there is a didactic—a teaching-through-feeling element in art.
> What I do know is that art can give meaning, can render meaningful areas of experience, and most certainly also enhances. But, teach? Contradict? State the opposite to what you believe and then lead you to accept it?
> In other words, can art *change* a man or woman?
> No.
> That is what life does.

These conversations with himself often lead to the kind of bons mots which could grace a book concerning writers on their craft or a playwright's handbook. "These periods," he writes, "between the finish of one play and the real start of the next one—these false starts, playing around with and examining ideas—are finally very important in their quiet and unobtrusive way. What they amount to, I suppose, is the equivalent of the training sessions and exercises of an athlete—keeping him fit for the next effort." Fugard chastises himself for talking about a work-in-progress: "I must guard against this and make silence an inflexible rule when working on an idea. Talk *always* dissipates." He later notes: "I don't think I live negatively—the impulse to write is a vigorous, affirmative one, but it never has its origin in the need for answers."

Throughout the notebooks Fugard reveals, in only a few words, the principles that define his dramaturgy: "I am very conscious of the 'Image' in playwriting. My new play was generated by one such image: 'Milly is unnerved at finding herself still in her nightclothes from the previous night.'" Virtually all of his plays have developed from exactly such a concrete particular rather than from an idea, a theme, or a detailed storyline. Fugard also anticipates the actual structure (and weakness) of some of his plays when he writes about *The Blood Knot* (1961): "We all know that our story only gets under way after interval." Having articulated to himself certain principles of his craft and structure, Fugard, however, soon distrusts them: "Dissatisfied and suspicious of what I feel is a 'stock' pattern, a 'formula' which I seem to have used in all my plays so far, i.e. *growing desperation* leading to *emotional crisis* leading to the *leap*."

These notebooks contain the seeds of most of Fugard's plays and, in a few cases, running commentaries on his struggle to get them right. Sometimes he does not, and he simply abandons the project—such as *Man Without Scenery*—or returns to it repeatedly despite several false starts, as with *A Lesson from Aloes*, as if determined to will a play into being.

The notebooks will surely be the source of thousands of footnotes in future dissertations and critical studies, but Fugard is not absorbed only with himself and his own writing. A dozen or so entries contain succinct critiques of what he has recently read or seen on stage. Most of these date to 1962 and 1963 at the beginning of his career when, perhaps, he was both impressionable and anxious to compare the quality of his writing with that of others. For example, Fugard finds the final statement of Lorraine Hansberry's *A Raisin in the Sun* comfortable: "The audience will leave feeling good and this makes me enormously suspicious. Not because making an audience uncomfortable is my aim, but because a man dreaming, or wanting, is the most painfully beautiful thing I know." John Donne, however, is deeply admired: "Sincerity, discipline, at times harsh, even brutal—all that is opposed to the morass of sentiment. Excellent instruction." T. S. Eliot fails to appreciate fully the role of poetry in drama: "Beckett is a greater poet in the 'theatre' that he (Eliot) has been or ever will be. Eliot goes on and on about blank-verse as if the poetic imagination in playwriting must drag this ball and chain. That is surely one of Beckett's greatest discoveries—that we can free the poetic imagination of this dead weight."

Samuel Beckett is highly revered. After reading *Malone Dies*, Fugard notes:

> Hard to describe what this book, like his *Godot*, *Krapp* and *Endgame*, did to me. Moved? Horrified? Depressed? Elated? Yes, and excited. I wanted to start writing again the moment I put it down. Beckett's greatness doesn't intimidate me. I don't know how it works—but he makes me want to work. Everything of his that I have read has done this—I suppose it's because I really understand, emotionally, and this cannot but give me power and energy and faith.

A second major influence is Albert Camus, the writer most frequently mentioned in the notebooks. Fugard may have made a personal connection with the man—another writer of European nationality transplanted to Africa, nurtured by the sun beside the sea—but most of all he responds to the writing:

> Resumed reading Camus's *Carnets*. I would be happy to spend the next ten years deepening my understanding and appreciation of this man—and rereading and again rereading everything he has written. Camus sounds out and charts the very oceans of experience, feeling and thought, on which I find myself sailing at this moment. His importance to me is monumental. Reading Camus is like finding, and for the first time, a man speaking my own language.

The notebooks of both Fugard and Camus also speak the same language as they focus upon man's search for intelligibility and consciousness.

Fugard's notebooks have been edited by Mary Benson so modestly that nowhere does she explain why previously published entries have been reworded, how decisions were made on what to cut and trim, and why fully half of the book is devoted to the first five of the eighteen years covered. The handful of notes at the back are helpful but leave one hungering for more. Indeed, the entire book does this, and we can eagerly await volume 2 as well as, some day, the complete text. Although Fugard stopped making entries in the late 1970's because he thought a self-conscious tone had crept into the notebooks, he has since returned to them.

The sensibility of Athol Fugard revealed in his notebooks is not essentially different from that implied in his plays. The discontinuous and eclectic nature of a notebook allows the reader to focus, however, primarily, on the sheer quality of the writing. Because there is so little mention here of the racial politics of South Africa, one presumes that it is simply a given element of Fugard's life as, indeed, it is in his plays—not *the* subject of the plays but a means to explore the universal struggle of all men for dignity, meaning, and community.

It is obvious from his plays that Athol Fugard has mastered stagecraft, that he knows how to create wonderfully palpable characters, and that he embraces mankind even while revealing the evil of man to man (that is, the malevolence within all people). What the discrete entries of the notebooks reveal is, simply, the sheer beauty of Fugard's language, images, and perceptions, as well as his ability to penetrate the onion layers that often cloak the essence of a person, a place, a received idea. Regardless of one's knowledge of Fugard's plays, or even one's interest in them, the notebooks are a fine book of and about writing.

Russell Vandenbroucke

Sources for Further Study

Kirkus Reviews. LII, February 15, 1984, p. 184.
Library Journal. CIX, June 1, 1984, p. 1124.
Los Angeles Times Book Review. April 8, 1984, p. 3.
The New Republic. CXC, April 9, 1984, p. 25.
New Statesman. CVII, January 6, 1984, p. 24.
The New York Times Book Review. LXXXIX, June 3, 1984, p. 42.
The New Yorker. LX, April 30, 1984, p. 120.
The Observer. March 18, 1984, p. 23.
Time. CXXIII, April 30, 1984, p. 76.

ONE THING LEADING TO ANOTHER

Author: Sylvia Townsend Warner (1893-1978)
Edited by Susanna Pinney
Publisher: The Viking Press (New York). 199 pp. $14.95
Type of work: Short stories
Time: 1944-1978
Locale: Great Britain

Twenty posthumous short stories of fine craftsmanship and style

When Sylvia Townsend Warner died in 1978, she left behind a number of uncollected stories and a few not previously published. Thirteen of these uncollected pieces and seven previously unpublished ones have been assembled by Susanna Pinney for inclusion in this, perhaps the last, volume of Warner's short fiction. Lovers of the genre and admirers of Warner will hope that there are still more awaiting publication, but if this is indeed her final book, it is certainly a fitting and worthy close to a long and distinguished career.

In an age jaded by sensationalism and overwhelmed by crises, Warner's brand of gentle, charming fiction may seem an anachronism at best, an irrelevance at worst. The stories in this volume seldom look at the world portrayed by the nightly news but focus on one that seems quaint, curious, remote. Of the twenty stories, only two deal with "significant" issues, and these are set during and immediately after World War II, a period now remote enough to seem nostalgic. The remainder deal with lonely spinsters, the Elfin world, and English village life. Three of these concern an eccentric family, the Finches; four are set in the arcane world of antique dealers and their customers. It seems damning with faint praise to say that much of the appeal of this volume lies in its humor, gentleness, and charm—in its insistence on the importance of the individual and its sensitivity to the plight of the lonely. If that is the case, so be it; there are still those, one hopes, for whom these qualities are virtues.

Warner's brand of wry humor and her understanding of people are revealed in the series of four stories centering on a village antique shop owned by the fastidious Mr. Edom and his discreet assistant, Mr. Collins. This is a trade actually practiced at one time by Warner, when her lifelong companion, Valentine Ackland, began dealing in Victorian bric-a-brac and silver. Warner's insider's knowledge gives the stories their authentic ring, but it is her insights into human nature and village society that make the stories worth reading. "A Saint (Unknown) with Two Donors" pokes gentle fun at the pretensions of the trade and the foibles of the pious. "A Pair of Duelling Pistols" turns on the observation that people can be induced to pay high prices for anything (including a pair of superfluous kittens) if the seller knows his wares and appeals to snobbery. Curing Mrs. Otter's alcoholism in

"The Three Cats" is made to seem almost tragic, for in place of the charming, vivacious, alluring, and brandy-nipping lady—"one of those women who are sent into the world to turn the heads of ageing men"—Mr. Edom and her other admirers are returned a woman of plain respectability and coarse voice. Psychiatry has gained a cure, but the world has lost a person. "Sopwith Hall" seems at first glance a casual, wandering tale with a Maupassant-like twist at the end. Reflection, however, reveals that Warner has deftly exposed the heartlessness of good taste, the limitations of the aesthetic, by focusing the conflicts of a marriage on the purchase of a Victorian china dessert set. Her skill in construction here is masterly.

One of Warner's great appeals is her finely tuned sense of tragicomedy. Many of the stories in this collection tread the fine line between wry comedy and wistful tragedy. The title story, for example, presents an overworked and underappreciated housekeeper employed by two Catholic priests. One day, accidentally, she throws a handful of snuff into what is supposed to be lamb curry and is dismayed to find that neither priest notices. Realizing that "to be relied upon is not the same thing as being attended to," she launches a series of culinary sabotages, each as ignored as the first. She resorts to wearing her hair down to attract attention but is simply given a lecture. Finally, she resigns, marries the only man who has paid her any attention, and establishes a successful shop. The housekeeper's eccentricities and the priests' obtuseness are in one sense comic, but the lack of male communication and caring is sad. This is the kind of ambivalence that Warner consistently evokes with great skill. "Some Effects of a Hat" is not quite as successful as "One Thing Leading to Another" because it hastens too rapidly to its conclusion, but the inclusion of one of Warner's letters, outlining the incidents on which the story is based, provides a case study in the transmutation of fact into fiction. "The Sea Is Always the Same" finds its tragicomedy in a triangular relationship involving a young married couple and the aged Miss Belforest, whom they drive to a seaside resort so that she can revisit scenes of her childhood. Warner's depiction of the hypocrisies and deceptions which they practice on one another during this one afternoon movingly captures the difficulties people experience in being honest with one another while simultaneously suggesting the usefulness of the white lie.

Warner's ability to make trivial events resonate with significance is best seen in "A View of Exmoor," one of three stories dealing with the Finch family. Perhaps the most remarkable feature of this delightfully perceptive study of freedom is the way in which she uses that most hackneyed of symbols, the bird escaped from its cage, as if discovering its possibilities for the first time. Moreover, as in another story of the Finches, "Chloroform for All," she shows a perfect eye for describing the surface details of her characters' lives and environment. For the stylishness and verve of their descriptive writing alone, several stories in this volume are noteworthy.

As might be expected of a collection of this sort, not all the stories are of equal quality. Miss Warner's lifelong interest in the supernatural manifests itself in two tales that might loosely be called ghost stories and four that deal with the Elfin world. Some readers will find these among the most successful in the collection, while others may be merely entertained by her suggestions of ghosts and poltergeists and by the clear parallels between the world of humans and that of fairies. Of these, "The Proper Circumstances" is the most successful, chiefly for the vividness of its characters. Set during World War II in a small town to which Londoners have been evacuated, it is narrated by a member of the Women's Volunteer Service (for which Warner herself worked). She takes in two bombed-out women, the enormously fat Mrs. Moor and her equally obese daughter, Evie. Mrs. Moor is a practical, talkative Cockney, overly fond of her daughter but an able worker and an amiable, if plaintive, companion. Her daughter, however, is lumpish and pouting, a brooding presence in the upstairs bedroom who nurses a weak heart valve and waits for letters from her boyfriend in India. The narrator— surely Warner herself, barely disguised—is pert and sparrowy, with a well-developed sense of humor and tolerance toward others. The clash of styles between the heavy, lugubrious Mrs. Moor and her sprightly hostess forms one of the attractions of the story. Under Evie's baleful influence, however, things begin to fall apart. First a drain stops, then a lintel sags, plaster falls, soot comes down, and moths invade the closets and magpies the garden. The narrator suspects a poltergeist is at work but hesitates to jump to conclusions. Still, she cannot help recalling a docile horse of her grandfather who kicked its stall to pieces because of thunder in the air.

The four stories about the fairy kingdom are akin to those collected in *Kingdoms of Elfin* (1977). Warner's fairies stand about a head shorter than humans, are very long-lived, use their wings only reluctantly, and they are given to venial rather than cardinal sins. There is much court intrigue, jockeying for social position, and concern for fashion. Many of the fairies' problems arise out of their encounters with humans, and it is thus that "Narrative of Events Preceding the Death of Queen Ermine" derives its significance. The Kingdom of Deuce awakens one day to find itself invaded by men seeking to mine the iron beneath the Pennines but is at a loss as to how to combat the intrusion. Sir Haggard, whose counsels are ignored, takes solace in righteous silence: "There is no pastime so engrossing as being in the right, and when it is crowned by becoming unpopular no person can withstand its charms." As the digging proceeds, the fairies can do little more than marvel at the ways of men. They rescue a desperate young fellow who tries to hang himself, and they suffer from the noise and loss of water caused by the mining. A hilarious passage describes the fairies' attempts to understand Anglican church services. One group hopes to work from within and places a fairy on the board of directors of the mine; another observes the working conditions and lives of the miners and concludes that rebellion is inevitable. What happens is that a particularly deep shaft strikes an underground river, flooding the fairies and drowning Queen Ermine. The parable is clear: What once was a beautiful and peaceable kingdom has degenerated into ugliness through "mere materialism," and a native culture has been destroyed. The story suffers from the weaknesses of its parable form but is rescued from limp moralizing by Warner's sophisticated wit and elegant style.

The other stories of this group are less successful. "Queen Mousie" follows the struggles of Queen Ermine's successor, a plain, quiet woman who copes for a time with the responsibilities of leadership and then calmly commits suicide. "An Improbable Story" and "The Duke of Orkney's Leonardo" have great charm, as Warner never fails to create an entertaining surface or to touch on some element of human nature; still none of these fairy stories strikes a deep or resounding note.

Warner's first successful character was the protagonist of *Lolley Willowes* (1926), and throughout her career she excelled in creating females of great individuality and strength, who were always vulnerable to the limitations of prefabricated social roles or afflictions of the heart. Appropriately, two stories in this collection continue the tradition. "A Widow's Quilt" is a simple story of a devoted wife who finds creative release and her own private world by secretly making a widow's quilt—a black-and-white, single-bed-size quilt for when her husband passes away. Ironically, she dies first of a heart attack suffered while fetching more thread. Her friend's remark that "there was something wrong with her heart" cuts two ways, but even more telling is the fact that her husband believed that she was making a "magpie" quilt. Communication fails to the very end and beyond. Perhaps the most touching story concerns Magda, a Polish refugee put to work on a British farm just after World War II. Deprived of her native language, she descends steadily to the level of a work animal, silent, sullen, isolated. Her pent-up grief is finally released at the funeral of a farmhand whom she barely knew, but neither the preacher nor the others can help. "Her outcry was of no language," and the prayers of the vicar are empty, for "he had only words."

Nothing could be more fitting to end Sylvia Townsend Warner's distinguished career than these stories about language and communication. She enriched and enlivened the language of fiction by the care and originality with which she used it. Like her contemporaries. H. E. Bates and V. S. Pritchett, she had complete control of the plain style, with a painter's eye for surface detail and a poet's word-hoard of metaphor. Who but she would have a character say, "There's such a nice buttony cat on your doorstep," or describe a man's clothes by remarking, "his cravats seemly as collects appointed for Sundays after Trinity"? The publication of this volume raises hopes that more stories in manuscript await Pinney's editorship or, if not, that a volume of collected stories will not be far behind.

Dean Baldwin

Sources for Further Study

Booklist. LXXXI, September 15, 1984, p. 110.
Kirkus Reviews. LII, September 1, 1984, p. 824.
Library Journal. CIX, October 15 1984, p. 1960.
Newsweek. LV, January 14, 1985, p. 70.
Publishers Weekly. CCXXVI, September 28, 1984, p. 99.
Punch. CCLXXXVI, May 2, 1984, p. 60.
Times Literary Supplement. March 18, 1983, p. 278.
Times Literary Supplement. August 24, 1984, p. 953.

ONE WRITER'S BEGINNINGS

Author: Eudora Welty (1909-   )
Publisher: Harvard University Press (Cambridge, Massachusetts). Illustrated. 104
pp. $10.00
Type of work: Memoir
Time: The late nineteenth and early twentieth centuries
Locale: Mississippi, Ohio, and West Virginia

A distinguished author's reflections on her early past as it shaped her creative talents

> *Principal personages:*
> EUDORA WELTY, a distinguished American author
> CHRISTIAN WELTY, her father
> CHESTINA ANDREWS WELTY, her mother

The Harvard University Press has printed many lectures delivered by distinguished visitors, but it has never until the publication of this work produced a best-seller. The wide appeal of this small volume rests on many of the elements that have made Eudora Welty one of the most respected of American fiction writers: her unerring ear for the cadences of human speech, her ability to draw extraordinarily vivid characters in a few words, her sensitivity to family relationships, and her rich insight into the interplay of experience and memory.

The three chapters that make up the book, "Listening," "Learning to See," and "Finding a Voice," explore Welty's own past and that of her parents in search of those experiences that molded her into a writer. These chapters are, however, more than a quest for the springs of her own creativity. They provide a window on early twentieth century American life, on an era when schoolteachers inspired awe and fear in small girls who committed the heinous offense of saying "might could"; a time when trains ran on time and car trips were perilous ventures on dirt roads and dilapidated ferries. It was a period, too, in which death seemed much closer at hand than it does today. Each of the author's parents lost a parent early, her father at seven, her mother at fifteen. The first of the four Welty children died at birth, nearly taking his mother with him. Christian Welty, Eudora Welty's father, fatally ill with leukemia, died at fifty-three, on a hospital bed while receiving a blood transfusion from his wife. Nevertheless, the picture Welty presents of the world of her youth is one of richness and vitality. Her adventurous parents were quick to take advantage of the opportunities available in the first three decades of the twentieth century, and they provided a near-ideal environment for the nurturing of their daughter and her two younger brothers.

Welty's story is as much her parents' as her own, and she acknowledges throughout the book their enormous influences on her life. Christian Welty left his family's farm in Ohio and joined a small but growing life insurance company in Jackson, Mississippi, a few years before his daughter's birth in 1909. He was a man who believed profoundly in the future, in progress, science, and facts. To prepare his children for the world he saw ahead, he provided them with blocks, tinker toys, erector sets, and electric trains, and taught them about astronomy and meteorology.

His wife, Chestina Andrews, was equally courageous but in some ways less confident in her approach to the world. Her early years will sound familiar to readers of *The Optimist's Daughter* (1972), in which Welty has given to Becky McKelva much of her mother's past: the West Virginia mountains, the close mother-daughter bond, the large, devoted, musical brothers, and the nightmarish journey of the fifteen-year-old daughter to a Baltimore hospital with her dying father and her return home with his body in a coffin. Chestina Welty is presented as a devoted wife and mother who instilled in her children her love of books, but she is also seen as a woman who felt herself somewhat exiled from her true home. She obviously considered the social life of a young Jackson matron, exchanging calling cards and small talk, a waste of time.

Welty explores in some depth her parents' relationship to each other and her own to them, musing affectionately and sympathetically about their characters and their idiosyncrasies. Her father, she notes, was essentially an optimist, but it was he who never went into a hotel without chains, rope, and ax to protect his family in case of fire. His pessimistic wife, on the other hand, could show unexpected courage. Her heroic dash into her burning home to save her set of the complete works of Charles Dickens, given her by her dead father, was a family legend. Both parents, perhaps as a result of their own childhood losses and of the death of their firstborn, were inevitably overprotective, and their daughter had to struggle for a long time to achieve independence from their sheltering love. She writes of the sense of guilt that often accompanied joyous occasions in her childhood, for her own pleasure usually depended on her mother's sacrifice. She could hardly relish the delights of the performance of *Blossom Time* when she thought of her mother at home missing them. Even as a young adult traveling to New York to show her stories and photographs to editors, she left home "with an iron cage around my chest of guilt," for she knew how much anxiety and apprehension her departure was to bring her mother. Both she and her brothers believed that their independent ventures had to be extremely successful to justify the pain they unwillingly inflicted.

For Welty, one way to handle this guilt was to transform it into art, and that revelation is the main theme of this work, which presents both her era and her family relationships primarily as the source of the attributes she needed to become a writer. Almost the first thing she learned was how to listen—to the chiming clocks in her home, the whistling duets of her parents, the conversations of neighbors. She tells a delightful anecdote of herself as a small child, seating herself in the backseat of the family car between her mother and a loquacious woman friend and saying, "Now *talk*." From this friend Welty developed a sense of scene; the woman's life was filled with crises that constituted small stories. Another source of endlessly fascinating narratives was Jackson's town seamstress, who reported—or invented—every family's latest scandal. Much to young Eudora's frustration, she rarely heard the climax of any story, for her mother would stop Fannie at the crucial moment: "I'd rather Eudora didn't hear that."

Welty's pleasure in listening helped her to develop two crucial gifts: an internal voice and an ability to distance herself from events as an observer. Reading was almost from the beginning an act of listening. "Ever since I was first read to, then started reading to myself, there has never been a line read that I didn't *hear*. . . . When I write and the sound of it comes back to my ears, then I act to make my changes. I have always trusted this voice." Observing came early as well. She recalls clearly the period when she was confined to bed for a heart problem at age six or seven. In the evenings she was allowed to rest on her parents' bed until she went to sleep. They would shade the lamp and talk quietly together at one end of the room while Eudora lay in the dim light and listened comfortably to the murmur of voices. "I suppose I was exercising as early as then the turn of mind, the nature of temperament, of a privileged observer; and owing to the way I became so, it turned out that I became the loving kind."

Listening also led Welty into her lifelong love of books that began with her mother reading aloud and progressed rapidly to the consuming of everything she could lay her hands on. Taste, she notes, is much less important than the instant gratification of the "devouring wish to read." She was equally happy with fairy tales, Jules Verne, or *Bunny Brown and His Sister Sue at Camp Rest-a-While*.

Her formal education was apparently much less significant in Welty's development as a writer than her personal experiences, but she does provide vivid glimpses of her life at the Jefferson Davis Grammar School, the Mississippi State College for Women, and the University of Wisconsin. The highlight of her secondary school years was Latin grammar, which "thrust me into bona fide alliance with words in their true meaning, . . . fed my love for words upon words, words in continuation and modification, and the beautiful, sober, accretion of a sentence." College added the joy of finding poetry a living thing, for which one can feel real passion. The other major legacy of Welty's formal education is her memory of the schoolteachers who became the models for "the longest list of my characters."

Another important source of creativity for Welty was the family trips by car and train to visit relatives in Ohio and West Virginia. Traveling through towns, noting the distinctiveness of each one, and reflecting on scenes glimpsed fleetingly through the window of a train aroused in her the desire to know and fantasize about the lives of others. Resting in the stillness atop a West Virginia mountain gave her a sense of independence and a desire to strike out on her own. This trait was to serve her well in later years, though its first manifestation sent her tumbling down a log chute, much to the amusement of her mother and her stalwart young uncles. The trips, like earlier experiences, contributed to her sense of what a story is; each journey was a whole, unified experience that changed her in some way, and she reflects that it is no accident that she began her first novel, *Delta Wedding* (1946), with a child riding on a train.

Welty's first full-time employment as an adult added one last essential element in her preparation for a career as a writer. As a publicity agent for the Works Progress Administration, she traveled all around the state of Mississippi as a photographer. What she learned was to look attentively for the right moment to snap the shutter. "Making pictures of people in all sorts of situations, I learned that every feeling waits upon its gesture.... And I felt the need to hold transient life in *words*—there's so much more of life that only words can convey—strongly enough to last me as long as I lived."

Like Welty's fiction, her memoirs lead the reader from the particular stories she tells to a deeper understanding of the meaning of human experience. She begins her book with clocks—the chiming oak grandfather clock in the hall of her family home, the smaller one in her parents' bedroom that echoed the grandfather's gongs, the cuckoo that chirped in the dining room. These were treasures of her practical, future-centered father (perhaps a reminder of his Swiss heritage), and from them she gained the skill in handling chronology that a fiction writer must have. As she grew older, however, she came to recognize time as something different and larger, a "confluence."

Past and present, she believes, continually interact, so that experiences today cast new light on the past, and moments from the past reappear unexpectedly to change one's perceptions of what is occurring now. "As we discover, we remember; remembering, we discover." Lives separated in time, divided by death, converge in memory. The beloved parents, whose living presence sometimes created barriers, can be better understood as their daughter hears their youthful voices in the letters they exchanged during their courtship and holds the worn book that was her father's tie to his dead mother. Looking into their past and her own, she can "glimpse our whole family life as if it were freed of that clock time which spaces us apart so inhibitingly, divides young and old, keeps our living through the same experiences at separate distances." Near the end of the book, Welty quotes a moving passage from *The Optimist's Daughter*, in which her heroine, Laurel, reaches the conclusion the author is discussing here: "For her life, any life, she had to believe, was nothing but the continuity of its love."

Perhaps in this line lies the real secret of the popularity of *One Writer's*

Beginnings. It is a book filled with love: Love of human eccentricities (in the Jackson librarian who refused to check out books to any young girl whose skirts she considered too thin; in Miss Duling, the school principal, who considered it her prerogative to tell any former pupil, be he mayor or chief of police, exactly how his job should be done; in her Grandfather Welty, who met visiting relatives silently but talked ceaselessly as he transported them to the station on their way home); love of words and books, those she has read, those she has written; love of her family, not uncritical but deeply sympathetic and appreciative of the courage, the anxiety, the devotion of her parents, the humor and camaraderie of her brothers, the affection shown her by her grandmother and her uncles; love, in short, of the whole world out of which her experience came. "The outside world," she writes, "is the vital component of my inner life. My work, in the terms in which I see it, is as dearly matched to the world as its secret sharer." Here, as in her fiction, she has transformed life into art, and the book is a joy to read from beginning to end. One only wishes that the distance between the two were much longer.

Elizabeth Johnston Lipscomb

Sources for Further Study

The Atlantic. CCLIII, March, 1984, p. 132.
Boston Review. IX, June, 1984, p. 25.
Choice. XXI, July, 1984, p. 1611.
Christian Science Monitor. LXXVI, March 12, 1984, p. 26.
Library Journal. CIX, February 15, 1984, p. 371.
Los Angeles Times Book Review. February 19, 1984, p. 1.
Ms. XIII, July, 1984, p. 24.
The New York Times. February 18, 1984, p. 13.
The New York Times Book Review. LXXXIX, February 19, 1984, p. 7.
The New Yorker. LX, February 20, 1984, p. 133.
Newsweek. CIII, February 20, 1984, p. 72.
The Sewanee Review. XCII, July, 1984, p. R75.

THE ONLY PROBLEM

Author: Muriel Spark (1918-   )
Publisher: G. P. Putnam's Sons (New York). 179 pp. $14.95
Type of work: Novel
Time: The early 1980's
Locale: St. Dié, France

A novel which explores the religious and philosophical issues raised in the Book of Job

> *Principal characters:*
> HARVEY GOTHAM, a Canadian millionaire who is writing a treatise on the Book of Job
> EFFIE GOTHAM, his wife
> EDWARD JANSEN, an actor who is an old college friend of Harvey
> RUTH JANSEN, the wife of Edward and sister of Effie
> NATHAN FOX, a friend of Edward and Ruth
> AUNTIE PET, Harvey's aunt

Muriel Spark's interest in the religious and philosophical issues present in the biblical Book of Job began with her first novel, appropriately entitled *The Comforters* (1957), and forms the central concern of *The Only Problem*. In this work, Spark explores "the only problem" of suffering, of why the enormous amount of human suffering so far exceeds any rational cause or explanation. In typically Spark fashion, however, she treats her profound subject matter in an elliptical and whimsical manner which initially appears to contradict the importance of the novel's major theme.

The novel's central character, Harvey Gotham, is a Canadian millionaire who has abandoned his beautiful young English wife Effie because she stole two bars of chocolate during a vacation trip in Germany. Harvey has retired to a cottage in the French countryside where he is engaged in writing a commentary on the meaning of the Book of Job, focusing in particular on how the question of human suffering is treated. Harvey, a quiet, studious man almost obsessed with his project, desires only the peace and solitude in which to complete it. Instead, like Job in the Bible, his serenity and fortunate circumstances are torn apart by external events over which he has absolutely no control.

In the meantime, Ruth Jansen, Effie's sister and the wife of Harvey's close friend Edward Jansen, has moved in with Harvey along with Effie's baby, Clara, who has been fathered by a friend of Effie. Effie has become a member of an anticapitalist terrorist group called the Front de la Libération de l'Europe (FLE), which begins by robbing supermarkets and progresses to Effie's murder of a Parisian policeman. With Effie being sought by the French authorities, Harvey himself falls under suspicion and surveillance and must undergo hours of intimidating, repetitive questioning by the police. Finally, Effie is shot and killed by the Parisian police in a raid on the

FLE's apartment, and Harvey manages at last to finish his work on the Book of Job.

Harvey's initial situation in *The Only Problem* is that of a man who, although interested in the question of human suffering, has not actually undergone severe trials himself. His treatise on the Book of Job is a means to explore this question in the abstract, but events force him to experience in concrete fashion the issues he has long grappled with in his mind. Harvey believes that "the only problem" in terms of philosophy and religion is the difficulty of facing "a benevolent creator" who can "condone the unspeakable sufferings of the world." Although Harvey attempts to rationalize this problem by saying that man has perhaps "contracted" for suffering before he is born and that full human development involves suffering, he never discovers a satisfactory solution to this philosophical dilemma. Unlike Ruth Jansen, who argues that Job only truly suffered when he developed boils and was touched personally by pain and as a result deserved what he got, Harvey sympathizes with Job's belief that he did not deserve the pain inflicted on him, that suffering is never in proportion to what the sufferer deserves.

During the press conference in which reporters ask Harvey questions about his wife's terrorist activities and whereabouts, he begins to opine that Job's main problem was his lack of knowledge. Job, says Harvey, was without any system of study which could enlighten him about the reason for his afflictions; although everyone wanted to talk to him, no one could enlighten him about his plight. Harvey tells the reporters, who simply want information as salacious as possible about his wife and are angered and bored by his philosophical reflections, that "our limitations of knowledge make us puzzle over the cause of suffering, maybe it is the cause of suffering itself. . . . As I say, we are plonked here in the world and nobody but our own kind can tell us anything. It isn't enough." This lack of knowledge is closely related to the character of God both as He appears in the Book of Job and in *The Only Problem*: God allows suffering and asks questions but refuses to provide any answers. Harvey observes that when Job said, "I desire to reason with God," he fully expected God to state His case "like a man"; in reality, God remains silent and inaccessible, offering no explanations. God's performance in the Book of Job is not one of His best in the Bible, according to Harvey, who believes that God emerges as power hungry and full of bluster and pomposity.

The inscrutability of God and the irrationality of suffering are the themes that dominate *The Only Problem*, and the desire to understand pain is in itself a form of suffering. Harvey notes that Job not only argued the problem of suffering; he also suffered the problem of argument, and in both instances explanations failed to appear. Harvey admits that his analysis of the God of Job leads him back "to the Inscrutable" and that if the answers to the questions raised in Job seem to be valid, "then it is the questions that are all cock-eyed": "It is God who asks the questions in Job's book." He believes that the attempts of scholars to rationalize the text by rearranging verses which appear to make no sense are a perversion of the very essence and meaning of Job, for, like suffering, the biblical book eludes rational analysis. The Book of Job, laments Harvey, "will never come clear."

In the end, Harvey can only extrapolate less monumental meanings from the text and must content himself with studying effects rather than causes of the "problem." Suffering, he decides, may have a beneficial effect in that it makes the world more interesting and significant, and in this sense all human beings need suffering. In addition, Harvey meditates upon the role of the comforters; he believes that they helped Job simply by conversing with him and served as psychoanalysts while Job enacted the role of a "patient on a couch." The relationship between Job and the comforters also underscores the "futility of friendship in times of trouble"; this is a revelation not about the nature of friends but about the nature of friendship itself, which can function properly only in times of happiness. Harvey's relationships with his friends during his sufferings are a reflection of the same motif, for they fail to provide anything other than conversation and occasional diversions from his problems.

Harvey, although he resembles Job in many ways, is not a mere stand-in for Job, for Muriel Spark is too fond of irony and complexity to create any simple one-to-one correspondence between Job and her own character. Harvey's problem is that he is too insulated, too protected from trouble; rather than being afflicted with boils he is shielded from the truth about his wife and left in partial ignorance about her activities. Spark, however, does wish to make the point that suffering can take myriad forms: Harvey's troubles, though less overt and dramatic than Job's, are genuine and painful. The interruption of his work on the Book of Job is a real and agonizing experience for him, and he conjectures that "*Job*, my work on *Job*, all interrupted and neglected, probed into and interfered with: that is experience, too; real experience, not vicarious, as is often assumed. To study, to think, is to live and suffer painfully."

In *The Only Problem*, Spark uses elements of the style that have characterized her fiction throughout her career. Her narrator-novelist Fleur Talbot in *Loitering with Intent* (1981) admits that she treats her characters "with a light and heartless hand, as is my way when I have to give a perfectly serious account of things." The narrator's cool detachment from the events described (despite their seriousness or intensity) is typical of Spark also, but in *The Only Problem* the flippant narrative tone creates too great a discrepancy between style and content. Although the whimsical, witty style of the novel is quite successful in comic scenes, it is inadequate when the novel begins to deal with weightier issues. Spark's fragmented, elliptical structure, which was manipulated so delicately in novels such as *The Comforters* and *The Driver's Seat* (1970), is less successful here; readers may find themselves annoyed by her failure to provide a minimum of information or emotional context for characters and events. *The Only Problem* has a fragmented, disconnected quality that at times makes it appear to be merely a series of notes for a short novel rather than a finished product.

At the same time, the novel, like Harvey's project, is also a very serious commentary on the Book of Job. Standing before Georges de La Tour's painting *Job visité par sa femme*, Harvey observes that the painting of Job is more provocative of meaning than many of the scholarly commentaries on the subject. The painting, Harvey reflects, "was eloquent of a new idea, and yet, where had the painter found justification for his treatment of the subject?" The same question can be asked of Spark's novel, and her treatment of the subject matter is, like the painter's, unconventional for a purpose. Art, she implies, is superior to analytical criticism as a means of understanding Job's story; an aesthetic approach to the inscrutability and mystery of human suffering yields better results than will any attempt to "fix" the meaning through a reductive "interpretation." One can only *add* meanings to a story as bizarre as Job's. Spark's novel is a creative exploration of the philosophical issues present in the Book of Job; it does not attempt any resolution of "the only problem."

Angela Hague

Sources for Further Study

The Atlantic. CCLIV, August, 1984, p. 113.
Kirkus Reviews. LII, May 1, 1984, p. 427.
Library Journal. CIX, June 15, 1984, p. 1252.
Ms. XII, June, 1984, p. 34.
The New York Times Book Review. LXXXIX, July 15, 1984, p. 1.
The New Yorker. LX, July 23, 1984, p. 104.
Newsweek. CIV, July 2, 1984, p. 77.
Publishers Weekly. CCXXV, May 11, 1984, p. 261.
Time. CXXIV, July 16, 1984, p. 68.
The Wall Street Journal. CCIV, July 13, 1984, p. 17.

THE PAPER MEN

Author: William Golding (1911-   )
Publisher: Farrar, Straus and Giroux (New York). 191 pp. $13.95
Type of work: Novel
Time: The 1980's
Locale: Primarily England, Switzerland, and Rome

A famous author finds himself pursued by an academic researcher determined to become his official biographer

> *Principal characters:*
> WILFRED BARCLAY, an English novelist
> RICK L. TUCKER, an American academic
> MARY LOU, Tucker's wife
> LIZ, Barclay's wife
> JOHNNY, Barclay's homosexual friend

William Golding's ninth novel, *The Paper Men*, was not especially well received on its publication in 1984. To some extent this may have been the result of a kind of critical jealousy. Golding had received the Booker McConnell Prize for Fiction in 1981 for his immediately preceding novel, *Rites of Passage* (1980). In 1983, he had been awarded the Nobel Prize for Literature. After these accolades, the temptation for reviewers to insist that they, at least, were not impressed, that they were not the slaves of popular opinion, that this book was not up to the standard of its predecessors (and so on) must have been considerable. Nevertheless, there is something more deeply and individually irritating in *The Paper Men*, which may also account for the critical pique it created. It is a comic novel, much of the time, but its comedy is malicious. On several levels at once, it reads as an attack on academics and critics and reviewers of literature, simultaneously parodying and provoking them. It is, again in several ways, a prolonged tease.

Thus, it is notoriously one of the worst errors a critic can make to confuse a character in a novel with the author. Writing "Jane Austen says, . . ." when really it was Elizabeth Bennet or Emma Woodhouse, will always be reproved. Such a mistake leaves the critic open immediately to allegations of insensitivity, failure to perceive irony, naïveté, and so on, all of them very damning. All the same, and in full awareness of the risks involved, one has to say that the protagonist and "I-narrator" of *The Paper Men*, Wilfred Barclay, does look and sound a lot like William Golding. Their names have the same number of letters—a trivial point, but exactly the kind of detail that the academic students of the fictional Barclay would notice: At one point in *The Paper Men*, Barclay finds himself listening to a paper in which his great persecutor, Professor Rick L. Tucker, has counted all of his relative clauses. The number of letters in a name would be perfectly good evidence to Tucker.

There are other more substantial connections. Golding's career, it is probably fair to say, was marked by the instant success of his first book, *Lord of the Flies* (1954), which reached a level of sales and of popularity matched by none of its successors. In the same way, it is clear from what Barclay says about himself that he too was launched by his first book, *Coldharbour*, which he describes as a "one-off," adding rather defensively, "But the books that followed hadn't been bad either." Barclay believes that no one has appreciated these later books properly, but his recognition that this is so has only a bad effect on him. Sitting in his hotel room, reading imperceptive critical papers about himself, he decides that if no one understands what he is doing, he may as well write economically rather than in strain and anguish. So, he says, "I wrote *The Birds of Prey* in next to no time, with no more than five per cent of myself" to be sent to his agent simply for profit. Does the fictional novel *The Birds of Prey* have an analogue in Golding's works, in the same way that *Coldharbour* parallels *Lord of the Flies*? One hopes not. Still, one cannot help remembering that Golding went through a long unproductive spell of some twelve years between publication of *The Pyramid* (1967) and *Darkness Visible* (1979). What was the problem? How did he get restarted? Did he decide consciously to operate on a different level? These are all questions that people have asked about Golding. To find a character in Golding asking and answering very much the same questions about himself must be at least suggestive.

This, however, is where the tease comes in. If a review starts to identify Wilfred Barclay with William Golding, the reviewer can hardly avoid the further parallel: between himself and Barclay's great antagonist, the critic and would-be biographer Professor Rick L. Tucker. Tucker is a blockhead and a figure of farce. On his first appearance in the novel, he is found by Barclay surreptitiously rifling the contents of Barclay's dustbin, or ash can, for evidence or old letters or scraps of paper. Hearing the noises of disturbance, Barclay's first thought is that Tucker is a badger—and he is right, in a way, for Tucker's vocation is precisely to "badger," to irritate, pester, and hound Barclay until Barclay agrees to make him his "official biographer" (when, of course, Tucker will only badger him even more). Tucker's university, meanwhile, is the University of Astrakhan, Nebraska, which he refers to jocularly as "Ole Ashcan." He even has a sweater with the joke knitted into it. So Tucker is from the outset portrayed as a digger of dirt who is prepared to go to almost any lengths for the mostly valueless scraps of information from which he proposes to build a career. On one level, the story of *The Paper Men* consists of Barclay investigating just how far Tucker is prepared to go. He is certainly ready to steal from dustbins. He also lies cheerfully: The professorship he claims at the start is self-awarded, and later on, at a literary conference, Barclay hears Tucker claiming complete intimacy with him on no ground other than that of the dustbin episode. As matters become more urgent, Tucker sends his wife, Mary Lou, to seduce Barclay into signing a statement of permission; near the end, Barclay makes Tucker get down on his knees and lap wine from a saucer to prove he is Barclay's dog. There seems to be nothing that the academic will not do to gain status from proximity to the creative artist.

Nevertheless, the Barclay-Tucker relationship is not completely one-sided. Though Barclay, like Golding, has a low opinion of the academic world (for Golding's opinion of American universities, see the essay "Gradus ad Parnassum" in *The Hot Gates and Other Occasional Pieces*, 1965), he is still in a way afraid of it. Critics "make or break" the writer, declares Tucker in chapter 3. Tucker's opinion is completely unreliable, but a friend of Barclay says rather the same thing more convincingly later, when he talks about the reviews of another late Barclay novel, *Horses at the Spring*. Barclay knows that this was an insincere and "economical" book, but according to his earlier theory, the critics should not have noticed. They have, though. Barclay can hear their doubts even when they are trying to be complimentary. It seems that, for all the excesses of the Tuckers and the follies of earnest conferences, writers are bound to face a collective judgment in the end, and that judgment on the whole is likely to be correct. Maybe, then, Barclay and Tucker ought to cooperate. They need each other. This is the insidious thought that haunts Barclay throughout the book and makes his baiting of Tucker seem increasingly neurotic, unmotivated. One may say that if the novel is on one level a prolonged taunting of Tucker, by Barclay, and on another level a long defiance by Golding of an academic world he has come to despise, it is on yet other levels a work of nagging self-doubt, a kind of apology for the artist's life.

Another literary issue to surface in *The Paper Men* is that of plagiarism. Shortly after the Nobel award, Golding himself was accused, by Auberon Waugh, of at least unconsciously plagiarizing a little-known novel of the 1920's, W. L. George's *Children of the Morning* (1926), when he wrote *Lord of the Flies*. Most highly successful writers are accused of plagiarism at one time or another. The accusation is rarely true (and certainly appears baseless in the case of *Lord of the Flies*), if only because plagiarism on any but the most easily detectable level is so hard to prove: It is not the ideas that count but the similarity in the written versions. Barclay is therefore at one point properly scornful of the academic notion that everything in any book must have come from some other book and that what a critic has to do is identify his author's "sources." He must also admit to himself, however, that he did indeed once plagiarize, lifting a good idea from an unpublishable manuscript. A plausible accusation against *The Paper Men* is that it looks at times like a work of "self-plagiarism," with Golding (perhaps in a dry spell) lifting ideas from his own earlier books to try to give a kind of gravity, a hint of deep significance, to what would otherwise be mostly broad comedy. *The Paper Men* in several respects recalls *Pincher Martin* (1956): Both are self-discoveries by characters seen with increasing criticism and blame. Both end unexpectedly with death (for Martin, the reader discovers, has been drowning all the time, while Barclay at the end realizes that what Tucker is pointing at him is "a gun"—though the last word is never completed). Both have at their center scenes of terrible perception of God. One could, of course, remark that these similarities (and others, with Golding's other novels) are only to be expected in the work of any individual author and are one of the elements that help to create an oeuvre, but are the scenes in *The Paper Men* justified, or are they here (as they were not in *Pincher Martin*) for padding?

It must be admitted that the metaphysical scenes in *The Paper Men* are hard to integrate with the comedy that surrounds them: There are perhaps three such main scenes, the fall, the stroke, and the stigmata. The first of these might pass muster more readily, if it were not for the ones that follow. What happens in it is that Barclay (having resisted the temptation of Mary Lou) goes for a walk with Tucker along an Alpine path in fog. He leans over a railing, it breaks, and only a prodigious effort by Tucker hauls him back from the mountainside to the path. In one way, this scene remains comic, part of the Barclay-Tucker duel. It gives Tucker a stronger hold on Barclay than if Barclay had taken his wife. Actually, however (as Barclay realizes to his fury years later), Tucker saved him from nothing: What seemed a terrible fall in the fog was no more than a gentle drop to a meadow. Tucker (who had been along the path before) knew all the time that Barclay was in no danger. There is something compelling, however, about the image of the author poised over fog and death and oblivion but hauled back by the critic—especially if one reflects that Barclay and Tucker have previously seemed very much like Christ and Satan in the Wilderness (see Matthew 4:1-11), with Tucker tempting Barclay with fame, and with flesh, looking out over the world from a mountaintop.

The identification of Barclay with Christ becomes obvious when he begins to suffer stigmata, pains in his hands and feet analogous to those of Christ on the Cross. The question remains, is the identification convincing? Barclay is not much like Christ. The persecution he endures from Tucker may be a social nuisance, but it is hardly a crucifixion. Is Barclay not taking himself far too seriously? The answer "yes" is compellingly given when a vicar, in the final chapter, astonishes Barclay by reminding him, "There were three crosses." In other words, Barclay is suffering the pains, not of Christ but of a thief—and he *is* a thief, as he has admitted. If the stigmata, like the fall, are a delusion, then, what is one to make of the stroke, precipitated for Barclay by a vision of Christ, and succeeded by his confusion of *colpo* (the stroke) with *culpa* (sin)? Barclay thinks that he has been struck by sin, but to the reader's eye, one has to say that his sins seem trivial, mere mistakes or embarrassments. The turn of the novel from literary comedy to metaphysical depth looks awkward, as if from habit rather than conviction.

There may, admittedly, be deeper patterns in *The Paper Men* than have been drawn out so far. Golding certainly works with insistent symbolism, from the ambiguity of the badger in the beginning to the scene at the end, when Barclay provokes a brawl with Tucker beneath a statue of Psyche. The reference is to the legend of Psyche lighting a lamp to see the face of her lover Cupid and by that act losing him forever. Psyche, the reader is meant to see, is the critical faculty whose light is death to creation. Still, the symbol may be true, and be understood, without ever becoming convincing. On one level, *The Paper Men* is an amusing social comedy; on another, it may be a statement about the role and nature of the artist. It is hard to resist the opinion, though, that its main function to William Golding was to present himself, through his character Wilfred Barclay, as a man on the run, a man guarding essential privacy—as he put it in his 1982 collection of essays, *A Moving Target*.

T. A. Shippey

Sources for Further Study

The Atlantic. CCLIII, April, 1984, p. 142.
Library Journal. CIX, March 15, 1984, p. 596.
Los Angeles Times Book Review. June 3, 1984, p. 3.
New Statesman. CVII, February 10, 1984, p. 23.
The New York Times Book Review. LXXXIX, April 1, 1984, p. 3.
The New Yorker. LX, May 21, 1984, p. 132.
Newsweek. CIII, April 30, 1984, p. 77.
Publishers Weekly. CCXXV, February 24, 1984, p. 127.
Time. CXXIII, April 9, 1984, p. 98.
The Wall Street Journal. CCIII, April 19, 1984, p. 28.

A PARTISAN VIEW
Five Decades of the Literary Life

Author: William Phillips (1907-   )
Publisher: Stein and Day (New York). 312 pp. $19.95
Type of work: Memoir
Time: The 1920's to the 1970's
Locale: The United States and Western Europe

A memoir of Phillips' career as editor of the Partisan Review, *recording his participation in the events surrounding the literary and cultural politics of New York intellectuals*

Interest in the New York intellectuals of the 1930's, 1940's, and 1950's has steadily increased in recent years, as surviving members take the occasion of their advancing age and, one presumes, increased leisure to produce memoirs and autobiographies in which they claim to set the record straight, defend themselves and their friends from the unwarranted vilifications of rivals, and wearily reflect on the spiritual debasement into which their heirs on the contemporary scene have fallen. The tone of these memoirs generally is elegiac, occasionally, as with Norman Podhoretz, combative and hectoring, less often, though Irving Howe is a notable exception, hopeful. None is likely to make its way into the canon of classic autobiographies. Even now, the interest generated by these works is largely confined to the participants themselves, that surviving stratum of the New York literary world that has not been completely submerged in the profit and loss sheets of multinational corporations, and scholars whose research on these figures demands that their memoirs be digested thoroughly and, one hopes, critically. The constant temptation when reading their work and writing about it is to value their place and importance in shaping the cultural environment of the United States as highly as they do themselves.

Reading William Phillips' recent collection of reminiscences gives one the sense of a man at the center of things intellectual. Phillips was among the founders of *Partisan Review*, which, in 1985, he continues to edit. Phillips' own view of the journal's place in setting the agenda for debate over culture and politics emphasizes the Partisans' central but fiercely independent role among American intellectuals. He tries to show that they maintained a delicate balance between iconoclasm and swimming in the mainstream, and that when individual writers stepped beyond the boundaries, the aberration was either temporary or ultimately led to their leaving the fold. At the center of it all is Phillips himself, *l'homme moyen sensuel*, a voice of reason and restraint amid the cacophony of competing intellectual postures, who held the ship of *Partisan Review* on a steady course, skillfully navigating between the Scylla of Stalinism and the Charybdis of neoconservatism. There will be occasion to return to the politics of the journal and the function it performed among what was until quite recently the most important segment of extra-academic literary intellectuals in this country.

First, however, something must be said about Phillips' self-image as truth teller, the man who comes before readers to correct the errors, bad faith, and tendentious misrepresentations of previous chroniclers of the New York intellectuals. *En passant*, Phillips takes swipes at Lillian Hellman, Francis Mulhern, Robert Coover, E. L. Doctorow, Dwight Macdonald, Alfred Kazin, and Norman Podhoretz, among others. Lengthier, more venomous attacks are launched against Simone de Beauvoir, William Barrett, and, most of all, former coeditor of *Partisan Review* Philip Rahv. This reviewer is not in a position to dispute many of the accounts that Phillips gives of controversies and conflicts among the New York intellectuals, although competing versions of many of the stories exist (Phillips invariably disputes them, presenting his own as the more accurate, objective, unbiased). In two instances, however, about which this reviewer does know something, Phillips' memory has played him false. In the midst of narrating the story of his first visit to Europe in 1949-1950, Phillips remarks upon making the acquaintance of Stuart Hall, who is identified for the uninitiated as the editor of *New Left Review*. Since this journal did not even exist until the early 1960's, it is unlikely that Hall could have been editing it in 1950. Moreover, Hall has never, to this reviewer's knowledge, edited the *New Left Review*, which was, until quite recently, edited predominantly (although not exclusively) by Perry Anderson. A small point, perhaps, but in the light of Phillips' sharp (and unsupported with any evidence other than Phillips' own word) indictment of Mulhern for participating in the "steady erosion of truth on the left" because of the latter's claim against *Partisan Review*'s "accepting the political premises of McCarthyism," it seems worthwhile to note that Phillips' command of the history of rival publications is not always certain.

A more consequent lapse of memory concerns a controversy which flared up in the pages of *Partisan Review* in the late 1930's. It is cited here, not merely to demonstrate the fallibility of Phillips' memory but to illustrate as well the political bias that has dominated his thinking from the 1950's to the 1980's. In thinking about this episode, the reader will possibly wonder if Phillips is as innocent of the charge of supporting the premises (if not all of the specific practices) of McCarthyism as he avers. The incident involves Kenneth Burke, whom Phillips brands (along with Granville Hicks and Malcolm Cowley) a "fellow-traveler" of the American Communist Party. Sidney Hook, one of the few figures who emerges from Phillips' indictment of Left intellectuals unscathed, had attacked Burke's *Attitudes Toward History* in the December, 1937, issue of *Partisan Review*, charging Burke with, among other things, being too sympathetic toward the Soviet Union. For Hook, as later for cold warriors of the 1940's and 1950's, being soft on Communism was the one unpardonable sin of American intellectuals. Phillips' account of what transpired is as follows:

> I had stayed late one day and was alone in the *Partisan Review* office when Kenneth Burke arrived unexpectedly. We had just printed a critical review by Sidney Hook of a recent book by Burke. And Burke had apparently come in to complain about it. We argued a bit but got nowhere, for Burke wanted some kind of restitution. All I could do was to suggest he write a reply, which we would print. He thought for a few minutes, then said he didn't think "they" would like his appearing in any form in *PR*. "They," so far as I could make out, referred to the editors of *The New Masses*.

It is perfectly true that Burke was writing for *The New Masses* at this period, and since he supported himself and his family almost entirely with earnings from his writings, he may indeed have hesitated to jeopardize this relationship by becoming associated with what was, after all, a stridently anti-Communist organ of opinion. Phillips, however, insinuates that Burke's loyalty to the Party overrode his intellectual integrity and (in this reviewer's reading of Hook's egregious and *ad hominem* attack) understandable anger. What Phillips has omitted, or forgotten, is that Burke overcame his scruple about publishing his work in *Partisan Review* and wrote a reply to Hook that appeared in the January, 1938, issue of the journal, along with a rejoinder by Hook. Perhaps "they" changed their mind. In any event, one does not come away from Burke's piece (or indeed from any of Burke's major published work of this period) with the impression that it was written either by a duped "com symp" or by a loyal Party hack. Phillips has, in effect, smeared Burke in a way that was to become familiar in the late 1940's and early 1950's, and not only at the hands of the junior senator from Wisconsin. Any sympathetic remark about the Soviet Union, however qualified, was taken as a symptom of Communist Party brainwashing, and one could count on anti-Communist ideologues such as Hook and Phillips to man with vigor the ramparts against the infiltration of American intellectual life by agents of Joseph Stalin and the Comintern.

Phillips' anti-Communist credentials are scarcely open to question. He wears them as a badge of honor and presents them as the writ of execution which empowers him to drub old enemies (Rahv, de Beauvoir, Hellman) as well as more recent opponents (Louis Althusser, Frederick Jameson, Mulhern) for their confusion, naïveté, and equivocation about the real nature of the Communist menace. His early break with the Communist Party was the watershed moment in his intellectual development, an instant conversion to the way, the truth, and the light. Like other converts to orthodoxy, he is without tolerance for those who remained infidel, and knowing their imperviousness to the message, he sets out to damn them to the deepest pits of the inferno.

Most astonishing, to this reviewer's mind, is Phillips' apparent blindness to the role his and others' anti-Communism has played in legitimating the most brutal imperialist aggression abroad for an American audience eager to believe that the slaughter of Vietnamese or Central American peasants is justified by the threat posed to freedom, democracy, and the American way of life by godless Communism. Phillips himself undertook a world tour under the auspices of the State Department in 1962, hopping through Asia and the Middle East, where he felt out of place, threatened, and generally hostile toward the nations and their people, before recovering his equilibrium in the more familiar climes of Western Europe. He disingenuously claims that he was "not a representative of the American government," while taking every opportunity to confirm in his readers their native sense of superiority over the backward and ignorant masses of the Third World. The State Department functionary who approved Phillips' self-proclaimed independence prior to the trip, while hoping that Phillips "might have some good things to say about [his] country," perfectly understood that this pose presented no threat to the image of American power which the government wished to project abroad.

In at least one instance, Phillips abandons the persona of disinterested spectator of the political scene. It is a noteworthy moment because of the hegemony this view enjoys among the New York intellectuals as a group. Their political differences and personal squabbles vanish as if by miracle when the question of Palestine arises. Phillips' apologies for the State of Israel are of interest, not for their originality but for their being so utterly predictable and familiar:

> I am aware of the arguments by concerned figures like Chomsky and the Peace Now Movement that an Israeli intransigent nationalism alone cannot solve the problems of Israel or of the Near East as a whole. But neither can they be solved, it seems to me, solely by Israeli concessions. True, Israel is far from an ideal state, and many of its positions are not defensible, but we cannot expect this little, beleaguered state to be the only country in the world to behave in an ideal moral fashion. We cannot demand that an ideal democratic or socialist state be built in one small country, surrounded by hostile nations whose irrational and aggressive policies are justified on the grounds of nationalism, which masks their true purpose, the destruction of Israel.

This "little, beleaguered state" has, in fact, been victorious in every major military conflict in which it has engaged since 1948, with no Arab state even remotely rivaling it in military might. Nor, in the present conjuncture, is it likely that the supposedly "hostile nations" said to be irresistibly bent upon the "destruction of Israel" will be able to act in concert to overwhelm the Israelis in some primitive upwelling of Islamic fanatacism, as apologists for Israel such as those gathered around *Commentary* and *The New Republic* never tire of predicting. Neither the ideologues of imperialism in the American government nor the ruling powers in Israel itself are so ingenuous as to believe that Israel is the weak sister among the nation states of the Middle East. This reviewer supposes that Phillips, however naïve he appears in this passage, is no fool about the relative strengths of Israel and the Arab nations either. Which is why the pitch that Israel must continually make to maintain unwavering support among the American electorate for its brand of imperialism (Americans do not know much about the Middle East anyway, and they certainly are not otherwise inclined to look favorably on Zionism as a democratic ideology) always involves more than the implausible claim that Israel is constantly threatened with imminent destruction. The current bogeyman is Hafiz al-Assad's Syria; previous to Anwar el-Sadat, it was Egypt, but the demon lurking behind all the "radical" Arab regimes is, *mirabile dictu*, godless Communism. Israel sustains itself in the eyes of the United States as yet another island of democracy amid a hostile sea of Soviet satellites. Thus one has, in a symbiosis of virtually classical form, Phillips' historic anti-Communism easily cohabiting with his more recent pro Zionism. Small wonder that his criticism of Podhoretz's and Midge Decter's conversion to neoconservatism is muted and hedged round with praise for their honesty, intelligence, and political perspicacity. Once the patina of the Old Left has been lifted, Phillips' politics, like that of Hook, Lionel Trilling, and the *Partisan Review* group as a whole, appears more nakedly for what it is: classical Cold War liberalism, the popularity of which has hardly diminished since its heyday from Harry S Truman through the Kennedys. As a coda to this account of Phillips' past and the politics he has consistently pursued, it should be recalled that that patron saint of the liberal establishment (on whose behalf Phillips proudly recalls he campaigned in 1968), Robert F. Kennedy, cut his political teeth, not in a righteous crusade against Jimmy Hoffa's Teamsters but as an assistant on the Joseph McCarthy committee. Only to a willed and self-serving naïveté do the bedfellows made by politics seem unduly strange.

Michael Sprinker

Sources for Further Study

Best Sellers. XLIII, March, 1984, p. 450.
Booklist. LXXX, January 1, 1984, p. 651.
Choice. XXI, May, 1984, p. 1308.
Christian Science Monitor. LXXVI, March 29, 1984, p. 20.
Kirkus Reviews. LI, December 1, 1983, p. 1248.
Library Journal. CIX, January, 1984, p. 92.
Los Angeles Times Book Review. February 12, 1984, p. 8.
National Review. XXXVI, March 23, 1984, p. 40.
New Leader. LXVI, December 12, 1983, p. 5.
The New Republic. CXC, February 6, 1984, p. 30.
The New York Times Book Review. LXXXIX, January 8, 1984, p. 28.
Publishers Weekly. CCXXIV, November 25, 1983, p. 56.

THE PERIODIC TABLE

Author: Primo Levi (1919-   )
Translated from the Italian by Raymond Rosenthal
Publisher: Shocken Books (New York). 233 pp. $16.95
Type of work: Memoirs

Reminiscences by the author about his development as a man and as a writer, viewed from the vantage point of his trade as a chemist

Primo Levi is best known for his memoirs of the concentration camps, *Survival in Auschwitz* (1961) and *The Re-awakening* (1965). *The Periodic Table* (published in Italy in 1975 as *Il sistema periodico*) is, in Levi's own words, an attempt to write "a micro-history, the history of a trade and its defeats, victories, and miseries." The trade is chemistry, and Levi, a lifelong practitioner, succeeds admirably in describing the unique characteristics of his vocation. Gifted with the imagination of a fabulist as well as with the analytic mind of a chemist, Levi also succeeds in doing much more. He pays tribute to the peculiarly human determination to wrestle with matter, as desperately as Jacob with the angel, so as to obtain the blessing of order in a world of apparent disorder. Accordingly, Levi's brilliant ability, demonstrated throughout this book, of animating lumpish matter is not mere whimsy or rhetorical dash but a most serious effort to humanize the world, to see primal and primeval matter as irrevocably altered by the impress of human history. Levi's passion for order is also a search for meaning, an enterprise made all the more urgent by the facts of Levi's personal history as a Jew and as a survivor of Auschwitz and by the horrors of recent world history, which call into question the meaning and value of human existence.

The structure of the book is an appropriate one. Each chapter takes its name from an element on the periodic table: In some chapters, this element merely serves as a reminder of some incident in Levi's life, but in others the element serves as a foil, metaphor, or symbol to illuminate a distinct period in Levi's past. Because Levi's work as an analytic chemist has focused on problems presented by particular elements, each chapter is problem-centered, simultaneously revealing Levi the chemist wrestling with a chemical problem and Levi the man grappling with a personal problem. Much of the energy, wit, and playfulness of these narratives proceeds from Levi's consideration of how these two aspects of his life intersect.

Levi's narrative begins not with his life but with a kind of prologue in a brief account of the Jewish community in Piedmont, Italy, into which he was born. In this chapter, "Argon," Levi describes the insular, static life of Piedmontese Jews, which was similar to the inert gas argon. As Levi describes them, they were "inert in their inner spirits, inclined to disinterested speculation, witty discourses, elegant, sophisticated, and gratuitous discussion." They enjoyed the evanescent security of a time which tolerated independence and eccentricity, the time before the rise of Fascism. Levi lovingly re-creates their feeling of interrelatedness in their calling every older member of the community either "aunt" or "uncle," and in their unique dialect, a mixture of Piedmontese and Hebrew, distinct from Italian in being rich not in curses but in "not very decent" terms, which offered the virtue "of relieving the heart without abrading the mouth." The rich detail of this chapter gives it a particular poignancy in commemorating a culture now long dead.

The first chapter about Levi himself is "Hydrogen," the first element on the periodic table and the first chemical element that Levi makes in a lab. The young Primo of this chapter sneaks into a laboratory at night to conduct his first chemical experiment, the formation of hydrogen and oxygen from water. Although his product explodes, he is triumphant in his newfound knowledge. The young experimenter is the prototype for the unquenchably inquisitive grown man. This chapter reads like the first chapter in a *Bildungsroman*: The only difference—if it is a difference—is that the talented young man whom the reader follows will develop into a scientist rather than an artist.

The reader follows Primo from the *liceo* to the Chemical Institute. In "Zinc," the young chemistry student tries to solve two problems: to prepare zinc sulfate from zinc and to win over his cold, indifferent lab mate, Rita. Characteristically, he personifies his laboratory endeavor, describing his experiment in imagery befitting his other pursuit. With delicious wit, he describes his laboratory work in sexual terms as an encounter with "the so tender and delicate zinc, so yielding to acid which gulps it down in a single mouthful." Rita, however, proves to be made of a more unyielding substance, and he spends so much time talking her into letting him walk her home that he ruins his experiment.

In "Zinc," he clarifies for himself as well some important ideas. Observing that zinc, when it is very pure, steadfastly resists combining with other elements, he notes that one can use this property to illustrate two conflicting morals, the praise of purity or the praise of impurity. He decides upon the necessity of impurity, telling himself "for life to be lived, impurities are needed.... Dissension, diversity, the grain of salt and mustard are needed: Fascism does not want them, forbids them, and that's why you're not a Fascist; it wants everybody to be the same, and you are not." Thus he comes to pride himself on his distinctiveness.

In one of the most moving chapters in the book, "Iron," Levi recalls his friendship with a remarkable young man named Sandro. His friend, a man of action rather than of words, was a great lover of nature and an extremely adept mountain climber. Sandro constantly urged the bookish Primo to accompany him on his rambles. These excursions into the mountains, arduous and dangerous as they were, proved wonderfully exhilarating, for they helped the young men to prove themselves and to prepare themselves "for an iron future, drawing closer month by month."

By January, 1941, Levi and his friends, lacking both the money and the initiative to escape from the lengthening shadow of German domination, lived by blinding themselves to the extent of the threat. Levi subsisted on a series of odd jobs as a chemist, from which he extracted not only necessary chemicals but also guidelines that would prove useful for his life. First he was hired as a lab assistant. Asked to perform a distillation with sodium, he decided to use the more easily obtainable potassium, sodium's apparent twin. When the experiment catches fire, he learns that "one must distrust the almost-the-same... the practically identical, the approximate," observing that the chemist's trade often consists of detecting small differences. He pointedly adds, "And not only the chemist's trade."

The chapter "Nickel" finds Levi working to extract nickel from the waste products of an asbestos mine. Working for some time unsuccessfully, he comes up with a hypothetical method for extracting the metal. He is so exhilarated at his brilliance that he temporarily forgets that this process, if successful, will greatly help the German war effort. Fortunately his hypothesis is incorrect, and the procedure fails.

During this period, Levi turned to writing fables in his spare time to escape the anxiety and danger of his daily life. *The Periodic Table* includes two curious fables written during this period. Read as allegories, they pay tribute to two opposed traits that combine in the talented chemist. The first, "Lead," is a tribute to dogged persistence. It follows the wanderings of Rodmund, a lead-smith, who tries his hand at many trades, only to return to the one he was born to and loves, knowing that it will result in his early death. He resigns himself to this consequence of his toxic vocation, marrying just in time to ensure the survival of his trade in the child his wife is carrying. The second, "Mercury," honors the ability to adapt to change. In it, a couple living on a remote island are visited by four adventurers who propose that they all make a living by distilling the mercury to be found there. One of the new arrivals also takes a fancy to the wife. First they import four more females, so that all may marry. Then the husband and the wife change partners and embark on their new occupation, leaving behind their former stable but dull existence.

In a final period of fear and waiting, described in "Phosphorus," Levi worked without conviction in a laboratory to test the groundless hypothesis that phosphorus is a cure for diabetes. Equally fruitless at the time was his crush on his lab partner, Giulia, engaged to another man. At her request, he carries her, tantalizingly out of reach on the handlebars of his bicycle, to the home of her future in-laws to resolve their differences. Knowing this to be his last chance, Levi nevertheless is unable to tell her how he feels about her. Years later, they meet again and speak of what almost was, agreeing "that a veil, a breath, a throw of the dice deflected us onto two divergent paths, which were not ours."

In 1943, Levi joined the partisans to fight against the Fascists. Shortly thereafter, Levi was captured and imprisoned by the Germans, who sent him to Auschwitz. The chapter "Gold" tells of his encounter in a holding cell with another prisoner, a gold prospector and seller of contraband, who is about to be released. He urges Levi to try prospecting for gold when he gets out, and Levi thinks of the gold of life itself, so much of which he has yet to experience and may never live to experience.

The most disturbing chapter of the book is "Cerium," which recalls Levi's stay in Auschwitz. Suffering from overwhelming hunger, Levi, working as a chemist in a chemical laboratory, tried eating all sorts of indigestible substances: fatty acids, glycerine, and fritters made of sanitary cotton. He soon realized that he had to learn to steal in order to survive. Mastering with difficulty the skills necessary for theft, he looked desperately about him for something worth stealing, something that could be traded for food in the intricate underground market of the death camp. He found a bunch of small rods, which proved to be iron-cerium, an alloy used to make flints for cigarette lighters. These he and his lab partner managed to sell to the makers of clandestine cigarette lighters in exchange for food: one flint for one day's bread ration. Thus he and his friend were able to buy for themselves enough bread to survive for two months, until Soviet troops entered and liberated the camp. In this instance, Levi's knowledge of chemistry was literally lifesaving.

After the war ended, Levi's great task was to recover from his experiences at Auschwitz. He was helped in his recovery by his meeting with a vital young woman who was to become his wife, and by his new job as a chemist-sleuth hired to find out why a certain batch of paint in a paint factory had "livered"—that is, turned to a thick, useless, liver-textured substance. Armed with past lab notebooks and files, he renewed once more his battle with matter. In "Chromium," he notes that "the adversary was still the same, the not-I . . . stupid matter, slothfully hostile as human stupidity is hostile." Through an admirable process of detection, Levi finds the faulty entry in a lab notebook and restores the texture of the defective paint by the addition of ammonium chloride. Years later, he learns that his addition of this substance, needed only one time, has been incorporated into the basic formula for the paint. So, quite needlessly, ammonium chloride, for long-forgotten reasons, is still systematically incorporated into every new batch of paint.

In the postwar years, scrambling frantically to make a living, Levi took on all kinds of strange chemical tasks. In partnership with a friend, he worked in a makeshift lab in the home of his friend's long-suffering parents. There, in a cramped apartment filled with demijohns of hydrochloric acid, they worked to turn tin into stannous chloride to sell to mirror manufacturers; to detect arsenic in a pound of sugar sent to a shoemaker by his jealous and unsuccessful rival; and to correct the lipstick formula of a mafioso lipstick manufacturer whose cheap imitation of a Paris product had an unfortunate tendency to bleed.

Finally Levi left the lab for a customer-service job. The chapter "Vanadium" finds Levi at this job, undertaking to answer a larger and far more difficult question than any he has yet asked. He asks for the answer from his former enemy, now his counterpart at a chemical factory in Germany.

The episode begins with a correspondence between Levi and a Dr. Müller over a company dispute. The company Levi represents has received a batch of varnish that will not harden, and Levi asks the German company to make good on the order, but the German firm denies responsibility for the problem. Then Levi, employing his well-honed sleuthing skills, begins to suspect from a consistent and peculiar spelling error that his correspondent is the same Dr. Müller who managed the laboratory in which Levi worked at Auschwitz. Levi, exhilarated to confront his former enemy (albeit one who had shown some kindness by getting him a pair of shoes), begins a personal correspondence with him. Levi demands in essence that Müller accept responsibility for Auschwitz, but Müller's reply is neither that of a penitent nor of an unregenerate Nazi. Rather, Müller shows himself to be "neither infamous nor a hero," but "a typically gray human specimen, one of the not so few one-eyed men in the kingdom of the blind." To relieve his conscience, Müller pleads for a personal meeting, to which Levi reluctantly consents. Before the meeting takes place, Müller dies unexpectedly. The meaning of Müller's death and the extent and nature of his responsibility—the answers to these questions is silence. Implicitly, the book acknowledges that there are questions outside the scope of the laboratory that are perhaps unanswerable.

In "Carbon," a marvelously playful final chapter which serves as a kind of antidote to the previous one, Levi traces the history of a carbon atom from its long imprisonment in a limestone rock, to its liberation into the air, its inhalation into the lungs of a falcon, its exhalation into the air again, and its penetration into a leaf, where, with the aid of sunlight, it enters the chain of life as part of a glucose molecule stored in a bunch of grapes which are made into wine, drunk by an individual, stored in his liver, and exhaled in the form of carbon dioxide. The atom, airborne again, lodges in a cedar in Lebanon, which is burrowed into by a woodworm, is formed into a pupa, and becomes part of one of the moth's thousand eyes. The moth dies, and the atom reenters the earth until 1960, when it reenters the life cycle through photosynthesis. It is located in a glass of milk which is drunk by the writer Levi, travels through his bloodstream, and enters his brain into the very nerve cell which is in charge of his writing, guiding his hand over the paper. Then, "a double snap, up and down, between two levels of energy, guides this hand of mine to impress on the paper this dot, here, this one."

Thus, with characteristic elegance and wit, Levi ends his book with carbon, the element of life, in a paean to life itself. The chapter, "Carbon" celebrates life in all of its infinite variety, adaptability, and renewal, looking back briefly to pay tribute to the specific, vanished life form of the Piedmontese Jews, with which the book opened, and looking ahead to the other specific life forms which will emerge, forms as specific as that of the highly individual author of *The Periodic Table*.

Carola M. Kaplan

Sources for Further Study

Book World. XIV, December 30, 1984, p. 7.
Booklist. LXXXI, December 1, 1984, p. 476.
Library Journal. CX, January, 1985, p. 81.
Los Angeles Times Book Review. December 9, 1984, p. 1.
The New York Review of Books. XXXI, January 17, 1984, p. 8.
The New York Times Book Review. LXXXIX, December 23, 1984, p. 7.
The New Yorker. LX, December 24, 1984, p. 88.
Publishers Weekly. CCXXVI, November 2, 1984, p. 69.
Time. CXXV, January 28, 1985, p. 81.

PLACES IN THE WORLD A WOMAN COULD WALK

Author: Janet Kauffman (1945-   )
Publisher: Alfred A. Knopf (New York). 132 pp. $11.95
Type of work: Short stories
Time: The 1980's
Locale: Rural Michigan

A poet's first collection of short stories draws on the tradition of regionalism to evoke the lives of working women

The regional tradition is strong and persistent in American short fiction, particularly in fiction written by women; the phrase "local colorist" is often used condescendingly to describe writers such as Sarah Orne Jewett or Kate Chopin who seem to be outside the main stream of their period's culture. The tradition is, indeed, congenial for outsiders—and, perhaps, especially for women—because it encourages looking very closely at the particular and concrete, and thereby generates evidence that can be used to question widely accepted cultural assumptions. Thus, the form draws those women writers whose generalizations and observations, rooted in daily life (whatever the region), may resist abstraction—or, more likely, whose abstractions are at odds with the dominant intellectual tradition.

Both regionalism and the short story are currently experiencing a revival. In Janet Kauffman's first collection of stories, as in Bobbie Ann Mason's *Shiloh and Other Stories* (1982), the writer's uncompromising examination of particular individuals supplies not only the pleasure of knowing a people and a region unfamiliar to most urban readers but also support for a message: that individuals are worth noticing, even in an age of mass culture and mass humanity, that individual life has value, and that—even in a literary climate which seems largely to deny it—meaning and values are worth writing about.

In these twelve short stories (some of which have appeared in *The New Yorker* and in little magazines), Janet Kauffman introduces the reader to rural and semirural Michigan and to people who seem rooted in a Yankee tradition of laconic talk and hardworking self-sufficiency, though the farms no longer provide an adequate income. Most of Kauffman's characters are (at least for the present) still engaged in physical labor and have the consciousness of life and death that controls the agricultural year; they do not share the restless unrootedness of Mason's Kentuckians with their transitional lives and their traditions overlaid by K-Marts and shopping malls.

Kauffman's Michigan, like Jewett's New England, is largely a female world. The men work for wages, often at seasonal occupations such as construction that take them away during planting and harvest. Agricultural labor has again become women's work; women drive the combines and backhoes, make the hay, kill rats with a garden fork, and feel the pleasure of muscling up in the sun. The small towns also are emptying. Often the men have drifted off, discouraged, leaving reality to the women. "Going away is tempting, of course," says one of the narrators, "easy as walking away in a blizzard, or losing your mind. You go out, and you don't come back."

The essence of regional writing is not merely that it gives readers from the outside world a guided tour to the peculiar lives and customs of people in an unknown territory. The regionalist is also, almost always, pointing out that even the most thoroughly ordinary lives and objects take on value and interest if they are examined accurately from a perspective that takes care to see. Kauffman might well be describing her own method in the story "Harmony," when she describes the efforts of one of the characters to make a meaningful map of Jackson, the Michigan city which (according to the story) *Life & Living* has described as the state's worst place to live:

> She wants each pin to mark a place you can sit and sit for a long time and not get tired looking. She gave me instructions about finding angles where the light is especially good, where buildings come together in interesting ways, where colors of plants and smells and everything combine to make some whole thing worth looking at. The first red pinhead on Sherry's map was the view from a slab in the vacant lot opposite Francis and Cortland, where a bricked-up six-story building marks the end of the mall. Four stories up, a mission church from around the corner has painted its name in huge blue cursive letters. You sit on the slab and you see the bricks and the blue letters, and the morning sun's on your back.

Kauffman uses a spare, laconic, concrete narrative voice which is also the voice of most of her characters. Though the stories are trimmed to the bone, they are not allowed to become meatless; like an imagist, Kauffman presents objects that suggest whole realms of feeling. Furthermore, one of her techniques is to show objects in a raw and unsparing light that cuts beneath the conventional associations, frustrates the reader's expectations, and gives the meaning a wry twist. At the beginning of many stories, abrupt prose plunges instantly into the middle of an unfamiliar context. The title story begins: "The day the tornado hit Morenci was the day Lady Fretts finally put her mind to the slaughter of Susie Hey Susie and her Babies." The first sentence of "At First It Looks like Nothing" is, "It's dark here now, and how long it will be before anybody says *Jesus sweet Jesus* to me I don't know." The voice is a part of the stories' authenticity; people who live in a relatively underpopulated world generally assume that anyone they speak to will understand their references and know the people they talk about. Kauffman's puzzles are therefore engaging, rather than appearing to be merely tricks of authorial invention.

The other striking feature of Kauffman's style is her ability to coin aphorisms and descriptive phrases that sound like folk wisdom and force the reader to halt while considering the truth in new light: "He's the middle of three brothers, the only one blessed with the talent of health," for example, or "Doll guards the world's crust as one would blown glass; her instincts require keeping boys and men light-footed and shushed, so the world does not crack." Another narrator supplies some modern weather lore about the aluminum-sided houses of Michigan:

> When a freeze touches houses, it's winter for good. The metal contributes to cold, and in a couple of months Michigan houses help pull down the air in those low bitter ground systems that hit Lake Erie and finally push off across New York. The state's a significant factor in weather.

The stories in the collection have an assortment of subjects (widowhood, abusive marriage, comradeship with people of the same or the opposite sex, the satisfaction of hard work in the sun, remarriage, parents and children, sexual exploration, patriotism) and a variety of central characters. Kauffman finds her truest voice, however, in the stories narrated in the first person by working women in their middle years; here the voice and the tone and the story merge within a worldview rooted in the familiar, where it seems natural for a detail to signify the whole.

Underlying the specifics, in most cases, is a kind of gritty optimism which grows from examining characters who survive and, even more surprisingly, can sometimes change and take control despite the inevitable disasters of both natural and human worlds. "Who Has Lived from a Child with Chickens" expresses the theme in comic terms. Colleen is a chicken named after a bland, traditional, and judgmental woman the narrator knew briefly at college in 1973—an obvious evocation of the kind of chicken-chick many women once were. Ratzafratz the rat eludes capture in the goat shed, and his depredations not only damage the walls but also interfere with the milk and egg supply. Various other plagues denude the garden. Amid the disaster, Colleen gradually takes on a new character; the chickens, allowed to roam free because there is nothing left for them to destroy, eat up the thistles that are ruining the lawn and eventually, under Colleen's disciplined leadership, even manage to destroy Ratzafratz. At the story's end, Colleen again looks blank and drooping, as if only a fool would think a chicken could kill a rat.

Many of the stories about humans also reveal the growth of strength under catastrophe. In the title story, Lady Fretts emerges from twelve years of mourning, kills the useless cow and calves she had kept because they were associated, emotionally, with her husband and his death, and abruptly goes off to Greece to learn about sculpture. In summary, the sequence sounds merely bizarre; told by an appropriate narrator, in evocative detail, it seems to reveal natural forces at work.

Kauffman is strongest at delineating character and finding the images that imply widening circles of meaning. Marabelle, the hairdresser of "The Alvordton Spa and Sweat Shop," lives in one of the basement houses one sees dotted throughout the Midwest; her husband left for the Sun Belt before the upper stories got built. Although Marabelle is bitter, her windowless room, snug with heavy old furniture, becomes a place of rest and healing for other women—including some who are educated and "rising in the world." There are resonances here of dens in the earth, of the settlers' first sod refuges, of the seasonal urges city dwellers lose. Finally, however, Kauffman has created—most essentially—a series of narratives about women one is glad to know.

Sally H. Mitchell

Sources for Further Study

Chatelaine. LVII, April, 1984, p. 4.
Christian Science Monitor. LXXVI, February 9, 1984, p. 28.
Kirkus Reviews. LI, October 15, 1983, p. 1104.
Library Journal. CVIII, November 15, 1983, p. 2172.
Los Angeles Times. January 19, 1984, V, p. 2.
Ms. XII, January, 1984, p. 15.
New Directions for Women. XIII, September, 1984, p. 23.
The New York Review of Books. XXXI, May 31, 1984, p. 35.
The New York Times Book Review. LXXXIX, January 8, 1984, p. 23.
Publishers Weekly. CCXXIV, November 11, 1983, p. 42.
Saturday Review. X, January, 1984, p. 52.
Virginia Quarterly Review. LX, Summer, 1984, p. 95.
Washington Post Book World. February 5, 1984, p. 6.

THE POEMS
A New Edition

Author: William Butler Yeats (1865-1939)
Edited by Richard J. Finneran
Publisher: Macmillan Publishing Company (New York). 747 pp. $19.95
Type of work: Poems
Time: 1889-1939
Locale: Ireland

A hypothetical reconstruction of the contents and order of The Collected Poems of W. B. Yeats *with additional poems*

Why should there be a new edition of the poems of William Butler Yeats? Should a scholar or a librarian who has on the shelf *The Collected Poems of W. B. Yeats* (definitive edition, with the author's final revisions, 1956) purchase this new edition? The answer will depend on the reader, specifically on the reader's interest in the history of the publication, revision, selection, and reordering of Yeats's poems.

In compiling this new edition, Richard J. Finneran, editor of the *Yeats Annual* and one of the editors of *Letters to W. B. Yeats* (1977), has written ninety-five pages of annotations to the poems, and, to establish accurate texts, he has consulted manuscripts, typescripts, corrected proofs, and the correspondence pertaining to publication. Finneran has chosen to print the later, revised versions of poems rather than the versions first published. He has also chosen to regularize very minimally Yeats's punctuation and spelling, a decision that alters the texts long familiar to Yeats scholars. He divides the familiar group of late poems, which in earlier editions began with "The Gyres" and ended with "Under Ben Bulben," into two distinct collections, the first now labeled *New Poems* (1938), and, for five of those poems, he includes musical settings. He substantially rearranges the very last poems Yeats wrote, not following chronology, but according to the poet's final ordering, as Finneran interprets it from the correspondence and manuscripts. The major change, in this new edition, is the inclusion, in an appendix, of 125 additional poems which Yeats himself had chosen not to publish in his own *The Collected Poems of W. B. Yeats*.

As might be expected, this new edition does not substantially alter the reputation or the stages in the career of the poet. Yeats published his poems over a span of some fifty years; his fame grew during his lifetime and has not diminished significantly since his death. His poetic life can still be divided into four major periods: the Celtic twilight, the nationalist violence, symbolism, and the origins of art. His concern with Irish folklore, mythic history, and occult mysteries dominates his early poems. During the early twentieth century, he wrote extensively on the conflict between personal history and public history, and his poems from that second period comment movingly on the nationalist violence in Ireland. During World War I, he began drafting "The Second Coming," and his poems published after the war explore the interrelations between personal history and symbolic historical cycles. His last poems celebrate the origins of imaginative art in carnal knowledge of real life. The impressive beauty, power, and complexity of his verse remain evident in this new edition, and his sound critical judgment is evident in his choosing not to reprint the 125 poems Finneran has added.

The additional poems echo the themes of Yeats's better-known poems. The major ideas within Yeats's body of poetry remain his fascination with the approaching end of the world; his melding together of Eastern religious, Rosicrucian, Celtic, and Christian images; his desire to portray reincarnation; his belief that a soul can become changeless and eternal; and his fervent exploration of individual, personal ethics. Yeats, who in his late career became fascinated with the nature of art, reshaped his earlier poems to emphasize the artifice of creation. By choosing to reprint Yeats's revisions in place of his earlier versions of poems, Finneran homogenizes the poetry.

The revisions and reshaping do, however, seem appropriate for the posthumously published *Last Poems*, now dated by Finneran 1938-1939. In the earlier *The Collected Poems of W. B. Yeats*, there were actually several different collections grouped together under the title *Last Poems*, then dated 1936-1939. Finneran wisely separates *New Poems* (1938) from *Last Poems* (1938-39). *New Poems* follows the same order as the earlier edition, from "The Gyres" through "Are You Content," but Finneran substantially reorders the final group of poems.

Last Poems (1938-39) now presents to the reader Yeats's own final work of art, carefully structured to be a self-portrait of the dying artist. This ordering begins with "Under Ben Bulben," in which Yeats writes his epitaph. The earlier edition, by concluding with "Under Ben Bulben," had emphasized his paradoxically sentimental and stoic approach to death. This new edition, by beginning with the same poem, sets up the pattern of antithesis that governs the altered order of poems. In their revised order, the poems recapitulate Yeats's career in a formal, carefully structured pattern of juxtaposition. "Under Ben Bulben" alludes to the legendary supernatural creatures who inhabit the Irish landscape and thus recalls not only Yeats's Celtic twilight period but also reaffirms his identity as an Irish poet. "Three Songs to the One Burden" reminds one of "Easter, 1916," Yeats's most famous poem on the nationalist violence, and concludes with a grim acceptance of bloodshed and death. "The Black Tower" portrays soldiers loyal to the British king who scorn an old man's suggestion that their own Irish king deserves their loyalty; counterpointing this drama is a refrain suggesting an apocalypse. "Cuchulain Comforted" takes up the legend after the great hero has been mortally wounded and is near death. "Three Marching Songs" celebrates Irish rebels of the past, as they go defiantly to their deaths. "In Tara's Halls" narrates the king's old age, his hundred and first year, concluding in his willed death. "The Statues" offers a breadth of perspective which connects Irish culture to Greek and emphasizes the ancient heritage, now neglected in the modern age. "News for the Delphic Oracle" grounds mystical truths in carnal sighs and sexual moans. The "Long-legged Fly" becomes an image for speculative meditation, linking a Caesar, a Helen, and a Michael Angelo. "A Bronze Head" explores the human mystery of identity: what is, what is to come, and what might have been. "A Stick of Incense" seems almost frivolous, or irreverent, but it, too, questions a central mystery of the Western tradition: the Incarnation, God's son born to a virgin. "Hound Voice' identifies the speaker as one who rejected the dullness of work in a city office, who likewise rejected the settled labor on a farm, but who chose to hunt, to roam freely with the hounds, to kill and to chant wildly of victory. "John Kinsella's Lament for Mrs. Mary Moore" shifts to another voice, neither the mystic poet nor the wild Irish hunter, but an ordinary, working-class drinking man voicing his grief. "High Talk" gives voice to Malachi Stilt-Jack who makes stilts for traveling performers, but who shares in the grandeur of the legendary giant heroes of Ireland. "The Apparitions" is a genial ramble about the privileges and joys of old age, set against a refrain reminding the speaker of his terror of physical decay. "A Nativity" speculates on artistry, craftsmanship, practical skill, gestures of human pride, gestures of awesome divine power, and returns to the human response to incarnation: mercy and terror. Yeats employs dramatic dialogue in "Man and the Echo" to explore the dying poet's responsibility for actions inspired by his art.

This revised sequence establishes, more clearly than the earlier collection, the paradoxical questions asked by a poet approaching the end of a long, productive career. Next to the last poem in this group stands one of Yeats's most frequently anthologized poems, "The Circus Animals' Desertion." It has been popular with editors because it reviews and sums up Yeats's poetic career, and it deserves the increased emphasis it receives here. The first line suggests that this is a poem about the old poet's inability to write. The conclusion, however, is deliberately ambiguous; the poet may be lying down to begin again. The paradoxes of this poem are strengthened by the context of the collection's revised order. While contemplating the strange turns his career has taken, the poet questions the artificiality and acknowledges the inspiration of his art. In the second, or the central, section of this poem, Yeats alludes to the themes of the Celtic twilight (the old heroes, the romance tradition), then to the themes of Irish nationalist politics (the Countess Cathleen, Maud Gonne), and finally to the theme of art itself. His poetic images seem to consume him, then to leave him expiring. The tone of the final section forbids grief, asserting instead an affirmation of the body and heart as source of the mind's and soul's images. This shift in tone prepares one for the poem now found at the end of *Last Poems* (1938-39): "Politics." Whether the poet is compelled to respond to contemporary historical events is the question raised when Yeats quotes Thomas Mann as an epigraph to his poem: "In our time the destiny of man presents its meanings in political terms." As if contradicting Mann, Yeats adopts a naïve voice, and the speaker in "Politics" distinguishes himself from a traveled man and from a well-read politician. The foremost and the final image in Yeats's final poem is that of a girl, the poet's beloved, whose attractions compel him to respond, even though he is no longer young. Behind Yeats's "But O that I were young again/ And held her in my arms" readers are expected to hear an anonymous sixteenth century poem, familiar long before Yeats reprinted it in his edition of *The Oxford Book of English Verse* (1934):

> O western wind, when wilt thou blow
> That the small rain down can rain?
> Christ, that my love were in my arms
> And I in my bed again!

In his final two lines, by deliberately echoing this verse, Yeats proclaims his allegiance to the poetic tradition rather than political history and asserts the supremacy of love poetry over political poetry, specifically celebrating poetry based in "the foul rag and bone shop of the heart" ("The Circus Animals' Desertion"). This revised ordering of Yeats's final poems has the effect of deemphasizing Yeats's 1930's involvement in the politics of order and strong leadership as well as sentimentalizing his powerful responses to Irish nationalist politics.

Finneran does not, in his annotations, note the echo of the "western wind" poem, but perhaps he omits it in keeping with his decision not to offer interpretive commentary in his notes. Many of Finneran's annotations are invaluable to readers unfamiliar with Irish history, mythology, and literature. A few of his annotations, however, seem superfluous: It is not necessary, for example, to explain an allusion to Rembrandt by giving in full his name, Rembrandt Harmensz van Rijn, and by telling readers that he was a Dutch painter and etcher. This is, after all, a scholarly edition, not one designed for inexperienced college undergraduates. Finneran acknowledges his indebtedness, in writing his annotations, to A. Norman Jeffares' *A Commentary on the Collected Poems of W. B. Yeats* (1968). Since the publication of Finneran's edition, Jeffares has published *A New Commentary on the Poems of W. B. Yeats* (1984), containing some criticism of Finneran's work.

It is as a canonical edition that Finneran's work has been most sharply criticized. Though most scholars welcome the reordering of *Last Poems*, several disagree with the decision to adopt the revised versions of early poems. For the scholar who wishes to consult all of Yeats's revisions, there is *The Variorum Edition of the Poems of W. B. Yeats*, edited by Peter Allt and

Russell K. Alspach (1957). For the reader who wishes to follow Yeats's development throughout his long career, the first published versions of his early poems would be more valuable than his late revisions.

Minor objections can be raised to Finneran's decision to correct silently some of Yeats's punctuation and spelling but in some cases to return to manuscript punctuation that had been corrected in most of the earlier editions of the collected poems. In "Politics," for example, at the end of the fourth line, Finneran has restored a comma in place of a logical question mark, with the result that the speaker does not pause very long at all but continues directly to his "Yet" at the beginning of line five. The restoration makes the poem less reflective and more didactic. Finneran's change has the effect of interpreting the poem, whether he intended that effect or not. His annotation to this poem does not comment on the restoration.

Quite serious objections are raised to the inclusion of 125 additional poems which Yeats himself had excluded from his canon of collected poems. Few of these poems can be defended as equaling the quality of the collected poems. They are of interest to the specialist in Yeats, but all are available elsewhere, and they do not merit inclusion in this edition.

The archival evidence supporting Finneran's decisions is self-contradictory, and to choose accurate texts requires interpretation not only of various manuscripts but also of the correspondence among the literary executor and poet's widow, Georgie Hyde-Lees Yeats, the publisher Harold Macmillan, and the publisher's assistant Thomas Mark. The archives to be examined are found in twelve different locations. Clearly, the task undertaken is not a simple one. Finneran explains his editorial decisions in his *Editing Yeats's Poems* (1983); the clearest and best-documented attack on Finneran's decisions may be found in Warwick Gould's review in the *Times Literary Supplement*.

The publication of this new edition has provoked considerable controversy, but, because it is not likely that Macmillan will publish another edition of the collected poems in response to the criticisms raised, the general reader might choose this new edition for Finneran's helpful annotations on Irish names, and the scholar might choose this edition to supplement the 1956 collection.

Judith L. Johnston

Sources for Further Study

Choice. XXI, March, 1984, p. 982.
Christian Science Monitor. LXXVI, April 19, 1984, p. 22.
Library Journal. CIX, January, 1984, p. 97.
The New York Review of Books. XXXII, January 31, 1984, p. 29.
The New York Times Book Review. LXXXIX, March 18, 1984, p. 1.
Times Literary Supplement. June 29, 1984, p. 731.

POSTSCRIPT TO *THE NAME OF THE ROSE*

Author: Umberto Eco (1932-   )
Translated from the Italian by William Weaver
Publisher: Harcourt Brace Jovanovich (San Diego, California). Illustrated. 84 pp.
   $8.95
Type of work: Literary criticism and autobiographical essay

A renowned semiologist discusses how he wrote a best-selling detective novel set in the year 1327 and assesses the historical novel in the postmodern period

Even before the publication of *Il nome della rosa* (1980; *The Name of the Rose*, 1983)—which won for its author Italy's two most prestigious literary awards, the Premio Strega and the Premio Viareggio—Umberto Eco enjoyed an impressive reputation in Europe and the United States. He was known, however, primarily in scholarly circles and almost exclusively as the author of a number of books on literary theory and aesthetics, including such studies as *A Theory of Semiotics* (1976) and *The Role of the Reader: Explorations in the Semiotics of Texts* (1979). *The Name of the Rose*, his first and only novel to date, catapulted him to worldwide fame. With the monographic *Postscript to "The Name of the Rose"* (published in Italy in 1983 as *Postille a "Il nome della rosa"*), the author refocused his attention on the scholarly preoccupation with signs, readers, and the Middle Ages that preceded (and culminated in) his writing a detective novel set in November, 1327, and peopled with such Sherlock Holmesian monks as William of Baskerville (a Franciscan and the story's principal sleuth) and Adso of Melk (his Benedictine sidekick). The wit and irony ubiquitous in the novel find equally free expression in *Postscript to "The Name of the Rose."*

Postscript to "The Name of the Rose" is divided into fifteen sections, including "Notes." Eleven pages of illustrations accompany the text and consist largely of photographs of architectural details of twelfth century churches and of medieval miniatures in commentaries on the Book of Revelation. Below each of the eleven pictures appears a passage from *The Name of the Rose*; the illustrations greatly assist the reader in visualizing the novel's narrative descriptions of the abbey and the macabre events that occur therein. Eco's comments on his best-seller, on the other hand, will hardly satisfy the reader who expects definitive or straight answers to why things happen the way they do in the novel. The author-commentator prefers to provide a few, often tantalizing, details on the background of the novel's composition and then allow the reader to draw his own conclusions.

In the first section, "The Title and the Meaning," Eco states that no novelist should supply interpretations of his own narrative. To do so would greatly limit a novel's purpose, which is, according to a somewhat tongue-in-cheek Eco, to generate interpretations. While he readily admits that almost any title, nevertheless, constitutes an interpretive key provided by the author, he claims that in his own case the title for *The Name of the Rose* came to him partially by chance (no further explanation); he hopes, moreover, that it disorients the reader and muddles his ideas. Eco continues in this ironic vein by concluding his opening remarks with the recommendation that the author "die once he has finished writing" in order "not to trouble the path of the text." In fact, however, he is determined to do exactly the opposite: to live and to trouble his text's path as much as possible. He begins the next selection, "Telling the Process," by observing that, while the author must not interpret his own works, it is nevertheless permissible for him to satisfy his readers' curiosity by relating "why and how he wrote his book." Eco, however, does not explain how such "why's" and "how's" can be clearly distinguished from interpretive authorial comments. How, then, does he justify *Postscript to "The Name of the Rose,"* which many readers will take, despite his protestations, as a form of interpretation? The remainder of the book does not answer that question as much as it demonstrates that Eco the Cat greatly enjoys playing with Reader the Mouse.

The game continues in "Naturally, the Middle Ages," in which the author makes such startling revelations as this: He wrote a novel because he "felt like poisoning a monk." The psychological implications, while ostensibly astonishing, should be taken *cum grano salis*. Much more valuable to the cultivated (and perhaps even to the unsophisticated) reader are the sections entitled "The Mask" and "The Novel as Cosmological Event." In these, Eco explains his desire not only to tell *about* the Middle Ages but also to narrate, as much as possible, *in* and *through* the period by means of an invented contemporary chronicler. To prepare to write historical fiction, he had, therefore, to read and reread chronicles of the time in order to acquire their style and tempo. In so doing, he claims to have "rediscovered what writers have always known: . . . books always speak of other books, and every story tells a story that has already been told." Having offered a plausible rationale for the multiple frames of his own Gothic tale, Eco then proceeds to undermine, at least in part, the seriousness of what he has said by stating that a novel has less to do with words than cosmology. Citing Genesis as a perfect example, he immediately undercuts it with an irreverent if humorous reference to Woody Allen ("we all have to choose our role models"). The chief point that emerges from such banter is that *The Name of the Rose* seeks to re-create a world long dead. Notwithstanding the text's numerous intertextualities and allusions to modern (for example, Heideggerian) philosophy and recent literary theory (for example, Eco's own beloved semiotics) few would deny that the author succeeds in proving once again that well-established constraints of setting in fiction or poetry often result in increased creativity on the part of the writer.

In "Who Speaks?" Eco offers readers James Joyce's *Ulysses* (1922) and Thomas Mann's *Der Zauberberg* (1924; *The Magic Moutain*, 1927) as models of "a concentrative universe" such as he wished to create. The author, both in this section and in "Preterition" and "Pace," explains with great insight the value of having the eighty-year-old Adso function as a "mask." By having the aged Adso speak of his youthful experiences with Brother William, the author can capture, at will, the innocent voice of youth or the wisdom of a man possessed of a long lifetime of experience. Rather than long-winded authorial interjections, the novel's digressions exemplify "the style of the medieval chronicler, eager to introduce encyclopedic notions every time something was mentioned."

"Constructing the Reader" displays Eco the literary theoretician at his prime. According to Eco's reader-oriented theory of criticism, detailed in *Opera aperta* (1962) and *The Role of the Reader*, any work in progress always contains a dialogue between the author and his ideal reader. Who was Eco's model reader for *The Name of the Rose*? The answer, once more, is neither simple nor straightforward. He claims to have imagined an accomplice who would play his game and who would become (along with the author) thoroughly medieval. He also wanted someone, however, who would become his prey and who would experience a transformation as the text evolved, someone who would take pleasure in "the metaphysical shudder" that only the detective novel can offer.

The concluding sections—"The Detective Metaphysic," "Enjoyment," "Postmodernism, Irony, the Enjoyable," "The Historical Novel," and "Ending"—constitute, in large part, exercises in literary criticism or excursions in metaphysical reflection. Eco equates, for example, the fundamental question of philosophy and psychoanalysis with that of the detective novel: "Who is guilty?" He compares the labyrinth in his novel to abstract models of conjecture and insists that the reader should not only amuse himself (as he explores the world of the novel) but also learn at the same time. He categorizes the historical novel as one of three ways of fictionally narrating the past—the other two being the Gothic novel or romance and the swashbuckling novel or cloak-and-dagger story. For all of his scholarly assessments and philosophical commentary, however, he returns, in the end, to the pose with which he began. Eco wrote *The Name of the Rose* because of an obsessive idea; it remains for the reader to decipher for himself the meaning of that idea's realization in print.

Madison U. Sowell

Sources for Further Study

The Atlantic. CCLV, January, 1985, p. 100.
Booklist. LXXXI, January 1, 1985, p. 613.

Library Journal. CX, January, 1985, p. 87.
Los Angeles Times. November 30, 1984, V, p. 30.
The New York Times Book Review. XXXI, December 20, 1984, p. 49.
Times Literary Supplement. November 16, 1984, p. 1310.

THE PRIVATE WORLD
Selections from the Diario Íntimo and Selected Letters, 1890-1936

Author: Miguel de Unamuno (1864-1936)
Publisher: Princeton University Press (Princeton, New Jersey). Illustrated. 358 pp.
$32.50
Translated from the Spanish by Anthony Kerrigan, Allen Lacy, and Martin Nozick
Annotated by Martin Nozick with Allen Lacy, with an introduction by Allen Lacy
Epilogue by Luis Portillo
Type of work: Diary and letters
Time: 1890-1936
Locale: Primarily Spain

The diaries and letters of the great Spanish author chronicle his inner struggles and his rejection of comfortable orthodoxies, whether rationalistic or religious

This book may be mistitled, Miguel de Unamuno did not make any distinction between his private and public worlds. He joined a handful of other philosophers, including Saint Augustine, Blaise Pascal, and Søren Kierkegaard, in maintaining that an understanding of an author's personal history is indispensable to an understanding of that author's work. As he says in his introduction to *Del sentimiento trágico de la vida en los hombres y en los pueblos* (1913; *The Tragic Sense of Life in Men and Peoples,* 1921):

> In most of the histories of philosophy that I know, . . . philosophic systems are presented to us as if growing out of one another spontaneously, and their authors, the philosophers, appear as mere pretexts. The inner biography of the philosophers, the men who philosophized, is assigned a secondary place. And yet it is precisely that inner biography which can mean most to us.

The *Diario íntimo* constitutes a part of the author's "inner biography." Its themes will be familiar to those who know Unamuno's philosophical works; nevertheless, the book illuminates a five-year period during which Unamuno endured an intense spiritual crisis.

This crisis was precipitated by the severe illness of his third son, Raimundo. In November, 1896, Raimundo, age ten months, contracted acute meningitis. The disease left the child hydrocephalic, partially paralyzed, and virtually unconscious until he died in 1902. At the onset of his son's illness, Unamuno fell into a deep depression and began to fear for his physical and mental health. One night in march, 1897, his wife awoke to find Unamuno weeping. To comfort him, she spoke two words—"My child!"—that were to have a profound effect on the course of his life and thought.

Raimundo's illness was only the catalyst for a spiritual crisis that had been building in Unamuno for years. Apparently he found in his wife's words the beginnings of a resolution for both the immediate and the long-term crisis.

The latter, a crisis of faith dating in a sense from Unamuno's own childhood, is another part of his "inner biography." His devoutly religious parents had raised him as a Roman Catholic; as a youth he often dreamed of becoming a saint. In his adolescence, however, he developed an intense interest in rationalistic philosophy that in time led him to abandon the faith of his family. Orthodox philosophers, such as the Catholic apologist Jaime Balmes, who had previously fascinated him, came to seem intellectually shallow and narrowly dogmatic. Later, at the University of Madrid, where he arrived in 1880 at age sixteen, he stopped attending Mass and began avidly reading works of positivistic philosophy and physiological psychology. (He also began his lifelong practice of learning foreign languages in order to read authors in the original: German for Georg Wilhelm Friedrich Hegel, English for Herbert Spencer and Thomas Carlyle. At age twenty, he knew eleven languages. Twenty years later, he taught himself Danish so that he could read Kierkegaard.)

By the time he was graduated in 1884, Unamuno appeared almost totally committed to positivism. His doctoral thesis was a pioneering effort to apply scientific method to the question of the origin and history of the Basque people. (He had been born in Bilbao, in Spain's Basque country.) He denounced all previous treatments for their failure, in his opinion, to define the Basque question with sufficient clarity. As further evidence of his predilections during this period, there is a scrap of manuscript in which he wrote, "Seek the kingdom of science and its righteousness, and all the rest will be added unto you."

Unamuno, however, never disposed of the religious-scientific conflict in the fashion that many other people do—that is, by coming down squarely and permanently on one side or the other. By the late 1880's, he had begun to encounter problems that neither rationalistic philosophy nor orthodox faith could resolve. For example, he wrote to his then fiancée, Concepción Lizárraga, about a dream that turned out to have been prophetic: "I dreamed that I was married, that I had a child, that this child died, and that over its body, which seemed to be made of wax, I said to my wife: 'Behold our love! Shortly it will decay: this is the way everything ends.'" This presented a question particularly disturbing to a person deeply concerned with words and their import: How does one committed to the concrete language of science and positivism express what is significant about a tragedy that besets a loved one? Unamuno was still confronting limitations such as this more than seven years later, when illness struck Raimundo and the strange dream became a reality.

It was at this point—1897—that Unamuno began the *Diario íntimo*. Both this journal and a handful of his letters bear evidence that Concepción's words—"My child!"—eventually induced her husband to identify her with Mary and to see himself as symbolically her child and as literally a child of God. This was to open the door for him to view Christian faith in a new and wholly personal way. The diary, for example, contains many references to "Padre nuestro" ("Our Father") and meditations on Mary, "the node of Christian life."

Unamuno's initial impulse, however, was not to embrace any such organic concept of Christianity but to retake his childhood faith by storm. Although implicitly he was striving to accept the tragedy that had befallen his son, most of the diary passages deal explicitly with Unamuno's attempts to resolve the dilemma into which his philosophical wanderings had led him. At times, this struggle is beautifully expressed, as in this passage: "He who wants everything to happen that does happen brings it about that everything happens as he wishes. Human omnipotence, by means of resignation. But I did not understand that such resignation is reached only through grace, through faith and love." At other times, he can only manage a wistful tone: "If I come to believe, what better proof of the truth of faith? It will be a miracle, a true miracle." "But now that I am back in the Christian community, I find myself with a faith which consists in wanting to believe, rather than in believing."

Unamuno rejects his former dispassionate scientific, rationalistic approach as a vain and shallow pursuit: "Human reason, left to itself, leads to nihilism." "To rationalize faith. I wanted to become its master and not its slave—and thus I fell into slavery instead of gaining freedom in Christ." "Intellectualism is a terrible disease, and all the more terrible when one lives in it in unknowing tranquillity."

Attempting to force himself back into an old mold, he often finds himself in a psychological doldrums. One Holy Wednesday, he laments, "A deathly calm, an enormous aridity. I see my case only intellectually. All of my feeling has dried up." At other times, simply the quest for faith is enough: "We ask for signs, ignoring the fact that the most evident sign is that we ask for them." In still other passages, he is able to rejoice in his progress: "Every day I make new discoveries in the old faith." Later in the journal, he asks in wonder, "How is it that suddenly, today, the 9th of May, 1899, in the midst of my studies, I am overcome by a craving to pray?" The last passage of the diary, dated January 15, 1902, ends: *"Thy will be done."*

Despite his belief in the connection between the "inner biographies" of authors and their published work, Unamuno's own *Diario íntimo* was only circulated privately among a few friends between 1898 and 1901; it then disappeared until 1950, when it was rediscovered by a Peruvian scholar and critic examining Unamuno's papers in preparation for his doctoral thesis. Though discussed in scholarly journals as early as 1957, the full text of the diary was not published in Spanish until 1966, and not in English until this translation appeared in Princeton University Press's selected edition of Unamuno's works.

The unpolished, often strident and repetitive meditations of the *Diario íntimo* lack the literary force of Saint Augustine's *Confessions* or Pascal's *Pensées*, yet they are important for two reasons. First, they introduce themes that were to become prominent in Unamuno's later works, especially *The Tragic Sense of Life in Men and Peoples* and *La agonía del Cristianismo* (1931; *The Agony of Christianity*, 1928, 1960). Unamuno kept his gaze on man's common end in death and "the whole point: whether or not there is a life beyond the grave." That, he asserts, is the only valid basis for philosophy.

Second, the *Diario íntimo* is important because it demonstrates the growing organicity of thought within this intellectual-in-spite-of-himself. He was never fully able to return to the neat simplicities of his abandoned faith—"Under the impact of that inner blow [Raimundo's affliction] I returned, or tried to return, to the ancient faith of my childhood"—but it helped Unamuno develop a new philosophical fluidity which ultimately led him to reject orthodoxies of all types, despite the discomfort of doing so.

In the diary, Unamuno reports, "In this calm, I seek inner agitation," and years later, in *The Tragic Sense of Life in Men and Peoples*, he was to write:

> But the truth is that my work—my mission, I was about to say—is to shatter the faith of men, left, right, and center, their faith in affirmation, their faith in negation, their faith in abstention, and I do so from faith in faith itself. My purpose is to war on all those who submit, whether to Catholicism, or to rationalism, or to agnosticism. My aim is to make all men live a life of restless longing.

One of Unamuno's vehicles for attacking orthodoxy—political, religious, or philosophical—was his extensive correspondence. This volume includes sixty-four letters (out of some forty thousand): They begin in 1890, when he was surviving on odd tutoring jobs while he vainly sought a university teaching post; they end in 1936, the year of his death, when he was an internationally famous author but had also recently lost his beloved Concepción and was under house arrest for his vehement protests against the new regime of Generalissimo Francisco Franco.

In his letters, more than in his diary, Unamuno kept open the channel between his private and public lives. The sheer volume of his letters aside, many were never published in Spain because of his outspokenness against the succession of despots who seized control of that country during the final years of his life. As it was, Unamuno was exiled to the Canary Islands in 1923, when an unidentified professor thoughtlessly published in Argentina one of Unamuno's most scathing letters: It denounces the dictator Primo de Rivera, who had recently staged a coup d'état, and calls King Alfonso XIII a "Royal Gander, . . . a cricket-brain, . . . a sack of vile abject passions."

Although politics is his main subject in many of these letters, Unamuno still applied a spiritual yardstick to political systems. To him, the measure for any form of government was the extent to which it allowed the people to make spiritual progress in their private lives. Indeed, this was what justified civilization itself. On May 25, 1898, he wrote to Pedro Jiménez Ilundain:

> The entire point of civilization is to protect the evolution of the Christian soul, to help it loosen the impure bond to the pagan past; if civilization does not serve this end, why then it serves no human end at all. The Christian soul must rid itself of the warlike impulses of military heroism, of narrow patriotism, and of all earthly attachments. Heroism must give way to sanctity, and patriotism to brotherly compassion.

He defined living faith in ways inimical to despotic government, whether civil or ecclesiastical: "Faith, true faith, is the enormous drive of the soul which engenders dogma, a living, moving, flexible dogma, a dogma that evolves, not that poor dead scrap of flesh, that mummified corpse which is handed down by tradition."

Unamuno's last public act was also a highly personal act—and one of despair. It was his "Last Lecture," delivered at the University of Salamanca on October 12, 1936, and reported by Luis Portillo (then a young professor of civil law) in an appendix to this volume. Unamuno spoke in response to an address in the same forum by the Fascist General Millán Astray, a supporter of Franco. In July, 1936, the Spanish Civil War had begun with Franco leading an army revolt in Morocco. By the time of Unamuno's speech in October, Franco's insurgents controlled a large part of Spain, including Salamanca. Before the faculty and other important personages at Salamanca, he told Millan Astray:

> You will win, but you will not convince. You will win, because you possess more than enough brute force, but you will not convince, because to convince means to persuade. And in order to persuade, you would need what you lack—reason and right in the struggle. I consider it futile to exhort you to think of Spain. I have finished.

For this speech, Unamuno was condemned to death, but the sentence was never carried out—perhaps because Franco's government realized that such an act would destroy whatever support the nascent "Movement of Salvation" had been able to garner. Instead, Unamuno was placed under house arrest. He died at home of a brain hemorrhage on December 31, 1936.

Thomas Rankin

Source for Further Study

Library Journal. CX, May 1, 1985, p. 57.

PROBLEMS OF DOSTOEVSKY'S POETICS

Author: Mikhail Bakhtin (1895-1975)
Translated from the Russian and edited by Caryl Emerson
Introduction by Wayne C. Booth
Publisher: University of Minnesota Press (Minneapolis). 333 pp. $35.00; paperback
$14.95
Type of work: Literary criticism

Mikhail Bakhtin's treatise on Dostoevski's poetics is now duly recognized as a major landmark in twentieth century literary theory because of its broad revaluation of literature in terms of the quality of polyphony, and this newly translated and thoroughly annotated edition of his masterwork should greatly enlarge the circle of Bakhtin's admirers

The Russian literary critic Mikhail Bakhtin was born in 1895 and died in 1975. Although an earlier version of the volume currently entitled *Problems of Dostoevsky's Poetics* had been published in 1929, Bakhtin was little known either inside the Soviet Union or elsewhere until the 1960's. Falling under the cloud of ideological suspicion during the paranoid Stalinist era, he was compelled to live in personal obscurity in a succession of provincial towns for most of his adult live. At the same time, the book that he had written on Dostoevski was totally withdrawn from circulation. His fortune, however, improved markedly during the post-Stalin period as a result of emergence of a less repressive intellectual climate within the Soviet Union. A revised and greatly expanded edition of his treatise on Dostoevski was published in 1963, and a previously unpublished book called *Rabelais and His World* appeared in 1965. Both of these works were translated into English and other Western European languages shortly thereafter, and Bakhtin's preeminence as a literary scholar was soon recognized by an international body of scholars. More recently, four of his essays were published in English translation under the title *The Dialogic Imagination* (1981). In addition, a long-standing need has finally been fulfilled with the publication of the biographical study *Mikhail Bakhtin* (1984), by Katerina Clark and Michael Holquist. Issued concurrently is a newly translated version of Bakhtin's *Problems of Dostoevsky's Poetics*. The present edition of this work should completely supplant the one previously published in 1973 by virtue of its extensive critical apparatus and its superior translation of the original text. Caryl Emerson's efforts on both counts can only be described as definitive. In the introduction, Wayne C. Booth, for his part, seeks to clarify Bakhtin's analysis of the role of narration in the novel by relating it to the position that he himself had formerly espoused in works such as *The Rhetoric of Fiction* (1961). In the process of making this comparison, Booth freely concedes that he has modified his views significantly as the result of having studied Bakhtin's arguments pertaining to the form of the novel.

The most important critical proposition to appear in Bakhtin's *Problems of Dostoevsky's Poetics* is the claim that Fyodor Dostoevski was the first truly "polyphonic" novelist in literary history. In essence, Bakhtin contends that the fictional characters created by Dostoevski have been endowed with autonomous voices to such an extent that the reader can no longer discern any authorial control over their utterances or actions. The genesis of original ideas is ultimately an inexplicable phenomenon, but Bakhtin's concept of polyphony must stem in part from the cultural stimulation that he experienced when his family moved from Orel to Vilnius. He was born in Orel, a Russian city of some sixty thousand inhabitants located several hundred miles due south of Moscow, and spent the first nine years of his life in an environment of linguistic and religious homogeneity. Upon moving to Vilnius, where his father had been reassigned as a bank manager, Bakhtin was exposed to cultural pluralism for the very first time. Approximately sixty percent of the 200,000 people who lived there used Polish as their mother tongue, and more than a quarter of the inhabitants were Yiddish-speaking Jews. At the same time, the city served as the capital of the Baltic province of Lithuania, and its official language was Russian. The city was called "Vilnius" by the Lithuanians, "Wilno" by the Poles, and "Vilna" by the Russians and the Jews. None of these disparate groups had much inclination to communicate with one another and were content simply to co-exist, but the five years that Bakhtin spent in Vilnius opened his eyes to the advantages of cultural polyphony in society. A subsequent move by the family to the port city of Odessa on the Black Sea only served to reinforce Bakhtin's appreciation of the ethnic and religious diversity to which he had been exposed in Vilnius.

Bakhtin remained in Odessa for four years before deciding to join his elder brother as a student of classical philology and history at Petrograd University in 1914. Suffering from chronic osteomyelitis, he was physically unfit for military service and was therefore permitted to continue his studies after the outbreak of World War I. The severe economic hardships that followed in the wake of the October Revolution obliged Bakhtin to seek employment in the provinces. From 1918 to 1924, he earned his livelihood as a teacher in educational institutions in Nevel and Vitebsk. In addition to writing several important essays dealing with problems in aesthetics during these years, he managed to convince his landlady's daughter in Vitebsk to marry him. Bakhtin was less fortunate in terms of personal health, however, for his osteomyelitis gradually worsened to the point where he qualified for a state pension as a handicapped person. (The inflammation of the bone marrow in his right leg eventually became so acute that he agreed to have it amputated in 1938.)

Since he no longer had to work, Bakhtin returned to Petrograd (present-day Leningrad) and devoted himself to various research projects. There, as elsewhere, he formed a circle of like-minded intellectual friends. During this period, several important studies of Freudianism, Formalism, and Marxist linguistic theory were published under the names of members of the so-called Bakhtin Circle; among these works was *The Formal Method in Literary Scholarship: A Critical Introduction to Sociological Poetics*, which was published in 1928 under the name P. M. Medvedev and appeared in English translation in 1978 with Bakhtin and Medvedev both named on the title page. The authorship of this book and other works of the Bakhtin Circle is a matter of ongoing critical debate; some scholars believe that these works were written entirely by Bakhtin, while others argue that they merely reflect his influence or, to a greater or lesser degree, his collaboration. In any case, Bakhtin's treatise on Dostoevski, published in 1929 under the title *Problems of Dostoevsky's Creative Works*, was his first book to appear in print under his own name.

Bakhtin claims to be the first literary critic to have grasped the essential polyphonic structure of Dostoevski's fictional works, and he attempts to establish this priority at the very outset of his treatise by conducting a survey of the views propounded by several of the foremost contemporary specialists on the Dostoevskian novel. In each case, he permits these literary scholars to speak with their own voices by quoting them directly at length. This exercise in polyphony concludes with a summary judgment to the effect that these critics have been so overwhelmed by the ideological content of Dostoevski's novels that they eventually select a single voice from all of the competing points of view as being the true surrogate for the author and relegate the others to an unjustifiably inferior status. For Bakhtin, on the other hand, the hallmark of Dostoevski's major novels lies precisely in the fact that each of the protagonists within any given work has been endowed with a full quotient of self-consciousness and that the ensuing dialogues are thereby analogous to conversations in real life. While some characters may express opinions that are actually shared by Dostoevski himself, those holding opposing ideologies are allowed to argue their own cases so fully that the reader cannot detect any authorial manipulation or supervision of their discourse whatsoever. There are, Bakhtin observes, no disembodied ideas in Dostoevski's fictional universe: Two ideas call for two persons. Clearly, Bakhtin's concept of polyphony is simply a synonym for dialogism. Despite the fact that he devotes much space to classifying the various forms of discourse to be found in Dostoevski's narrative writings, the basic form for dialogue in these works is quite simple: It is the opposition of one person's consciousness to another's. So strong is the opposition of "I" to "the other" in Dostoevski's writings that it even manifests itself in the monologues that he puts into the mouths of his characters. As a case in point, Bakhtin calls attention to part 1 of Dostoevski's *Notes from the Underground*, where the nameless protagonist delivers a lengthy diatribe to a nonexistent audience from the isolation of his own humble abode and is constantly responding to imagined objections.

In establishing the nature of the polyphonic novel, Bakhtin underscores the extent to which many of its qualities were anticipated in two ancient Greek genres: namely, the Socratic dialogue and the Menippean satire. In the case of the Socratic dialogue, such as those written by Plato and Xenophon, he contends that the essence of the genre lies in its systematic search for truth by means of a free-spirited exchange of ideas or opinions among individuals. This distinguishing characteristic is, in Bakhtin's view, to be found only in those dialogues that Plato wrote during his early and middle periods. During the late period, he goes on to argue, Plato uses the figure of Socrates solely as a teacher of truth rather than as someone actively engaged in an open-minded search for it. What impresses Bakhtin most about the early and middle dialogues is the way that Plato uses a cast of characters whom he invests with autonomous voices as the bearers of ideologies, in much the same manner that Dostoevski does in his major novels.

When Bakhtin revised his treatise on Dostoevski for publication in 1963, he added much new material pertaining to the Menippean satire as a forerunner of the polyphonic novel. None of the writings of Menippus, who founded this genre during the first half of the third century B.C., has survived. The characteristics of the genre are best preserved in the satires by the Latin writers Varro (116-27 B.C.) and Seneca (4 B.C.-A.D. 65) as well as those by the Greek writer Lucian (c. 120-180). Even though these imitations of Menippus' satires differ greatly in terms of form from the Socratic dialogues, both genres have the common goal of testing ideas and their carriers. One of the qualities that Bakhtin most admires in the Menippean satire is the seriocomic mockery of conventional wisdom and social custom. Although he cites many specific examples of Menippean episodes in the works of Dostoevski, Bakhtin makes no claim that the Russian novelist had any direct knowledge of this genre; instead, he asserts that these parallels are largely the result of the fact that both Menippus and Dostoevski lived in historical epochs during which their respective cultures were experiencing profound crises of confidence and that their works accordingly reflect the intense rivalry between competing religious and philosophical systems.

Bakhtin also regards the Socratic dialogue and the Menippean satire to be, in large measure, literary manifestations of the perennial carnival tradition that has its roots among the common people. As he perceives this tradition, the carnival is a season when the masses can escape the regimentation of the official order and enjoy a brief period of variety and change in which social roles are reversed and dominant ideologies challenged. Although the phenomenon of the carnival is examined more fully in *Rabelais and His World*, Bakhtin uses his treatise on Dostoevski as an occasion to connect the carnival spirit with many disparate genres, including the early literature of Christianity and the narrative works of Dostoevski. Like the carnival itself, the Christian Gospels and the novels of Dostoevski are seen as violating generally accepted social norms. Hence, in his view, they lead readers to the ultimate questions in life. In a number of essays written during the 1930's and 1940's, Bakhtin carries his admiration for the Socratic dialogue, the Menippean satire, and the carnival tradition to its proper conclusion and insists that a work does not even qualify as a novel unless it tests the limits of the doctrines that society regards as sacrosanct. True novels, such as those of Dostoevski, force the reader to confront a reality that is incomplete and imperfect. Those novels which seek to depict a world that is complete and perfect are, in his view, really epics.

To the extent that the polyphonic novel is based on dialogue, it would appear to have many of the formal properties which are found in the dramatic genre. In view of his thorough background in classical literary theory, it is surprising that Bakhtin never makes any attempt to address the arguments set forth in Aristotle's *Poetics*. There is a decided need to do so, for Aristotle himself attaches a major significance to the aesthetic consequences of the narrative factor (that is, one's awareness of the authorial presence in a literary work). In his analysis of the epic and dramatic techniques in the *Poetics*, Aristotle argues the case for the superiority of the drama chiefly on the grounds that it is able to dispense with narration entirely and that it thereby permits the characters to interact among themselves directly. It must be emphasized, moreover, that the superiority of this genre is, for Aristotle, in no way dependent upon properties derived from its staging. Students of the *Poetics*, for some strange reason, frequently fail to take note of two passages in chapter 26 where Aristotle explicitly states that plays still retain their dramatic vividness in reading as well as in actual performance. It is, accordingly, tempting to conclude that the dramatic genre is inherently polyphonic by virtue of its formal structure. Without challenging the authority of the *Poetics* directly, Bakhtin, for his part, simply asserts that drama is by its very essence incapable of achieving genuine polyphony since it can never be truly multi-voiced. From his perspective, it is the hero of each play who supplies the only valid voice. He even goes as far as to deny that any of William Shakespeare's plays may in itself be deemed polyphonic, although he is willing to concede that the entire body of the bard's dramatic works may possess this quality if viewed collectively. While such notions may be correct, they clearly stand in need of validation.

Bakhtin was arrested sometime around January 7, 1929, for reasons unrelated to his views on literature. It was his involvement with a number of religious associations which caused the Soviet authorities to regard him as an enemy of the state. His treatise on Dostoevski was actually published several months after his arrest, and the fact that it received a favorable review from Anatoly Lunacharsky, a high-ranking scholar in the Bolshevik bureaucracy, was instrumental in influencing the courts to impose a lighter sentence than otherwise might have been the case. He was, consequently, sent into exile—first to Kazakhstan and later to cities lying to the west of the Ural mountains. Once having been politically rehabilitated during the late 1960's, Bakhtin was allowed to settle in Moscow and he lived there until his death on March 7, 1975. Perhaps the supreme irony of his life was to have preached the virtues of polyphony in a society attuned solely to monophony.

Victor Anthony Rudowski

Sources for Further Study

Book World. XIV, July 8, 1984, p. 12.
Choice. XXII, December, 1984, p. 564.
Commentary. LXXVIII, November, 1984, p. 39.

PROVIDENCE

Author: Anita Brookner (1928-   )
Publisher: Pantheon Books (New York). 183 pp. $13.95
Type of work: Novel
Time: The 1980's
Locale: London

A part-French, part-British lecturer in Romanticism at a small college is about to embark on two projects: performing her lecture such that she will gain a permanent appointment and winning the heart of the art historian with whom she is infatuated

> Principal characters:
> KITTY MAULE, a lecturer in Romanticism
> MAURICE BISHOP, a well-born, chic art historian on the faculty
> CAROLINE, Kitty's next-door neighbor and companion
> LOUISE, Kitty's French grandmother and a fashion designer
> VADIM, Kitty's grandfather

With the publication of *Hotel du Lac* (1984) and its subsequent reception of the Booker McConnell Prize for Fiction, one of England's most prestigious literary awards, Anita Brookner has come into her own, it would seem. She has garnered considerable notice since that point, including an interview on National Public Radio's "All Things Considered." All of this attention means that she will be known to a much wider Stateside readership than she has enjoyed in the past. This prospect is a fortunate one for both author and readers—indeed, providential.

Prior to this most recent coup, Brookner had published several novels, including *Look at Me* (1983) and the novel under review, *Providence* (published in Great Britain in 1982). It is useful to consider *Providence* in the light of *Look at Me*, for one thereby sees in sharper relief many of the elements which are combined with greater complexity in the later work. One is even tempted to dub *Providence* a sort of "dry run" for the subsequent novel, but there are too many special properties attaching to this work for that assertion to be true.

The most striking similarity between *Providence* and the later work is the "spurned woman" plot mechanics that drive this narrative. Kitty Maule, the heroine, is the victim of her own deluded love for a man who, it is quickly evident to the reader, cares little if at all for her. Kitty, like the protagonist of Brookner's earlier novel *The Debut* (1981), is simply not beautiful enough to seize the amorous prize that she desires. To make matters worse for Kitty, she is part French and must make her way through the intricacies of insular British manners, being always too cautious and correct, a shade too impeccable for her own good. Even her stylish dresses, a legacy of her grandmother's skill as a fashion designer, are always just a bit too stylish; they are tasteful (or, to use a recurrent word in the novel, "suitable"), but finally they make it harder for her to fit in, harder for her to place.

Kitty's object of desire is Maurice Bishop, a cool but dashing figure whose pullover sweaters impress the fashion-conscious Kitty, especially when set against the backdrop of shabby-genteel dowdiness which marks the rest of her colleagues at the unnamed university where she hopes to make her temporary appointment into something more permanent. The sartorial emphasis given seemingly every description of Maurice Bishop led one critic to lament that, rather than a genuine character, what Brookner was giving the reader was "part-icon and part-knitting pattern."

Bishop, however, is more than a knitting pattern by far. He is also a title, inherited wealth and breeding, social assurance, academic prominence, and even—however unlikely in modern-day secular England—religious faith. These are all attributes which, it is implied at one or another stage, Kitty wishes to possess and does not. The religious motif is especially insistent with respect to Maurice: His last name implies a transmitter of supernatural truth, his specialty—Gothic cathedrals—confirms it, and he even wears a signet ring. Kitty, whose specialty is Romanticism, exists firmly in the here and now of everyday reality but longs, like so many of the men she studies, for the splendors and the spiritual certitudes of the Middle Ages. Perhaps the key word here is "certitude," however, since that is what a belief in providence entails. Bishop represents less religious faith or certitude in the narrow sense than the quality of certitude as such: a faith that the social world which has been so kind and generous in the past will inevitably be so in the future, a faith that is hard to distinguish from faith in oneself.

Indeed, Bishop's belief in his own charm verges on narcissistic hubris. His public lectures on cathedrals have poetic leaps of inspiration and assumption that leave people such as his perennial antagonist, called only "the Roger Fry professor," incredulous with contempt. The ladies (the wife of the Roger Fry professor included), however, and most of the gentlemen admire the lectures anyway. He seems to feel capable, despite a paucity of evidence on a given medieval topic, of virtually communicating with the dead themselves. The ability to do this would be especially desired by Kitty, whose life has been very early overshadowed by death. Her father—a British captain and an idealized figure—died before she was born, and her weak mother, Marie-Thérèse, expired suddenly one night at her grandparents' dinner table. In another striking parallel to Frances Hinton, the heroine of *Look at Me*, Kitty Maule is thus orphaned, her life bordered by the somber hues of death; and her orphanhood makes her even more aware of her marginal, misfit status.

One doubts it will be betraying anything to say that Kitty's designs on Maurice Bishop are not fully realized—although the precise way in which they are compromised, as revealed in a stroke of theater on the final two pages of the novel, is astounding in its farcical reversal of expectations yet satisfying in its confirmation of the reader's deepest suspicions about

Maurice's true level. Nevertheless, the reader is in on the cruel joke long before the protagonist, to the point where the reader risks feeling that Kitty is somewhat dim: a fatal prospect in a text that depends so heavily on reader sympathy with the heroine. Kitty's blindness may arouse consternation in much the same way that Frances' choice of James Anstey in *Look at Me* causes perplexity. There is one respect, at least, in which *Providence* is different from, and better than, its later counterpart. The reader is given enough information to know, finally, what it is that Kitty sees in Maurice Bishop and why what she sees has so little to do with what is actually there.

In *Look at Me*, the reader is apprised neither of James's inherent qualities nor of Frances' reasons for being drawn to him in particular rather than someone else; one has the sense that the entire affair is built merely to fall apart, so to speak, because James is such a hazy figure throughout. Instead of images of James in that affair, the reader sees the changes in Frances: One chapter even closes with a photograph of Frances taken during her time with James. Such features suggest a strong element of narcissism in Frances' interest, a suggestion which the book's title also carries, but there are so many machinations at her expense in the narrative that this hint is a muted one. Frances is so clearly more sinned against than sinning that those ways in which she is complicit in her own victimization seem less significant than they really are. In *Providence*, perhaps partly because it is a journeyman work with a more schematic setting of scene, the self-concern of the heroine is more starkly posed. The reader of *Providence* sees quickly why Kitty is attracted to Maurice Bishop, and why considerations of character, even of details of physical appearance, would not matter very much.

Kitty's interest in Maurice Bishop derives not from who he is but from where he is—and ironically, it is the very outsider status which both makes Kitty long for Maurice and also makes it harder for her to judge whether he reciprocates. Really, it is above all his position—at the academic pinnacle, within the British class system, along the grid of fashion—that Kitty desires in desiring him. Put a slightly different way, Kitty desires him because he is desired, because everyone else desires him or desires to be him, and because what he is and possesses is presumed to be what everyone desires to be or to possess. Kitty affects to scorn her duties at the university, with the attendant pretensions to an academic career, in part because she does them so effortlessly that she cannot take them seriously. In fact, she works quite hard at her post, and much of the book is taken up with her anxious anticipation of a maiden university lecture on which her permanent appointment is said to hinge. One especially unkind, and generally imperceptive, Stateside reviewer for a weekly magazine did, not without some justice, remark that Kitty often seems less concerned for Maurice than for her lecture.

The point, however, is that Kitty sees gaining Maurice and gaining the appointment as the dual culmination of her ambition. She sees them as linked in time (Maurice's dinner party, which she feels will be pivotal is to occur within a week after her lecture) but also in purport. Through each she hopes to gain the "place" in British society that she has always felt the need to acquire. One realizes that for Kitty, Maurice stands as both the reward for accomplishment and the complement to accomplishment: icing on the cake of respectability. Indeed, she views Maurice much the way arriviste men of means are said to view their highborn wives, as the emblem of achieved legitimacy. Maurice's flaws as a person—the fact that he sees her only for dinners she prepares, for example—are never clear to Kitty because Maurice's personhood as such is not of interest to her.

Despite this fact, one cannot resist feeling a certain sympathy for the heroine, just as one does for Frances Hinton in *Look at Me*. Kitty's state has been rendered so well, and her past history so effectively culled, that she solicits the reader's regard. She is clearly an admirable person who deserves well and cannot afford to be disappointed too many more times. It would be difficult to deny one's rooting interest in a heroine of whom this is written, during the period immediately preceding her maiden lecture: "For two days she sat in the garden or walked about the streets, and she would remember those two days as a curious interval, when all things seemed possible, an almost mystical time of promise and anticipated fulfillment."

Yet while in one major respect, *Providence* is better than *Look at Me*, in most others, it does not come up to the level of the latter book. Some of the strongest pleasures of Brookner's more recent work are here, but in still developing form. The dry, piquant style is still being shaped, and the tone vacillates between satire and lyricism in a way that is better modulated in her subsequent fiction. Minor characters abound here: Professor Redmile, the dean who bores to tears with false heartiness and endless talk of the college's forthcoming new building; a fortune-teller whom Kitty consults to find out whether she will land Maurice; the neurasthenic, brilliant young Larter, her student who, when not explicating Benjamin Constant's *Adolphe* (a guiding motif of the novel), skulks around local schoolyards. These characters, along with the social background against which they move, are drawn so well that one wishes for more, even if, as in *Look at Me*, the lushness of the vegetation threatens at times to obscure the principals. Brookner is so good at the novel of manners that it may even defeat her darker designs in *Providence*, and the schematic quality of the book makes the split between these two tendencies more apparent. (The tone of the ending, for example, is hard to figure: The revelation is shockingly laughable, yet given the reader's investment in Kitty, one realizes that she has been betrayed as much by the text itself as by Maurice.)

In its essentials, however, *Providence* presents a solid achievement for Anita Brookner. Happily for the reader, it is also a great pleasure to read. The spare but pregnant style, the wonderful portraits of Kitty's French grandparents in their defiant suburban London exile, the Jane Austen-like sense of social ritual and the sadly but predictably huge weight everybody gives it, and above all, the constant Brookner bass note of lonely, quiet desperation—all of these are presented in a way that holds the attention, and the memory. If it is true that *Providence* lacks the complexity, control, and delicacy of later Brookner fiction, it also, perhaps for that very reason, allows the reader to see more vividly the outlines of psychological mechanisms, such as narcissism, that operate more submerged elsewhere in her writings. For that reason, it may be of use to read this book before reading the others. In addition, there is no such thing, apparently, as an Anita Brookner novel that fails to delight, and *Providence* is certainly no exception to the rule.

Mark Conroy

Sources for Further Study

Booklist. LXXX, February 1, 1984, p. 803.
Christian Science Monitor. LXXVI, May, 1984, p. 24.
Kirkus Reviews. LI, December 15, 1983, p. 1259.
Library Journal. CIX, January, 1984, p. 108.
Los Angeles Times. February 8, 1984, V, p. 16.
The New York Times Book Review. LXXXIX, March 18, 1984, p. 17.
The New Yorker. LX, April 9, 1984, p. 144.
Newsweek. CIII, February 27, 1984, p. 71.
Publishers Weekly. CCXXIV, December 16, 1983, p. 66.
Washington Post. March 9, 1984, p. D3.

RALPH WALDO EMERSON
Days of Encounter

Author: John McAleer (1923-   )
Publisher: Little, Brown and Company (Boston). Illustrated. 748 pp. $27.50
Type of work: Literary biography
Time: 1803-1882
Locale: The United States, Europe, and Egypt

*A detailed biography which traces influences upon Emerson's thought, his writing,
and his lecturing; which portrays the milieu that nourished him; and which reveals his
relationships with and influence upon many people in his long life*

> *Principal personages:*
> RALPH WALDO EMERSON, a minister, essayist, poet, and lecturer
> ELLEN TUCKER EMERSON, his first wife
> LYDIA (LIDIAN) JACKSON EMERSON, his second wife
> AMOS BRONSON ALCOTT,
> HENRY DAVID THOREAU, and
> NATHANIEL HAWTHORNE, his Concord neighbors and friends
> MARGARET FULLER and
> CAROLINE STURGIS, his two close bluestocking friends
> THOMAS CARLYLE, his British friend and longtime correspondent

Ralph Waldo Emerson was looked upon by many of his contemporaries as a foolish optimist who seemed unaware of the social ills of his time or who was unmoved by them because he lived too much in an ideal world of his imagination. He was attacked as a radical by conservatives and traditionalists, who saw him as a danger to the youth of the nation, whom he advised to rebel against well-established customs of religious belief and action. He was mocked as a borrower of other men's ideas who had no philosophic system and who wrote and spoke nonconsecutively and often in a "transcendental" style which hid whatever meaning he was trying to convey. Nevertheless, Emerson lived long enough so that for many years before his death at seventy-nine he was esteemed as one of America's most impressive speakers and one of its finest essayists. He was honored not only for what he said but also for what he was.

Many biographies and memoirs of Emerson have been published since his death in 1882. Gay Wilson Allen's *Waldo Emerson* (1981) portrayed the poet-philosopher as a much warmer man than he seems in his essays and his poetry. Now, three years later, John McAleer looks at the sage of Concord during his "'days of encounter' which constituted for him spiritual, ethical, ideological, emotional, or physical crises advancing the progress of the soul."

For the most part, McAleer avoids detailed analyses or commentary on Emerson's individual works, but he devotes considerable attention to "The Method of Nature," a neglected oration originally delivered at Waterville

College, in Maine. Although "The Method of Nature" is, as McAleer says, a companion piece to the famous Harvard Divinity School address, the Waterville oration aroused little interest when it was delivered at the small Baptist college. This contrasts strongly with what Emerson called "the storm in our washbowl" that followed the Harvard address, when Andrews Norton in a Boston paper assailed Emerson as a man attempting to subvert Christianity and as being possibly an atheist.

Many of McAleer's eighty brief chapters are restricted to Emerson's relationships with members of his family, close personal friends, or other people who sought him out or to whom he was drawn at various stages during his long life.

As a young man, Emerson said of himself, "What is called a warm heart, I have not." In middle age he wrote, "Even for those whom I really love I have not animal spirits." In between these two assessments of his lack of feelings, he wed and lost a young wife after less than seventeen months of marriage; he married a second wife who bore him four children; and he lost at five years of age the first of these children, Waldo, whose death inspired the beautiful elegy "Threnody," in which the father tries to console himself for the loss of his beloved son.

That Emerson was capable of intense emotion is evident in his courtship of and his brief marriage to consumptive Ellen Louise Tucker. He kept her letters; he invited his second wife, Lydia (Lidian) Jackson, to read them; and he wrote poems commemorating his and Ellen's love (there were none to Lidian).

After Ellen's death, Emerson wrote, "There is one birth & one baptism & one first love & the affections cannot keep their youth any more than men." He concluded that what he had experienced once could never be repeated. He made no pretense of feeling toward Lidian, whom he married more than four years after Ellen's death, as he had toward Ellen. The amazing letter of proposal to Lidian (included in Gay Wilson Allen's *Waldo Emerson* and quoted in part by McAleer) surprised her, since it was totally unexpected. She asked him to visit her; she quizzed him about various matters; she confessed her own inadequacies; then she accepted his offer.

The forty-seven-year marriage of Emerson and Lidian (whom he called Queenie) seems to have been marked by mutual respect and some affection, but there is little indication in McAleer's biography that there was much more. One wonders how much jealousy Lidian felt during two long visits of Margaret Fuller to Bush, the Emersons' Concord home. Perhaps Fuller's homeliness may have lessened any jealous feelings Lidian had about her visitor's chances of alienating Emerson's affections. Fuller, an intense young intellectual, did seemingly fall in love with Emerson; when she tried, however, to penetrate the ice which he confessed was a part of his nature, she found it too thick to break. They remained friends, though, until after a European trip she drowned in a shipwreck off the American coast, along with her young Italian husband and their baby son.

After a spell of ill health in 1832, Emerson sought a cure in a voyage to Europe. McAleer remarks that he was also seeking a guru who might set him on the right path in life. A visit to the poet Walter Savage Landor in Florence quickly convinced him that Landor was not the one. Emerson's disillusionment with two more English poets, whom he sought out when he reached England, is well-known, but McAleer gives some details which show a brash young American expecting too much of two famous but aging men. He found Samuel Taylor Coleridge and William Wordsworth very different from what he had imagined.

At Coleridge's home, Emerson arrived in the morning and was told to return after noon since the poet was still abed. On the return, Emerson was treated to a lengthy monologue which he occasionally tried to interrupt. McAleer thinks that Emerson was ungrateful after Coleridge gave him an hour's time for his visit, only to be criticized for having produced what Emerson termed "rather a spectacle than a conversation."

When Emerson reached Rydal Mount, Wordsworth's rural home, the poet's daughters called him in from the garden where he had been composing the last of four sonnets on Fingal's Cave after a visit to Scotland. Wordsworth, like Coleridge earlier, talked while Emerson mostly listened. He also recited the three sonnets he had completed. Writing later of the experience, Emerson thought Wordsworth made "the impression of a narrow and very English mind; of one who paid for his rare elevation by general tameness and conformity."

The one British author who made a deep and lasting impression on Emerson was Thomas Carlyle, at whose farm home at Craigenputtock he was invited to stay overnight. They stimulated each other in their extended conversation in the home and while walking about the Scottish hills. Each later sponsored the books of the other in his respective country. Also, they established a correspondence that lasted nearly forty years, a remarkable series of letters revealing their deep friendship, their disagreements, and their very different characters.

After study in Harvard Divinity School, Emerson became a Unitarian minister in 1826, but his reading and the development of his own thought led him increasingly to rebel inwardly against the restrictions of his profession. He concluded, "It is the best part of the man . . . that revolts most against his being a minister." He resigned as minister of his Boston church, causing some church members to think that he had lost his mind.

From this time onward, though for several years he occasionally delivered sermons in various churches, he was an independent moral lecturer, principally on the Lyceum circuit. As a speaker, he avoided the flamboyant oratory used by many others in the nineteenth century. He spoke simply and naturally, using many illustrations from common life. One listener, describing him as he appeared on the platform, said "he had but one gesture, a downward thrust of his clenched right hand, held contorted and tense at his side, and used with unconscious earnestness in driving imaginary stakes." A striking portrait by David Scott, which McAleer includes among his illustrations, shows Emerson the lecturer with his clenched right hand.

As Emerson became well recognized beyond his Concord-Cambridge-Boston home area, he increased the geographical range of his lecturing, giving sixty lectures in Ohio alone in the years 1850-1867 and eighty lectures in fourteen states in 1867. McAleer lists the dismaying travel troubles which Emerson endured on these lecture tours: a lake boat fire, a hotel fire, cold, mud, scheduling errors, hostile journalists, inquisitors, poor housing, noisy and unheated lecture halls, a power failure the night he was to lecture on power in Cincinnati, even cholera outbreaks in St. Louis and on a riverboat. One wonders how Emerson, whose health had been delicate in his early years, managed to survive the rigors of his traveling and his lecturing. His belief in the principle of compensation in life—a loss here, a gain there; a pain here, a joy there—must surely have helped to keep him going.

Though Emerson was regarded as a reformer, he differed from lesser reformers of the time who attacked such specific evils as industrial exploitation and child labor. He believed that only when man was reformed from within could society be reformed without, and he preached this gospel throughout his career. Nevertheless, he did become a supporter of women's rights and he spoke out against slavery. Of the Fugitive Slave Bill, which he considered "Mr. Webster's law," he wrote in his journal: "This filthy enactment was made in the nineteenth century, by people who could read and write. I will not obey it, by God." In 1854, he delivered in Boston an attack on the law, which he deeply resented because it represented an invasion of the personal rights of Northerners, making them submit to the will of Southern slaveholders.

Emerson did not harbor for Abraham Lincoln the contempt he showed toward Daniel Webster, but he did at first view Lincoln as a vacillating politician because he delayed the emancipation of the slaves. After Lincoln was killed, Emerson realized that he had underrated him. Lincoln had waited till the time was ripe before freeing the slaves. Preserving the Union was the primary objective and only after the tide of war clearly favored the North following Robert E. Lee's defeat at Antietam did Lincoln issue the Emancipation Proclamation.

Oncoming age began to take increasing toll as Emerson moved into his middle sixties. Speaking at Harvard in July, 1867, he had trouble seeing his manuscript. By 1872, he was beginning to lose his memory. Having trouble developing new lectures, he began cannibalizing from earlier ones. A series of talks on literature in Boston was designated as "conversations," a name deemed more appropriate to their rambling content.

In July, 1872, Bush burned, and the excitement and pain of seeing his home on fire brought on a stroke. From this time until his death ten years later, Emerson's memory was so poor that he could not remember people's names and sometimes even his own name. In 1878, he planned to read "Education" with his daughter Ellen standing by to prompt him. He said, "A funny occasion it will be—a lecturer who has no idea what he's lecturing about, and an audience who don't know what he *can* mean!" His last visit away from Concord was to attend his friend Henry Wadsworth Longfellow's funeral. He did not recognize the man he saw in the coffin.

There is pathos in these closing scenes of Emerson's life, but one is struck by the way he accepted his infirmities. He had observed nature, he had spoken and written about it for many years, he had urged his listeners and his readers to realize the part they play in a natural world dominated by what he termed an Over-Soul. His physical "days of encounter" were reaching an end now. He did not rage against what was happening. Walt Whitman, seeing him seven months before he died, sat in Franklin Sanborn's Concord home and observed "the well-known expression of sweetness" in the face of the man who, many years before, had with his essays inspired the writing of *Leaves of Grass* (1855).

Students seeking a better knowledge and appreciation of Emerson's life and work would do well to read R. L. Rusk's *The Life of Ralph Waldo Emerson* (1949), long regarded as the standard biography, and to add both Gay Wilson Allen's *Waldo Emerson* and McAleer's biography. Though McAleer says less about Emerson's writings than either Rusk or Allen, he supplies many details about Emerson's connections to a large number of his contemporaries. From his own area, he knew Nathaniel Hawthorne, Henry David Thoreau, Longfellow, Oliver Wendell Holmes, James Russell Lowell, Margaret Fuller, and Amos Alcott. He knew the Henry Jameses (father and son) and Walt Whitman, from New York. He knew W. D. Howells, a New Englander transplanted from the Midwest. He charmed John Muir, of California, whom he met late in life. He knew Thomas Carlyle and Arthur H. Clough from Great Britain. All of these the reader meets, and many others, among the large cast of figures in McAleer's *Ralph Waldo Emerson: Days of Encounter*, whose portraits re-create the milieu that produced and then nourished one of America's earliest major writers.

Henderson Kincheloe

Sources for Further Study

Book World. XIV, September 16, 1984, p. 7.

Booklist. LXXX, August, 1984, p. 1591.
Choice. XXII, November, 1984, p. 426.
Kirkus Reviews. LII, May 1, 1984, p. 441.
Library Journal. CIX, July, 1984, p. 1328.
Los Angeles Times Book Review. August 26, 1984, p. 1.
The New York Review of Books. XXXI, November 22, 1984, p. 19.
The New York Times Book Review. LXXXIX, September 30, 1984, p. 41.
Publishers Weekly. CCXXV, May 25, 1984, p. 55.

READING FOR THE PLOT
Design and Intention in Narrative

Author: Peter Brooks (1938-   )
Publisher: Alfred A. Knopf (New York). 363 pp. $17.95
Type of work: Literary criticism/psychoanalysis

Applying psychoanalysis to a number of French and English novels of the nineteenth and twentieth centuries, Peter Brooks argues that the death instinct and therapeutic transference provide a model for narrative plot

Students of literature are often taught that "reading for the plot" is a low and undignified way to approach literature, appropriate perhaps to the consumption of popular works such as Peter Benchley's *Jaws* (1974) but certainly not to the higher appreciation of Henry James. In his last book, *The Melodramatic Imagination* (1976), Peter Brooks showed that Henry James himself owed much to the popular tradition of melodramatic plotting. In this lucid and elegant sequel, he makes another, more theoretical attempt to restore the dignity of plot. In analyses of canonical narratives, ranging from Honoré de Balzac's *La Peau de chagrin* (1831; *The Wild Ass's Skin*) and Stendhal's *Le Rouge et le noir* (1830; *The Red and the Black*; 1898) to Joseph Conrad's *Heart of Darkness* (1902) and William Faulkner's *Absalom, Absalom!* (1936), with excursions into the fairy tale, Eugène Sue's *Les Mystères de Paris* (1842-1843; *The Mysteries of Paris*, 1843) and Sigmund Freud's "Wolf Man" case, Brooks argues that, far from being an atavistic vestige of more primitive levels of storytelling, plot is an inescapable human universal, essential to the mind's structuring of reality and, more important, a model of the structure of the mind itself.

Human beings can only make sense of the world, Brooks asserts, by making up stories about it, organizing the chaos of experience into orderly narratives with beginnings, middles, and ends. Even criticisms of those stories are themselves further stories. So, for example, Jean-Jacques Rousseau, appalled by the story of his false accusation of Marion in the *Confessions* (1782, 1789) and vowing never to say another word about it, can only respond to the horror it reveals about himself by revealing more, by producing a succession of further narratives. Everything, for Brooks, is narrative. He has little interest in debating the philosophical question of whether all meaning must take narrative form—whether, as Fredric Jameson claims in *The Political Unconscious* (1981), narrative is the unique, paradigmatic instance of how meaning is produced. The real center of his concern is psychological. Plot is a universal, first and foremost, because its basic mechanism duplicates the dynamics of the psyche. Freud's theory of the self, Brooks concludes, is also the "masterplot" of human narrative.

This thesis immediately distinguishes *Reading for the Plot* from the two approaches that come closest to it and from which it has learned the most:

narratology and psychoanalytic criticism. In his appeal to psychoanalysis, Brooks turns away from what he sees as the "formalism" of narratology, whose search for elementary units of narrative has made it blind to the dynamics of time and to human desire. In contrast, however, to the better-known proponents of Freudian criticism—for example, Marthe Robert in *The Origins of the Novel* (1981)—Brooks does not simply apply Freud's theory to the analysis of characters, authors, or even readers. For him, as for the New Criticism and for Jacques Lacan's reading of Edgar Allan Poe's "The Purloined Letter," the text itself can be seen as a libidinal system of desires and resistances analogous to that of the psyche. As such, each of the classic nineteenth and twentieth century texts he examines is shown to be, simultaneously, a critical commentary on its own plottedness.

This project remains an application of Freud; Brooks does not claim that narrative teaches one anything about Freud that one did not already know but only that the Freudian model generates fresh insights into the texts of the canon. This claim is abundantly substantiated. In the novels of the early and middle nineteenth century in particular, which Brooks refers to as the "Golden Age" of narrative, his perspective reveals an admirable and unexpected self-consciousness about plots and plotting. In the indifference to worldly marriage, the abdication of worldly ambition, and the return to the maternal embrace of Madame de Rênal that end *The Red and the Black*, for example, Brooks finds not merely material for a case study of Julien Sorel's psychology but also a throwing into question of the transgressive energies of plot itself. Much the same point is made about the conclusion of Charles Dickens' *Great Expectations* (1861). Again, the end of the plot coincides with the death of desire, "a life that has outlived plot, renounced plot, been cured of it: life that is left over. . . . Plot comes to resemble a diseased, feverish state of the organism caught up in the machinery of a desire which must eventually be renounced. Plot, we come to understand, was a state of abnormality or deviance." In Balzac, Stendhal, and Dickens, where plot and desire had seemed so powerful and straightforward, what Brooks discovers and praises is this understanding of an ultimate quiescence which waits beyond all desire and all plot.

To that extent, however, he is not so much praising plot as revealing modernist misgivings about plot even in its realist exemplars. This raises the problem of precisely what plot Brooks is reading for. He uses the term in two contradictory senses. When he speaks of "its potential for summary and retransmission: the fact that we can still recognize 'the story' even when its medium has been considerably changed," he is clearly identifying plot with what narratologists call "story," which the Russian Formalists call *fabula* and Roland Barthes in *S/Z* (1970) calls the "proairetic code" or the simple order of events as they occurred. It is for the defense of this unlikely and unfashionable object that his title implicitly takes credit. Brooks's explicit account of plot, however, is quite different. Like R. S. Crane's defense of Aristotelian plot in "The Concept of Plot and the Plot of *Tom Jones*," Brooks's defense works by expanding the definition of the term. Plot is not simply the order of events, he says, but the tension or play between the order of events and how they are arranged and presented in narrative discourse ("discourse" or, in Formalist terms, *sjužhet*). The detective story—an important reference point throughout the book—thus becomes the paradigm of all narratives, even the simplest. Citing a study of oral narratives by inner-city adolescents, Brooks argues that even the most brutally linear, episodic sequence generates questions and enigmas which require evaluation and interpretation. In short, this concept of plot combines "story" with "discourse," *fabula* with *sjužhet*, Barthes' proairetic code with his "hermeneutic" code. If plot, however, includes the questioning and interpretation of events as well as the low, atavistic sequence of events itself, then there is much less credit to be claimed for defending it.

In "Story and Discourse in the Analysis of Narrative," Jonathan Culler argues that it makes as much sense to think of events being generated by the mode of recounting them as of the mode being determined by the events recounted. Neither has priority; *fabula* and *sjužhet* cannot be synthesized without contradiction. For Brooks, the contradiction between *fabula* and *sjužhet*, the "double logic" from which Culler says narrative suffers, is the very definition of plot. As a way into realism, this definition produces a new and valuable emphasis on the dark suicidal backdrop of nineteenth century ambition and on the complex reflexivity of narratives that have often seemed to revel naïvely in the onward rush of events. As it applies to modernism, on the other hand, it comes very close to the banality of received opinion. Between realism's enthusiastic plotting and modernism's suspicion of plot, the familiar hinge is Gustave Flaubert: "No longer can the reader espouse the protagonist's desire, no longer can he read in the forward-moving expectation created by the force of that desire. The binding, totalizing work of Eros seems to have reached a halt." The extended contrast between Balzac and Flaubert, between a world charged with the character's desire and a world disinvested of desire, distanced by the *style indirect libre*, made over into an aesthetic spectacle for the invisible observer, will be of more use to introductory students than to those already familiar with the field. In *Heart of Darkness*, Brooks explains, Marlow's "loyalty to Kurtz is perhaps ultimately the loyalty of *sjužhet* to *fabula*: the loyalty of telling to told, of detective to criminal, follower to forerunner, repetition to recollection." Despite the narratological vocabulary, no significant new insights are yielded by this view of modernism.

Indeed, on the whole, the book's forays into literary history are not very convincing. Given Stendhal's notoriously slapdash habits of writing and his well-known refusal to go back over his work, it seems unlikely that he could have carefully planned the dating of *The Red and the Black* so as to make the final catastrophe a displaced version of the Revolution of 1830, which, in fact, the text never mentions. Brooks's tendency to think in ahistorical psychoanalytic universals makes it difficult to allow for real historical discriminations. Can Odysseus' desire to return home, the picaro's scheming to feed, clothe, and shelter himself, and the ambition of the nineteenth century "young man from the provinces" all be usefully grouped under the single heading of "desire"? Does the supposed preference of children for plots with beginnings, middles, and ends really prove that Aristotelian plot is a universal?

Brooks's use of the universal "we" has a more serious consequence. It performs the same quarantine on female sexuality that Brooks accuses prostitution of performing in nineteenth century France. In a book whose aim is to bring together plotting and sexuality, the chapter on *The Mysteries of Paris* is the only place where specifically female sexuality receives any attention. Elsewhere, the sexuality that is offered as a universal is quite clearly male. In his discussion of Balzac's *The Wild Ass's Skin*, the premise that the fulfillment of desire through the magic skin is equivalent to death is linked by Brooks to Freud's argument in *Beyond the Pleasure Principle* (1920) that what lies beyond the pleasure principle is the death instinct, the drive toward extinction. This is male fantasy, as Brooks's own vocabulary suggests. It depends on seeing "desire as erection, as the tumescence of a self in a state of domination, an imperious and imperial self. Yet this magic skin retracts and shrinks with the realization of desire, in a kind of postcoital quiescence." "It is characteristic of textual energy in narrative," Brooks generalizes, "that it should always be on the verge of premature discharge, of short-circuit. The reader experiences the fear—and excitation—of the improper end." This may be true of (some) male readers, but it seems foolhardy to take these sexual anxieties as human universals. This is especially true in that the extensive feminist literature on Freud and Lacan has taken such pains over the past decade to demonstrate the inescapable specificity of gender within any psychoanalytic account of the individual's development.

What Brooks claims to be adding to narratology is attention to "temporal dynamics," to "the play of desire in time that makes us turn pages and strive toward narrative ends." What exactly does he mean by time? He does not, like Stanley Fish, break reading down into the stages of a temporal process. On occasion, time indicates mortality, which is brought in to rescue the old-fashioned notion of transmissible narrative meaning from modern doubters. Brooks cites Walter Benjamin's suggestion in "The Storyteller" that death gives to an individual life the visible coherence that no one can glimpse while still alive; narrative, he suggests, may be synonymous with obituary. Nevertheless, this sense of time is only an adornment of the main argument. In effect, what Brooks means by time is the principle of detour or postponement. All desire, he asserts, is desire for the end, for the end of desire, for a return to preorganic quiescence. "The desire of the text is ultimately the desire for the end, for that recognition which is the moment of the death of the reader in the text." The delay of that inevitable end, then, is what constitutes narrative. Thus Shahrazad, who substitutes her string of stories for the violence of the Sultan's deathly desires, curing those desires by prolonging them and reinvesting them in a detour, an intermediary or "dilatory" space of premortem events, provides the model for all storytelling. Narrative, our hero, saves us from the disorders of desire.

What of the fact that Shahrazad is a woman? Though the pulsing, ceaseless rhythm of her storytelling, like Penelope's nightly weaving and unweaving, scans very differently from the anxious measure of one-shot tumescence and fear of premature discharge, the supposed universality of desire leaves no room for gender difference. Brooks does, however, add one crucial term to his characterization of ungendered desire. About halfway through the book, the equation of desire with the death instinct quietly takes a backseat to an explanatory account of Shahrazad's "detour." Desire is also, Brooks writes, the desire to narrate, to be heard, recognized, and understood. Going back to Balzac's *Le Colonel Chabert* (1832; *Colonel Chabert*, 1897)—this shift does not coincide exactly with the transition from realism to modernism—Brooks identifies the desire to narrate with the model of transference in Freudian therapy. If desire in narrative itself is a desire to die, an urge to pull out of emotional investments in order to return to an infantile calm of mind, the desire for a hearing shows loyalty not to death but to life. As the analysand transfers blocked feelings to the listening analyst, thereby working them through, so all narrative enlists the reader in a transference of desire from past to present objects. Following Quentin in *Absalom, Absalom!*, Brooks makes not a "triumphant apology for narrative" but "an apology for narrating, an enterprise apparently nostalgic, oriented toward the recovery of the past, yet really phatic in its vector, asking for hearing."

At this point it is not clear that Brooks is speaking about what anyone would call plot. Indeed, one might as well, like Edward Said in *Beginnings* (1975), use Freud's endless, palimpsestic analyses as a model not of plot but of freedom from plot's simplifying foreclosure. Yet if *Reading for the Plot* works its way through the self-consciously nostalgic subject of "plot" to a more modern focus on "narrative," it may also demonstrate to skeptics how seductive plot can be.

Bruce Robbins

Sources for Further Study

Antioch Review. XLII, Fall, 1984, p. 507.
Booklist. LXXX, May 15, 1984, p. 1287.
Kirkus Reviews. LII, April 1, 1984, p. 333.
Library Journal. CIX, July, 1984, p. 1327.
Los Angeles Times. August 10, 1984, V, p. 10.
The New Republic. CXCI, July 9, 1984, p. 36.
The New York Times Book Review. LXXXIX, July 22, 1984, p. 31.
Publishers Weekly. CCXXV, April 13, 1984, p. 55.

REASONS AND PERSONS

Author: Derek Parfit (1942-   )
Publisher: Oxford University Press (New York). 543 pp. $29.95
Type of work: Moral philosophy and metaphysics

An attempt to establish a nonreligious basis for impartial benevolence, arguing that there is no enduring self to which one can be partial

Rarely does a long and densely argued philosophical work come to the attention of the general reader. Reviews of such books are generally restricted to academic journals; it is assumed that they will be of interest only to specialists. Occasionally, however, wider claims are made for a work of philosophy, and such has been the case with Derek Parfit's *Reasons and Persons*. Writing in *The New York Review of Books*, the distinguished British philosopher P. F. Strawson praises Parfit's book not only for its "intellectual illumination and delight" but also for its potential practical effect; *Reasons and Persons*, he suggests, "may point the way to the emergence of a satisfactory theory of rational beneficence, and this might, in the long run be capable of influencing political behavior." Samuel Scheffler, in the *Times Literary Supplement*, writes that "*Reasons and Persons* may be the greatest work of substantive moral philosophy in the utilitarian tradition" since Henry Sidgwick's classic study *The Methods of Ethics* (1874). These are large claims indeed, and they demand a close reading of Parfit's book.

Parfit describes himself as one who by temperament is a revisionist: "Philosophers should not only interpret our beliefs; when they are false, they should *change* them." The fundamental ideas that Parfit thinks we ought to abandon are "beliefs about our own nature, and our identity over time." In short, Parfit contends that we have no good reasons to believe that we exist throughout our lives as the same person.

Unlike many revisionists, however, Parfit does not write merely to shock. Instead, he writes as a champion of that venerable moral principle—impartial benevolence. His argument, although somewhat complex, is ultimately straightforward: Impartial benevolence is the most rational principle to guide one's life choices and decisions, because the only plausible alternative—the principle of enlightened self-interest—falsely assumes that an individual remains the same person throughout his life. Without this assumption, self-interest theorists would have to recommend a life of unrestrained sensual gratification. All but the crassest of Philistines, however, realize that while an evening of wine, women, and song may be enjoyable, the costs paid on the day after almost certainly cancel out the benefits of the previous night's pleasures, and even if there were some cases of pleasure without payment, there can be no doubt that an entire life so spent would not be the most conducive to an individual's own happiness.

Suppose, however, that there is only a tenuous or nonexistent connection between the intemperate adolescent and the prematurely old man dying of kidney failure. If this is so, the principle of enlightened self-interest loses its appeal. Part 3 of *Reasons and Persons* argues that there are only these tenuous or nonexistent connections between individuals over time.

Does this mean that if we are presently in the full flower of youth, we simply ought to abandon any concern we might have for that prematurely old man? Parfit is sure that we should not. "Some outcomes are *good* or *bad*, in a sense that has moral relevance: it is bad for example if people become paralyzed, and we ought, if we can, to prevent this." Thus, it is wrong for anyone to act in a way which leads to an early death, even if it is his own. What Parfit believes his revisionist theory of personal identity shows is that we have no better reason to be concerned with our own future well-being than we have to be concerned with the future or present well-being of someone else. Thus, the long-range partiality to self that is recommended by enlightened self-interest is impossible to implement because there is no enduring self to which a person can be partial.

This conclusion is one which almost all moralists can welcome. Moreover, Parfit carefully makes room for the entitlements and individual rights upon which many contemporary critics of utilitarianism insist. Nevertheless, many philosophers would say that this is not the book that solves what Sidgwick regarded "as the profoundest problem of Ethics"—the conflict between self-interest and morality. These philosophers would argue that Parfit's denial of an enduring self pays too great a price, especially because there are less costly ways of solving the problem.

Aristotle, Bishop Joseph Butler, and those in the twentieth century who refer to themselves as "descriptivists" are among those who think that there is a less costly way. Instead of appealing to the "metaphysical fact" of a nonexistent self, these philosophers appeal to less esoteric facts which can be discovered through shrewd observation and inculcated by good sermons. As Butler wrote and preached, "Surely that character we call selfish is not the most promising for happiness," and again, "Surely the man of benevolence hath as great enjoyment as the man of ambition." Butler and others argue that impartial benevolence is reasonable because in the long run it coincides with a person's own happiness. Partial benevolence is impossible because it is self-defeating. If a person asks, Why should I not devote myself to a life of enlightened self-interest? Peter Geach observes that an "obviously relevant sort of reply . . . is an appeal to something the questioner wants, and cannot get if he does so-and-so." Furthermore, Geach adds, "only such a reply is relevant and rational."

Parfit would disagree, and his objections are found in part 1 of his book. His argument focuses on what has come to be known as "the Prisoner's Dilemma." Two thieves are caught, and while the prosecutor has sufficient evidence to win a two-year conviction, it is impossible to win the stiffer ten-year sentence which they both deserve without the testimony of one of the thieves. The prosecutor therefore questions them separately and makes the following offer to both: If you confess and give evidence for the state while your partner remains silent, you will go free and he will receive a twelve-year sentence. If you both confess, you will receive a ten-year sentence.

One might at first think that the prosecutor's offer of freedom contingent upon the other's silence too generous an offer. The prosecutor, however, is convinced that all thieves operate under the principle of enlightened self-interest and is therefore sure that neither will go free. Suppose either thief is a gambler and opts for freedom. If so, he will confess and hope his partner remains silent. On the other hand, if one opts to play it safe and minimize his loss, no matter what the other partner does, he will confess. The dilemma arises when we remember that if there were honor among thieves, the prosecutor's case would virtually collapse, and both would only receive a two-year sentence.

In such cases, Parfit argues, we see the fundamental weakness of self-interest theories and the need for impartial benevolence. Furthermore, such cases make it clear that enlightened self-interest and impartial benevolence do not coincide. If one thief is an egoist and the other honorable, the egoist wins big and the honorable man gets the fool's reward. Thus, Parfit writes, "Prisoner's Dilemmas need to be explained. So do their moral solutions. Both have been too little understood."

One wonders, however, how many times individuals actually find themselves in a prisoner's dilemma where there can be no communication and hence no reciprocity. The possibility of reciprocity is crucial for those who maintain that self-interest and benevolence coincide; certainly, that calculating secularist Benjamin Franklin would not have recommended honesty as the best policy in a world where reciprocity was impossible. "Outside prisons, or the offices of *game-theorists*," Parfit admits, this crucial condition is rarely met. Parfit admits that even the much-discussed arms race between the United States and the Soviet Union is not a true Prisoner's Dilemma because "the choice made by each may affect the later choices made by the other."

Why, then, even discuss such artificial problems? Parfit writes, "Though we can seldom know that we face a Two-Person Prisoner's Dilemma, we can very often know that we face Many-Person Versions. And these have great practical importance. The rare Two-Person Case is important only as a model for the Many-Person Versions." For example, in cases where "wages depend on profits, and work is unpleasant or a burden," says Parfit, "it can be better for each if others work harder, worse for each if he himself does." Another example involves soldiers: "Each will be safer if he turns and runs, but if all do more will be killed than if none do." A third example involves fishermen: "When the sea is overfished, it can be better for each if he tries to catch more, worse for each if all do." In all of these cases, we "need moral solutions. We must be directly disposed to make the altruistic choice." As Parfit asserts, these solutions will often involve self-denial where each person does for moral reasons what he knows will be worse for him. Thus, self-interest and morality do not always coincide.

Why is this? Cannot union workers, soldiers, and fishermen communicate with one another? Is there no possibility of reciprocity in such situations? Is there no camaraderie in these professions? It may be true that in these professions, if one does what is morally right, while others do not, he is at a distinct disadvantage. If, however, we suppose that a person acting selfishly may influence others to act similarly, it may also be the case that someone behaving unselfishly may have a beneficial effect on the actions of others. What we have is something similar to William James's "faith which creates the fact."

Suppose a person meets someone with whom he would like to be friends. The reasonable thing to do is to make some sort of friendly gesture. Of course, one may be spurned, and one's feelings hurt, but if one succeeds in making friends, one has demonstrated how kindness and self-interest can coincide. An exceptionally cautious person might wait for the other person to make the first move. This would indeed eliminate some risk of being hurt, but such a "safe" course of action may prevent a friendship from ever developing.

While Parfit does not directly address this possibility, he does implicitly provide a way around it:

> Each of us could sometimes help a stranger at some lesser cost to himself. Each could about as often be similarly helped. In small communities, the cost of helping might be indirectly met. If I help, this may cause me to be later helped in return. But in large communities this is unlikely. It may here be better for each if he never helps.

Why the difference between small and large communities? "When there are few of us," says Parfit, "if we give to or impose on others great total benefits or harms, we must be affecting other people in significant ways, that would be grounds either for gratitude, or resentment." The argument must go something like this: While it is true that sometimes I may help a person only to have him kick me in the shins, it is morely likely that an act of kindness will dispose the recipient, or even an observer, to respond in kind. Thus, in a small community, where everyone knows everyone else, an act of kindness has an escalating effect. In a large community, however, an act of kindness done to A and observed by B is likely to be totally unknown by X, whose help I now require. Therefore, in a large community it is unreasonable, as far as my own self-interest is concerned, to help A when it is unlikely I will call upon either A or B for help in the future. Here, self-interest and benevolence do not coincide.

While it seems clear that Parfit must have some such argument in mind, this interpretation is not without problems. It commits the very mistake in "Moral Mathematics" that Parfit goes to some length to refute; namely, the belief "that an act cannot be wrong, *because* of its effects on other people, if this act makes no one perceptibly worse off. Each of our acts may be *very* wrong, because of its effects on other people, even if none of these people could ever notice any of these effects. Our acts may *together* make these people very much worse off."

One can almost hear a contemporary Butler or Franklin addressing Parfit: We should cease to think that an act of kindness cannot redound to one's own favor if this act makes no potential benefactor perceptibly better off. Each of our acts may be very rational as far as self-interest is concerned *because* of its effects on other people, even if our act of kindness goes unnoticed by our future benefactor. Our acts of kindness may improve the moral climate of the community and thus *together* make everyone very much better off.

Part 2 develops a remark of Sidgwick into a full-fledged argument against self-interest theories. The crucial lines from Sidgwick take the form of a question:

> If the Utilitarian has to answer the question, "Why should I sacrifice my own happiness for the greater happiness of another?", it must surely be admissible to ask the Egoist, "Why should I sacrifice a present pleasure for a greater one in the future? Why should I concern myself about my own future feelings any more than about the feelings of other persons?"

One reply is that desires are temporally neutral, that "while there is great rational significance in the question *who* has some desire, there is no such significance in the question *when* the desire is had."

As Parfit notes, this reply cannot be correct as it stands, for clearly one should not, and does not, try to fulfill all of his past desires, yet Parfit makes too much of what seems to be little more than an oversight on Sidgwick's part. A contemporary Butler would simply say that inasmuch as the ultimate aim of all men is happiness, it follows that all desires are conditional upon the belief that they would bring us happiness if fulfilled. Thus, if I believed as a child that being a fire fighter was the best sort of work for me, whereas now I believe a life of philosophical contemplation would be better, I am in no way obligated to try to fulfill my past desires.

While Parfit admits that some desires are conditional, he maintains that other desires are not.

> Suppose that I meet some stranger on a train. She describes her life's ambitions, and the hopes and fears with which she views her chances of success. By the end of our journey, my sympathy is aroused, and I strongly want this stranger to succeed. I have this strong desire even though I know that we shall never meet again, and that my desire will not

last. My desire that this stranger succeed would not be implicitly conditional on its own persistence.

Is this example coherent? How can I have a strong unconditional desire that this stranger succeed "even though I know that we shall never meet again?" Parfit does not say why we would not meet again, yet the answer is crucial. It cannot be the normal reason strangers who chat on trains do not meet again—namely, that neither party has the desire to carry on the conversation when there are other possibilities. It must be the case that there is some impediment that is preventing Parfit from acting on his desire. Say he is to be shot at dawn. Now the example is coherent, but it will no longer serve Parfit's purpose—to embarrass self-interest theorists with the question, Why should I not try to fulfill this past desire? If I am dead, the question has no sense.

It is on questions of personal identity that Parfit has done most of his previous work. Part 3 of *Reasons and Persons* is an exposition and defense of his conclusions on these matters; it is also a section where the dust-jacket comment—"The book does not assume any previous knowledge of philosophy"—must be taken with a grain of salt. Philosophical discussions of personal identity are highly esoteric and technical, but several general observations are in order.

Part 3 begins by describing a "Teletransporter," a machine that destroys a person's brain and body while recording the exact state of all of his cells. It then transmits this information at the speed of light to a "Replicator" elsewhere in the universe which re-creates a brain and body identical to the one destroyed. Parfit asks, "What can we learn from this imaginary story?" Though some believe that we can learn little, Parfit thinks that by considering this and even odder thought experiments, we can "discover our beliefs about the nature of personal identity over time." Parfit is by no means alone in this conviction, as anyone who glances at the literature in the field soon discovers: Imaginary examples are part and parcel of almost all discussions regarding personal identity. Therefore, it seems that one must admit with W. V. O. Quine that "the method of science fiction has its uses in philosophy," but one can wonder with him "whether the limits of the method are properly heeded." Only two cases will be mentioned where doubts might be raised, but first Parfit's conclusions will be given.

First, Parfit contends that there are cases where the answer to the question asked, Is X the same person as Y? would be indeterminate, neither true nor false. A decision to call X the same person as Y, or not, would be purely arbitrary. Second, he argues that it is not "personal identity" that is important but rather the amount of psychological continuity and connectedness (memories) that exist between X and Y. Furthermore, psychological continuity and connectedness are matters of degree and not all-or-nothing affairs. Third, Parfit asserts that it is an empirical fact that the psychological connections which exist between any two points of an individual's life weaken as the temporal distance increases. Therefore, we can have no more reason to be concerned about our own future well-being than we do with the present well-being of others.

Let us consider the question of indeterminacy. Parfit asks us to imagine some callous neurosurgeon who step-by-step replaces a few of the cells in Parfit's brain and body with those of Greta Garbo as she was at age thirty. This continues until, with the exception of a few cells, there is nothing left of Parfit on the operating table, but what lies there is "both physically and psychologically, just like Greta Garbo." Parfit's question is: When the surgery is fifty percent complete, who is lying on the operating table: Parfit or Garbo? His answer is that this would "be an empty question," with no right answer; we could call it Parfit or we could call it Garbo; both responses would be equally correct.

Suppose I have a Chevrolet and a Ford. The first gets rear ended, though from the driver's seat forward it is unharmed. The Ford gets hit from the front, though from the driver's seat back it is unharmed. Suppose I cut the two cars in half and weld the front end of the Chevrolet to the rear end of the Ford, taking care that all vital connections—brakes, drivelines, electrical circuits—are properly connected. If someone then asked, What kind of car do you drive? I would without hesitation and quite correctly respond: a Chevord. It seems equally possible to provide the correct answer to the question of who is on the operating table at the halfway point: Parbo.

Perhaps, however, this is not a simple yes or no to Parfit's question, Would the resulting person be me? Nevertheless, if the question, Who is on the table? is a little puzzling to Parfit, he might do well to consider some of its less puzzling cognates. Suppose the neurosurgeon stops at the halfway point, and his patient takes up an acclaimed acting career. The answer to Who is that acting? would clearly be Greta Garbo. If the patient, however, begins to write: ". . . the change from A to B therefore gives to the B-people an average net gain . . ." the answer to Who wrote that? would clearly be Derek Parfit.

In order to undermine further the notion of personal identity, Parfit argues that there is no immaterial self or Cartesian Ego upon which personal identity is based. While Parfit's conclusions are widely accepted by other philosophers, his use of imaginary examples appears to lead him astray once again.

One of his arguments against Cartesian dualism involves what he calls "My Division." The story goes like this:

> My body is fatally injured, as are the brains of my two brothers. My brain is divided, and each half is successfully transplanted into the body of one of my brothers. Each of the resulting people believes that he is me, seems to remember living my life, has my

character, and is in every other way psychologically continuous with me. And he has a
body that is very like mine.

How many people survive the accident? "For Cartesians," says Parfit, "this
case is a problem with no possible solution."

It is not clear, however, why a believer in a Cartesian Ego must respond to
this example. He may simply say that if this sort of thing happened, we
should be forced to give up, or greatly modify, our position, but this sort of
thing does not happen so you have proved nothing. Does such a reply violate the rules of philosophy as a nonempirical science involving conceptual
analysis? If one is not willing to answer hypothetical questions, some philosophers would say, then one simply is not doing philosophy.

For a philosopher who believes that his only job is conceptual analysis,
this may be a cogent reply. Parfit, however, is not one of these philosophers.
"Some writers," says Parfit, "claim that the concept of a Cartesian Ego is
unintelligible. I doubt this claim. And I believe that there might have been
evidence supporting the Cartesian View." Suppose that a person claimed to
remember burying a bronze bracelet shaped like two fighting dragons beside
a specified megalith. Furthermore, suppose that much later another person
then dug up this very bracelet in soil that had remained undisturbed for at
least two thousand years. If this sort of occurrence were commonplace,
Parfit says, "we might have to assume that there is some purely mental
entity... which has continued to exist during the thousands of years that
separate the lives of these two people. A Cartesian Ego is just such an
entity."

Of course, there is not this sort of evidence, but suppose that a Cartesian
insisted that Parfit answer such "what if" questions and added that failure to
respond would be tantamount to forfeiting one's claim to being a philosopher. What could Parfit say except, If this sort of thing happened, I would
have to give up my beliefs, but this sort of thing does not happen, so you
still have not proved anything, have you?

Parfit's third conclusion is that since there is no Cartesian Ego, a person's
identity depends upon psychological connectedness, but because connectedness, on any view, weakens over time, it is not irrational to be less concerned about what happens to our future self.

In many cases this is surely true, but it in no way contradicts self-interest
theory. Future trials are uncertain: As Calvin Coolidge observed, "Never go
out to meet trouble. If you will just sit still, nine cases out of ten someone
will intercept it before it reaches you." To this we might add the Parfit Cor-
ollary: Never go out to meet trouble. If you will just sit still, nine cases out
of ten you will not even care about it when it reaches you. This is good
advice. A boy of twelve might be quite concerned to hit a baseball better
than any of his peers because the thought of being anything but a profes-

sional baseball player might be very painful to him. It is so painful that all he does is play baseball, leaving no time for the ordinary joys of childhood.

Certainly, as Parfit argues, such actions may be less than wholly rational. The boy may very well grow up to be a philosopher and wonder why he spent so much time playing baseball as a child. Parfit explains this as being the result of the fact that the boy and the philosopher may literally be two quite different individuals. The self-interest account, however, seems simpler and more plausible: Do not worry too much about future disappointments—they may never arrive.

Following the end of part 3, Parfit still has one hundred more pages in which he demonstrates his philosophical virtuosity. This section discusses questions concerning justice between future generations. While part 4 is well worth reading, it constitutes a book in itself and will not be discussed here.

Parfit writes as a revisionist who paradoxically defends rather traditional conclusions about how we ought to act morally. The last few lines of *Reasons and Persons* reveal his motivation and hopes:

> Disbelief in God, openly admitted by a majority, is a very recent event, not yet completed. Because this event is so recent, Non-Religious Ethics is at a very early stage. We cannot yet predict whether, as in Mathematics, we will all reach agreement. Since we cannot know how Ethics will develop, it is not irrational to have high hopes.

Ric S Machuga

Sources for Further Study

Commonweal. CXI, October 5, 1984, p. 538.
Listener. CXI, April 26, 1984, p. 26.
New Statesman. CVII, May 4, 1984, p. 25.
The New York Review of Books. XXXI, June 14, 1984, p. 42.
The Observer. June 24, 1984, p. 21.

REFUGEE SCHOLARS IN AMERICA
Their Impact and Their Experiences

Author: Lewis A. Coser (1913-   )
Publisher: Yale University Press (New Haven, Connecticut). 351 pp. $25.00
Type of work: Intellectual portraits
Time: 1933-1984
Locale: Europe and the United States

A brilliantly researched collection of intellectual portraits of representative refugee scholars and thinkers, mostly Jewish, who fled Hitler's Europe in the 1930's and 1940's and found asylum in America

Fifteen years ago, Donald Fleming and Bernard Bailyn edited an important collection of essays by prominent refugee scholars and scientists entitled *The Intellectual Migration: Europe and America, 1930-1960* (1969), and two years ago Anthony Heilbut published his arresting interpretation of refugee experience, *Exiled in Paradise: German Refugee Artists and Intellectuals in America, from the 1930's to the Present* (1983). Indeed, an understanding of the refugee contribution to American life and thought has been fed by dozens of memoirs, eulogies, and biographies. Although Lewis Coser's book represents a milestone in refugee scholarship, it is unlikely that the impulse to assess and reinterpret this remarkable moment in history will diminish in the near future. The last of the greatest refugee scholars are now quite up in years, and those a generation younger, born after World War I, are largely past their prime. When they finally do fade away, like Douglas MacArthur's "old soldiers," their contribution to the maturation of American culture will probably seem even more impressive than it does in the mid-1980's.

Why? One has to go back to the dispersion of Greek scholars, scribes, and tutors throughout the Roman world to find an intellectual migration of comparable importance. America was not in cultural darkness before the refugees arrived, any more than Rome needed the Greeks to become itself, but in both cases the contact served to legitimize the intellectual authority of the receiving culture—to grace supplanting power with the best that the older culture had to offer. There is great irony in the fact that Adolf Hitler divested Europe of the one resource America needed to achieve cultural parity: theoretical and scholarly superiority in the humanities and sciences. Was America sufficiently aware of the advantage Hitler's insane bigotry had given her? Yes and no. Himself a refugee and an eminent American sociologst, Professor Coser has done a masterful job of recording the intellectual, social, and personal experiences of dozens of prominent European émigrés. He illuminates not only their trials and accomplishments but also the development of the several disciplines in America with which they became involved.

This book does not touch on the stellar contributions of refugee physicists, but the natural and physical sciences are adequately presented in earlier works such as the Fleming and Bailyn volume. Coser concentrates on the psychological and social sciences, but he also has important vignettes on humanists and writers. He chose to omit artists and experts in international law. The refugee contribution is simply too subtle and extensive to summarize in one book. The introduction stresses the "marginality" of the refugee intellectuals and notes how their being "wanderers" somehow gave them the power "to throw a novel and more searching light on American society and scholarship" than their American-born counterparts. They could not help but think "otherwise" and used their privilege as immigrants in a free country to become innovators and gadflies, to challenge American optimism and "present-mindedness" with their own deeply felt and often tragic sense of history and tradition.

The social marginality of the refugees was often reflected in their interdisciplinary approaches. As thinkers, they seemed at home in crossing from one discipline to another to flesh out their intricate sense of intellectual history, what they called *Geistesgeschichte*. The great psychoanalyst Erik Erikson and his famous explorations in psychohistory (*Young Man Luther*, 1958, and *Gandhi's Truth*, 1969) brought together historical and psychoanalytical interpretation. The economist George Katona developed a theory of consumer behavior based on economic theory and Gestalt psychology. Another economist, Fritz Redlich, merged entrepreneurial and business history, in the German tradition of Max Weber and Wilhelm Dilthey, with American sociology and organizational studies in his magisterial *The Molding of American Banking, Men and Ideas, 1781-1840* (1951). Ernst Kris, a Viennese art historian turned psychoanalyst, published an important collection of essays entitled *Psychoanalytical Explorations in Art* (1952), and Rudolf Arnheim used Gestalt psychology and its pattern history in his books on art appreciation. The great literary comparatists Erich Auerbach, Leo Spitzer, and René Wellek not only established comparative literature as a viable field of study in the American university, but they also set new standards for breadth *and* depth in learning and theoretical flexibility. Leo Spitzer's textual criticism relied equally on linguistics, psychology, and aesthetics.

Refugee art historians, like refugee physicists, writes Coser, "came at the right time." He might also have added psychiatrists. American art history and psychoanalysis had reached a degree of sophistication by the 1930's which made them particularly receptive to European talent. Walter W. S. Cook found permanent chairs for prominent refugee art historians at the Institute of Fine Arts of New York University. Erwin Panofsky, the most renowned of all émigré art historians and the father of iconology, an elaboration of iconography that went far beyond the authenticating theories of Bernard Berenson, recalled that Cook used to say, "Hitler is my best friend; he shakes the tree and I collect the apples." Roughly a hundred European art historians came to America in the 1930's and later. They brought a new brilliance to the cultural criticism of art and trained a generation of American art professors and museum curators. Refugee art historians helped introduce art history to regional universities in the South and Midwest. More than half of the contributions to W. Eugene Kleinbauer's anthology *Modern Perspectives in Western Art History* (1971) are by refugee scholars.

Even more impressive than the success of the art historians is the dominance of refugee psychiatrists. Between 1933 and 1941, about forty European psychoanalysts immigrated to the United States. In a short time, almost all of them rose to high prominence in the field. Because they had either studied with Sigmund Freud or were close to his major disciples, the refugees had an aura native Americans could not match. Coser produces an impressive chart which documents the ascendancy of refugee analysts as both leaders and trainers over any other group or faction in the profession.

Not all fields and disciplines were friendly to the refugees. American psychology was dominated by behaviorism in the 1930's and 1940's and did not take kindly to the Gestalt tradition of European psychology. Classical studies in America was a socially elitist field which had declined from its Germanic thoroughness in the nineteenth century to a genteel—and exclusively gentile—club more interested in the "study of artifacts" (archaeology) than the "study of texts." The sudden arrival of internationally recognized classicists, most of them Jewish, embarrassed American classics departments, which had successfully excluded American Jews from the professorial ranks. At first, the refugees were thought of as interlopers and job stealers, but eventually they were accepted, stimulated interest in *Geistesgeschichte*, and, by being tenured, made it impossible to refuse tenure to native-born Jews.

Perhaps because he himself is a sociologist, Coser seems most interested in the fate of the many social scientists—other sociologists, economists, political scientists, and historians—many of whom had a dramatic impact on American thought. Many of these thinkers were invited by the farsighted American scholar and administrator Alvin Johnson to join the New School of Social Research, an adult education institution which attracted a variety of liberal and radical students and thinkers. Others struggled to make their way slowly up the academic ladder. What shines through most of them and seems to characterize their best work is unusual sensitivity to the nuances of social existence. Their own precarious lives had alerted them to the difficulties and challenges of "group" experience everywhere. They seemed driven to philosophize social reality. Kurt Lewin single-handedly revitalized social psychology in America. His theoretical work is behind the fruitful concept of group dynamics; he is the originator of leadership training and his ideas have entered the vernacular in phrases such as "level of aspirations" and "life space." Paul F. Lazarsfeld became the "founding father of American social research" and pioneered political and marketing surveys. He was always relating behavior, of individuals or aggregates, to "the latent social structure." Not widely known during his lifetime but now highly venerated, Alfred Schutz devised a phenomenological social psychology that parted from Edmund Husserl, the founder of phenomenology, in its concern with intersubjectivity rather than mere subjectivity. Jacob Marschark, the "pioneer of econometrics," did important work on "information theory and the analysis of decision-making, particularly in groups or teams." It is, however, in the thought of the maverick economic historian Karl Polanyi that the full philosophical weight of the refugee's concern for a moral world order is felt most keenly. More to the left than most of the refugee economists, who leaned toward the liberal and laissez-faire tradition of the Austrian school, Polanyi argued that market-guided economies are not "normal" but exceptions in the course of human history: "In past times, the economy was embedded in society; in capitalism the reverse occurred—society became embedded in the economy."

Polanyi's calling capitalism to account by reminding it of its obligation to a culture larger than its economic assumptions is redolent of the same humanism that appears in the neoconservative thought of Leo Strauss. A political philosopher who hated all forms of ethical relativism, positivism, and historicism, he insisted on reviving the purity of classical Greek thought. Hannah Arendt, who reveled in being a "self-proclaimed pariah" and believed that her marginality kept her honest, nevertheless had a great passion for the "public sphere" and insisted that true freedom was attainable only through political action. She too admired the Greek polis.

All of these thinkers, no matter what their politics, embraced the social imperative. Strangers in the land of their adoption, they held to an ideal of social possibility beyond their time. Fleeing from a terrible persecution, they settled in Edens of the mind. We are fortunate that they let *us* in.

Peter A. Brier

Sources for Further Study

Christian Science Monitor. LXXVI, December 10, 1984, p. 36.
Kirkus Reviews. LII, September 15, 1984, p. 888.
Library Journal. CIX, December, 1984, p. 2292.
Los Angeles Times Book Review. September 23, 1984, p. 9.
The New York Times. CXXXIV. September 24, 1984, V, p. 19.
Publishers Weekly. CCXXVI, August 31, 1984, p. 428.

THE RENAISSANCE *HAMLET*
Issues and Responses in 1600

Author: Roland Mushat Frye (1921-   )
Publisher: Princeton University Press (Princeton, New Jersey). Illustrated. 398 pp.
   $28.50
Type of work: Literary criticism

By placing Hamlet *in its Renaissance contexts—aesthetic, cultural, and historical—Roland Frye explains how Shakespeare's audience responded to those elements that create problems for modern readers*

If a nineteenth century student of Shakespeare had been asked to name William Shakespeare's greatest drama, he would almost certainly have replied *Hamlet*; in the twentieth, the answer would probably be *King Lear*, although *Hamlet* still ranks among the greatest dramas ever written. An important reason for the relative decline in favor is that *Hamlet* has grown increasingly remote from modern attitudes and values; there is, for example, the acceptance of revenge as a legitimate motive for action, a viewpoint questionable to most readers. Further, more than any other Shakespearean play, *Hamlet* re-creates, not always accurately, an aura of Renaissance Catholicism, with references to purgatory, with specific rites, and with a legalistic approach to ethical questions. There is the important question of real or feigned madness of the hero—never, it seems, adequately resolved. While critics generally agree that Hamlet is not mad in the modern sense, it is difficult to account for his behavior by any other assumption and still remain sympathetic, as when he appears to Ophelia and terrifies her, or when he leaps into her grave to struggle with Laertes, later explaining to Laertes that he was experiencing a bout of madness. Roland Mushat Frye attempts to resolve some of the pressing ambiguities and problems by explaining how Shakespeare's contemporaries would have reacted to them. To this end, he draws upon the history, philosophy, and art of the Renaissance, citing analogies and clarifying responses to them.

Editions of Shakespeare's plays normally include illustrations depicting Elizabethan culture—from objects such as ordinary tools, weapons, and instruments to the most elaborate civil and religious ceremonies. These contemporary artistic representations of reality enhance readers' understanding of the dramas. Frye, however, raises this method to a much higher plane, perhaps a unique one, by including eighty-seven illustrations intended to resolve problems and ambiguities in *Hamlet*. Further elucidation of the cruxes comes from his use of historical and polemic sources of the Renaissance, as he ranges over the sixteenth and seventeenth centuries for parallels to Shakespeare's tragedy.

According to Frye, Shakespeare's plays reflect the "form and pressure of the time"—that is, Shakespeare sought the universal in the particular and the particular in the Elizabethan era. A dramatist for all time, he remains firmly rooted in his own time, and therefore it is not surprising that modern responses to *Hamlet* differ from those of Shakespeare's contemporaries. Nevertheless, Frye acknowledges that Elizabethan audiences would not have experienced a uniform response. On some subjects, such as incest, they would have agreed; on others, such as the justification of tyrannicide, they would have differed among themselves; on still others, such as the "maimed" funeral rites of Ophelia, they would not have agreed with the interpretation offered in the play.

Frye begins with the initial problem of the drama—reactions to the Ghost. Eleven sightings by four different characters make the Ghost seem real enough, yet the characters as well as the audience would have entertained the possibility that the Ghost represented a demonic apparition. Protestant theology tended to encourage this interpretation of ghosts, since it did not accept belief in purgatory, as citations from theologians make clear. Ghost reports of the time were not normally associated with revenge; those few linked to vengeance were particularly suspected of demonic origin. Thus, the audience would have shared the characters' fear and doubt of the Ghost, while accepting the possibility of its authenticity. At best, the Ghost is ambiguous, a conclusion that leaves the problem unsolved, for it does not account for Hamlet's vacillation. To do this, the critic must get beyond Shakespeare's time by drawing upon psychological theory. Frye's conclusion that "Shakespeare requires us to be confused" represents an acknowledgment that the problem remains, even after one has viewed it from an Elizabethan perspective.

Since the Ghost incites Hamlet to revenge against Claudius for adultery, incest, and fratricide, its appearance raises questions about the acceptability of vengeance and tyrannicide. In speculations based upon biblical sources, Renaissance thinkers drew a distinction between revenge by private individuals, universally forbidden, and by princes and magistrates—allowable under specific conditions. Frye proceeds to explain how King James VI of Scotland was publicly incited to avenge his father's death at the hands of the Earl of Bothwell, who shortly after the murder married the widowed mother of James, Mary of Scotland. Even though Bothwell died before the young prince James grew to manhood to carry out the revenge urged by his grandparents, the incident represented a precedent for princely revenge.

It is one thing to justify revenge against a nobleman such as Bothwell, another to sanction it against a king such as Claudius. Elizabethan theory permitted the removal of tyrants, and Claudius, with his mercenary Swiss guards and spies, qualified as a tyrant to the Shakespearean audience. Although both Catholic and Protestant writers on the Continent believed assassination of tyrants justifiable under some conditions, Anglican thinkers were more judicious. In an effort to justify total opposition to foreign monarchs who represented England's enemies and yet permit only passive resistance at home, Thomas Bilson produced a treatise on tyranny for Queen Elizabeth I, stating among other things that elected monarchs might justifiably be overthrown, whereas hereditary ones must be endured passively. Frye's long discussion convincingly demonstrates that Hamlet would have acted against Claudius only after overcoming grave doubts, thus representing a credible reason for his delay. Nevertheless, invoking theory to justify tyrannicide reveals more about the audience than about Hamlet or his motivations. Although Claudius is demonstrably a tyrant and murderer, Hamlet would not have slain him for his tyranny alone, however acceptable the tyranny made the slaying to the audience. Further, when considered apart from the question of revenge, tyrannicide does not represent a significant problem for modern audiences.

In his first appearance in the tragedy, Hamlet wears a mourning suit and experiences deep grief, often regarded as an extreme reaction to events at the court of Denmark and attributed to excessive melancholy. It appears that Hamlet is disturbed by a marriage which the other characters accept, that of Claudius and Gertrude. Frye reminds the readers that English law forbade marriage of a brother-in-law and sister-in-law as incestuous, a law that remained in effect until 1907. The audience would have shared Hamlet's revulsion at the marriage, especially since it occurred within two months after the first husband's death. Formal mourning was taken seriously during the Renaissance, and most responsible people heeded a custom, upheld by law, forbidding a widow to remarry earlier than a year following the death of her husband. With his suit of black, complete with mourning cloak and hood, Hamlet followed the expectations of the audience.

Turning to a significant plot element in *Hamlet*, Frye devotes a major portion of the book to explaining how the audience would have reacted to problems arising from intrigue, involving the efforts of characters to influence others. Confronted with the choice between wisdom and fortune, Rosencrantz and Guildenstern choose fortune and side with Claudius. To the audience, fortune suggested chance, opportunism, peril, and an inevitable fall—associations reinforced by references in the drama to the wheel of fortune, so that destruction of Rosencrantz and Guildenstern came as no surprise. With their departure, Claudius incites Laertes to wrath and revenge against Hamlet. According to Frye, the audience would have found Laertes' impulsiveness a sign that he was a moral simpleton rather than a villain. His reaction to the death and hasty burial of his father, Polonius, would have been understood. The "maimed rites" of Ophelia following her suicide further inflame Laertes against Hamlet. As for Hamlet, his major effort at intrigue occurs when he attempts to reveal to Gertrude her guilt for incest. He uses a mirror which the audience would have recognized as associated with concealed guilt. By forcing the queen to confront and acknowledge the evil, Hamlet moves her to repentance.

Following his analysis of intrigue, which creates one form of suspense, Frye devotes the final third of the book to the character and role of Hamlet, whose angst and development create the kind of suspense that probes the ultimate mysteries of human nature and destiny. In a chapter concerning the soliloquies, Frye acknowledges that the audience would have been unclear on many points about Hamlet's proposed course of action. Attempting to balance the soldier and philosopher within his character and to sort out his own guilt and responsibility, Hamlet engaged in trains of thought well understood by his audience. Accustomed to associating melancholy and introspection with a studious nature, they would have recognized the character type, and Hamlet's feigned madness was commonplace in fiction and only slightly less so in history. The soliloquies raise familiar debate questions and employ familiar terms. As he explores the state of his inner being, Hamlet inevitably postpones his revenge.

In the chapter titled "The Prince amid the Tombs," Frye examines the contribution of the cemetery milieu in the fifth act, often seen as gruesome by modern audiences, to the development of Hamlet's character. It represents the setting for Hamlet's coming to terms with his own mortality. Surrounded by the graves, reflecting on the fate of Yorick, whose skull he holds, and grasping the brevity and fragility of life as he meditates on death, Hamlet achieves a measure of calm and resignation that is interrupted only when he becomes overwrought at the burial of Ophelia. The Elizabethan audience, as Frye asserts, would have found the setting appropriate to bring about Hamlet's growth. The skull was an almost universally accepted symbol of *memento mori*, as numerous illustrations reveal, particularly those portraits of young men that feature skulls as grim intrusions. In addition, graphic details of bodily decay in a variety of forms were included in painting and sculpture during an age when people faced death squarely and at close quarters.

When analyzing the scene at Ophelia's burial, Frye sheds light on Hamlet's leaping into the grave to struggle with Laertes, an action that to modern readers appears so inexplicable. An early quarto stage direction, Frye points out, refers only to a "corse," not a coffin, indicating that Shakespeare may originally have conceived of the burial as in a shroud. If so, the Elizabethan audience would have understood, for it was usual for the nearest kin or chief mourner to embrace the body before it was lowered into the grave. Hamlet's action may reasonably derive from his wish to assume this role with Ophelia, although this hypothesis does not account for his frenzied speech to Laertes. On the whole, however, it makes evident the value of Frye's method.

By drawing such numerous parallels and analogies, Frye weaves *Hamlet* into the fabric of its time. The result is that the reader can now better understand how Shakespeare's audience reacted and can infer at least some of Shakespeare's assumptions about their reactions. To be sure, Frye's method has its limitations. As he himself acknowledges, on many questions the audience would have been divided. One cannot be certain that the works of art and events of history cited in the text were familiar to the audience, especially those that were remote in time and setting. While many of the analogies are to England, others are to Europe, making their familiarity to the audience even more doubtful.

At times Frye, like other critics, must interpret somewhat arbitrarily. One point of ongoing controversy concerns the play-within-the-play, used by Hamlet to ascertain the king's guilt. The play is preceded by a dumb show, with the characters miming the murder of the player king, action which closely follows details of the elder Hamlet's murder, yet Claudius, seated as a member of the audience, betrays no sign of guilt. When the action is repeated a few moments later, however, he rises in terror, calls for lights, and rushes out, behavior that convinces Hamlet and Horatio of his guilt. Why does he not react thus at the first showing? Among possible explanations, two stand out: Either he was not watching the dumb show (perhaps ignoring it as an archaic device or engaging in silent conversation with someone nearby), or he maintained his composure while viewing it. Modern directors usually prefer the first interpretation, but Frye chooses the second as more revealing of Claudius' character, even though he finds no evidence to confirm it. This is one of many ambiguities which remain to perplex readers after the most searching criticism. Even so, Frye's method of placing *Hamlet* in its Renaissance context produces numerous corrections of flawed impressions that arise from modern misreadings.

Stanley Archer

Source for Further Study

Times Literary Supplement. February 22, 1985, p. 208.

REQUIRED WRITING
Miscellaneous Pieces, 1955-1982

Author: Philip Larkin (1922-   )
Publisher: Farrar, Straus and Giroux (New York). 328 pp. $17.95; paperback $9.95
Type of work: Anthology of interviews, reviews, and critical essays

A collection of articles, reviews, interviews, talks, and introductions done for the past generation by one of England's most noted poets

In his quiet, modest fashion, Philip Larkin has established himself as one of the six or seven best poets currently writing in English, along with his fellow Britons Thom Gunn and Ted Hughes, the Irishman Seamus Heaney, and the Americans A. R. Ammons, James Merrill, and John Ashbery. Larkin's first collection of verse, *The North Ship* (1945), showed an infatuation with William Butler Yeats's verbal music, which he abruptly abandoned in the early 1950's, converting instead to the autumnal-wintry terrain of Thomas Hardy, distrustful of complex gestures and mythic postures, stressing the narrow human limits of a nontranscendent universe. *The Less Deceived* (1955), Larkin's next collection, stressed his newly rediscovered sense of a native English tradition of stepped-down possibilities and simple, discursive statements. He maintained his deliberate pace of issuing slim collections of his poems once a decade with *The Whitsun Weddings* (1964) and *High Windows* (1974). Asked about the sparseness of his poetic production by a *Paris Review* interviewer in 1982, Larkin contented himself with replying, "It's unlikely I shall write any more poems."

Required Writing contains not only the conversation with the *Paris Review* writer but also one with an *Observer* representative in 1979; together, these talks reveal much about a man who has devoted his adult years to constructing the persona of an intensely private person, affecting surprise that anyone should be remotely interested in whatever he might have to say, running himself down perhaps to build up the reader's confidence in him. "I don't want to go around pretending to be me," he responds when questioned why he does not accept poet-in-residence invitations or read from his canon on the lecture circuit.

Philip Larkin was born in Coventry to the city treasurer, who could afford to send him to "public" (that is, private) schools and then to Oxford University. He characterizes his schoolboy career as "unsuccessful": He was afflicted with extreme myopia, and an equally extreme case of the stammers, which lasted until he was thirty; listening to jazz and reading were his chief outlets. After he was graduated from Oxford in 1943, he wrote, in quick succession, his only two novels: *Jill* (1946) and *A Girl in Winter* (1947), both dealing with ineffectual people leading desolate working-class lives in featureless provincial towns. Why did Larkin then stop writing fiction? "Novels are about other people and poems are about yourself. . . . I didn't know enough about other people, I didn't like them enough."

Larkin is too self-effacing to advertise the disciplined energy required to accomplish his writing in his spare time while working full-time as a librarian. He began in Birmingham's municipal system (1943-1946), graduated to the library of the University College, Leicester (1946-1950), then Belfast University (1950-1955). Since 1955, he has been university librarian at Hull, heading a staff of more than one hundred, working a five-day-a-week schedule. In his interviews, Larkin defends the desirability of an author having a full-time nonliterary occupation, like Anthony Trollope. Yet he *does* drop his defenses by stating, "Sometimes I think, Everything I've written has been done after a day's work, in the evening: what would it have been like if I'd written it in the morning, after a night's sleep? Was I wrong?"

The clear implication is that Larkin's spare-time writing routine deprived him of the opportunity to produce more poems, if not better ones. "I like [Hardy] because he wrote so much. I love the great *Collected Hardy* which runs for something like 800 pages." Larkin, however, quickly assumes his mentor's determinism to squelch any inner rebellion about his choice of life: Subsidies for authors are wrong; he could never have made his living from writing; he lacks the mind and temperament for teaching; people envy whatever they do not have; choice is an illusion; happiness is unlikely for most humans.

Will reading Larkin as critic help one read Larkin as poet? He assumes his sour, gruff façade to emphasize that his criticism and poetry differ distinctly in the motivation and attitude with which he composed them: His articles and reviews were produced on the request of editors, and he "rarely accepted a literary assignment without a sinking of the heart, nor finished it without an inordinate sense of relief." Yet one can make a solid case for the proposition that *Required Writing* is, in significant respects, the prose equivalent of such hardheaded, hard-hitting, empiric poems as "This Be the Verse," "A Study of Reading Habits," and "Love." Both Larkin's poetry and his prose are characterized by economy, plainness, dry wit, precision, lucidity in style and disillusioned skepticism, parochialism, antimodernism, and pervasive sadness in substance.

The reigning god in Larkin's critical pantheon is Thomas Hardy as poet. Larkin did not read him with understanding until he was twenty-five, but then

> I was struck by... the sense that here was somebody writing about things I was beginning to feel myself.... What I like about him primarily is his temperament and the way he sees life.... He's not an Eliot; his subjects are men, the life of men, time and the passing of time, love and the fading of love.

Hardy, continues Larkin, gave him the confidence to go his own poetic way, to use the stuff of his life guiltlessly for his art, and to make sadness his touchstone: "Hardy was peculiarly well equipped to perceive the melancholy, the misfortunate, the frustrating, the failing elements of life." The dominant cadence in his work is "the sometimes gentle, sometimes ironic, sometimes bitter but always passive apprehension of suffering." Sadness and passive suffering are Larkin's favored attitudes, as the speaking voices of his poems register resignation, frustration, pathos, bitterness, and, sometimes, fellow feeling in face of irremediable circumstances. Larkin concludes that Hardy's poetry is "many times over the best body of poetic work this century so far has to show."

While Larkin shares an impressive capacity for emotional penetration with Hardy, he outdoes his master in professing and practicing the flaw of mean provinciality, or plain ornery insularity. He loves to proclaim his philistine, antimodernist convictions, as in the notorious section of his introduction to *All What Jazz* (1970), a collection of his journalistic articles on jazz, wherein he excoriates the twentieth century experimental artist for engaging in "mystification and outrage":

> Piqued at being neglected, he has painted portraits with both eyes on the same side of the nose, or smothered a model with paint and rolled her over a blank canvas. He has designed a dwelling-house to be built underground. He has written poems resembling the kind of pictures typists make with their machines during the coffee break, or a novel in gibberish, or a play in which the characters sit in dustbins. He has made a six-hour film of someone asleep. He has carved human figures with large holes in them. And parallel to this activity ("every idiom has its idiot," as an American novelist has written) there has grown up a kind of critical journalism designed to put it over. The terms and the arguments vary with circumstances, but basically the message is: Don't trust your eyes, or ears, or understanding. They'll tell you this is ridiculous, or ugly, or meaningless. Don't believe them.

These are claims the sheer cantankerousness of which constitutes silliness: Did Pablo Picasso paint cubist art because he was "piqued at being neglected"? Are Samuel Beckett and Henry Moore to be indiscriminately lumped with the most exhibitionistic showmen of action painting or concrete poetry? Has modernist art truly severed all connection between artist and audience? In jazz, the dismal Fall occurred for Larkin somewhere between Louis Armstrong and Fats Waller, with Charlie Parker bridging to the "inhuman" era of Thelonius Monk, Miles Davis, and John Coltrane. The last made jazz *"ugly on purpose"*; after Coltrane, "all was chaos, hatred and absurdity. . . . It was fearful."

It is sadly regrettable that Larkin's blinkered insularity prevents his mind and imagination from recognizing the avant-garde achievements of hundreds of composers, choreographers, performers, writers, painters, sculptors, and architects who have expanded and intensified our aesthetic responses. Moreover, his parochial mind-set isolates him from all literatures but England's, with the single surprising exception of a review of Henry de Montherlant's tetralogy, *Les Jeunes Filles* (1936). This energy and affection are instead engaged by British writers who have a strong feeling for English national characteristics; if they have been overlooked and underrated by the current critical mainstream, the more stimulating his mission. Hence his fondness for John Betjeman, Stevie Smith, Barbara Pym, Gladys Mitchell, and even Ian Fleming, while the cosmopolitanism of James Joyce, Yeats, Ezra Pound, and T. S. Eliot enrages him. As for the great masters of modern Continental letters—Thomas Mann, Franz Kafka, Marcel Proust, Rainer Maria Rilke, André Gide, Osip Mandelstam, Boris Pasternak, André Malraux, and others—not one word. Whereas Eliot's 1921 essay on Andrew Marvell constituted a canon-changing reevaluation which aligned Marvell with the European culture of Catullus, Propertius, and Ovid, Larkin's 1978 essay is characteristically local: It emphasizes Marvell's eighteen-year career as Member of Parliament for Kingston-upon-Hull. While Larkin admires Marvell's virtuosity as a metrist and versifier, he is skeptical of the permanence of Marvell's reputation as the poet of dissociated sensibility, of enigmatic, concealed, and contradictory meanings: "Every poet's reputation fades in so far as his language becomes unfamiliar, . . . and despite the iron lung of academic English teaching Marvell is no exception." One may disagree with Larkin's judgment, but one can only admire the terse wit with which he expresses it and the precise aim of his critical cudgel.

Probably the most misplaced and characteristic evaluation in this volume is that of John Betjeman's poetry. "It Could Only Happen in England" is the chauvinistic title of Larkin's introduction to the American edition of Betjeman's *Collected Poems* (1971). He obviously regards Sir John as a brother in arms and attitudes, hailing his "self-abasing sense of ridicule, [and] defiant advocacy of the little, the obscure, the disregarded, all backed up with an astonishing memory and an outstanding gift for phrasing." Larkin adds with affectionate satisfaction that Betjeman would have been out of his proper sphere in the cosmopolitan circles of Gertrude Stein and Jean Cocteau. He celebrates his subject's cultural insularity: "For him there has been no symbolism, no objective correlative, no T. S. Eliot or Ezra Pound, no reinvestment in myth or casting of language as gesture." Instead, Betjeman is fundamentally concerned with the particulars of individual lives in a well-defined society; his poetic aesthetic is interchangeable with his social aesthetic; "he is a robust and responsive writer registering 'Dear old, bloody old England' with vivacious precision"; and he has succeeded in establishing a direct relationship with a wide reading public. In what seems to be all seriousness, Larkin calls Betjeman a true descendant of Thomas Hardy and asks rhetorically, "Can it be that, as Eliot dominated the first half of the twentieth century, the second half will derive from Betjeman?"

What is one to make of Larkin's harsh antimodernist scriptures, his bashing of the previously Sacred Untouchables? This reviewer prefers to take the reactionary aesthetic with a heavy dose of skeptical salt, for at least two reasons: Larkin's poetic practice often contradicts his prose-bound diatribes, and the tone with which he vents the latter is often playful and lighthearted. He is clearly parodying his role as philistine when, asked whether Jorge Luis Borges is the only other distinguished writer who is also a librarian, he retorts, "Who's Jorge Luis Borges?" or when he defends his xenophobia by saying, "I wouldn't mind seeing China if I could come back the same day" or when, asked about his reading habits, he replies, "I read almost no poetry. I always thought the reading habits of Dylan Thomas matched mine—he never read anything hard."

More persuasively, Larkin's poetry often fails to limit itself to his narrow critical track. *High Windows* has many poems that derive from Yeats's symbolist and visionary impulses, such as "Solar," "To the Sea," and the final stanza of the title poem. "An Arundel Tomb," from *The Whitsun Weddings*, meditates on the voyage of two effigies through time with a contemplative resonance that concludes in a superbly lyric burst of affirmation:

> Time has transfigured them into
> Untruth. The stone fidelity
> They hardly meant has come to be
> Their final blazon, and to prove
> Our almost-instinct almost true:
> What will survive of us is love.

While there is much in Larkin's coarsely grained and sometimes boorishly censorious criticism to provoke dismay, the majestic excellence of his best poetry demands that he be forgiven his prosaic trespasses. Despite his professed distaste for most of them, he will find himself placed in the pantheon of English poetry's modern masters, alongside not only Hardy but also—no kicking and gouging, now!—Yeats, Pound, Eliot, and W. H. Auden.

Gerhard Brand

Sources for Further Study

Library Journal. CX, May 1, 1985, p. 57.
The New York Times Book Review. LXXXIX, August 12, 1984, p. 9.
The New Yorker. LX, August 13, 1984, p. 93.
Publishers Weekly. CCXXV, April 13, 1984, p. 54.

THE RETREAT

Author: Aharon Appelfeld (1932-   )
Translated from the Hebrew by Dalya Bilu
Publisher: E. P. Dutton (New York). 164 pp. $12.95
Type of work: Novel
Time: The late 1930's
Locale: The Austrian countryside near Vienna

In provincial Austria, a Jewish horse trader converts a mountaintop hotel into a retreat for aging Jews who are no longer wanted by their assimilated children

Principal characters:
> LOTTE SCHLOSS, a dismissed actress who, to avoid burdening her daughter's household, seeks refuge in the retreat
> JULIA, Lotte's daughter who has married an insensitive Gentile
> BALABAN, the retreat's founder, whose character deteriorates
> HERBERT ZUNTZ, a formerly distinguished journalist, who befriends Lotte in the retreat
> ISADORA, a retreat inmate who commits suicide
> BRUNO RAUCH, the senior resident of the retreat
> BETTY SCHLANG, a frustrated would-be actress who comes into her own as a cook
> ROBERT, the retreat's quiet Gentile janitor
> MAX HAMMER, a disillusioned, stoic resident of the retreat
> LANG, an anti-Semitic Jew who devotes his energy to physical exercise

Aharon Appelfeld is a survivor whose writing is stamped by a melancholy sense of the doom he managed to elude. Born in Czernovitz, Bukovina (then Rumanian, now within the Soviet Union), he was eight when the invading Germans sent him to a labor camp in 1940. His mother was killed, his father died in the camp; the boy managed in 1941 to escape into the inhospitable countryside, working as a shepherd and on farms for three years, hiding his identity from hunters of Jews, growing up without a proper adolescence. In 1944, he became a field cook for the Soviet army, after the armistice made his way to Italy with a small tide of refugees, and from there migrated to Palestine in 1946. Though he knew no Hebrew before the age of fourteen, he writes exclusively in his adopted language and is admired as a polished stylist. His published works in Israel include six collections of stories, eight novels, and one book of essays. *The Retreat* is Appelfeld's fourth novel to be published in the United States.

The first, called *Badenheim 1939* when David R. Godine, Publisher issued it in 1980, was titled *Badenheim, 'ir nofesh* in Hebrew, which translates literally as Badenheim, resort town. Badenheim is a Jewish summer resort near Vienna, clearly resonant of the existing Baden, whose visitors are middle to upper-middle class, addicted to rich pastries, strawberries, readings from Rainer Maria Rilke's lyrics, concerts, and flirtations. The climate of mild skies, self-indulgent appetites, and idle conversation promises a Continental social comedy. It is, however, darkened by the Cassandran moods of the local pharmacist's wife, herself ill, who has hallucinatory visions about her native Poland. Then the local sanitation department ominously extends its authority, registering all summer vacationers, preparing genealogies, festooning its walls with travel posters proclaiming that "The Air in Poland Is Fresher." Most of the guests remain smugly optimistic about the prospect of leaving for Poland, whose cultural standards are said to be high, while porters unload rolls of barbed wire and cement pillars. The novel's final paragraph savagely moves the Jews to a freight train headed east while a Panglossian entertainment impresario, Dr. Pappenheim, blindly asserts his faith in a rational and benevolent world. The author's theme seems to be the inability of the bourgeois imagination to understand the total disaster of totalitarianism.

In *Tor-ha-pela'ot* (1978; *The Age of Wonders*, 1981), trains also play a crucial role: The first and longer book of the novel begins in a first-class train compartment, only to conclude in a cattle car. The narrator is a twelve-year-old boy whose return trip with his mother from a summer holiday is marred by an unscheduled stop far from any station. Politely, "all foreign passengers and all Austrian passengers who were not Christians by birth" are requested to register with the "security forces." Reluctantly, a diversity of passengers file out to record their Jewishness; an elegant lady disdains to admit her kinship with what she regards as vulgar, lower-class Jews. Evidently, the *Anschluss* of March, 1938, has enfolded Austria within Adolf Hitler's Germany. Nevertheless, Appelfeld refrains, here as in his other fiction, from direct allusion to historic events. All the boy knows is that "nothing would ever be the same again." He finds his parents and their friends arguing obsessively about the nature of Jews and Judaism as anti-Semitic stresses increase by a series of incremental tremors.

The boy's father is a famous Austrian writer, called "A." in Kafkaesque fashion, whose lofty reputation is attacked by a sequence of articles calling his characters "Jews who . . . were now useless, corrupt, perverted; parasites living off the healthy Austrian tradition." The critic, himself Jewish, dies, but his anti-Semitism is adopted by the father, who desperately advertises his assimilated Austrian outlook, curses the Jews "infesting Austria like rats," and drifts into madness, writing pamphlets excoriating the Jewish petite bourgeoisie. Eventually he abandons his wife and son, fleeing to a Gentile mistress in Vienna; mother and boy are rounded up for a final journey on a "cattle train hurtling south."

In book 2, about twenty-five years later, the reader discovers that the boy—now named Bruno—has somehow, like his creator, survived the Holocaust; his parents did not. Like Thomas Mann's Tonio Kroeger, he returns to his native town, only to dawdle aimlessly in parks, bars, and eating places. He encounters several living relics from his boyhood, climaxing with a Jewish bachelor who married his Gentile housekeeper, became a cattle farmer, and grew to hate Jews, and who now tells Bruno to leave town and is assaulted by him. Bruno then departs, emotionally desolate, "empty of thought or feeling." Despite this relatively weak coda, *The Age of Wonders* is the most impressive of Appelfeld's books that have to date been translated into English. It is a chilling, plangent, remorselessly pessimistic study of Jewish self-denial, self-estrangement, self-hatred, of flawed human beings pushed into tight corners of base self-betrayal by circumstances whose enormity overwhelms description.

Tzili: The Story of a Life (1983) is a simpler tale than the first two, with the protagonist's wanderings an approximate outline of Appelfeld's own during and after World War II. Tzili is a slow-witted East European girl, neglected and abused by her large, impoverished Jewish family. When the Nazis come, the family flees but leaves Tzili behind to guard the house, rationalizing that no harm will come to a simpleminded child. Harm consumes many others, but somehow Tzili survives the slaughter, mistaken as the bastard daughter of a Gentile village whore. Execrated as one of the devil's brood, she is tormented by the peasants with sticks and ropes until she meets Mark, a wandering Jew, whose articulate cleverness contrasts with her intuitive, inchoate feelings. Mark impregnates her but then leaves their mountain refuge for death among the peasants in the plain. Toward the close of the war, Tzili joins a small band of camp survivors, delivers a stillborn child, and embarks for Palestine without regarding it as the Promised Land. Her last desire, aboard ship, is for a pear; it is not available. Appelfeld has written here a bleak folktale depicting the survival—on a level of minimal expectations—of the simpleton with animal strength, opposed to the destruction of self-conscious intellection and reflection.

In *The Retreat*, Appelfeld returns to the provincial Austria of the late 1930's, again with no explicit reference to Nazis, concentration camps, or the imminent world war. The featured personage—though hardly the protagonist—is Lotte Schloss, an actress in late middle age who has pursued her career with a grim determination that precludes love for her husband or daughter. In 1937, she is dismissed by her theatrical company for being Jewish; she retreats to her daughter Julia's home, only to find her parsimonious Gentile son-in-law hostile and Julia docile to his wishes. What further refuge? The retreat itself, organized by a Jewish horse trader, Balaban, who has bought an old mountaintop hotel near Vienna, and issued a prospectus to aging Jews in the district offering, at first, a kosher kitchen as well as bracing mountain air and peace of mind. The mention of "kosher" alienates potential guests, so Balaban revises his brochure to emphasize sports and calisthenics but above all "assimilation into the countryside" and painless eradication of "embarrassing Jewish gestures and ugly accents." This proves to be the right lure, and soon the establishment is filled with Jews who have been spurned by their assimilated offspring.

Balaban himself, however, begins to adopt such "Jewish" characteristics as overeating, arguing, smoking, and card playing. He finds himself unable to forget his Jewish origin in a Polish village where he had a clever sister called Tzili. (It is unlikely that she is the primitive Tzili of Appelfeld's previous novel, but one then wonders why he gave her the same name.) Occasionally, Balaban descends to the plain's village—Appelfeld's recurring metaphor for Jewish immersion in Gentile culture—only to return drunk and enraged, calling Jews "loafers, cheats, liars, money-grubbers and gamblers. There was no hope for them but a forced labor camp." Several months after Lotte's arrival, Babalan becomes ill, reverts to the Yiddish of his youth, assumes the appearance of a simple Jewish laborer, and dies. His death puzzles the other inmates: "They would recall him as a riddle which refused to be solved."

Lotte entered the retreat in a mood close to suicide: "If nobody wants me any more—I'll go to the Jews." Nevertheless, she is befriended by Herbert, a journalist also dismissed for his Judaism, who hews to the integrity of the great Viennese satirist Karl Kraus. Herbert arranges an acting grant for Lotte despite her awkward poetry recital at another inmate's funeral service. In return, she matures to the realization that her theatrical talent had never exceeded mediocrity, "that she had never plumbed the depths of a single role."

Appelfeld's characters are flat in this parable, characterized by no more than two or three traits, deficient in motivation and ambiguous in development. Each represents a stage in life, a status or an attitude toward the issue of Jewish fate and identity. By spreading the narrative fairly evenly, the author precludes the reader's strong response—let alone attachment—to any of them. Thus, the reader encounters the ambitious-for-her-child Jewish stage mother (Lotte's); the mousy husband-father (also Lotte's); the denier of his Jewish self (Adolf Wolf); the self-hating Jew who detests Judaism (Isadora); the anti-intellectual pretender to Gentile identity (Lang); the intuitively good, stable peasant (Robert, the janitor); the troubled, unstable Jewess who fantasizes about Gentile lovers (Betty Schlang); the modest defender of Judaism (Lauffer); the disillusioned, pragmatic Jew who insists that his sons convert to Christianity and reject him (Max Hammer).

The Retreat ends on a baffling note. Negatively, the men who descend to the village are beaten and bring back scant provisions. The world narrows down to simple dimensions of cooking and eating. Affirmatively, the retreat's quarrels become muted and die quickly; the residents help one another, so that "If a man fell or was beaten he was not abandoned." Nevertheless, the supply of goods and money is drying up; people are afraid at night; and the reader knows—without authorial warning—that European

Jewry's encounter with tragic history is about to reach its climactic stage. A retreat, alas, is no escape.

Do Appelfeld's novels belong to the subgenre called "Holocaust Literature?" Not literally, since they never mention the monstrous reality of deaths almost beyond reckoning in the "Final Solution." Symbolically, however, they surely do. For Appelfeld's artistic strategy is to produce fiction whose structure, imagery, and tone meditate harrowingly on the meaning of contemporary Judaism. He struggles with the culture of self-rejection to which many Jews succumbed in Western and Central Europe. In his flat, understated manner he passes a scorching judgment on the spiritual and psychological meanness of Jewish assimilation to a dominant Gentile society. Like Gustave Flaubert, he flays his Bouvards and Pecuchets for their banal and narcotized acceptance of monstrously irrational hatreds. Like Marcel Proust, he depicts bizarre intra-Jewish snobbery and status-scoring. Like Franz Kafka, he ponders whether being Jewish is an incurable disease. Aharon Appelfeld lacks the intensity, range, and imaginative power of these literary ancestors, but he shares with them the honesty of refusing to proffer any didactic or dogmatic solutions to fundamental problems of ethnic and cultural identity. His sadness at man's capacity for victimization and cruelty is almost inexpressible. He bears witness to a chapter in human history for which no explanations can fully account.

Gerhard Brand

Sources for Further Study

Kirkus Reviews. LII, February 15, 1984, p. 151.
Library Journal. CIX, March 1, 1984, p. 508.
Los Angeles Times Book Review. July 8, 1984, p. 2.
The New York Times Book Review. LXXXIX, May 20, 1984, p. 38.
The New Yorker. LX, June 4, 1984, p. 133.
Publishers Weekly. CCXXV, February 17, 1984, p. 72.
Quill and Quire. L, August, 1984, p. 37.
Time. CXXIII, May 28, 1984, p. 86.
Washington Post Book World. April 18, 1984, p. 1.

RILKE
A Life

Author: Wolfgang Leppmann (1922-   )
Translated from the German by Russell M. Stockman in collaboration with the
  author; verse translations by Richard Exner
Publisher: Fromm International Publishing Corporation (New York). 421 pp. $22.50
Type of work: Literary biography
Time: 1875-1926
Locale: Europe

*A major new biography, drawing upon Rilke's voluminous personal correspondence
and featuring extended commentary on his principal poetic and prose works*

> *Principal personages:*
> RAINER MARIA RILKE, an Austrian poet
> SOPHIE ENTZ, his mother
> LOU ANDREAS-SALOMÉ, a writer and Rilke's lover
> PAULA MODERSOHN-BECKER, a painter and source of poetic inspiration for Rilke
> CLARA WESTHOFF, a sculptor and the wife of Rilke
> AUGUSTE RODIN, a sculptor and Rilke's employer
> BALADINE KLOSSOWSKA, a painter and Rilke's lover
> PRINCESS MARIE VON THURN UND TAXIS-HOHENLOHE, Rilke's friend and benefactor

From the recent explosion of publications on the subject of Rainer Maria Rilke (1875-1926) which has brought readers Stephen Mitchell's excellent translations of Rilke's poems and *Letters to a Young Poet* comes this translation of Wolfgang Leppmann's 1981 *Rilke—Sein Leben, seine Welt, sein Werk*, the first full-length biographical study to appear in many years. Rilke was a singularly private man, incompletely known even to persons biographers would have to consider his intimates. As such, he presents no small challenge to his would-be biographer. Leppmann, fully aware of this dilemma, chooses therefore to opt for speculation about many of the particulars of the poet's life, and must turn instead to the work, the result being an example of that currently conspicuous genre of literary publishing, the so-called literary biography. Its patchwork design leads the reader now into what can be recovered of the writer's life, now through the complexities of the literary output, as if to acknowledge and attempt to compensate for the fact that the writer is almost by definition the man or woman who resigns from life in order to write, that most solitary of activities.

This very separation between the life and the work is in fact a function of the aesthetic modernism of which Rilke, the heir of literary symbolism, is so exemplary. Rilke, no less so than Stéphane Mallarmé or Marcel Proust, elevated art to the status of a cult, if not of religion itself. It has become a commonplace to observe that this effort springs in part from the need to fill the void left by the removal of traditional belief. Many of Rilke's most moving poems are infused with a longing for God which persists in the face of post-Nietzschean pessimism with regard to such a quest. Such a *crise de foi* alone, however, does not account for the modernist quarantine of art from other aspects of life, for Rilke's symbolist, *fin-de-siècle* world intensified the romantic aloofness toward bourgeois culture. The sanctity of art was increasingly proclaimed against the real or perceived Philistinism of bourgeois society. The artist, by definition, was not like other people, and this isolation was at once his punishment and his liberation.

As Leppmann makes clear, Rilke endured multiple forms of differentiation. Born in Prague as a subject of the Austro-Hungarian dual monarchy, his identity with the German-speaking minority of what was later to become Czechoslovakia constituted his original estrangement. He was to be even more reduced within that narrow circle, for the circumstances of his upbringing bordered upon the outrageous. Apparently to console herself for the death of the infant daughter whose birth preceded his, Rilke's mother had him christened René Maria Rilke and dressed him as a girl until he reached the age of seven. His hair was arranged in long ringlets. Then, at the age of ten, his stereotypically cold, absent father enrolled him in a military school. That Rilke's developing personality survived the shock of these incongruities is nothing short of a miracle, although Leppmann advises the reader that the military academy's regimen fell far short of the degree of harshness which the poet later ascribed to it. In fact, Leppmann argues, having lived the two extremes of culturally sanctioned gender experience, Rilke was better suited than nearly anyone else of his time to empathize with the experiences of the opposite sex. Leppmann even sees Rilke as a man "before his time" in his enlightened sexuality, but his would seem to have been a theoretical, not a practical, form of sexual liberation. Leppmann, for example, acknowledges Rilke's failures as a husband and as a father. His daughter, Ruth, received only intermittent attention from the father who apparently regarded her as an occasional visitor with no permanent claim on either his affection or his responsibility.

Sensitive and frail, Rilke would appear to have been the sort of boy that is singled out for special persecution by his schoolmates. Leppmann, however, at some pains to present the military academy as a moderate example of such institutions, argues that Rilke was appreciated by the other students precisely because of his poetic nature. He was frequently called upon to read his poems aloud in classes, and such occasions apparently did not lead to derision. Others found compelling Rilke's own early determination to become a poet or, better, to make himself into one. This quest toward the perfection of a chosen craft, rather than an innate gift, becomes the central drama of the biography, culminating in a breathtaking climax as Leppmann recounts the weeks late in the poet's life during which he wrote most of *Duineser Elegien* (1923; *Duino Elegies*, 1930) and all of *Die Sonette an Or-*

pheus (1923; *Sonnets to Orpheus*, 1936), generally considered to be his two greatest books. Rilke's process of growing into his vocation and preparing for the challenge of his greatest poetic statements provided the sense of purpose which seemed at times to be denied by his nomadic wanderings across Europe. In a very real sense, his work was his only home.

Wolfgang Leppmann is unexcelled as a literary biographer, as one who must navigate the difficult middle course between straight biography and textual analysis. Into his narrative, he skillfully interweaves poems and fragments of poems which illuminate the biographical episodes he must recount—and vice versa. The chapter on Duino, replete with passages quoted from Rilke's breathless bulletins to friends and lovers as he reports on the long-overdue visit bestowed upon him by his muse, is the most successful realization of this style. Leppmann's stance toward his subject is at times surprisingly deprecating, as when he reiterates Rilke's appalling lack of reading, a condition the poet blamed on his education. According to Leppmann, Rilke only read many of the great German-language poets and authors very late in his life, the works of Johann Wolfgang von Goethe and Heinrich von Kleist constituting huge gaps in his poetic education. Leppmann especially writhes in agony whenever he contemplates Rilke's ignorance of Goethe and clearly would wish to remind his English-language reader of the analogy between this situation and the hypothetical English or American author's ignorance of William Shakespeare.

The elegant interplay between lines of Rilke's poetry and sections of biographical narrative, nevertheless, falls short of the biographer's goal of bringing the poet to life for the reader. As Leppmann himself is forced to admit, Rainer Maria Rilke was something of a mystery even to his closest friends and must remain so for readers today. Rather than accepting the suggestion of a greater-than-usual degree of complexity or inscrutability on the part of this artist, however, the reader should see this as evidence of the dubious claims of those who would insist on the unproblematic link between the author and his/her oeuvre. The road from the text to the author is not the easiest road for the critic to travel. Similarly, despite Leppmann's tendency to explain to the reader that Rilke was probably experiencing some thing or other at the time of a poem's composition, biographical details concerning a phase of the poet's life do not suffice to situate a particular poem for the reader, nor need such an objection betoken an uncritical acceptance of a formalist, New Critical, or structuralist poetics.

This biography can certainly be faulted on feminist grounds, especially since Leppmann continually claims for Rilke a modern feminist stance, *avant la lettre*, without according any space to the many modern-day feminist critics and scholars who have done so much to illuminate such attitudes as found in either men or women. More crucially for the biography as a readable book, the women in Rilke's life, including his wife (the sculptor

Clara Westhoff), Princess Marie von Thurn und Taxis-Hohenlohe (who made the Duino castle available to him), and Baladine Klossowska (Rilke's "Merline" and mother of the French painter Balthus), emerge in many ways as more interesting as biographical subjects than Rilke himself. Much as the great sculptor Auguste Rodin and fellow poet Paul Valéry contributed to Rilke's artistic and personal development, these strong women may well have played a greater role. Compared to their strengths, and in some cases to the financial support they offered Rilke, the poet himself seems weak and ineffectual.

Still, no woman stands out more than the brilliant, enigmatic Lou Andreas-Salomé, the great love of Rilke's life and an important writer and early champion of psychoanalysis. That she has traditionally been remembered as the object of Friedrich Nietzsche's affections, as Rilke's lover, and as Sigmund Freud's friend and patient is explained by the long-standing tendency to regard women solely as players of supporting roles for men. She contributed enormously to Rilke's intellectual development, and, as a native of Russia, she introduced him to the chief geographical inspiration for his poetic vision. This is analogous to the role Rilke's wife played by introducing him to his great aesthetic master Rodin, and there is every indication that Lou provided Rilke with much more than she gained from their relationship, despite her affection for him.

Perhaps the unavoidable contradictions of Leppmann's book can be summarized in this way: Faced with the almost impossible task of making his biographical subject appear to the reader in full, three-dimensional clarity, Leppmann, when not relying on the poems themselves, in their problematic relationship with the life, must throw into relief Rilke's character against the background of a large circle of friends, lovers, and aesthetic influences. Like the theatergoer who feels greater sympathy for one who is not the lead actor, the reader may well be distracted by one or more of these supporting characters. Add to this the problems of the genre of literary biography, whose distinctions from literary criticism are far from clear. Still, it must be acknowledged that Leppmann uses the form of literary biography very much to stylistic advantage, producing a book that is highly readable if less than totally convincing. Using his own extensive knowledge of modern European literature, Leppmann, who, for example, compares Rilke's efforts in *Duino Elegies* to attempts by writers such as Thomas Mann, James Joyce, Marcel Proust, or T. S. Eliot to preserve or recapture a world in time though the careful crafting of a literary work, is able to enhance our understanding of the literary modernism that has done so much to enshrine that notion of the inviolable, transcendant aesthetic creation in isolation from the world it renounces.

James A. Winders

Sources for Further Study

Book World. XIV, July 8, 1984, p. 1.
Kirkus Reviews. LII, April 15, 1984, p. 400.
Library Journal. CIX, July, 1984, p. 1327.
Los Angeles Times Book Review. October 14, 1984, p. 4.
The New York Review of Books. XXXI, September 27, 1984, p. 17.
The New York Times Book Review. LXXXIX, October 7, 1984, p. 24.
The New Yorker. LX, October 8, 1984, p. 133.
Publishers Weekly. CCXXV, April 27, 1984, p. 76.
Time. CXXIII, May 28, 1984, p. 86.

RIVER

Author: Ted Hughes (1930-   )
Publisher: Harper & Row, Publishers (New York). 79 pp. paperback $6.95
Type of work: Poetry

A seasonal account of a river and its creatures

Ted Hughes, named England's poet laureate in 1984, has always written about nature, especially animals, and *River* is no exception. The river in this book is both stage and major character in a play whose plot is controlled by the seasons from winter to fall, whose other characters are a variety of animals and man himself, and whose themes are death and renewal.

As a stage and the props that go with it, the river in this book is not ordinary. In Hughes's view in "Flesh of Light," it has an origin that smacks of the divine; it comes from the "boiling light" of "The mill of the galaxy." It can also be decked out as Hell with its "furnace boom," the human actors on it "possessed/ By that voice in the river,/ And its accompaniment/ Of drumming and flutes" ("The Gulkana"). More sinister than this, the river, visited by "the snow princess" of winter in "Japanese River Tales," can be transformed into "a gutter of death." In addition to these, the river is the machinery behind its scenes, the "Engine of earth's renewal" cranking up in the spring, repairing itself, and a summer wine that "Swells from the press/ To gladden men."

As a character in the play of the seasons, the river is cast in several female roles. It is Eve in "Torridge," "A novelty from the red side of Adam.// She who has not once tasted death." It is a young girl eloping while her father the landscape "Claws weakly at her swollen decision" ("Fairy Flood"), "a beautiful idle woman" ("Low Water"), and a bride ("Salmon-taking Times"). It is a maternal character with a "Heavy belly" in "River Barrow" and the gruesome victim of a cesarean with no issue in "New Year." It is both male and female, "the swollen vent/ Of the nameless/ Teeming inside atoms," whereby it says "Only birth matters" ("Salmon Eggs").

The fluidity, so to speak, of the river's guises extends to the supernatural. In "Last Night," it is an "evil" presence, in "The Gulkana," it is the "deranging cry" of a monster, "A stone voice that dragged at us," while in "River," it is a god "uttering spirit brightness/ Through its broken mouth."

A great variety of animal characters have roles to play in and about the river. There are the land animals. The mink embodies play, gluttony, and lust in "The Merry Mink." In "Salmon-taking Times," the pigs are "Tumbling hooligans ... / Piling in the narrows," and in "That Morning," the bears are almost human, joining the fishermen and "Eating pierced salmon off their talons," taking their nourishment from the river as the ewe in "Four March Watercolours" does, stepping into the river "to replenish her udder," playing a sort of allegorical character who stands for spring. There are birds, too. The kingfisher is a dazzling irritant, a spirit of chaos, in "The Kingfisher." In "Last Act," the damselfly is a "dainty assassin," and the cormorant is both the antagonist who outduels the fisherman narrator in "A Cormorant" and the cold-blooded figure of death itself in "A Rival." Finally, there are fish, perhaps the most important characters in the book besides the river itself. Of these, the eel is "The nun of water," a predator which is almost beyond relating to because it is so old and single-minded, and the cock minnows are anchorites who "have abandoned contemplation" to have "A stag-party, all bridegrooms, all in their panoply" ("Under the Hill of Centurions"). Sea trout enter the scene, too, playing the part of happy morons.

By far the most important characters among the fish, however, are the salmon. Hughes sees them as tragic, even godlike. Their one aim is to procreate, and they accept the challenge of all obstacles to do so. Somehow, enough survive to lay and fertilize eggs, though "forty-odd thousand" of these may be "milked" by humans, and those fish which manage to make it to the spawning grounds are doomed once they do their job. The patience and endurance of the salmon inspires the narrator of "Four March Watercolours" to see them as miners "Under the mountain of water," and their undeviating sense of purpose moves him in "October Salmon" to refer to them, after their journey of "two thousand miles," as "simply the armature of energy" which drives them to their "doom"—a fate to which they remain "loyal." The salmon which the poet looks at in "An August Salmon" accepts the river like a tragic hero; it is "the ceaseless gift/ That unwinds the spool of his strength." The salmon becomes in this way "A god . . . / With the clock of love and death in his body."

It is true that Hughes comes close to the pathetic fallacy when he describes animals and things in nature, and sometimes he outright (and with thumping energy) personifies them, as when he calls the river a woman and snowy hills the "bosom" which "wears this river/ Like a . . . jewel" ("Dee"). He seems to have, though, a firsthand knowledge of landscape and its creatures, and his intimacy with the parts of nature featured in *River* is dramatized by the pervasive image of the fisherman, who is a major character in the book.

Sometimes Hughes presents the fisherman in a metaphysical light. He links him to the reader in "Go Fishing," as he says, "Join water, wade in underbeing." The flowing water is a "plasm" which restores health to the fisherman who enters it, as though the river were his own blood. This empathy with the river as an ontological source is continued in "After Moonless Midnight"; his "blood easy/ As this river," the narrator-fisherman says, "The whole river . . . / held me . . . / With its blind, invisible hands"—which are life itself. Hughes wants readers to see the poet in the fisherman in these two poems: At times, as in the first poem, the poet must give up words to understand their basis, and at other times, as in the second poem, the poet is caught fast by his subject. The fisherman, like the poet, is linked not only to the river but also to its creatures—the salmon in it and the bears that come to catch them: "So we stood, alive in the river of light/ Among the creatures of light, creatures of light" ("That Morning"). The fisherman seems to stand for the poet inspired here, just as the seasoned fisherman in "Eighty and Still Fishing for Salmon" is like the poet, remaining "Loyal to inbuilt bearings"; he is "indifferent" to human distractions and "holds/ The loom of many rivers" (that is, that aspect of nature by which it creates). Summarizing the poet as fisherman, Hughes says, "I lean and watch the water, listening to water/ Till my eyes forget me// And the piled flow supplants me" ("Salmon Eggs"). He is, in short, reeled in by what he has come to fish and so repeats the Romantic idea of the poet's imagination and feelings absorbed into nature.

The dark side of this encounter is the modern element in it. The poet goes fishing in a remote and primordial part of the river. It overawes him with its inhuman power, and when a fish hits his line, it terrifies him, as though he had come in contact with a savage monster. The poet realizes that he is projecting, for the fish turns out to be "only a little salmon," but before this, the otherworldly quality of the fish is clear to the poet when he says, after the fish abandons the bait, that it "sank disembodied" ("Milesian Encounter on the Sligachan"). The effect of this event is to make the poet feel insubstantial ("I faded from the light of reality") in much the way that the Existentialists used to describe the feeling. The more primitive, indeed, the kind of river with which the poet comes in contact, the more frightened he becomes. He feels like an adventurer in an alien environment which makes him doubt himself. In "The Gulkana," he confesses, as he fishes the wild river, "my fear. . . seemed to live in my neck," and the fish he catches gives him the creeps, for it is "small, crazed, snake-like."

Such is the partial lot of the poet playing the role of the fisherman, perhaps especially in these times. The farther away that nature is from human control and comfort, the smaller the poet who comes to it may feel. At least Hughes has a sense of humor about his vulnerability, and it is as though he were talking about the poet having a frustrating time writing when he tells of the bad luck he had one day on a fishing venture; even trying to find a spot was a disaster, "my net, long as myself, . . . // infatuated/ With every twig-snag and fence barb" ("A Cormorant").

Hughes is hooked, one might say, on first and last things dramatized by nature. The river itself is the godlike director of the play, and it is sometimes disguised as a human player. The other characters—from the buffoon mink and bears and pigs to the villain cormorant, from the maddening kingfisher to the tragic salmon—help develop the themes of death and renewal, and their corollaries of rot and ripeness, in the plot of the seasons. The play itself has a mythic force for Hughes, which he tries to render, as in his previous books, in muscular rhythms and diction that recall Anglo Saxon verse. To be sure, he is at his best when he does not push the mythic element in his subjects into abstraction but lets their physical details speak for themselves—when he does not ride the horse of his pride in seeing the meaning of things but goes unobtrusively on foot among the creatures and events of nature.

Mark McCloskey

Sources for Further Study

American Poetry Review. XIII, September, 1984, p. 38.
Booklist. LXXX, June 15, 1984, p. 1433.
Christian Science Monitor. LXXVI, October 5, 1984, p. B4.
Guardian Weekly. CXXIX, September 25, 1983, p. 21.
Library Journal. CIX, July, 1984, p. 1330.
Listener. CXI, January 12, 1984, p. 23.
The New Republic. CXCI, September 3, 1984, p. 39.
The New York Times Book Review. LXXXIX, September 30, 1984, p. 45.
The New Yorker. LX, December 31, 1984, p. 66.
Publishers Weekly. CCXXV, April 27, 1984, p. 76.
Times Educational Supplement. November 11, 1983, p. 22.

766

ROSS MACDONALD

Author: Matthew J. Bruccoli (1931-   )
Publisher: Harcourt Brace Jovanovich (San Diego, California). Illustrated. 147 pp.
$14.95
Type of work: Literary biography
Time: 1915-1983
Locale: Canada; the United States

The first in a series of compact illustrated biographies, HBJ Album Biographies, of modern American writers

> Principal personages:
> KENNETH MILLAR (ROSS MACDONALD), an American detective novelist
> MARGARET MILLAR, his wife, also a novelist
> RAYMOND CHANDLER, an American detective novelist
> DASHIELL HAMMETT, an American detective novelist
> ALFRED A. KNOPF, an American publisher

With the publication of *The Underground Man* in 1971, Ross Macdonald received unusual attention for a writer of detective fiction: a front-page review (by Eudora Welty) in *The New York Times Book Review* and a cover story in *Newsweek*. Twenty-two years after publishing his first Lew Archer novel (*The Moving Target*, 1949), Macdonald finally seemed to have achieved what he had been striving for through more than twenty books and many short stories: recognition as successor to Dashiell Hammett and Raymond Chandler in the hard-boiled school and acceptance as a serious novelist. His professional odyssey (including the metamorphosis of his name from Kenneth Millar originally to John Macdonald and then to John Ross Macdonald and finally to Ross Macdonald) was matched by a nomadic personal journey (from birth in California to upbringing in western Canada to college in Ontario, graduate study in Michigan, World War II naval service in the Pacific, and permanent residence in Southern California), and both odysseys are reflected in his characters' identity crises and rootlessness.

All of this and the novels themselves are the subject of Matthew J. Bruccoli's *Ross Macdonald*, the first in a series entitled HBJ Album Biographies, for which Bruccoli also serves as editor. Focusing upon modern American authors, the series aims to provide brief studies that are extensively illustrated. The Macdonald volume, presumably typical, has forty-one pages of pictures and seventy-eight of text (exclusive of those devoted to an appendix, notes, and a bibliography). Necessarily, then, the attention paid to each novel is scanter than the extensive analyses in Peter Wolfe's *Dreamers Who Live Their Dreams: The World of Ross Macdonald's Novels* (1976) and Jerry Speir's *Ross Macdonald* (1978). Bruccoli, in fact, gives short shrift to most of the novels—briefly summarizing plots (for some), identifying themes, quoting from reviews—and seems to be more interested in publishing histories and sales figures than in the substance of the books. This, then, is not a work for the serious student of literature, who should go to Wolfe or Speir. It will be useful, though, for Macdonald buffs, who will find here a good overview of the author's life and career as well as lucid capsule judgments of the novels.

As a first step toward a Kenneth Millar/Ross Macdonald biography, Bruccoli's effort also merits attention, because he had access to Macdonald material at the University of California, Irvine, and consulted manuscript collections elsewhere. Margaret Millar, Macdonald's widow and herself a prizewinning mystery writer, also apparently cooperated. The result is a biographical sketch that is informative about many aspects of Macdonald's early life, including his emergence as a writer of detective fiction and his attempts to be recognized as a serious novelist. For insights into the early life and career, however, Macdonald's own eight-page introduction to Bruccoli's *Kenneth Millar/Ross Macdonald: A Checklist* (1971) is more revealing, while Macdonald's eminently readable pieces in the 1973 *On Crime Writing*, "The Writer as Detective Hero" and "Writing the Galton Case," are preferable to Bruccoli's exposition of the influences on Macdonald, his writing methods, and the conception of Lew Archer.

In his fourth novel, *The Three Roads* (1948), Macdonald introduced the quest motif, the California locale, the "pastness of the present" idea, and the Oedipal theme, all of which were to become omnipresent in his subsequent novels. Not until *The Moving Target*, a year later, however, did he introduce Lew Archer as his private eye and narrator. (Archer was to star in seventeen more novels and two collections of stories.) Bruccoli calls *The Moving Target* Macdonald's "first breakthrough novel," primarily because of Archer, who functions for the first time as a necessary "distancing character" providing a "layer of insulation between writer and material" and causing "things to happen and extend[ing] the web of causality." (This also was the first Millar novel published under a pseudonym and the only time he used "John Macdonald.") While Bruccoli does refer to Archer's mythical links and connections with such predecessors as Philip Marlowe and Sam Spade, he does not develop them adequately nor does he elucidate Archer's singular qualities to the point that he emerges as a truly distinctive series detective, and while criticizing Macdonald for doing "very little to fill in Archer's personal history in the subsequent novels . . . almost as though Archer has no life between cases," Bruccoli stresses Archer's role as "observing participant," not hero; this suggests a confusing double standard on the part of the critic, especially because in discussions of later novels, Bruccoli focuses upon ways in which Archer indeed does evolve and thus is seen as a fluid character, unlike most series detectives.

Curiously, Bruccoli disposes of Macdonald's next three novels—*The Drowning Pool* (1950), *The Way Some People Die* (1951), and *The Ivory*

Grin (1952) in merely two pages (most of which are devoted to quotations from reviews and Macdonald himself), despite the fact that the Archer persona is greatly expanded in these books, particularly his moralizing and sermonizing tendencies. An equally significant lapse in the singularly cursory treatment of *The Drowning Pool* (which gets merely seven lines) is Bruccoli's failure to mention that central to it are the themes of corporate greed and environmental destruction—themes that figure prominently in Macdonald's later novels, mainly the important *The Underground Man* and *Sleeping Beauty* (1973); it was at about this time that both of the Millars became actively involved in environmental causes.

A major turning point in Macdonald's career was the writing of *The Doomsters* (1958), a book which he said, "marked a fairly clean break with the Chandler tradition, which it had taken me some years to digest, and freed me to make my own approach to the crimes and sorrows of life." A Thomas Hardy poem supplied him with his title, and Archer's concluding thoughts in the book echo the poet: ". . . men and women were their own doomsters, the secret authors of their own destruction. You had to be very careful what you've dreamed." *The Doomsters* was Macdonald's most complex novel to date; it has a plot (not merely a succession of scenes in the Chandler manner) that develops a family saga as a means of dramatizing theme, and, as Bruccoli says, Archer for the first time "is personally involved in the events and might have prevented three of the murders," a departure from the usual detachment of a private eye. *The Doomsters*, therefore, foreshadows *The Galton Case* (1959), which Bruccoli properly regards as Macdonald's "second breakthrough book." His discussion, however, is superficial, largely devoted to a reconstruction (via quotations from an essay by the author) of the composition of the book, a reprinting of dust-jacket blurb copy that Macdonald himself wrote, an analysis of reviews, and a three-paragraph plot summary. Why is *The Galton Case* a significant work in Macdonald's development? Bruccoli again relies on the author: "I learned what every novelist has to learn: to convert his own life as it grows into his fiction as he writes." In writing this novel, his thirteenth, Macdonald delved into his own past while maintaining the necessary aesthetic distance, and he gave a new dimension to what had become his customary concerns: the identity quest, greed, alienation, and the "pastness of the present."

During the next decade, Macdonald produced eight novels, all Lew Archer novels but one (*The Ferguson Affair*, which followed *The Galton Case* in 1960). Bruccoli calls this period "a time of consolidation and mastery," and he traces the growth of Macdonald's art, primarily in plotting, while recognizing the continuing superficiality of his characters, the latter weakness "mainly the result of the requirements of form—the novel of 250 to 280 pages." Bruccoli's discussions of the individual novels, however, except for that of *The Far Side of the Dollar* (1965), are perfunctory, and such, unfortunately, is also true of his treatment of the landmark *The Underground Man* and the last two books, *Sleeping Beauty* and *The Blue Hammer* (1976).

The Underground Man is generally recognized as Macdonald's major achievement. In it, the Oedipal roots and other motifs of earlier books recur, and there is increased emphasis upon the environment and ecology. Macdonald skillfully develops the novel's multiple plots, unifying the work not only by his tight organization but also by relating all the key events to the moralistic worldview that emerges from the characters' suffering and pain. Not the least of the messages in the book is that which a minister's letter conveys: "The past can do very little for us—no more than it has already done, for good or ill—except in the end to release us. We must seek and accept release, and give release." Bruccoli calls the statement ironic and says that neither Macdonald nor his characters "can accept this sound advice"; Wolfe and Speir, however, think otherwise, and the evidence of the novel and Macdonald's life supports them. (Linda Millar Pagnusat, the only child of Kenneth and Margaret Millar, died the year before the book was published; she was thirty-one and had led a troubled life since her involvement in a vehicular homicide in 1956. These problems affected her father, who in 1956-1957 underwent psychotherapy.)

After *The Underground Man*, Macdonald wrote only two more novels: *Sleeping Beauty*, a kind of sequel because of its focus on the environment (an oil spill is its central symbol), and *The Blue Hammer*, which had its genesis fourteen years earlier in notebook entries and which is a fully realized delineation of the double motif and the need for self-realization. Some of the reviewers notwithstanding, these books show Macdonald to be at the height of his creative powers, but not long after finishing *The Blue Hammer*, he started to exhibit the symptoms of Alzheimer's disease. He died on July 11, 1983.

Ross Macdonald is an attractively designed book and an admiring tribute to the most important American writer of detective fiction since Hammett and Chandler. Its many pictures, spanning the full range of Macdonald's life and career, complete the text, but in a work that is filled with scholarly apparatus, it is surprising that not even approximate dates are given for most of the Jill Krementz candids. Notwithstanding Macdonald's comment (certainly hyperbolic) that W. H. Auden was "the most important single influence" on his life, a full-page photograph of the poet seems to be excessive, as do the twenty-seven reproductions of book jackets and paperback edition covers. Bruccoli amply demonstrates that Millar/Macdonald was almost as complex a person as the characters he created, but even within the limited parameters of the HBJ Album Biographies format, he should have offered more substance regarding the novels and their themes. The readers at whom *Ross Macdonald* is aimed certainly are more interested in what the man wrote than in his annual earnings and the idiosyncracies of the publishing world. Nevertheless, this book serves a useful purpose, and it whets a reader's appetite for a full-scale Millar/Macdonald biography still to be written.

Gerald H. Strauss

Sources for Further Study

Booklist. LXXX, April 1, 1984, p. 1096.
Choice. XXII, September, 1984, p. 92.
Christian Science Monitor. LXXVI, September 25, 1984, p. 22.
Kirkus Reviews. LII, January 15, 1984, p. 74.
Library Journal. CIX, May 1, 1984, p. 892.
Los Angeles Times Book Review. April 8, 1984, p. 1.
The New York Times Book Review. LXXXIX, April 1, 1984, p. 20.
The New Yorker. LX, April 30, 1984, p. 122.
Publishers Weekly. CCXXV, February 10, 1984, p. 183.

SARAH PHILLIPS

Author: Andrea Lee (1953-   )
Publisher: Random House (New York). 117 pp. $12.95
Type of work: Novel
Time: 1959-1974
Locale: Philadelphia, Pennsylvania; Cambridge, Massachusetts; and Paris, France

> *Sarah Phillips moves toward a sense of self in a novel made from stories that crystallize the experiences of an intelligent and privileged young black woman*

Principal characters:
> SARAH PHILLIPS, a Harvard University graduate from suburban Philadelphia
> THE REVEREND JAMES FORREST PHILLIPS, her father, minister of a prosperous Baptist congregation and active in the civil rights movement
> GRACE RENFREW PHILLIPS, Sarah's mother, who teaches sixth grade in a small Quaker school

The time is 1974. Sarah Phillips, like many another young American over the years, has graduated from college with vague literary aspirations and fled to Europe, where she is living an aimless and fairly meager existence in a Paris apartment shared with several Frenchmen. "The dollar was down that year," she reports, "and it was harder than ever to live on nothing in Europe, but scores of Americans were still gamely struggling to cast off kin and convention in a foreign tongue." As so often happens when Americans go abroad in order to free themselves from home and family and class and country, to discover their true selves, one of the first things that she learns is that she is an American. In Sarah's case, there is an added fillip: She is a particular kind of American, a middle-class, Harvard-educated black American, and the stories that illuminate her roots and her sense of self show, with a detached and ironic clarity, the experiences that have formed a new generation of privileged young black people who are heirs of a civil rights movement which they can barely remember.

This is Andrea Lee's first novel. Her *Russian Journal* (1981) was nominated for a National Book Award and praised for its vivid description of the incongruities in Soviet life. In *Sarah Phillips*, sharp observation and emotional distance remain the hallmarks of Lee's writing. The novel is created from a series of short stories, many of which have appeared in *The New Yorker*. The first records Sarah's moment of recognition in Paris; the rest of the stories, without any linking narrative, record rather systematically the incidents and experiences that shape Sarah's—and the reader's—knowledge of who she is.

Each story has a narrow focus; most cover a single incident at a specific time. Their sequence is thematic as much as chronological: The second story centers on Sarah's connection to her father; the third is about her mother; the next about the neighborhood in which she grew up; and then so on through Sarah's school experiences and through a group of incidents that refine and illustrate aspects of race and class and way of life. Though the plot reaches no real conclusion—one closes the book with little sense of what Sarah might do next in leading her life as an adult black American—it resolves thematically in the story entitled "A Funeral at New African," which supplies a reprise of earlier material. Despite the ironies and contradictions that grow from their curious intersections, family, civil rights, church, the stuffy gentility of the old black bourgeoisie, and the freedom of a safe suburb gave Sarah a secure and happy childhood—and provided her with a fine perception of the ironies and contradictions in the world at large. At the novel's end, Sarah is on a train, in motion. Staring out the window, she places herself among the many people of various colors and conditions who are in transit, moving away from anything they have ever known with only a faint idea of where they are going, but hoping for the moment that motion is enough.

The cool detachment of the first-person narrator lets Andrea Lee give Sarah Phillips a sharply detailed individual background which, at the same time, symbolizes the making of a whole new social group. Even though Sarah is heir to generations of education and relative privilege, the essential nature of upper-middle-class black life is changed for her generation. Sarah's father is pastor of the New African Baptist Church, a Philadelphia congregation founded in 1813 by free blacks and now filled by prosperous, conservative, light-skinned parishioners who were able to move into the suburbs during the 1950's; they return on Sundays to a church now surrounded by grimy, litter-filled streets. Sarah, like all suburban children, is uncomfortable and embarrassed by the inner-city neighborhood and distressed by those elements in the ritual of worship that come to seem increasingly primitive. She also has a sharp eye for the gentility and formality that mark the older generation. She recalls that, in 1963, when white students from Philadelphia universities began attending New African to hear the Reverend Phillips preach sermons on civil rights, the women of the congregation were quite distressed by their visitors' casual clothes and hatlessness.

Even though the civil rights movement took place during Sarah's grade-school years, it touched her only as a dim background: something adults talked about, "a necessary burden on my conscience, like good grades or hungry people in India." At ten, she found it quite embarrassing to have a father who openly admitted that he had gone to jail in Alabama. The bitter jokes made by her father and her uncle (an NAACP lawyer) are only confusing. Allowed to go to Washington with her father in the summer of 1963, her primary feeling is joy at having him all to herself while her mother is in Europe and her brother at camp. When she discovers that he is gone all day at meetings, she happily throws herself into friendship with a girl cousin. For one brief moment, she has a vision of the march he is helping to organize and asks to be part of it, but in the end she and her brother have to watch on television because of their mother's practical fear of "stampedes and what she called 'exposure'—by which she meant not sun and wind but germs from possibly unwashed strangers."

Sarah represents a curious irony that disturbs many middle-aged blacks who work in education and public service. The traditionally black colleges, in years past, provided not only education but also an ethic of concern and service; they trained teachers, preachers, lawyers, doctors, politicians, and civil servants with a sense of mission toward the less privileged. Many others in the black middle class who went to integrated schools outside the South experienced, twenty years ago, enough incidents of brutal prejudice, closed doors, and restricted opportunity to channel their lives into advancing the black community at large. As a consequence of the activism of such women and men whose life experiences were bent by segregation and prejudice, their children have been able to grow up in a world almost totally free of actual barriers. As graduates of preparatory schools or good suburban high schools and Ivy League colleges, they compete for the same corporate jobs as their white classmates and measure achievement by the same standards. Is it a success or a failure that the civil rights movement drained the black community of its most talented people?

Andrea Lee raises questions such as these by indirection and telling detail. "Servant Problems" portrays Sarah's experience as the first black girl to attend an exclusive preparatory school. Her minor miseries over personal slights are a far cry from incidents of oppression that would have an effect on life beyond adolescence. More significant is her difficulty in feeling any sense of identification with the servants who do the school's cooking and janitorial work. Class is clearly a major part of the issue, but so also are values. In "The Days of the Thunderbirds," Sarah is as disturbed as everyone else by the irresponsible and amoral behavior of the street kids who are invited to visit the carefully integrated and ecumenical summer camp attended by the children of professors and clergymen. The impulse that she and her friends have to sing the gang's song—once the troublemakers are safely inside their bus getting ready to leave the camp—only demonstrates that shared emotions do not begin to bridge the real barriers between people.

Most disturbing of all is the story "An Old Woman," in which Sarah and her mother's argument about a pair of French jeans the teenaged Sarah wants to buy at Saks Fifth Avenue is interrupted to visit an old woman in a convalescent home. Together they hear her story of rape (at age twelve) and childbirth and working for white folks while the baby lies in a basket in the dining room. Neither Sarah nor her mother can discover the words or the willingness to discuss the incident, although it must certainly be taken as the archetype of a certain kind of black female experience.

The strengths and the contradictions in the character of both parents become increasingly apparent as Sarah's narrative voice takes her up to the edge of maturity. The child Sarah feels wicked, frightened, and unreasoning when she is unable to step forward and accept baptism: "One phrase struck me newly each time: 'This is my beloved son, in whom I am well pleased!' Daddy sang out these words in a clear, triumphant tone, and the choir echoed him. Ever since I could understand it, this phrase had made me feel melancholy; it seemed to expose a hard knot of disobedience that had always lain inside me." As an adult, Sarah believes that her father gave her freedom by not applying religious pressure. She does not, however, draw any other conclusion about the cause or consequences of the incident.

Sarah's mother, Grace Renfrew Phillips, has "all the fussy little airs and graces of middle-class colored girls born around the time of World War I." She played the piano, went to church and to Girls' High, became a schoolteacher—but her life also included Quaker work camps and Communist Party meetings. She is adored by the sixth graders she teaches, swims miles every summer, and cooks with a truly consuming passion, disdaining convenience and modern appliances. Sarah's parents and her neighborhood are displayed with a sharpness and, perhaps, an impulse to preserve that has something in common with Grace Phillips' cooking; Lee's ironic distance prevents sentimentality yet permits her to re-create the happy childhood that produced such an independent and fortunate adult.

It was once generally agreed that the short story was, for all practical purposes, dead; young writers continued to produce short stories because the form appealed to people who were as yet unable to sustain a novel, but there were few outlets other than campus-based literary magazines. Short-story collections were held to be virtually unmarketable. In the early 1980's, there has been a surprising resurgence of the form and a number of novels have appeared, such as this one, which seem to be novels only nominally—because they are more than a hundred pages long, and because all of the stories are about the same character or the same place. For some readers, this is a very welcome phenomenon—the short but well-crafted and absorbing tale certainly fits crowded lives, and a whole book of them provides the added pleasure of becoming better acquainted with a person or place.

Sarah Phillips is rich with lucid phrases that fix a moment or an attitude. It is also very slender. There is not much sense of cause and consequence or any major pattern of development to connect the stories; each presents more information about Sarah Phillips and therefore a fuller portrait. The primary interest is largely biographical—the stories are pleasing because she is an interesting person, but the reader has no driving sense of discovery or meaning. Furthermore, the emotional distance in the narrator's control of tone—that very distance which allows her to craft the crystal phrases— keeps readers from sensing emotional depth in Sarah Phillips. As a coming-of-age story presumably based on autobiographical materials, the book is far better than many first novels. Lee is an intelligent writer with the ability to make her ideas clear without making them unduly explicit. One would like to see her next work move beyond *The New Yorker* compass and style.

Sally H. Mitchell

Sources for Further Study

Book World. XIV, November 4, 1984, p. 1.
Booklist. LXXXI, October 1, 1984, p. 192.
Essence. XV, December, 1984, p. 44.
Kirkus Reviews. LII, August 15, 1984, p. 772.
Library Journal. CIX, October 1, 1984, p. 1862.
The New Republic. CXCI, November 9, 1984, p. 41.
The New York Times Book Review. LXXXIX, November 18, 1984, p. 13.
Publishers Weekly. CCXXVI, October 5, 1984, p. 82.
Saturday Review. XI, February, 1985, p. 74.
Vogue. CLXXIV, October, 1984, p. 270.
Women's Review of Books. II, March, 1985, p. 3.

SAUL BELLOW, VISION AND REVISION

Author: Daniel Fuchs (1934-   )
Publisher: Duke University Press (Durham, North Carolina). 345 pp. $35.00
Type of work: Literary criticism

A broad-ranging analysis of Saul Bellow's works, primarily his novels, based upon the study of Bellow's manuscripts and emphasizing his liberal humanist view of both man and art

According to the annual Modern Language Association Bibliography, forty-nine critical and/or scholarly articles and books about Saul Bellow's work were published in 1980, forty-two in 1981, forty more in 1982, and sixty-three the following year—all in addition to numerous sketches, profiles, and articles that appeared in newspapers and magazines during the same four-year period. Clearly Bellow has become, in fact has long been (even before receiving the Nobel Prize for Literature in 1976) a literary institution as well as (among academic critics) a literary industry. Just as clearly, much of the critical commentary is superfluous, either reductive or redundant, sometimes both. Daniel Fuchs's *Saul Bellow, Vision and Revision* is distinguished from the bulk of these studies both by its appeal to serious readers outside the academic world and by its analysis of Bellow's manuscripts: Fuchs was granted sole permission to quote from the Bellow materials housed at the University of Chicago, where the great majority of Bellow's manuscripts are held, and at the Humanities Research Center of the University of Texas.

Fuchs's first two chapters deal with Bellow's "vision," while the remaining nine (as well as a brief epilogue on *The Dean's December*) involve critical studies of individual works. Although the "vision" chapters break no substantively new ground, they do provide a convenient, at times incisive, summary of Bellow's philosophy and his aesthetic. Fuchs rightly sees Bellow as an "essentialist" who rejects not only existentialism but also the modernist aesthetic that has been linked to it. Although Fuchs calls Bellow "the postmodernist par excellence," what he actually means is that Bellow is the major antimodernist of his age, a liberal humanist who detests the aesthetic detachment of Gustave Flaubert and James Joyce, the "stylized misery" of the existentialists, and the determinism of Sigmund Freud and others to deny the autonomy and the worth of the individual that Bellow chooses to affirm. Linking Bellow to the great nineteenth century Russian novelists, Fyodor Dostoevski and Leo Tolstoy, and to such twentieth century social theorists as Raymond Aron and Edward Shils, Fuchs claims that "The central thrust of Bellow's fiction is to deny nihilism, immoralism, and the aesthetic view." Bellow wants to prove that there is more to human life than modernism allows; to do this he does not write didactic thesis novels but instead novels based on his characters' groping efforts to discover their essential humanity. Their gropings, Fuchs insists, parallel the author's own as he writes and revises his work. "The main reason for rewriting," Bellow has said, "is not to achieve a smooth surface [the Flaubertian ideal], but to discover the inner truth of your characters."

It is fitting, therefore, that a study of Bellow's vision be coupled with the study of his revisions, of the composition process through which Bellow's novels have come to fruition. The reader learns, for example, that although there is little difference between early and late versions of *Seize the Day*, the few changes that there are are significant, the several versions of the novel's opening and closing scenes, in particular. Fuchs also explains the way in which Bellow slowed the pace of *Henderson the Rain King* and eventually created that novel's distinctive narrative voice—less realistic and more lyrical than it first had been. Examining the more than four thousand manuscript pages for *Henderson the Rain King* (there are six thousand each for *Herzog* and *Humboldt's Gift*), Fuchs comes upon an important source, the writings of neurophysiologist Paul Schilder, who is mentioned by name in a draft but not in the published version. In revising his characters, Bellow did more than merely flesh them out; he often altered them to a considerable degree. As Fuchs explains in his analysis of *Humboldt's Gift*, for example, "Generally speaking, the earlier descriptions of Humboldt are acerbic, neutral to negative; the later ones forgiving, elegiac, neutral to positive." Just as Bellow struggled with his characters in *Humboldt's Gift*, so too did he struggle with the novel's form, fusing together what had originally been two separate works, subsequently paring one and expanding the other in order to achieve a balance between the Chicago and New York stories as the finished novel gradually took shape, and painstakingly reworking the novel's important opening passage until it became "a tempered elegy, with retrospective youthful effusiveness present but not [as in earlier versions] out of hand."

Unfortunately, such analytic descriptions of Bellow's revisions are, considering the book's size, relatively few in number. *Saul Bellow: Vision and Revision* thus proves to be a less valuable addition to Bellow studies than it promised to be, for the textual analysis that is its strength is often relegated to secondary importance (and often buried in the extensive endnotes) as Fuchs the scholar-critic metamorphosizes into Fuchs the apologist. Fuchs is undoubtedly right to claim that "No American writer since the war has given us as level-headed, vibrant, and true a description of contemporary life as Saul Bellow, and no one has delineated so clearly and so deeply the relationship of the way we live now to what we read now, of character to ideas, of personality to books." Yet such a large and entirely plausible claim must be weighed against the persistent complaints of critics concerning the formlessness of Bellow's novels, the arbitrariness of his endings, and his inability to make his essentialist vision convincing. Fuchs acknowledges these issues but does not address them other than perfunctorily.

Indeed, for Fuchs, Bellow's having revised his work is proof positive that the author himself foresaw reviewers' objections and remedied all problems in advance. In one of his *Herzog* chapters, for example, Fuchs writes, "That *Herzog* is one of Bellow's most rewritten novels may not by itself dismiss the charge of formlessness, but it does undermine that point of view." It undermines nothing of the kind. To refute the charge of formlessness, Fuchs needs either to demonstrate conclusively that Bellow was concerned with structural problems during the revision process (on the basis of the evidence offered in *Saul Bellow: Vision and Revision*, one would have to conclude that in general he was not) or that the standards for form by which Bellow's novels have been judged do not in fact apply to Bellow's antimodernist novels—any more than they apply to Robert Coover's postmodernist novels—a sound enough view that Fuchs at times seems almost ready to put forth. Fuchs notes, for example, that Bellow was deeply moved in writing the final chapters of *Henderson the Rain King*. "Were most readers similarly moved in the reading? Whether they were or not, we see [in the novel and in the readers' responses] the familiar formal problem of a novelist whose subject is the comic spiritual seeker. The manuscripts shed a unique light on these issues." So far so good, but then Fuchs once again backs away: "In addition to showing that not only the reader, but also the writer had some struggling to do before a necessary illumination was achieved, they show, in some ways more clearly than the novel itself, that the dramatic parts of the novel express a meaning far less enigmatic than is commonly supposed."

Although in a footnote Fuchs rejects the role of textualist scholar, preferring to play the part of "critic," the plain fact is that it is precisely as a textualist that Fuchs could have done Bellow studies the most good. While it is true that Fuchs deftly weaves manuscript material together with passages from the published works to support his readings of these works, it is also true that he makes it difficult for the reader to gain a clear idea of the manuscripts in general and the revisions in particular apart from his selective use of them.

Equally troubling is the fact that Fuchs raises an interesting textual matter in his chapter on Bellow's play, *The Last Analysis*, that Bellow's revisions here may speak less about his intentions as author than about the dramatic work as a collective rather than an individual effort. Instead of pursuing this matter, however, as George H. Jensen has done so exhaustively in "The Theater and the Publishing House: Joseph Heller's *We Bombed in New Haven*" (in *Proof 5: The Yearbook of American Bibliographical and Textual Studies*, 1977), Fuchs writes a fairly conventional character analysis. More puzzling is Fuchs's chapter on Bellow's stories: Why discuss only nine of them? Why none later than 1968? Why make such large claims for what are arguably minor works? Why discuss them at all since what little manuscript material there exists for these works runs counter to Fuchs's vision-revision thesis? Finally, why, except to create the illusion of completeness, discuss Bellow's most recent novel, *The Dean's December*, in a hastily prepared five-page epilogue when Fuchs has obviously not examined any manuscript material and has nothing interesting or, surprisingly, even good to say about this novel, which he faults for many of the same reasons that earlier, previous reviewers and critics have faulted the earlier novels.

Saul Bellow, Vision and Revision is a valuable addition to Bellow studies insofar as it sheds light on the unpublished manuscripts and insofar as Fuchs, at times a very perceptive critic of Bellow's work, sprinkles his text with those "crushing one-liners" of which Albert Corde and other Bellow characters are so fond. Given Fuchs's access to and permission to quote from the abundant manuscript materials, however, *Saul Bellow: Vision and Revision* is not the book it could and should have been.

Robert A. Morace

Sources for Further Study

American Libraries. LVI, October, 1984, p. 446.
Choice. XXI, June, 1984, p. 1465.
The New York Times. CXXXIII, March 3, 1984, V, p. 15.
Times Literary Supplement. June 22, 1984, p. 688.
University Publishing, New Books Supplement. I, Summer, 1984, p. 13.

SECOND MARRIAGE

Author: Frederick Barthelme (1943-   )
Publisher: Simon and Schuster (New York). 217 pp. $15.95
Type of work: Novel
Time: The 1980's
Locale: An unnamed Southern city

In this novel, the principal characters languidly attempt to repair the breakdowns in their personal lives

> Principal characters:
> HENRY, the narrator
> THEO, his wife
> RACHEL, Theo's thirteen-year-old daughter
> CLARE, Henry's first wife
> JOEL, Clare's boyfriend

The last names of the principal characters in *Second Marriage*, Frederick Barthelme's first novel, are not given. Neither is the name of the Southern city, or even the state, in which they live. They have jobs, but they are not shown doing them, nor do they talk about them. Virtually nothing is said about their pasts. Though the narrator does evidently have feelings, he is profoundly reluctant to reveal them, even to himself. Plot, defined as a causally related sequence of events leading to the resolution of a conflict, barely exists. All of this is to say that Barthelme has deliberately divested himself of most of the tools which traditional realists use to build the house of fiction. Nevertheless, *Second Marriage* is nothing if not realistic. This book presents the odd spectacle of a skilled craftsman, at the height of his powers, working hard to produce something small and quirky. It might equally be viewed as a very thin, understated novel or a very long *New Yorker* story. In fact, according to a note on the copyright page, "portions of this book first appeared in different form" there. It is to the readership of that magazine that *Second Marriage* is most likely to appeal.

Such plot as there is can be summed up in a few sentences. Henry, the narrator, has married Theo after a long period of living with her, and they have bought and moved into a house, along with Theo's thirteen-year-old daughter Rachel. Theo is on good terms with Clare, Henry's first wife, who, as a result of problems with her boyfriend, moves in with Theo and Henry. After awhile, Theo asks Henry to move out, which he does, and drifts into and out of several brief, not-very-satisfying sexual affairs; then Clare moves to Colorado, and Henry moves back in with Theo. The novel could as easily be half as long or twice as long; it is a question simply of how many episodes Barthelme chooses to include.

If the emphasis so far has been on what *Second Marriage* is not, this is to suggest that Barthelme's canvas is more shadow than highlight. Actually there are many brief, sharply realized scenes; the point is that, from the perspective of most readers and writers, the emphasis is deliberately skewed. Henry's courtship of Theo is summarized in several sentences, their wedding disposed of in less than a page. In neither instance is there any indication of what anyone is feeling; what the reader does learn instead (and this is a typical kind of detail) is that "Jerry played the Wedding March on his horn and passersby slowed their Buicks and Oldsmobiles to watch the ceremony." The scenes that most writers would emphasize—the wedding, the reconciliation at the end—are muted almost to the vanishing point. Barthelme chooses rather to focus on minor events which reveal the surface of everyday life. Thus, pages and pages are devoted to Henry and Theo's squabble with their neighbors, stemming from an altercation between the family dogs. A considerable amount of attention is paid to the interiors of the bravely tacky houses and apartments and motel rooms in which the characters live, or at least pass their days and nights. The characters eat but hardly ever cook. If *Second Marriage* has an organizing principle, it is a random circular journey by automobile; if a central image, it is a fast-food joint.

The characters go to Pie Country and Long John Silver's and Burger King, and there random encounters take place. (Almost all encounters in this novel are random; little is planned more than a few minutes ahead of time.) At Pie Country, Henry and Theo and Rachel run into Clare and her boyfriend. Later, at Long John Silver's, Henry and Rachel strike up a conversation with Kelsey, a nubile college student, who then follows them home and becomes peripherally involved in the action. What Barthelme does and does not do with these scenes is instructive. In the first, "Clare led us across the restaurant to her table so she could introduce her boyfriend, Joel, who was a smallish guy with more muscles than he really needed." Nevertheless, the sexual tension implicit in Henry's snideness (one can imagine Ernest Hemingway's Jake Barnes making the same sort of wisecrack) never develops. In fact, there is virtually no conversation between Henry and the other adults. Theo chats with Clare and Joel at one table, Henry with Rachel at another. In contrast with Jake's keen awareness of Brett in *The Sun Also Rises* (1926), Henry apparently pays no attention to what is going on across the way. Characters have been brought onstage; in their physical grouping there is merely a hint of Theo's later alliance with Clare at the expense of Henry, but of what Henry might be feeling about this situation almost nothing is revealed. "You were looking pretty rocky there for a minute," Rachel says, having dragged him away from the others—but whether or not he was feeling rocky, Henry does not say.

The question then arises: What purpose does this very typical scene, which might stand as an emblem of Barthelme's method throughout the novel, serve? Its function in terms of plot and character development is minimal. Only when viewed not as part of a larger entity but, primarily, as a discrete unit, complete in itself, does it begin to make sense. Its purpose, in that light, is simply to show what Pie Country is like. The skinny, gum-chewing waitress (who is perhaps the most important character in the scene, and who never appears again) has on "a pink waffle-textured uniform"; her brown apron has "a lot of discouraging spots on it." The menu offers items such as "Pineapple Crunch Pie Supreme" (virtually synonymous, in Henry's view, with "Pineapple Upside Down Pie" and "Pineapple Meringue") and "Pumpkin Cinnamon Escape"; when Henry asks for plain chocolate he gets "Double-Boiled Chocolate Rollover"; and so on. It is this tawdry plastic world, in which everything is mass-produced and disposable, which really catches Barthelme's eye and engages his imagination. Relationships are also disposable—that is a central point, insofar as the story has one—but what matters most is Pie Country's menu. *Second Marriage* is a satire at heart.

Through this fast-paced world the characters drift. Remarkably passive, without ambition except to muddle into relationships with which they can live, they collide, cling briefly, ricochet off—but all in slow motion, as if under water. Henry is in advertising ("In and out," he says); at one point, he shows Rachel several signs that he designed, which is the sole indication of what his job actually entails. Aside from that, he is an out-of-work academic who makes no discernible effort to find employment in his field. Only when an opportunity is actually thrust at him does he apply for a one-year instructorship in biology; only at this point, almost three-quarters of the way through the novel, does Barthelme reveal that Henry is a biologist. Science is hardly a passion with him—he never talks about it, and, when offered the job, he never does decide whether to accept it. Neither is there anything to indicate whether he likes or dislikes his advertising job. The same is true of Theo and her public-relations job for the university. In Barthelme's schema, the world of work, along with all the pressures and struggles it normally involves, is insignificant. Nor is money—the lack of it, the desire for it—of particular importance. That the characters have enough to meet their needs is simply a given.

What Henry does care about is getting back together with Theo. So few details are given about their earlier life together that one can only guess how or why their relationship developed in the first place, as, also, one must guess why they split up. Theo's vague dissatisfaction, never openly discussed, at one point manifests itself in digging a large hole in the backyard. When she abandons Henry in favor of Clare (whether the women have a physical relationship is another moot point), he is clearly unhappy. Once he cries, once he has a small breakdown, but he does nothing to try to repair the relationship. He simply drifts, not content exactly to let events take their course but temperamentally incapable of doing anything else. He is at any rate a step ahead of Clare, who at one point says, "I don't know what I want." She finally wanders back to the man for whom she abandoned Henry in the first place. The conflicts in this novel, which insofar as it is about human conflict at all resembles a very languid game of musical chairs, are necessarily muted. (The only character who could really be called lively is thirteen-year-old Rachel.) As the characters ramble around in circles, so also does the novel itself. With little momentum, little development of tension, it consists essentially of a series of discrete set pieces.

A point of great significance about *Second Marriage* is that it is told in the first person by an exceptionally reticent narrator. Even Hemingway's Jake Barnes is forthcoming by comparison. This point of view is realistic, in the sense that it mimics the way in which any given individual receives information about the world; we are all people locked into a single consciousness. The corresponding problem, from the writer's perspective, is limited access to information. The reader can know only what Henry knows and is willing and able to divulge—and that, aside from details about the spots on the waitress' apron, is not very much. Barthelme may be making a point about the essential aloneness of all human beings: an important idea, but it is undercut by his not having chosen a more active and communicative speaker. (The reader learns not all that *can* be known about the characters but all that *Henry* knows and chooses to tell.) Similarly, the point may be that language, radically limited in its uses, fails at the point where people really begin to hurt—an idea which, once again, this fiction does not properly test. Or Barthelme may think that he is revealing everything that really matters about his characters, in which case the obvious response is that he has not chosen very interesting characters to write about. Finally, he might be regarded as withholding vital information by hiding behind Henry. The effect in any case is to distance the reader from the characters and events. Because it is difficult to identify with any character except Rachel, such appeal as the novel has is almost entirely to the intellect.

Second Marriage does not contain many passages in which events or physical details are emotionally charged. At one point, Henry's memories of Theo—"Theo and me in the car going to the grocery or the drugstore, on an evening just after the summer, one of those first nights of fall when the heat evaporates suddenly and you click off the air conditioner, roll down the car windows, and let the air flood in"—are moving. Also, there is a touching moment when, parting from Clare for the last time, he takes her hand: "Her fingers were dry and stubby. I'd never thought about her fingers." For the most part, however, the novel is deliberately flat. Because the characters' pasts are hardly delineated at all, there is little sense of personal history bearing down on them; because they are concerned only with the present and the immediate future, there is little sense of the pressure of time. Their emotional range is limited. What remains are surfaces, effectively and at times even brilliantly rendered. Barthelme, fully in control throughout, has written an admirably crafted novel.

At the same time, it is a fashionable sort of book—a fashion formed at least in part by the enormous influence of *The New Yorker*—and therefore likely to be overpraised. It takes few risks: Emotionally guarded, it could not possibly be called sentimental; morally ambiguous, the author's vision hidden behind a character who himself reveals no clear vision, it could not be called didactic. Mimesis in the simplest sense—writing which reveals an accurate eye and ear—is also popular, and Barthelme's physical details are vivid and convincing, his dialogue flawless. On a deeper level, however, the reticence of *Second Marriage* limits its value. The fictive world, upon whose weight and integrity the author's illusion and in turn the reader's lasting pleasure depends, is here oddly light. The effect is something like early Hemingway, lacking the nightmarish central vision. That is a crucial lack. And so this novel raises a final question: Well written as it is, was it worth writing to begin with?

Edwin Moses

Sources for Further Study

Booklist. LXXXI, December 1, 1984, p. 480.
Kirkus Reviews. LII, July 15, 1984, p. 632.
Library Journal. CIX, September 15, 1984, p. 1769.
Los Angeles Times. September 28, 1984, V, p. 14.
The New York Times Book Review. LXXXIX, September 30, 1984, p. 1.
Newsweek. CIV, October 1, 1984, p. 87.
Publishers Weekly. CCXXVI, August 3, 1984, p. 51.
Vogue. CLXXIV, September, 1984, p. 575.
Washington Post. September 19, 1984, p. B1.

SECOND WORDS

Author: Margaret Atwood (1939-   )
Publisher: Beacon Press (Boston). 444 pp. $18.95; paperback $9.95
Type of work: Essays

Essays and lectures on Canadian culture, on Canadian and American literature, on being a writer, and on the writer's political relationship to society

Margaret Atwood's novels, short stories, and poetry have won for her many readers south of the Canadian border; Americans interested in literary and cultural history will find both discriminating analysis and a consistently lucid voice in Atwood's *Second Words*, a collection of lectures and essays. The chronological arrangement creates a portrait of the developing artist from 1960 through 1982; indeed, one can read this book as an intellectual autobiography. Through the essays, one meets a precocious undergraduate who once took a course in John Milton from an unintimidating Northrop Frye, a Harvard University English graduate student who studied American Romanticism with Perry Miller, an author coping with the popular success and hostile literary reviews of her landmark study of Canadian literature, a published poet and novelist whose work has firmly established her literary reputation, and an activist for human rights. In these essays, Atwood examines recurrently three topics: Canada's nationalistic responses to cultural imperialism (British and American), the voices created by literary women, and her own passionate dedication to writing, both to renew language and to make a moral and ethical critique of society. Defining the interrelationships among these three topics, Atwood offers a map, or perhaps an anatomy, of her literary culture. *Second Words* sketches a personal literary history of the 1960's and 1970's.

Atwood divides her collection into three parts. Part 1, 1960-1971, includes student essays written for the literary magazine at Victoria College, University of Toronto, and book reviews written by a beginning novelist for academic, popular, and avant-garde periodicals. Part 2, 1972-1976, records, in impressive diversity, Atwood's response to her growing reputation as a poet and her scandalous success as a critic of Canadian literature, and documents her increasing awareness of women writers' significance in literary culture. Part 3, 1977-1982, reveals Atwood's dedication to human rights, her commitment to appropriate critical reviews of Canadian and women writers, and her reflections on literary influence.

In her earliest essays, Atwood expresses her fascination with Canadian literature. Praising the barren solemnity of Margaret Avison's poems, Atwood, in 1961, writes in a collegiate style stuffed with figures of speech. Her prose style improved dramatically over the next twenty years, but her discriminating intelligence is evident even in her first published essays. Her 1962 review of J. P. Matthews' *Kangaroo & Beaver: Tradition in Exile*, a comparative study of two "colonial" literatures, Australian and Canadian, reveals both her bias and her analytic brilliance. Although she praises the book's comprehensiveness and documentation, she faults Matthews for preferring Australian literature to Canadian. Succinctly, she explains that the gaps in Matthews' categories and his uneven selection of certain Canadian authors have undercut the value of his conclusions. This review was one of several which Atwood published in *Alphabet*, a little magazine that specialized in Canadian literature. James Reaney, poet and editor of *Alphabet*, was one of Atwood's mentors; she pays tribute to Reaney in three separate essays. The magazine lasted for nineteen issues and eleven years, and, on the occasion of *Alphabet*'s final issue, Atwood wrote a discriminating analysis of the Canadian habit of mind, contrasted with the English and the American. Her analysis assumes the importance of historical and cultural roots for any writer, and her perspective on Canadian writers commands critical respect. In "Nationalism, Limbo and the Canadian Club" (1971), she further describes her own generation of Canadians, who received a public school education in British imperial history and a popular education in the cultural and economic dominance of the United States. Atwood remembers that Canada defined itself negatively, as failing to be the United States. Re-creating her years of graduate study at Harvard University, she diagnoses the self-defeating attitudes of Canadian students at Harvard Business School, who imbibed too much Canadian whiskey, earnestly discussed whether they should pursue profitable careers in the United States, and repeatedly played a record of "The Star Spangled Banner." Atwood chose another path. As an undergraduate at Toronto University, she had studied English and American literature in her classes, but outside class she discovered Canadian writers whose work was being published in the little magazines. As a graduate "studentess" at Harvard, she was barred from the English and American texts kept in Widener Library for male students, but in the library annex where she could read freely she found Canadian literature. During her years in the United States, she rejected narrow, self-centered cultural horizons; she chose instead a broader worldview against and within which she could struggle for cultural identity. She, and many others in her generation, did struggle against the attitude that placed Canada second, did return home to Canada.

Included in part 2 of this collection is "Mathews and Misrepresentation," Atwood's detailed response to Robin Mathews' attack on her book, *Survival: A Thematic Guide to Canadian Literature* (1972), which was a popular success but was, she writes, sneered at by academics. As she corrects Mathews' misreadings, she again asserts her belief that the individual writer and society have an interdependent relationship. This belief unites the diverse essays of part 2. In explaining her position, she offers a politically strategic analogy between the dilemma of Canadian artists in a colonial culture and the position of women in a sexist society. Women may ignore their victimization, blame biological necessity, or struggle to change society. Clearly, Atwood chooses the third response: rage against the identifiable oppressor, accompanied by a vision of a more equitable and productive culture. Until the culture is changed, she reminds Mathews, neither women nor colonial artists can act as liberated individuals but must act against cultural oppression together, in a community.

The same clear-eyed, creative vision characterizes Atwood's criticism of women writers. She praises Adrienne Rich's poetry for forcing readers to think about themselves, for heroically exploring the myths and truthfully imaging the bond between the powerless and the powerful. She praises the fiction of Audrey Thomas for depicting, with technical and psychological brilliance, a woman's quest for cultural rituals of grief. She praises Erica Jong's poetry for mocking the contempt that a male-dominated culture directs toward women. She praises Marie-Claire Blais for creating, in *St. Lawrence Blues* (1974), a social satire on Quebec's uneasy transition from a repressive order to a confident, free society. Atwood imagines a personified French-Canadian culture, laughing bitterly at itself.

Atwood comments on that bitterness in her essay on English-Canadian humor, asserting that concealed in the laughter of a colonized culture is a self-deprecating assumption: I am not provincial; that is to say, I am not Canadian. Surveying Canadian literary monsters, she traces a history in which early writers imagined monsters associated with the forces of nature, while contemporary writers imagine monsters produced by human passions. That progressive alienation and self-hatred Atwood correlates with Canadians' shifting self-image; her literary analysis consistently places writing in a cultural context.

Atwood's "On Being a Woman Writer: Paradoxes and Dilemmas" expresses cogently and without simplification the contradictions that she perceives within feminist critical and creative literature. As she notes, her questions and responses are not unique, but she thoroughly analyzes the attitudes with which women writers contend. To discuss sexual bias in the language of reviews, Atwood creates six subtopics: "Assignment of Reviews," "The Quiller-Couch Syndrome" (defining style as masculine or feminine), "She Writes like a Man," "Domesticity" (as a literary theme), "Sexual Compliment-Put-down," and "Panic Reaction." She identifies four distinct "Media Stereotypes." She acknowledges the various forms of rivalry among women writers, contending for one coveted position within a male-dominated culture. Her carefully subdivided categories assume the authority of a comprehensive catalog; having named and classified the oppressors, she reduces their power over her. In her personal statement, she dismisses the combat against sexual bias, to reclaim the writer's true arena, the imagination, and to arm herself with the writer's tool, language.

The breadth and variety of Atwood's cultural interests are most clearly displayed in part 3. Atwood champions the feminist work of Tillie Olsen, Sylvia Plath, Canadian prairie women, and black American women writers, but she also praises the political fiction of Nadine Gordimer and E. L. Doctorow, the technical virtuosity of the fiction writers Timothy Findley and W. D. Valgardson, and the classical achievement of the poet Jay Macpherson. She describes the gentle influence of Northrop Frye on her own intellectual development, and she makes an eloquent appeal to intellectuals on behalf of Amnesty International. Four major essays demonstrate Atwood's essential good humor, analytic and synthetic intelligence, and passionate dedication to her vocation. These are: "Witches," "An End to Audience?" "Canadian-American Relations: Surviving the Eighties," and "Writing the Male Character."

In "Witches," Atwood identifies herself with one of her New England ancestors, a woman convicted of witchcraft and condemned to be hanged; she survived. Analyzing the politics of witch-hunts in a larger context, Atwood warns her audience to recognize the dangerous power of authority to eliminate threatening subversives. Exiled from the Anglo-American literary culture as a Canadian, excluded from Widener Library as a woman, examined by critics as a woman writer, not simply a writer, Atwood transforms her experience into a positive identification with other outsiders. She brilliantly observes the connection between an old cultural attitude that judges women to be witches and a contemporary cultural attitude that assumes female writers acquire power not by developing their technique or style or ideas but by being unnatural women.

In "Writing the Male Character," Atwood puts her audience at ease, makes them laugh, and cleverly defuses their fear and anger. She sketches a history of women writers portraying aggressive male characters, men portraying passive or bitchy female types, and women portraying female victims and rebels, but then she envisions a culture in which the full range of characters, male and female, appear in the literature of writers, male and female. She articulates a plea for tolerance, understanding, and an inclusive portrayal of humanity.

"Canadian-American Relations: Surviving the Eighties" addresses again the imbalance of power between the two cultures. It is an important essay in Atwood's development, revealing her changed perspective. She looks back over the two decades with a historian's insight. For the first time, she acknowledges that in *Survival* she addressed English-Canadian, not Canadian, nationalism. That movement, she notes, reached its turning point in 1975. In the 1980's, she is ready to let her concern range "beyond cultural nationalism." She broadens her scope to address oppression that crushes the imagination. She defines the writer as a witness, inevitably involved in politics, observing and giving testimony to readers in a shared culture.

As a writer, Atwood communicates hope to her readers. Even in her most grim portrayals, she argues, she envisions the possibility of the world being other than it is. In "An End to Audience?" Atwood stresses the power of fiction to criticize the ethics of a community. Exercising that power, she acknowledges, makes her a political novelist.

Atwood presents herself in *Second Words* as an intelligent literary critic and a passionately committed writer. Her prose is witty, entertaining, and enlightening. Her ideas provoke significant revision of American and Canadian cultural assumptions. One finishes reading this collection reluctantly, for literary and cultural essays as good as these are rare.

Judith L. Johnston

Sources for Further Study

Canadian Forum. LXII, February, 1983, p. 26.
Choice. XX, April, 1983, p. 1133.
Kirkus Reviews. LI, December 1, 1983, p. 1231.
Library Journal. CVIII, February 1, 1983, p. 208.
Los Angeles Times Book Review. March 25, 1984, p. 7.
Macleans. XCV, December 6, 1982, p. 64.
Ms. XI, April, 1983, p. 32.
Publishers Weekly. CCXXV, January 6, 1984, p. 81.
Quill and Quire. XLIX, February, 1983, p. 34.
Washington Post Book World. March 4, 1984, p. 3.

SECRETS AND OTHER STORIES

Author: Bernard MacLaverty (1942-   )
Publisher: The Viking Press (New York). 130 pp. $13.95
Type of work: Short stories
Time: The 1970's
Locale: Northern Ireland, Ireland, and England

Fifteen stories of everyday life in Northern Ireland

With the American publication in 1983 of *Cal*, a novel depicting the complexities of the Protestant-Catholic-British conflict in Northern Ireland, Bernard MacLaverty became the best-known Ulster writer on this side of the Atlantic. Following *Cal*, *Lamb* (1980), his first novel, and *A Time to Dance and Other Stories* (1982) is *Secrets and Other Stories*, a collection of fifteen stories published in Ireland and Great Britain in the 1970's. The stories avoid the political context of *Cal*, with only an occasional reference to British soldiers. Written in a simple, straightforward style, these stories examine the everyday lives of working-class people whose joys and sorrows are so universal they could be living almost anywhere. That they are citizens of Northern Ireland makes their situations seem even more desperate, the frequent humor of these situations unexpected and all the more effective.

At their best, MacLaverty's stories resemble those of James Joyce and Frank O'Connor, his obvious models. The stories, however, are uneven, too often merely sketches, clearly the work of a writer still learning his craft. Some are pleasant but insubstantial. In "A Pornographer Woos," the opening of which recalls Leopold Bloom spying on Gerty MacDowell in James Joyce's *Ulysses* (1922), a writer, inspired while watching his wife on a beach, creates a mildly pornographic sketch; she reads it, and they return to their hotel room to make love. In "The Miraculous Candidate," a schoolboy prays for help during an exam, levitates, and receives divine assistance. MacLaverty has a talent for whimsey, but the best stories in this collection deal with the more commonplace.

Dick, the protagonist of "The Bull with the Hard Hat," has eight noisy children and a ninth on its way. Unfortunately, he is more successful at impregnating his wife than at his job: the artificial insemination of heifers. He can get no peace at home and none at work since increasingly (despite ten years' experience) he fails to impregnate the cows and knows that he is to blame. Even if he were good at his job, he would find it an ordeal: "The long rubber glove, the cow's hot insides, the constant prevailing smell of dung, the muck and clabber yards he had to tramp through. It was either that or home, he didn't know which was worse." Dick finds happiness only in his fantasies. Driving from job to job, he imagines he is Grand Prix champion Emmerson Fittipaldi. Pulled over to the side of a road to eat the bland lunch his wife has prepared, he imagines having sex with Carmel, one of the women in his office. Carmel represents not only the prospect of sex but also something even less likely—an ordered life: "With Carmel it would have been so different. They could have had two nice children and she would be there crisp and clean for him when he came home, the house immaculate, the toys tidied away." In his pathetic retreat from the chaos of his life, Dick is typical of MacLaverty's characters.

The nameless protagonist of "Between Two Shores" has a happy home life threatened by the fulfillment of his sexual fantasies. He thinks about the mess he has made of things while on a boat returning to Belfast from England where he has gone to work for a time. Hospitalized to have his appendix removed, he falls in love with a nurse. He is sexually attracted to her but also needs company in this alien land. He acquires a venereal disease from her and spends his passage home both worrying about what to do about it, afraid to tell his faithful wife, and trying to forget about it by approaching a pretty student. Unable to resolve his problem, he tries to wish it away. MacLaverty does not seem to be implying anything about England infecting Ulster but is simply presenting a man's inability to deal with loneliness, guilt, and despair.

"Anodyne" is a lighter, more ironic look at loneliness. James Delargy, a teacher, has been devoted to his invalid mother. After she dies, a doctor suggests that he go away and begin rebuilding his life: "He must begin to see himself as an adult." James goes to a seaside, hoping to meet people, especially females. He has spent most of his time with his mother, who once threw away his copy of Thomas Mann's *Death in Venice* because she killed a fly with it, and knows few people. Like Aschenbach in Mann's novel, James discovers a vision of pure loveliness at the beach and makes a date. Her father arrives instead, informing James that the girl is only fifteen. The father is a professor of English at Trinity College, and the two spend the night discussing literature. James is much happier than he would have been with the girl. After meeting the professor's charming wife, James thinks "how sad it was that his mother would never meet these lovely people. He was sure she would have approved."

"Hugo," the longest and best-written story in the collection, underscores MacLaverty's debt to Joyce. As a boy, the narrator develops an attachment to one of his widowed mother's tenants, Hugo, a pharmacy student. Hugo, who resembles Joyce, helps cure the boy's stammer. He is also a Joyce expert and devotes his spare time to writing a novel. When the narrator goes to university, Hugo asks him to read the novel, and he is shocked: "It was all too embarrassingly bad. He had not even grasped the first principles of good writing." After he tells Hugo, "as kindly as I could," what he thinks, his friend shuns him. Some time later, Hugo hangs himself.

The narrator interrupts this story halfway through to explain how difficult it is for him to write about his friend, to give some sense of this man's tragic life, "to swell a few fragments into something substantial." This, of course, is what MacLaverty is attempting to do in each of these stories, and in "Hugo," he succeeds well in connecting his themes of desperation, responsibility, guilt, and people's ineffectual efforts to help one another, to save themselves.

In "St. Paul Could Hit the Nail on the Head," a housewife visits her husband at his work, a demolition site. Walls ripped away, the interior of a house stands exposed: "Mary felt she shouldn't look, seeing the choice of wallpapers: pink rosebuds, scorned in her own family, faded flowers, patterns modern a generation ago. She felt it was too private." MacLaverty clearly disagrees since he is exposing the private moments of everyday lives in these stories. Like Mary, one may occasionally want to turn away, but MacLaverty's skill and compassion keep the reader's attention where he wants it to be.

MacLaverty's talent, like that of so many Irish and British writers, is quiet, understated. In "Hugo," the title character explains what his creator is trying to achieve:

> Literature is the science of feeling. The artist analyses what feelings are, then in some way or other he tries to reproduce in the reader those same feelings. . . . Nuances. That's the secret. The lines in the spectrum between pity and sympathy. Literature is the space between words. It fills the gaps that language leaves.

There are enough such nuances in *Secrets and Other Stories* to make reading it a moving experience.

Michael Adams

Sources for Further Study

Booklist. LXXXI, October 1, 1984, p. 192.
British Book News. August, 1984, p. 192.
Christian Science Monitor. LXXVI, October 4, 1984, p. 24.
Kirkus Reviews. LII, August 1, 1984, p. 707.
Library Journal. CIX, October 1, 1984, p. 1860.
The New Republic. CXCI, November 26, 1984, p. 39.
The New York Times Book Review. LXXXIX, November 11, 1984, p. 12.
Newsweek. CIV, January 14, 1985, p. 70.
Times Educational Supplement. June 8, 1984, p. 32.

THE SELECTED ESSAYS OF CYRIL CONNOLLY

Author: Cyril Connolly (1903-1974)
Edited, with an introduction, by Peter Quennell
Publisher: Persea Books/A Stanley Moss Book (New York). 307 pp. $17.95
Type of work: Essays

Reviews and essays on literature, art, and travel, with a selection of satires and parodies, drawn from three previously published collections by the prominent English critic

When Cyril Connolly was at Eton, the Master in College, J. F. Crace, wrote that the sixteen-year-old Connolly was "in danger of achieving nothing more than a journalistic ability to write rather well about many things." That this prediction proved accurate was both the triumph and failure of Connolly's life. He became one of England's leading literary journalists but was dissatisfied with being merely a critic. This dissatisfaction emerges in several of the pieces in *The Selected Essays of Cyril Connolly*, but so do his wit and insight. As his friend Peter Quennell writes in the introduction to this collection, Connolly was a reluctant journalist but, nevertheless, a born critic.

Connolly began his career as a regular reviewer for the *New Statesman* in 1927, founded, with Stephen Spender, the literary magazine *Horizon* in 1939, edited it until its demise in 1950, and became the main book critic for the London *Sunday Times* in 1951. He also published one novel, *The Rock Pool* (1935), and two highly regarded, partly autobiographical works, *Enemies of Promise* (1938) and *The Unquiet Grave* (1944). The thirty pieces in *The Selected Essays of Cyril Connolly* are taken from three previous collections: *The Condemned Playground* (1945), *Ideas and Places* (1953), and *Previous Convictions* (1963). Divided into sections dealing with travel, life and literature, and satires and parodies, the essays reveal Connolly's passion for literature, art, and several sacred shrines of art and literature and his equally passionate disgust for nationalism, tourists, snobs, "the increasingly illiterate rich," philistines in general, and, frequently, his native England. Only true genius meets with his approval, and there is too little of that around.

Despite Quennell's claim that Connolly is the finest satirist-parodist since Max Beerbohm, the final section is the weakest in the collection. In "Felicity" and "Felicity Entertains," Connolly pokes fun at the Bright Young Things of the period between the world wars and those who wrote about them, but he is much less amusing than Evelyn Waugh in *Vile Bodies* (1930). In "Bond Strikes Camp," Connolly captures Ian Fleming's style only in the catalogs of trivial details. Once he gets Bond into drag, he does not know what to do with him. Funnier are "Told in Gath," an Aldous Huxley parody, and, especially, "Where Engels Fears to Tread," purportedly the memoirs of a pseudointellectual who abandons going to parties for the Party: "I realize I shall never understand eclectic materialism but I'm terribly terribly Left!" Connolly is at his best when he simply stoops to Wodehousean silliness: "There were beaches where summer licked me with its great rough tongue. Ah, summer! There's a crypto-fascist for you!"

The travel pieces combine appreciations of England, the Continent, and Egypt, focusing mainly on their art works, with complaints about the travails of sightseeing. Travelers too often have the wrong attitudes, acting as if they were cramming for exams or clocking "into a museum like an office, arriving fresh and leaving with jangled nerves and a furious hunger, still several rooms behind schedule." Another annoyance is other tourists, as when Connolly visits Saqqara and the Pyramids: "Surrounded by honking cars and Sunday crowds, they are more like two indestructible film stars signing autographs. If only one could get them alone!" Despite the tourists, the hectic pace alternating with boredom, the occasional revolution, Connolly must continue to travel, pursuing the spirits of famous travelers of the past such as Henry James, searching for some sort of revelation, perhaps even a rebirth.

Connolly most often fulfills his quest through works of art. The cave paintings at Lascaux represent "holy ground" for "all who have not quite given up hope for mankind." Unfortunately, the sacred quality of most art is diminished by its being too accessible: "Great paintings should be kept under lock and key and shown as seldom as wonder working images." For Connolly, "life has no moral, and the moral of art is that life is worth while without one." A major problem with art is that society, which tolerates the artist without appreciating him, cannot perceive the same magical qualities as does Connolly. The capitalist sees not beauty but an object to be possessed. Culture as a whole is "precarious, like a match lit in the surrounding darkness that everyone is trying to blow out." It is difficult for any form of culture to win a place in a society motivated entirely by "money, sex, and social climbing."

Literature possesses the same spirituality as art: The memory of

> giants like Henry James and Flaubert, or Baudelaire and Mallarmé, [must be] always before us, even if we never read them, for they are the saints of modern bourgeois art, whose virtues—sensibility, intellectual courage, renunciation, and consecrated devotion—emanate even from the mere storing of their books in our rooms. They are sacred relics which we need not too often disturb.

Connolly, however, does not easily bestow sainthood upon supposed literary giants. Marcel Proust and James Joyce, for example, are writers of enormous talent "crippled" by "elephantiasis of the ego." Joyce failed to achieve greatness because he concerned himself with the mediocre lives of mediocre men: "He fed his queen bee of a mind with inferior jelly." Oscar Wilde failed because he preferred to talk about art rather than produce it, having the gifts of a great writer but not the conscience of one. The writers Connolly truly loves elicit not only his praise but also some of his most evocative writing, as with Laurence Sterne's *Tristram Shandy* (1759-1767): "Slow though the action moves, he will always keep his balance and soon there will follow a perfect flow of words that may end with a phrase that rings like a pebble on a frozen pond."

Regardless of the subject, Connolly's love-hate relationship with England seems always to be on his mind. He loves the "superb wretchedness of English food": "What a subtle glow of nationality one feels in ordering a dish that one knows will be bad and being able to eat it!" The young Connolly writes in 1929 that "England is a problem: parts of it so beautiful, a few people in it so intelligent, yet never can I manage to fit in." He continues to feel an outsider in his native land because of the "smug hostility" of the English to all forms of art. He wishes that "our philistinism (which also expresses the English lack of imagination and fear of life)" could be made a criminal offense. Still, he occasionally feels an unexpected rush of affection for his country, "just as we may suddenly prepare to forgive someone who has deceived us before the memory of their infidelities swarms in on us again."

Connolly has similarly mixed feelings about his work. He calls reviewing "the white man's grave of journalism": "The work is grueling, unhealthy, and ill-paid, and for each scant clearing made wearily among the springing vegetation the jungle overnight encroaches twice as far." The reviewer "may simply wear out in praising or abusing—(it matters not which)—the never-ceasing flow of second-rate and worthy productions—but eventually the jungle claims him." He considers the artist to be striving for greatness, art to be eternal, while the critic's work is, in Connolly's bitter self-estimation, ephemeral. The work of the critic who takes his task seriously, however, who attempts to elucidate entertainingly, can be more lasting. When Connolly is at his best, as he is in "Writers & Society, 1940-3" and "Beyond Believing," he is more than simply a critic; he is a witty, impassioned witness to the best and worst Western culture offers. As long as this culture exists, Connolly will not be claimed by the jungle.

Michael Adams

Sources for Further Study

Christian Science Monitor. LXXVI, March 2, 1984, p. B2.
Library Journal. CIX, January, 1984, p. 91.
Los Angeles Times Book Review. February 15, 1984, p. 3.

The Nation. CCXXXVIII, April 21, 1984, p. 484.
The New York Review of Books. XXXI, March 15, 1984, p. 6.
The New York Times Book Review. LXXXIX, February 19, 1984, p. 3.
The New Yorker. LX, September 3, 1984, p. 92.
Newsweek. CIII, March 19, 1984, p. 93.
Publishers Weekly. CCXXIV, December 9, 1983, p. 46.
The Wall Street Journal. CCIII, March 12, 1984, p. 26.

SELECTED ESSAYS OF JOHN CROWE RANSOM

Author: John Crowe Ransom (1888-1974)
Edited, with an introduction, by Thomas Daniel Young and John Hindle
Publisher: Louisiana State University Press (Baton Rouge). 354 pp. $30.00
Type of work: Essays

John Crowe Ransom's essays demonstrate his adherence to the New Criticism and reveal his efforts to develop a theory of criticism, philosophically based, for the movement he championed

John Crowe Ransom, poet, teacher, and literary critic, became known as the father of the New Criticism. The primary formative influences upon his attitudes and thought appear to have been his Southern background and his education at Oxford University as a Rhodes Scholar studying classics of philosophy and literature. His career spanned sixty years, first at Vanderbilt University, where he had been an undergraduate, and later at Kenyon College, where he edited the *Kenyon Review*. Thomas Daniel Young and John Hindle have selected twenty-four pieces, including addresses, articles, and chapters from books, to represent Ransom's critical thought; they have also added portions of a letter as an appendix and have provided an introduction. Presented chronologically and ranging over a period of thirty-five years, the selections reveal Ransom's development as a critic and thinker and illuminate the changes in his opinions. Among the subjects treated in the collection are social criticism, theory of criticism, analyses of particular poems or passages, and evaluations of individual poets.

In reading through Ransom's work, one is struck by a mental cast resembling that of two important predecessors in both poetry and literary criticism, John Dryden and Matthew Arnold, whom he sometimes echoes. Like them, he thinks largely in polarities or dichotomies, expressed in opposing terms which are encountered in abundance: art-science, classic-Romantic, poetry-prose, texture-structure, intension-extension, tenor-vehicle, ego-id. Even some of his essay titles—"Forms and Citizens," "Honey and Gall," "New Poets and Old Muses"—reflect his penchant for dichotomies. Closely allied to this inclination is a generous use of analogies: the poem to the human body, to music, or to architecture. A critic who uses this approach to analysis sharply delineates his basic terms, creating powerful and clear differences between them, and he is able to organize ideas and value judgments around a simple framework, but a major weakness arises when the writer is tempted to oversimplify one of the juxtaposed terms, as Ransom does, for example, with *science*, which he defines as "the mind devoting itself exclusively to the attainment of a practical purpose." A further weakness may be a degree of instability in the structures, leading those who think in dichotomies to change their views, as Ransom did about his social and literary criticism and, more frequently, his evaluations of other poets.

A second prominent feature of his thought is the pervasive influence of philosophy from many sources. At Oxford, where he studied under F. H. Bradley, Ransom was steeped in the philosophy of Immanuel Kant and his followers, especially Arthur Schopenhauer and Georg Wilhelm Friedrich Hegel. Their influence is apparent in his quest for philosophical bases for aesthetic judgments. Ransom accepts as basic the Kantian distinction between the interior moral life and the external world of objects, of those things-in-themselves which cannot be fully understood, and like the philosopher, Ransom frequently chooses to create his own terms, although they are not so esoteric as those found in philosophical treatises. In these and in numerous other ways, the reader is reminded that the aesthetic ideas of Ransom emerge from and are weighed against a philosophical background.

Although the selections include little of Ransom's social and economic criticism, the portion that is there reveals something significant about his thought—his inclination to abandon previously held views. He belonged to a group centered in Nashville, Tennessee, known as the Southern Agrarians, who flourished in the 1920's and 1930's. They held the view that man lived the best life in harmony with nature in a rural agrarian setting that provided economic self-sufficiency and promoted the extension of aesthetic values to work as well as leisure. Their ideas are outlined in *I'll Take My Stand: The South and the Agrarian Tradition* (1930), the opening chapter of which, "Reconstructed but Unregenerate," was Ransom's contribution. In "The Aesthetic of Regionalism," included by Young and Hindle among their selections, Ransom applies similar values and insights to the Pueblo Indians of New Mexico, praising their culture for its economic success despite a harsh environment and for its aesthetics in the form of rituals. He believed that aesthetic sense emerges naturally in a society once the people have established a harmonious relationship with their surroundings. It is worth noting that Ransom developed his economic and social ideas in a book-length manuscript entitled "Land!," a work he destroyed when it failed to find a publisher, but perhaps by then he had changed his views. In the essay "Art and the Human Economy," he refers to his previously held views as agrarian nostalgia, and he expresses an attitude far different from his earlier one on industrialization: "Without consenting to a division of labor, and hence modern society, we should have not only no effective science, invention, and scholarship, but nothing to speak of in art . . . ." Writing of a plan by the Allies to turn Germany into an agrarian nation following World War II, he concludes that what he had formerly considered a desirable goal for all would constitute a heavy punishment for the German people.

To turn to the literary criticism, by far the greatest concern of Ransom, it might be useful to show his areas of agreement with the major trends in the New Criticism and then to suggest how he differs from other critics of that school. When one thinks of the criticism of Ransom and his intellectual allies—Yvor Winters, R. P. Blackmur, I. A. Richards, Cleanth Brooks, Allen Tate, and Robert Penn Warren—one thinks of emphasis upon the poem as a thing-in-itself, a unique artifact, what Ransom calls "the living integrity of the poem," to be understood and appreciated on its own terms. A fitting approach toward understanding the poem consists of a close reading of the text, with a view toward explicating obscure passages, exploring the symbolic and connotative meanings, and describing the effects of the meter. Because many of the New Critics were practicing poets, they were often well prepared to undertake analysis of this kind. With this emphasis Ransom appears to be in agreement. He gives clear analytic readings of passages from William Shakespeare, Thomas Hardy, John Milton, and William Wordsworth, among others, and systematically attempts to clarify their meanings.

A second general area of agreement occurs with the New Critics' generally negative attitudes toward other kinds of literary analysis. In his essay "Criticism, Inc." Ransom attempts to define the proper role of criticism so as to exclude historical scholarship, the ethical emphasis of the New Humanism, synopsis, paraphrase, emotional response, and studies of language. Instead, he believes, the critic should attempt to clarify those qualities that make poetry different from prose, to explain "what it [poetry] is trying to represent that cannot be represented by prose." His emphasis upon the individual poem suggests that to him the poem itself contains the elements necessary to reveal the meanings. Among other critical movements of his time, Ransom finds none that provides much useful theory to the critic. In "The Literary Criticism of Aristotle," he specifically rejects the Chicago School for its reliance upon the *Poetics*, for in Ransom's view Aristotle placed too much emphasis on logical form and predetermined, though unclear, effects upon the audience. He suggests that the critic's task of understanding the text will not be lightened by reliance upon critical theorists of the past or schools of the present.

While Ransom was in agreement with two major emphases of the New Criticism, he differed from its general tenets through emphases of his own, and these may represent the area of his unique achievement. First, his work reflects, to an unusual degree, an emphasis upon theory. In numerous essays, Ransom calls for the development of a theory of criticism adequate to the tasks that confront a critic; particularly notable is the magnificent essay "Wanted: An Ontological Critic." If "ontology" to Ransom does not mean quite what it means in philosophy—the science of being—it means something very close, probably the science of the poem's being, an approach adequate for clarification of the poem's manifold meanings. Ransom suggests that a critic regard the poem as a conflict between meaning and meter and give the closest attention to indeterminate meaning, that part which takes shape "under metrical compulsion." In other contexts, he emphasizes irony, tropes, schemes, and imagery as appropriate concerns of the critic, yet one is left with the impression that he never perfected a critical theory to his own satisfaction.

In part, this uncertainty was a consequence of Ransom's emphasis upon polarities, inherent in his early definition of a poem as "a *logical structure* having a *local texture*." By "logical structure," he comprehends the meanings of the poem that can be expressed in prose, captured in a paraphrase. By "texture," he appears to mean ornamentation—such elements as diction, meter, figures of speech, schemes of repetition, and imagery. These elements give a poem its integrity and aesthetic uniqueness, and thus they are the critic's major concern. Initially, Ransom paid greater attention to meter than to the other elements, but later he analyzed such elements as ironic understatement and imagery.

The view of the poem as a thing-in-itself held for Ransom a dimension that other New Critics hardly acknowledged, for included in his category of *texture* are *images*, words representing physical objects. New physical objects, as Kant observed, can never be fully understood; one gets only a partial understanding of them at best. By naming them in the poem, the poet creates a dimension that neither he nor his readers can fully comprehend, try as they may. To the ambiguity inherent in an image, the readers add further complexities by bringing their individual associations with the term. Ransom explains, "We think we can lay hold of image and take it captive, but the docile captive is not the real image but only the idea, which is the image with its character beaten out of it." Further, he believes the poet to be consciously aware of the ambiguity surrounding imagery. Thus, even in an epistemological sense, a poem retains something of a mystery, and no critical system capable of exhausting its meanings has yet been devised. Even if a critic manages to account for all of the aesthetic choices that form the poem's structure, meter, and tone, the images will remain elusive.

Having developed the structure-texture dichotomy to some length, Ransom later abandoned it as inadequate, for the dichotomy may conceal or muddle more than it illuminates. It is never clear what belongs in a paraphrase *(structure)* and what belongs to the poem's texture. Images and symbols, for example, clearly may be included in a paraphrase; are they then no longer a part of the texture? Ransom's dichotomy does not adequately distinguish prose from poetry, but it creates an even greater problem where the New Criticism is concerned, for it invites one to view the poem as a loosely connected bipolar structure made up of the rational and the aesthetic. In the view of the New Critics, a poem represents a unified whole, an organic creation, and a major purpose of the critic is to show the poem incorporating diverse elements into a unified whole. Ransom was not inclined to approach analysis in this way, and more often than not his analysis seems intended to test theoretical concepts. Ransom's later position comes nearer to that of his colleagues, a view of poetry highly influenced by Samuel Taylor Coleridge: that a poem is an organism, a unified product incorporating intellectual language, affective language, and rhythmic language. Thus, Ransom's divisions for criticism became three—the intellectual, the imaginative, and the metric.

Ransom, like many other thinkers of a philosophical bent, found it easier to discover the limitations of other theories than to develop a coherent theory of his own. Some of his most subtle thinking was occasioned by critical analysis of positions held by other New Critics; in a long and complex essay in opposition to W. K. Wimsatt, for example, Ransom shows why Hegel's concept of the concrete universal does not work well when applied to poetry. Nevertheless, Ransom's own critical system was not developed beyond generalizations and a few stimulating insights. For years he worked to lay the foundations for a theory of criticism, but, as with his earlier work on social and economic thought, he destroyed his book manuscript when he could not bring his ideas to satisfactory fruition.

If he could not solve the problems involved in understanding a work of art, Ransom at least helped to define them and shed some light upon their complexity. For this, as well as for his insightful evaluations of other poets and for a style that conveys dignity and grace, he holds a secure and respected place among the critics of his time.

Stanley Archer

Sources for Further Study

Booklist. LXXX, February 15, 1984, p. 840.
Choice. XXI, July, 1984, p. 1608.
Christian Century. CI, May 16, 1984, p. 532.
Library Journal. CIX, February 15, 1984, p. 376.
The New Republic. CXC, June 25, 1984, p. 32.
The New York Times Book Review. LXXXIX, May 20, 1984, p. 11.
Publishers Weekly. CCXXV, January 13, 1984, p. 61.

SELECTED POEMS

Author: Octavio Paz (1914-   )
Translated from the Spanish by Eliot Weinberger et al.
Edited by Eliot Weinberger
Publisher: New Directions Publishing Corporation (New York). 147 pp. $14.95
Type of work: Poetry

This selection from Paz's vast body of work is usefully wide-ranging, and the variety of translators keeps any one English voice from "colonizing" the originals

Eliot Weinberger has carefully selected from four previous collections of the poetry of the great Mexican poet Octavio Paz and produced a valuable and manageable introduction to the work of this vital and transcendent writer. Although most of these poems have already appeared under the New Directions imprint, several have been newly translated for this book, and in a small number of cases, Paz's own revisions have been taken into account. Weinberger provides many of the translations, a useful if fulsome introduction, and a few notes at the end. It is especially fortunate that permission has been available to reprint several of the best translations of these poems; among the eleven distinguished poet-translators in this book are Elizabeth Bishop, Paul Blackburn, Denise Levertov, Charles Tomlinson, and William Carlos Williams. Except for rare cases of unusual skill and sympathy, this approach is "fairer" to the originals than collections done entirely by a single translator; if one is unable to be sure when a poet-translator is giving in too much to his own tendencies, one at least has a chance to see these tendencies shift from one sensibility to another.

On May 16, 1984, at the annual ceremonial of the American Academy and Institute of Arts and Letters, Octavio Paz delivered the Blashfield Foundation Address. This brief lecture provides a few useful insights into Paz's understanding of his role as a poet and as a spokesman for Latin American literature and culture. Having noted the remarkable rise of Latin American literature in the last half of the twentieth century, Paz said:

> There is one feature that unites the literatures of the United States, Brazil and Spanish America: the use of a European language transplanted to the American continent. This fact has marked the literatures of America in a deeper and more radical way than any economic structure or any changes in technology and politics. . . . [There emerged,] as the critic Philip Rahv put it: two breeds of writers, the "palefaces" and the "redskins," the Henry Jameses and the Walt Whitmans. In Spanish-speaking America these two attitudes are represented by a tradition that stretches, on one side, from Sarmiento to Vallejo, and on the other, from Darío to Reyes and Borges.

With the quickness of wit and vision that characterize his poetry, Paz went on to reveal the artificial side of this classification and to turn a phrase or two suggestive of his own way of doing things: "Our great authors have been, at the same time, cosmopolitan and American, with their feet on the earth and their heads among the clouds. Or the other way around: some have practiced upward flight and others downward, some have been miners of the heights while others have soared the depths."

Selected Poems suggests the poet's slow but steady progress toward such an all-encompassing vision; the first third of the book consists of small selections from each of seven books that appeared originally between 1944 and 1961; with the exception of the major "Sun Stone" and poems from *Eagle or Sun?* (1951), these generally have the flat prosiness which characterizes translations of poetry that are both surrealistic and openly philosophical. Even in *Eagle or Sun?* one finds occasional examples of this problem, as in this passage from the prose "Toward the Poem":

> *Words, phrases, syllables, stars that turn around a fixed center. Two bodies, many beings that meet in a word. The paper is covered with indelible letters that no one spoke, that no one dictated, that have fallen there and ignite and burn and go out. This is how poetry exists, how love exists. And if I don't exist, you do.*

It is important to emphasize that much of the trouble here arises from the translator's impossible task; he (Weinberger, in this instance) has conveyed what can be paraphrased, but not such musical qualities as may make these statements more pervasive in the original. The reader is given too much freedom to doubt what is being said, because the ingredients which make the passage compelling have been strained out.

On the other hand, with the remaining prose passages from *Eagle or Sun?*, whether excerpts from a long sequence of paragraphs entitled "The Poet's Works" or self-contained items for which the unfortunate term "prose poem" may suffice, both Paz and Weinberger have been much more successful. Most of these pieces belong to the tradition of prose poetry as exemplified by Charles Baudelaire: The language is dense with "poetic effects," but what truly carries the reader along is the narrative force of brief, dreamlike visions that often burst into surrealism or at times even begin with it.

The four passages from "The Poet's Works" are wittily various in their treatment of usual poetic obsessions, from the Word that will say it all to the frustration of needing a fresh pack of cigarettes. By giving in to quite plausible bursts of near silliness, Paz undercuts the portentousness that usually afflicts this kind of writing:

> It hovers, creeps in, comes close, withdraws, turns on tiptoe and, if I reach out my hand, disappears: a Word. I can only make out its proud crest: Cri. Cricket, Cripple, Crime, Crimea, Critic, Crisis, Criterion? A canoe sails from my forehead carrying a man armed with a spear.

"Sun Stone" is, in every sense, the largest poem of the first third of Paz's career. Readers are fortunate that Muriel Rukeyser's translation is able to sustain itself. As Paz explains in an endnote, the poem takes its structure and theme from the Aztec calendar, which measured a period from one conjunction of Venus and the sun to the next—a period of 584 days. The poem is composed of 584 lines of eleven syllables each—though it must be noted that Rukeyser has wisely allowed herself to range between ten and twelve syllables per line.

The poem alternates between recollection and meditation on the nature of time and its susceptibility to the power of love. Put thus baldly, the subject sounds pedestrian, but as in many major poems, the abstract content is not among the forces that make it go. Rukeyser has been able to maintain control over the poem's headlong sentence structure: There is an almost total absence of periods, the clauses tumbling one after the other in a breathless recitation of scenes, names, recollected moments, and pronouncements on the passage and meaning of time. For example, following a catalog of laws, customs, and their enforcers—"the mad and decaying masks/ that are used to separate us"—there comes a moment of vision and philosophizing:

> they are thrown down
> for an enormous instant and we see darkly
> our own lost unity, how vulnerable it is
> to be women and men, the glory it is to be man
> and share our bread and share our sun and our death,
> the dark forgotten marvel of being alive. . . .

This way of confronting directly the abstract qualities of a thought or an experience does not translate very well into interesting poetry, at least as contemporary taste defines it. Too often, such translation sounds like the work of a poet going mostly on willpower, forcing the significance into his work with something like a bicycle pump. Such passages, however, are rare in "Sun Stone"; more commonly, the abstract nouns such as "being," "life," and "death" find contexts that do not deflate so readily. The result is a powerful exploration of the human need to dream of transcending time and of the equally important need to recognize that such transcendence can only be imagined.

The next several years of Paz's career, from 1957 to 1966, are represented in this book by twenty-seven poems taken from four collections. The tendency toward direct statement is still there, but the variety of starting points is notable; during this period, for example, appear several poems based on the mythology and theology of India, where Paz was for a time Mexico's ambassador.

In 1966 appeared "Blanco," perhaps the culmination of Paz's attempts to synthesize Aztec and Tantric backgrounds, as well as those symbolist and surrealist techniques and ways of seeing which Paz owes to the French. "Blanco" means, primarily, "white," but it also conveys, as Paz tells the reader in an introductory note, "blank; an unmarked space; emptiness, void; the white mark in the center of a target." The note continues to explain the poem's slightly unusual typographical arrangement; in its original edition, it appears to have been printed on a single page that unfolded vertically, like the fanfolded paper fed into computer printers (a simile which was not readily available in 1966). It was, then, partly a Tantric scroll, partly an Aztec screen, as Weinberger tells the reader in his introduction. The poem is further set off into sections which begin at one of three left margins. The reader is told that he may read the poem straight through or as a set of individual poems, depending on the order in which he reads the sections on the left, in the center, or on the right. Weinberger adds that this fragmentary way of approaching the poem "owes much to Mallarmé and to Pound's ideogrammatic method. . . ." The procession of images and lines is supposed to provide a series of discrete experiences and an overall experience of the poem as a whole. Clearly, to carry off something as cerebrally designed as this, yet as disjunctive in its texture, requires magisterial control, almost impossible to judge in translation. Weinberger has struggled valiantly with the challenge of producing English lines which can connect either with the line to the right or with the line below, and Paz has made the syntax of the poem open enough to allow this to happen most of the time. It may be argued that if the syntax is loose enough, mere proximity will not necessarily cause one phrase to connect with another, but in this poem, the central idea of passion's power to dissolve seemingly hard boundaries is enough to carry the associations. "Blanco," in the present English version is arresting and provocative.

This attention to large "masterpieces" is not meant to suggest that the small poem, even the "slight" poem, is beneath Paz's notice. Even in this tight selection from a large body of work, there are many very short poems, such as the early epigrammatic poems mentioned at the beginning of this review and which appear throughout to the end of the book, by which time several of these have that earned good luck that comes of long practice.

In 1974, Paz published "Pasado en claro," here translated as "A Draft of Shadows." Weinberger explains that this is a way of leaning toward some of the original title's ambiguities; it denotes "clean copy," as that phrase is used of manuscripts, but "pasado" (past, passed) and "claro" (clear, bright) have considerable resonance. Taking his epigraph from William Wordsworth's *The Prelude* (1850), Paz follows what he hears toward some conclusion about what the words are and where they come from: "I drift away from myself,/ following this meandering phrase,/ this path of rocks and goats."

Through recollection of childhood and adolescence ("land of clouds"), and through speculation on the "swarm of signs" everywhere evident to him who can see them, "A Draft of Shadows" becomes a moving testament of the poet's desire to pursue the attractive phantoms that may lead to the right words. It is a chancy business, as most writers know:

I am where I was:
I walk behind the murmur,
footsteps within me, heard with my eyes,
the murmur is in the mind, I am my footsteps,
I hear the voices that I think,
the voices that think me as I think them.
I am the shadow my words cast.

Work such as this is ambitious in a way that has become unfashionable in the United States; many American poets revel in the hopelessness of doing much of anything beyond reporting, however elegantly, on specific small emotions and experiences.

There are passages in this collection which will confirm these poets in their idea that poetry is not the place for some kinds of utterance, but at other times, the difficulty of what Paz is attempting is so striking that it almost ceases to matter whether he succeeds. It is a matter for gratitude that he succeeds most of the time, and that some of the time he has been able to take his translators with him.

Henry Taylor

Sources for Further Study

Booklist. LXXX, July, 1984, p. 1512.
Library Journal. CIX, May 15, 1984, p. 984.
The New York Times Book Review. LXXXIX, August 19, 1984, p. 13.

SEMIOTICS AND THE PHILOSOPHY OF LANGUAGE

Author: Umberto Eco (1932-   )
Publisher: Indiana University Press (Bloomington). Illustrated. 242 pp. $25.00
Type of work: Philosophy and literary theory

An erudite but lively theoretical and historical discussion of semiotics in relation to the philosophy of language

At the Second Congress of the IASS, an international meeting of semioticians held in Vienna in 1979, author Umberto Eco called for a reexamination of the history of philosophy and linguistics to chart the origins of semiotic concepts. Semiotics is the study of signs, but interpreted broadly, signs are everything that signifies, ranging from language to patterns of etiquette to traffic signals. Eco's *Semiotics and the Philosophy of Language* represents his own response to that call: This work is a historical reexamination of general semiotics, understood to be one of a number of possible philosophies of language. Fans of *The Name of the Rose* (1983), Eco's brilliantly written and surprisingly popular detective story set in the Middle Ages, will not necessarily find this work appealing, but its appeal is not limited to semioticians, philosophers of language, and theoretical linguists; in particular, readers interested in literary theory will find much of value in this demanding volume.

Defining general semiotics as "a philosophy of language which stresses the comparative and systematic approach to languages (and not only to verbal language) by exploiting the result of different, more local inquiries," Eco is taking the controversial position that general semiotics is not a science. In contrast, specific semiotics, Eco argues, is a science that attempts to provide the grammar of a particular sign system: traffic signals or the phonemic features of spoken language. Because it is scientific, specific semiotics will not only provide an objective description of phenomena but will also exercise a predictive power. General semiotics, like philosophies of language, enables one to organize experience into a coherent form. This means of organizing and explaining experience can change the course of events, but it cannot predict them, because the very pattern of coherence posited transforms the object examined.

Chapter 2, "Dictionary vs. Encyclopedia," is the only one of the seven chapters that has not previously appeared in print in an earlier version. This chapter is particularly worth reading with care because of its combination of historical insight and semantic exactness. In his comparative discussion of the interpretive efficacy of the dictionary and of the encyclopedia, Eco makes use of two classical images: the tree and the labyrinth. Of these two images, Eco regards the concept of the labyrinth as the more appropriate for representing human culture or the world of semiosis. The labyrinth conceptually allows the interpreter to take into account an infinite and indefinite network of "interpretants"; because it resists the either/or approach of searching out what is definite and true, the labyrinth takes account of literary truths and beliefs about truth. Moreover, the conceptual approach of the labyrinth resists ideological bias by refusing to posit that its system is "global," "unique," and "complete." The dictionary, based upon the construct of the Porphyrian tree, can, Eco concludes, be useful as a tool, but only if one recognizes that the semantic universe is a labyrinth of encyclopedic meanings.

In chapter 4, "Symbol," Eco offers a surprisingly superficial account of the symbolic interpretation of the Holy Scriptures during the Middle Ages. Regarding the relationship between the Old and New Testaments, he says that Origen decided that the two Testaments should be read as parallel texts in which the Old Testament was the "signifier" or "letter" while the New Testament was the "signified" or the "spirit." This system of reading the two Testaments as parallel texts is called typological. Typology developed during the Middle Ages, and it remained important throughout the Renaissance because of the parallel reading of the two Testaments, both of which were supposed to be divinely inspired. Typology came to be recognized as a mode of signification in which both the type—that is, the Old Testament signifier—and its antitype—the New Testament fulfillment of the Old Testament foreshadowing—were historically real events or entities. Allegory, on the other hand, involved the invention of fictions or symbols to represent an underlying truth or reality. Origen, whom Eco rightly cites as an important influence on symbolic interpretation of the Scriptures, states in his *De principatibus*, that "anyone who reads the stories with a free mind, who wants to keep himself from being deceived by them, will decide what he will accept [as the literal truth] and what he will interpret allegorically, searching out the meaning of the authors who wrote such fictions." Allegorical interpretation allows for a flexibility and freedom on the part of the interpreter that typology resists. The differing philosophical and psychological perspectives of typology and allegory and their very different attitudes toward the text amount to differing systems of interpretation. While the distinctions were indeed blurred in medieval hermeneutic practice, the specific psychological attitudes toward the texts are important if one is to understand clearly the history of medieval exegesis.

George Puttenham, the author of a sixteenth century English treatise entitled *The Arte of English Poesie* (1589), identifies two kinds of allegory: full allegory and mixed allegory. Mixed allegory occurs when the author tells the reader how to interpret his fiction, while in full allegory the meaning is obscure. In short, there is evidence that modern conceptions of allegory and symbolism are not in accord with those which prevailed in the Middle Ages and the Renaissance. Edmund Spenser, the author of the sixteenth century English epic *The Faerie Queene* (1590, 1596), also comments about allegory in his letter to Sir Walter Raleigh: "To some, I know, this Methode will seeme displeasaunt, which had rather have good discipline delivered plainly in way of precepts, or sermoned at large, as they use, then thus clowdily enwrapped in Allegoricall devises." Spenser thinks of allegory in terms of fictional devices, rather than in terms of the precepts which can be deduced from the encyclopedic or cultural frame.

Eco, like most contemporary critics and scholars, shares a post-Romantic aesthetic bias that symbolism is more interesting and more complex than allegory. He explains the symbol as a "semiotic machine" which signifies to the reader that it has something to say but something that cannot be spelled out—because then the symbol would cease to say it. This conception of the symbol as resisting paraphrase or translation resembles that of Eliseo Vivas, who describes the "constitutive symbol" in precisely these terms, except that Vivas acknowledges that the textual context does afford a code for interpretation. Eco insists that the symbol brings the reader face to face with the uncoded.

In chapter 5, Eco discusses the notion of "code," an important term in the work of such twentieth century scholars as Roman Jakobson, Morris Halle, Claude Lévi-Strauss, and Roland Barthes, which is extremely illuminating. Eco observes that "codes were introduced to put events under the control of structures," but when linguists and sociologists perceived that the code might produce and create society and individuals, that the code might not be the product but the shaper of human culture, then it became unmanageable. Eco, however, believes that it is possible to conceive of the code or the encyclopedia as an open matrix, a labyrinth which may be culturally produced, but which may also be described. This view should not be misinterpreted as a rejection of logical models or systems of coherence; the rules are very important to Eco.

Identifying himself as a follower of Charles S. Peirce and crediting Peirce with outlining the discipline of semiotics, Eco regards semiotics as an analysis of the relationships of systems of signs, ranging from language to writing to symbolic rites to military signals. His own philosophical and historical approach to this analysis is also a response to certain questions which Eco believes general semiotics must confront: First, is it viable to approach many ostensibly different kinds of phenomena as though they were all part of systems of signification or communication? Next, is there a unified approach to explaining these different semiotic phenomena which suggests that they can be understood by the same system of rules? Finally, are the approaches of the semiotician scientific?

Each of these questions is examined and then reexamined from a different perspective in Eco's *Semiotics and the Philosophy of Language*. That Eco ranges widely in the types of examples he introduces as a means of stating problems or illustrating theoretical observations demonstrates that he does believe semiotics can approach many different phenomena as systems of sig-nification. He examines social codes (chivalry and etiquette) and scientific disciplines (astronomy and biology), as well as linguistics, literary texts, and film, the more traditional materials of the semiotician.

In response to the problem of a unified approach to account for different kinds of semiotic phenomena, Eco offers the model of the labyrinth, a con-struct which gives coherence to the encyclopedia of one's cultural context. In arguing for the labyrinth over the Porphyrian tree, the encyclopedia over the dictionary, Eco astutely refuses to reject the earlier models: They are useful as long as they are not perceived as stable and universal; they can exist within the open matrix that he posits.

It is in his introduction that Eco most explicitly responds to the question of whether the approach of the semiotician is scientific; this issue and its im-plications for explaining human culture become the organizing frame for *Semiotics and the Philosophy of Language*. Like Ernst Cassirer, in *The Philosophy of Symbolic Forms* (1923-1929), Eco is examining the coherent principles which enables one through comparison and contrast to describe the basic forms, or systems of signs, in one's culture. Cassirer, however, in *An Essay on Man* (1944), arrived at the conclusion that mathematics, the tightest and most potentially closed of systems, is the highest form of sym-bolizing. It may be that Cassirer's desire for a complete system with predict-able coherence led him to affirm this kind of hierarchy.

While acknowledging that aspects of specific semiotics are scientific and that some of the problems posed today by general semiotics may have sci-entific answers, Eco insists upon regarding the inquiry into language and human culture as philosophical rather than scientific. This insistence informs his discussion of the dictionary and the encyclopedia, the tree and the laby-rinth. *Semiotics and the Philosophy of Language* is not intended to provide a final answer to the problem of whether language and culture should be approached as science or as philosophy; Eco's chapters on code and isotopy conclude with "provisional conclusions." His work, however, belongs to the tradition of rigorous and humanistic inquiry.

Jeanie R. Brink

Sources for Further Study

Choice. XXI, June, 1984, p. 1479.
The New York Times Book Review. LXXXIX, May 13, 1984, p. 17.

THE SEPARATE NOTEBOOKS

Author: Czesław Miłosz (1911-   )
Translated from the Polish by Robert Hass and Robert Pinsky with the author and
    Renata Gorczynski
Publisher: The Ecco Press (New York). 212 pp. $17.50
Type of work: Poetry

*A bilingual selection of poems by the 1980 Nobel Prize-winner, including work
from earlier decades as well as recent poems*

The poetic work of Czesław Miłosz, the 1980 Nobel Prize laureate and arguably the greatest living Polish poet, has been made more or less accessible to English-speaking readers over the past decade thanks to the assiduity of numerous, mostly American, translators, including the author himself— Miłosz, a resident of the United States since 1961, often shares in his translators' labors. *The Separate Notebooks*, his third American collection following *Selected Poems* (1973) and *Bells in Winter* (1978), is the fruit of just such a collective endeavor, with two prominent American poets, Robert Hass and Robert Pinsky, acting as translators in close collaboration with the Polish-American critic Renata Gorczynski and Miłosz himself. The results of this concerted effort are impressive; the translations sound stylistically fluent and unconstrained, while being, at the same time, semantically exact and faithful to many of the poems' original characteristics. Unlike the previous two collections, this is a bilingual edition, which offers the Polish-speaking reader the special pleasure of observing how ingeniously the originals' difficulties have been overcome by the translating team.

One misfortune the Nobel Prize for Literature holds for its recipients is that the laureate, subjected to public scrutiny and faced with exorbitant expectations, more often than not finds it impossible to continue his work. This rule certainly does not apply to Miłosz, who has not allowed his poetic development to be disturbed by trivial accidents like this or that literary prize; on the contrary, the line of his artistic growth has risen steadily in the five years following his Nobel Prize. *The Separate Notebooks*, however, provides proof not only of Miłosz's most recent achievements but also of the consistency of his lifelong evolution. As were the two previous collections, this is actually a cross section of the poet's entire output, from the earliest phase of his career, represented here by poems of the 1930's, such as "The Song" or "Slow River," to the World War II period, among others, the famous poem "Campo dei Fiori" and the extensive lyrical sequence "The World (A Naive Poem)," to the postwar years. Within the latter phase, Miłosz's work from the late 1970's and early 1980's is illustrated, first of all, by his long poem, or rather collage, composed of poetic and prosaic fragments, which has lent its title to the entire collection.

Miłosz has often been described as a poet formed, first and foremost, by the experience of twentieth century history—by the catastrophic mood of the 1930's, World War II, which he spent in Nazi-occupied Warsaw, and the observation of Communism at work in postwar Eastern Europe. This is certainly, if only partly, true; in particular, the powerful poem "Campo dei Fiori," which speaks of the extermination of the Warsaw Ghetto and "the loneliness of the dying" when faced with the indifference of the external world, gives credence to the view that Miłosz's ethical system was built on the foundation of his historical experience. There is, however, another perspective from which Miłosz's poetry must be viewed simultaneously. It is highly significant that during the war years he wrote not only poems such as "Campo dei Fiori" but also "The World," a poem of a completely different type, deliberately ahistorical. The poem is an attempt to reconstruct the metaphysical basis of the world's Being as seen through the eyes of a child; the war is absent here or rather present only insofar as it provides the unspoken reason for why the world's foundations must be raised anew. These two poems' proximity in time—both "Campo dei Fiori" and "The World," were written in 1943—offers an important clue to Miłosz's poetry. In fact, what is most characteristic in him is exactly this peculiar fusion of two perspectives—the poet has always viewed human existence in both its historical and metaphysical dimensions. Miłosz's skill in blending these two dimensions culminates in his most recent work, of which the long poem mentioned earlier, "The Separate Notebooks," is a prime example; the autobiographical content serves here to demonstrate how an individual life can be molded by the course of History while still being subject to unchangeable laws of Existence.

Miłosz's own system of metaphysics and ethics is an extremely complex one, and it cannot be elucidated by referring to his poetry alone; an indispensable key is provided by his essayistic writings, first of all by his recently published book *The Land of Ulro* (1984; reviewed in this volume). To put it simply, one might say that the bottom line of his poetic philosophy is the dissonance or antinomy created by the clash of two contrary convictions. On the one hand, his poetry is an ecstatic hymn to the beauty of objectively existing things, of everything that *is* (see, in particular, the poem "Esse"); this, incidentally, has tremendous consequences for Miłosz's concept of poetic language, which strives for utter concreteness in naming things and reflects, by means of stylistic polyphony, the bewildering richness of various "voices" with which the world speaks. On the other hand, this ecstatic admiration comes into conflict with Miłosz's sober awareness that reality is marked by the constant presence of evil. In that, he is clearly a Manichaean: Evil is for him the ineffaceable shadow of all that exists, including, perhaps above all, the poet's own ego. Hence the unique tension produced in Miłosz's poetry by the contrast between his ever-present fascination with the world's beauty and the equally ubiquitous tone of dissatisfaction, disappointment, or even bitterness. It is the dissatisfaction of the speaker with himself; looking back at his own past (as in the poem "Account"), he perceives it as "the history of my stupidity," an irritating accumulation of errors, violations of his own conscience, and manifestations of his shortcomings and weaknesses. Evil, however, can be "my own and not my own"; it is not only the responsibility of the individual but is also an inseparable constituent of what Miłosz (in "The Separate Notebooks") calls "the truth of the earth." In his constant Manichaeanism, the poet is indeed very far from the Romantic myth of Nature's innocence; for him, Nature is by no means a quiet and serene retreat—on the contrary, it is marked by violence, brutality, and innate injustice.

Nature, however, although no less evil and sinful than Man, is at least stable and self-assured, devoid of any uncertainty or doubt. Compared to this, the human being stands as a solitary example of ceaseless self-torment. He is constantly compelled to question not only the moral justness of his actions but also, so to speak, the very necessity of his existence. One needs only to see oneself against the background of the stable, solid Being of the outer world to ask the basic question, To what extent is my own existence necessary at all, since without it the world would exist anyway? This question leads naturally to another: Since my existence is a fact, why is it that I exist in this particular form, enclosed in this particular body and life? Why am I myself and what does it actually mean "to be oneself"? Miłosz asks these questions with increasing frequency as his work progresses, and it is no accident that in his latest phase—witness poems such as "City Without a Name" or "The Separate Notebooks"—the issue of his own identity plays such a dominant role. First, it is consistent with a perspective he has often assumed—that of looking back at his own life's experience. Second, the question of the ratio between chance and necessity in one's own identity is absolutely crucial, because on it depends one's idea of the meaning of existence. If one imagines blind chance as the prevailing element, only a short step remains to nihilism and despair. Miłosz apparently seems to favor such a vision of human predicament; whatever he says about Man in the contexts of both Nature and History points toward the conclusion that an individual existence is not rationally justified and that human nature is inevitably branded by evil. There is, though, a recurrent "however" in Miłosz's work, a "however" that could be compared with Blaise Pascal's famous "Wager." Miłosz seems to be saying, yes, one's existence on earth is erratic, sinful, and senseless; *however*, there are individual acts that defy this senselessness. Just as Christ assumed human form in order to suffer with human beings, Man is able—through acts of sacrifice—to overstep the boundaries of human existence and imbue it with some kind of divine sense. Such is the meaning of Miłosz's invoking specific—supposedly actual—persons in his poems (for example, in "The Separate Notebooks," the painter Mieczysław, who during the Nazi occupation "used his workshop to help people/ and hid Jews there, for which the penalty was death"). Such is also the meaning of the poem "Incantation," which is ostensibly an unconstrained hymn in praise of the triumphs of human reason—and only the title indicates that the poem is not an assertive statement but rather a magical invocation of things as they should be, despite all odds and all of man's experience.

Miłosz's unique stature among contemporary poets lies not only in the fact that he copes with metaphysical dilemmas in a rather antimetaphysical age. Even more important, he has proven able to transfer philosophical problematics into the domain of private, personal, and autobiographical experiences and reflections. Or perhaps the reverse is true; he has been able to elevate the autobiographical material to the rank of a universal vision of human existence. While speaking of all-embracing problems of human nature, he never loses sight of the individual's entanglement in various contexts at once—in his bodily form, in surrounding space, in historical time, in society, in the world of Nature. Miłosz's lyric hero exists simultaneously in all of these conflicting dimensions, and he is perfectly aware of their mutual incompatibility. As a consequence, Miłosz's is a poetry that offers no ready solutions, no comforting utopias. "Sensing affliction every minute, in my flesh, by my touch, I tame it and do not ask God to avert it, for why should He avert it from me if He does not avert it from others?" says the author in the poem "A Poetic State." This is a significant statement that leads in many directions at once. It implies the conviction that affliction is an unavoidable companion of human existence. It asserts that trying to avert affliction is somewhat immoral, since it involves demanding special rights for oneself. It also states, however, that it is possible to "tame" affliction, if not avert it. One means of "taming affliction" is through poetry—through giving the world its true name—and the effort itself is enough to dispel the idea that the world is senseless. The opposition between individual existence and universal Being is thus suspended rather than resolved, but even this suspension gives worth to human fortitude, to the persistent striving that is more real—and therefore more valuable—than the unattainable goal.

Stanisław Barańczak

Sources for Further Study

Choice. XXII, October, 1984, p. 276.
Hudson Review. XXXVII, Autumn, 1984, p. 498.
Los Angeles Times Book Review. September 2, 1984, p. 8.
The Nation. CCXXXIX, December 22, 1984, p. 686.
The New Yorker. LX, March 19, 1984, p. 138.
Times Literary Supplement. July 13, 1984, p. 778.

THE SEVEN MOUNTAINS OF THOMAS MERTON

Author: Michael Mott (1930-   )
Publisher: Houghton Mifflin Company (Boston). Illustrated. 690 pp. $24.95
Type of work: Biography
Time: 1915-1968
Locale: France, England, and the United States

A major biographical study emphasizing Merton's conversion to Catholicism, his complex attitudes toward monastic life, and the development of his literary career.

> *Principal personages:*
> THOMAS MERTON, a Trappist monk, essayist, poet, and social critic
> OWEN MERTON, Merton's father and a landscape painter
> ROBERT GIROUX, a book publisher and close friend of Merton from their days at Columbia University
> JAMES FOX, Abbot of Our Lady of Gethsemani Monastery

Thomas Merton died in Bangkok, Thailand, on December 10, 1968. He accidentally electrocuted himself on a large floor fan that had been faultily wired. Had Merton lived another six weeks, he would have reached his fifty-fourth birthday. Exactly one-half of his life had been spent at the monastery of Our Lady of Gethsemani, a Trappist foundation in rural north-central Kentucky, near Bardstown. As early as 1953, Merton sensed that he needed to live as a hermit, and in 1965 his abbot officially recognized Merton's retirement into complete solitude in a small cinderblock on the grounds of the monastery.

A poet, novelist, and professor of English at Bowling Green State University (Ohio), Michael Mott has produced a meticulous biography, the text of which runs to nearly six hundred pages. Confronted with a volume of this size, the potential reader will want some preliminary justification. How much can one say about a life devoted mainly to godly *silence*? Merton was a remarkably prolific poet, essayist, theologian, and social critic. His writings might then necessitate an *intellectual* biography, but Mott insists that this is not what he has written. Thus questions remain: Can there be a history of a Cistercian cenobite who gradually became an anchorite? If so, can this be anything more than a chronicle of spiritual mood changes and "monastery politics"?

The answer to both questions is yes. If anything, Mott's book is too short. His account of Merton's first twenty-seven years makes up only one-third of the book, and these years are truly fascinating ones. Nevertheless, Mott's strategy here is excusable because this is the very period covered in Merton's famous autobiography *The Seven Storey Mountain* (1948), perhaps the finest spiritual life writing of the twentieth century. The story is so unusual and provocative that even Mott's two-hundred-page effort is not quite enough. By the end of his life, Merton was as close to being the "universal human" as one is ever likely get, and the seeds of this universality were sown early in his life.

Merton's father was a New Zealander and his mother was American. His upbringing took place in France, the United States, Bermuda, and England. To his native bilingualism Merton gradually added competencies in Latin, Italian, German, Spanish, Portuguese, Russian, and Chinese. At Columbia University—where he went after a chaotic sojourn at Cambridge University—most of his friends were Jewish. Reared a Protestant, he went through a long period of religious indifference which even included a flirtation with Marxism. His upper-middle-class standing did not completely protect him from economic realities, for his father's vocation as a landscape painter brought little income. Merton's mother died when he was only six years old, and by age fifteen he was an orphan. He rarely enjoyed long stretches of good health; in 1941, he failed the military-service examination because he had too few teeth. Unlike most undergraduates of his day, he was sexually experienced and may even have fathered an illegitimate child.

Such inherently dramatic settings and tensions furnish rich material for the biographer, but to his great credit Mott manages to make the post-conversion, "hidden life" of Merton no less interesting. For readers unfamiliar with monastic life in general, and Trappist practice in particular, Mott's account of life at Our Lady of Gethsemani provides revelations. Merton chose the Cistercian Order of the Strict Observance over the Benedictines and the Franciscans precisely because the Cistercians seemed to require of him the greatest sacrifice. He was not disappointed.

Committed to silence (except during worship, community business meetings, and certain work situations), Merton had to learn to use Trappist sign language for ordinary social interaction. He was allowed no "Particular Friendships" with other monks, yet he nevertheless lived in the closest proximity with his brothers in Christ. In tiny cells created by curtains, the men slept in their woolen habits on straw-filled pallets. To fulfill the Cistercian demand for penance, each monk kept a small whip, to be used on the bare back every Friday. Mirrors were forbidden. All mail, incoming or outgoing, was read. Eggs, fish, and meat were not served in the refectory. Travel was almost completely ruled out, even to the funeral of a parent. Worship consumed nearly one-third of the monastery day. Because the monastery attempted to support itself through various farming and manufacturing activities, the physical work load was considerable.

Remarkably, Merton still found the time to continue his career as a writer. His autobiography became a huge best-seller in 1948, and the monastery received the royalties. This fact helps explain the latitude Merton was given to do his own work, and since that work was largely an explanation and defense of monasticism and the *vita contemplativa* to an increasingly receptive world, Merton's special position within the order could certainly be justified. Thus, in the succeeding two decades, a tidal wave of writing moved out of Merton's narrow enclosure. More than fifty books and hundreds of articles and essays appeared. Victor A. Kramer usefully places the material into five categories: autobiography, devotional writing, essays, fiction, and poetry. Besides *The Seven Storey Mountain*, the works which stand out in each of these genres are *Conjectures of a Guilty Bystander* (1966), *Seeds of Contemplation* (1949), *Raids on the Unspeakable* (1964), and *Selected Poems of Thomas Merton* (1959).

Michael Mott wisely does not attempt to include lengthy summaries of Merton's major works in the biography. Rather, he discovers the genesis and evolution of the writings, situates them in their historical context, and reviews their central themes. He also shows how vital to Merton's literary vocation were his letters and journals. Mott states that Merton probably began keeping a journal as a teenager at the Oakham School in England. At present, the Merton archives contain an incomplete set of journals from 1939 to 1968. Access to the journals written in the last twelve years of Merton's life has been reserved to the official biographer (until 1993). The renowned Catholic author John Howard Griffin was to have fulfilled that role, but ill health forced him to allow the responsibility to pass to Mott.

As a letter writer, Merton certainly must be ranked with Mahatma Gandhi, Bertrand Russell, or Virginia Woolf. Mott reports that in 1941 Gethsemani monks could only send out and receive mail four times a year; four half-page letters was the limit on each occasion. This regime somehow relaxed itself, for by the time of his hermitage Merton's incoming mail filled a briefcase each day. The enthusiasm engendered by his autobiography brought to him a considerable number of permanant friends-by-correspondence. Letters nurtured the deep friendships he had established at Columbia (with Mark Van Doren and Robert Giroux, among others). Significantly, one of his most important writings on race relations in the United States was the lengthy "Letters to a White Liberal" series.

Thus, journals and letters spawned books and articles, these in turn linking Merton to an ever-widening circle of correspondents. The Word directed Merton to a life on silence and isolation, but in response, his hermit's cell became a veritable telegraph station, sending out words in all directions. D. T. Suzuki, the great explicator of Zen Buddhism, Ernesto Cardenal, the Nicaraguan poet-priest; Aziz Ch. Abdul, the scholar of Sufism; Jacques Maritain, the French Thomist; Boris Pasternak, the Russian novelist—they joined less celebrated persons around the world to carry on extended epistolary dialogues with Merton. A surprising number of Merton's correspondents came to visit Gethsemani. Walker Percy, Daniel Berrigan, John Howard Yoder, A. J. Muste, Joan Baez, and Czesław Miłosz all made the pilgrimage. Martin Luther King, Jr., intended to see Merton after his fated campaign in Memphis, Tennessee.

These contacts provide much material for Mott's chronicle. The book, however, is not an exercise in name-dropping. Mott tells of a wonderfully zany correspondence between Merton and an effervescent California teenager. He also carefully reports on what the journals and letters reveal about Merton's relationship with "S.," a young Louisville nurse with whom he fell in love in 1966. It will certainly astonish many readers to learn that fifty-one-year-old Merton—the very embodiment of the monastic ideal in modern times—came very close to leaving his order and marrying. Furthermore, there was nothing of restrained Thomistic rationalism in the way Mertain managed what can only be called his "affair." Mott writes sensitively of how the relationship sprang from Merton's long struggle to turn himself from an excessively pious and rigid monk "into a vulnerable human being." While Mott regrets the way in which Merton ended the liaison, he understands the lovely transformation it wrought in Merton's life: "He loved greatly and was greatly loved. He was overwhelmed by the experience and it changed him forever."

Writing about Thomas Merton continues to cascade from academic, religious, and secular presses. One may be certain, however, that no new biography of Merton on this scale will be attempted for decades. The thoroughness of Mott's work is dauntingly impressive. The "Notes and Sources" section of the book runs on for almost eighty fine-type pages. Morever, Mott has written with tact (perhaps a bit too much), and grace. That he chose to structure the biography around the seven mountains which figured so importantly in Merton's life is only one evidence of the literary quality of the work. Mott's work will surely not be the last on Merton's life, but it will long be the most important.

The shortcomings of Mott's work derive from a problem that admits of no good solution—the problem of a differentiated audience. Many people know about Thomas Merton, but they do not know of the same things. Some are drawn to the Merton of *The Seven Storey Mountain*, the rake whose progress landed him in a Trappist enclosure. Others fasten on him as a religious poet and devotional writer, a provider of sacred images of the contemplative inner desert. Then there is the social activist Merton, who had a role in the civil rights movement and anti-Vietnam War movements. Finally, Merton reaches out to students of comparative mysticism and Eastern spirituality. Mott attempts to describe all of these facets of Merton, and thus he does speak effectively to the several audiences attracted to Merton.

Still, this is not enough. It is also necessary to try to show how these facets express a single personality or tendency of mind. Too often, Mott's persistent and patient discussions of Merton's literary efforts function as disconnected episodes in the biography. The impression one is tempted to accept is that Merton was very much the dilettante. One learns that Merton simultaneously wrote about social injustice, pacifism and violence, Sufi mysticism, Zen spirituality, and cargo cults. What was the inner logic connecting these preoccupations? With what underlying problem was Merton struggling to come to terms?

Mott's quite magnificent effort is thus partially vitiated by his failure to step back from his subject occasionally and take stock. The biography would have perhaps been less clearly a biography had Mott included more synthesizing and interpretive material. Such an attempt, however, would have gone far to deal with the considerable problem of audience that he faced.

Leslie E. Gerber

Sources for Further Study

America. CLI, August 18, 1984, p. 346.
Book World. XIV, December 16, 1984, p. 1.
Commonweal. CXI, October 19, 1984, p. 560.
Kirkus Reviews. LII, September 15, 1984, p. 900.
Library Journal. CIX, December, 1984, p. 2272.
Los Angeles Times Book Review. December 30, 1984, p. 4.
The New York Times Book Review. LXXXIX, December 23, 1984, p. 1.
Publishers Weekly. CCXXVI, September 28, 1984, p.108.
Saturday Review. X, November, 1984, p. 88.
The Wall Street Journal. CCV, January 15, 1985, p. 32.

SHERWOOD ANDERSON
Selected Letters

Author: Sherwood Anderson (1876-1941)
Edited by Charles E. Modlin
Publisher: University of Tennessee Press (Knoxville). Illustrated. 260 pp. $24.95
Type of work: Letters
Time: 1916-1941

A collection of letters, many published for the first time, reflecting Anderson's personal and professional life from the beginning of his writing career until just before his death

One usually reads the letters of a famous author for two basic reasons: to gain some insight into his thought and art and to get an impression of his personal life, especially in terms of friendships and personal acquaintances. The assumption is that letters, because they are not written for publication, communicate an intimacy and honesty perhaps lacking in the author's other work. Although such indeed may not always be true, since established writers are often well aware that their letters will be collected and eventually published, this new collection of letters by Sherwood Anderson does indeed give at least the illusion of intimacy and straightforwardness.

Sherwood Anderson, however, may be a special case, since it has often been remarked that his writing generally is characterized by sincerity and a personal voice. Indeed, Anderson's *Winesburg, Ohio* (1919) has a lasting place in the history of American short fiction for breaking the mold of cheap tricks and popular devices which characterized the short story in the twentieth century before its publication. Because of its honesty and unaffected style, *Winesburg, Ohio* has had a positive influence on the American short story ever since the book appeared.

This is not the first collection of Anderson letters, nor is it by any means an attempt to be complete. Howard Mumford Jones and Walter B. Rideout edited *Letters of Sherwood Anderson* in 1953, and other letters have been published in various places, most notably letters to Van Wyck Brooks and Gertrude Stein. This does not mean, however, that Charles Modlin has here had to take insignificant "leavings" from an already well-scoured barrel. The Newberry Library owns more than five thousand Anderson letters, so many that the 401 letters published mainly from that collection by Jones and Rideout did not begin to exhaust the source. In addition to selecting letters from the Newberry collection, for which there had been no room in the Jones-Rideout volume, Modlin has also included letters from twenty-three additional libraries and from private collections. The most important of this last group, not made public before, are to Arthur Barton, a New York playwright with whom Anderson collaborated for a staged version of *Winesburg, Ohio*, in which the reader gets a more personal view of Anderson's feeling for the characters in that epoch-making book.

The purpose of this new selection—that is, in addition to making public a group of important letters never before seen in print—is to give a unified view of Anderson's life from the beginning of his career until his death. Thus, there is a certain poignancy in opening the collection with January, 1916, letters from Anderson to Henry Mencken, then editor of a New York magazine, and Theodore Dreiser, an established writer at the time, asking them to read the manuscript of his first novel, *Windy McPherson's Son*, published later that year, and ending it with a letter two months before his death to his old boyhood friend, Herman Hurd of Clyde, Ohio (the real town fictionalized as Winesburg), asking him to check if the Clyde library needs copies of any of his books.

In between these early letters of a mature man of thirty-nine, who struggled to leave the advertising work in Chicago that he hated, and become a writer, and the final letter of a man of sixty-four, asking an old friend if the story were really true that an old-maid librarian in Clyde had once burned his books, one finds a wide spectrum of Anderson insights and observations about American industrialized society, about literature, about his rural life on a farm in Virginia, and, of course, about his own life and work. As to be expected in collections of letters by literary figures, one finds here the usual complement of letters to editors, critics, and other writers. In addition to the letters to Dreiser and Mencken, there are letters to Upton Sinclair, Carl Sandburg, Waldo Frank, Jean Toomer, F. Scott Fitzgerald, Ernest Hemingway, Thomas Wolfe, and Hart Crane.

Perhaps because he received help from older writers when he was beginning, Anderson was particularly encouraging to younger writers such as Toomer, Crane, and Hemingway. For example, he advises Crane in 1919 that his poetry should give something of himself, "the bone and flesh and reality of you as a man," and invites Crane, if he can afford to spend the money, to come to Chicago and see him. He tells Jean Toomer, who was writing *Cane* (1923) at the time, that his work is of special significance to him because it is the first "Negro work I have seen that strikes me as really Negro." In 1924, after reading *Cane*, he urges Toomer not to let the white men get to him, to stay by his own.

There are only a few letters to, or concerning, Ernest Hemingway included here; the more detailed letters Anderson wrote to Lewis Galantière and Gertrude Stein, introducing Hemingway to Paris literary society with glowing words of praise, are included in the Jones-Rideout collection. There is, however, one interesting letter of June, 1926, in which Anderson, obviously hurt by Hemingway's parody of him in *The Torrents of Spring* (1926), responds to that rather brutal and sophomoric joke at the expense of Anderson's *Dark Laughter* (1925). Anderson scolds Hemingway for speaking to him as a master to a pupil and says that he still packs a little wallop: "I've been middleweight champion. You seem to forget that." Anderson tells Hemingway that *The Torrents of Spring* will do more harm to Hemingway than to himself and accuses it of having a "smarty tinge," saying that Fitzgerald and John Dos Passos must have baited him. Finally, even though Anderson was obviously hurt, he invites Hemingway to visit him at Ripshin Farm in Virginia.

One real disadvantage in reading the letters of an author is the fact that one does not have at the same time the letters of the correspondent; for example, if would be instructive to read the letters of Hemingway alongside the letters of Anderson concerning *The Torrents of Spring*. Although Modlin does a good job of providing footnote identification of the various people to whom Anderson wrote, as well as explanations for many of his references, it is still not the same as reading the letters of both correspondents. For example, in a March, 1923, letter to Fitzgerald, Anderson mentions a review Fitzgerald did of Anderson's *Many Marriages* (1923) and asks him if Thomas Boyd, literary editor of the Saint Paul *Daily News*, has told him the story of how he went about saying that Fitzgerald's style bothered him and his characters seemed insignificant. (Fitzgerald, in his review of *Many Marriages*, had written the same things about Anderson in the same words.) If one checks Andrew Turnbull's *The Letters of F. Scott Fitzgerald* (1963), one finds Fitzgerald's reply, in which he says that he has just been asking a woman at *Vanity Fair* to save him an autograph of Anderson if one comes along with his letter. He obviously does not understand Anderson's ironic story, for he says, "I don't quite get you about Tom Boyd—he's a great fellow, incidentally, and a strong admirer of your work."

One finds in this collection many repeated common preoccupations of Anderson concerning both his life and his work. Although he says at one point that he never really wanted to make a lot of money, a common theme in the letters is indeed his lack of it—his regret especially to his children that he could not provide them with the money he would have liked; his gratitude to the wealthy Burton Emmett, a New York advertising executive, for lending him five thousand dollars to buy two small-town newspapers in Virginia and allowing some of his manuscripts to forgive three thousand dollars of that debt; and his occasional whimsical wish that some patron would release him from financial obligations and allow him to write. A related theme is his hatred of the lecture circuit, a task he needed to perform to supplement his income, the funds from which allowed him to buy his much-loved Ripshin Farm.

Anderson also felt quite personally the repeated accusation of critics that after *Winesburg, Ohio* he had died as an author. In 1927, he admits that the Sherwood Anderson of *Winesburg, Ohio* has died, but that he has spent too much time already over the man's funeral. "Well, let him die." He says that he is more concerned with whether another Sherwood Anderson is coming to life. Critical opinion seems fairly agreed that a more significant Anderson never really did come alive—that with the exception of some excellent short stories, particularly in *The Triumph of the Egg* (1921) and *Death in the Woods and Other Stories* (1933), the title stories of which were two of Anderson's personal favorites, Anderson never again achieved artistic success. A predominant theme of the letters is Anderson's absolute need to write, both for his own expression and as a fulfillment of his professional life, and his disappointment at the often unenthusiastic reception of work for which he had such high hopes.

Throughout the letters, one finds Anderson's repeated affirmation of his belief that art requires the best of oneself. He advises aspiring writers not to be "writey," to beware of manufactured smartness, and to realize that fame is not good. He worries about becoming a hack, reminds the critics that he is more conscious of technique than they think he is, and insists that he has tried to write a kind of prose that has a singing quality about it. "I wanted a loose rhythmic prose," he says in a letter to a German friend, with laughter buried down under the words, a prose so simple that only a master would know what "I had buried in it."

The basic impression one receives of Anderson as a man and an artist from this selection is of his wholehearted dedication to his art, his generosity to other authors struggling in their youth as he had in his maturity, his sadness at the "muddle" of his personal life, especially his three unsuccessful marriages, and his genuine puzzlement at his failure, with few exceptions, to recapture the critical and popular successes he achieved with *Winesburg, Ohio*. Frequently, one sees here the sense of loneliness that made possible Anderson's identification with the lonely grotesques of his fiction, and one hears his frustration with his work and his yearning for friendship and intimacy. In one particularly poignant letter in 1931 to Charles Bockler, a young painter whom he had encouraged, Anderson describes a "dead blank place" that he is in again and speaks of the difficulty of trying to sustain a flight of creativity. He confesses how hard it is for him to live with anyone and worries that he has been an egotist who has used the women in his life. He yearns for a man's friendship.

This is indeed a full and rich collection of letters which allows the reader to gain a deeper insight into the life and work of one of the most influential American short-story writers of the twentieth century. Because of their honesty and clarity, the letters are alive with the spirit and vitality of the man and the artist. In a 1930 letter to Burton Emmett, who was collecting his manuscripts, Anderson says that he cannot always remember not to burn his originals. If William Shakespeare were alive and were to write him a dull letter, he says, he would throw it away, but if an utterly unknown farm woman were to send him a letter full of sense and feeling, he would preserve that. "These are my instincts." As these letters prove, they are good instincts. There are no dull letters here, and the reader is truly glad that they were not thrown away.

Charles E. May

Sources for Further Study

Library Journal. CIX, January, 1984, p. 81.
The New York Times Book Review. LXXXIX, April 22, 1984, p. 1.

THE SIREN
A Selection from Dino Buzzati

Author: Dino Buzzati (1906-1972)
Translated from the Italian by Lawrence Venuti
Publisher: North Point Press (Berkeley, California). 160 pp. paperback $10.50
Type of work: Short stories
Time: 1933-1972
Locale: Primarily Northern Italy

In the stories of this collection, Dino Buzzati shows his skill at varying fantastic with realistic settings, as also in moving from pastoral to satire during his observation of Italian life pre- and postwar

Dino Buzzati's writing career was long and prolific. His first work was the novella *Bàrnabo delle montagne* (1933; *Bàrnabo of the Mountains*, 1984), his last, the collection *Le notti difficili* (1971). In between, he produced hundreds of poems, short stories, and plays, while working indefatigably as a journalist and bringing out many essays and travel pieces. How can this diversity be presented within a single volume? This was clearly the main problem for Lawrence Venuti, when he set about producing a successor to his first volume of Buzzati translations, *Restless Nights* (1983). He was guided in solving it, he says in the preface to *The Siren*, by a remark in one of Buzzati's notebooks, to the effect that every writer or artist has "only one thing" to say, only one scene or landscape to paint. Naturally it may not appear so. Beneath superficial diversity, a true, a sincere artist will display deeper unity and integrity. Venuti says that he decided to use this remark as his criterion for selection and accordingly to offer the fourteen pieces in *The Siren* as a study in preoccupations and reverberations. From the long novella which opens the collection, through the twelve short stories that follow (some fantastic, some realistic), and on to the concluding autobiographical travel piece, the reader is asked to draw continually a sense of personality and of coherence.

This proves in fact to be a rewarding task. The opening piece, "Barnabo of the Mountains," appears at first sight to come from an almost vanished world—one of "mountain pastoral," set in the tiny enclosed communities of the Northern Italian forest, where everyone is known by name and reputation, and where life is (or was) not only innocent but also sparse, uncrowded even with objects. When the title character, Barnabo, is forced to leave the forest service, for example, it takes him only a few minutes to pack, and the list of possessions he leaves—some cards, a bandage, an old pistol barrel—is pathetically small. By contrast, several of the later stories are set in the postwar consumer boom of Milan and Turin, where people drive cars, catch planes, break relationships, and accumulate possessions in a way entirely alien to the world of Barnabo. Nevertheless, there are themes to connect both early and late works: "otherness," inhibition, the pursuit of happiness, but above all, time.

The passing of time is the leitmotif of "Barnabo of the Mountains," but Buzzati's attitude to it is a complex one. In a sense, and by modern standards, his characters are hardly aware of it. When Barnabo, disgraced, is forced to leave the foresters and go to work in the plain, he waits for more than four years before trying to make any contact with his former life, even to find out whether the brigands whom he failed to resist have been caught. Nor does he show any sign of impatience; he seems to live in stasis, without aging or changing. On a larger scale, the mountains themselves appear to represent changelessness, opposing to the dynamic forces of modernity and government, and the plain, a kind of stubborn passive resistance. Almost the first thing the reader is told in the novella is the story of how the authorities tried to build a road through the mountains, with contractors and explosives. The project failed, in the face of local opposition and inertia, but the explosives remained; military officers therefore had a powder magazine built and detailed the foresters to guard it, which they then continue to do in a routine that becomes itself unchanging. The very agent of disruption, the gunpowder, thus becomes itself an emblem of stasis, something not to be used, but to be kept, stored, preserved inviolate.

Still, change creeps in. At the start of the novella, the foresters are moving from their old dilapidated quarters, the Casa dei Marden, to a "new house" (it never acquires a name), more conveniently placed. Their leader, Del Colle, though, typically goes back for a last visit to the old house, surprises brigands investigating it, and is shot dead. The rest of the story then becomes, at one level, a search for vengeance, while there is no doubt that Del Colle is dead, that authority within the foresters must shift, and that *some* things can never be the same again. How deep does change go, and how should one react to it? These questions are answered within the novella by the story of Barnabo.

This is easy to summarize, because it is once again less a story of events than of nonevents. Barnabo tries to catch the murderers of Del Colle, driven by dreams of fame and status; not only does he fail, however, when the brigands attack the powder magazine, but he also gives way to fear and fails to join in. Typically, no one notices his cowardice, but his absence from the fight is itself enough to get him dismissed. He leaves the mountains, goes to the plain, but after some years returns to try to regain his old position and his old happiness. He forms a plan, too, to ambush the brigands; and his plan is successful. At the moment that he has them under his gun, he hesitates, decides not to act, and lets them go. The story ends with silence, tranquillity, the unmoving mountains.

For an English-speaking reader, it is hard not to draw the obvious comparison to Joseph Conrad's *Lord Jim* (1900). There, too, a would-be hero failed to spend the rest of his life trying to expiate failure. Conrad's character, however, in the end meets death and reaches at least a kind of heroic status. Buzzati's Barnabo not only repeats his inaction but also escapes its consequences. The reader is meant to think, furthermore, that his inaction the second time is right, that his years of exile have brought him a kind of wisdom which shows itself in forfeiting the urge to "be somebody," even at the expense of others' lives. Barnabo moreover is presented to the reader not merely as a man who has learned reverence for life but also as one who has learned a more evasive truth, about the way time passes.

This is expressed most clearly within the novella by a group of visually precise but morally ambiguous images, all in some way to do with change and permanence. Del Colle, for example, is dead. His men bury him in a mountain cave. As soon as they have done so, one of them climbs an inaccessible spire. Why? To plant on it, driven in with a nail, Del Colle's old beret with the bright feather in it. After that, Del Colle is quickly forgotten, his famous gun is passed on to other hands, his murderers remain uncaught. The beret and the feather remain, summer and winter, as a witness of his existence, though they, too, like his bones, wear, fray, and decompose. There is a sense, however, that the mountaineers as a whole have a power over time, expressed in symbolic gestures, and that they are therefore unaffected by it. When another of them dies in a spot so inaccessible that no one can reach his body, Del Colle and the others are content merely to mark the spot; it is the dead man's father who comes up from the plain and insists on being taken to the body, on having something *done*. It is accordingly he who suffers a sense of failure (for the body still cannot be reached), which is not shared by Del Colle and the others.

Barnabo's sense of failure, over the brigands' raid, associates him with the grieving father; one may extend the parallel to say that when he returns from the plain, puts on his old uniform, returns to the old house, and prepares his plan to reestablish himself, he is once more striving for the inaccessible. Like the bones of Darrio, the past is in a place that no man can reach. It is realizing *that* which makes Barnabo in the end content to leave things as they are. His decision, though, is deepened by a further sense, throughout the story, that leaving things as they are never quite works. Time may appear, in the mountains, to have stopped; but, in fact, change comes in as powerfully as imperceptibly, like dust settling, rust spreading, brightness fading. Perhaps all one can say in the end is that time remains beyond one's control; what can be controlled is human reaction to it, with as a model, a kind of passive, watching, aware acceptance.

The connection with some of Buzzati's later stories is then easy to establish. One of the more fantastic pieces translated in *The Siren* is "The Time Machine." In this, an inventor discovers a way of slowing time within the field of a generator, so that rich people can come and live in a special city until they are two hundred. As one might expect, though, the genera.or breaks, the field reverses itself, and all the potential double centenarians accelerate to death and dust within seconds. Barnabo, one sees, would have resisted the time machine's temptations. In the same way, he would not have fallen into the trap of "The Five Brothers," in which also lives are wasted by a futile, preoccupied search for security. What connection is there, though, between "Barnabo of the Mountains" and the other stories of this collection? What else do the latter reveal of the single "landscape" which, according to Buzzati's notebook, should be at the core of the artist's vision?

Briefly, one may say that many of the later stories move physically down into the plain; and they become, accordingly, the generic obverse of "mountain pastoral," which is "urban satirical." "The Plague" speculates comically on how tragic all the city dwellers would think it if their cherished automobiles were to catch contagious diseases; but the tragedy is a false one, viewed wryly. Rather grimmer is the last story here, "A Difficult Evening," in which the close relationships of the Italian family have given way to an international bourgeois nightmare, of children coming to kill the parents for their accumulated wealth. In "The Prohibited Word," a point is further made about how, in cities, people can be conditioned. Once a word has been abolished, no one will say it, or hear it, or write it, or read it even if it has been written. To make the point, words are blanked out of the story; you, too, (Buzzati tells his readers) are as conditioned as the characters.

This story brings forward another theme, which is that of literature's "self-reference" (to use the modern term). Buzzati sports with this in "An Interrupted Story," "Confidential," and "Duelling Stories": In each of these, the boundary between life and literature is shifted, so that stories come true, or become autobiographical, or, if interrupted, wither away. Is this fantasy? It is. As with "Barnabo of the Mountains," however, there is a feeling that fantasy can be acted out and become reality; or, as in the satires, that real life in the cities is by nature dull, if frenetic—no competitor for the insidious truths and images that steal in from folk wisdom and folktale.

Buzzati's last clearly identifiable theme in *The Siren* is that of haunting. Several of his characters, such as those in "The Bewitched Bourgeois," find themselves transported from mundane surroundings to a strange world or visited *within* their mundane surroundings by an ominous, gnawing, blackmailing outsider. In his concluding travel piece, "Kafka's Houses," Buzzati himself confesses to have been haunted all of his life by comparisons with the Czech writer Franz Kafka. Buzzati's trip to Prague becomes an attempted exorcism.

Like Barnabo's exile in the plain, however, it proves a failure. Memory, in the work of Buzzati, is not so easy to assuage. It is appropriate that his own stories should be so memorable, aiming, as they do, not at complex narration or heavy analysis of character but at striking images varied and repeated within a simple frame. Simplicity makes especially heavy demands on a translator, however, and it should be recorded that a great part of the growing reputation of Buzzati within English-speaking countries is a result of the unobtrusive skill of his translator, Lawrence Venuti. *Ars est celare artem*, as the maxim says; but if Venuti has concealed his own art, he has displayed that of his subject to a wider world. Appropriately, the title of this collection refers not to the sirens who strove to trap Odysseus but to the siren a ship sounds to indicate its departure. Buzzati's aim is to transport his readers across boundaries and frontiers, whether of language or genre or literary expectation.

T. A. Shippey

Sources for Further Study

Book World. XIV, September 23, 1984, p. 12.
Choice. XXII, January, 1985, p. 688.
Kirkus Reviews. LII, August 1, 1984, p. 692.
Library Journal. CIX, October 1, 1984, p. 1859.
The New York Times Book Review. LXXXIX, October 28, 1984, p. 32.
Publishers Weekly. CCXXVI, August 10, 1984, p. 75.

SLOW LEARNER
Early Stories

Author: Thomas Pynchon (1937-   )
Introduction by the author
Publisher: Little, Brown and Company (Boston). 193 pp. $14.95
Type of work: Short stories

A collection containing five of Pynchon's six previously published short stories

Thomas Pynchon does not exactly rush into print. After the publication of his monumental *Gravity's Rainbow* (1973), he remained silent for a decade—except for the blurbs he occasionally contributed to the books of other writers. His introduction to a new printing of Richard Fariña's *Been Down So Long It Looks Like Up to Me*, published by Penguin in 1983, may have marked a turning point in his publishing habits, since it was followed the following year by *Slow Learner* and by an essay in *The New York Times Book Review*.

Given the paucity of new Pynchon writing, the most significant aspect of *Slow Learner*, his collection of early stories, may be the author's introduction. A piece of some length, it is witty and surprisingly candid. Readers enjoy playing hide-and-seek with this reclusive author, and he rewards them here with some intriguing hints about his personal life, notably that he may now be a father (whether in the biological sense or not is, typically, left ambiguous). He hints, too, that he has been in analysis (or so one interprets the reference to a time "before I had access to my dreams"). He also discusses the writers and thinkers by whom he was influenced as a young man. He mentions Henry Adams, certain nineteenth century scientists, Norbert Wiener, and Jack Kerouac and the Beats. For the most part, he confirms the source studies of his critics.

In commenting on his stories (and, incidentally, on his novel *The Crying of Lot 49*, 1966), Pynchon uses a tone of bantering self-disparagement, pointing out what he now considers to be embarrassing or merely funny infelicities of style, plot, and characterization. He emphasizes that only one of the stories ("The Secret Integration") is, in his eyes, anything more than "apprentice work." Nevertheless, *Slow Learner* has been politely received by critics in the popular press, most reviewers cheerfully accepting the rhetorical ploy of the introduction. Only the occasional critic has been so churlish as to quote the negative evaluations in the introduction and conclude that the stories are every bit as bad as Pynchon suggests they are. More typical are the confirmations of the respectful judgments of earlier, scholarly critics—observations that, yes, the stories are flawed but that the reader takes pleasure in them nevertheless. Michael Wood, for example, notes the authorial disclaimers but insists that "what Mr. Pynchon doesn't talk about is how extremely good the stories are for all their faults." Christopher

Lehmann-Haupt, similarly, says of the collection that "if it is as much of a failure as Mr. Pynchon insists, then it makes failure positively inviting." Whether one should attribute these critics' generosity to the success of Pynchon's introduction ("forewarned is disarmed," admits Lehmann-Haupt) or to a collective sense that critical discourtesy might forestall the appearance of this author's more recent efforts (presumably the fruit of eleven years' labor), one must conclude that the creator of *Slow Learner* remains a critical favorite.

Indeed, the collection merits critical approbation, for the five stories included abound with Pynchon's characteristic imagination and humor. A sixth story, "Mortality and Mercy in Vienna," does not appear in the book, and one is at a loss to explain the omission. The author does not refer to it in his introduction. Though this story is arguably Pynchon's weakest, its shortcomings do not seem much graver than those of the stories which the author does include.

Pynchon makes up for the omission by including a rarity, a story entitled "The Small Rain," which appeared in the *Cornell Writer* in 1959 and marked the author's fictional debut. The story, which concerns an alienated soldier who participates in the relief effort after an especially destructive hurricane, suffers a little from undergraduate pretentiousness, but it is interesting to see a great writer learning to deploy motivic and symbolic detail. Pynchon introduces references to the Bible, the *Book of Common Prayer*, and *The Waste Land*. His protagonist, Nathan Levine, is one of T. S. Eliot's hollow men, deracinated and spiritually dead. To heighten the bleakness of his vision of the Waste Land, Pynchon leaves in a thematic thread of sexual sterility. More than once he characterizes Levine as a "plowboy" but never allows him to rise above the more trivial or vulgar meanings of this appellation (which potentially links Levine mythically to the earth and its cycles of death and rebirth). Instead, the story closes with Levine copulating woodenly, like "the young man carbuncular" in *The Waste Land*. The fact that the hurricane and its aftermath have been covered by photographers from *Life* magazine inspires him to a sardonic postcoital pun on the familiar prayer-book phrase for "The Burial of the Dead": "In the midst of *Life*. We are in death." One of his army buddies likens him to the seed that falls on stony ground. He will, in other words, share in no vernal efflorescence; like the rest of his generation, he resists resurrection.

The Waste Land also makes its presence felt in the second story in the collection. In "Low-lands," Pynchon continues to present images of a vitiated culture. Dennis Flange, the main character, has reached affluent middle age, with an expensive house, a thousand-dollar stereo, Mondrians in the belvedere, and an expensive psychiatrist. Thrown out by his unsympathetic wife, Flange retreats with some disreputable companions to a surreal garbage dump, a Sargasso Sea in which the detritus of a civilization comes at last to rest (one recalls the junk sculpture Pynchon describes and reflects on in his article "A Journey into the Mind of Watts"). The dump is also, symbolically, the culture itself—a culture full of consumer goods such as refrigerators, tires, mattresses, washing machines, and other dead things. Beneath the dump, in interlacing tunnels built by anarchists in the 1930's, dwell a shadowy group of outsiders, an alternative society undreamed of by the well-adjusted folks back at Flange's law firm. Here Pynchon was experimenting with the idea of surface and subsurface realities in America—an idea that would eventually become *The Crying of Lot 49.*

"Low-lands" ends with a dream sequence in which Flange encounters a gypsy named Nerissa, a kind of fairy-child who is at once an emblem of his ambivalence toward the opposite sex and a fantasy of female complaisance. Nerissa is associated with all the projections of Dennis' anima: wife, mother, the sea (with which Flange, a navy veteran, has a mystical affinity). Only three and a half feet tall, she is also the child he regrets never having had, and finally she is the projection of Flange's immaturity—which, Pynchon wryly concedes, may have been his own immaturity at the time the story was written.

Though Pynchon jokes about the shortcomings of this story, he maintains its relative superiority to "Entropy," which follows it in the collection, yet "Entropy" may strike less captious readers as the most durable of these early fictions. It has its lapses into undergraduate humor (a complaint of critics throughout Pynchon's career), but the story also reveals a growing competence with fluid prose and with structure. Pynchon may disparage it simply to combat the tendency of some of his critics to overemphasize the theme of entropy in his work.

"Entropy" unfolds at two levels, with two complementary narratives—set on contiguous floors of an apartment building—going on simultaneously. On the upper floor, a strange man and woman in a sealed, ecologically balanced hothouse observe what they think may be the signs of incipient entropic collapse. The man, Callisto, is obsessed with entropy, which is the progressive dissipation of heat energy. His thoughts and remarks provide the thematic substance of the story. He broods over the cosmic-heat death that will one day come, and he spins out a cultural analogy: Western society, and especially contemporary America, suffers its own version of entropy (again, an anticipation of the theme of *The Crying of Lot 49*). Meanwhile, in the apartment below Callisto's, a "lease-breaking party" heads into its third day, increasingly chaotic. The cumulative breakdown of order in the wild party provides a comic illustration of entropy taking its course.

The story ends with an ironic reversal. The downstairs host, Meatball Mulligan, resolves to set about restoring order—thereby reversing entropy in his immediate sphere. Upstairs, simultaneously, Callisto fails in an attempt at literal heat exchange. He has been trying to save a dying bird by sharing with it his own body heat, but the bird dies, its little "system" lapsing into miniature heat death. Callisto's companion underscores the implied ecological dissolution by breaking a window of their hothouse. Though there is a sense in which increased order in one place (the party) must be compensated for by increased disorder elsewhere (upstairs), Pynchon seems to be exposing the folly of entropic obsession (the very obsession with which he has implicitly been charged), for the reader sees that Callisto is irrational in his rationality. In contrast, Meatball, downstairs, handles snowballing disorder with commonsensical resourcefulness.

Entropy, in the sense of a gathering, fearsome disorder, also figures in the collection's penultimate story. "Under the Rose," which appears in altered form as chapter 3 of *V.* (1963), is a spy story set in the Egypt of 1898, a time when British and German operatives jockeyed for position as the Great War loomed on the international horizon. The story's premise is that the British spies must try to keep hostilities from breaking out between their nation and France as a result of the crisis caused by an encounter between French and British armies at Fashoda, a remote outpost on the Nile. The German spies act as agents provocateurs, hoping to bring off an assassination that will start a war disastrous to their chief European rivals. The British spies prevail, though their leader perishes, and the story ends with a glimpse of his surviving colleague in the crowds at Sarajevo in 1914, hoping once again to forestall apocalypse.

Pynchon admits to finding this story less objectionable than the earlier ones, and indeed it is masterfully constructed. The local color—cribbed from an 1899 edition of Baedeker's guide to Egypt—is nicely handled, and the allusions, unlike those in "The Small Rain" and its immediate successors, add depth rather than pretentiousness to the story (a pattern of allusions to the opera *Manon Lescaut* highlights the English spymaster's inner struggle with the ethics of his profession). The mature Pynchon claims to have intended his heroes as authentic Englishmen—he is therefore embarrassed at their clichéd "pip-pip, Old Chap" banter—but the miscalculations of a writer such as Pynchon often prove serendipitous: His "stage Englishmen" provide a delightful variety of campy humor which heightens rather than undercuts the serious theme of Armageddon-in-the-making.

The reader who is impressed by Pynchon's meditation on the paradoxes of purity and impurity among spies will find even more impressive the related inquiry into innocence and experience in his last story, "The Secret Integration." This is a coming-of-age story, a tale of childhood innocence struggling comically against a corrupt adult world. It is a story in which a winsome—perhaps too winsome—group of kids resist the racism of their parents and their community by small gestures of defiance and by the adoption of an imaginary black playmate. "The Secret Integration" evokes the clandestine world of preadolescent children with great brilliance and with a comic resourcefulness that recalls some of Frank Conroy's stories. What is especially deft in Pynchon's handling of the theme here is the gradual modulation from comic and infantile rebellion—sodium bombs in the toilet and such—to the doomed expression of a more meaningful rebellion: the resistance to racism.

The alleged puerility of Pynchon's humor is cushioned by his point of view, by the fact that the story's humor seems of a piece with its "puerile" milieu. As the author sketches the gulf between the innocence and virtue of the children and the hopelessly complex world of the adults, however, the narrative takes on a fine, sad, elegiac quality. If anything is missing, it is perhaps some clearer indication of the actual scope of the adult world's complexity. Though the story closes with the hint that these children have begun to acquire knowledge, it never quite manages to hint that they must also fall—become as capable of error, as passionately wrong, on occasion, as their benighted parents. Nevertheless, as Pynchon himself realizes, this is his most accomplished piece of short fiction.

The authorial judgments alluded to here, all from Pynchon's introduction, should be compared with those of more objective critics. These stories have been discussed since Pynchon first began to attract systematic critical attention, and consequently there are a number of worthwhile treatments of them in books and articles on Pynchon. Of the individual stories, "Entropy" has attracted the most attention, with an important discussion by William M. Plater and essays by John Simons, this reviewer, and others. For a comparison of "Under the Rose" to chapter 3 of *V.*, see David Cowart's *Thomas Pynchon: The Art of Allusion* (1980). The most comprehensive treatments of the stories are those of Joseph W. Slade and Tony Tanner.

David Cowart

Sources for Further Study

America. CLI, July 7, 1984, p. 16.
Kirkus Reviews. LII, February 1, 1984, p. 106.
Los Angeles Times Book Review. May 6, 1984, p. 3.
National Review. XXXVI, November 16, 1984, p. 53.
The New Republic. CXCI, July 16, 1984, p. 36.
The New York Times Book Review. LXXXIX, April 15, 1984, p. 1.
The New Yorker. LX, April 23, 1984, p. 130.
Newsweek. CIII, April 9, 1984, p. 100.
Publishers Weekly. CCXXV, February 17, 1984, p. 72.
Time. CXXIII, April 23, 1984, p. 81.

SNOOTY BARONET

Author: Wyndham Lewis (1882-1957)
Edited, with a critical essay, by Bernard Lafourcade
Publisher: Black Sparrow Press (Santa Barbara, California). Illustrated. 313 pp.
$20.00; paperback $12.50; deluxe edition $30.00
Type of work: Novel
Time: The 1930's
Locale: London, southern France, and Persia

A satiric novel which describes the bumbling actions of its windup-doll characters in an energetic and highly idiosyncratic style

> Principal characters:
> "SNOOTY" SIR MICHAEL KELL-IMRIE, the narrator and protagonist
> VALERIE, his mistress
> HUMPHREY COOPER "HUMPH" CARTER, his agent
> ROB MCPHAIL, a poet

This handsome new edition of *Snooty Baronet*, a novel originally published in Great Britain in 1932 but never available in the United States except as a library-bound photographic reprint, is a welcomed part of a renewed interest in Wyndham Lewis, an important but controversial figure in twentieth century art and letters. Lewis was a painter, novelist, philosopher, literary and social critic, and sometime dramatist and poet. The ultimate value of his contributions in each of these areas is debatable, and *Snooty Baronet* serves well to illustrate the nature of that debate.

Snooty Baronet, as with all of Lewis' fiction up to that time, raises the question of the relationship between style and content in his work. Is Lewis primarily a prose-producing machine that cranks out pages of intriguingly idiosyncratic and highly intellectualized prose, the value of which is largely formal, or does he at the same time, as one expects of all first-rank writers, also offer a vision of life that is compelling?

A brief review of the course of events in the novel indicates that the answer to this basic question is not to be found in the plot. It is so arbitrary and peripheral to the focus of the novel as to be largely irrelevant. Snooty is a writer whose books (like many of Lewis') are difficult to categorize, neither anthropology nor philosophy nor culture-criticism but partaking of all those disciplines. Snooty's agent, Humph, prevails upon him to travel to Persia so that he can be captured by a cooperative bandit, who will ransom him back to a British public enthralled (so the plan goes) with this heretofore little-known baronet. Reluctantly dragging his mistress along, he stops in southern France to try to enlist a poet friend on the expedition. The poet is killed in a bullfight before he can make up his mind, and Snooty, Valerie, and Humph proceed to Persia for some random misadventures.

No less arbitrary than the plot, but of infinitely greater interest and significance, is the characteristic Lewis prose style in *Snooty Baronet*. There is no need to look any further than the opening sentence: "Not a bad face, flat and white, broad and weighty: in the daylight, the worse for much wear—stained, a grim surface, rained upon and stared at by the sun at its haughtiest, yet pallid still: with a cropped blondish moustache of dirty lemon, of toothbrush texture: the left eye somewhat closed up—this was a sullen eye." Such prose activates one's intellect at the same time that it straight-arms emotional involvement. The reader is not invited to be intimate with this or any other character but to join Lewis in a detached, withering, often coldly comic observation of human behavior.

Such observation requires paying great attention to the seemingly trivial, because that is where the human puppet reveals its true nature. Snooty, the Lewis-like puppet master of this show, therefore renders in great detail, for example, the inner struggle which he perceives in Val as she tries to answer a telephone in the most socially advantageous way. Or he records a simple kiss as only Lewis, the master of the antierotic could do: "'Mike darling!' she said between two sunbursts of intoxicated kiss-stuff, and close-ups screwed down like thermos-stoppers. . . ."

Such a style awakens the reader to the almost infinite possibilities of language in service to an omnivorous intellect. One marvels at the intricate verbal constructs which arise out of pure intelligence hovering ruthlessly over human activity. Whether one ever really cares, however, about any of Lewis' characters, whether it matters to the reader what happens to them is another question and a clue to the controversy over the ultimate worth of Lewis' fiction.

If there is more to this novel than an exercise in style, it begins with the notion of the Wild Body that informed all of Lewis' fiction into the 1930's. Lewis is the great champion of consciousness and the intellect as the source of anything that might be of value in human beings. The human body is essentially comic, a great puppet or machine that careens wildly and purposelessly about unless it is controlled, as in a handful of cases, by the ghost within the machine—the human intellect. In *Snooty Baronet*, this deflating vision of humanity is apparent on almost every page. Even a simple reaction to the name of another character, for example, is portrayed as a lockstep mechanical sequence: "As I had said *Ritter* his face had undergone a violent change, as if a series of shutters of different sorts and sizes were being swiftly operated upon it—shutting off one expression after another, as soon as each flashed up."

Lewis might argue that rather than deflating, this view of the human condition is simply realistic. If so, it is the realism of the satirist, one that often employs exaggeration, caricature, and invective in service, it affirms, of truth and right. In *Snooty Baronet*, there are more specific satiric targets than the general human condition. Lewis spends part of the novel in a somewhat wearisome attack on a familiar antagonist—D. H. Lawrence, apologist for the visceral, the instinctual, the primitive, and therefore the perceived enemy of much that Lewis values.

Perhaps the novel's best claim for a respected place in Lewis' work and in modern fiction is its self-consciousness as a novel and its exploration of the many levels of ambiguity inherent in storytelling. Two paragraphs after the novel's opening line quoted above, one finds the following: "The face was mine. I must apologize for arriving as it were incognito upon the scene. No murder has been committed on No. 1040 Livingston Avenue—I can't help it if this has opened as if it were a gunman best-seller." This introduces themes which surface regularly throughout the novel, among them the idea of writing as disguise, illusion, parlor game, and joke, not to mention a readily apparent bitterness on Lewis' part that his novels have never enjoyed anything near the popular success regularly accorded to worthless pulp fiction.

Although there are precedents for novels which constantly refer to their own fictiveness, even in early English fiction, *Snooty Baronet* predates most of the modern works which use this device to question traditional assumptions about the nature of reality. Events take a disturbing turn near the end of the novel, when Snooty casually murders his agent and infects his mistress with smallpox. He informs the reader not long after, however, that his mistress claims he is lying about both the murder and the smallpox and that her very different version of events is more generally believed.

Is one to take Snooty's version seriously and reach conclusions about the acts people are capable of if they allow intellect to destroy normal human emotions? Is one to see the differing accounts as indicating something profound about the ambiguous nature of reality? Is Snooty/Lewis simply giving readers that exciting, farfetched, pulp-fiction ending that the reading world he has been grumbling about throughout the novel expects? Or is he doing all this and more at the same time? More important, has the reader been sufficiently drawn into the novel at whatever level—through style, character, theme, or any other element—to care if the work has any larger significance?

Bernard Lafourcade, the editor of this edition, believes that the work has great significance indeed. As part of the many scholarly accoutrements included, he provides a fifteen-page essay which attempts to link Lewis and the novel with every significant novelist since the eighteenth century. This greatness-by-association strategy is not particularly convincing, even to one already convinced of Lewis' overall importance.

One also has mixed feelings about the other fruits of modern scholarship found in this edition. Twenty-four pages are devoted to listing and discussing variant readings from the different manuscript forms of the novel, a wearisome addition even to those few novels that profit from it, but of very dubious value in a work such as *Snooty Baronet*. One is also asked to be thankful for little flags within the text, which send the reader to the back of the book to find, for example, Snooty's observation, "You can bring a stallion to the riverbed but you cannot always make him sip," compared with "One man may lead an ass to the pond's brink but twenty men cannot make him drink." This particular case of the common attempt of scholars to make themselves indispensable to literature may in a sense be fitting. It un-intentionally creates a mock-heroic air around the novel which is in keeping with the spirit of the work itself.

These reservations about the possible excesses of scholarship notwith-standing, this edition is beautifully put together. From the fine-quality paper and type, to the wonderfully appropriate Lewis drawings, to the very attrac-tive cover, this is a model for how a book should look and feel. If there is some overkill in the editing, it is the sort of killing with kindness that Lewis received too little of in his own lifetime.

Snooty Baronet is ultimately a rather minor work, even within Lewis' own oeuvre, yet the majority of all novels are minor works, and this one is more interesting than most. If one takes any joy in inventiveness with language, in the verbal acrobatics and mental projections of a powerful sensibility, then this book, as with anything created by Lewis, will be worth reading whether one finds larger meanings or not.

Daniel Taylor

Sources for Further Study

The Observer. August 12, 1984, p. 19.
Punch. CCLXXXVI, June 20, 1984, p. 57.
Quill and Quire. L, June, 1984, p. 37.
Times Literary Supplement. July 6, 1984, p. 762.

SOLZHENITSYN
A Biography

Author: Michael Scammell (1935-   )
Publisher: W. W. Norton and Company (New York). Illustrated. 1051 pp. $29.95
Type of work: Literary biography
Time: 1918-1980
Locale: The Soviet Union and the United States

A massive volume that offers not only a biography of Alexander Solzhenitsyn but also an introduction to a wide range of Soviet phenomena and personalities

> *Principal personages:*
> ALEXANDER I. SOLZHENITSYN, a Soviet author and polemicist
> NATALIA RESHETOVSKAYA, his first wife
> NATALIA SVETLOVA, his second wife

In a comment to refer to himself, Anton Chekhov advised: "... write how this youth squeezes the slave out of himself drop by drop, and how, waking up one fine morning, he feels that in his veins flows no longer the blood of a slave but that of a real man." Alexander I. Solzhenitsyn has undergone much the same process, although cast in a much different context, and Michael Scammell's biography of the exiled Soviet author and polemicist records the tests of character and physical ordeals which led Solzhenitsyn from an ideological position of comfortable conformity to one of uncompromising opposition.

This is a big book (1051 pages) about a person who seems larger than life; both Solzhenitsyn's virtues and vices, almost Homeric in scope, are recorded in detail and with objectivity. In fact, Scammell prefaces his work by stating that both opponents and supporters of Solzhenitsyn will probably criticize this book. The author visited Solzhenitsyn at his Vermont estate for a week, although the biography is not authorized, and he has recorded the work habits of the reclusive Solzhenitsyn as he labors to complete his cycle of historical novels.

As befits a biography, Scammell treats Solzhenitsyn's life chronologically, weaving biographical detail with copious background information concerning the Soviet Union and critical reaction to Solzhenitsyn's fiction and nonfiction works. Scammell is really writing a much broader work than the title might suggest; Solzhenitsyn holds center stage, but he is also the means by which the reader is introduced to all sorts of Soviet phenomena and personalities.

Solzhenitsyn's early life was made difficult by poverty and the fact that his social origins were of the wrong sort in proletarian times. After doing well at school, he matriculated at Rostov University to study mathematics and physics, a decision which, years later, would prove beneficial, as it saved him for a time from being sent to a hard-regime labor camp. He also studied

Marxism-Leninism and, in his own words, "was carried away." Solzhenitsyn remained a Marxist until the latter half of the 1940's, defending Lenin while blaming Stalin for the excesses and shortcomings of the Soviet system. In April, 1940, he married his fellow student, Natalia Reshetovskaya; in June, 1941, they were graduated as the Germans invaded the Soviet Union.

In the fall, Solzhenitsyn entered the Soviet army as an enlisted man; after a series of semicomic adventures within the army bureaucracy, he completed artillery school and was commissioned an officer. For two and a half years, he fought at the front, becoming a captain in the process. He recalls that he enjoyed the privileges of an officer, an attitude which he seems now to regret, but by all accounts was popular with the men in his command. During this time, he corresponded with Nikolai Vitkevich, a friend from school and university days, who was also an officer in the Soviet army. In these letters, Solzhenitsyn criticized Stalin for his conduct of the war, and in February, 1945, he was arrested by the counterespionage service, Smersh. This arrest began an odyssey through the Soviet camp system, the gulag, which would be the basis of much of Solzhenitsyn's fiction. After interrogations in Moscow, Solzhenitsyn worked briefly on construction projects in Moscow, then spent about three years in a *Sharashka*, a prisoner-staffed scientific-technical institute, housed in what was formerly a theological seminary on the outskirts of Moscow. This period of relative calm allowed Solzhenitsyn to prepare himself, mentally and physically, for the rigors of the hard-labor camp in Central Asia to which he was transferred in 1950.

Despite the privations of Solzhenitsyn's incarceration, the period from 1945 to 1953 was a time of tremendous intellectual and spiritual growth for him. The disgraced officer began his prison career in a state of confusion, completely bewildered by the course of events, confident that a mistake had been made and would soon be rectified. As time went by and expected amnesties did not materialize, Solzhenitsyn buckled down and learned the complex routines of camp life, sometimes as a result of painful mistakes and miscalculations. He even briefly became an informer, which he later regretted and considered the low point of his prison life.

At the same time, Solzhenitsyn began his unofficial education, meeting forcibly returned émigrés, imprisoned scientists, vocal Christians, and political dissidents, all of whom began to shake his faith in Leninism. During long and free discussions, all sorts of topics were discussed: religion, Marxism, life in the West, and life in Russia before the Revolution. Solzhenitsyn gradually shed his belief in Marxism-Leninism and began his journey toward his present belief in Russian Orthodox Christianity. By the time of his release in March, 1953, Solzhenitsyn was thoroughly prison-wise and completely convinced that his survival depended solely upon his own efforts, an attitude which led to secretiveness even with his friends and allies.

Throughout the book, Scammell pays great attention to the relationship between Solzhenitsyn and his first wife, Reshetovskaya. During his stay in the camps she divorced him, although the suggestion first came from Solzhenitsyn himself in order to protect her from persecution as the wife of an enemy of the people. Her remarriage, however, hurt him, and he was profoundly jealous of her second husband, calling him a scoundrel "for tempting into marriage a wife whose husband was still among the living."

From 1953 until 1956, Solzhenitsyn lived in exile in Kazakhstan, working as a physics and mathematics teacher in a local secondary school. By all accounts, he was an excellent teacher, clear in his explanations and devoted to his students. He was extremely lonely, however, and was looking for a wife, although he seemed to go about it in a way which would guarantee that no woman in her right mind would marry him. Solzhenitsyn was looking for a wife who would be completely devoted to him; he asked prospective candidates to read Anton Chekhov's story, "The Darling," a tale of a woman's mindless devotion to her various husbands and lovers.

Solzhenitsyn also used this period to begin his writing. Although a student of the sciences, he was keenly interested in literature and had taken a correspondence course in that area while a student at Rostov University. He decided to write a series of works about life in the camps and then a series of historical novels which would demonstrate the deterioration of Czarist Russia into Stalinist Russia. He began to hoard his time in order to write these works—thus his interest in a wife who would help him in this great task. Since children would be a hindrance, the prospective wife would have to agree to remain childless, a sore point between Solzhenitsyn and Reshetovskaya even before his arrest in 1945.

In 1956, Solzhenitsyn was permitted to resettle in European Russia, and in 1957, during the era of de-Stalinization, he was completely cleared of all charges. He obtained another teaching position and continued his writing. Reshetovskaya left her second husband, Solzhenitsyn moved to Ryazan where Reshetovskaya was employed, and the couple remarried.

In November, 1962, *Odin den Ivana Denisovicha* (*One Day in the Life of Ivan Denisovich*, 1963) was published. In a short time, Solzhenitsyn was transformed from an obscure physics teacher in provincial Ryazan to a lionized author, known all over the Soviet Union and, because of the rapid translation of his novel, all over the world. He was able to leave his teaching position and devote himself to his writing, while his wife acted as his secretary.

Two powerful stories followed the success of the novel, and Solzhenitsyn was recommended for a Lenin Prize in literature. The political winds were changing, however, and after Nikita Khrushchev's fall from political grace in 1964, Solzhenitsyn's star began to dim. Hard-liners in the Soviet literary establishment disliked his treatment of camp themes, his association with the liberal literary journal *Novy mir*, and his growing independence. His personal habits did not stand him in good stead; his singular devotion to his work led Solzhenitsyn to omit the usual meetings and social activities which are part and parcel of being a famous Soviet writer. Scammell details the subsequent difficulties in publishing *V kruge pervom* (1968; *The First Circle*, 1968) and *Rakovy korpus* (1968; *Cancer Ward*, 1968) and their eventual illegal publication in the West.

As Solzhenitsyn's public life became more troublesome, so did his private life. His relationship with Reshetovskaya soured as he sought to spend more and more time away from their house in order to devote uninterrupted time to his work. Reshetovskaya felt slighted and suspected her husband of extramarital affairs; when he admitted that her fears were correct, she insisted upon separate bedrooms, thereby making further infidelities almost inevitable. Scammell treats the situation objectively, presenting both points of view, but Solzhenitsyn comes out the worse as he tries to justify his affairs as a necessity for an author to discover life and, further, maintains that writers should not be held to the same norms as ordinary mortals. The couple eventually was divorced when Solzhenitsyn discovered that he was to become a father by Natalia Svetlova, his present wife. The entire episode, replete with a suicide attempt, teary confrontations, and attempted reconciliations, reads like a soap opera; combined with increasing difficulties in the public arena, the domestic drama made Solzhenitsyn's life difficult and reinforced his habitual secretiveness. Even his close friends and allies were kept guessing as to his location, activities, and intentions; he would go to great lengths to disguise whence a letter was being mailed. Some of his stealth was justified by intrusions of the KGB upon his life, especially as he became more active in the dissident movement and manipulated the publicity about himself in order to receive maximum coverage throughout the world and thus a certain amount of protection from arrest. In such a manner, he was able to survive the illegal publication of *Avgust chetyrnadtsatogo* (1971; *August 1914*, 1972) in the West, the award of the Nobel Prize for Literature, and increasing defiance of the Soviet establishment.

The final blow to the Soviet government seems to have been the publication abroad of *Arkhipelag gulag* (1973-1975; *The Gulag Archipelago*, 1974), which led to Solzhenitsyn's arrest and expulsion from the Soviet Union. Scammell records all the details of these events, including several contradictory accounts of the arrest and interrogations.

Solzhenitsyn's life in the West is treated objectively here, as Scammell traces the changed perceptions of the author by the public as he began to speak out on non-Soviet topics, such as the future of the West, democracy, freedom of the press, and unbridled materialism. Scammell maintains that Solzhenitsyn does not understand the West, that he regards American freedom, especially freedom of the press, to be a sign of weakness and anarchy. This view of Solzhenitsyn is now shared by many in the West, especially in the United States, and there is some truth to it. One should balance this view, however, with the realization that Solzhenitsyn sees little of the United States on his Vermont estate, where he continues to follow his Herculean work habits and tries to marshal time by avoiding trips and visitors. What he does see is superficial, especially the consumerish aspect of American society, which perhaps should be reexamined in the light of ideals based upon considerations other than conspicuous consumption. In any event, Scammell correctly points to the vagueness of Solzhenitsyn's proposals for an alternative and draws a distinction between the great writer and the mediocre polemicist who does not brook opposition to his ideas.

This book is aimed at the popular market and presupposes little knowledge of the Soviet Union. Scammell introduces the uninitiated reader to large chunks of Soviet history, to the dissident movement, and even to the inner workings of a Soviet literary journal. He depends upon other books for much of his information, quoting extensively and widely. In a sense, this is one of Scammell's achievements; by putting so much into one volume, a sort of anthology of recent events on the Soviet literary scene, he saves the reader from having to read numerous other works. Errors are minor and inconsequential; for example, Wilbur Mills was not a senator but a congressman. The book will probably remain the authoritative work on Solzhenitsyn for some time, unless the exiled writer comes out of seclusion to refute it or write his own complete memoirs.

Philip Maloney

Sources for Further Study

The Atlantic. CCLIV, September, 1984, p. 124.
Kirkus Reviews. LII, July 1, 1984, p. 625.
Los Angeles Times Book Review. September 23, 1984, p. 3.
The New Republic. CXCI, October 15, 1984, p. 35.
The New York Review of Books. XXXI, October 11, 1984, p. 13.
The New York Times Book Review. LXXXIX, October 28, 1984, p. 1.
Newsweek. CIV, December 17, 1984, p. 95.
Publishers Weekly. CCXXVI, July 13, 1984, p. 39.
Vogue. CLXXIV, September, 1984, p. 575.
The Wall Street Journal. CCIV, October 2, 1984, p. 28.

SOMETHING OUT THERE

Author: Nadine Gordimer (1923-   )
Publisher: The Viking Press (New York). 203 pp. $15.95
Type of work: Nine short stories, one novella
Time: The 1980's
Locale: South Africa

A richly varied collection by South Africa's most accomplished fiction writer

With strikes and riots against apartheid once again making headlines all over the world, Nadine Gordimer's newest collection of stories, *Something Out There*, takes on a special urgency and relevance. Unlike sociopolitical extremists, however, Gordimer refuses to be led into the simplistic thinking that lies behind political slogans. In this respect, her ninth collection of stories resembles her previous eight, although if one compares *Something Out There* with her prize-winning collection, *Friday's Footprint* (1960), an intensifying of political concern becomes evident. In *Friday's Footprint*, nearly all the characters were white, and the tensions of the stories were those between man and wife, or between individual white characters and white society. *Something Out There* looks more directly at blacks within white South Africa. Nevertheless, Gordimer never deals in abstract political problems and still less in abstract or ideal solutions; rather, she sees all such issues and all those affected by them as complex. This is not to say that she waffles on the moral issues—apartheid is clearly repugnant to her—but she is an artist first and a propagandist not at all. She refuses to identify supporters of the present system with evil or its opponents with good. In Gordimer's fiction, the human dimension is more important than the political.

The lead story, for example, "A City of the Dead, a City of the Living," appears for most of its length to be a casual, even aimless description of life in Number 1907, Block C—a government-housing development for blacks. Into the lives of Nanike Moreke and her husband, Sampson, comes Nanike's cousin Shishonka, a black revolutionary hiding from the authorities because of his participation in the bombing of a police station. Nanike cooperates fully in Shishonka's precautions against discovery and, then suddenly, on the pretext of going out to buy milk for her baby, reports him to the police. The story is stunning in the casual, meandering way that it leads to this devastating ending, a conclusion that rings true because it is so quintessentially, irrationally human. No motives for Nanike's actions are offered, though each reader may supply plausible explanations of his own. Such behavior is illogical yet completely understandable. Gordimer risks incurring the reader's irritation in thus pursuing her truth; she gambles on the ability of her art to transcend racial issues and political propaganda.

In sharp contrast to the naturalistic style of the preceding story is "At the

Rendezvous of Victory," written in the manner of a political fable. The story could be subtitled "A Myth for Our Time," because the characters and situations are twentieth century archetypes. The protagonist is Sinclair "General Giant" Zwedu, a resourceful bush fighter who succeeds in driving the white colonial government from his African homeland. Like so many revolutionary figures, however, he lacks the political sophistication of lesser men, and after the revolution he is outmaneuvered and relegated to a minor role in the new government, reduced in the process from a man of dignity and bravery to a petty dissolute. His story is emblematic on several levels, reminding the reader that the simple hero—direct, honest, outspoken, slightly naïve—has no role in a world run by wily bureaucrats and political expediency. Whether the citizens of a nation are black or white, their leaders turn out to be gray. This story, incidentally, bears comparison with Gordimer's novel, *A Guest of Honour* (1970).

The human effects of the systematically oppressive governments headed by these gray men are explored in "Crimes of Conscience," reminiscent of John le Carré's novels in its atmosphere of moral nullity. Alison Ross is a correspondence-school teacher, an occupation that suggests isolation, but her profession is misleading, for Alison is active in a South African civil rights group, not violently revolutionary but motivated by a respect for human dignity and a passion for justice. At a political trial she meets Derek Felterman, recently returned from five years abroad, where he had been recruited by the secret police. Their relationship grows from friendship to intimacy, though he is spying on her. In spite of himself, he becomes sympathetic to her point of view, and one night after making love to her he confesses his treachery. Gordimer's description of the moment is intensely moving:

> Her face drew into a moment of concentration akin to the animal world, where a threatened creature can turn into a ball of spikes or take on a fearsome aspect of blown-up muscle and defensive garishness.
>
> The moment left her face instantly as it had taken her. He had turned away before it as a man does with a gun in his back.
>
> She shuffled across the bed on her haunches and took his head in her hands, holding him.

This passage is especially moving because it is the one moment of emotional heat in a story otherwise detached, cool, and matter-of-fact. Her commitment, his spying, their love life are all presented as parts of the coldly manipulative world in which secret police recruit spies to report on citizens whose only crime is an acute conscience. Though obviously set in South Africa, the story could occur anywhere in the modern world, wherever men and women of principle are assumed to be threats to the existing order. Regrettably, a certain impersonality weakens the impact, for the characters are shown from the outside only, as emblematic rather than individual figures. Shadowy as they are, they make a potent statement, though as more complex characters they might have made a powerful one.

"Blinder" looks at oppression from the black point of view, not by directly attacking government policies but by describing quietly and sympathetically the plight of Rose, a black servant whose lover, Ephraim, is killed in a bus accident. Rose is an alcoholic and lucky, therefore, that her mistress is compassionate and enlightened, concerned enough for her welfare to have tolerated Ephraim and encouraged Rose to attend Alcoholics Anonymous. The lady of the house, as Gordimer calls her, is sensitive and understanding during Rose's mourning, and in fact the whole family could be called exemplary. Rose is loved and respected by them all—in the same sense that black mammies were in the United States. The evils of this paternalism are not visible through most of the story because the main problem seems to be Rose's alcoholism, and that appears only tangentially related to race or politics. The reader eventually learns, however, that Ephraim was killed because he had to return to his native village to oversee his family's interests in a dispute over ancestral lands that the white government suddenly claimed. Thus, the story of Rose and Ephraim turns out to be one of a million incidental tragedies of the white man's presence in Africa. No one is to blame for the fact that Ephraim had to leave his wife and children, his tribe and traditional homeland, in order to find work in the city, just as no one is to blame for Rose's alcoholism or the situation which led to her illicit but tacitly approved relationship with a married man. Nevertheless, it is appropriately ironic that in the end, Rose decides to leave her white "family" and join Ephraim's wife in Umzimkulu.

Some commentators on Gordimer's fiction have noted the recurrence of betrayal in her works, and indeed it is a unifying link in all the political stories of *Something Out There*. Behind this theme, however, lies another which seems closer to the heart of these stories—the evils of "the system." Gordimer does not use this term, but she dramatizes it, making it so much a part of the moral landscape that no character can escape its influence. Apartheid in her fiction resembles atmosphere in Joseph Conrad's, an indefinable but palpable presence affecting everyone. Gordimer does not naïvely reject all organization, but she subtly exposes the impersonal and mindless way human relationships are damaged by the inevitable conflicts between an unjust social order and its citizens, whether they are among the oppressed or the oppressors. Readers are thus moved to anger or fear in a story such as "A Correspondence Course." Here again, Gordimer moves indirectly, in this instance examining the lives of Pat Haberman and her daughter Harriet. They are quiet and conscientious, liberal in their sympathies. Harriet's innocuous article on "Literacy and the Media" draws the attention of Roland Carter, a political prisoner with whom she subsequently corresponds for more than a year. Then, Carter escapes, and suddenly

Harriet's innocent letters link her in police minds and files with a dangerous escapee. The two women secretly cheer his liberation and hope that he has found safety in a bordering country. The police do not even visit the house. Then one morning, Pat, looking for the newspaper, finds a bundle of clothes carefully hidden in the bushes: "In just this way [Harriet] had put out milk for the fairies (or stray cats?) when she was a little girl." A few evenings later, Roland Carter appears at their door. Recognizing him from a newspaper photograph, Pat retreats into her bedroom, to grieve "for what she had done, done to her darling girl, *done* for." In one swift and quiet stroke, Gordimer evokes the terror that accompanies any resistance of the state and its omniscient secret police.

The same nameless fear inhabits the longest and best of these tales, "Something Out There." Two plots are juxtaposed in this sometimes humorous but ultimately serious study of South African life. In one, a white couple exploits the racial stereotypes and assumptions of the ruling minority to rent a house in the country as cover for two black guerrillas intent on blowing up a power station. In the other, some animal (baboon? escaped chimpanzee?) terrorizes an affluent suburban neighborhood, killing pets, stealing food, scaring the inhabitants and their servants. The monkey is an effective symbol for the unspoken fears that give rise to the laws of apartheid, laws which the revolutionaries are attempting to destroy. The most chilling part of the story occurs after the power station has been damaged and the security police begin their investigation. While city police were unable to deal with the rampaging monkey, the security forces prove alarmingly thorough and effective in tracing the revolutionaries. Once again, much of Gordimer's effect derives from her ability to depict frightening events with the utmost in stylistic aplomb. The apparent indifference of her tone mirrors a world in which both terrorism and Draconian police have become part of everyday life.

Not all the stories in this collection touch on race and politics. "Letter from His Father" is a brilliant satire cast as a letter from Franz Kafka's father in response to Kafka's "Letter to His Father." Here, the ultimate Jewish father both spurns and takes credit for the accomplishments of his son. "Sins of the Third Age" resembles Doris Lessing's "To Room Nineteen" in depicting a marriage that appears to succeed by intelligence and common sense but in the end falls victim to the irrational. Other stories in the volume suggest that people have little control over their lives, personal or political, and that to expect human beings to be other than what they always have been is foolish. This idea is extended in a poignant way by "Terminal." An elderly man and his wife have always promised each other that in case of an incurable illness one would help the other to die quietly and painlessly. The wife, having survived an operation for bowel cancer, cannot tolerate the prospect of living with an unsightly bag at her side. She takes an overdose of sleeping pills, secure in the knowledge that her husband will honor their pact. He does not. Irrational love has overcome reasoned choice, just as in "Sins of the Third Age" it spoiled the retirement plans of Peter and Mania. Betrayal thus takes on a new dimension, becoming in this instance a higher form of loyalty.

Something Out There demonstrates once again that Gordimer is an intelligent, sympathetic, and alert interpreter of her times. How many of these stories will outlast their contemporary relevance? That will depend less on thematic concerns than on style and form, and here matters are not quite so clear. Gordimer has long since mastered short-story technique; her sense of form, rhythm, and timing is superb. In this collection, however, her style seems to have lost its edge a bit. She writes with grace and clarity, and her accustomed lyricism shines through in moments of emotional stress, but for some readers at least these qualities will not compensate for a certain thinness of texture. Explicit statement would sometimes profit from increased suggestiveness and subtlety, just as her admirably sketched characters would engage readers at deeper levels if they were developed in more detail. Perhaps for this reason, the characters in the title story are the most alive and convincing as individuals. Nevertheless, *Something Out There* demonstrates the vitality of the short-story form and the continuing growth of a significant voice in modern fiction.

Dean Baldwin

Sources for Further Study

Christian Science Monitor. LXXVI, August 9, 1984, p. 24.
Library Journal. CIX, July, 1984, p. 1346.
Los Angeles Times. July 31, 1984, V, p. 5.
Ms. XIII, July, 1984, p. 33.
The New York Review of Books. XXXI, August 16, 1984, p. 3.
The New York Times Book Review. LXXXIX, July 29, 1984, p. 7.
Newsweek. CIV, July 9, 1984, p. 71.
Publishers Weekly. CCXXV, April 20, 1984, p. 82.
Time. CXXIV, July 23, 1984, p. 95.
The Wall Street Journal. CCIV, July 9, 1984, p. 22.

SOMETHING TO BE DESIRED

Author: Thomas McGuane (1939-   )
Publisher: Random House (New York). 173 pp. $14.95
Type of work: Novel
Time: The 1980's
Locale: Deadrock, Montana

A novel dramatizing Lucien Taylor, a character struggling against the gravity of doom which McGuane typically assigns his leading male protagonist

> *Principal characters:*
> LUCIEN TAYLOR, a divorcé, painter, and outdoorsman
> SUZANNE, his wife
> JAMES, his son
> EMILY, a femme fatale, Lucien's lover

Thomas McGuane at his best writes about nature and animals with Ernest Hemingway's keen eye and about people with distinctive wit and humor. *Something to Be Desired* is a book aimed at the very degeneracy which, when exploited by McGuane in a book such as *Panama* (1978), discourages the reader and makes him feel, quite simply, bad. McGuane is not certain that he can exorcise the demon of depravity, but he sets out to look at it from a point of view at least informed by nostalgia for morality if not belief. McGuane's eye is as sharp as ever in describing the natural world, and throughout the novel he presents Lucien Taylor, the main character, in harmony with his surroundings as an escape from the disorder of human contacts. McGuane's writing is exceedingly clear and beautiful on such occasions, as when he describes Lucien cleaning ducks:

> He sat and plucked the birds, an easy job with their still-hot bodies. Down drifted and caught in the russet brush, and in a short time he had a pair of oblate units of food, the meat shining pinkish through a layer of creamy fat and pale dimpled skin.

Lucien reverences nature, but humanity, of which he is a painful example, urges only fight-or-flight emotions. For this reason, McGuane males are often vivid automatons equipped with perfunctory impulsiveness, self-mocking silliness, and high school rebelliousness. They would rather die than grow up and lead the dull life which being human requires. A reader will resist the slumming which is occasionally required of him in the tracking of such types. Do I, the reader asks himself, want to read this anecdote of Lucien and another man's wife at the drive-in—she with her period making Lucien reluctant in his advances but still willing—and the farce of Lucien driving out fast after mistakenly depositing the woman's tampon on the windshield of a big cowboy's car? The question is not prudish but betokens a suspicion that the anecdote is gratuitously gross. Will the tampon dangling between Lucien's thumb and forefinger "like a rodent" advance the story of Lucien, or is it merely registered for the sake of a good locker-room guffaw? As it turns out, on the following morning, Lucien is so "grossed out" by the event that suicide offers a plausible relief. He does not wish to live a life of dirty jokes.

In *Something to Be Desired* McGuane requires more of Lucien than dying to escape his monstrous failure to be pure. McGuane desires something, and Lucien desires something. The novel's title says this, as does the epigraph from Charles Morgan's *On Retrievers*:

> There is no question that the dog
> who is really ready for a big trial
> is on the threshold of committing
> grave mistakes.

Lucien talks to himself about being "on trial" and "ascending to a kind of rendezvous" with himself. What McGuane desires is advancement from Lucien and development beyond the static persona victimized by bizarreness and mirroring bizarreness. In Lucien, McGuane probes at the shell of the masculine outcast, a type he has focused on before sheerly for the attractive and entertaining qualities such characters possess. From Lucien, he succeeds in releasing a flow of humanity. Lucien's trial is not to discover how tough he is but how he will respond in the wider agonistics of relationships with a wife and son, given the allure of wildness in nature so beckoning to the potential hermit-escapist. McGuane's problem as a novelist is to sustain development in a character.

To establish Lucien as a vulnerable human being, McGuane opens the novel with a flashback to a boyhood outing with Lucien and his father, in about 1957. The author expertly draws the pain of a boy whose childhood is presided over by faithless people constitutionally incapable of love. Lucien and his father hike in the hills around Deadrock, Lucien's hometown and the locus of the book's action. The father has returned from Arequipa, Peru, where he had run away from his former wife and boy, Lucien, to participate in "The World Adventure Series," a program for male escape from stultifying homogeneity and boredom in America. Lucien wants to love this man but finds his father to be less than adequate at giving love, hung up as he is on himself, his desires, and his disappointment that life is not very adventurous. His father's real lack, from Lucien's vantage, is his dislike of the country through which the two are walking. To the father, they are "in the desert" and "lost" even though Deadrock's lights are clearly visible in the distance. The father's theatrical gloom isolates Lucien. The man shares nothing, no conversation, no stories, with the boy, and he offers nothing but criticism and ponderous announcements of guilt about "stealing" Lucien from school to go camping. When Lucien finds the campsite, his father decides to leave the tent and canned goods for whoever finds them, in order to return more quickly to a Deadrock motel and whore, whom Lucien meets in the middle of the night, waking from a restless sleep, as she is thrown out of the room by her customer. This emotional mess that Lucien has for a father subsequently reunites with his former wife, and before Lucien's cringing gaze, they fight bloodily, cuddle, and decide to remarry. They part permanently when Lucien's mother, instead of saying "I do," screams that the man she loves is dead in Peru, the Art Clancy who lured Lucien's dad there and who died from a bullet in the head at the hand of his Peruvian lover.

The phantasmagoric horribleness of Lucien's parents is a believable depiction, and the pity one immediately feels for Lucien alerts the reader that McGuane desires to do more in the book than flaunt life's nightmarishness, craziness, and murderousness, though these are the elements that make up the atmosphere into which Lucien is born. When the reader finds Lucien, thirty pages later, alone after abandoning his own wife and boy and abandoned by his own version of the Arequipa mistress, the reader is at least open to the possibility that Lucien's life has taken a tragic turn. He finds himself to be an image of the father whom he found so distasteful and ignorant.

Lucien learns early that men and women lie to one another and do not love their children. In college, his model for the faithlessness between the sexes is Emily, a "raving beauty with electrifying black eyes," who loves Lucien and a medical student. She arranges when possible for one suitor to observe the other taking the pleasure she provides. However untrue Emily may be, her shamelessness hypnotizes Lucien, and her wantonness is the equivalent of "The World Adventure Series." Her bestial sexuality is a testing ground for Lucien, who returns to her when he senses, married to Suzanne, "the lack of high romance in his life." Emily has shot her doctor husband and Lucien leaves his wife and son, James, to join her in Deadrock. The rationale for the murder is sketchy, intentionally so, hyping Emily as femme fatale. Her embodiment of wild allure and dangerousness contrasts with Lucien's wife's embodiment of chastity. Suzanne tolerates Lucien's sexual adventurousness while remaining true. Neither Emily nor Suzanne, however, will suffice as the living example of the woman he wants. After rejecting the boring normal life with Suzanne, a life of writing and vacationing in Central America, he is rejected by Emily. After he pays her bail, Lucien is deserted by Emily. She signs over her husband's ranch to the bemused Lucien and flies off with the ranch foreman.

The rest of the novel is a series of scenes depicting the essentially solitary Lucien pondering his fate, having an affair with Dee (another man's wife from Deadrock who, on the morning after, looks "like one of the monuments on Easter Island"), trying to paint the Montana mountains, growing depressed when the painting fails, rejecting suicide in favor of starting a business at the ranch, and temporarily reuniting with his wife. A metamorphosis of some sort in Lucien is McGuane's intention. Nevertheless, such a change will happen only in the heavy humorous lead of McGuane's sardonic tone. The author frequently resolves problems in his characters by putting them to death, or leaving them alive, after someone else is put to death, to grow more estranged. McGuane proposes that Lucien is a victim of a lack of love, who in turn victimizes others through his poverty of marital and paternal feelings. What Lucien is made to feel, alone on the ranch, is a heavy load of guilt. He would like to escape by seeing himself as victim and nothing more, and such would allow a self-induced reward of romantic death and escape from the miserable world. McGuane keeps Lucien alive and with admitted humor and irony rubs his nose in his deeds, forcing him to admit responsibility. McGuane has no easy solution to the problem of where Lucien is going to find the "right" emotions and actions which will make him able to love his boy and wife, but the author will, through the trial of self-loathing and character examination, make Lucien feel the absence in himself and will not equip him with a simple excuse.

It puzzles Lucien that he can resent his father's lack while not being anything more to his son, James. Love, apparently, is a responsibility. It is not a hopeless answering howl to the ephemeral siren Emily. Failure to submit to the ordinariness of marriage renders one alone, lonely. Nature will not be a surrogate paramour. Lucien fails as a painter, so he is twice lonely. Nature lures him because it is nonhuman and beautifully silent, inviting the eye to feast on contours of geography and patterns of water in streams. The animals lead their clear lives and are beautiful in motion and in the economy of their actions. When humans aspire to the conditions of nonhuman nature, they become Jack London parodies of nature, like Emily, and escape the human conditions of shared space and shared values through flight or murder. Lucien, sensing his groundedness, declares, "I am a family man," and eschews suicide for lightly parodic entrepreneurship. He turns the ranch into a health spa, utilizing the sulphur hot springs that he originally discovered on the boyhood hike with his father. McGuane anchors the enterprise, in which Lucien finds himself a flaming success, in comedic sideshow details, assuring the reader that life as it is lived by people is still pretty much a joke. Man's presence in nature is all irony. One wants to be here, but one really is not here, at least not nobly or seriously. Lucien, the serious businessman, is playacting. Sulphur (brimstone) rises from the center of his thriving brainstorm. Lucien's clients have the product of their bowels inspected daily by one Mary Celeste, who, watching the waste pass through the diaphanous plumbing in her "enema therapy center," can tell "booze from water, beets from a bleeding ulcer and bacterial diarrhea from bad cocaine."

McGuane's excessive irony in appraising life causes hesitation when he tries to "make a man" out of Lucien. One is not sure how serious McGuane can be about Lucien. For McGuane to be too serious would violate the irony in which all of his characters are conceived. Lucien is, as health-spa operator, Caliban in a tuxedo. The spa allows McGuane to assemble a host of bit players who perform episodic comedy through the last half of the novel. McGuane, however, uses the spa to give Lucien the specious respectability which will bring Suzanne and James back into his life. The reader has to contend with the humorous daydream of the spa alongside the clearly serious treatment of a family reunion. Suzanne, now divorced from Lucien, comes to vacation at the spa with James. She repels Lucien's advances but consents to Lucien's being with James, who is openly fearful of his father. McGuane now writes straightforward scenes devoid of irony. With the reverence which he reserves for characters who are in touch with nature, he describes Lucien and James on a hawk-banding adventure, atop a butte under a camouflage net, from which, prone, side by side, they offer a live pigeon through a slit to the hawks circling above. Much can be done to interpret this scene symbolically. McGuane is very cleverly sending the two "to church" as father and son:

> From underneath it [the camouflage], the wind seemed diminished and the sky behind the mesh harsh and clear, vast as a cathedral. The longer they stayed under the net, the more it seemed to curve high over them, as though its sides were somehow not far away and its center absolutely vertical overhead.

With forceful imagination McGuane puts the father in touch with the son just as nature is about to receive their offering. A prairie falcon dives to the bait, and the scene becomes a confirmation both of communion and isolation. Lucien holds the falcon, whose landing has spooked James, and cries: "It's a prairie falcon. It's the most beautiful bird in the world. I want to come back as a prairie falcon." Then, to the bird: "We're married at last." The bird, banded, flies "vertically from his glove and with hard wing-beats made straight into deep sky." James holds the dead pigeon, from which blood runs "down the domestic blue feathers of its narrow shoulders." McGuane, and Lucien, cannot reconcile "deep sky" and domesticity. The forces of "deep sky" kill whatever is tame. Lucien would like to be a father to James, but with his romantic and slightly hokey mysticism he isolates his son, just as Lucien's father isolated Lucien. McGuane, as observer, is on both sides of the fence but leans more toward the "deep sky" of inhumanity. Nevertheless, he is aware that humans make meager birds of prey, and his insertion of the line "I want to come back as a prairie falcon" is risky, injecting as it does a hip-mystical aroma just when the reader wants Lucien to be a human father to James. Yet it does underline the conflict McGuane is examining in the soul of Lucien, the romantic. On balance, the scene is successful and moving and portrays Lucien's effort of righteousness toward the boy.

To end the novel, McGuane flies Emily home to Deadrock, only to have

Lucien fly her out again. This is another consciously righteous act on Lucien's part and connects organically with the falcon scene. Emily has killed again, her latest pigeon being the ranch foreman whom she found to be the king of premature ejaculation. Lucien sends her back into deep sky, despite her feeling that banishment will end her life. Suzanne is happy with James's growing affection for Lucien, but she leaves as well, taking the boy. Though McGuane does not fully reconcile the marital breach, leaving as he does a possibility of final reunion, he does divorce Lucien from catastrophe. When Emily's plane leaves the ground, Lucien cannot distinguish its lights from the stars. The book has a positive ending. Driving Emily to her exit from his world, Lucien feels "suddenly uprooted, a feeling as violent as childbirth." The transformation that he experiences "could have come from some source thousands of years or thousands of miles away." What sort of conversion is taking place the reader is left to ponder. It may seem like an afterthought to readers of contemporary fiction, accustomed to the diet of hopelessness usually dished up. Lucien willfully puts a destructive power out of his life, and it is reflection upon his life as a "family man" that partially effects the change. Whether he will grow into a tolerance of conventionality sufficient to make life with a wife possible is open to speculation.

McGuane has, in *Something to Be Desired*, faithfully acknowledged and depicted the problems which a man of proud eyes and longing has upon collision with the humdrum path of life. It is to be assumed that McGuane writes novels to give everyone willing to read the book a respite from the ordinary, but the book is more than entertainment. McGuane's language is, in several instances, as powerfully evocative as one can hope for, straining to provide entry or witness for some grace "coming from thousands of years or thousands of miles away." If anyone lacks volition to be good on his own, as Lucien, as anyone alive, then the admission of such poverty may foreshadow some change "as violent as childbirth." It is such a hope with which McGuane intends to stick his reader against his own mountainous doubts.

Bruce Wiebe

Sources for Further Study

Book World. XIV, December 16, 1984, p. 10.
Kirkus Reviews. LII, August 15, 1984, p. 774.
Library Journal. CIX, November 1, 1984, p. 2080.
The New York Times Book Review. LXXXIX, December 20, 1984, p. 11.
The New Yorker. LX, December 24, 1984, p. 88.
Newsweek. LV, January 21, 1985, p. 71.
Publishers Weekly. CCXXVI, September 21, 1984, p. 89.
The Wall Street Journal. CCIV, December 24, 1984, p. 5.

THE SORROW OF ARCHITECTURE

Author: Liam Rector (1949-   )
Publisher: Dragon Gate (Port Townsend, Washington). 75 pp. $14.00; paperback
   $6.00
Type of work: Poetry

A first collection of poems which introduces a poet of rare maturity, inventiveness, and skill

Occasionally a book of poems appears which raises central questions about the place of poetry in American culture. For the past several decades, a general complaint has been that poets write mostly for one another; more recently, this charge has been refined to include the observation that prizes and awards are given to poets primarily by other poets, so the poet who knows what prizes he wants will be careful about choosing his audience. The general reader, it is assumed, is beyond the reach of serious poetry, so insularity becomes a means of self-preservation. This attitude appears to be vindicated by another cruel fact: It requires almost no sophistication whatever to be embarrassed by the work of best-selling poets such as James Kavanaugh and Peter McWilliams.

These remarks are prompted by a collection which seems intentionally designed to put off the general reader, whoever that may be; *The Sorrow of Architecture* has a distinctively "modern" title which will rapidly separate the literalists from those who go along readily with odd propositions in literature. The cover photograph is suggestive but not communicative: a black-and-white shot of four women facing away from the viewer, up a stone stairway whose bottom and top are both out of the picture. The women wear dark hats and dresses, slightly outmoded, and the longer one looks at the picture, the more firmly one is convinced that the picture is posed, that the women have not been snapped in the act of walking up the stairs but are posed in slightly different attitudes *suggestive* of walking up the stairs. Finally, the book carries a blurb from Richard Howard, pitched high and inside: "What 'works' in the vanguard poems of Liam Rector is the counter-valent impulse to put together, to enclose—what it countervails, of course, is all that vanguardism of taking apart, diffraction. One reads them over and over, wondering how he put so much together and left so much out . . . by repeating and by inventing, and by certain enormous repudiations, as of comfort, as of ease."

This assessment is balanced by two others, from David St. John and Jordan Smith, who speak of Rector's "raw, dazzling passion" and his poignancy, eloquence, and responsibility. As a rule, one ought not to review blurbs (Jordan Smith, for example, will perhaps want it known that he did not use the phrase "raw, dazzling passion"). The point here is that the outside of this book conveys strong impressions which will be borne out by a careless glance at the contents.

If these, however, are "vanguard poems"—and in many ways they certainly are, for these poems are obtrusively repetitive, evocative of the "still shots" in *Last Year at Marienbad*—they are also dependent on some of the oldest devices in Western poetry: narrative, echo, traditional form. Moreover, they often demand emotional responses fully as strong as those so badly aimed at by popular poets.

The opening of "Driving November," one of three longer poems in the collection, displays a few of the tendencies hinted at so far:

> We are driving November we turned
> October several towns back. We applaud
> the passing of all that is innocent we inherit
> the road as it is here. You speak of habit
> as if things do not change I speak
> of sweet repetition. We are driving November, from harm.

In this poem of little more than one hundred lines, it becomes less and less clear where the "we" might be; they may actually be driving, or they may be imagining driving. Things happen in ways which sometimes seem suggested merely by word association, as in: "We pass/ in the passing lane   An old woman/ passes out in the supermarket" and "we sleep it off here   We sleep it on and off here/ (Take your clothes off Johnny, it's time for bedlam)."

By the end of the poem, however, though it is hard to make a literal paraphrase of the "story line," there is a powerful sense of some deep effort of friendship having passed between the people referred to as "we." The poem is too long for a definitive demonstration of how well the ending is earned, but the ending is worth quoting:

> We didn't remain there the entire year. Odd jobs.
> Live fast, die young.   Many pass.
>
> You and I have dreamt November, from harm.
>
> I roll down this window you see
> I vote you this blue hello.

The oddity of the phrase "from harm," coming at the end of the line here and in the first passage quoted, will remind some readers of the sound of the sestina. It happens that there are three other stanzas scattered through the poem, using the same end-words as the first stanza; according to the word-order rules of the sestina, these other stanzas would be, respectively, the second, fourth, and third. They are separated by chunks of open verse, apparently random in length but in fact not. The passages between the sestina stanzas are unequal in length, but their lines are numbered in multiples of eleven. Why? The answer may be as simple as this: It is not nec-

essary that the reader discover this way of controlling the length of the poem's parts, but that control has nevertheless been exercised, with additional
benefits in precision of phrasing, in choice of episode, image, and echo.

This last point is of supreme importance. If the poem *required*, for effect
or understanding, that the reader notice these technical facts, the poem
would be no more than an act of literary dandyism. The repetitions of the
sestina, however, can operate on a consciousness unfamiliar with the rules of
that highly artificial form; what the poet may choose in addition, as a way of
giving himself a cage to rattle, or in which to find freedom, matters only in
terms of the result.

Rector has an uncanny ability to vary the uses of repetitive phrasing, so
that it reinforces poems having to do with boredom, desperation, nostalgia,
or the frenetic attack that civilization makes on one's senses. It is not surprising, perhaps, that several of his poems are cast in paragraphs, or even
that one of these prose items turns out to be a concealed sestina, somewhat
ragged in meter but flawless in its arrangement of the repeating end-words.
It is more surprising, however, in this "vanguard" context, to see how well
Rector writes in traditional forms.

"When Down by Long Boy's Lane," subtitled "a ballad for the old boy," is
a wonderful combination of odd diction and the traditional sound of the
ballad:

> A visionary bowler,
> gone down by Long Boy's Lane,
> a casually bitter stroller,
> a roller with the strain,
>
> went dancing dark through night-town
> (suggesting day was done),
> fell flat onto the sidewalk
> hardly lost but barely won.

W. H. Auden sometimes sounded like this: The odd arbitrariness that
"bowler" begins to take on as it is repeated—nine times in thirty-two
lines—is similar to the effects Auden created in poems such as "As I
Walked Out One Evening." Rector's control over this poem, the delicate
balance between the sentimentality of the drunkard's plight and the gentle
irony of the voice in its form, are, however, his alone. It is a high-risk poem,
but it pays off:

> If gods sing to the bowler,
> they toast a bitter cup.
> When he is looking down from stars
> they tell him to look up.
>
> The moonlight, often striking,

> as down by Long Boy's Lane,
> the bowler drinks the morning
> with vision, and in rain.

"In Snow" is another formal tour de force: A poem in trochaic tetrameter—a meter made all but impossible ever since "Hiawatha."

Indeed, Rector makes plain his indebtedness to earlier poetry; there are explicit references to T. S. Eliot, William Carlos Williams, Ezra Pound, Hart Crane, Arthur Rimbaud (a snide aside, actually), and echoes from poets as diverse as Robert Lowell and Michael Drayton.

Knowledge and technique are powerful tools, but their skillful use requires a sharp eye and a thoughtful attention to the world. Most of Rector's poems arise from situations that are not only familiar but also intrinsically important to us. The title poem, for example, gradually reveals itself to be concerned with a difficult moment in a marriage, but the potential tritenesses of a man walking out, thinking things over as he walks about the streets, visualizing a parting in a motion picture, and calling back to the apartment from a public phone are all made specific and immediate by the quality of Rector's observation and his ability to meditate, sometimes with epigrammatic brevity, on what he observes:

> . . . The snow pounds its thorough white
> all through the dark megadorm of the city
> where we each widow-walk the nighttime air
> by the river, outlived
> by any embrace that might hold us, outsmarted
> by the innocence that might send us home.

One might quarrel with the excessive ingenuity of "megadorm"—it seems a small violation of tone in the passage in which it appears—but Rector's tendency is to avoid the excessively solemn, even in poems not intended to be humorous in their overall effect. Furthermore, the word comes late in the book, by which time the reader is aware that one of the binding themes of the collection is the ironic tension between the human need for shelter and the constrictive nature of one's dwellings. "The sorrow of architecture" has its local meaning in the title poem, where a building surrounds the person staying behind in the apartment, while the speaker wanders around outside it, thinking of walls and doors that let sorrows onto the streets. Plenty of other poems in the book as well explore the possibilities inherent in the title phrase.

"The Carpenter," for example, is a long poem cast in the form of a recollection; a character named Rector is working with a builder, who gives him advice, teases him, and finally talks to him as a fellow; the italicized passages in which the builder speaks are interspersed with meditative, sometimes absentminded responses from the speaker of the poem. The effect is a little like that of Henry Reed's "Naming of Parts," except that the distance between the builder and Rector diminishes as the poem proceeds, and the poem reveals itself as an acknowledgment of indebtedness for valuable lessons learned.

Immediately following "The Carpenter," though, is "Apartment," which comes right out and laughs at the way people do things. "I walk into apartment," it begins, and there follows an account of the way the rooms have been conversing, complaining; meanwhile, "The ceiling sulks,/ jealous over nothing." The poem ends with a fine flourish:

> I cannot afford this place.
> The bill for the rent slides in under the door.
> It grins and lights a cigarette.
> This must be part of the glamor of Manhattan,
> what I came for—
> the animate detail of price.

This poem, like most of the poems in *The Sorrow of Architecture*, is remarkable for the aptness of its ending. Rector has a strong grasp of the curve of emotion generated by a poem and a sure sense of how to bring it to a conclusion. In a few cases, perhaps, the oddity of the subject and a certain arbitrariness in its treatment will make the effort seem a slight one, but there are fewer of these "filler poems" here than is usual in first collections. Liam Rector makes an impressive debut with this book; it is filled with far more than promise.

Henry Taylor

Sources for Further Study

Choice. XXII, October, 1984, p. 270.
The Georgia Review. XXXVIII, Fall, 1984, p. 628.
Hudson Review. XXXVII, Spring, 1984, p. 127.

STARS IN MY POCKET LIKE GRAINS OF SAND

Author: Samuel R. Delany (1942-   )
Publisher: Bantam Books (New York). 368 pp. $16.95
Type of work: Novel
Time: The very far future
Locale: The planet Rhyonon, the planet Velm, and other locations in space

The lone survivor of a destroyed planet undergoes rehabilitation as part of a scheme to ward off potential interstellar catastrophe and a developing intrigue between factions of humanity

> *Principal characters:*
> KORGA, a "rat," the sole survivor of the planet Rhyonon
> MARQ DYETH, an industrial diplomat, Korga's erotic partner
> JAPRIL, an agent of "the Web"
> SHOSHANA, Marq's human mother
> LARGE MAXA, Marq's nonhuman mother
> GEORGE THANT, a guest of the Dyeths

Stars in My Pocket like Grains of Sand is the first of a pair, or "diptych," of science-fiction novels, the second being promised for late 1985 under the title "The Splendor and Misery of Bodies, of Cities." Until the second volume appears, it is clearly impossible to form a final judgment of the first, and indeed, *Stars in My Pocket like Grains of Sand*, for all its considerable length, ends with many questions unanswered. At its heart is the erotic relationship of "Rat" Korga, the last survivor from the destroyed planet of Rhyonon, with Marq Dyeth, an industrial diplomat from the planet of Velm, while round its edges lies a tangle of maneuverings—between the two "parties" who dispute the six-thousand settled planets of Delany's universe, between characters competing for the coveted position of "Focus Family" on one world or another, between humanity as a whole and the Xlv, the only other intelligent race besides humanity to achieve star travel. Though all of these contests or relationships are set going during the course of *Stars in My Pocket like Grains of Sand*, none of them is resolved by its close. Instead, the reader is left wondering: Why have "Rat" and Marq been separated by "the Web"? What gives these characters their apparently focal position? What destroyed Rhyonon? Why is an Xlv armada closing on Velm? What is Cultural Fugue? Answers to these questions will, presumably, be forthcoming, yet one cannot be entirely sure, first because Delany has promised, not a sequel, but as it were an opposing panel, the other half of a "diptych," and second because, in spite of the questions it raises and the complexity of its plot, *Stars in My Pocket like Grains of Sand* is very far from being a "cliffhanger" or even a plot-dominated novel.

The concept that does dominate this novel is one which has undergone sharp semantic redefinition in recent decades—namely, "information." In the 1940's, this meant little more than "news" or "knowledge communicated," but with the coming of cybernetics, computers, and the new discipline of "information theory," the word has taken on radically new meanings, often technical and often susceptible only to mathematical definition. One of the many consequences is that it became possible to say not only that "people had information," or that "books held information," but also that "information" (in its new sense) was stored or communicated in quite unexpected and unintended ways, as, for example, in rules of syntax, electronic signals, and printing conventions. There has been a growing realization that there is far more information in the world than previously suspected and that human beings are spectacularly better at "processing" it than they realize (since the activity, until it became a matter of teaching it to machines, was largely unconscious). What Delany has done in *Stars in My Pocket like Grains of Sand* is to extrapolate this "information revolution" to a very much higher degree, creating a universe in which control of information is the major preoccupation, and in which, furthermore, nearly all the characters are intensely, almost morbidly, aware of all the sign systems and sense systems by which information can be carried.

Other concepts are then redefined in the light of the ruling one. Thus, the reader is told at one point that " 'stupidity' is a process or strategy by which a human, in response to social denigration of the information she or he puts out, commits him or herself to taking in no more information than she or he *can* put out." This is by no means a normal definition of stupidity, but it carries some conviction; it says (to use another modernism) that stupidity is caused by "negative feedback." Diplomacy, meanwhile, is another name for "the subconscious systems by which you decide whether other people possess a context for understanding what you want to say or not, and, if not, for adding appropriate contextual material to your own communication"—in other words, another information-processing skill.

Delany's redefinitions of these concepts not only affect the concepts but also create his characters. Marq Dyeth, as noted above, is an industrial diplomat from a "high-data" culture, unusually skilled in words and signs, while Korga, though Dyeth's perfect erotic partner, not only comes from a data-restricting culture but also (hardly realizing it) has volunteered for Radical Anxiety Termination and become a "rat"—something rather similar, in human terms, to volunteering for prefrontal lobotomy and ending up deeply, if artificially, stupid. "Rat" Korga and Marq Dyeth, then, are erotically close but virtually at opposite informational poles. This latter makes no difference to them, partly because Korga's operation is annulled by the rings that he has inherited from the ancient tyrant and poetess Vondramach Okk. Nevertheless, Korga *possesses* very little information, and the reader is furthermore left to wonder whether intelligence and eros would affect each other very much anyway.

The main point about Delany's novel, though, is that it can be seen at all levels, plot and character included, as an extended fantasia on information. It is a book of extraordinary density. At one point early in the story, for example, Korga, while still on his home world, is rescued from virtual slavery and taught to "read" data cubes by means of an instantaneous retrieval device. In quick succession, Korga reads, or experiences, *The Nu-7 Poems* (a lyric collection), *The Mantichorio* (traditional epic narrative), *The Sharakik Years* (a compilation of documents about a legendary outlaw), *The Lyrikz* of Megel B'ber, the collected novels of Sni Artif, a memoir called *The Sands*, a seven-volume psychoanalytic biography.... Delany's list goes on and on, each title being furthermore annotated in tantalizing depth to create, first, a sense of the overwhelming experience Korga undergoes but, second and more important, a vivid sense of the sheer plethora of any literate civilization. Real analogs of all of Delany's inventions could after all be found—any major library contains them—but who, even on our present single planet, can take in the resources of a major library? In a future universe of many thousand planets, it would seem that not only "rats" but also supergeniuses would be stunned and surfeited by information. How is anyone to cope?

It is this question which Delany is implicitly answering by the very density with which he writes. His solution, to reduce it to the simplest terms, is to say that the "rat" strategy of cutting down information flow must be rejected and replaced by an alternative strategy of openness to experience, coupled with extremely skilled information handling. All organs of sense, for one thing, should be pressed into service: People should not learn from eyes and ears alone. On Velm, the aboriginal "evelmi" have taught humans to lick and taste one another, and to learn even from such "samples"; Korga's alienness and individuality are fixed by taking tissue samples from him, cloning them, and eating the results. The major scene at the end of the book is set at a formal banquet, every aspect of which, including the food preparation, carries profound meaning—as is true, in a more restricted way, of the elaborate dining rituals of some cultures in present reality. Any form of patterning may be pressed into service: for example, mosaics made out of light-sensitive titles, or the multiple-tongued songs of evelmi hunters, or (in an extreme case) a writing system based on "shiftrunes," letters which are pronounced one way on first occurrence, another on second, another on third, and so on, resulting in a poetic technique of continual opposition between visual and phonetic effects.

There is no way for Delany to show how these systems work. He is able only to report them, but the reportage gains a certain conviction, both from Delany's unfailing inventiveness and from the analogs that one may continually draw between his fiction and one's own observed fact. Only in his universe, for example, does it make a critical difference (of formality, politeness, or scorn) whether one uses given name or surname first, but very similar effects of intimacy to one person and scorn to another are created by French use of *tu* and *vous*, while the question of whether one should begin a movement with the left foot or right is vital not only to evelmi dragon hunters but also to most army sergeant-majors. Delany, in short, is bringing into conscious focus semiotic systems of which most of his readers have already been dimly, or by analogy, aware. The effects that Delany so powerfully creates—of synesthesia, of hypersensitivity—are partly intended to suggest an older and richer civilization, but they also serve to remind one that human beings cope with many semiotic systems already, as a matter of daily routine, whether in assessing strangers' sexual potential or driving on the freeway.

There can be little doubt that *Stars in My Pocket like Grains of Sand* achieves its main aim of communicating a sense of rich and varied experience—admittedly only by samples, and in a way that defies further paraphrase, but with great bravura, and also with unusual range across physical, emotional, and intellectual reactions. Once one has recovered from the rather stunning effect of Delany's descriptions, further questions are bound to arise. What, after all, is all of this "information" for? Is there any direction, point, or moral in what readers are being so carefully and expansively told? These questions are not as simple to answer as one might expect, but some moral points do emerge (perhaps to be reinforced more strongly once the "diptych" is complete).

For one thing, it is striking that for more than half of the novel one remains uncertain about the sex of the two main characters. This occurs because, in Delany's universe, all humans are called "women," whatever their sex. The word "man" is hardly ever used. "He" is used, as well as "she," to refer to "women," but the distinction seems to be not by sex but by intention: "He" is used for a potential erotic partner, who will be referred to otherwise as "she." In fact, both Korga and Marq Dyeth are men. Korga's homosexuality is one of the reasons for his becoming a "rat." That operation is considered to be a barbarism, as is the sexual discrimination that led to it; Delany sees both as forms (one physical, one mental) of information blocking—in his terms, the ultimate sin. Parallel to his sexual intolerance, on Rhyonon, is a form of racial intolerance continually referred to as existing in other parts of Velm. At Dyethshome, humans and evelmi are united in a complex family known as a "wave" and continued by various forms of genetic interchange other than by "egg-and-sperm." This is clearly thought to be an ideal. Elsewhere on Velm, though, the humans and the aborigines practice a form of apartheid marked by intolerance, war, and murder. Again, Delany clearly believes that the exchange of DNA (a highly coded form of information) is entirely good, and that notions of species purity are as evil as ideals of sexual restriction. In a sense, the book is a plea for tolerance and for "manners." One of its climaxes is the realization, at the last formal banquet, that the guests of honor from another planet are talking about homosexual relations, and about interspecies relations, with exactly the disgust with which bestiality would be referred to today. The Thants' conversation is, to human beings, entirely familiar; to the other characters in the novel, it is almost inconceivable, incomprehensible. The gap between the two reactions is a measure of how hard Delany has worked to promote receptivity and—in the case of the main characters' gender—to deny his readers even the opportunity of making prejudiced judgments.

The point of the novel still remains, by intention, hard to state. Within an ethic of richness and diversity, compression is not a goal. It is clear only that Delany is arguing for, and trying to exemplify, the utmost development of human capacities, and that the poles of his novel are Cultural Fugue (when multiplicity goes too far and ends in worldwide panics) and Radical Anxiety Termination (when panic is made impossible at the expense of virtually all of one's humanity). The first half of the diptych has concentrated on the evils of one extreme. One might hazard a guess that the second half will move toward an examination of the other, developing, it may be, the comparison implicit in *Stars in My Pocket like Grains of Sand* between the problems of a six-thousand-planet humanity in the future and those of multiethnic and multireligious states today.

T. A. Shippey

Sources for Further Study

Kirkus Reviews. LII, September 15, 1984, p. 877.
Los Angeles Times Book Review. January 20, 1985, p. 4.
The New York Times Book Review. XC, February 10, 1985, p. 15.
Publishers Weekly. CCXXVI, November 9, 1984, p. 62.

STATION ISLAND

Author: Seamus Heaney (1939-   )
Publisher: Farrar, Straus and Giroux (New York). 123 pp. $11.95
Type of work: Poetry

A summary of the author's life as a poet connected to and isolated from the sources of his experience

Seamus Heaney's main concern in *Station Island* is the spiritual life of the poet that he is. Spread out over three sections, this theme expresses itself in several motifs: Part 1 takes up the isolation of the poet; part 2, "Station Island," his return to the past and back to the present; and part 3, "Sweeney Redivivus," his exile. As symbols and words are important to the first section, so are ghosts and spiritual revival to the second one and the uses of exile to the third.

"The Underground," the first poem of part 1, shows the narrator cut off from someone he loves, yearning for her but unable either to catch or forget her. The "lives in their element" that hold onto his memory in "Away from It All" make him wish that he could be rid of them, for he is a loner and so cannot be defined by them. As a poet, he cannot even belong to the community of exiles—the prisoners whose guard regards him as "a silhouette not worth bothering about" ("Sandstone Keepsake"). Anton Chekhov, Heaney says, may have gone further in identifying himself with prisoners ("Chekhov on Sakhalin"), but he is still an artist, still moved by that fact, still isolated from the most isolated of humans by it. There are those, too, in the poet's memory who stand for the very isolation that he feels; Brigid in "A Migration" must not only survive as an outcast constantly on the move (which is how the poet seems to feel about himself), but her connection with the poet is brought to bear when he calls her fetching water "a spill of syllables." The dead Irishman in "Last Look" also becomes an image for the poet as one apart, beyond even the attention of a beautiful and legendary woman.

Not that the poet is dead to sex; in fact, the female part of it symbolizes life itself and, having "nothing to hide," lets him do what he wants with it as his batlike soul follows its bent for distractions. The sexual is, after all, domestic and social, and though it bids the poet to " 'look at me to your heart's content,' " it also bids him to " 'look at every other thing' "—that is, to be free and thus a loner ("Sheelagh na Gig").

The truth is, as "The King of the Ditchbacks" states, the poet is like the Prodigal Son, "leaving everything he had/ for a migrant solitude." Unlike the Prodigal Son, however, the poet, in returning to his roots (which he cannot help doing if only in memory), must "resist/ the words of coming to rest" ("The Birthplace"). When he says, "your voice slips back into its old first place/ and makes the sound your shades make there" ("The Loaning"), he emphasizes the pull of what no longer exists except in words and in this sense guarantees his isolation.

The poet is actually a paradox in the world of humans and nature: His loyalty to words makes him a kind of pariah, but the things from which his calling cuts him off (the rural settings and people he knew when he was young) give birth to his words. The objects in that world become symbols which words convey: Chips of granite mean both moral callousness and mental sharpness, an iron means the satisfaction of hard work, a railroad spike even means the distance between things and what the poet wants them to mean ("Shelf Life"). Heaney, indeed, often looks back over his origins, rummaging in the "limbo of lost words," which are the countryside—its vehicles and roads, its shelters, its "throats," its earth and sky ("The Loaning"). He remembers when words were magical in his childhood, part of the "sizzling wires" of the telegraph, and remembering the carved boat that was made for him for Christmas when he was a boy, he calls "speech all toys and carpentry" ("An Ulster Twilight"). In "Changes," he wants his exile in the city to be refreshed by the memory of simple things and their sounds.

So the poet has his words to keep him company and believes it, it seems, when he is told to "be dialect,/ tell of this wind coming past the zinc hut" ("Making Strange"). It is right and comforting for him to do this, but the strangeness of it never leaves him, making him an alien, as exotic (if lovely) as the music made in "Widgeon" by blowing on a dead bird's windpipe.

The guilt which Heaney seems to feel for being a man apart moves him to make up for it somehow. His narrator humbles himself to the past in which he participated mostly as an observer, and it is in this vulnerable mood, in the title poem, that he meets the ghosts from that past. The twelve sections of "Station Island" suggest, in concentrated form, an epic on the scale of the *Aeneid*, as does its trip to—in effect—the land of the dead. Here the ghosts give the narrator advice or wisdom or insight. Simon Sweeney, "an old Sabbath-breaker," a spirit of isolation and rebellion and the prototype for the Sweeney of part 3, "Sweeney Redivivus," shouts at the narrator to "'Stay clear of all processions!'"—meaning the herd of the guilt-ridden, the penance seekers. Carleton the "old fork-tongued turncoat" says, "'you have to try to make sense of what comes./ Remember everything and keep your head.'" In section 5, the ghost of an old teacher insists that the source of poetry is "'*Feeling, and/ in particular, love.*'" Wisdom such as this is accompanied by insights. The dead priest of section 4 becomes an image of isolation without the freedom and warmth of the poet; as a missionary, the priest was repelled by "'Bare-breasted/ women and rat-ribbed men.'" In the presence of the ghost of his old girlfriend, the narrator remembers "Haunting the granaries of words like *breasts*"—seeing in this way a source for poetry in sex. He sees that a quiet isolation does not save one from sudden death, as his dead friend the archaeologist makes clear, nor does it save the narrator from being accused, for his cousin, a political murder victim, tells him that he was with the poets the whole time and " 'saccharined my death with morning dew.' "

Other encounters with the dead put the narrator in a repentant mood. To the murdered shopkeeper in section 7 he says, " 'Forgive the way I have lived indifferent—/ forgive my timid circumspect involvement.' " To the terrorist in section 9 he says, " 'I repent/ My unweaned life that kept me competent/ To sleepwalk with connivance and mistrust.' " He even goes so far as to say, " 'I hate where I was born, hate everything/ That made me biddable and unforthcoming.' " Here his anger at being vulnerable and his guilt for being withdrawn fuse.

At this point, the narrator begins to save face by finding an image for himself that merges endurance and passion: His metaphor is a mug on a shelf, and he concentrates on "its patient sheen and turbulent atoms." The narrator seems strong enough now to disburden himself to the ghost of the monk confessor, who assures him that what has failed him in his life will be renewed and gives him what turns out to be a penultimate piece of advice: " 'Read poems as prayers.' " The rest of section 11 is a litany which makes the advice ironic, for the refrain insists on the unnameable power behind all things, which turns both prayers and poems into nothing.

Emptied now, the narrator returns to the present. He is like an epic hero without the trappings coming back to the shore from the underworld. He is unlike the survivor of such a journey in that his guide (his Sibyl, his Vergil) shows up only now. The narrator's guide, his final source of advice, is the arch-poet James Joyce, brandishing his ashplant stick like the Sibyl's Golden Bough. Joyce's blindness as well gives an added touch, for it alludes to the prophet Tiresias. He says, " 'The main thing is to write/ for the joy of it' " and " 'Let go, let fly, forget.' " He adds that mooning over political oppression is " 'infantile,' " and that the poet-narrator must listen to the poet alone in him, exploring whatever interests him without guilt or the need for others' approval.

The poet is now in a good position to see his isolation as a blessing. He is like Sweeney, the medieval Celtic king, whose penance was exile, but whose exile had its uses. For one thing, old assumptions fall away: "from there on everything/ is going to be learning." This is the view of "Unwinding," near the beginning of part 3. Sweeney sentimentalizes nature in "Drifting Off" (perhaps because he has been turned into a birdman), but his intimacy with it allows him to see beyond the commonplace. Religion is useful, too, for it forces a character such as Sweeney, or the poet, into rebellion, isolation, and self-discovery ("The Cleric"). For the exile, old maxims have a power that they did not have before ("The Master"). In "In the Chestnut Tree" and "Sweeney's Returns," the reader is shown how the solitary adventurer is always drawn back to the domestic world or the female; the difference is that the adventurer cannot really return, and woman becomes for him not only the secret of the domestic but also magical. Finally, exile teaches endurance: The artist in "An Artist" may hate "his own embrace/ of working" at his art—this being the activity that has the greatest value for him—but, as the poem says, "his fortitude held and hardened/ because he did what he knew." Sweeney may have to "roost a night/ on the slab of exile"—in short, keep moving and never have a home; still his "spirit," worn out as he himself is, can break out of the mortality by which it is captured.

Seamus Heaney has gone to much trouble in *Station Island* to define what it means for him to be a poet. He finds that his experience of where he comes from, whom he knew, and what he did there, is a problem because he is a poet. Because he must write about these things rather than assume them, he is drawn to them while refusing to give in to them. He explores as many facets as come to him of being in the middle like this, and he decides, using a time-tested versification as honed as it is resonant, that the poet must love the world in the only way that he can: through the words that the world itself has given him with which to love it.

Mark McCloskey

Sources for Further Study

America. CL, June 23, 1984, p. 60.
Book World. XV, January 27, 1985, p. 1.
Library Journal. CIX, December, 1984, p. 2285.
The New Republic. CXCII, February 18, 1985, p. 37.
The New York Review of Books. XXXII, March 14, 1985, p. 19.
Time. CXXV, February 25, 1985, p. 91.
Times Literary Supplement. October 19, 1984, p. 1191.
World Literature Today. LVII, Summer, 1983, p. 365.

STONES FOR IBARRA

Author: Harriet Doerr (1910-   )
Publisher: The Viking Press (New York). 214 pp. $14.95
Type of work: Novel
Time: Approximately 1960-1966
Locale: Mexico

Sara and Richard Everton leave San Francisco to rebuild an abandoned copper mine in Mexico; Stones for Ibarra *describes their surrender to a new culture in a primitive and isolated mountain town*

Principal characters:
SARA EVERTON, an American housewife in her early forties
RICHARD EVERTON, the owner of a deserted home and mine in northern Mexico, husband of Sara

Sara and Richard Everton, Americans somewhere near the presumed middle of their lives, leave their San Francisco home and everything that is familiar to them, borrow on their insurance, and drive to a remote village in Mexico where they have decided to spend the rest of their lives. Standing on the cracked porch of the house that she will occupy for the next six years, with lizards basking at her feet and hornets swarming about, Sara Everton finishes a thought begun on the dusty road the night before. "I wonder," she says aloud to the empty landscape, "if we have gone out of our minds."

This accomplished and satisfying first novel by Harriet Doerr, published when the author was in her middle seventies, makes the answer to such a question almost irrelevant, for the life the Evertons lead in Ibarra confounds both their expectations and those of the reader. The values and assumptions that sustain the townspeople in this remote village are so different from their own that Sara and Richard seem alien and bizarre. They are, the Mexicans decide, *mediodesorientado*, half disoriented in this primitive world, like laughing blindfolded children spinning beneath a piñata. Rejecting superstition and an all-pervading religious faith that blurs distinctions between present and past, Sara and Richard live for six years on the periphery of the town and the culture and learn only gradually that their own perceptions are blurred and that they, like their neighbors, finally exist only on faith.

Stones for Ibarra has a clarity and precision of style rare in any fiction, let alone a first novel. Eight of the eighteen chapters appeared before publication in various journals. Although each chapter has a self-contained quality that makes this episodic appearance appropriate, *Stones for Ibarra* has the unity and continuity of a single exhaled breath. It is a story about death and imagination, filled with the best kind of descriptive metaphors, those that extend the theme of the novel and define its tone. The desert and the poverty of the village never simplify the process of perception; instead, they seem to isolate moments of existence, making the most violent incidents seem at once unique and unremarkable, part of an endless, inevitable sequence of events.

Like Malcolm Lowry's *Under the Volcano* (1947), D. H. Lawrence's *The Plumed Serpent* (1926), and other works of fiction that depict the juxtaposition of the two conflicting cultures in this southern section of the Northern Hemisphere, *Stones for Ibarra* throws into relief the differences between the cold rationality of the North Americans and the harsh simplicity of the Native Americans and Spaniards. The Evertons and their neighbors come to accept but not really to understand one another. Communication remains imperfect; the disorientation is permanent. There is in this novel, however, no sense of defeat. When Sara leaves Ibarra, she has gained more than she has given: She and the villagers become part of the same memory.

The Evertons are people of impulse. They leave their box-hedged house, with its glimpse of San Francisco Bay, in pursuit of an illusion engendered by a packet of old photographs and a few old letters in a bundle marked "Mexico." Richard's grandfather had owned and worked a copper mine in Ibarra. His father had played there in the dusty roads with the Mexican boys. The wallpaper of the old house had been imported from France; there were polished dance floors and grass tennis courts, orchards and flower beds, all left behind in the Revolution of 1910. Seduced by these fragments of a past, Richard and Sara sell their possessions and pack their station wagon, marking with a red line on a creased map the road to a town so far from civilization that it had no cinema, no airport, no telephones, a town of "a hundred burros, half as many bicycles, one daily bus, and two automobiles." The two of them, drawn by the faded sepia images, will replant the flower beds, drain the water from the tunnels in the mine, order new machinery, polish the floors. Out of the past, they plan to create a future.

Whatever may have been in their minds originally is forgotten when, halfway through the first year, Richard Everton is diagnosed as having leukemia. He will live, they are told, perhaps six years. Time then loses its ordinary meaning, as each of them devises strategies to cope with this knowledge. Richard, absorbed in his work of re-creating and restoring the mine, adjudicating the conflicts between his men, and watching the copper market, views life as an act of will. All death is suicide, he believes, but he begins to mark off his time, measuring, counting the days and months left. Sara tells stories to herself and to Richard, stories about the town and about the nuns and priests and children who surround them, hoping somehow to fill in the empty spaces by imagination and to prevent death by refusing to imagine it.

In Ibarra, however, death is constant and often brutal. Stories only soften the blow. Death touches the innocent and the uncomprehending as well as the vicious, and the villagers see it with a clarity that the North Americans deny themselves. A nineteen-year-old, saddled with a retarded younger brother who prevents his marriage and encumbers his life, hesitates a moment before reaching out from the edge of a dam, and the child is drowned in cement tailings, his rolling eye and hand visible to the last. Two men are killed by a drunk whom they had taunted and nearly destroyed. A young man, shooting wildly, trying to save his girlfriend and his beloved truck, kills the younger brother he had reared, perhaps on purpose. In Ibarra, Richard and Sara's refusal to acknowledge his illness in public seems as fantastical and irrational as the villagers' superstitions.

The Americans do not pray, the villagers observe; they do not believe in a heaven or a hell; they encourage the doctor to teach contraception, taking away God's gift of children, yet they feed stray dogs and spend money on flowers. The Evertons are furious when they find among their possessions evidence that spirits have been invoked to bring them success and health: a thorn left on a lamp, three beans folded into the linen. Nevertheless, Sara's faith in the doctor, in her desperate and increasingly frequent phone calls from the nearby town, seem to her neighbors no less unjustified or peculiar. Myth and magic, religion and science, in this landscape seem to lose their distinctive shapes. In a wonderful chapter near the end of the book, "The Doctor of the Moon," Sara's flight for help, through the flower-laden countryside on the eve of All Souls' Day in the back of a red taxicab with an interior light that never goes off and a driver at once compassionate and untruthful, becomes a magical (and hilarious) journey into a world where time has stopped.

Novels set in Mexico have built into them a supernatural dimension. To North Americans, the Mexican fascination with death seems frightening, morbid. It is a measure of Doerr's skill that she makes this cultural obsession seem a natural response to the uncertainties of life. At the beginning of *Stones for Ibarra*, the Evertons must drive their car across a chasm on two narrow boards. Sara keeps her eyes tightly closed. By the end of their time in Ibarra, however, both she and Richard have learned to accept the imminence of danger, neither fearing the future nor dwelling on the past.

As this brief outline of the plot might suggest, time and the perception of time are important parts of Doerr's story; the narrative structure reflects this concern. Distinctions between past, present, and future are intentionally tense, allowing the reader to see Richard and Sara as they experience the dangers and tensions of their new life. The movement toward Richard's death is inexorable, yet the chapters of the book seem to follow no necessary sequence. From the beginning, the reader is told of the future: "Richard and Sara Everton will be the only foreigners in the village and they will depart in order, first Richard, then his wife." The past, on the other hand, is invented, embodied in stories and embroidered by Sara's imagination. The old nun who teaches Spanish grammar to Sara hides from her student the details of her own former life, as Sara hides the truth about her husband and about her future from herself and those around her. The women skirmish and come to a standstill, each resigned to what is told, what is said. Learning verb tenses becomes an act that is freighted with significance.

The effect of this concentration on time is to diminish its importance. Every event has its own weight and every moment its interest. At the end of *Stones for Ibarra*, Sara, returning after her husband's death to empty the house, remembers everything. The ghost of her teacher, Madre Petra, bids her to "conjugate the radical-changing reflexive verb, to recollect."

"*Me acuerdo*," Sara answers. The piles of stones that have been dropped by the open gate by passersby to show that they remember Richard's death grow higher. The empty house, still lit, looks unchanged and alive.

Stones for Ibarra is not a conventional novel. The reader is left knowing little about the Evertons. Their love for each other is unquestioned, and only their differing attitudes toward the future distinguish them from each other. The villagers, though given names and vivid personalities, act as members of a chorus, watching and commenting on the strange acts of these outsiders. What makes the book remarkable is the sense of restraint and control that permeates it, despite the bloody and often horrifying deaths and mutilations that form the substance of nearly every chapter.

Harriet Doerr was born in 1910. *Stones for Ibarra* was written in part while she participated in the graduate fiction program at Stanford University in 1978. Although she has spent time in Mexico, Doerr claims that the book is not autobiographical. Like her heroine, she seems to have filled in the silences between her imagined characters with accounts that have been "half heard and half invented" but are as convincing as any reality. Evoking in precise and vivid language the heat, poverty, and beauty of the mountainous landscape of Ibarra, the author has created from a slight and sad story a polished, elegant, and haunting work of art. *Stones for Ibarra* won the 1984 American Book Award for First Work of Fiction and the Bay Area Book Reviewers Association Fiction Award; in addition, Doerr's novel was nominated for the National Book Critics Circle Award for Fiction.

Jean W. Ashton

Sources for Further Study

Christian Science Monitor. LXXVI, January 6, 1984, p. B6.
Kirkus Reviews. LI, October 15, 1983, p. 1102.
Los Angeles Times Book Review. January 1, 1984, p. 4.
Ms. XII, January, 1984, p. 12.
New Directions for Women. XIII, July, 1984, p. 10.

The New Republic. CXC, April, 1984, p. 40.
The New York Times Book Review. LXXXIX, January 8, 1984, p. 8.
Publishers Weekly. CCXXIV, November 4, 1983, p. 57.
The Wall Street Journal. CCIII, January 23, 1984, p. 20.

THE STORY OF HENRI TOD

Author: William F. Buckley, Jr. (1925-   )
Publisher: Doubleday & Company (Garden City, New York). 254 pp. $14.95
Type of work: Novel
Time: 1961
Locale: Berlin

In the fifth of Buckley's spy stories, set at the time of the erection of the Berlin Wall, Blackford Oakes is caught between the conflicting interests of a secret German nationalistic society and the policies of the United States and the CIA

Principal characters:
  BLACKFORD OAKES, a CIA agent
  RUFUS, Oakes's control
  HENRI TOD (HEINRICH TODDWEISS), the leader of the *Bruderschaft*
  CASPAR ALLMAN, a nephew and aide to Walter Ulbricht
  CLAUDIA KIRSCH, Caspar's lover
  JOHN F. KENNEDY, President of the United States, 1961-1963

The artistic temperament is not usually considered to be a particularly disciplined one, but when William F. Buckley, Jr., puts on his novelist's cap he is ordered indeed. Every two years, amid other obligations as editor, columnist, television personality, Conservative guru, and yachtsman, Buckley produces a spy story. He began in 1976 with *Saving the Queen*, then followed *Stained Glass* (1978), *Who's on First* (1980), *Marco Polo, If You Can* (1982), and now the present work, *The Story of Henri Tod.*

With this fifth novel, certain patterns and devices become apparent. It is clear that Buckley prefers to present his fictional hero and his adventures against the backdrop of recent moments of political crisis. *Saving the Queen* has as its background the attempts of the Soviets to acquire, in the early 1950's, the requisite knowledge to produce the H-bomb. *Who's on First* is set against the race for space and the Hungarian Revolution in the mid-1950's, while *Marco Polo, If You Can* is Buckley's rewriting of the incident in 1960 in which a U-2 pilot crash-landed in the Soviet Union. The present work, finally, is concerned with the erection of the Berlin Wall in 1960. Only *Stained Glass* does not have as its background any specific high point of East-West relations; even so, it does take place against a background of West German politics in the late 1940's and early 1950's.

It will be observed that what these historical events share is that they are commonly regarded as "defeats" of the West by the Russians and their allies. There is a common theme here, and Buckley plays it for all it is worth: The West, and specifically the United States, has been guilty of cowardice and a failure of will for not standing up to the Russians—if necessary, with force. This theme is reinforced in the present work, because CIA agent Blackford Oakes has just come to his new assignment—to find out what Nikita Khrushchev plans to do in Berlin and when—from some sort of unspecified involvement in the events of the Bay of Pigs. In his series of novels, Buckley emphasizes the theme of betrayal; the suggestion is clear that the United States has betrayed its values and even Western civilization, just as governments betray their operatives and as individuals betray their countries, their friends, and their comrades. Oakes himself is frequently forced into situations of conflicting loyalties where he must make choices which can easily look like betrayals.

This setting of stories against well-known historical events is both an advantage and a disadvantage for an author. It is an advantage to know what happened ahead of time so that one can make one's own plot fit the events, but it can be a disadvantage in that suspense is lost, because the average reader probably already knows, for example, that the Berlin Wall *was* erected and that the Western Allies did *not* choose to make an issue of the event. In a similar manner, there are advantages and disadvantages in sprinkling one's novels with real people (Dwight D. Eisenhower, John F. Kennedy, John Foster Dulles, Dean Acheson, and others). With this technique, one appeals to the general curiosity about the famous and acquires a certain amount of instant believability while, at the same time perhaps, confusing the reader concerning the actual line between fact and fancy. In *The Story of Henri Tod*, for example, Buckley provides several interior monologues by President Kennedy. They certainly look and feel as though they might well be the real thing (which is an effect that a good novelist strives to achieve), but there is presumably no documentary authority behind them.

Spy novels by William Buckley, then, present certain problems for the reader and reviewer which are not found in dealing with the works of novelists who are not public figures associated with specific social and political philosophies. Certainly, a spy novel by Buckley is bound to attract attention regardless of its innate quality. A novel by Buckley is more noticeable, though not necessarily more notable. Given that Buckley's hero, Blackford Oakes, is born into well-to-do Establishment circumstances, is a veteran of World War II and a Yale graduate recruited by the CIA, and is possessed of traditional conservative and patriotic views, the reader should not be surprised to discover the same pattern in the life and career of the author. Because of Buckley's connections with influential political and social personages, one continually wonders whether Buckley is creating fiction or, perhaps, revealing the *real* inside story. Such concerns, however, while they may attract readers to Buckley's books, would seem to undercut the power of his stories to stand on their own *as* stories.

In many ways, *The Story of Henri Tod* is a traditional and conventional spy story. The hero, Blackford Oakes, is distressingly handsome, attractive and attracted to women (each novel has the requisite sex scene). He has the usual personal problems which he must resolve in addition to the greater issues and crises in which he is involved for his government. There are the agents on the other side, who have more freedom of action because they are not limited by conventional morality, neither personal nor political. There is also the familiar convention of the dangerous venturing into the enemy's camp and the hero's survival—even if for no other reason than to continue as the hero of the next book.

Unlike previous novels in the series, this work does not display Oakes at his best. In the first place, he is simply not onstage very much in the novel. Second, he shows here as a rather dull chap, not particularly good at his chosen profession of spying. In point of fact, Oakes discovers little in the course of the book, spending most of his time brooding and speculating on broad issues, moral and political. If anything, Oakes is more of an observer than an actor in the events depicted. The central mission assigned to Oakes, to find out what Khrushchev is planning for Berlin and when it will occur, is accomplished, but Oakes has little to do with it. It comes about mainly by chance.

Indeed, there is a considerable amount of chance involved in the incidents of the story, or perhaps it would be more precise to call it coincidence. It is pure chance that occasions the wounded Tod to stumble into the apparently deserted railroad car, which is used by Walter Ulbricht's nephew and his girl as their lovers' rendezvous, and escape from the gray world of East German Communism. Caspar and Claudia become attracted to Tod and begin giving him information direct from the office of Ulbricht. Thus is the desired information acquired; ironically, the West does not choose to contest the division of the city, and thus the West loses ground in the great struggle and displays its lack of moral conviction. Thus, too, is Oakes once again frustrated, for his sympathies are all with the Germans who wish the United States to take a stand.

The Story of Henri Tod is similar to all the other Oakes novels in having as one of the central characters an attractive man, usually young, for whom Oakes has great sympathy and understanding, but whose eventual ruin it is Oakes's fate to accomplish, even if unintentionally. In this work, even more than in the others, the story revolves around such a character, Henri Tod— and therefore the novel is appropriately titled. Really, Tod claims a greater share of the reader's attention and sympathies than does Blackford Oakes. Tod is the leader of an underground West German group called the Bruderschaft (brotherhood) which is militantly anti-Communist and which has informants, safe houses, agents, and supporters capable of providing any required special service or talent. It performs political assassinations as required and generally bedevils the Communists. Oakes (like Buckley, it is clear) admires Tod and his group. *Tod* means *death* in German, and it is left to the reader to discover how appropriate a name this is for Henri.

It is a convention in the reviewing of mystery and spy novels that the ending of the story not be revealed, but as history has unveiled, the Berlin Wall was built, and the reader of previous Buckley novels will not be too surprised to discover a frustrating and even tragic conclusion to the events described here. This is perhaps the most serious, as well as the most grim, of all Buckley's novels to date.

Though the novel may be grim, there is still plenty of range for some of the good things one has come to expect from Buckley in these novels. Above all, the style is vintage Buckley—witty and sophisticated, particularly in the conversational passages. The occasional puns, though sometimes outrageous, are welcome and suggest, through all the gloom and moral dithering, that Buckley enjoyed writing the book. He clearly enjoyed writing the passages in which Kennedy appears, recalling those in *Marco Polo, If You Can* in which Eisenhower is featured. Such passages are intended as counterpoint to the labors of Oakes in the field and, surely, as political comment by Buckley.

Buckley also has a knack for creating the occasional striking scene, often one of high comedy. Though he has never, since his first novel, written so hilarious a scene as that describing the bedding of the Queen of England by Blackford Oakes, there are still some interesting elements here. The scenes between Walter Ulbricht and his nephew Caspar offer an amusing as well as interesting commentary on the Communist and bureaucratic mind. Perhaps best of all are the scenes in the fancy railroad car named Berchtesgaden, once Adolf Hitler's private car and now shunted to a siding in an East Berlin station and forgotten. Here Caspar and Claudia love and live in a sort of dreamworld that in its warmth and creature comforts suggests both the capitalist world and a fantasy realm where the strife and trouble of the outside do not intrude. Buckley also manages to work in the by-now expected reference to himself, having Oakes refer to a column in the *National Review* by Buckley.

This novel, then, has weaknesses in plotting and in the presentation of the ongoing character of Oakes. It is either helped or marred, depending on one's biases, by sizable dollops of political hindsight. It has an attractive style and wit as well as some of the sense of fun which Buckley can provide. Overall, it does not attain to the stature of the first two novels of the series and, on some counts, may be the poorest of the five.

Finally, if one can ignore that these novels are by William Buckley, a public figure of a certain eminence, where do they rank in the minor pantheon of spy novels? Buckley's works in this genre are probably to be found in the second rank. They are entertaining and certainly worth reading, but they do not attain to the level of John le Carré for plotting and realistic, modern spy work or of John Buchan for sheer narrative drive and adventure. They are, however, much less silly than the James Bond stories or the later adventures of Tommy Hambledon. They are, perhaps, almost as good as the novels of

Eric Ambler or the equal of the spy stories of Hammond Innes or the early Anthony Price. This is no mean company in which to find oneself.

Gordon N. Bergquist

Sources for Further Study

Best Sellers. XLIII, March, 1984, p. 444.
Christian Science Monitor. LXXVI, February 24, 1984, p. 22.
Library Journal. CIX, March 1, 1984, p. 508.
Los Angeles Times Book Review. January 22, 1984, p. 2.
National Review. XXXVI, February 24, 1984, p. 56.
New Statesman. CVIII, July 13, 1984, p. 28.
The New York Times Book Review. LXXXIX, February 5, 1984, p. 22.
Publishers Weekly. CCXXIV, November 25, 1983, p. 57.
Saturday Review. X, January, 1984, p. 37.
The Wall Street Journal. CCIII, January 17, 1984, p. 28.
West Coast Review of Books. X, March, 1984, p. 29.

SUPERIOR WOMEN

Author: Alice Adams (1926-   )
Publisher: Alfred A. Knopf (New York). 368 pp. $16.95
Type of work: Novel
Time: 1943-1983
Locale: Palo Alto, California; Cambridge, Massachusetts; New York; Washington, D.C.; and rural Georgia

Superior Women *traces the intertwined lives of four young women and their friends from Radcliffe College in 1943 to New York, Washington, D.C., and Georgia in the 1980's*

> *Principal characters:*
> MEGAN GREENE, a Californian; at first a shy observer, later a successful literary agent
> LAVINIA HARCOURT COBB, a wealthy and beautiful socialite from Washington, D.C. who enjoys money and power
> CATHY BARNES, a Midwestern Catholic, devout and serious, who becomes an economist
> PEG SINCLAIR, a large and motherly young woman from New Jersey who marries and divorces a Texas businessman

"Did you ever read those really old books about girls' boarding schools?" one character asks another in Alice Adams' *Superior Women*, ". . . there were always four girls. One beautiful and rich and wicked, and one big and fat and jolly. . . . I think one was poor and virtuous and the other one was very smart."

Alice Adams' great strength as a writer of fiction has always been her ability to depict the emotional bonds that can exist between women—mothers, sisters, daughters, friends—as they move in and out of the erotic relationships with others that determine the direction of their lives. In *Superior Women*, her fifth novel, this subject moves from the periphery to the center of her field of vision. The story of four young women who meet at Radcliffe for an accelerated college course during World War II and remain friends, more or less, for the next forty years, *Superior Women* is Adams' "boarding-school book," her contribution to a popular genre of fiction exemplified in the past by Mary McCarthy's *The Group* (1963) and Rona Jaffe's *Class Reunion* (1979).

Megan Greene, naïve, bookish, plump, and lusty, provides the point of view through which the reader observes the antics of rich Lavinia, inscrutable Cathy, and boisterous Peg as they develop (or fail to develop) into the "superior women" of the title. All privileged, if only by virtue of their opportunities, and all, the reader is told, extremely intelligent, they prove to share the weaknesses of ordinary mortals, suffering unhappy marriages, intertwined love affairs, and unwanted pregnancies like other female members of their generation.

Adams' previous novels, in particular *Listening to Billie* (1978) and *Rich Rewards* (1980), conveyed with great skill and charm the sense of growing up in the 1940's and the 1950's and of being an adolescent or young adult in milieus so rich in atmosphere that they impressed themselves upon the memory and became inseparable from experience: New York jazz clubs, San Francisco frame houses, cottages in Maine. The author has an eye for significant detail and the ability to create characters who are at once interesting and sympathetic.

Although Adams' gifts have not entirely deserted her, admirers of her earlier fiction are likely to be disappointed by *Superior Women*. There is a certain slickness and superficiality here that is not evident in her previous works. The author is still able to evoke effectively a crowded Greenwich Village apartment or a Cambridge coffee shop, but the characters are finally too stereotypical to be believable and their interactions so predictable that they become annoying. Novels that follow a group of people for several years are inherently episodic. In this case, the conventions of the work undermine it.

Megan Greene, often referred to by her friends somewhat inexplicably as "little Megan," meets her fate in a Palo Alto, California, bookstore when a Harvard premed walks in, bringing to her starved sensibilities an exotic atmosphere of New England autumns, Cape Cod clamming parties, and preppie tweeds. Madly in love, Megan somehow arranges to start college at Radcliffe in the following year. (The ease with which people are able to arrange such transformations is one of the more dubious aspects of the novel.) Her motivation is partly to see more of the soon-faithless George and partly to live out her own highly charged fantasies of Eastern college life.

Megan, the reader is told, is good at imagining other people's lives. She is also an inveterate fantasizer, hearing waltzes when debutantes are mentioned and envisioning herself and her friends in novels that increase in complexity as her literary taste develops from popular fiction to Henry James and Marcel Proust. She is selected by sophisticated Lavinia as a confidante and thus becomes part of a tight select group that excludes the other girls in the dormitory. "She's just so—so Jewish," says Lavinia of one aspirant with whom Megan traitorously remains friends.

Quite plausibly, it is never clear what draws this particular group together. Lavinia, with her silk bathrobes and quick scorn, dominates the group, gossiping about the quiet Midwestern Cathy and allowing herself to be given back rubs by Peg, the noisy, maternal one, but it is Megan who has the incredibly satisfying sex life ("You're a living sexual fantasy," says her afternoon lover. "Do you have any idea how extraordinary you are?") and graduates summa cum laude, feeling only slightly chagrined when she is excluded from Lavinia's fancy wedding. Peg gets pregnant and married, Cathy breaks up with her rich but vulgar boyfriend and becomes a grind, Janet—the "so—so Jewish" girl, drops her plans to go to medical school to marry a crazy Irish playwright.

The comment about boarding-school novels quoted above seems to indicate an ironic detachment from this conventional material, a comment about the relationship between art and life, but the reader is not convinced that profundities lie beneath the surface. The stereotypes fail to become rounded characters and the extended destinies worked out for the four women are not really very different from the perfunctory summaries tacked on the boarding-school books. This is partly because the characters seem to be conceived one-dimensionally, as elements of a contrived plot that is designed to allow the author to reflect on bits and pieces of history as they touch upon individual lives, and partly because of a technical choice that calls attention to the shallowness of the contrivance. If Adams had allowed all of the novel to be told from Megan's point of view (as in a sense it really is, since she clearly sets the standard of judgment and is the moral norm for the plot), one might have accepted the superficial characterization of her friends, attributing it to the heroine's naïve perception. Adams, however, switches from one point of view to another and fails to find voices for the lesser characters that are at all convincing. Lavinia in particular evolves into a caricature; like the villainess of a television soap opera, she is the sum of her outrageous statements.

Women as vain and self-serving as Lavinia or as sexually energetic as Megan do of course exist and they often say things that seem extraordinarily in character. The challenge in a novel of this sort is to provide the illusion of depth, so that clichés sound like revelations. Here plausible situations and statements sound exaggerated and implausible because they are not embedded in the fabric of experience. Megan, for example, picks up a black jazz trombonist in a bar in New York during her junior year and has sex with him from time to time for the next thirty years, whenever they happen to be in the same town or feel the sudden need. Their rapport is instantaneous, and their sexual encounters are always tender and exciting—no ambivalence or regrets. A whole novel could be written about this relationship and the difficulties that might be expected, but as presented, it occupies a very small and cheerful corner of Megan's existence. Jackson Clay, the musician, is charming, but the reader does not believe in him for a minute.

Indeed, the omission of social, cultural, and even emotional context is a recurring weakness of the novel, which appears to be informed by the conviction that character must unfold in certain ways, whatever the environment. The novelist's description of events thus becomes a kind of shorthand, indicating in brief the gist of a love affair or event rather than a long exposition so that the reader can discover quickly what the episode means or what effect it has in speeding up or retarding a character's preordained end. This makes sense, in a way, but as it works out in *Superior Women*, so much is left out that portraits seem like cartoons. Grossly exaggerated features turn individuals into types, and types, although they can compel recognition, can seldom evoke an empathetic response.

Megan's postcollege years are predictably happy. After a year in Paris, where she loses her baby fat, she becomes a popular New York literary agent, svelte and chic—although never quite as chic as Lavinia, now Mrs. Potter Cobb, makes a point of being. Megan has a messy Greenwich Village apartment where she entertains her always satisfying lovers and eventually falls in love with one of Lavinia's cast-off beaux, who turns out to be also a friend of Peg, now the mother of four, who has left her husband so that she can register voters in Georgia. Cathy, an unwed mother impregnated by a priest, dies of cancer in California, causing Meg the one great sadness of her life, a sadness assuaged by a week in a Hawaiian hotel with Jackson Clay. In the end, Lavinia loses her lovers, surrenders to the plastic surgeons, and throws a fabulous party for her thirtieth wedding anniversary, while Megan, Peg, and an assortment of sympathetic friends, lovers and relations, including Jackson Clay, establish a luxurious halfway house in rural Georgia for the homeless. (They pick people up on the streets of Washington, D.C., and drive most of the night to get back to Georgia.)

All of this sounds somewhat preposterous—and indeed it is. It is the stuff of cheap fiction, and it is sad to see an author capable of sensitive discriminations succumbing to the temptation to skim over surfaces and wallow in melodrama. It must be possible to summarize the experience of a generation without mentioning all the symbolic touchstones: the McCarthy investigations, the voter-registration drives, the drugged-out flower children, the Richard Nixon candidacy, Christopher Street, Watergate, the new conservatism, lesbianism, the plight of the aged, the homeless. It is not that these elements did not affect the lives of people educated as these "superior" women were. The problem results from their predictable appearance and too obvious function. Like the old calendar pages used in motion pictures to indicate the passing of time, they are signs, not events, and their use seems to suggest that the author is less than serious.

At the end of *Rich Rewards*, the heroine embarks on an affair with an elegant Frenchman, an idol of her youth. This was the weakest aspect of an otherwise strong book, for the happy ending, the rich reward, seemed unlikely, a wish-fulfilling fantasy. The element of fantasy is even stronger in *Superior Women*. Megan, overweight and on the periphery of the group at the beginning, eventually has a happy life, a gorgeous body, and a successful career. Lavinia, beautiful and mean, suffers in isolation and does not even know that she is suffering. Peg inherits money, falls in love with a Mexican social worker, and fulfills the demands of her nature by caring for the homeless and the needy. Cathy—like Beth in Louisa May Alcott's *Little Women* (perhaps another model for this book about grown-up girls)—dies without betraying her lover and manages to inspire noble thoughts. The communal home at the end where all of the good characters are rewarded for their suffering seems right out of the Brothers Grimm. The serious literary model that the girls cite, and which, sadly, invites comparison by being mentioned, is *Remembrance of Things Past*, but Lavinia is no Duchesse de Guermantes, and Adams, for all of her ability, no Proust.

There are good things in this book: Meg's sensitivity to the trivial details of her environment, for example, and Cathy's bleak, knowing letters from the hospital in California. *Superior Women* is predictable but not boring, and it may well appeal to people who want a quick read with a happy ending that makes few demands on their intelligence. There is some satisfaction in learning that even brilliant women can have daughters with acne. One hopes, however, that Adams will return to the less ambitious but more credible terrain of her earlier novels and short stories. There are too few writers able to convey successfully the texture of friendship, of family relations, and of female experience as well as Adams does at her best, and all too many who can perform for the popular market.

Jean W. Ashton

Sources for Further Study

Glamour. LXXXII, October, 1984, p. 240.
Kirkus Reviews. LII, July 1, 1984, p. 581.
Los Angeles Times Book Review. September 30, 1984, p. 1.
Ms. XIII, September, 1984, p. 28.
The New York Times. September 7, 1984, p. 24.
The New York Times Book Review. LXXXIX, September 23, 1984, p. 9.
The New Yorker. LX, November 5, 1984, p. 160.
Newsweek. CIV, September 24, 1984, p. 82.
Publishers Weekly. CCXXV, June 22, 1984, p. 87.
USA Today. III, October 5, 1984, p. 3D.
Vogue. CLXXIV, September, 1984, p. 570.
The Wall Street Journal. CCIV, September 21, 1984, p. 28.

TESTING THE CURRENT

Author: William McPherson (1933-   )
Publisher: Simon and Schuster (New York). 348 pp. $15.95
Type of work: Novel
Time: 1938-1939
Locale: The Upper Midwest of the United States

An eight-year-old boy's experiences as the youngest son of a socially prominent family in a small manufacturing town

> *Principal characters:*
> ANDREW THOMAS "TOMMY" MCALLISTER, a sensitive, innocent eight-year-old
> EMMA MCALLISTER, Tommy's forty-three-year-old attractive mother
> JAMES "MAC" MCALLISTER, Tommy's father, owner of the local chemical plant
> JOHN MCALLISTER, Tommy's twenty-year-old brother who attends Northwestern University
> DAVID MCALLISTER, Tommy's nineteen-year-old brother who lives at home
> LUCIEN "LUKE" WOLFE, a wealthy bachelor attracted to Tommy's mother

One of the most widely reviewed first novels of the year, William McPherson's *Testing the Current* is a portrayal of life in the Upper Midwest in 1939, immediately preceding the beginning of World War II. In part, this widespread response developed from McPherson's reputation as a journalist: He founded the *Washington Post Book World* in 1972 and won a Pulitzer Prize for distinguished literary criticism in 1977, and he is currently on the editorial staff of the *Washington Post*, where he is one of that paper's most highly regarded journalists. The more important reason for the critical attention, however, is the considerable artistic merit of the novel. *Testing the Current* does not display many of the characteristic limitations and flaws of a first novel; McPherson, in his fifties when the novel was published, has an intimate knowledge of the art of fiction, and in *Testing the Current* he has been very successful in converting that knowledge into the "concrete philosophy" which John Gardner believed was the special providence of the fiction writer.

The primary focus in the novel is on the experiences of a gentle, innocent eight-year-old, Tommy McAllister, and McPherson creates his character with extraordinary skill. The novel, however, is more than the presentation of a single character; on the periphery of Tommy's experiences is the constant presence of the social world in which he lives. McPherson's oblique portrayal of that social world—very similar in method to James Joyce's portrayal of the larger social world in his early *Dubliners*—continually calls into question its morals and mores. Often in the novel, a tension exists between what the eight-year-old knows from his experiences and what McPherson suggests to the mature reader; thus, McPherson provides an ironic commentary on the ways of society, in particular on the ways of those more privileged members of the higher social circles. This ironic commentary is balanced by McPherson's basically compassionate view of his protagonist, and the dual impulses of compassion and irony create a complexity of tone upon which the artistic merit of the novel rests.

Structurally, McPherson employs a rather deceptive, traditional approach, moving from scene to scene through Tommy's eighth year, in what Russell Banks terms a "Proustian logic of association, carried forward by a gentle, scrupulously precise narrator." McPherson is a stylist, and his tightly controlled language and technique have caused critics to compare his methods to those of Edith Wharton and Henry James. The pace of the novel is even, as steady as that of a weaver of an Oriental rug, wherein the details—the epigram is a quote from Stendhal on the necessary relationships between detail and originality and truth in writing—create the overall pattern, so that the completion of each carefully constructed sentence, like the precise tying of each knot in the rug, works toward the end of the overall design. The close exploration of Tommy's consciousness—through the great abundance of detail—requires a commitment on the part of the reader, for as William Pritchard has noted, the novel "runs the risk, not always successfully, of narrative claustrophobia." That claustrophobia is the same as many readers find in a story such as Joyce's "The Dead"; like Joyce, McPherson continually balances the inner life of his protagonist against the larger social life in which the protagonist moves, and like Joyce, McPherson's concern for language and its relationship to the thought process is constantly on the edge of the character's consciousness. If the strategies of the novel seem familiar, however, it is because such strategies are inherent in a certain kind of novel, the realistic novel of psychological portrayal. McPherson has used those strategies to develop his own artistic vision of the world, for as Stefan Kanter has noted, "The author's imagery and style are wholly his own; from here on, it is his turn to be analyzed and imitated."

In the character of Tommy, McPherson presents a child who has all the advantages—not only material comforts, but also a mother who is loving and sympathetic to his needs and desires; an older brother who cares deeply for him; a housemaid who allows him to do most everything he wishes and yet who provides guidance; a father who, although driven by his management of his factory, loves and creates a place for Tommy in his life; and a whole neighborhood of families who view him as a valued member of the community and who respond favorably to his gentle, innocent nature. In this age of current ills—the aftermath of the Holocaust, nuclear armaments—such advantages as those of Tommy, such protection is often viewed with either nostalgia or impatience, but McPherson's compassion toward the

world of the child—the fresh world of new experiences and strange words—
is rendered with such commitment that one does not grow impatient with
the character. At the same time, the novel does not invite a sentimental
longing for its era; McPherson's ironic commentary guards against cheap
nostalgia. David Lehman sees the novel as a "stunning evocation of—and
elegy for—a vanished age of American innocence," but Tommy's innocence
is not matched in the larger social world in which he moves, and the novel's
strength resides in the tension between those two poles.

If Tommy is not immediately threatened by the uncontrollable forces that
bedevil many of his schoolmates, he is a sensitive child who knows of his
privileged position in a subtle, vague way. Much of the novel is concerned
with Tommy learning the subtleties of his upper-class society, with its attitudes toward people who make a living with their physical labor, with its
attitudes toward Jews and Native Americans and blacks. Such attitudes contain prejudice, and although Tommy does not readily grasp the significance
of this prejudice, the reader feels McPherson's condemnation of it in the
irony. Such attitudes, though, are not easily defined; they are an outgrowth
of the very circumstances that have created the structure of the society in
which Tommy lives, and those circumstances, as the overall pattern of the
novel suggests, are extremely complex.

Indeed, if the events in the novel seem straightforward, almost simple—
Tommy's birthday, Thanksgiving dinner, a summer day at the country club,
Christmas Day, his parent's twenty-fifth wedding anniversary—there is a
tension between the daily details of these events and their larger significance. One of Tommy's friends is a black woman who is a steward at the
country club, and he has learned that "the word 'Negro' was never used in
her presence, because the condition it described was thought to be embarrassing at best and irreversible in any case"; in the same way, he knows that
it is not polite to stare "at cripples on the street" or at "the stump where the
plumber's thumb used to be."

Such ironic, understated comments develop from the very pattern of the
novel's events. The area in which the novel is set is populated by a number
of Native Americans; they provide the common labor for the summer
homes of the privileged, which are a short distance from town on a group of
small islands. The McAllister housemaid, Rose, is Native American; when
she catches her husband in an adulterous situation, she physically beats him,
and he is driven to the hospital with his injuries. This situation is viewed
with considerable amusement by the adult members of Tommy's world. The
nature of that humor, however, is not based on compassion; instead, it reflects the paternalistic attitude of the group. Their reaction is quite different
when Tommy's mother engages in an affair with Luke Wolfe, an adventurous Canadian bachelor; there is a general disapproval and dismay. Class
differences are responsible for these contrasting responses, but this analysis

is never made explicit in the novel; instead, it arises naturally from the sequence of the novel's events.

Tommy is not consciously aware of his mother's affair. Unseen, he views Luke Wolfe fondling his mother's leg, and he tells the neighbors of an incident when Luke accompanies his mother home from a rendezvous while his father is out of town, but Tommy does not grasp the significance of such behavior. The reader does, however, and the discrepancy between Tommy's awareness and the reader's contributes to the complexity of the novel's tone.

Although he does not understand what is happening, Tommy is vaguely troubled by his mother's new emotional dimension, and one afternoon, when he unexpectedly comes upon Luke and his mother alone in the summer cottage, he attacks Luke verbally. Tommy's mother is wise enough not to respond negatively to his behavior. In her compassion for her son, she talks to Tommy about his behavior, and she then takes him in her arms, suddenly realizing how her actions have affected Tommy's emotional well-being. If her character were not so fully developed, this situation would seem melodramatic, but in McPherson's rendering of the scene, Tommy's emotional relationship to his mother becomes, instead, as complex as the situation demands. One measure of a novelist is his ability to create characters of emotional depth, and by this standard, McPherson measures up well.

McPherson's in-depth development of character, wherein the character is viewed both as an object of irony and as a complex person capable of compassion, is also found in the characterization of Tommy's father. On one level, Tommy's father is the typical male chauvinist who "didn't like women to swear, to wear pants, or shorts, to dye their hair, or to contradict him. He especially didn't like to be contradicted. . . ." He favors his oldest son, John—one of Tommy's two older brothers—for John has adopted his father's ideals of success; attending Northwestern University, he is engaged to one of the wealthy members of their social set. In contrast, Tommy's father is intolerant of David, his second son, who has dropped out of college and who lives at home and works in his father's chemical plant. David cannot do anything right in his father's eyes, and Tommy is puzzled by his father's attitude toward David. On another level, however, Tommy's father is the conscientious owner-manager of the town's chemical plant. He devotes his life to the success of the plant; it not only provides wealth and prestige to the family but also work for many of the townspeople. Tommy and the other members of the town have great respect for his father's technical expertise and his managerial abilities. When there is an explosion at the plant and three workers are killed, the blame is not directly attributable to Tommy's father, but he reacts as if it were. In his own way, he feels responsible, and this complex response—which contains his deep feelings for the families of the men—elevates his character, as Tommy's mother is elevated in her response to Tommy's attack on Luke Wolfe. Such portrayal of character is possible only when a writer has a certain vision of humankind; if these characters display prejudice and destructive attitudes toward other people, they are yet capable of compassion.

That vision is particularly evident in the creation of the character of Tommy: McPherson creates the child's world with rare fullness and insight. Tommy often wonders about language—words that suddenly take on mystery or a new meaning. One of these words, appropriately enough, considering the circumstances of the novel, is "adultery"; Tommy assumes that it is "one of the mysteries of the adult world, else why the name?" The "adult"-"adultery" connection is the kind of serious language play that James Joyce continually displays in his work. Tommy asks an adult friend of his at the country club the meaning of the word, and a subtle irony develops from this situation in that the man whom Tommy asks will discover before the conclusion of the novel that his wife is having an adulterous affair. Words can be strange: The word "pinfeathers," Tommy thinks, "was another queer word." Or goose bumps. When Tommy goes wild-geese hunting with his father, he experiences "goose bumps" when the geese suddenly appear, and he thinks, "So this was what they meant by goose bumps." The geese are honking "as if they had the croup—which his mother had said he'd surely get if his father took him out at that hour, in this weather." Sure enough, the next morning, Tommy does come down with the croup: The inner world of words and their relationship to the thought process are a constant concern of a stylist such as McPherson. Such concern with language and its mystery is also reflected in Tommy's great love of song—lullabies, hymns, popular tunes, nursery rhymes. One particular line from a hymn seems strange to Tommy as he sings it: "*Sing praise to His Name, He forgets not His own.*" Tommy wonders how "could God possibly forget his own name?" For "God was everywhere and knew everything—too much. . . . It was preposterous that he might forget his own name." The confusion in Tommy's mind over the connotation of "His own" leads to the seemingly offhand comment that God knows "too much"; from such a small detail as this mistaken meaning, McPherson, in the tradition of a Gustave Flaubert or a Joyce, goes to the thought-provoking idea that God's omniscience seems "too much" for humankind. The significance of this thought is, however, for the reader; it is beyond Tommy's understanding. Tommy also struggles with the word "hate," which, he knows, is a "terrible word; it was forbidden." His thoughts on the word in relationship to specific people lead to conversations with his mother on the nature of hate and love, and in these scenes McPherson displays the insight and power of a very talented novelist.

In Tommy's character, McPherson has found the perfect vehicle to enable him to explore the very nature of personal and social experience. Tommy not only wonders about words but also about people and their ways, and in this speculation, McPherson explores such topics as the role of custom, the concept of decorum and its advantages and hypocrisies, the world of the senses, and the nature of cause and effect. Such topics are those of the significant novelist, and although this novel has flaws—occasionally, one experiences, the claustrophobia that Pritchard identifies; occasionally, the accumulation of detail does not achieve the significance it requires to redeem its abundance, and it becomes merely tedious—the overall achievement is of such considerable artistic merit that the novel seems destined to become a classic.

Ronald L. Johnson

Sources for Further Study

Kirkus Reviews. LII, January 1, 1984, p. 11.
Library Journal. CIX, April 15, 1984, p. 824.
Los Angeles Times Book Review. May 6, 1984, p. 6.
The New Republic. CXC, April 30, 1984, p. 39.
The New York Times Book Review. LXXXIX, March 18, 1984, p. 3.
Newsweek. CIII, May 14, 1984, p. 77.
Publishers Weekly. CCXXV, January 13, 1984, p. 63.
Time. CXXIII, April 2, 1984, p. 86.
Washington Post Book World. April 15, 1984, p. 5.

THE THEATER OF ESSENCE

Author: Jan Kott (1914-   )
Translated from the Polish by various hands, with an introduction by Martin Esslin
Publisher: Northwestern University Press (Evanston, Illinois). 218 pp. $19.95
Type of work: Dramatic criticism

Essays on nineteenth and twentieth century dramatists by an influential critic who values drama both as literary text and as theater

Jan Kott is a Polish-reared, internationally seasoned critic whose vast knowledge of world drama puts him in the select circle of Eric Bentley, Robert Brustein, Maurice Valency, and very few others. In his preface to this volume, Martin Esslin calls him a representative of the vanishing category of *homme de lettres*, at home not only in literature and the theater but also in politics, philosophy, linguistics, and anthropology.

Kott was born in Warsaw, wrote surrealist poetry as a young man, received a doctorate in literature from the University of Lodz, and belonged to an extreme left-wing resistance group battling the Germans during World War II. In the postwar period he came to reevaluate his Marxist thinking and, allied with the brilliant philosopher Leszek Kolakowski, broke with Stalinism in 1956. In the mid-1960's, Kott migrated to the United States. Since 1969, he has held a professorship at the State University of New York at Stony Brook.

Kott's first important book, *Szkice o Szekspirze* (1962; *Shakespeare Our Contemporary*, 1964), has also been his most famous. In it, he interprets the Shakespearean historical cycle, the Roman plays, and the tragedies as akin to the twentieth century's Theater of the Absurd. The book's best-known essay, "*King Lear* or *Endgame*," inspired Peter Brook's direction of a distinguished production starring Paul Scofield as Lear. It also caused many Shakespearean specialists in academic halls to denounce Kott as a licentiously adventurous, ahistorical critic willing to stretch a text's meaning beyond its proper bounds and argue his case with rhetorical extravagance.

In *The Eating of the Gods: An Interpretation of Greek Tragedy* (1973), Kott tries to show that Greek drama belongs not only to the ancient but also the modern stage, with Sophoclean spectacle and ceremony as contemporary as Jean Genet's. Kott views Attic tragedy against his own background of European violence, its cruelty in the light of today's totalitarianism. What he addresses is a central problem with works of antiquity: how to have them speak to our eyes and ears and hearts yet respect the nature and context of their original culture. He thus views Ajax, Oedipus, and Antigone as isolated and self-consciously absurdist protagonists, while Euripides' *Alcestis* (438 B.C.) is a very dark *pièce noire*.

In *The Theater of Essence*, Kott has collected sixteen of his essays, translated with varying competence by thirteen different hands. (Kott's own version of English, heavily flavored with Polish and French words, is called "Kottish" by Esslin.) The range is from Oriental and European theater to American, from Nikolai Gogol to Jerzy Grotowski. The tone is lively to the point of rhapsodic; the argument is bold, sometimes arcane, occasionally subtle; the orientation is toward production considerations in the theater, with Kott consistently analyzing the playworthiness of plays—yet his learned love of reading frequently solidifies his comments.

The longest and most probing critique deals with Gogol's *The Inspector General* (1836), which Kott reads as a descendant of ancient comedy and the *commedia dell'arte*, but also as a forerunner of Buster Keaton, Charles Chaplin, and Marx Brothers comedies. Kott stresses the work's archetypal conflict between a house of virtue and a house of ill repute, with Gogol's tragicomedy anticipating the dark farces of Samuel Beckett, Eugène Ionesco, and Harold Pinter. Gogol's play is a graphic daytime nightmare whose grotesque clarity foreshadows Franz Kafka's. Kott even links Gogol's denial of his own work's satiric thrust with the denial practiced by the newspeak propaganda of present-day police states.

A reader unfamiliar with modern Polish writers may find Kott's half-dozen essays on them the most valuable in the book. The study of Stanislaw Witkiewicz—who preferred the name Witkacy—regards him as a premature prophet of today's drug culture and yesterday's student rebellions, who nevertheless strikes Kott as "a dazzling relic from the very beginning of the Twentieth Century who had strayed into the present." Poland's most eminent author between the wars, Witkacy also painted the kinds of portraits that were later to be called psychedelic and dabbled eloquently in both philosophy and poetry. As a dramatic theorist, he shares many grand and grandiose visions with Antonin Artaud, whom he never met. Curiously, Kott barely mentions such important Witkacy works as *The Madman and the Nun* (1923) and *The Water Hen* (1921). Kott's primary emphasis is on his subject's affinities and resemblances rather than artistic achievement.

The younger Polish novelist and playwright Witold Gombrowicz reminds Kott of François Rabelais and Molière in his stress on comic role-playing. More currently, he recalls to Kott's memory a party in German-occupied Warsaw where he saw two gifted young writers, Jerzy Andrzejewski and Czesław Miłosz, devoting hours to competitive grimacing learned from Gombrowicz's novel *Ferdydurke* (1937). Gombrowicz's fascination with mocking ceremonies, shame, and debasement points backward to Alfred Jarry and forward to Genet. In another comedy, *Operetta* (1966), he reminds Kott of Aristophanes but also anticipates his compatriot, Tadeusz Kantor.

Kantor gets most of Kott's attention in the title essay, "The Theater of Essence." He analyzes Kantor's best-known plays to date, *The Dead Class* (1975) and *Wielopole Wielopole* (1979), which disturbed and puzzled audiences at the 1984 Olympics Arts Festival in Los Angeles. In *The Dead Class*, the dead return to their former school benches and confront mannequins that represent their student past. In *Wielopole Wielopole*, Kantor also depicts the dead as ghosts, concentrating on World War I; the living are corpses which remain alive. This is the kind of stage that Kott calls "theater of essence," defining it in these words:

> In Sartre existence precedes essence. In Kantor's vision essence is the aftermath. Existence is freely created through a series of choices, but essence, as final as the Last Judgment, is what remains of us. Essence is the human drama freed of accident and of the illusion that there are choices. Essence is a trace, like the still undissolved imprint of a crustacean on a stone.

The analogues Kott draws are to *Everyman* (c. 1500), a morality of Christian essence, and William Shakespeare's *Macbeth* (1623), also dramatizing a situation of stark doom. The mass graves of twentieth century warfare constitute history's theater of essence.

The dreadful theater of totalitarianism leads Kott to eulogize another brilliant Polish artist, Tadeusz Borowski, who survived and wrote about Auschwitz, then took his life in his twenty-ninth year. Kott regards him as his generation's most gifted Polish writer, whose first volume of poetry, published by Warsaw's underground press when he was in his early twenties, "predicted in classical cadences the extermination of mankind." After the war, his collection of stories, *This Way for the Gas, Ladies and Gentlemen*, dazzled as well as shocked readers. Set in Auschwitz, the cycle of tales features a "Kapo" slave worker to whom Borowski gives his first name and who, assigned the duties of a low functionary, finds himself executioner as well as victim. Borowski portrays Auschwitz as a microcosm of the outside world, with the ovens devouring lives while both Ludwig van Beethoven and soccer are being played. "Between two throw-ins in a soccer game, right behind my back, three thousand people had been put to death." Kott interprets Borowski's suicide as a despairing act by a man who accepted his share of responsibility for the world constituting one large concentration camp.

In essays such as this one, Kott clearly demonstrates the social concerns of his humanistic perspective. He may be a disillusioned former Marxist, but he still fantasizes about a City of Man on Earth and responds to a literary or theatrical work, whenever feasible, in the context of his own conditioning by the unhappy history of his country during the postwar generations. Such a sociopolitical stance probably explains Kott's two attacks on Jerzy Grotowski's avant-garde Laboratory Theatre. Kott is astonished that, despite the intensely political awareness of Poland's post-World War II artistic atmosphere, Grotowski should have advocated a mystic theater of apolitical religiosity that considers the actor "holy" and seeks to dramatize archetypal experiences. He consequently dismisses Grotowski's influential work, *Apocalypsis* (1968), as a mistaken attempt at catharsis by way of flagellation and other physical degradations. "In Grotowski's theater," Kott charges, "liberation comes only through death, the torture of the body, and the humiliation of the spirit.... Why should I take part in the sacred dance?"

Kott shows his catholic interests by writing on Nō drama and the Bunraki and Kabuki theaters. He compares the tense stasis of Nō's dramatic structure with Jean Racine's, the system of its rigorous and frozen gestures to the ceremoniousness of calligraphy. Bunraki theater has puppets manipulated concurrently by three persons, while its plot is sung-recited by a narrator who doubles as a chorus. Kott is fascinated by the metaphysical aspects of a drama that bares the mechanism of its illusion-creating process rather than concealing it. Kabuki is a theater of miming which exaggerates its dramatic signs. Its female roles are enacted by males; its plots are drenched in morbidity, cruelty, and erotism. Kott notes the effect of these strategies on the dramaturgy of Artaud and Grotowski, Brecht and Genet. Surprisingly, Kott fails to note Ariana Mnouchkine's dazzling *Théâtre du Soleil* (1979), which presents Shakespeare's plays in Kabuki style.

A thirty-page essay on Henrik Ibsen furnishes many fresh insights: Kott reads *A Doll's House* (1879) as an inversion of Molière's bitter comedy *The Misanthrope* (1666), with the woman exiting into the world instead of the man into a social desert. Ibsen's play also inverts Pierre de Beaumarchais' *The Marriage of Figaro* (1784), in which the husband rediscovers his wife in the guise of a stranger; here the wife discovers the stranger in the guise of her husband. In *Ghosts* (1882) and *The Wild Duck* (1884) Ibsen uses classical tragedy's pattern of homecoming descended from Sophocles' *Electra* (c. 414 B.C.) to Shakespeare's *Hamlet* (1603) to Pinter's *Homecoming* (1965). *Ghosts* is, to be sure, a tragedy, with the father's "sin" of syphilis symbolically killing the son. It, however, also enacts a comic pattern of the daughter dominating the mother, as Regina leaves the Alving household, "free of remorse and of the ghosts of the past." In *The Wild Duck*, the son returns to avenge his mother, only to sacrifice his half sister, Hedvig, whose death also reenacts the mythic pattern of Iphigenia as she gives her life to regain her father's love. The wild duck's multivalent meanings inspired Anton Chekhov's equivalent use of a water bird in *The Sea Gull* (1896).

Kott interprets the last cycle of Ibsen's plays, from *Hedda Gabler* (1890) to *When We Dead Awaken* (1900), as repetitions of the theme of sexual frustration leading to self-destruction. He regards Hedda Gabler as Ibsen's double, with the tragedy dramatizing a lifelong "conflict between the Father/superego and the id. By shooting herself, Hedda kills the shadow of her Father and the child she never wanted. The 'shadow' of the father kills the daughter."

Kott reverses the consensual estimates of Ibsen critics by denigrating *The Master Builder* (1892), while calling *John Gabriel Borkman* (1896) the master's greatest play. He ignores the first work's meaning as an allegory of artistic creativity and destructiveness, instead stressing a biographical and historical reading: Not only is Hilde Wangel modeled after the eighteen-year-old Austrian Emilie Bardach, but Hilde also resembles August Strindberg's ambitious second wife, Frida Uhl, and Edvard Munch's mistress, Dagny Juel—all belonging to the first generation of emancipated European women who shocked propriety by casting off their corsets and stockings. The drama's ending, with its protagonist's fall from the tower he erected, strikes Kott as a displacement of Ibsen's fear of impotence with regard to Emilie Bardach, hence as an artificial climax, leading to "unearned tragicality." Kott's chief reason for admiring *John Gabriel Borkman* seems to be its anticipation of Beckett's *Endgame* (1957); he also stresses the similarities between both these works and *King Lear* (1623), enabling him to retrace some of the steps he took in his study of Shakespeare. In Ibsen's tragedy, Borkman leaves his eight-year self-imprisonment inside his house to seek a mountaintop through deep snow and freezing cold. Like Lear, he sinks into madness outdoors; unlike Lear, his heart fails to break, he develops no compassion. Kott quotes Ibsen's explanation of Borkman's death: "It was a freezing hand of metal that seized his heart."

These essays represent a major interpreter of modern drama at both his best and worst. His failings are clearly evident: indiscriminate use of any and all critical methods, a tendency to take undue liberties with a text, a weakness for striking, but not always supportable, parallels and speculation. Nevertheless, his virtues are also evident: a passionate enthusiasm for his subject, erudite scholarship, eagerness to absorb and communicate ideas, responsiveness to the broadest spectrum available of artistic and social experiences. On the whole, Jan Kott is an estimable figure on the critical landscape.

Gerhard Brand

Sources for Further Study

Library Journal. CX, January, 1985, p. 87.
The New York Review of Books. XXXII, March 14, 1985, p. 3.
The New York Times Book Review. XC, February 10, 1985, p. 18.
Publishers Weekly. CCXXVI, November 9, 1984, p. 54.

THOREAU'S SEASONS

Author: Richard Lebeaux (1946-   )
Publisher: University of Massachusetts Press (Amherst). 410 pp. $28.50
Type of work: Psychological biography
Time: 1845-1862
Locale: New England

The second and final volume of a psychohistorical biography, tracing Thoreau's development during his mature years from the beginning of the Walden experiment to his death in 1862

> *Principal personages:*
> HENRY DAVID THOREAU, an American author and naturalist
> JOHN THOREAU, JR., his older brother
> HELEN THOREAU, his older sister
> SOPHIA THOREAU, his younger sister
> JOHN THOREAU, SR., his father
> CYNTHIA DUNBAR THOREAU, his mother
> RALPH WALDO EMERSON, an American philosopher and essayist
> LIDIAN EMERSON, Emerson's wife
> BRONSON ALCOTT, an American Transcendentalist
> MARGARET FULLER, an American Transcendentalist
> ELLEN SEWELL OSGOOD, a young woman courted by Henry and John Thoreau
> HORACE GREELEY, a New York newspaper editor

In *Thoreau's Seasons*, Richard Lebeaux has written a sequel to his *Young Man Thoreau* (1977), continuing his psychohistorical biography of Thoreau through his mature years, from 1845 to his death in 1862. Lebeaux outlined the major premises of his study in the introduction to *Young Man Thoreau*, and because *Thoreau's Seasons* continues where the earlier book left off, it is essential to read both books in conjunction in order to appreciate fully Lebeaux's accomplishment. His approach is based upon the assumption that there is in Thoreau a fundamental conflict between the self-assured, confident voice of the writer and the troubled, self-doubting personality of Thoreau the man. Too often, the self-created, mythic personality in the writing has been accepted uncritically as being identical with the more complex and elusive personality of the writer. "It behooves us to see Thoreau as a 'complex and tortured man,'" Lebeaux argues, "even if this is not what we want to see." The confident, optimistic voice that one hears in *Walden* (1854) masks the often intense and prolonged self-doubt, conflict, and continual personal struggle that Thoreau experienced in resolving the issues of identity and vocation through his writing. The mature Thoreau that one finds in Lebeaux's rich and provocative study is neither as confident nor as self-assured as the literary "voice" at the end of *Walden*.

To a large degree, Lebeaux's approach is based upon psychoanalyst Erik Erikson's model of the eight stages of the human life cycle, first developed in *Childhood and Society* (1950) and later applied in *Young Man Luther* (1958) and *Gandhi's Truth* (1969). These stages involve conflicts between trust and mistrust, autonomy and shame or doubt, initiative and guilt, industry and inferiority, identity and identity confusion, intimacy and isolation, generativity and stagnation, and finally integrity and despair. According to Erikson, at each stage of human development, it is necessary that these conflicts be resolved in order to achieve a healthy and productive maturity. Lebeaux has adapted the conceptual framework of Erikson's humanistic psychoanalytic theories and has applied these insights to interpret Thoreau's creative development throughout his life. As Lebeaux cautions, however, Thoreau did not simply "resolve" each stage of development and then move on to the next. Instead, each "life-crisis" builds upon previous stages; thus, Lebeaux's psychobiography demonstrates the ways in which Thoreau's experience had a cumulative effect upon his development as a writer and a person and shows "how he *continued* to struggle throughout his life with issues first encountered in earlier developmental stages."

The major question with which Thoreau wrestled throughout his life was, "How shall I live?" This central issue of economy, vocation, and identity serves as a unifying theme in *Walden*, in which Thoreau purports to give a "simple and sincere account" of his life and of what he has learned through his Walden experiment, though the autonomous and self-reliant persona that one finds in *Walden* was often considerably at odds with Thoreau's actual experience, both during the Walden years and after. As Lebeaux demonstrates, the actual psychological conflicts that motivated Thoreau's Walden experiment were more complex than the economic issue of how he could earn his living as simply and self-sufficiently as possible. Thoreau's pretense of self-reliance, in fact, belied his much deeper sense of guilt and resentment concerning his considerable dependence upon his parents and family, as well as his ambiguous mentor-disciple relationship with Ralph Waldo Emerson, and his unresolved sense of guilt for his older brother John's death from lockjaw in 1842. These were the psychological forces that sent Thoreau to Walden Pond from 1845 to 1847, and the degree to which he was able to resolve those issues there profoundly influenced his later years. That the Walden experiment was not the unequivocal success that Thoreau pretended it was should not come as a surprise, since his account in *Walden* has the quality of a self-consciously embellished myth. The *Journal* accounts of the post-Walden years tell a story considerably at variance with the tone of *Walden*, and it is this conflict between the man and the myth that Lebeaux addresses in *Thoreau's Seasons*.

As Lebeaux's title indicates, the cycle of the seasons became increasingly important to Thoreau during the years after 1845, both as a creative metaphor and as a framework for personal adjustment and renewal, especially as he struggled to resolve the issues of generativity versus stagnation and integrity versus despair during these last years. When Thoreau went to Walden Pond to take up residence on July 4, 1845, a week short of his twenty-eighth birthday, he realized that he was no longer in the springtime of his youth. Thoreau's decision to go to Walden was by no means as simple as he pretended, and his reasons were not entirely unequivocal; instead, he went, as Lebeaux suggests, out of a "complex mix of motives and opportunity." He was at least in part symbolically declaring his independence from his family and townspeople, separating himself from the example of his unsuccessful father and domineering mother, resolving his guilt concerning his brother's death, and putting to rest his local reputation as an idle loafer and a "woodsburner," stemming from the accidental fire that he had set outside Concord in the spring of 1844, which had burned more than three hundred acres before it was finally extinguished by the townspeople. Indeed, in the years from 1837 to 1845, he had spent much of his time wrestling with the issues of identity, vocation, and separation from family. His time since graduating from Harvard University seemed relatively unproductive, except for the two years he had spent teaching school with his brother, John. Both brothers had been rebuffed in their courtship of Ellen Sewell, and Thoreau may privately have begun to feel some uneasiness about Concord's judgment of him, though outwardly he remained defiant and unconcerned about town opinion.

Going to Walden, then, permitted him to redeem himself through a noble experiment in living and to erect tangible foundations for his dreams of independence and purpose. Walden Pond and the natural cycle of the seasons would provide the nurturing presence that Thoreau needed in order to forge a mature identity. He experienced a confidence and reassurance through his intimacy with nature. His springtime of hope had not passed after all, he discovered, and there might yet be some noble work for him to accomplish. Thoreau's two years at Walden showed him that he could set up a household and live independently of the domestic atmosphere of his mother, aunts, and sisters. He left Walden with his sense of identity confirmed, sufficiently freed from the burden of guilt and self-recrimination which he had suffered that he could act now on his own behalf, without Emerson's assistance, to find a publisher for his manuscript titled *A Week on the Concord and Merrimack Rivers* and also to try to launch his own literary and lecture career.

It is interesting here to examine the woods-burning accident as indicative of Thoreau's pre-Walden state of mind. In April, 1844, Thoreau and Edward Hoar, who had been fishing on the Concord River, kindled a fire in a dead stump, surrounded by dry grass, in order to cook their mess of fish. The grass suddenly caught fire and rapidly spread toward the woods, out of control. That so careful a woodsman as Thoreau could have been responsible for so careless an act, and then refuse to help put out the fire, raises some interesting questions of motivation. Could he have unconsciously wanted to strike back at the forces of respectability that he believed were thwarting him? Did he imagine that some of the townspeople would have preferred to see him dead instead of his brother, John? What is most revealing is Thoreau's arrogant refusal to help put out the fire once it had started, preferring instead to watch it from a nearby hill as it spread and others struggled to extinguish it. The woods-burning incident was a public humiliation for the proud and sensitive Thoreau, one that he could not even bring himself to mention in his journal until six years later. Lebeaux argues that Thoreau's behavior here reflects his guilty and unsettled mind after his brother John's death.

John Thoreau, Jr., was Henry's talented and personable older brother, with whom he often felt in competition. There had been a falling out between the brothers concerning their schoolteaching venture and their rivalry in the courtship of Ellen Sewell. Then, in January, 1842, as Lebeaux recounts, the brothers "were brought together again under the most tragic of circumstances." John had cut his ring finger while stropping his razor blade, and he carelessly folded the skin back over the injured finger without cleaning it or letting it bleed. Two days later, the skin had begun to mortify around the finger, and John began to feel acute pain in his joints. By the third day, he complained of stiffness of the jaws, as with seizures the lockjaw set in. A doctor was called, but by then the patient was beyond cure. Henry stayed beside his brother constantly and devotedly nursed him during the last two days before his death. Thoreau was devastated by his brother's sudden death, though for about a week and a half he remained outwardly calm until he, too, developed a near-fatal case of sympathetic lockjaw. The death of his brother coming so unexpectedly soon after a period of rivalry and estrangement between them must have awakened in Henry intense guilt over their Oedipal and post-Oedipal rivalries. Lebeaux speculates that Thoreau may have believed that he was being "punished" for his rivalry and competition with his older brother, and this intense guilt may have prolonged and intensified the normal grief reaction.

In time, Thoreau would begin to transfer some of this intense feeling away from the memory of his brother and toward a feeling of empathy with his "brothers" the Native Americans and toward the publication of *A Week on the Concord and Merrimack Rivers* (1849), which he envisioned as a memorial to his brother and a record of the trip they had taken together in 1839. As Lebeaux indicates, "Thoreau went to Walden at least partially to 'conduct some unfinished business'—the writing of *A Week*." That work completed, he felt free to return to Concord and resume the other lives he had yet to live. Nevertheless, Thoreau was slowly discovering during the 1840's that it was not so easy to find one's own way in the world, particularly if one chooses an unconventional path. Throughout the decade, the Thoreau family's pencil business had been thriving, thanks to Henry's discovery, in 1838-1839, of an improved manufacturing process, though he obviously resented the time that he had to spend helping his father with the family business, referring to himself repeatedly in his *Journals* as Apollo bound to King Admetus. Gradually, Thoreau had been developing his surveying skills as a way of supporting himself and enjoying the outdoors at the same time, but a series of personal disappointments after he left Walden tested his new-found optimism and self-confidence.

According to Lebeaux, the publishing failure and lack of critical response to *A Week on the Concord and Merrimack Rivers* in 1849 touched Thoreau deeply, since he had intended the book as a memorial to his brother, John. The book's failure decisively ended his hopes of earning a living through a literary career and left him deeply in debt. Obligated to buy back 706 unsold copies, he reluctantly returned to the family pencil business, but his resentment concerning Emerson's failure to help publicize his book led to a tension in their relationship later that same year. Thoreau continued to work on revisions of the *Walden* manuscript during this difficult period, though in a moment of discouragement, he remarked in his journal, on July 19, 1851, shortly after his thirty-fourth birthday, "Here I am thirty-four years old, and yet is my life almost wholly unexpanded. How much is in the germ! There is such an interval between my ideal and the actual in many instances that I may say I am unborn." Nevertheless, as Lebeaux indicates, this was the "seedtime" that eventually led to the publication of *Walden* three years later.

One of Thoreau's greatest disappointments after he returned from Walden was the gradual estrangement from Emerson. Thoreau had returned to the Emerson household during Emerson's second trip to Europe in 1847-1848, but he soon realized how uncomfortable his position there was, compromising his independence. Indeed, much of the anger apparent in Thoreau's essay "Civil Disobedience" was animated by his sense of betrayal in his friendship with Emerson. He complained in his *Journals* of not being able to trust his "fair weather friends" and of being "stifled" by genteel Concord society. In protesting against the injustice of the Massachusetts poll tax, he may well have identified the state with the family as a repressive entity from which the individual must free himself. A famous anecdote has Emerson and Thoreau confronting each other after Thoreau had gone to jail rather than agree to pay the tax. Emerson asked Thoreau what he was doing in jail, and Thoreau quickly replied by asking Emerson what he was doing outside jail. The coolness in Emerson's attitude toward his former disciple is evident in his journal entries, his lukewarm review of *Walden*, and even in his eulogy at Thoreau's funeral. With the loss of this friendship, Thoreau experienced an increasing loneliness during the last decade of his life, only partially compensated for by his new admiration for Walt Whitman, John Brown, and the Maine Native American guide Joe Polis.

A different kind of conflict emerged for Thoreau in 1854 with the publication of *Walden*. He had been working on successive revisions and expansions of the manuscript since 1849, but in the winter of 1854 he completed the seventh draft of *Walden*, adding chapter titles and establishing the cycle of the seasons as the dominant structural principle. The manuscript of *Walden* was accepted by Ticknor and Fields in March of that year and published in August, but its publication brought on a different kind of struggle for Thoreau, one associated with emptiness and loss following the completion of a sustained and intensive creative endeavor. Once *Walden* was finished, he experienced a kind of "postpartum depression" that sapped his energies and left him anxious about the future. What could he write after *Walden*? What future directions would his creativity take? His loss of vitality in the months after the publication of *Walden* brought on a lingering illness that left him without energy or purpose. He felt the sudden onset of middle age and a sharp sense of his own mortality and impending death. It took him more than a year to resolve this generativity crisis and to get on with his autumnal work.

The last decade of Thoreau's life was marked by consolation and acceptance, as he struggled with the conflict of integrity versus despair. His deepening awareness of the correspondence between the cycle of the seasons and the "seasons" of his own life helped him to resolve the generativity crisis and to prepare himself for the eventuality of his own death. There is a renewed vitality in his *Journals* after 1855, evident also in his trips to Cape Cod and Maine and his return to lecturing. He began studying nature more systematically and scientifically, so that many of his entries took on a less metaphorical, more impersonal and objective style. Becoming involved in the Fugitive Slave Law controversy, he wrote an impassioned "Plea for Captain John Brown," identifying Brown's fate with that of his own generativity. Conservation and preservation also became increasingly important to him, as he looked ahead to posterity, and he wanted to see Walden set aside as a park. The metaphor of "tracking" assumed significance for him as he looked back over his life and evaluated what he had done. The essay "What Shall It Profit?" later entitled "Life Without Principle" reaffirmed his fundamental values.

In December, 1860, Thoreau contracted a severe cold that later developed into bronchitis and kept him indoors all winter. In the spring of 1861, he went to Minnesota in an attempt to regain his health, but by late 1861-1862, Thoreau showed the signs of advanced tuberculosis. Nevertheless, he seemed cheerful and accepting, as is often the case with consumptive patients. Though he knew that his family was susceptible to tuberculosis, he showed great serenity and courage during his final illness. According to one tradition, when Thoreau was asked whether he had made his peace with God, he answered that he did not know that they had ever quarreled. On

May 6, 1862, he died peacefully at the age of forty-four.

In *Thoreau's Seasons*, Richard Lebeaux has done an admirable job of re-interpreting Thoreau's literary accomplishments within a framework of personal growth and development that helps to account for their genesis. His use of the Eriksonian model of the eight stages of human life offers a rich and insightful analogue to the "seasons" of Thoreau's own interior life. Lebeaux's Thoreau is a more complex and interesting figure than that of previous biographers. *Thoreau's Seasons*, along with *Young Man Thoreau*, marks a major event in Thoreau scholarship.

Andrew J. Angyal

Sources for Further Study

Best Sellers. XLIV, August, 1984, p. 183.
Choice. XXII, October, 1984, p. 269.
Library Journal. CIX, March 15, 1984, p. 585.
Publishers Weekly. CCXXV, February 10, 1984, p. 185.

TIME AND NARRATIVE
Volume I

Author: Paul Ricoeur (1913-   )
Translated from the French by Kathleen McLaughlin and David Pellauer
Publisher: University of Chicago Press (Chicago). 274 pp. $25.00
Type of work: Philosophy

This first volume of Ricoeur's two-part study critiques twentieth century theories of historical knowledge and attempts to integrate Saint Augustine's theory of time with Aristotle's theory of plot to develop a thesis about the temporality of narrative

Although the title of this work by modern philosophy's most eminent phenomenologist might suggest that its focus is on literary theory, readers searching for a study of fictional narrative will be disappointed. That task Ricoeur is reserving for the second volume. In volume 1 of *Time and Narrative* (published in France in 1983 as *Temps et récit*), he is primarily concerned with the narrative nature of history. In fact, more than half of the book is devoted to a survey and a critique of historiography, including the philosophy of history, to develop his thesis that the ultimate character of history is indeed narrative. The other half makes use of Saint Augustine's study of time in the *Confessions* and Aristotle's study of plot in the *Poetics* to develop Ricoeur's central thesis that time only becomes human when it is articulated by means of narrative, and narrative is meaningful only when it is mimetic of temporality.

As opposed to the semioticians, who, following upon the popularity of structuralism, seem to hold to the day in modern criticism, Ricoeur is concerned with the level of meaning beyond the sign. In *The Rule of Metaphor* (1977), his focus was not on signs but on discourse—that level of language-acts equal to or higher than the sentence, the level which Ricoeur says is synthetic and cannot be reduced to a combination of signs. In that work, Ricoeur was concerned with the semantic level of discourse—that is, how metaphor makes meaning. In *Time and Narrative*, he moves to the level higher than the sentence—to plot—but he is still concerned with semantics, and, as opposed to structuralist theorists of narrative who have struggled with the abstract syntax of narrative, he is concerned with the semantic relationship between narrative and that which narrative takes as its structure and subject: the paradoxical nature of time itself.

Ricoeur seems to be fighting a rear-guard action against the modernist and postmodernist dogma that has dominated literary criticism and theory at least since the French Symbolists, according to which the primary poetic function of language is the self-referential focus on language for its own sake. Ricoeur's study of the semantic nature of both metaphor and narrative is a return to mimesis, a return to the study of art as referential to the external world. This does not mean, however, that Ricoeur defends a naïve realism which understands imitation as a photographic duplication of external reality. Rather, he is concerned with the ability of narrative plot to reconfigure man's confused and unformed experience of time itself. "What then, is time?" asks Saint Augustine. "I know well enough what it is, provided that nobody asks me; but if I am asked what it is and try to explain, I am baffled." Plot for Ricoeur is a means of dealing with what cannot be explained in ordinary discursive language, the temporality of experience.

The critiques of Saint Augustine and Aristotle which make up the first two chapters form an introduction to the basic thesis of the reciprocity between narrativity and temporality, a thesis developed more thoroughly in chapter 3. Ricoeur chooses Saint Augustine and Aristotle because in both the essential dichotomy between concordance and discordance (which is also the essential tension of time and narrative) is most clearly laid bare. Saint Augustine focuses on the human desire for concordance in spite of discordance in temporal experience, while Aristotle emphasizes the dominance of concordance over discordance in the plot. In his effort to show that narrative deepens and humanizes time, Ricoeur also battles against the more accepted modernist thesis that the art work dechronologizes narrative or spatializes it and that therefore the critic's job is to lay bare the logic or rules which the narrative creates out of the merely temporal.

Ricoeur's "return to Aristotle" might, at first glance, resemble a similar attempt to resurrect the mimetic nature of plot to combat formalism by the so-called Chicago or Neo-Aristotelian school in American criticism thirty years ago. Ricoeur's Aristotelianism, however, is not so thorough-going; he is only concerned here to focus on the implications of the basic Aristotelian notion of emplotment or *muthos*—that is, the organization of events. He wishes to explore whether the paradigm of order which Aristotle establishes for tragedy can be extended and transformed to apply to the whole narrative field, including history as well as fictional narrative. For Ricoeur, mimesis aims at the universal reconfiguring power of *muthos*, not merely the configuring of a particular story. To make up a plot, says Ricoeur, is to make the intelligible spring from the accidental, the universal from the singular, the necessary from the episodic. The Aristotelian notions of tragic reversal and recognition go beyond tragedy; they are essential to every story or history where meaninglessness threatens the meaningful.

Mimesis, as Aristotle defines it, is not simply the imitation of some preexisting reality, says Ricoeur, but rather a creative imitation, a reconfiguring which produces what the Russian Formalist critics call the "literariness" of the work. Since the study of literariness is precisely the field the semioticians have made their own, and by doing so have ignored both the referential nature of literature as well as its impact on the reader, Ricoeur establishes three definitions, or moments, of mimesis, which he names mimesis$_1$, mimesis$_2$, and mimesis$_3$. Whereas the semioticians suggest that a science of a text can only be based on the internal laws of mimesis$_2$, Ricoeur says that that such "literariness" is only intelligible because of the intermediary position it maintains between mimesis$_1$ and mimesis$_3$.

Drawing from the work of Ernst Cassirer, Ricoeur characterizes mimesis$_1$ by showing that human action is a quasi-text already articulated by signs, rules, and norms. Before action can be imitated or represented, it must be preunderstood in its semantics, its symbolic system, and its temporality. Mimesis$_2$, or emplotment, is the process that configures simple succession so that we can ask what is the "thought" of the story. We are mistaken, however, if we take such a thought or theme to be atemporal. Instead, Ricoeur says, a new quality of time emerges. Instead of understanding time as flowing from the past to the future, we can, because of the configuration of emplotment, read the ending in the beginning and the beginning in the ending and thus learn to read time backwards to reveal temporal causality.

In arguing that mimesis$_3$ marks the intersection between the text and the reader, Ricoeur takes up the area of study of the reception of critics such as Roman Ingarden, Robert Jauss, and Wolfgang Iser, for whom the text is a set of instructions that readers execute in various ways. Ricoeur, who says that he will critique the theories of these critics in more detail in volume 2, says that an aesthetic of reception cannot deal with the problem of communication without also dealing with the problem of reference. On the level of the sentence or beyond, language is inevitably oriented beyond itself; it says something *about* something. All reference is coreference, Ricoeur argues; it is dialogical. Following the thesis he developed in *The Rule of Metaphor*, Ricoeur asserts that poetic works refer to the world in their own specific way, that of metaphorical reference rather than descriptive reference. Instead of producing weak images of reality, as proposed by Plato, or producing images that refer only to themselves, literary works *augment* reality with means that depend on metaphoric devices or the devices of emplotment.

The second half of *Time and Narrative* may be more interesting to historians than to students of literary narrative, for it is primarily an extended summary and critique of historiography since the 1930's. Ricoeur's thesis here is that history belongs to the field of narrative—that, indeed, if history were to break all connections to the basic competence of readers to follow a story, it would cease to be historical. Ricoeur sets himself three tasks in the second half of the book: first, to correlate the "eclipse of narrative" by French historiography, which denies the narrative character of history by arguing that the social fact rather than the active individual is the object of history, and the similar eclipse by the logical positivists, who deny narrative by arguing for an epistemological break between historical explanation and narrative understanding; second, to survey and integrate those twentieth century theorists who have defended the narrative nature of history; and third, to examine why the connection between history and narrative competence must be an indirect rather than a direct one. Ricoeur warns that these three chapters constitute only a preparatory analysis of the relationship between historical *explanation* and narrative *understanding*. Only in the second volume, which is devoted to fictional narrative, will he take up the total project—the reconfiguring of time by narrative, which he says is the joint work of history and fiction.

Ricoeur agrees with the historical narrativists that to narrate is already to explain, for narrative brings about a causal connection by means of the operation of emplotment. According to Ricoeur, however, the narrativist model disintegrates by moving explanation by emplotment away from story line to explanation by argument and by ideological implications. Thus, the narrative thesis, which Ricoeur has reworked to the point of becoming antinarrativist, has no chance of replacing an explanatory model of history. A gap remains between narrative explanation and historical explanation which Ricoeur takes as his primary task to bridge. His means of doing so is through the phenomenological methodology of Edmund Husserl of "questioning back" to arrive at the intentionality of historical knowledge. The key for Ricoeur is the fact that the world to which history refers is prestructured, because it is a world of action already configured through narrative activity—the world of mimesis$_1$. The entities of mimesis$_1$, however, the entities belonging to the sphere of action, can only be referred to by means of the strictly narrative category of characters, which is a concept that derives from the literariness of mimesis$_2$.

Ricoeur makes clear that in his concern to focus on the narrative nature of history he has set aside the issue of history's relation to the past and therefore its truth claim; he has only considered those aspects of time related to the configuration process that relates history to narrative. Moreover, he reminds the reader that volume 1 of his study is primarily preparatory—that all of the second half of the book is an investigation of the relation between the writing of history and the process of emplotment to make sure that history does indeed belong to the narrative field defined by the configuring process of emplotment.

In layman's terms, the basic issue Ricoeur is exploring is the seeming paradox of narrative which has been lamented by critics at least since E. M. Forster and C. S. Lewis—that is, that although narrative must tell a story, must indeed both reflect and exist in time, it is not the mere storyness that the artist is after. Rather, the point or theme of the story seems to be something that is timeless, something that exists all at once rather than as "one damn thing after another." Modernist writers since James Joyce have tried to escape this narrative trap by creating fictions that hold together in a spatial way by means of the structured repetition of metaphors and thematic motifs. According to many modern critics, one reads for meaning by reading spatially—that is, by breaking up the narrative into related groups of motifs and displaying them for interpretation in a spatial pattern. This formalist approach to fiction, which began with the Russian Formalists in the 1920's, has led ultimately to the structuralist approaches of Claude Lévi-Strauss and Tzvetan Todorov, who assert the primacy of the paradigmatic (or universal and atemporal) nature of narrative over its syntagmatic or time-bound process.

Ricoeur, being a good phenomenologist, wishes to return narrative to time, desires to regain the mimetic nature of art that the formalist-structuralist approach has abandoned. It is not clear, however, from this first volume of *Time and Narrative*, precisely how he intends to do this. That narrative or emplotment reconfigures time seems obvious enough. That there are indeed three dynamics to consider in dealing with mimesis—the "world" which the narrative takes as its subject, the work or text that reconfigures the world, and the reader who processes this reconfiguration— is a theme that informs much contemporary criticism. It is less obvious, however, how Ricoeur intends to integrate these three dynamics and thus "solve" the problem of the paradox of narrative by clarifying how narrative "explains" in a temporal way. Perhaps, as Ricoeur promises throughout the book, it will be with volume 2, when he tackles fictional narrative, that he makes clear how narrative constitutes an explanatory model by means of, rather than in spite of, the fact that it presents events as "one damn thing after another."

Charles E. May

Sources for Further Study

Library Journal. CIX, July, 1984, p. 1330.
The New York Times Book Review. LXXXIX, July 22, 1984, p. 13.
Publishers Weekly. CCXXV, May 4, 1984, p. 48.

TIRANT LO BLANC

Author: Joanot Martorell (d. 1468) and Martí Joan de Galba (d. 1490)
Translated from the Catalan by David H. Rosenthal
Publisher: Schocken Books (New York). 642 pp. $21.95
Type of work: Novel
Time: The fifteenth century
Locale: England, the Greek Empire, and North Africa

How Tirant lo Blanc, of Breton Saltrock lineage, knight of the Order of the Garter, liberated Rhodes, pacified North Africa, and became Imperial Caesar of the Greek Empire

> *Principal characters:*
> TIRANT LO BLANC, the protagonist, a knight
> CARMESINA, Princess of Greece and Tirant's bride
> FREDERIC, ruler of the Greek Empire; Carmesina's father
> DIABHEBUS, a cousin to Tirant
> STEPHANIE, Carmesina's friend; Diabhebus' wife
> PLEASURE-OF-MY-LIFE, Carmesina's confidante
> THE EASYGOING WIDOW, Carmesina's rival

An extraordinarily rich, complex, lively, and refreshing masterpiece has come to light. In *Don Quixote*, Cervantes rightly characterized *Tirant lo Blanc* as the best book of its kind in the world, a wealth of pleasure and a gold mine of enjoyment. The contemporary Peruvian novelist Mario Vargas Llosa places its author, Joanot Martorell, at the head of the lineage of God supplanters such as Henry Fielding, Honoré de Balzac, James Joyce, and William Faulkner, who create in their fiction an all-encompassing reality. Joanot Martorell's novel, however, has never before been accessible to the English-speaking world and has had few other translations (into Italian in 1538, French in 1737?, and Castillian in 1511 and 1969). When it was published in Catalan in Valencia in 1490, the Catalan language and its literature began a decline from which they have, outside the Catalan lands, barely recovered. *Tirant lo Blanc* is, then, a true "lost" masterpiece which has only recently been rediscovered, a masterpiece that ranks with the greatest medieval and Renaissance classics, such as Giovanni Boccaccio's *The Decameron*, Geoffrey Chaucer's *The Canterbury Tales*, and Cervantes' *Don Quixote* itself.

Joanot Martorell, the work's principal author, was above all a knight of Valencia who also wrote, not a writer who happened to be a knight, as David Rosenthal persuasively argues in his scholarly "Translator's Foreword." Martorell's firsthand experiences with duels and cartels of defiance, with the Moorish kingdom of Grenada, with a family history of crusades against the Saracens, and with the chivalrous code inform and suffuse the novel and ring truer than the obligatory citation of authorities (such as Aristotle, Scipio, Vergil) in some of the formulaic speeches of the characters. Martí

Joan de Galba, another knight, who edited the novel sometime between Martorell's death (1468) and its publication (1490), may have composed as much as a quarter of the work and is responsible for many of the obvious bridges of some of the later episodes ("Here the book leaves the king . . . and returns to the six vessels . . ."). De Galba's contributions extend beyond simple editing to include, in the opinion of most scholars, Tirant's pacification of North Africa and his final succor of the Byzantine Empire, though it does appear that de Galba followed a plan set forth by Martorell. De Galba's wide-ranging passion for geography and his cartographerlike penchant for exact physical locations in the North Africa section of the novel turn up a remarkable mention of the kingdom of Bornu, a place generally believed to have been discovered by eighteenth century Europeans.

The novel itself is everything that late-medieval, early-Renaissance novel of chivalry should be: Tirant, the hero, is as wonderfully superhuman in war and gloriously human—if a bit obtuse—in love as one could wish, while Carmesina, daughter of the emperor of Greece, is as perfect as any high-minded, well-spoken, well-read, and hot-blooded damsel of fourteen years could be. Together, they act as perfect foils to each other, as their protracted, furtive, and somewhat ill-starred romance forms the center of much of the novel's action. That the course of true love never did run smooth is, in their case, an understatement. Thwarted by the disparity of their respective positions in society until near the end of the novel, when Tirant is designated to succeed the emperor and to wed the princess he has already won, foxed by the cunning of the Easygoing Widow, from whom the Wyf of Bath could have learned a trick or two, separated by conventional morality and then by shipwreck, they finally unite in a joyously sportive celebration of sexuality, and then reunite, once their future earthly union is duly assured, in death.

As the love story of Tirant and Carmesina is central to much of the novel's forward movement, so the true education of a knight, his induction into the code of chivalry, his Herculean performance time and again against all odds, and his making virtues not only of necessities but also of adversities form a second important dimension of the novel. Informed by the Crusader history of the Martorell family, Tirant's military exploits reflect the wars between Christendom and the Muslim world which remain unabated in their fierceness in present-day Lebanon, holy wars that once had the elaborate justifications of chivalry to legitimatize them but now seem as boyish as any other war. Like most medieval romances and the Renaissance epic poems of dynasty, *Tirant lo Blanc* contains superb examples of tournament fighting, duels of honor, and full-scale battles. One notable difference in this regard is that Martorell's novel contains a wealth of detail that reinforces its realism. This realistic element pervades the entire work, not only the grim and gory battle scenes. The level of detail in descriptions of places, physical geography, architecture, furniture and adornment, costume, customs, characters and their situations and speech helps to establish the work as a novel rather than an episodic romance. Indeed, the individualization of character this realism serves to produce makes the novel a novel and sets it apart from much work contemporaneous with it.

Tirant, for example, is not merely a fighting machine with some feelings; rather, he is a genuinely human character trying to better himself, to serve the causes of truth and right as he sees them, and to better the lot of his companions and those he serves. He is also a complex character who must contend with a full array of emotions ranging from anger to pity to self-pity to love. The object of his love and cause of some of his self-pity is herself a fully developed character, the princess Carmesina. The princess and her close companions are among the few women in literature of the fifteenth century (and later as well as earlier) who exhibit, in the portions Martorell wrote, a range of feelings, a depth of understanding, and a sense of equality with, if not superiority to, their male counterparts.

One aspect of reality rarely presented explicitly and in any depth in the earlier romances and generally confined to the fabliaux of such writers as Chaucer and Boccaccio is the open and frank treatment of sexuality. This treatment includes but moves beyond the sly and ribald comments and innuendo common to the fabliaux and the prevailing moral climate, to explore the often confusing and complex issues of sexuality, including physical performance, and subsumes it in stages: unrequited love (a staple of chivalric epic and romance), the fear of rejection, the fear of acceptance and surrender, the peak moments of pleasure, and the romance and emotional involvements and ambiguities that attend loving and being in love. One important element of sex in the novel is the conscious choice on Carmesina's part that triumphs over compulsion; another is the free and natural enjoyment of pleasure in a context of genuine affection and a demonstrated commitment. If one test of a classic is its enduring relevance to successive ages and tastes, then the treatment of sex and sexuality in *Tirant lo Blanc* qualifies it as a classic with a modernity which speaks to the late twentieth century about current obsessions, compulsions, and sources of complicated dilemmas, satisfactions, ideals, and discontents.

Another "modern" aspect of the work, one which has much in common with what has been termed the literature of exhaustion, is Martorell's and de Galba's piling up of fact upon fact, detail upon detail, so that the reader is thoroughly immersed in the fictional situations and is led to feel embroiled in the action while being firmly directed to take the protagonist's part. Clear instances of this abound as the reader is instructed, for example, how to burn ships, how to prepare a siege and how to resist one, how to gather military intelligence, and how to deceive the enemy about one's numerical advantage. At times the level of detail can be stultifying and impede the progress of the plot, especially in some of the sections that treat physical geography and the technicalities of warfare; at other times, however, the detailed descriptions are richly satisfying.

Tirant lo Blanc is, surprisingly, accessible to a wide modern readership—surprisingly, because although it has all the trappings of medieval and Renaissance literature, it also has a strong story line and credible characters. Some of the trappings will be foreign to modern readers: The vast store of learning about classical literature, heraldry, medieval customs, and everyday life which Martorell and de Galba include may cause many readers to stumble. For others, these are precisely some of the points of attraction to the literature of this period. Part of the novel's charm is that it can satisfy those who do not care for the historical background and literary sources as well as those who do care about them. The language is formal and archaic, though Rosenthal avoids the intentional archaisms which have been widely identified with the medievalism that nineteenth century writers who rediscovered the Middle Ages made up as they went along. Indeed, the translation has been criticized for being entirely too modern and upbeat and for using words that did not enter the English language for centuries after the time of the novel's composition and publication, yet to so criticize is to miss one essential component of translation, the temporal dimension: The novel is translated into English (American English, at that) for twentieth century readers, few of whom have read Chaucer and Sir Thomas Malory in their original versions. Rosenthal's translation is not aimed at producing a full-dress academic text, replete with exhaustive notes on sources and analogues, textual variants, longish disquisitions into military campaigns, and the usual *apparatus criticus*. Rather, this is a popular translation which will provide a wide readership for "the best book in the world" and which also points students and scholars in directions they can pursue for further information in a superb "Translator's Foreword," fourteen pages of interesting, informative notes, and nearly two pages of judiciously selected bibliography.

John J. Conlon

Sources for Further Study

Booklist. LXXX, May 1, 1984, p. 1226.
Choice. XXII, November, 1984, p. 431.
Christian Science Monitor. LXXVI, August 3, 1984, p. B1.
Library Journal. CIX, July, 1984, p. 1348.
Los Angeles Times Book Review. July 8, 1984, p. 1.
The Nation. CCXXXIX, August 4, 1984, p. 85.
The New York Times Book Review. LXXXIX, July 15, 1984, p. 10.

The New Yorker. LX, July 30, 1984, p. 87.
Publishers Weekly. CCXXV, May 4, 1984, p. 50.
The Wall Street Journal. CCIV, August 7, 1984, p. 30.

TOUGH GUYS DON'T DANCE

Author: Norman Mailer (1923-   )
Publisher: Random House (New York). 229 pp. $16.95
Type of work: Novel
Time: The 1980's
Locale: Provincetown, Massachusetts

A metaphysical murder mystery, firmly rooted in the reality of Provincetown and full of fascinating characters, concerning a writer who must confront the worst in himself in order to conceive of a new basis on which to live

> *Principal characters:*
> TIM MADDEN, a writer, the novel's narrator-protagonist, and a murder suspect
> PATTY LAREINE, Madden's missing wife who has conducted herself like a character out of F. Scott Fitzgerald's *The Great Gatsby*
> LAUREL OAKWODE, a Patty Lareine look-alike with an assumed name (Jessica Pond), who is also missing
> LEONARD PANGBORN, a man who accompanies Jessica Pond to Provincetown and also disappears
> ALVIN LUTHER REGENCY, Provincetown's acting police chief and Madden's arch rival
> HENRY "SPIDER" NISSEN, a Provincetown local, a writer, and another one of Madden's rivals
> MADELEINE FALCO, Madden's former flame and Regency's wife
> MEEKS WARDLY HILBY III, Madden's wealthy school chum, Patty Lareine's former husband and murder conspirator
> JOSEPH "BOLO" GREEN, a black stud and "bad nigger" who takes up with Patty Lareine and Beth, Spider's girl
> "DOUGHY" MADDEN, Tim's father, confidant, and exemplar
> "STOODIE," a man who collects bets for "Pete the Polack" Petrarciewisz
> SVEN "HARPO" VERIAKIS, a psychic and madman

Norman Mailer has a considerable reputation for being the tough guy of American letters. Attacked by Kate Millet and others for his misogyny, he has come to seem, in many reviewers' minds, the incarnation of male chauvinism. His writings are studded with analogies between boxing matches and literary performances, and his much-publicized personal life—including the stabbing of his second wife—has been conflated with novels such as *An American Dream* (1965), in which Steven Rojack gets away with murdering his spouse. Mailer's often flamboyant and controversial public persona—most recently on view in his support of the murderer Jack Abbott—has further eroded, for many readers, the distinctions which might be made between the person and his prose.

Mailer's latest novel, a murder mystery featuring two decapitated women, will do nothing to lessen feminist criticism of his work. The tough-guy strain in his writing, however, is almost always balanced by great tenderness and self-doubt—as it is in this first-person fiction of a faltering writer who is at least as tentative as he is tough. Like the Mailer of *Advertisements for Myself* (1959), Tim Madden questions his talent even as he tries to promote and cultivate it. He worries over a tendency toward timidity, connected in his mind with his defeat in the only Golden Gloves bout he ever fought. More or less kept by his prized wife, the apparently wealthy Patty Lareine, he cannot write when she deserts him.

As her name suggests, Lareine has been Madden's imperious queen, and he seems at a loss when he is not in her service. At the same time, however, he has clearly chafed under her rule, for he regrets having broken his code of male self-sufficiency. As a result, the couple's marriage has been alternately turbulent and harmonious; in the latter stages of their relationship, they share murderous inclinations toward each other.

Thus it is that Madden must confront the possibility that he has murdered his missing wife in a drunken spree which he can barely recall. As his name suggests, Tim Madden is a divided man—on the one hand subject to insane energies that he can hardly control, on the other hand inhibited by a timorousness that arouses self-contempt. The novel's real mystery—aside from an intricate plot that should not be divulged for devotees of the genre—is Madden's metaphysical concern about existence, about how thoroughly dualistic it is—right down to the creaturely level of his dog sensing the proximity of a severed human head: "his voice now raised in a mixture of elation and fright as if, like us, he could call upon two deep and divided halves of himself."

The first two sentences of the novel emphasize the somber setting of winter in Provincetown, a fitting image for the waste of a life that Madden will redeem only by recovering the courage to accept his human vulnerability: "At dawn, if it was low tide on the flats, I would awaken to the chatter of gulls. On a bad morning, I used to feel as if I had died and the birds were feeding on my heart." He remains throughout his story perilously poised between life and death and in desperate need of a new code by which he can be reborn, for he has reservations about the seemingly simpleminded macho injunction by which his father has lived. In pondering the anecdote to which the remark "tough guys don't dance" refers, Madden comments:

> Surely my father had meant something finer than that you held your ground when there was trouble, something finer that doubtless he could not or would not express, but it was there, his code. It could be no less than a vow. Did I miss some elusive principle on which his philosophy must crystallize?

Madden never does offer a definition of his father's remark, but given the behavior of both father and son, the key to what Madden calls his koan, "tough guys don't dance," has to do not so much with toughing things out— which implies a kind of static defense of what one already is—but with recognizing the elusiveness of principles and perceptions that inevitably change in the course of time. Madden's father, Doughy, admits that, in some ways, he has not been as tough as his son supposes, and thereby Doughy gains toward the end of the novel an impressively supple strength on which his son—always somewhat abashed by his father's macho superiority—can rely. In other words, Doughy, who faces the prospect of his own death by cancer, is willing to shatter the stereotype of toughness in which his son has invested so heavily.

Readers who prefer taut, spare plots and prose may bristle at the complications of Mailer's syntax and philosophizing. Evil, however, has many sources that are not easily linked up in the satisfying way of many murder mysteries. The heads and bodies buried in different locations are indicative of the splits in the human psyche that Mailer has pursued in much of his writing. As Tim Madden has it: "We live with not one soul but two," souls which are often as unequal as two badly matched horses. Usually Mailer is able to finesse the shifts between the novel's ideas and events, and his delineation of characters through clipped dialogue is convincing, but sometimes his transitions and asides are awkward and forced: "This is no exposition of dualities, but. . . ." At such times, his narrative loses momentum, perhaps because he has tried to do too much, to integrate characters, ideas, and plot simultaneously in a single narrative voice.

What is never in question, however, is Mailer's evocation of setting. Provincetown, past and present, is vividly portrayed through the novel in tantalizing vignettes. Each digression into Provincetown history is meant to give a concrete context for the narrator's divided soul. His house—Patty Lareine's house, he reminds himself—is built out of the very stuff of the "whoretown" or "Hell-Town" that thrived in the days of whaling:

Half of our holding of sills, studs, joists, walls, and roof had been ferried over from Hell-Town more than a century ago, and thereby made us a most material part of that vanished place. . . . Provincetown, then, was just far enough away to be able to keep up the Yankee proprieties of widows' walks and white churches. What an intermingling of the spirits, therefore, when the whaling ended and the shacks in Hell-Town were floated over to us.

Tough Guys Don't Dance is about the intermingling of spirits, about Laurel Oakwode (Jessica Pond) doubling for Patty Lareine, about Alvin Luther Regency's two names for himself, and about each character's counterpart or alter ego. Fortified by the strong presence of Provincetown as a place and as a paradigm of history, a paradigm of division between perversity and propriety, Mailer is able to create his characters and plot with considerable, if occult, persuasiveness.

As the novel's title perhaps suggests, there is also a sportive and amusingly combative tilt to Mailer's writing. Other titles—*Dead Men Don't Wear Plaid* and *Real Men Don't Eat Quiche*—come to mind. Apparently, the author is willing to have a little fun with the macho attitudes that he has been attacked for espousing. For some reason, reviewers have seldom been willing to praise Mailer for his playfulness, or it may be that they are temperamentally unsuited to appreciate the fact that, for him, even ideas about which he is deadly serious have their comic side. Even at his most intellectual, Mailer is rarely ponderous because he has the grace to puncture or at least to back away from his more inflated notions. This is surely one reason why he appends the definitions of comedy and tragedy to the end of his narrative. The humor of these definitions—so close in meaning to each other—is ironic, as is one of Madden's final remarks, that "all my present stability of mind rests on the firm foundation of a mortal crime." The difference between surviving and perishing, as between comedy and tragedy, is perilously slim, and Madden knows that he can never count himself safely sane.

Tough Guys Don't Dance, for all of its ruminations on telepathy and the occult, is a far more relaxed and measured performance than earlier Mailer novels such as *An American Dream*, which is perhaps the closest antecedent to his current fictional concerns. Certainly Mailer has mellowed in this book, which does not assault the senses in the frenetic fashion of *Why Are We in Vietnam?* (1967). As a consequence, however, *Tough Guys Don't Dance* seems less driven by the fierce contrarieties of that novel which is still his finest work of fiction. In *Barbary Shore* (1951) and *The Deer Park: A Play* (1955), he also made his first-person narrators into writers, both of whom were in doubt as to their true identities. Tim Madden, approaching forty, seems somewhat older than these earlier Mailer protagonists and more willing to settle for an incompleteness of character which his writing may never resolve: "I am so compromised by so many acts that I must try to write my way out of the internal prison of my nerves, my guilts and my deep-rooted spiritual debts." Such words suggest a writer of formidable experience, a writer of middle age who may be about to reach his prime, a writer, in short, similar to Norman Mailer himself.

Carl E. Rollyson, Jr.

Sources for Further Study

America. CLI, November 17, 1984, p. 329.
The Atlantic. CCLIV, September, 1984, p. 128.
Christian Science Monitor. August 1, 1984, p. 21.
Library Journal. CIX, July, 1984, p. 1347.
Los Angeles Times Book Review. August 19, 1984, p. 1.
The Nation. CCXXXIX, September 15, 1984, p. 213.
The New Republic. CXCI, August 27, 1984, p. 40.

The New York Times Book Review. LXXXIX, July 29, 1984, p. 1.
Newsweek. CIV, August 6, 1984, p. 67.
Publishers Weekly. CCXXV, June 29, 1984, p. 96.
Time. CXXIV, August 6, 1984, p. 66.
USA Today. August 24, 1984, p. 30.
The Wall Street Journal. CCIV, August 9, 1984, p. 26.

THE TRADITION OF RETURN
The Implicit History of Modern Literature

Author: Jeffrey M. Perl (1952-   )
Publisher: Princeton University Press (Princeton, New Jersey). 325 pp. $22.50
Type of work: Literary criticism

> *Examining the loyal attention that great modernist writers such as James Joyce and T. S. Eliot paid to their distant literary ancestors, this work argues that their indebtedness belongs to a larger modern pattern of "return" to beginnings*

Unlike the Renaissance, which took its title from a "rebirth" of classical learning, the modernism of the twentieth century was named for its aggressive modernity, its refusal of custom and precedent. For Jeffrey M. Perl, however, modernism is a misnomer. Like the Renaissance, the great explosion of creative energy in the early twentieth century should be pictured as a figure turned toward the past, draped respectfully in the authority of the classics. The apparent rebelliousness of both periods has hidden their common tendency to seek inspiration or legitimation from classical ancestors. Taken together, therefore, they form a "tradition of return," uniting modern literature in a will to escape from the forward rush of history by clutching at the anchor of privileged origins.

The raw materials out of which this argument is built will not be surprising to the student of any of the "modern" periods since 1500. Perhaps because today's reader is still so close to modernism, however, its particular return to sources has usually been seen as a minor interruption of its revolutionary drive, reassuring to some and troubling to others, but in any case secondary. *The Tradition of Return* breaks with received opinion by making this return central to the modernism of James Joyce, T. S. Eliot, William Butler Yeats, and Ezra Pound, among others. With polemical vigor and unabashed sympathy for his subject, Perl launches a full-scale defense of a retrospective or even regressive modernism. The reader should not be misled by occasional bits of more skeptical terminology, such as the appearance of the word "ideology" in the titles of the book's two parts and in the repeated phrase "*nostos* ideology." This latter phrase refers to Odysseus, whose return to Ithaca (*nostos* is the origin of "nostalgia") is discussed in the introduction. Perl chooses the homeward-bound Odysseus of *The Odyssey* for his hero, and not the adventurer of *The Iliad* (like many other readers, he judges the bloody heroics of the Trojan War to be a big mistake). He presents neither his own choice nor Odysseus' obstinate homing in on Ithaca as "ideological" in the ordinary sense of the word, nor does he define an extraordinary sense for "ideology" that would allow him to praise the return to roots and sources while also taking some critical distance from it. On the contrary, from the outset, Perl establishes Odysseus' homecoming as an unquestioned moral touchstone, which teaches, he says, "that life's signal adventure is the discovery of home."

The second chapter, devoted to Jean-Jacques Rousseau's *La Nouvelle Héloise* (1761), extracts from that novel much the same moral. The idealistic, antisocial passion of Saint-Preux and Julie is shown to be unwise; when Julie marries Wolmar and, contrary to everyone's expectation, is happier than before, Romanticism is checked and mated. Observing the "revolutionary normalcy" of the Wolmars' marriage, the erstwhile romantic Saint-Preux sees the error of his assault on social convention; he "realizes that the conventional and the ultimate are one." Conventionality does not exclude the ideal, as he had thought, but can be made to incarnate it. (Can it, though, if Julie must then die?) Moreover, there is no real alternative to home life. Outside conventions is nothing but "the Void."

This rediscovered indulgence toward social conventionality informs the rest of the book as well. The introduction distinguishes two attitudes toward modernity, each based on a nineteenth century attitude toward the Renaissance. Jacob Burkhardt's "nostalgia for the fifteenth-century Florentine revival," accompanied by "an urgent intuition that a new and lasting renascence might yet occur in the nineteenth or twentieth century," issues, however, in a "hatred born of disappointment." Burkhardt proclaims the final incompatibility between noble antiquity and the sordidness of the new bourgeois industrial order. Walter Pater, on the other hand, represents "a second line of *nostos* ideologists," whom Perl calls "theodicean"; in the view of such thinkers, "providence and the philosopher of history can agree: the battle of past and present is a fine way of bringing past and present into intense relation, and all is part of a theodicean design whose wholeness lends significance to every part." Though it falls short of the reactionary resignation of Burkhardt, the "theodicean" line is still a far cry from "progressive" or "romantic" thinking. In order to mount an attack on Romanticism, which seems to be his primary antagonist, Perl renews the rather tired debate between Romanticism and classicism. In chapter 3, he begins his discussion of modernism proper by denying the thesis that it is a further stage of the romantic revolution, as suggested by Northrop Frye, Harold Bloom, and Paul de Man. Perl does so not by confronting their arguments (they are dismissed in two sentences) but by reading sympathetically several works by T. S. Eliot (for example, Prufrock as the exorcizing of romantic personality) so as to support Eliot's repudiation of Romanticism and his identification of modernism with classicism. Eliot, the only figure to be treated in two chapters, is clearly a central inspiration. His lines from *Four Quartets* (1943) might have served as the book's epigraph:

> We shall not cease from exploration
> And the end of all our exploring
> Will be to arrive where we started
> And know the place for the first time.

His famous description of his religious and political beliefs may be as relevant to this book as his brand of classicism.

The rest of the book consists of self-styled case studies. Chapter 4, on the revival of traditional verse drama by Eliot and Yeats, is uncharacteristic, both in its confession that under modern conditions it could only fail to revive the nobility of the ancient theater and, more important, in its subversive hint that the assumption on which revivalism was based—the absolute contrast between the sordid commercialism of the present and the glory-that-was-Greece—was largely specious. Imperial Athens was nothing if not commercial. Chapter 5, looking back at the history of the novel from the vantage point of Joyce's *Ulysses* (1922), attempts to view the genre as a reincarnation of classical epic. Correcting Matthew Arnold's indifference to the novel, it briefly aligns Henry Fielding with an Arnoldian project of cultural regeneration, then brings out the Homeric Hellenism in Leo Tolstoy's account of battle, and finally discusses the psychologizing of epic war in the military vocabulary of Henry James's *The Ambassadors* (1903). Each of these novelists, Perl suggests, anticipated Eliot's "dissociation of sensibility" doctrine. What, however, does heroic combat have to do with Eliot's vision of history, beyond the fact that both celebrate a past superior to the present? Is the fact that Strether, who, like Odysseus, returns home at the end, or that James, who insisted on dividing *The Ambassadors* into twelve books, really evidence of any meaningful revival of ancient epic? By paying homage to any and all modern piety to the forms, ideals, or bric-a-brac of the past, Perl produces a scattershot effect which detracts from the seriousness of his enterprise.

Perl is on stronger ground in chapter 6 when he considers *Ulysses* as a theodicean rewriting of *The Odyssey*. The final "yes" of *Ulysses* gives Perl his happiest ending, reaffirming the urgency of pagan myth in the modern world, simultaneously criticizing other, facile myths of return, and in so doing also affirming the possibility of making do with modernity. His account is devoted not to the novel's experimental intricacies of form and allusion but, refreshingly, to the three main characters: Stephen, who is led through doubt to acceptance of the messy sensible world; Bloom, the new Odysseus who brings together Hebraism and Hellenism; and Molly, whose pagan earthiness reconciles all opposites. Together, they make up—at least in Molly's mind—the Holy Frame of modernism, proof that a natural home can still be reconstituted. Is this domestic group natural, or is it rather a new construction? More attention might have been paid to how much has been changed in this repetition of Homer. In Perl's account of the modern Odysseus, his triumph forfeits its social dimension; it no longer stands in for the restitution of an entire community. Indeed, it is so inward as to be nearly invisible. The psychological reenactment of epic, in which victory is not even the achievement of a paradise within but merely a passing configuration in a single character's mind, might be described as less a return to epic than a move away from it. In addition, if return is essentially "psychological," "a way of perceiving, or making sense out of, experience," if *The Tradition of Return* is an example of psychohistory, then how is it that it can omit any treatment of Sigmund Freud's "family romance," surely the central psychological paradigm of the literary *nostos*, or Freud's later discussion of the death instinct as a darker rephrasing of the imperative to return?

As *The Tradition of Return* draws to a close, it becomes more explicit about the terms on which affirmation of the modern world is conceivable. It suggests that the social order of modernity can perhaps be tolerated, on the one hand, if the psychological and theological order of premodernity is embraced, on the other hand. Chapter 7 unites psychology with theology. It treats Friedrich Wilhelm Nietzsche, Freud, and D. H. Lawrence as modern demythologizers who, in fact, were engaged in attempting to re-create pre-Christian myths for the post-Christian present. That is, they aimed at a reassociation of sensibility, a psychological reintegration, by making "the symbolic-mythic unconscious a benign and even a blessed part of psychic life." Here the guiding spirit is Carl Gustav Jung. The conclusion then takes up the problem of social order, notably in Pound. Inevitably, it evokes the connection between the return to classical glory and contemporary Fascism. It argues, however, that Pound was "at all times the artist first: the *homme politique* was always a subordinate persona." Contemporary writers can and should rehabilitate Pound's aesthetics while "being careful to dissociate themselves from Poundean politics." When translated into broader terms, this becomes a stance of political acquiescence: "the theodicean poet ... holds ... that 'Universality necessarily stipulates submission to an established order.'" In short, society must and can be left alone, both by the left and by the right, in order for modern man to benefit safely from the balm of spiritual regression.

As the word "regression" indicates, the main problem of the book's argument as a whole is its definition of the three-step, "A-B-A" scheme of historical return, whereby the present (A) attacks its immediate predecessors (B) by identifying itself with more distant and authentic ancestors (also A). Can one really go home again? In speaking of Rousseau, Perl makes a concession of some importance. "'Process of return,' then, may be a slight misnomer—the process is actually one of growth, dislocation, and reintegration." Reintegration, unlike return, implies the creation of a new synthesis. Judging from Perl's own examples, it would seem that the final, synthetic A in his A-B-A scheme should be an A' or, even, a dialectical C. While texts are circling backward, that is, they are also spiraling upward. In his discussion of Joyce, Perl uses the figure of the spiral, but he has not fused it with his definition of return or extended it to the book as a whole. In his eagerness to show that there exists a rearward movement, he makes little effort to graph this extra vertical dimension. Perhaps one reason is the further concession this move would require: His scheme would closely resemble the upward Hegelian spiral that M. H. Abrams has discovered precisely in Romanticism, about which Perl has less good to say than about any other period. When one considers the appeal to Rome by French revolutionaries and the appeal to Greece and to folk culture by romantic writers, the line dividing Romanticism from classicism seems blurred. To be fair, Perl is not especially interested in periodization. What is more serious is the confusion that is never dispelled from the second A, the final step of the three-step scheme. After a "rebellion against the convention" in step two, this "apocalypse of the clichéd convention," involving "neither acceptance nor negation but revelation and rededication," is difficult to distinguish from a simple return to the homely virtues that had been rebelled against. When Perl calls it "a technique for revealing the ultimacy that is latent in the mundane," the vagueness of his vocabulary seems to lead back into areas beyond the reach of rational discussion.

Among the historical differences that are flattened by Perl's scheme, the most important is perhaps that between Eliot and Joyce. Perl notes correctly that Eliot misread *Ulysses* in his own image, taking its Homeric framework as a parallel to his own Burkhardtian pessimism and missing its affirmative impulse to sanctify or at least make a new dwelling place in drab Dublin for modernity, but then Perl seems to reconcile them after all, and on Eliot's terms: "Joyce might well have subtitled *Ulysses*: Tradition and the Individual Talent." If Eliot and the Burkhardtian line seem to prevail over Joyce and the theodicean line, it is because Perl has pulled the latter's teeth. At best, promodernity for him is only a weak version of antimodernity. His sense of the present offers it nothing to defend. Postmodernism gets only two pages, devoted largely and strangely to Iris Murdoch and Jean-Paul Sartre. Equally significant is Perl's reliance on the ubiquitous adjective "bourgeois." Melting T. S. Eliot and Karl Marx into a seething, undifferentiated mess of antimodernity, the term "bourgeois" is surely not the most precise or most useful way of conceiving how one lives now. Like a set of terms used with equal frequency, the opposition of "real" and "ideal," it has no bite, makes no distinctions, forces no choices. If this is all there is of the present, then modernity possesses nothing worth affirming—except, indeed, its saving continuities with the past.

In defending modern literature by displaying those continuities, *The Tradition of Return* is itself an example of the theodicean line it defines, but this is where history stops. Since coming full circle, there is nowhere to go but back, or around again, nothing to do but return to the tradition of return. In the quarrel between the Ancients and the Moderns, to show the dependence of the Moderns upon the Ancients is not a new move. At this late date, if the quarrel is worth taking up again in the old terms—which is not sure—then it will be necessary to make it newer.

Bruce Robbins

Source for Further Study

World Literature Today. LIX, Winter, 1985, p. 163.

TRAVELING LIGHT

Author: Bill Barich (1943-   )
Publisher: The Viking Press (New York). 226 pp. $15.95
Type of work: Essays
Time: The early 1980's
Locale: California, the Pacific Northwest, Long Island, London, and Florence

Barich's second book is based on travels in the early 1980's in the United States and Europe and presents a record of his preoccupations with friends, family, fishing, horse racing, history, and art

Perhaps the most useful thing to say at the beginning is that this book is not to be confused with the novel of the same title written in 1980 by Lionel Mitchell, which is described as a spiritual odyssey of a young black man in New York's East Village. This collection of travel pieces may also be in some ways a spiritual odyssey for the author, but for the reader that is not the most important or enjoyable element of the book. This is Bill Barich's second book (after *Laughing in the Hills*, 1980); with the exception of one essay, all the contents first appeared in *The New Yorker* between 1981 and 1984. Portions of Barich's first book were also first published in *The New Yorker*.

The volume contains ten essays, divided into three parts: Part 1 is mainly about fishing and horse-racing on the East and West Coasts, while part 2 deals with London and Florence, also emphasizing horse racing; part 3 is a single essay, again about fishing on the West Coast. The individual essays range from eleven to thirty-six pages in length, and all but three treat horse racing or fishing in some form. The horse-racing pieces continue the theme of Barich's first book, which dealt exclusively with the author's experiences at various California racetracks. The pieces in *Traveling Light* are arranged chronologically, but the author tells the reader that there is really no need to read them that way.

The book is ostensibly travel literature and in most libraries will be found in the travel section, but the real antecedents and parallels for the work are rather to be found in the tradition of the informal essay. Barich's true niche is not to be found with Ring Lardner or even Izaak Walton, but with Charles Lamb or E. V. Lucas or Max Beerbohm. The individual pieces are true essays, displaying the best qualities of that genre, and it is in virtue of this that they may well be read as independent works. *Traveling Light* would in truth make a good bedside book.

Additionally, the book has very little to say on the actual subject of travel; travel, by itself, is, in fact, never discussed. What the essays *do* discuss are places and people. With an eye for significant detail, Barich makes a California trout stream, a London pub, and an Italian racecourse come alive. He does not so much visit these places as live there or become a regular. He enters into the life afforded instead of observing from the outside in the usual manner of the tourist. In fact, tourist is the furthest thing from what Barich becomes.

People, too, are central to the work, and the emphasis is always on people in their natural habitat—whether it be pub or racetrack or trout stream. Barich is attracted to secure, relatively unsophisticated people, to competent people who know what they are about and operate with a minimum of fuss. Examples from the book would be his fishing companion in California, Paul Deeds; Dorothy Wharton-Wheeler, whom he meets at a racecourse in England; or O'Neill, the proprietor of a tackle shop on Long Island. These are only a selection; there are many others, some the subject of lengthy, developing descriptions, some neatly realized in a page or a paragraph.

Along the way, Barich offers a great many other pleasant and delightful things; again, in this, he models himself on the essay tradition, creating the relaxed, conversational tone so important in that form. In the midst of an account of fishing in California, there are brief bits on the history of early Russian involvement in California, the distinctions between kinds of trout, and Zane Grey. The essay "J. D. Ross's Vision" not only tells the reader much of attempts to dam rivers in Washington for power but along the way presents neat bits of Seattle politics. A visit to Saratoga Springs for the annual yearling sale also provides readers with the history of that spa and racecourse and some insights into tax shelters and investment. These are only a few of the random bits that are likely to spring unannounced from the pages. Barich does not introduce these topics in order to show off but brings them in naturally as they might turn up in good conversation. He has the knack of being interesting on a subject, however recondite (such as Florentine painting), even if the reader initially knows or cares little about the topic.

It is clear that Barich not only likes to talk to people but also has the ability to put them at ease and enter into their concerns, whether he be in California, England, or Italy. This trait is particularly evident in the best (and longest) essay in the book, "At The Fountain"—a record of Barich's entry into the life of a pub of that name in the London suburb of Islington. He becomes a "regular," as the official term is, enjoying the pub's "air of domesticity, the way the lovely insistence of family life kept intruding upon the solitary world of the drinker." As with a family, it is the individual persons who make the difference. While Barich provides along the way insights into brewing history, distinctions between varieties of British beers, and a plea for "real ale," he is mainly concerned to describe the people who give a pub its particular character and who constitute its particular family. It is John the cellarman who guides Barich through the mysteries of the various types of beer and for whom, because of his skill and professional principles, Barich develops a great affection. A very different pair of characters are Simon and Juliana, an unmarried couple squatting illegally in the attic of a house near the pub. Their attraction for Barich is that their lives are simple and uncomplicated, and the friendship eventually develops to the point where the young couple exchange dinner invitations with Barich and his wife. These are only a few of his acquaintances from the pub; Barich himself is so impressed with the variety of people to be met at The Fountain, and with the release of the hidden human desire for intimacy occasioned by Burton beer, that he provides a list of some of the other people he came to know there: The list ranges from a pen salesman to a solicitor to a girl who sold naughty underwear in a boutique.

Perhaps one of the most important elements of the traditions of the informal essay is style, for it is style that attracts and holds, it is style that conveys attitude and personality. Barich's style is quiet and understated, with plenty of room for significant detail. He is intimate and subtle, with an attractive sense of humor that is often appealingly self-deprecatory. He has the ability of all good stylists to find exactly the right word or comparison: Italian firemen wear "elaborate brown uniforms that made them look like gnomes from the Tyrol"; the despised sucker fish "have chubby humanoid lips and appear to be begging for cigars"; Guinness stout has for Barich "all the attraction of thirty-weight motor oil." Barich can also slide into his prose the deceptively simple, thought-provoking sentence: "Language pales in comparison to the syntax of nature"; "One of the secret terrors of the age is that we are all dying slowly of complacency." In one of the book's most evocative passages, in the essay "O'Neill Among the Weakfish," Barich recreates, in less than a page, the sound, sight, and smell of the boyhood memories of family vacations spent in a Minnesota fishing shack with aunts, uncles, cousins, and beer. If one of the excellences of style is to be able to capture concisely the central and essential nature of a place or a person, Barich possesses it.

In *Laughing in the Hills*, Barich was much given to philosophizing and agonizing about the shape and direction of his life. This book is pretty much free of such passages, though there is a theme in many of the essays of complexity versus simplicity, the complexity usually being caused by the mind of man. Barich does frequently wonder (especially in betting at tracks) why he is making such a simple thing complex. The first book frequently saw horse racing as a sort of metaphor for human life, and this book continues some of the same, only in a more relaxed and less obtrusive way.

While this book may be read, as the author suggests, simply as a collection of individual pieces, there are features of it that encourage its reading as a consecutive whole. One of the patterns which emerges is that of balance and circularity. Not only do the style and the repeated topics of horse racing and fishing create a sense of unity, but also the larger organization of the book conveys its message. The book begins and ends in California, the author fishing with Paul Deeds; after his trips to New York and Europe, he has come full circle. In addition, the opening and closing essays are both set in fall and early winter, providing a rounding-off suggestive of Henry David Thoreau's scheme in *Walden* (1854). The contents are further balanced by the three horse-racing locales: Golden Gate Fields in California, Kempton Park in England, and Ippodromo Le Cascine in Florence. Each park is different, each has its characters and touts, but there is a sense of familiarity and continuity nevertheless. The circularity, the returning to where he began, suggests something of the possibility of a search or "spiritual odyssey" on the part of the author. It would be unwise to push this theme too far, however, and it is certainly not a dominant element in the book.

There is a final minor theme in the book, one of which the author himself may not be entirely conscious but which is still enjoyable for the reader— food. In his accounts of the many places that he writes about, the author does not fail to mention distinctive foods: From various kinds of fish prepared various kinds of ways, to venison and beer in England, to a pork pie at Kempton Park (described as heavy enough to have been flung from a catapult at the Visigoths), to more exotic wines and espresso and olives and fava beans and pasta in Italy, Barich has a sharp palate and a skill for rendering such tastes for the reader.

Traveling Light is a thoroughly enjoyable book. The author and his style are friendly, soft-spoken, amusing, and interesting. There are sufficient suggestions in the book of weight and depth to prevent it from being merely a lightweight, summer afternoon's reading. It is an advance, especially in sensitivity to the objective, outside world, over his first volume. Bill Barich is a skilled writer whose next book will be looked for by many readers.

Gordon N. Bergquist

Sources for Further Study

American Libraries. XV, May, 1984, p. 284.
Best Sellers. XLIII, March, 1984, p. 446.
Booklist. LXXX, November 15, 1983, p. 467.
Kirkus Reviews. LI, November 15, 1983, p. 1186.
Library Journal. CVIII, December 1, 1983, p. 2250.
Los Angeles Times Book Review. January 15, 1984, p. 8.
The New York Times. CXXXIII, January 17, 1984, p. 25.
The New York Times Book Review. LXXXIX, February 5, 1984, p. 19.
Publishers Weekly. CCXXIV, November 25, 1983, p. 53.
Time. CXXIII, February 6, 1984, p. 72.

THE TRUE ADVENTURES OF JOHN STEINBECK, WRITER

Author: Jackson J. Benson (1930-   )
Publisher: The Viking Press (New York). 1116 pp. $35.00
Type of work: Literary biography
Time: 1902-1968
Locale: Primarily the United States; also Western Europe and the Soviet Union

A comprehensive, probably definitive biography of the distinguished American writer

> *Principal personages:*
> JOHN STEINBECK, an American writer
> JOHN ERNST STEINBECK, his father
> OLIVE HAMILTON STEINBECK, his mother
> CAROL HENNINGS, his first wife
> GWEN, his second wife
> ELAINE, his third wife
> EDWARD F. RICKETTS, his friend, a biologist
> TOM and
> JON, Steinbeck's sons by his second wife

For the general reader, Jackson J. Benson's massive and richly satisfying biography provides a trove of documented material, but for the specialist the book offers few important new insights and only one mystery. The mystery concerns the title itself: *The True Adventures of John Steinbeck, Writer.* In the commonly understood meaning of the word, Steinbeck's life was hardly "adventurous," at least in comparison with that, say, of Ernest Hemingway. To be sure, during World War II Steinbeck picked up a rifle and fought briefly in the Italian campaign, violating the stipulations of his journalist's contract, yet his wartime services to the country, at least creditable and perhaps heroic, did not climax a life of rugged adventure. Nor were Steinbeck's numerous sexual liaisons typical of the picaresque lover-adventurer. Basically monogamous, Steinbeck was on the whole a faithful husband to his three wives, although he neglected his first wife, Carol, toward the end of their decaying relationship. As for the writer's casual affairs with a few Hollywood stars—or starlets—between marriages: His attachment to them was cautious, just as his youthful flings before his first marriage had been brief and inconsequential. Although Steinbeck traveled widely rather late in his life, beginning in the 1940's, his view of the world was that of a tourist and reporter rather than that of an adventurer. In fact, he was a working journalist, or a part-time diplomat with a job to accomplish. By most tests of romantic adventure, one might argue that Steinbeck's life was curiously flat: Not until the late 1930's did he attain to a considerable popular reputation. During the years of his obscure toil as well as those three years of celebrity afterward, he resolutely fought for his privacy, eschewing as much as possible the adulation that often attaches to a famous writer. Nevertheless, in one respect Benson's title accurately describes the focus of his biography. Steinbeck's adventures were those of a writer. In his craft as an artist he experienced the true adventures of his spirit. According to Benson, Steinbeck "didn't write for fame, although occasionally he enjoyed being famous; he didn't write for money, although there were times when he needed money; he wrote because he loved to write, because he was addicted to it."

Stated so simply and directly, the biographer's statement appears to be a truism applicable to many, perhaps most, serious artists. After all, George Orwell's famous description (in "Why I Write") of the reasons why a writer undertakes the labors of composition seems to cover all possible points: to revel in sheer egotism, to express aesthetic enthusiasm, to follow some historical impulse in order to store up facts for posterity, or to serve as partisan for a political purpose. None of these reasons quite covers Steinbeck's case. As Benson views the writer, he did not work for any of these reasons, although he certainly had an ego to express, certainly enjoyed describing beautiful (or terrible) subjects, certainly wished—in most of his novels—to mirror the sociopolitical images of his time, and certainly professed beliefs that he needed to give form. None of these reasons, however, Benson helps the reader to understand, fully explains Steinbeck's devotion to the hard work of creating literature. "What he cared about," Benson says, "was writing itself." To Steinbeck, living was less intense than writing.

For such a person—a type rare even among the most compulsive of authors—the activities of a lifetime are adventures only to the extent that they allow him source material as well as time for reflection and composition. So from a certain point of view—the reader's point of view—the external episodes of Steinbeck's life are far less interesting than those internal struggles that shaped his craft. These internal forces, however, remain mostly hidden, despite the great weight of documentation that Benson brings to bear on his subject. To be sure, the fault is not the biographer's. Steinbeck was, on the whole, reluctant to discuss with others or reveal in print the matter of his creative struggles. Throughout his long, stubborn years of apprenticeship, culminating at last with the critical and popular successes in the 1930's of *Tortilla Flat* (1935), *In Dubious Battle* (1936), *Of Mice and Men* (1937), *The Long Valley* (1938), and *The Grapes of Wrath* (1939), Steinbeck changed very little from his essential nature. Somewhat more genial in social relations, somewhat more controlled in his manners, more assured, he nevertheless rejected, for the most part, the glamorous values that often go with success. Fame and money allowed him greater scope to travel, to meet and influence people in a wider stratum of society—including his friend Adlai Stevenson and American presidents John F. Kennedy and Lyndon B. Johnson, yet the later years of his life failed to bring him the satisfaction he craved as a writer. Although he continued to publish, and most of his fiction commanded top positions on best-seller lists, he was aware of the fact that he was unable to concentrate as well as earlier upon the craft of writing. When he received the Nobel Prize for Literature in 1962, most critics savagely attacked his selection, and Steinbeck felt crushed. The award seemed to discourage rather than encourage his efforts.

In telling Steinbeck's life story, Benson generally avoids psychoanalytic interpretations. Although as a young man, Steinbeck on a few occasions behaved erratically—even violently—his conduct in the long view was not that of a neurotic personality. One occasion, however, that deserves some attention was Steinbeck's irrational behavior toward Polly Smith, who was then in her early twenties. Steinbeck had been intermittently dating Polly (while he was more deeply involved romantically with Carol Henning, later to become his wife). After an evening of drinking, Steinbeck made a pass at Polly, who refused his overtures and, the writer supposed, started to tease him. "In a rage of drunken frustration," Benson reports, Steinbeck "hauled her to the second-story window of the bachelor quarters, . . . grabbed her by the ankles, hung her head down out the window, and began shaking her." This ugly scene came to an end when a friend rushed upstairs and rescued the girl. Several other violent incidents during Steinbeck's youth seem to show signs of a troubled personality, but Benson rarely ascribes psychological motives for the behavior; and, to be sure, the mature years of the writer's life offer little evidence of irrationality, although Steinbeck was certainly capable at times of terrible jealousy, rage, and depression. Without dismissing the notion that many artists are motivated to create because of a psychological "wound," Benson writes of the special case of Steinbeck: ". . . that [he] was, with all his problems, an unusually healthy man helps to explain both what is missing from his work and that special quality that makes it distinctive. His greatness, if one is willing to call it that, comes not from his wound, but from his wholeness."

Turning aside from analysis, therefore, Benson centers his investigation of Steinbeck's character on a great accumulation of data gathered mainly from interviews but also from letters, unpublished and published material by the writer and also by others who knew Steinbeck. In a labor that spanned thirteen years of researching and composing the book, Benson uncovered many facts, for he believed that his "first job in writing this book has been to get the facts straight." In this respect, the biography succeeds. Indeed, some readers may object to the lengths to which Benson will go to provide even trivial facts that might, in some small way, illumine his subject. For example, Benson pays attention to such minor details as the color of a handkerchief—"singularly nauseous purple"—that Elaine, Steinbeck's third wife, selected as a souvenir on the island of Saba. Or he will recall that, in 1962, Elaine purchased for her husband a paperback entitled *John Steinbeck* by Frank William Watt; Steinbeck's reaction was: "This book doesn't seem to be about me but it's pretty interesting about somebody." With the wealth of details in Benson's study, few if any readers would have the same objection about this book. Clearly the biography is about Steinbeck, all about him—from the slightest anecdote to the dramatically insightful actions or statements that reveal the man.

Judged from a positive point of view, Benson's grasp of details reveals not only his subject in sharp focus, but also the background scene. One learns, for example, about Steinbeck's classes at Stanford University, about the idiosyncrasies of his teachers, even about the contents of his courses. One learns an extraordinary amount of information concerning his family, his neighbors at Salinas, his friends through the years of the Depression, and his many acquaintances during the crowded final decades of his life. One learns this information not superficially but with ample (some would say, excessive) documentation, so that Steinbeck is captured: his actions, his gestures, his moods, his words.

Benson provides so much information about people who knew and influenced Steinbeck that, on occasion, those in the background thrust themselves forward to center stage. For example, Benson devotes a chapter (and long passages throughout) to biologist Edward F. Ricketts, Steinbeck's closest and most important friend during the years of his conspicuous creative activity. This information, carefully documented and scrupulously fair in its assessment, constitutes a mini biography of Ricketts. Moreover, Benson's extended treatment of other persons, some famous and others not, provides far more useful information than one would expect. In addition to collecting facts concerning their impact upon Steinbeck, one learns a considerable amount about the character and attitudes of George Albee, Nathaniel Benchley, Katherine Beswick, Pascal Covici, Elia Kazan, Burgess Meredith, Elizabeth Otis, Carlton Sheffield, Webster Street, and others. Finally, one learns much—perhaps too much, in terms of Steinbeck's personal reticence in dealing with his family and with other intimates—about the writer's wives and his sons.

As a documentary account of Steinbeck's life, Benson's biography is not likely to be surpassed. His second objective in writing the biography, however, is not entirely realized. He declares that his intention "has been to try to bring a man alive, a very complicated man who led a very vivid and eventful life." Without question, Steinbeck was complicated, but much of his early life can scarcely be considered either vivid or eventful. A taciturn, grimly humorous man, Steinbeck in his youth had few "adventures" different from those of most sensitive, tenaciously dedicated young writers. Indeed, his early apprenticeship to the craft of writing was one of dogged self-criticism and very hard work; of writing, rewriting, and discarding ineffective prose; and of managing to stay alive, to remain moderately companionable while perfecting his work. Only later in life did he emerge as a complete personality: a tough, resilient, mostly tolerant, mostly decent, straight-talking man who had come to terms with his early illusions about romantic writing and romantically inclined women. His later years were, indeed, vivid. For readers patient enough to follow Benson's account of the generally unadventurous early life of Steinbeck and to stay with him until his middle years, there is the reward of seeing Steinbeck come into his own as a real human being, a man of character. One likes him. One forgives his few remaining illusions. One forgives—and understands—as well his growing political conservatism (particularly his hawkish stance toward the war in Vietnam), his failures to write great novels after *The Grapes of Wrath*, and his deepening sense of failure. The reader understands that Steinbeck's life and work were in the American vein and that ultimately he did not fail. As a corrective to Steinbeck's detractors, Benson's biography offers a man whose main "adventures" were to keep trying, to write craftsmanlike novels, to continue growing intellectually, and to maintain the abiding love of his life—for ordinary people struggling to be loyal to their better selves. The death of Steinbeck, as Benson details the writer's slow decline from successive strokes, is of tragic proportions. Benson achieves his major goal: One comes to admire Steinbeck the man.

Leslie B. Mittleman

Sources for Further Study

America. CLI, July 21, 1984, p. 37.
Christian Science Monitor. LXXVI, March 6, 1984, p. 22.
Los Angeles Times Book Review. January 1, 1984, p. 1.
Macleans. XCVII, February 20, 1984, p. 58.
New Statesman. CVII, April 20, 1984, p. 27.
The New York Review of Books. XXXI, February 16, 1984, p. 25.
The New York Times Book Review. LXXXIX, January 22, 1984, p. 1.
The New Yorker. LIX, February 6, 1984, p. 127.
Newsweek. CIII, February 6, 1984, p. 80.
Time. CXXIII, January 23, 1984, p. 69.
Virginia Quarterly Review. LX, Summer, 1984, p. 87.

T. S. ELIOT
A Life

Author: Peter Ackroyd (1917-   )
Publisher: Simon and Schuster (New York). Illustrated. 400 pp. $24.95
Type of work: Literary biography
Time: 1888-1965
Locale: The United States and Europe

A thoroughly researched and sympathetic treatment of Eliot's life that synthesizes more material than any previous Eliot biography

> *Principal personage:*
> THOMAS STEARNS ELIOT, an Anglo-American poet, critic, and play-
> wright, winner of the Nobel Prize for Literature in 1948

Interest in Eliot's life has become very strong recently, culminating in Michael Hastings' play *Tom and Viv*, staged in London in 1984. The play is about Eliot's first, tragic marriage to Vivien Haigh-Wood; prolonged correspondence about the play was published in the *Times Literary Supplement* and other British periodicals, debating its demerits and merits. The biography of Peter Ackroyd, too, is a sign of this new interest; perhaps it had to wait for Eliot's critical doctrine of impersonality—his view that poetry is an "escape from personality" rather than an expression of it—to lose its force. Eliot's own reticence when he was alive (he died in 1965) also served to hold this interest in check. Eliot left instructions in his will that there should be no official biography, and his estate has consistently refused permission to quote from his unpublished correspondence—this permission was refused to Peter Ackroyd, among others. It is known that still, at the present date, much information is being withheld; for example, some two thousand letters exchanged between Eliot and Emily Hale will not be available until the year 2020. Inevitably, both the public and the critics have come to think that much of Eliot's fascination lies in his concealments. This attitude has greatly increased in the two decades since Eliot's death. Part of the interest has been gossipy and perverse, as in *Tom and Viv* and other biographies of Eliot (by Robert Sencourt, T. S. Matthews, and James E. Miller, Jr.). On the other hand, with the passage of time, an understanding has grown that Eliot's life was important, even very important—and this being the case, why should it be ignored when readers try to understand his difficult poetry? Indeed, is it possible to understand his poetry without knowing more about his life?

Ackroyd's biography of Eliot is not gossipy or perverse in any way. It makes use of all of the published material about Eliot's life, which is considerable; Eliot was one of the strongest literary influences in the English-speaking world during the period from 1920 to 1960, and the sheer bulk of the materials about Eliot—his poetry, criticism, drama, and his life—is both voluminous and intimidating. Ackroyd's account is sober and largely sympathetic to his subject. The account of Eliot's first marriage is judicious and seems relatively complete: A broad variety of sources are quoted, ranging from the acutely psychological to the medical, from friends of Eliot to members of Vivien's family. By page 200 of Ackroyd's book, when Eliot has finally separated from his increasingly insane wife, some readers may well wonder why this did not happen earlier. The year of this event was 1933, relatively early in Eliot's life, yet the apparently disproportionate amount of space devoted to the relationship is probably justified. Most of Eliot's important poetry and his most innovative criticism had been written before the break, and if a "life" of an author is relevant to an author's work, then it would be Eliot's life prior to 1933.

Curiously, despite the many virtues of this biography, a surprising number of professional critics have been dissatisfied with it. Few have faulted its scholarship, the thoroughness of its research, or its objectivity. The notes are abundant, accurate, and usually quite apt; they reflect a broader range of sources than do most critical books. Although it is natural that critics should disagree with some of Ackroyd's often tentative interpretations, the problem seems to lie elsewhere. One critic, for example—Barbara Everett—has been unwilling to accept the subtitle of this book for what it is— "A Life," arguing at length that the book does not formulate adequate criticisms of Eliot's work. Ackroyd is modest and consistent; he never claims that he is giving readers more than he does, that is, "A Life," and the work should not be confused with a critical study. It will be of great value to all those interested in Eliot, just as lives of other great figures—artists, politicians, or generals—are important. They are not a substitute for an analysis of works or deeds, but they can contribute much else to aid readers in their understanding: a knowledge of historical background, of family influence, and the very concrete, specific social and professional milieux in which the subject lived and worked. The striking quotations of perceptions of Eliot by his friends, many of whom were highly articulate writers such as Virginia Woolf, Osbert Sitwell, and Aldous Huxley, help to provide a full, three-dimensional sense of Eliot the living and breathing man, with all his shyness and reticence. True, Eliot wrote that poetry "is an escape from personality." A good biography, however, such as this one, can help readers to understand why he made the statement, and readers can understand more clearly the nature of the man who held this doctrine and why he held it. Eliot had good reasons for his belief, which was by no means defensive: It was part of a highly ambitious aim to embrace the world in its objective reality. Thus, Eliot was not contradicting himself when he also wrote that the critic should be a master of fact, and facts include biographical information about a writer, and that "we also understand the poetry better when we know more about the man."

The book raises a number of essential questions about Eliot, that are far from being answered. First, Eliot came to have extraordinary authority during his lifetime but to what was this due? Can it be attributed to his own personality and his work, or did this authority have more to do with his audience and his times? Ackroyd describes how Eliot became a "cultural totem" late in his life, and how in 1956 he gave an address on "The Frontiers of Criticism" at the University of Minnesota; fourteen thousand people gathered in the baseball stadium to listen to him, presumably more because he was T. S. Eliot than to learn about literary criticism. Eliot must have corresponded to a need of his age. Thus, the question naturally arises, is it a legitimate need of the 1980's, too? Or was it period bound, a fad?

Another question is related to Eliot's personality: Did he have a single identifiable voice in his poetry, or was he a "plethora of voices?" As Ackroyd demonstrates, this is a very difficult question to answer. In Eliot's early poems, there are many different voices, often conflicting or unresolved. *Prufrock and Other Observations* (1917) had no identifiable single voice behind it, and as Ackroyd observes, Eliot found his own voice by first reproducing that of others. Edmund Wilson explained Eliot's behavior by suggesting that within him there were a number of different characters; V. S. Pritchett described him as "a company of actors inside one suit." Which voices were those of the "real" Eliot?

This ultimately leads to a pointed question about *The Waste Land* (1922): Who was the real author of this poem? The question is more serious than it may appear at first sight. All the books which contain this poem state that it is "by" Eliot and then proceed to give the epigraph and the dedication to Ezra Pound, "il miglior fabbro," and yet Pound's contribution to the poem was much greater than that of the usual editor; indeed, he left an indelible stamp on it. The facsimile and transcript of *The Waste Land*, published in 1971, shows that the version before Pound worked on it was strikingly different from the 1922 poem. In 1921 and 1922, Eliot, unable to impose an adequate organization on the poem, virtually abandoned it to Pound. As Ackroyd writes, "Pound had an extraordinarily good ear, and he located in the typescripts of *The Waste Land* the underlying rhythm of the poem—the music of which Eliot was so distrustful and which he surrounded with more deliberate and dramatic kinds of writing." Ackroyd goes on to say that it was this music which affected the first readers of the poem and which is a major source of its impact. Pound located it; Eliot himself was unable to locate it. This plays havoc with any notion of Eliot's evolution as poet, because he had intended the poem to be a dramatic interplay of parodied voices that was entirely different from the resulting poem. Shortly after its publication, Eliot was to continue his experiments with voices in his project for a dramatic version of *Sweeney Agonistes*, and this line of evolution was to lead to his interest in plays in the 1930's and 1940's. Should it not be admitted that *The Waste Land* was a product outside of Eliot's evolution as a poet and that Pound is the virtual coauthor of the poem?

Another essential question about Eliot is raised: What was the true nature of his faith? During his lifetime, he was sometimes accused of embracing Anglo-Catholicism as a refuge or an escape. Eliot himself had suggested that John Donne was the kind of man who "seeks refuge in religion from the tumults of a strong emotional temperament which can find no complete satisfaction elsewhere." There is no question that Eliot's faith was at least in part related to his own personal problems: "These were the unhappy months in which he placed his new faith around him like a carapace." Lawrence Durrell once suggested to Eliot that he was not a Christian at all but more like a Buddhist or a primitive. To this, Eliot replied only with a question, "Perhaps they haven't found me out yet?"

Another question relates to literary history and Eliot's contribution to modernism. Anglo-American modernism in literature is a movement that is difficult to define. Early modernists such as Pound, James Joyce, Eliot, and Wyndham Lewis were united by their pessimism and their revolt against the optimistic idealism of late nineteenth century figures such as George Bernard Shaw and H. G. Wells. Two results of this revolt were Imagism in poetry—the reliance on the individual image—and the desire to create works of art that would be on their own terms self-sufficient, capable of communicating their own values. Eliot was one of those who helped to build modernism, but as the mixed nature of *The Waste Land* indicates, Eliot was also working in other directions. He had difficulty in making the voices in his poems cohere; they were not naturally self-sufficient, and as Ackroyd indicates, it was Eliot who helped bring down the modernist tradition and "assisted at its burial." He came to assert the public role and social usefulness of the writer in an almost nineteenth century manner. If one is to continue to apply the epithet "modernist" to Eliot's poetry in a meaningful way, it must be with careful qualifications.

An additional problem with Eliot's critical doctrines, only touched upon by Ackroyd, has to do with Eliot's early concept of "subjectivity" and the need to combat it. Eliot adopted this notion almost entirely from Irving Babbitt, his Harvard University professor who waged a polemical battle against Jean Jacques Rousseau's cult of the emotions. Still, Eliot can be called antisubjective only with difficulty—he attributed great power and above all, danger, to the emotions. He associated them with evil, darkness and chaos, and sin. In a sense, he was paying them a backhanded compliment and even magnifying their importance. These attitudes, never clearly avowed, were probably the source of the most successful imagery and rhythms of his best-known poetry written during the period from 1915 to 1922.

The great virtue of Ackroyd's biography is that it presents the reader with a broad amount of objective information about Eliot in a highly readable form, and this in turn permits the reader to ask questions such as these without prejudging them. Other questions inevitably arise: for example, the strange fact that Eliot never really became an Englishman but adopted a hyper-Tory position that seemed unnatural to many of his new compatriots; the "Bolo poems," some of them pornographic, which Eliot once wanted to publish; Eliot's fascination with music halls, boxing, and sensational murders; and the tangled problem of Eliot's political identity—his distaste for democracy (it was not one of the "traditions" he admired) and his temporary admiration for Benito Mussolini. Ackroyd presents all of these aspects of Eliot's personality in the full context of his concrete life. The book is biography at its best, closely allied to history. The complex personality of Eliot comes alive and becomes understandable in a way that most readers can grasp. A "legend" of Eliot developed during the 1940's and after his reception of the Nobel Prize in 1948, that legend assumed epic proportions, was highly uncritical, and often threatened to distort a true understanding of his work. The biography of Peter Ackroyd presents readers with something quite different, finally taking the place of the legend: a very concrete, and unique, man.

John Carpenter

Sources for Further Study

Book World. XIV, December 9, 1984, p. 1.
Library Journal. CIX, November 15, 1984, p. 2145.
Los Angeles Times Book Review. December 2, 1984, p. 1.
The New Republic. CXCI, December 17, 1984, p. 38.
The New York Review of Books. XXXI, December 20, 1984, p. 31.
The New York Times Book Review. LXXXIX, December 20, 1984, p. 9.
Newsweek. CIV, November 26, 1984, p. 110.
Publishers Weekly. CCXXVI, October 5, 1984, p. 77.
Time. CXXIV, December 3, 1984, p. 80.
The Wall Street Journal. CCIV, December 3, 1984, p. 32.

T. S. ELIOT
A Study in Character and Style

Author: Ronald Bush (1946-   )
Publisher: Oxford University Press (New York). Illustrated. 287 pp. $25.00
Type of work: Literary criticism and biography

An investigation of the relationship between psychological developments in T. S. Eliot's life and the nature of his poetry

In his *T. S. Eliot: A Study in Character and Style*, Ronald Bush provides several valuable services to Eliot scholarship. The first is as organizer and synthesizer of a tremendous amount of primary material and received opinion about T. S. Eliot and the general outline of his career. In this capacity, Bush's work is not strikingly original. His overall view of both Eliot's life and the nature and merit of individual poems is largely consistent with and indebted to existing scholarship. The value of Bush's book lies in his thoroughness, his grasp of the wholeness of Eliot's diverse efforts (Bush skillfully uses Eliot's criticism, for example, to enlighten both his poetry and temperament), and in the most complete attempt to date to illuminate the link between the psychological contours of Eliot's life and his changing poetic style.

Bush's subtitle indicates the primary focus of his work. His approach is largely a combination of psychological biography and close reading of individual poems, though he does just enough deconstructionist criticism to show that he is up-to-date. Eliot's reticence about making public the details of his life, reflected in his refusal to authorize a biography and the many restrictions on his existing private papers, has hindered attempts to explore fully relationships between his life and work—relationships that, in Eliot's case, are unusually significant. In the past, one had to be content with the reminiscences of friends and acquaintances and the generalities of scholars. Recent books such as Lyndall Gordon's *Eliot's Early Years* (1977) have begun to correct that situation, and Bush's efforts are another significant step in that direction.

The basic picture Bush presents of Eliot is not a new one, but it is rendered in greater detail and made to serve new ends—an exploration and explanation of the changing course of Eliot's style. Eliot is seen as the archetypally reflective person, struggling all of his life with the conflicting romantic and classic sides of his nature, the former having the upper hand up to the time of *The Waste Land* (1922) and the latter thereafter, but with the tension between them never fully resolved at any time. Bush's treatment is much more subtle than this, but it is essentially an elaboration of a common view of the tenor of Eliot's life.

What is uncommon is the attention Bush pays to the relationship between Eliot's life and the style of his writing. It has long been observed that Eliot's poetry after *The Waste Land* is more discursive, philosophical, and less concrete than before (see, for example, Floyd C. Watkins' *The Flesh and the Word: Eliot, Hemingway, Faulkner*, 1971), but Bush both develops this notion in greater depth than before and ties it more intimately to the spiritual and psychological struggles of Eliot's life.

Bush portrays the changes in Eliot's style as a reflection of his ongoing battle between the desire to make contact with and express a deeper self that was more authentic and energizing than the conventional self and the impulse to control and order the potentially destructive and egotistic nature of that deeper self. Ezra Pound's Imagism and the increasing spareness and directness of William Butler Yeats reinforced the young Eliot's own deep suspicion of rhetoric and convention in favor of a poetry that eschewed eloquence for presentation of concrete images charged with emotional power.

Bush follows Gordon and others in portraying the early Eliot struggling with the contradictory forces of self-denial, service of others, emotional and intellectual control, the need to succeed, and so on that were the legacy of his patrician American upbringing, and the fear that all of this was artificial, constrictive, and life-denying. Eliot was equally unnerved by the prospect of being a Prufrock or Gerontion on the one hand, trapped in a web of social and rhetorical convention, unable to express and perhaps even feel genuine emotion, and a vulgar and earthy Sweeney on the other. This conflict can be seen even in Eliot's famous advocacy of impersonality—which, Bush contends, was simply a way to bypass the superficial, acquired self so as to reach the more authentic self below.

Bush's greatest interest, however, is in the later Eliot and in what happened in the 1920's that signaled the great change in his poetry. Bush argues that Eliot's use of the seemingly impersonal to reach the personal had worked too well in *The Waste Land* and that Eliot came to believe that he had revealed more in that work than he had intended or ever wanted to reveal again. Bush speculates that Eliot's breakdown at the time lowered longstanding barriers against forces from his buried self—forces which therefore appeared more directly than they had before. The poem was made to look more impersonal and objective than it really is, Bush claims, by the late addition of the mythic structure, more illusory than actual, and the red herrings of Eliot's infamous notes.

The heart of Bush's thesis is that changes in Eliot's life after *The Waste Land* led him to new conceptions about poetry and subsequently to a new kind of writing. These changes were both professional and personal. The general success of *The Waste Land* and his growing stature as a poet and man of letters gave Eliot increased confidence. Similarly, the launching of the *Criterion* provided a sense that he had an opportunity to affect the course of European culture.

This was also a time of new resolve to bring order to his greatly troubled domestic life. Bush brings together pointed recollections from different sources to indicate exactly how necessary (and ultimately impossible) such healing was between Eliot and Vivien. Indeed, in Bush's view, the desire for order became the driving force in Eliot's life from this point on, both leading him to and defining the nature of this experience with God and the Church.

All of these factors contributed to a move in Eliot's poetry toward the overtly spiritual, social, and philosophical. No longer concerned primarily with the relationship between the buried and conventional self, or with the struggle between rhetoric and the concrete image, he was preoccupied instead with the ability of poetry to convey the feelings of belief (not the propositions) and the emotional colorings of spiritual struggle and intellectual thought.

The extent of this new resolve in Eliot is clear when one considers equally significant changes in his critical writing. Bush records the entrance into Eliot's literary criticism of conservative ideology as early as 1923. In the mid-1920's, Eliot revised his opinion of writers such as John Donne, whom he criticized for qualities that he had previously admired. At the same time, Eliot increasingly prized Dante as a poet who could transform theology and philosophy into the highest kind of art. Eliot's admiration for the cool irony of a Jules Laforgue faded in proportion to his growing esteem for Paul Valéry's success in subsuming Symbolist evocation to formal control.

Eliot's criticism written during this period reveals an increasing appreciation for a kind of meditative poetry that is concerned to record the *pattern* of feelings, especially the feelings of a person of faith in an unbelieving age. The result, Bush maintains, was a poetry which, after *The Hollow Men* (1925), foregoes the concentration and concreteness of an Imagist sensibility for discursiveness, incantation, liturgical elements, and musical elaboration. At its best, Eliot's later poetry returns to a Symbolist aesthetic of the musical evocation of highly charged but indeterminate symbols. At its worst, it degenerates into painfully unpoetic prosaicness.

Bush offers two of Eliot's own phrases in a 1926 essay, "Sir John Davies," as keys to his later poetry. Eliot thought of the poet as "a man reasoning with himself in solitude," looking for ways of "turning thought into feeling": The culmination of this movement was *Four Quartets* (1943). One of the longstanding debates about Eliot is whether *Four Quartets* represents his crowning achievement or simply marks the end of his decline. The answer to this question is often determined on other than aesthetic grounds. Those unsympathetic with Eliot's Christianity and conservative ideology are predisposed to finding his later work unsatisfactory, especially if they are also not inclined to locate the source of poetry in "reasoning" or "thought"; others are predisposed to praising the later poetry precisely because they are pleased by Eliot's ideological shift. Bush comes down somewhere in the middle, finding undeniable lapses of emotional intensity and craft in *Four Quartets*, and yet discovering also a powerful and unique realization of Symbolist techniques in service to an expression of religious struggle and belief. The power of the poem derives in part from its paradoxical nature, at once intensely personal yet distanced and controlled. It is the power of great emotion restrained rather than released—or released only obliquely in the suggestiveness of indeterminate symbols.

T. S. Eliot: A Study in Character and Style is an important book in Eliot criticism, impressive in its synthesizing and analytic accomplishments and in its use of previously unpublished material. These strengths also contribute to its stylistic faults. The book is overdocumented and relies too heavily on quotations to be anything but laborious to read. The more than 550 endnotes testify to Bush's thoroughness but also clutter his writing with an almost unbroken string of introduction to quotation, quotation, evaluation of quotation, critical citation, and introduction to another quotation. (Nearly half of the words in chapter 4, for example, are someone else's.)

Stylistic infelicities aside, Bush's book is an important overview of Eliot's life and work, providing many insights into the complex relationship between the two.

Daniel Taylor

Sources for Further Study

The Atlantic. CCLIII, April, 1984, p. 145.
Booklist. LXXX, January 15, 1984, p. 711.
Choice. XXI, July, 1984, p. 1604.
Library Journal. CIX, January, 1984, p. 91.
Los Angeles Times Book Review. March 11, 1984, p. 7.
The New York Review of Books. XXXI, June 28, 1984, p. 5.
The New York Times Book Review. LXXXIX, April 8, 1984, p. 10.
Virginia Quarterly Review. LX, Summer, 1984, p. 86.

TWENTIETH CENTURY PLEASURES
Prose on Poetry

Author: Robert Hass (1941-   )
Publisher: The Ecco Press (New York). 308 pp. $17.95
Type of work: Essays

A wide-ranging collection of essays on poets living and dead, American and European, and on such varied topics as the nature of poetic form and the cultural renaissance of the San Francisco Bay Area

To write about poetry in an intelligent and engaging way is no simple matter. Much of what is published in academic journals is certainly intelligent, but such essays are engaging only to specialists—and then only occasionally. Moreover, academic writing about poetry tends to distance poetry from the business of daily life. Review criticism, on the other hand, often suffers from an amateurism that is unable to educate readers. Of opinion there is no shortage, but real knowledge and sensitivity are hard to find. Furthermore, most review criticism is either too brief or too partisan or both. Before a reader can be intelligently engaged, a subject must be given sufficient space for the mind of the critic to reveal itself in the process of engagement. Robert Hass may not be the most important critic writing today. He is certainly not the most learned. Still, the intensity and scope of his engagement with poetry, the relaxed yet purposeful shapes of his essays, and the clarity of his style make him among the most rewarding. He has found an angle of approach and a manner which will reward specialist critics, poets, and the general reader for whom poetry is a genuine interest.

Because Hass is an accomplished poet, his observations have a built-in authority. He is successful, however, far beyond the measure of other poets of his generation who have set out along similar paths. Few have made good sense, in prose, on the very subject that they supposedly know so much about and cherish. Among those few are Robert Pinsky, Jonathan Holden, and Robert Hass. Writing of Hass's second collection of poems, *Praise* (1979), Peter Davison commented on the "architectural grandeur" of the whole and the severe discipline ("limits . . . as stern as gravity") of the individual poems. The uncanny thing about Hass's work, whether it be in poetry or the prose essay, is how formal discipline and spontaneity coexist. Few writers seem so relaxed within the limits they have set for themselves.

Twentieth Century Pleasures: Prose on Poetry includes assessments of major American moderns such as Robert Lowell and James Wright; living Continental masters such as Joseph Brodsky, Tomas Transtromer, and Czesław Miłosz; more distant but more imposing figures such as Rainer Maria Rilke; and such forceful critical and poetical personalities as Yvor Winters, Robert Creeley, and James McMichael. Hass treats individual works, books, or entire careers of these varied talents, and he pays a very special homage to Stanley Kunitz—a poet whose work has not received the attention it deserves. In all of these essays and reviews, Hass manages a fine balance between the general and the particular. He is always patient with his evidence, knowing when and what and how much to quote. The tone is warm, even friendly; the penetration is deep and sharp.

Surprisingly, Hass has much to say about form. Not only does he treat formal issues in dealing with most of the poets named above, but he also sets aside special investigations of formal problems. Hass's sense of form is catholic; he is at home dealing with metrical issues, but he does not tie form to metrics in a narrow sense. He can write about rhythm and meter without ending up seeming to write about mathematics. Better yet, Hass writes about such matters without connecting them to the repressed, the anal, or the archaic. Hass's projection of a healthy, relaxed, committed, celebrative, and alert sensibility allows him to be successful (again, "engaging") where so many others fail. He is at home in these essays. The clothes of his language and his ideas fit. Knowing who he is, he knows what to wear.

Representative of Hass's method is the pleasantly meandering meditation "One Body: Some Notes on Form." He begins by telling how thinking about form in poetry led him to remember some episodes in the lives of his children which exemplified the power of daily patterns and the freshness of perception. "Wonder and repetition," Hass observes, comingle in one's experience of life, and their interaction "is the psychological basis for the power and the necessity of artistic form." Hass sidles past references to or quotations from R. D. Laing, Arthur Rimbaud, Theodore Roethke, Ezra Pound, Gary Snyder, Randall Jarrell, and the anonymous poet of "Western Wind," all the time pursuing an argument about form in poetry. Each poem and passage which Hass quotes is illuminated by his response, and each illumination adds to the others like so many small waves building to a crescendo. Gathering momentum, Hass's wave picks up Pablo Picasso, Ingmar Bergman, Sylvia Plath, Charles Simic, more Pound, Wallace Stevens, William Wordsworth, and Louise Gluck. By now, Hass has won the right to assert; "The form of a poem exists in the relation between its music and its seeing; form is not the number or kind of restrictions, conscious or unconscious, many or few, with which a piece of writing begins." A dozen more amplified quotations from current writers back to the Renaissance and up through Walt Whitman to the Beats, and finally Hass lets go of his subject—reluctantly. Hass's intimacy and his clarity of vision and expression make it difficult for the reader to let go. Luckily, there are many more essays.

In his foreword to Hass's first collection of poems, *Field Guide* (1973), Stanley Kunitz observed that "Robert Hass is a poet who sits easy in his skin." Kunitz found the rewards of Hass's poetry to include "the satisfactions of an art committed to making 'felt connections' between words and body, between body and world." The same man whose poems Kunitz has characterized so effectively is the easy yet committed fellow bringing readers *Twentieth Century Pleasures*. At bottom, Hass's concern with form has to do with connections between the nature of language and the pulse of life and of the world. He is most alert to poets whose poems make these connections click.

"Listening and Making" is, mainly, a meditation on Gary Snyder's "August on Sourdough," but it is also an important discussion of the way prosody operates in contemporary free verse. Though Hass is not the first to observe that patterns of stressed syllables constitute one major formal element in recent poetry, he is one of the few to have presented an attractive and compelling demonstration. Early in the essay, Hass reminds readers that "rhythm is always revolutionary ground. It is always the place where the organic rises to abolish the mechanical and where energy announces the abolition of tradition." Hass discusses Oriental poems of leave-taking, Native American chants, and William Butler Yeats's "The Second Coming" to build his context for Snyder's brand of free verse. Hass writes cogently about the way in which free-verse poems, assuming openness or chaos, insist on "sensual attention"—a state of awareness not provoked by the metrical poem's immediate presentation of order. Hass also takes up the special way in which free-verse poems find appropriate closure. Always quick to move from abstraction to concrete demonstration, Hass handles prosodic issues vividly, giving them unexpected life.

Hass's review of *The Collected Poems of Robert Creeley: 1945-1975* (1983) is called "Creeley: His Metric." Here, Hass, in tracing the influence of William Carlos Williams on the young Creeley, develops an understanding of Creeley's line that goes far beyond the usual technical matters and into contemporary language theory as transmitted by Claude Lévi-Strauss, Jacques Lacan, and Jacques Derrida. As ever, Hass takes what he needs from his wide reading in an easy manner, applying it plainly, concretely, and without haste to the task at hand.

The concern with poetic form which Hass reveals in these essays is but a part of his concern with the relationship between poetry and the business of living. He is a poet who is truly delighted over the work of other poets, and he has found, repeatedly, an accessible critical language through which to share their excellences and sometimes their fascinating failures. This sharing is always to the end of anchoring poetry in life and life in poetry. In a way, these writings are a kind of autobiography: Hass is holding communion with his fellow poets and with his readers, expressing himself as an informed *personality*, not as the executor of a critical system. Hass the man is all over these pages; he does not appear at the expense of his subjects, but neither will he vanish in their service. His quest after the inner processes of Lowell's "The Quaker Graveyard in Nantucket" is a personal journey, as is the more obvious searching in the essay titled "Looking for Rilke." It is not surprising, then, to find among Hass's critical explorations a piece called "Some Notes on the San Francisco Bay Area as a Culture Region: A Memoir." For Hass, discovering Kenneth Rexroth is part of discovering himself.

Perhaps the most striking essay in this collection is the long concluding one, "Images." Its shape is the least traditional in a book full of such shapes. It is an essay about seeing: how images form in the imagination, how they are held and transformed by memory, and how not only the sensory field but also the excitement of its impact can be, in the special terms of poetic art, created anew for the reader. In part, the essay is a recollection of private moments: the sensation of Hass's child's weight in his arms; the image of an excited woman, skillet and scouring pad dropped to her sides, following a memory. Hass is after what these private moments hold—these images charged with feeling. In part, the essay is a field of bright quotation: jottings from Anton Chekhov's notebook, excerpts from Denise Levertov, passages from Walt Whitman.

Hass is concerned with the image unfettered by metaphoric weight, and so he turns to Eastern tradition. He addresses the work of Issa, Li Po, Buson, and Matsuo Basho—all the while adding to a portrait of himself, among family and friends, living and working in the California mountains, attentive to his senses as they register everything that the setting has to offer. This interpenetration of a deeply felt animal life, the intellect and imagination playing over it, and the possibilities of language is Hass's theme. "Images" is a meeting of East and West, past and present, body and world and word.

Robert Hass is a "laid back" Californian in the best sense. These unhurried considerations which make up *Twentieth Century Pleasures* have much in common with Hass's poems, poems that Stanley Kunitz found to be "as much an expression of an organic principle as the activities of which they are an extension—walking, eating, sleeping, lovemaking—and they are equally pleasurable, equally real." Of course, the essays are not about these actions in the same way that the poems are. Still, there is a connection. Hass's vision of the poem's importance has to do with its getting people back in touch with themselves. His essays do that, too.

Philip K. Jason

Sources for Further Study

Booklist. LXXX, March 15, 1984, p. 1023.
Kirkus Reviews. LII, February 15, 1984, p. 186.
Library Journal. CIX, April 1, 1984, p. 722.

Los Angeles Times Book Review. November 18, 1984, p. 8.
The New York Times Book Review. XC, March 3, 1985, p. 37.
Poetry. CXLV, March, 1985, p. 345.
Publishers Weekly. CCXXV, February 10, 1984, p. 185.

TWO WINGS TO VEIL MY FACE

Author: Leon Forrest (1937-   )
Publisher: Random House (New York). 296 pp. $15.95
Type of work: Novel
Time: The 1980's, with recollections extending to the 1800's
Locale: Illinois

A young black man's attempt to understand himself by coming to understand his own history in terms of his grandmother's past

Principal characters:

NATHANIEL WITHERSPOON, a young man, aged twenty-one, who tries to understand a complex and ambiguous past and his role in it

GREAT MOMMA SWEETIE REED, his grandmother, who promises to fill in all the blanks of her history when Nathaniel reaches his majority

JUDGE JERICHO WITHERSPOON, her husband, a runaway slave and forty years her senior

ARTHUR WITHERSPOON, their son

I. V. REED, Sweetie's slave father, who sleeps on a pallet beneath his white master's bed

ANGELINA, Sweetie's mother

ROLLINS REED, the "master," Sweetie's grandfather, who raped Angelina

SYLVIA REED, Rollins' wife, whose diamonds connect past and future

REESE SHANK HAYWOOD, a man who loved Angelina and tried to kill Rollins

ANTIE FOISTY, the woman who put Rollins back together and adjusted some of his behavior patterns

CANDY CUMMINGS, a young woman not yet ready to accept the ambiguities of life

In his third novel, *Two Wings to Veil My Face*, Leon Forrest continues to exhibit the force and eloquence of a major black writer schooled in a literary tradition that helps to shape his work. As a kind of foreword, Forrest quotes passages from Homer, James Joyce, and Ralph Ellison. Throughout the novel, references to William Shakespeare, Herman Melville, Richard Wright, and other writers abound; at the same time, Forrest's method of storytelling reveals a writer attuned to the oral tradition. *Two Wings to Veil My Face* is a better novel even than his first two, *There Is a Tree More Ancient than Eden* (1973) and *The Bloodworth Orphans* (1977), both praised as major literary achievements.

In *Two Wings to Veil My Face*, Forrest tells the story of a strong black woman, Sweetie Reed, who tries to come to terms with her past as she prepares for a future judgment day. Though the details of the story primarily concern Sweetie, however, it is only in the telling of that story to her grandson Nathaniel that the events take on meaning. From Nathaniel and his acceptance of his complex heritage, Sweetie learns to abandon her self-righteous pride in an act which unveils her soul and prepares her for the redemption that she seeks. Just as important as Sweetie's redemption is Nathaniel's role in it, and perhaps more important is the revelation that the whole story of the "American curse" is something with which all Americans will have to deal as they try to come to terms with their nation's history.

The novel is told through the consciousness of Nathaniel Witherspoon, who, at age twenty-one, the time of his majority, comes to hear the whole story of his Great Momma Sweetie Reed. At age ninety-one, Sweetie is willing to fill in the blanks of her history both for the edification of her grandson and for a final act of contrition. Nathaniel has been the recipient of bits and pieces of the story from his earliest memories, but there are things that have been left out, mysteries, which cast over the whole story an aura of wonder and of the incomprehensible. He has been aware, also, through all of his life, that his grandmother has been preparing him to become her hearer, that he must be a re-creator of her story, so that he can create himself from "history, ancestors, lovers, and the demons and gifts of living." Black history is oral history, but Great Momma Sweetie Reed, spurning a tape recorder, makes Nathaniel take down her story in longhand so that he will remember it better—in effect, to sear it on his soul. To keep his aged grandmother's attention focused and to stimulate her expressive tongue and gift for language, Nathaniel gives her periodically a jigger of scotch dashed over boiling sassafras leaves. Thinking of himself as Sweetie's Boswell, Nathaniel wonders about his role in the storytelling. He does not view himself as a mere recorder. He must be true to her words, but he must also be a great illuminator, "spinning" out the story and thus transforming it into an "eternal goal beyond the radiance of the here and the now." For Nathaniel, Sweetie is not only a bard but also an actress who has often rehearsed the promised story long into the nights and pursued pieces of it into her dreams.

Forrest's emphasis on storytelling and the method of transcription is tied to the fact that much history never gets told. Sweetie's insistence on *telling* the story suggests an ultimate dissatisfaction with print and lack of trust because of what has not been printed. The emphasis in the novel on Sweetie's learning to read and her skills with words, on her mother's gift for language, on the muteness of her half sister, along with all the stories told by various people throughout the narrative and all the references to writers both black and white, past and present, parallels language with mysteries to be resolved, blanks to be filled in. The method of accretion of detail as the novel progresses also underlines this theme. Constructed from bits and fragments, the novel is an elaborate maze through which readers must, with Nathaniel, make their way. Essential images and details are established and then repeated with additional details augmenting the story, extending it to include not only Nathaniel but also all readers whose history has somewhere in it hidden facts, blank spaces.

For Nathaniel, Sweetie has been both queen and priest. She is the reigning matriarch of the family. When he helped her as a boy, he was more altar boy than when he served at Mass. The food which she dispenses to the poor is, in Nathaniel's mind, a sacrament. The biscuits, dripping in butter and honey, which she feeds to Nathaniel are closer to being Host than the wafers served at the Mass.

As he sits by her bed during the times when she is sleeping, waiting for her to awaken to continue her story, Nathaniel reflects not only on his role in the storytelling process and on his relationship to his grandmother but also on his relationship to his grandfather Witherspoon, on the occasion of his grandfather's death, and on his own relationship to a young woman, Candy Cummings. These reflections on Candy are much briefer than Nathaniel's reflections on his grandfather, beginning with a few details at the beginning of the novel, accumulating details as the novel progresses, and ending with the revelation that Candy was sent away from Nathaniel by Sweetie.

Nathaniel's reflection on his grandfather Witherspoon's life and death take up considerably more space, becoming juncture points for extensive memories. These memories focus on events related to his grandfather's death at the age of 117 and on Sweetie's initial refusal to participate in the burial rites. One of the mysteries surrounding Sweetie is her relationship to her husband, Jericho, forty years her senior, from whom she had separated in 1905, not divorcing but taking back her maiden name. All Sweetie has said about the situation is that Jericho is prideful first and above all, though she acknowledges the debts that she owes him and has never objected to Nathaniel's or his father's close relationship with Jericho.

For Nathaniel, Jericho has been king. Jericho placed upon Nathaniel his slave tunic as a mantle and a mark of remembrance. Jericho encouraged Nathaniel to question, gave him concrete information concerning the flight North from slavery when Jericho assumed varying disguises and costumes. He has been a lawyer and then a judge. Nathaniel can identify his own physical features in those of his grandfather and his father. Though Jericho was not himself a believer, Nathaniel invested his grandfather with godlike powers and stature, and the young man finds himself torn between grandfather and grandmother in a purgatory of confusion, not clarified by the various religious beliefs (Protestant and Catholic) present in his own family. Bothersome to Nathaniel is the blank spot in history related to the place in the family Bible which records the apparent date of his father Arthur's birth, though Arthur celebrates his birthday a month sooner than the date indicates.

During her narration, Sweetie has her own juncture points, places in her narrative that recur and provide the underlying structure for her story—the kidnaping of herself and her mother when Sweetie was seven; the rape, consequent death, and burial of her mother; her mother's song; Sweetie's rescue, paralleled with her sitting on her grandfather Rollins' knee and her father I. V.'s scratching at the door; her meeting with her bridegroom consequent to his purchase of her; and the conversation she had with her father prior to his death. As the novel concludes, two other juncture points are revealed: the loss of her own children and the arrival of Jericho with the baby Arthur, borne by Lucasta Jones, and Sweetie's hypothesis that perhaps the whole of humankind springs from a series of rapes and that, if God is a man, then women have no alternative but to protect themselves against men.

Sweetie's mother, Angelina, is tied to most of the juncture points that prod Sweetie's memory. Daughter of the slave, Jubell, and her white master, Rollins Reed, Angelina was a house slave working for, trained by, and emotionally bound to Sylvia Reed, Rollins' wife. Angelina's song, including the lines: "Angel got two wings to veil my face./ Angel got two wings to carry me away," provides the title for the novel and a series of recurring images concerning physical and mental survival and flight to safety as well as a redemptive, spiritual flight to Jesus. Using the metaphoric wings to hide her face, Sweetie assumes a haughtiness and pride designed to maintain her dignity against the painful memories of her past and allow her to cope with the psychological devastation attendant upon master-slave relationships, whether they involve physical or mental bondage. Finding it necessary for her own survival and identification to cleave to her mother, in spite of the fact that she has reason to be jealous of Angelina, Sweetie turns against the men who have used or desired her or her mother, refusing them any compassion or understanding.

A large portion of Sweetie's narration is taken up by an apparently verbatim conversation between Sweetie and her father, I. V., who on his deathbed tries to explain the reasons for his behavior and to justify his actions to his daughter. This dialogue is placed at the center of the novel and holds the answers to many of the questions Sweetie has had throughout her life. Though I. V. is mendacious, tricky, and selfish, his reasons for his behavior make sense in context of the total novel, and his answers to Sweetie's questions provide her with more images and details to fill in the story that she is trying to tell Nathaniel.

I. V.'s narration provides another set of juncture points relevant not only to him but, insofar as they help to fill in the blanks, also relevant to Sweetie and eventually to Nathaniel. Dominant in I. V.'s story are images concerning Rollins, the slaver; Reese Shank Haywood, the black slave driver for Rollins who, at I. V.'s instigation, almost killed Rollins; Antie Foisty, the black woman who put Rollins back together again as if by magic; the pallet under

Rollins' bed on which I. V. was condemned to sleep; Sylvia Reed and her diamonds; the loss of Angelina; the sale of Sweetie to Jericho; and slingshot shoes and a mask in the shape of wings, which then become metaphors for I. V.—talismans to be buried with him.

Angelina is a pervasive figure in I. V.'s narration, too. Her birth was the result of Rollins' rape of Jubell, for which Haywood almost killed the white man. When the Yankees were coming, Rollins' wife, Sylvia, gave Angelina some of her diamonds to hold, and the spilling of the diamonds saved Angelina from the Yankees. I. V. married Angelina at fifteen to help make up for his participation in the death of Haywood; Angelina's quickness to conceive kept I. V. out of her bed for long stretches of time, and since all the children died except Sweetie, I. V. resented them, including Sweetie, because he had been denied sex for no good reason. Finally, he sold Sweetie to Jericho, who had been in love with Angelina.

Sweetie's rejection of I. V., the lying man of many voices, is similar to her rejection of Jericho, the eloquent man of many costumes, and is caused by a similar rejection of her by the men. Earlier, it was not the baby Arthur she rejected but Jericho, for his "philandering"; she left him, taking the baby with her. These facts, coming at the culmination of Sweetie's story to Nathaniel, fall on him with the impact of severe blows, but he realizes that he remains tied to Sweetie, if not by flesh. His knowledge of his strong psychological and historical ties helps him to accept the truth, even when, at the climax of the novel, Sweetie gives him a picture of his real grandmother Lucasta and a packet of diamonds saved by Sylvia Reed from the Yankees because they were taped inside her rectum.

Nathaniel can accept the truth in all of its horror, and he pleads with Sweetie that she accept the truth also and without rancor. Nathaniel says that he has "No two wings to hide the riddled features upon my fated American face." Falling to his knees, he prays not only for himself and Great Momma Sweetie Reed but also for all Americans bound to their past. Throughout her life, Sweetie's struggle has been to remain human—proud and dignified—in a system that dehumanized master and slave alike, and she does not give in without a struggle. Gradually, however, her curses, prayers, and denunciations give way to gestures, as two wings unveil her soul, and she allows redemption to occur.

Mary Rohrberger

Sources for Further Study

Booklist. LXXX, February 15, 1984, p. 845.
Essence. XV, August, 1984, p. 48.

Kirkus Reviews. LI, December 15, 1983, p. 1265.
Library Journal. CIX, March 1, 1984, p. 508.
Los Angeles Times Book Review. March 25, 1984, p. 6.
The New York Times Book Review. LXXXIX, February 26, 1984, p. 15.
Publishers Weekly. CCXXV, January 6, 1984, p. 77.

TWO-BIT CULTURE
The Paperbacking of America

Author: Kenneth C. Davis (1954-   )
Publisher: Houghton Mifflin Company (Boston). 430 pp. $18.95; paperback $9.95
Type of work: Publishing history
Time: 1939 to the 1980's

A study of American mass-market publishers since 1939, emphasizing the influence of social and economic forces and analyzing the cultural significance of popular books

Commercial mass publishing has been reinvented a number of times over the past two centuries. The basic idea is to discover what people want, produce it cheaply enough that a great many of them can buy it, and then rake in the profits. It happened with family newspapers and dime novels in the nineteenth century, with pulp magazines early in the twentieth, and then, most visibly to the contemporary eye, with the paperback revolution that began in the United States when the first ten titles Robert de Graff had chosen to appear as twenty-five-cent Pocket Books reached New York City newsstands on July 30, 1939. Like the earlier ventures in mass publishing, Kenneth C. Davis argues, the paperback phenomenon is no longer a revolution; it ended in the mid-1970's when conglomerates swallowed the individual publishers, cover prices escalated, and the basic goal of cheap books for everyone vanished once more.

Davis has worked for *Publishers Weekly* and made good contacts inside the trade. His detailed history is enriched with enough anecdotes and quotations to be thoroughly readable. It is also more ambitious than the other recent books on the subject. *Mass Market Publishing in America* (1982), edited by Allen Billy Crider, supplies individual accounts (with bibliographies) of sixty-eight separate publishers; *UnderCover: An Illustrated History of American Mass Market Paperbacks* (1982), by Thomas L. Bonn, is more general and much shorter. *Two-Bit Culture* is the first history of American paperbacks that also attempts serious cultural analysis. The analysis is less successful than the history, partly because the topic is massive and partly because Davis' own attitude—like that of the mass publishers he most admires—is somewhat ambiguous. He is excited by the idea of reading democratized books but troubled by commercial success that rests on mass taste; he believes that really massive best-sellers may indicate fundamental changes in social outlook but seems to prefer publishers who promote intellectual tastes and avant-garde writers.

Davis does demonstrate convincingly a number of ways in which mass publishing has reflected a time or a trend or an idea. In 1931, the whole of America had perhaps five hundred bookstores that carried any reasonable selection of titles. Even a relatively prosperous middle-class family that believed in education might keep its entire library between a single pair of bookends. Robert de Graff's decisions about price and format and titles were probably less important than his means of getting books to readers; Pocket Books not only made its own arrangements with bookstores, department stores, and the more important drugstore and five-and-dime chains but also had more than six hundred magazine distributors moving its wares into newsstands, cigar shops, groceries, bus depots, and train stations in virtually every small town and neighborhood in the country.

Davis is very good at explaining the complex relationship of publishing success to social forces, economic realities, cultural changes, personality quirks, enterprise, and luck. The early paperback years coincided with a struggle between the American News Company and the independent magazine distributors (whose original power grew from Moe Annenberg's control of the racing wire); Pocket Books generated so much income for the independents that American News gave financial backing to Avon Books in order to get a share of the book market. For many years thereafter, the publishers (such as Avon Books) that originated in the magazine trade featured genre fiction—Westerns, mysteries, science fiction, romance—and often depended on writers who had moved over from the pulps. In contrast, Pocket Books and the houses with ties to the hardcover trade were more likely to provide reprints of popular novels or books with proven backlist value.

The war years established the reading habit among men who had passed tedious hours with staple-bound Armed Services Editions in their pockets. Postwar times created a mammoth college generation ready to own books and produced an average of three-and-a-half million babies every year. War and college and economic opportunity and social mobility separated a great many of these babies from the grandparents who might have helped out. Several years earlier, however, Robert de Graff had asked a young pediatrician with psychoanalytic training to come up with something that would be easy to read and could be sold for a quarter. The book was delayed by the doctor's own military service, but in 1946—at exactly the right moment— Benjamin Spock's *Baby and Child Care* began to roll off the presses. De Graff arranged for a hardcover publisher as well, so that medical authorities would supply reviews, but the book was indisputably a creation of the paperback revolution and not simply its beneficiary. It eventually sold more copies than any other book ever printed in the United States except for the Bible. *Baby and Child Care* is by far the best evidence for *Two-Bit Culture*'s thesis that "*paperback* books have been responsible for significant changes in the American consciousness." It is also a good example of the difficulty in disentangling the social and economic forces, the combination of luck, timing, and distribution, and the interaction between author and publisher that produce a best-seller.

These interrelationships make the book fascinating to read but often weaken the contention that mass-market books are able to change society. Davis provides lists of best-selling and significant titles grouped by decade or half decade and also an appendix of fifty paperback books that he claims have influenced the United States in some significant way. These books range from Ruth Benedict's *Patterns of Culture* (1946; all dates which follow are for first paperback publications) to *Peyton Place* by Grace Metalious (1957) to *The Last Whole Earth Catalogue* (1971). The democratization of reading and the simple availability of titles in large quantities are certainly significant, but the question is often circular. A book cannot become a mammoth best-seller unless millions of people want to read it. Does the book then influence them, or do their interests and desires, which already existed, cause the book to be published? Davis' analysis of popular fiction is more superficial than his knowledge of the publishing trade, and, furthermore, for a writer whose subject is popular culture, he is curiously uncomfortable with the mass-market books that appeal to what he repeatedly calls the "lowest common denominator." He does attempt to demonstrate how a decade's characteristics are reflected in emblematic books. Among the subjects he treats are Erskine Caldwell, Mickey Spillane, *Peyton Place*, the spy novels of the middle 1960's, and the Harlequin phenomenon of the 1970's.

The real paperbacking of America, Davis suggests, took place during the decade between 1950 and 1960. At its opening, paperbacks were in danger of following some previous waves of mass publishing into tawdriness and disrepute. The magazine wholesalers wanted more sex and mystery for quick turnover; virtually every book in the racks flaunted a provocative cover, even when it was written by Sinclair Lewis or Nathaniel Hawthorne. At about the same time, however, highbrow magazines began to notice the paperback revolution and debate its significance. *New World Writing* offered an eclectic anthology of established and avant-garde high-culture writers. As the decade passed, the balance of power within the publishing industry shifted. Between 1959 and 1960, paperbacks passed adult hardcovers in annual dollar sales. Reprint houses vied for best-sellers and deemphasized their anthologies and nonfiction; the money they laid out for rights began to influence decisions about which authors would be published in hardcover. Stock in Pocket Books was offered to the public in 1960 and before long the era of corporate takeovers had arrived; control passed to business managers instead of people trained in the traditional "gentleman's business" of publishing.

Davis, himself in the gentlemanly tradition, approves most of the publishing trade when it does not simply feed public desire but rather uses mass resources to influence taste or pursue ends that he defines as socially responsible. It is perhaps surprising, given the potential, that the paperback industry has not more often used its marketing knowledge for deliberate manipulation. During the war, Penguin created specials around topics that would aid patriotic effort. In 1948, a publisher wanted people to buy John Hersey's *Hiroshima* and understand nuclear war:

> Realizing the difficulty of publishing a book so sympathetic to the Japanese in the postwar years, Bantam played its cards cautiously, if somewhat misleadingly. The cover of the first paperback edition showed a man and woman, looking anything but Oriental, walking away from a bright light. The woman wore completely Western clothing and neither she nor the man was tattered or injured. The copy read: "Six Survived to Tell What Happened." This cover approach had been tested and approved for Bantam by the Gallup organization. If the cover was deceptive, it was—to Ian Ballantine at least—a practical necessity. "We thought the book was important. We wanted people to read it. We couldn't very well just say 'wipeout.'"

Ian Ballantine later became head of his own house where he would produce Alan Guttmacher's *The Complete Book of Birth Control*—which, in 1962, overcame the Post Office ban on contraceptive information—and a series of ecological titles in conjunction with the Sierra Club. Dell made best-sellers of James Baldwin and Eldridge Cleaver. Barney Rosset at Grove Press not only expended a considerable amount of money defending obscenity cases and becoming the American publisher of D. H. Lawrence's *Lady Chatterley's Lover* (1962) and Henry Miller and the Marquis de Sade but also printed Frantz Fanon and *The Autobiography of Malcolm X* (1966).

Grove Press published a lot of other titles that were not quite so defensible. Even after the 1950's vogue for half-dressed women on the covers of all books—whatever their subject—had passed, many mass-market publishers retained a somewhat schizophrenic air. New American Library (NAL) made its reputation with quality titles aimed at the college market, was one of the first paperback lines welcome in hardcover outlets, and was publisher of William Faulkner, James Joyce, Virginia Woolf, and Ralph Ellison. NAL also published Mickey Spillane, and one third of its revenue in the middle 1960's came from James Bond books.

Davis' own ambivalence about popular culture surfaces in a curious complaint, in the book's final pages, that the sorry state of paperback publishing in the 1980's is indicated by the fact that 1982's top fifteen paperback titles are by what he calls "best-selling commercial authors, none of whom lays any claim to literary seriousness." It might, in fact, seem more surprising if best-sellers were anything else, but Davis' analysis of recent trends introduces some provocative ideas. The extremely high auction prices of the mid-1970's, he says (along with other changes brought about by corporate takeovers and bottom-line management), drove prices up and killed the concept of cheap books that everyone would read, which had been made possible by volume production, low overhead, and tiny per-copy profit margins. It would seem, too, that the concept of "everyone" has disappeared along with the "cheap books." Even blockbuster reprints are no longer the industry's mainstay. Following the lead established by Avon Books in the 1970's, houses increasingly depend on commissioning original works (some serious, even if most seem to be fast-buck imitations of successful cartoon and fitness titles). Other publishers have followed Harlequin's lead toward brand-name marketing of a product line. The readership is fragmented: The volume of books has long outgrown the drugstore and bus-terminal racks and has spawned chain bookstores—which, whatever else may be said of them, supply an extraordinary variety of titles to shoppers whose grandparents could not have found a bookstore if they wanted one.

Davis believes that the industry's response to this situation has been inadequate, and that although the really homogenized mass market of Eisenhower America is gone, the publishers have, ironically, homogenized themselves and their product. The era of conglomerates and safe financial management has diluted the individuality of imprints and muffled the publishers who once took innovative risks, trusted their own taste, and sometimes found a mass public that would respond.

Clearly, selling paperback books is not like selling automobiles or cake mix—and, apparently, it is not even very much like selling hardbacks. Davis' book is excellent for noting these differences, for understanding the peculiarities of the trade, and for speculating on the social and cultural aspects of product as well as text. Some of the literary analysis, however, is quite weak. The psychological speculations about thrillers and romances can only be superficial; Davis gives a paragraph or two to topics that are beginning to get their own excellent volumes of literary criticism. Nevertheless, he covers an extraordinary variety of material, much of it in specific detail— chronology, distributors, financiers, design, pricing, covers, the relationship of specific books to major contemporary movements (feminism, civil rights, nuclear issues, ecology, psychology, sexuality, varieties of self-help), instant books, pornography, fantasy and science fiction, marketing, distribution, and, above all, people—writers, editors, publishers and their interests, their innovations, their quirks and wisdom and luck. If Davis sometimes loses sight of the broad picture in wrestling with the mass of detail, his wealth of information will serve as the foundation for all studies yet to come.

Sally H. Mitchell

Sources for Further Study

The Georgia Review. XXXVIII, Fall, 1984, p. 654.
Kirkus Reviews. LII, March 15, 1984, p. 285.
Library Journal. CIX, July, 1984, p. 1322.
Los Angeles Times Book Review. August 12, 1984, p. 1.

New Leader. LXVII, May 14, 1984, p. 3.
The New York Times Book Review. LXXXIX, July 1, 1984, p. 21.
Newsweek. CIV, November 26, 1984, p. 113.
Publishers Weekly. CCXXV, March 2, 1984, p. 78.
Time. CXXIII, June 18, 1984, p. 88.
The Wall Street Journal. CCIV, July 16, 1984, p. 16.
Washington Post. June 6, 1984, p. 81.

THE UNBEARABLE LIGHTNESS OF BEING

Author: Milan Kundera (1929-   )
Translated from the Czech by Michael Henry Heim
Publisher: Harper & Row, Publishers (New York). 314 pp. $15.95
Type of work: Novel
Time: The 1960's and the 1970's
Locale: Primarily Czechoslovakia and Switzerland; France, Thailand, and the United States

A brilliant, perverse "novel of ideas"—although not in the usual sense of that term

> *Principal characters:*
> TOMAS, a surgeon and an incorrigible womanizer
> TEREZA, his lover and wife
> SABINA, a painter and one of Tomas' mistresses
> FRANZ, a professor in Switzerland and, for a time, Sabina's lover

When Milan Kundera's fourth novel, *The Book of Laughter and Forgetting*, appeared in English translation in 1980, few American readers were familiar with his work; indeed, few had so much as heard his name. By the time *The Unbearable Lightness of Being* was published, three and a half years later, Kundera had become one of the most visible figures on the international literary scene, the subject of many feature articles, interviews, and even (in France and England at least) television programs. *The Unbearable Lightness of Being* was a number-one best-seller in France (where Czech exile Kundera has lived for ten years) and appeared on best-seller lists in the United States. Kundera's novel was a critical success as well, widely and favorably reviewed, and was the winner of the *Los Angeles Times* Book Award for fiction in 1984.

Two striking features distinguish *The Unbearable Lightness of Being.* First, it is a novel in which reflective thought plays an unusually prominent role. Kundera offers not only many arresting "ideas" (aphorisms, *pensées*) but also extended exercises in thinking (arguments, "thought experiments," even brief essays). The second feature, related to the first, is what Kundera has referred to as the novel's "polyphonic" structure. Polyphony, as Kundera defines it, is the fusion of "philosophy, narrative, and dream" and "the specifically novelistic essay" into "a single music."

Ironically, the very features that give *The Unbearable Lightness of Being* its distinctive character have been ignored, downplayed, or misrepresented in most reviews of the novel. There are two reasons for this failure, one trivial and one not. The former is simply a matter of space; it is possible to do only so much in a short review. The latter, however, is a matter of widely held and generally unexamined assumptions concerning the role of ideas in fiction. While such issues cannot be pursued here, it must be noted that Anglo-American modernism (as opposed to the Central European modernism of Robert Musil and Hermann Broch) has as one of its ten commandments a prohibition against ideas in the novel. Many reviewers, like many critics and indeed many novelists, accept this dogma without question.

The Unbearable Lightness of Being is divided into seven parts: part 1, "Lightness and Weight"; part 2, "Soul and Body"; part 3, "Words Misunderstood"; part 4, "Soul and Body"; part 5, "Lightness and Weight"; part 6, "The Grand March"; and part 7, "Karenin's Smile." In turn, each part is divided into numbered subsections of varying length. (In a *Paris Review* interview, Kundera refers to these subsections as "chapters"; accordingly, that usage will be employed here.)

This structure, with its suggestion of theme and variation, seems to invite the reader to find a musical analogy—an invitation confirmed in Kundera's remarks on the novel:

> The chapters themselves must . . . create a little world of their own; they must be relatively independent. That is why I keep pestering my publishers to make sure that the numbers are clearly visible and that the chapters are well separated. The chapters are like the measures of a musical score! . . . Each part could have a musical tempo indication. . . .

Such musical analogies, insofar as they are supposed to correspond to the reader's experience of the text in more than the most general fashion, are notoriously dubious. Nevertheless, Kundera's remarks help to convey the feel of his novel in a way that most of the reviews have failed to do. As one reads the book, one is always aware of its intellectual structure. This is not a submerged symbolic structure such as students are taught to recognize in Joseph Conrad's *Heart of Darkness*; it is quite explicit. To summarize the "action" of Kundera's novel within the scope of a review, one must abstract the narrative from its structural context. The effect, whatever the reviewer's intentions, is to imply that what really matters in the novel is "the story."

Surely, however, what "really matters" in a novel that calls itself *The Unbearable Lightness of Being* is its illumination of being. In a brilliant essay in *The New York Review of Books* entitled "The Novel and Europe," Kundera suggests that the rise of science—"which, in reducing the world to an object of technical and mathematical investigation, . . . put *die Lebenswelt*, the world of concrete living, beyond its pale"—has been paralleled by the development of the novel: "Cervantes gave birth to a great European art which is nothing other than the perpetual investigation of the being ignored by science." The phenomenology of Edmund Husserl and Martin Heidegger, Heidegger's diagnosis of "the forgetting of being," was anticipated, Kundera says, in "four centuries of novel-writing."

While unhesitatingly affirming the cognitive authority of the novel to "shed light on existence" (he defines the history of the novel as *"the sequence of [its] discoveries"*), Kundera is, however, equally emphatic in his seemingly contradictory insistence that "The novel . . . is a territory where one does not make assertions; it is a territory of play and of hypotheses. Reflection within the novel is hypothetical by its very essence." In practice, though, what does this mean? In what sense is the reader of Kundera's novel intended to regard its various reflections as "hypothetical"? These questions are not extrinsic to the novel, imported from the classroom; rather, they are the very questions that must arise in any responsible reading of Kundera's text. It is not merely a matter of extracting the novel's ideas.

To read *The Unbearable Lightness of Being*, one must (whatever one makes of his paeans to Laurence Sterne, Denis Diderot, and the novel as play) take seriously Kundera's project for the novel as a form. To do so, one is not required to share Kundera's vision of human life and its place in the universe—not at all; one must, however, share his faith in the novel's unique capacity to observe "man's concrete being, his 'living world.'" Those who find such ambitions inappropriate to a work of fiction, or merely pretentious, should not read Kundera's novel.

If it is impossible here to follow Kundera's "investigation into existence" throughout the novel, it is at least possible to consider in detail a representative passage before summarizing the "love story" that constitutes the main plot line. The novel's opening chapter is a brief one, about a page and a half long. Here is Kundera's first paragraph:

> The idea of eternal return is a mysterious one, and Nietzsche has often perplexed other philosophers with it: to think that everything recurs as we once experienced it, and that the recurrence itself recurs ad infinitum! What does this mad myth signify?

This is an extraordinary way to begin a novel. The content is surprising, but this is not all that gives pause: Who is speaking? It seems that the novelist himself—not a character or a "narrator" in the conventional sense of the term—is speaking here, addressing the reader with a compelling directness, yet Kundera never resolves the uncertainty which the reader feels after the first paragraph concerning the status of such reflections. The remainder of the chapter—the answer to the question posed in the first paragraph—is vital to the whole overarching structure of the novel, yet hardly a single review so much as mentions this meditation on the notion of eternal return, let alone outlining its function in the novel and critically engaging the implications that Kundera draws from it.

What does Kundera make of Friedrich Nietzsche's "mad myth"? He begins with a dazzling dialectical trick:

> Putting it negatively, the myth of eternal return states that a life which disappears once and for all, which does not return, is like a shadow, without weight, dead in advance, and whether it was horrible, beautiful, or sublime, its horror, sublimity, and beauty mean nothing.

While the reader is still grappling with the question that concludes the opening paragraph, Kundera makes this stunning assertion—almost by the way.

At first, the reader is unlikely to appreciate what has hit him. The entire tradition of Western literature rests on the assumption that individual decisions, acts of human will, are invested with significance by the irrevocable flow of time. In the world of Western literature, profoundly influenced by Christianity, human beings are both blessed and burdened with an awesome power to choose, to exercise their freedom; it is no accident that Kundera plants references to *Anna Karenina* in the course of his narrative, for Leo Tolstoy's novel is among the supreme exemplars of the drama of irrevocable choice that can be traced all the way back to the *Iliad* of Homer.

Implicitly rejecting this tradition, Kundera maintains that only if events were to recur would they have significance, weight: "If the French Revolution were to recur eternally, French historians would be less proud of Robespierre. . . . There is an infinite difference between a Robespierre who occurs only once in history and a Robespierre who eternally returns, chopping off French heads." That which is "ephemeral, in transit"—in other words, "light"—cannot be submitted to moral judgment, Kundera asserts: "In the sunset of dissolution, everything is illuminated by the aura of nostalgia, even the guillotine." This move accomplished, Kundera gives his argument a final twist. He recounts "a most incredible sensation" that he experienced while leafing through a book about Adolf Hitler. Certain portraits of Hitler, Kundera says, reminded him of his own childhood, and he was touched:

> This reconciliation with Hitler reveals the profound moral perversity of a world that rests essentially on the nonexistence of return, for in this world everything is pardoned in advance and therefore everything cynically permitted.

Some readers may feel that it is Kundera's moral perversity that is revealed here; certainly the passage is characteristic of the deliberately provocative tone of his fiction. In any case, as noted above, this opening chapter is crucial to the novel's structure. It introduces the metaphorical opposition between "lightness" and "weight" that organizes much of the book, in particular the notion of "the unbearable lightness of being." The interlocking stories of the novel's main characters all are presented in terms of the conflict between traditional concepts of moral choice and destiny ("character is fate") and the radically opposed perspective that Kundera introduces here, summed up only a few pages later in the novel: "*Einmal ist keinmal.* . . . What happens but once, says the German adage, might as well not have happened at all. If we have only one life to live, we might as well not have lived at all." Finally, this brief opening chapter of a page and a half establishes the book's polyphonic structure, its capacity to embrace modes of thought normally regarded as foreign to the novel.

Such reflections, meditations, and arguments are as integral to the novel as the stories with which they are interwoven, and while it is not possible to discuss them all, or even most of them, one must at least acknowledge their existence, ranging from reflections on the word "compassion" and its cognates and on Ludwig van Beethoven's last quartet (part 1) to "A Short Dictionary of Misunderstood Words" (part 3), from an essay on kitsch (part 6) to a disquisition on man's treatment of animals (part 7)—not an exhaustive list.

Indeed, the characters themselves are schematically presented—explicitly so. "It would be senseless for the author to try to convince the reader that his characters once actually lived," Kundera writes, beginning the first chapter of part 2. Yet, by the grace of fiction, his characters live in the reader's mind—particularly Tomas and Tereza, the novel's principal pair.

Tomas, a surgeon, divorced, a Don Juan of the type familiar in Kundera's fiction, meets Tereza in a small town, where they talk for an hour or so before his train leaves for Prague. Ten days after that first casual meeting, Tereza (much to Tomas' surprise) visits him in Prague. They make love; she stays for a week, sick with flu, and then returns to her provincial town. After a time, she comes back to Prague and to Tomas, who rents a room for her: They are lovers, but he does not want to give up his independent lifestyle.

Tereza is "heavy": Her love for Tomas is exclusive, a kind of absolute. Tomas is "light," incorrigibly promiscuous. Although he eventually marries Tereza, and although he is well aware of the suffering which his infidelities cause her, he continues to be unfaithful to her. At the same time, he sacrifices much for her. After the Soviet invasion of Czechoslovakia in August, 1968, he falls out of favor with the government and is relegated to a provincial clinic. Even there, however, the political pressures are relentless, and he ceases to practice medicine at all. Finally, he and Tereza end up in the country, where they buy a small cottage from a farmer who is moving to town; Tomas drives a pickup truck for the local collective farm. He is driving that truck when he and Tereza are killed in an accident while traveling to a nearby town, where they occasionally go to dance and spend the night in the run-down hotel.

Kundera's telling of the story is richer than this summary suggests (not to mention the relation of their story to the novel's other plot lines). The reader learns of Tomas' and Tereza's death before the halfway point of the book (there are shifts in chronology throughout, and several times the same incident is related from two different points of view); the effect of this revelation, which is presented matter-of-factly, is to give their death a force that it would have lacked had it occurred at the end of the novel. At the same time, this device gives added resonance to that which follows, for the reader sees it all in the light of Tomas and Tereza's end.

This is particularly true of the novel's closing passage, which tells of

Tomas and Tereza's first trip to the town on the road to which, after repeated visits, they will meet their death. On this first night there, after dancing with friends from the collective farm, they go up to their room in the hotel; the last paragraph of the novel describes the scene:

> Tomas turned the key and switched on the ceiling light. Tereza saw two beds pushed together, one of them flanked by a bedside table and lamp. Up out of the lampshade, startled by the overhead light, flew a large nocturnal butterfly that began circling the room. The strains of the piano and violin rose up weakly from below.

This passage has an odd, almost whimsical beauty; it is a reminder that, along with his well-advertised affinity with the Enlightenment spirit of Diderot, Kundera also has an affinity with Franz Kafka and with the Czech Surrealist poets. The tenderness of this concluding paragraph—surprising, perhaps unearned, but nevertheless welcome—brings to mind Kundera's injunction against taking any one of the novel's many voices as unequivocally that of the author.

John Dugdale Wilson

Sources for Further Study

Christian Science Monitor. LXXVI, August 8, 1984, p. 25.
Commonweal. CXI, May 18, 1984, p. 298.
Library Journal. CIX, May 1, 1984, p. 915.
The Nation. CCXXXVIII, May 12, 1984, p. 582.
New Statesman. CVII, May 25, 1984, p. 26.
The New York Review of Books. May 10, 1984, p. 3.
The New York Times Book Review. LXXXIX, April 29, 1984, p. 1.
Newsweek. CIII, April 30, 1984, p. 77.
Publishers Weekly. CCXXV, March 9, 1984, p. 97.
The Wall Street Journal. CCIII, April 27, 1984, p. 26.

A VERY PRIVATE EYE
An Autobiography in Diaries and Letters

Author: Barbara Pym (1913-1980)
Edited by Hazel Holt and Hilary Pym
Publisher: E. P. Dutton (New York). Illustrated. 358 pp. $19.95
Type of work: Diaries and letters
Time: 1932-1980
Locale: Primarily England; Italy, Portugal, Germany, and Central Europe

A lively, poignant, and entertaining record of a writer's life

> Principal personages:
> BARBARA PYM, a novelist
> HENRY HARVEY, an older contemporary at Oxford University with
> whom she fell in love
> ROBERT (JOCK) LIDDELL, a mutual friend at Oxford, later a novel-
> ist, critic, and travel writer
> PHILIP LARKIN, a poet, instrumental in Pym's rediscovery
> HILARY PYM, Barbara's younger sister

A Very Private Eye adds another chapter to the marvelously improbable and still ongoing saga of Barbara Pym. Published in the summer of 1984 to excellent reviews, this collage drawn from diaries, working notebooks, and letters had forty-five thousand copies in print by the fall of that year. Essential reading for students of Pym's novels, it is also a fascinating document in its own right.

The Barbara Pym who emerges from these pages has all of the qualities that have attracted readers to her fiction, especially a quirky sense of humor and a spirited delight in the commonplace, yet the picture of her personality and her career is now much fuller, more nuanced and complex. Because she was almost thirty-seven when her first novel was published, in 1950, and because she was (mistakenly) said to have given up writing fiction for the duration of the long hiatus between the rejection of her seventh novel, in 1963, and her "rediscovery" in 1977, reviewers have sometimes condescended to Pym even while praising her, implying that she lacked the resolve, the single-mindedness, the ambition of the serious writer. *A Very Private Eye* should correct this misperception, for it reveals the extent to which Pym's was truly a writer's life.

The volume begins with a useful preface by coeditor Hazel Holt. Holt, Pym's literary executor and for many years her coworker on the staff of the International African Institute in London, recounts the origin of *A Very Private Eye* and places it in the context of Pym's work. In 1931, when she was about eighteen, Pym began to keep a diary, which she maintained, with some breaks, through World War II. "After the war," Holt explains, "she gave up keeping a formal diary, writing instead in a series of small notebooks, from 1948 until her death in 1980." In these eighty-two spiral-bound notebooks (which, like the diaries and all of Pym's manuscripts, including several unpublished novels, repose in the Bodleian Library at Oxford University), Pym "recorded not only events but random thoughts and ideas for her novels, so that they are, in effect, working notebooks." *A Very Private Eye*, then, consists of selections from the diaries and notebooks, in chronological sequence, mixed with letters by Pym to various correspondents; each chronological section is informatively and wittily introduced by Holt.

Also helpful—and frequently amusing—is the superb index. From the biographical notes in the index, for example, one learns the subsequent fate of some of the people who figured largely in Pym's Oxford years; quotations of poetry are indexed, as are references to Pym's fictional characters. Some readers will be particularly grateful for another service provided by the index: definitions of slang. Thus, when one reads that "After supper Honor and I Baldwinned our legs," one can turn to find that a "Baldwin" is "a glove made of emery paper to defuzz legs." Similarly, the reader who is baffled by a description of certain undergarments—"blue celanese trollies—pink suspender belt—pink kestos—white vest"—will find enlightenment in the index.

Hilary Pym, Barbara's sister and Holt's coeditor, has provided a brief background chapter, "The Early Life," sketching her sister's life up to the time she entered the university. Barbara Mary Crampton Pym, the eldest of the two daughters of Frederic Crampton Pym and Irena Spenser Pym, née Thomas, was born on June 2, 1913, in Oswestry, Shropshire, near the Welsh border. Frederick Pym, a solicitor, was the illegitimate son of a domestic servant—a fact which Hilary Pym uncovered only after Barbara's death. The Pym family was reasonably prosperous; in Hilary's account, theirs was "a happy, unclouded childhood," with animals and music and amateur theatricals and much churchgoing. When she was twelve, Barbara was sent to a boarding school, Liverpool College, Huyton; she went up to Oxford, where she read English, in 1931.

The main text of *A Very Private Eye* is divided into three parts: "Oxford" (1932-1939), "The War" (1940-1945), and "The Novelist" (1948-1980; there is a gap in the immediate postwar years). In one important respect, the sequence of these headings is misleading, for although, as noted above, Pym's first novel, *Some Tame Gazelle*, was not published until 1950, she was nevertheless a novelist long before that time. In fact, although revised after the war, *Some Tame Gazelle* was written at Oxford—Pym was twenty-two when she first sent it to a publisher—and indeed, as Holt notes in her introduction to the Oxford section, Pym had completed her first attempt at a novel, "Young Men in Fancy Dress" (unpublished), when she was only sixteen. Through the rest of her life, there was never a long period in which she was not at work on a novel; she finished her last one, *A Few Green*

Leaves, only two months before her death and had already outlined another novel which she did not live to write.

Thus, even when she began her diary as an eighteen-year-old undergraduate, Pym was already writing consciously *as a writer*. It is true that the diary as a form, despite its apparent directness and relative freedom from artifice, requires the diarist, in Walter Ong's words, to "fictionalize the reader": The diarist "must construct in his imagination, clearly or vaguely, an audience cast in some sort of role." To whom is a diary addressed? After all, "the diarist pretending to be talking to himself has also, since he is writing, to pretend he is somehow not there." Still, if the diary as a form demands an imaginative projection akin to that required by fiction writing, it remains the case that Barbara Pym as a diarist was from the beginning exceptionally aware of these demands. In her diary as much as in her fiction, she was writing with a consciousness that her seemingly private words would one day be read by others; in an entry for February 20, 1941, she went so far as to anticipate their eventual destination, writing of "this diary, this sentimental journal or whatever you (Gentle Reader in the Bodleian) like to call it."

If the girl who went up to Oxford in 1931 was in some ways exceptional, she was in other ways very much a child of her time and her class. On a trip to Germany in 1934, she saw Adolf Hitler: "I thought he looked smooth and clean, and was very impressed." Politically naïve, she was more concerned with flirting with German men; indeed, her principal preoccupation while at Oxford was romance, and the diary's record of her various affairs is by turns lyrical, poignant, cloying, and comic. Her great love was unrequited: In 1933, she fell in love with a student two years her senior, Henry Harvey, whom she dubbed "Lorenzo." (Before they met, she followed him, learned all she could about his background; she had a lifelong passion for such unorthodox amateur detective work, which she called "research into the lives of ordinary people.") When, in 1937, he married a Finnish girl, she was devastated.

This unhappy love established a pattern which was to recur throughout her life, and yet side-by-side with her unabashed romanticism, the diary reveals Pym's delightful and extraordinary capacity for comic observation of herself and others, including the objects of her love. In *Some Tame Gazelle*, the twenty-two-year-old lovestruck girl imagined herself and her sister Hilary as middle-aged spinsters, with Harvey transformed into a rather pompous archdeacon whom one of the sisters (Barbara's counterpart) loved in her youth and still loves out of habit. This striking metamorphosis—how many twenty-two-year-olds are capable of imagining themselves as women well advanced into middle age?—suggests some of the fascination of *A Very Private Eye*, the interplay between Pym-the-observer and Pym-the-observed.

By the end of 1940, Pym had completed three novels in addition to *Some*

Tame Gazelle and had done the first draft of another, her "spy novel," as she called it; one of the three, *Crampton Hodnet*, written in 1939-1940, was published in 1985. In 1941, required to register for war service, she chose a job in censorship in Bristol, where Hilary was working for the BBC. During this period, Pym had another unhappy love affair, "very serious on her part, perhaps less so on his," with a radio writer and broadcaster whose estranged wife (a divorce was in progress) was a good friend of Pym. In 1943, Pym joined the Women's Royal Naval Service (WRNS), working in naval censorship; in 1944, she was posted to Naples, Italy, returning to England in July, 1945.

In 1946, Pym joined the staff of the London-based International African Institute, where she served as assistant editor of the Institute's journal, *Africa*, and performed other related editorial tasks. As readers of her novels know, this work was a fertile source of inspiration. Many of Pym's portraits of anthropologists are wickedly funny, and her eye for the pretensions of the academic world was unerring, yet there was also a genuine correspondence between the discipline of anthropology and her own "research"—a parallel noted in her books, as when one of her fictional anthropologists asks: "Haven't the novelist and the anthropologist more in common than some people think?" It was at this time, in the early stages of her work at the Institute, that, as foreshadowed in *Some Tame Gazelle*, she began to share an apartment with Hilary, who had separated from her husband; the sisters were to live together until Barbara's death.

Pym's life after the publication of *Some Tame Gazelle*—the series of beautifully crafted and richly comic novels of the 1950's; the bitterly discouraging years in which, as numerous publishers told her, her kind of writing was out of fashion; the fairy-tale rediscovery of her work and the novels that followed to great acclaim; the growing Barbara Pym cult, flourishing especially in the United States—all of this has been documented in many feature articles. Still, neither the articles nor the novels prepare the reader for the courage, the pathos, but above all the wonderful individuality, the fresh idiosyncratic vision of the notebook entries and letters of these later years.

In her preface, Holt notes that "It is now possible to describe a place, a situation or a person as 'very Barbara Pym'. She is one of that small band of writers who have created a self-contained world...." The notion of a writer "creating a world" is a cliché, and an unfashionable one at that, but *A Very Private Eye*, along with Pym's novels, gives life to this worn-out tribute.

John Dugdale Wilson

Sources for Further Study

Christian Science Monitor. LXXVI, August 23, 1984, p. 21.

Library Journal. CIX, June 1, 1984, p. 1126.
Los Angeles Times Book Review. August 5, 1984, p. 1.
Ms. XIII, July, 1984, p. 21.
The New York Review of Books. XXXI, August 16, 1984, p. 15.
The New York Times Book Review. LXXXIX, July 8, 1984, p. 3.
The New Yorker. LX, July 16, 1984, p. 91.
Newsweek. CIV, July 23, 1984, p. 64.
Publishers Weekly. CCXXV, May 4, 1984, p. 46.
The Wall Street Journal. CCIV, July 3, 1984, p. 22.

VICTOR HUGO AND THE VISIONARY NOVEL

Author: Victor Brombert (1923-   )
Publisher: Harvard University Press (Cambridge, Massachusetts). Illustrated. 286 pp. $20.00
Type of work: Literary criticism

Critical readings of key Hugo novels designed to take current literary theory into account and to show just how "current," in terms of style and preoccupation with questions of writing, Hugo can be, as 1985 marks the centennial of his death

In a celebrated response to a question concerning the state of French literature in the generation that preceded his own, André Gide replied, "Victor Hugo, *hélas!*" Hugo may have lacked a Rodin to sculpt a tribute to his magnificence, as Auguste Rodin did for Honoré de Balzac, but Hugo looms large above the landscape of nineteenth century French culture. His funeral in 1885, followed by entombment in the Pantheon, was truly a state occasion, outstripped only by the transferral of the remains of Napoléon I to Les Invalides. Familiar to all students of French literature and to the legions of readers of such imposing novels as *Notre-Dame de Paris* (1831; *The Hunchback of Notre Dame*, 1833) and *Les Misérables* (1862; English translation, 1862) is the figure of Hugo towering over his contemporaries, just as he preferred to write standing up and facing the sea in his own "tower" atop his famous place of exile, Hauteville-House on the island of Guernsey. Unforgettable as well is the high-flown language, as if Hugo spoke on behalf of God—or the other way around. The grandeur of such language, like that of Hugo's contemporary, the historian Jules Michelet, is something of an embarrassment in the twentieth century. Gide, whose generation stood on the other side of Symbolism and several other waves of the literary avant-garde from *le maître* Hugo, articulated in his "*hélas!*" the discomfort "moderns" experience in the presence of such strong authorial confidence in one's mission and in the steadfast belief that one will be read; that literature "matters."

All of which means that Victor Brombert, with a number of distinguished books behind him, including much experience in writing of Hugo, has his work cut out for him when it comes to making Hugo "new" and immediate for a late twentieth century literary public. Much of the difficulty Brombert has faced simply comes with the territory. To begin with, there is the impossibility of reducing the vicissitudes of such a complex life, spanning the periods of Empire, Restoration, July Monarchy, short-lived Second Republic, Second Empire, and beginnings of the Third Republic, to some general formula of characterization. Hugo triumphed in every literary genre: There is the young poet and dramatist, writing under the spell of Romanticism, whose play *Hernani* premiered in 1830 on one of the most tumultuous evenings in the history of the French theater. There is also the energetic author of novelistic epics intended to move and revitalize the French reading public, awakening them to the nobility of the cause of *le peuple*. Politically, there is the young defender of monarchy and would-be "second Chateaubriand." In a much less typical trajectory for an admired author's personal political evolution, there is the Victor Hugo who scorned "Napoléon *le petit*," his scathing label for Napoléon III, and who chose exile rather than existence in a France that had betrayed the ideals of 1848. This same man would move much further to the Left, eventually championing the cause of the Paris Commune, expressing outrage at the massacre of the Communards in 1871.

Perhaps wisely, Brombert does not seek to resolve such contradictions with a too-neat summation, although his choice of the label "visionary" for Hugo is a strategic one which furthers his aim of winning over those who, having cut their teeth on Symbolism or Surrealism, have learned automatically to scoff at Hugo, or gleefully to quote Jean Cocteau's waggish epigram, "Victor Hugo was a madman who thought he was Victor Hugo." Use of the word "visionary" in referring to modern French literature places one along the register established by Arthur Rimbaud, who, in his famous letter of 1871 to Paul Demeny, insists that the poet must be a *voyant*, a prophet, a visionary. By usurping this label and applying it to such a seemingly forbidding precursor, Brombert forces readers who habitually take Rimbaud as the watershed figure in recent French literature to see Hugo in a new light. In addition, Brombert invokes the very kinds of literary theory and criticism commonly reserved in recent years for "difficult" modern texts following in Rimbaud's wake. Rimbaud's appreciation of the "poetic" qualities of Hugo's prose is cited, and Hugo is credited with creating the hybrid genre of the *roman poème*. This idea, considered through (post) modern textual strategies, means that Hugo's texts are "undecidably" either prose or poetry.

Brombert, after a preliminary chapter in which he sketches the general outlines of his "new" orientation to Hugo, proceeds chronologically (and often rather conventionally) through *explications de texte* of the most "visionary" novels: *Le Dernier Jour d'un condamné* (1829; *The Last Day of a Condemned*, 1840), *The Hunchback of Notre Dame*, *Les Misérables*, *Les Travailleurs de la mer* (1866; *The Toilers of the Sea*, 1866), *L'Homme qui rit* (1869; *The Man Who Laughs*, 1869), and *Quatre-vingt-treize* (1874; *Ninety-three*, 1874). Along the way, he then touches upon the many points that he wishes to make. For the reader interested in the theoretical questions which have helped to shape Brombert's reconsideration of Hugo, the cumulative effect of reading through these chapters is one of gradual recognition. It becomes clear that Mikhail Bakhtin, Michel Foucault, Roland Barthes, and Jacques Derrida have all contributed to Brombert's thinking in this book. There is a school of thought which recommends the procedure of beginning with examples from texts and then moving into theoretical questions, and such is Brombert's preference. Still, one cannot help but wonder whether, in this case, Brombert would have been better served by establishing his theoretical orientation to Hugo's "visionary" texts in a longer first section. Then he could proceed to the novels that lend themselves most to "new" readings. One suspects that Brombert has a hidden agenda: that of persuading readers to return to the novels which are less often read. Still, the most exciting chapters (not surprisingly?) are those devoted to the two books by which the author is best known: *The Hunchback of Notre Dame* and *Les Misérables*.

The following sample of new theoretical insights into the reading of Hugo will demonstrate how Brombert's book threatens to fly off in all directions at once: Hugo's texts accomplishing the "decentering" of the human subject; use of laughter in Hugo as illustrative of Bakhtin's theory of the "carnivalesque" in literature inspired by peasant sources; Hugo's metaphoric treatment of prisons as an equivalent of Foucault's discursive examinations of the "carceral" project of modern society; God as both author and protagonist in *Les Misérables*, who writes the text of history, and to whom the only proper response is more writing; Hugo's rhetorical usage of antitheses and oxymorons, building tropological conflicts and conundrums into the text; and Hugo's scoffing characterization of the institution of "literature" as a "Tower of Babel." In addition, a physical feature of the volume deserves comment along these lines: Brombert's volume reproduces twenty-seven of Hugo's drawings, which are often bizarre in the extreme and which serve as something of a foil for the books themselves. Many of Hugo's drawings make use of the letters of his own name, which sprawl contortedly over nightmarish landscapes, calling to mind poststructuralist critiques of the ideology of the author's name (what Foucault called "the author-function") as a kind of inscription in the text of culture.

Instead of developing extensive arguments along at least some of these theoretical lines, Brombert, while never thoroughly disappointing the reader, is content to use them as the "exotic" flavorings for his workmanlike explications. Moreover, having locked himself into a chronological sequence and wishing to comment on such an array of texts, he must pass up the opportunity to dwell exhaustively on any one interpretive problem, however interesting it may prove to be. To appreciate the critical difference between what Brombert has elected to do in his book and what can be accomplished by a critic on intimate terms with Hugo's texts and well versed in literary theory, the reader is advised to seek out Jeffrey Mehlman's *Revolution and Repetition: Marx/Hugo/Balzac* (1977). Mehlman carries out a reading of *Quatre-vingt-treize* that is a tour de force, and while no less attentive than Brombert to the nuances of the text, he engages the reader at the level of theory at the outset, drawing upon Derrida's *Glas* (1974), Foucault's *Surveiller et punir* (1975; *Discipline and Punish*, 1977), and the lectures on the Freudian concept of anxiety by French psychoanalyst Jean Laplanche.

The objection that it is unfair to contrast Brombert's more ambitious book with one in which a Hugo novel is singled out in order to demonstrate the power of theory must be met with the reminder that Brombert himself has written much more effectively and convincingly of Hugo in a previous book: *The Romantic Prison: The French Tradition* (1978). In that book, Brombert explores a powerful theme, glimpsed repeatedly in the present book, in concentrated chapters, including a brilliant chapter on Hugo. The influence of Michel Foucault's historical investigations of prisons and penology is also much more in evidence in *The Romantic Prison*.

Brombert almost, but not quite, buries his many themes in *Victor Hugo and the Visionary Novel* by pursuing a somewhat ill-advised chronological sequence of readings and perhaps also by handling the Hugo legend with kid gloves when taking the bull by the horns would produce a more exciting book. At this rate, one may still be saying "Victor Hugo, *hélas!*" in the years to come. At least Brombert provides some important suggestions for the reconsiderations that the Hugo centennial is sure to bring. In such circumstances, it is often better to have the first, rather than the last, word.

James A. Winders

Sources for Further Study

Book World. XIV, October 14, 1984, p. 5.
Choice. XXII, January, 1985, p. 678.
Kirkus Reviews. LII, June 15, 1984, p. 558.
The New York Review of Books. XXXI, January 17, 1985, p. 41.
The New York Times Book Review. LXXXIX, December 23, 1984, p. 9.

VICTORY OVER JAPAN

Author: Ellen Gilchrist (1935-   )
Publisher: Little, Brown and Company (Boston). 277 pp. $15.95
Type of work: Short stories
Time: World War II to the 1980's
Locale: New Orleans and other Southern locations

A collection of stories about Southern women and their adventures, winner of the American Book Award for Fiction in 1984

Ellen Gilchrist is good company. She is the sort of raconteur one would like to have along on a boring automobile trip or a slow afternoon at the beach. Her tone is intimate—there is an "I really should not be telling you this" sound to the prose—and her material is so entertaining as to be almost gossipy. She presents the details of her stories in a casual, offhand manner, often mentioning in passing a character whom she develops more fully in a later piece. By the end of *Victory over Japan*, a collection of Gilchrist's stories which won the 1984 American Book Award for Fiction, the reader has come to know and delight in an extended family of mostly female cousins and their friends, Southerners all, tales of whose outrageous antics Gilchrist recounts with energy and wit.

The women in *Victory over Japan* are a richly varied assortment, interested in men and more interested in themselves. Gilchrist's single characters long to be both thin and married; they fantasize about the "good girls [who] press their elegant rib cages against their beautiful rich athletic husbands." Her married women are dissatisfied too. Their marriages provide economic security, but their emotional confinement is sometimes destructive of sanity. The state hospital in Mandeville, otherwise known as the "Loony Bin," looms large in the minds of Gilchrist's restless protagonists. In two of her stories, women are physically confined by their husbands and psychiatrists, and one narrator alludes darkly to a woman "that ended up in Mandeville forever because she wouldn't be a proper wife." This treatment of the enclosure and confinement of women in marriage places Gilchrist squarely in an important tradition in women's writing, a tradition represented by such works as Charlotte Perkins Gilman's *The Yellow Wallpaper* (1899). Unlike Gilman's protagonist, however, Gilchrist's women are hardly victims. There is a heroic vitality in her females and not a trace of guilt or shame. As one of her most vivid characters, Nora Jane Whittington, says, "I've never been ashamed of anything I've done in my life and I'm not about to start being ashamed now."

Nora Jane is one of several characters who appear in more than one story. Her adventures in earlier volumes of Gilchrist's work are summarized in the author's note to the "Nora Jane" section of the present collection. A practical nineteen-year-old hedonist who has recently been graduated from the

Academy of the Most Sacred Heart of Jesus in New Orleans, Nora Jane is involved with two men, either of whom may be the father of the twins she is carrying. Her boyfriend Sandy is tied up in a Laetrile scam with a wealthy older woman who is always saying, "Energy. That's all. There's nothing else." The other paternity candidate is a bookstore owner who gives Nora Jane a baby-blue convertible and seduces her with quotations from "The Love Song of J. Alfred Prufrock." Nora Jane has decided to marry neither of these unreliable specimens; she plans instead to get a job in a day-care center where she can support herself and take care of her babies all at the same time. The reader last sees the pregnant Nora Jane in a station wagon on the Golden Gate Bridge; trapped there by an earthquake and awaiting rescue by the Coast Guard, she is comforting a hungry, frightened kindergarten car pool with her angelic singing.

The other memorable women in *Victory over Japan* are Rhoda and Crystal. Rhoda figures in the three stories that begin the book. Her father is the brother of Crystal's father, and, although the reader never sees the cousins together, it is clear that they are cast in the same mold. Spoiled, rebellious, and sensuous, Rhoda and Crystal stop at nothing to assuage their curiosity or to get what they want. As a third grader, in the collection's title story, Rhoda insists on befriending and then interviewing for the school newspaper a shy, tearful classmate who is undergoing treatment for rabies. Rhoda conflates these events with collecting newspapers for the war effort and with her memories of family arguments, her discerning naïveté offering a distorted but recognizable view of adult preoccupations. As an adolescent, in "Music," Rhoda is given to dramatic statements and grand gestures. She flaunts her disbelief in God, smokes Lucky Strikes to defy her parents, reads Dorothy Parker, and longs to lose her virginity; she is, as Gilchrist puts it, at "a holy and terrible age, and her desire for beauty and romance drove her all day long and pursued her if she slept." In the third Rhoda story, called "The Lower Garden District Free Gravity Mule Blight or Rhoda, a Fable," Rhoda is in her mid-thirties, in the process of divorcing her rich, boring husband and still in search of adventure. She finds it this time in her seduction of Earl Treadway, a black insurance agent with whose company Rhoda has filed a fraudulent claim. In this story, Gilchrist subtly reveals both Rhoda's and Earl's motives, arising from the long and sordid history of Southern racism, as they maneuver each other into bed.

Rhoda's cousin Crystal, whose doting father gives her a fur coat when she is ten, is the subject of the five stories that constitute the final section of the book. Four of these are narrated by Crystal's black maid, Traceleen, and one by Crystal's friend DeDe, maid of honor for both of Crystal's weddings. Like Rhoda, Crystal has married for money. To amuse herself, she plays tennis, takes lovers, gets involved in an improbable effort to crack a prostitution ring. Her companion and confidante during these adventures is

Traceleen, whose job it is to take care of Crystal's three-year-old daughter and to run her house. Traceleen is married to her third husband, Mark, a man "so sweet you wouldn't hardly know he is a man," but the reader catches only glimpses of her personal life. At Crystal's request, Traceleen is keeping a diary in which she records her employer's experiences. Confined to her bed after an "accident" in which her husband pushed her down a flight of stairs, Crystal needs a record of what is happening to her: "Traceleen," Crystal says, "write it down. You got to write it down. I can't see to read and write. So you got to do it for me."

Gilchrist takes risks with the narrative structure of the Crystal stories. The reader is being asked not only to accept the notion that Traceleen would agree to keep Crystal's journal but also to believe that Traceleen would write page after cheerful page about Crystal and almost nothing about herself. There is the further problem of authenticity in Gilchrist's distractingly inconsistent rendering of black vernacular language. Minstrelsy of this sort, with a white narrator in blackface, is embarrassingly familiar to Southerners; it often combines genuine affection with condescension and ridicule. Those readers who believe that Gilchrist is appropriating what she thinks is Traceleen's language primarily for the purpose of amusing her audience will undoubtedly be uneasy with the point of view that she has chosen.

On the other hand, Gilchrist is not insensitive to the nuances of relations between black and white women. At several points, she implies that Traceleen and Crystal are similar, and she has Traceleen say, "Miss Crystal . . . has been as good to me as my own sister." At the same time, Traceleen is sometimes surprised and put off by Crystal's behavior, as when, on a trip, Crystal climbs into bed with her baby daughter and Traceleen, and Traceleen writes, "First time I'd ever sleep with a lady I work for. That's how Miss Crystal is. Just act like she thinks she can make up the world." Certainly Gilchrist tries to convince the reader that Traceleen's unusual relationship with her employer is a plausible one. At the end of Crystal's most improbable adventure, she tells Traceleen, "I could never have followed my conscience today if you hadn't been there to help, you know that, don't you?" and Traceleen writes, "I accepted the compliment. I knew it was the truth. Nobody can get anything done all by theirself. That's not the way the world is set up." Despite the problems inherent in Gilchrist's portrayal of the relationship—both narrative and emotional—between Traceleen and Crystal, the sisterly camaraderie of women is an important theme in the collection as a whole. Often Gilchrist writes with tender humor about the loyalty of women to one another. Her pairs include Lady Margaret Lanier Sarpie and her cousin Devoie Denery in "Looking over Jordan"; Lilly and Fanny, allies in a long war with the wealthy families into which they have married; and Diane and Lanier in "The Gauzy Edge of Paradise," best friends and diet partners since the age of thirteen.

Diane's diet is the occasion for one of Gilchrist's most hilarious scenes. High on speed and alcohol, Diane joins a female impersonator onstage at a nightclub and begins entertaining the crowd with a mixture of popular songs such as "I Gotta Be Me" and instructions from her workout record. Gilchrist's confident handling of this sort of comedy is one of the pleasures of *Victory over Japan*: She knows how to bring together unlikely combinations of characters and events to create moments of high farce. Another wonderful passage occurs in "Traceleen's Diary"; the crowd of characters in Crystal's front hall already numbers eight when Queen Esther, the meter reader, appears on the scene, and Traceleen, in a droll understatement, observes, "There's enough going on in the hall to last us about a year." Crystal's revenge on her brother, Phelan, for a wrong he has done her in childhood is the occasion for a hunting trip and antelope escape that parody two of William Faulkner's most famous stories, "The Bear" and "Spotted Horses." The statement in "Looking over Jordan" that "anything can happen to anyone at anytime" certainly applies to Gilchrist's zany comedy. Even the few potentially violent incidents in these stories usually have a comic flavor: A disaster-threatening drug trip dissolves into a mildly disturbing dream; an attempted robbery becomes an occasion for a seduction; Rhoda's nightmares about World War II merge with her memories of her father yelling at her mother.

The violent events of Rhoda's adolescence include a fit of anger in which she smashes her grandmother's Limoges chocolate pot just for spite. As this incident suggests, Gilchrist can be flippant about Southerners' reverence for the past. As Traceleen is polishing a silver service that has been in Crystal's family for generations, she observes that "Miss Crystal she likes the modern world." Crystal's father, by contrast, has no use for it. Blaming Crystal for her son's running away, he says,

> "You moved him down here, Sister, and let him know all those poets and homosexuals and suicides and now you're paying for it. Well, your old daddy's still alive. Thank your stars for that. I've found him once this week. I'll round him up again. Get me a glass of sweet milk, Traceleen."

Vignettes such as this one, and the one in which Crystal's mother and future mother-in-law, their hands touching, exclaim over the comforts of rose gardening, demonstrate both Gilchrist's familiarity with earlier generations of upper-middle-class white Southerners and her ironic ambivalence toward them.

Although Gilchrist does occasionally reveal the long sweep of the past, she is usually more concerned in *Victory over Japan* with entertaining her audience in the present. There is little heavy symbolism in these stories, little "poetic" or "beautiful" language, but there is much to please and amuse the neighbor ready to settle down in the porch swing for a good gossip about the latest Weiss family wedding or the carryings-on of Cousin Baby Gwen Barksdale. Gilchrist's radio journals, currently being broadcast on National Public Radio, perfectly capture the conversational ease and artlessness of her prose style. She is, more than anything else, a voice—a witty, energetic, unmistakably Southern voice—ready to regale her listener with yet another of Rhoda's or Crystal's or Nora Jane's crazy and extravagant adventures. Traceleen puts Ellen Gilchrist's fictional purposes as succinctly as anyone could: "What's a story of this type for? What's any story for? To make us laugh I guess."

Carolyn Wilkerson Bell

Sources for Further Study

Christian Science Monitor. LXXVI, December 7, 1984, p. 38.
Kirkus Reviews. LII, August 1, 1984, p. 698.
The New York Times Book Review. LXXXIX, September 23, 1984, p. 18.
The New Yorker. LX, November 19, 1984, p. 190.
Newsweek. LV, February 18, 1985, p. 81.
Publishers Weekly. CCXXVI, July 27, 1984, p. 136.
Washington Post. September 12, 1984, p. B1.

THE WALL JUMPER

Author: Peter Schneider (1940-   )
Translated from the German by Leigh Hafrey
Publisher: Pantheon Books (New York). 139 pp. $11.95
Type of work: Novel
Time: 1980
Locale: West and East Berlin

A loosely structured narrative describing a writer's search for a representative fiction about the divided city of Berlin and containing his observations and insights on the absurdities of life in the shadow of the Berlin Wall

> *Principal characters:*
> THE NARRATOR, a West German writer living in Berlin
> ROBERT, an East German poet living in West Berlin, a friend of
> the narrator
> POMMERER, an East German writer living in East Berlin, also the
> narrator's friend
> LENA, the narrator's former girlfriend
> GERHARD SCHALTER,
> MR. KABE,
> LUTZ,
> THE TWO WILLYS,
> WALTER BOLLE, and
> MICHAEL GARTENSCHLÄGER, the "Wall jumpers"

Peter Schneider burst onto the West German literary scene in 1973 with the publication of the short novel *Lenz*. Although he was fairly well-known on the West German Left for his political writing and activism in the 1960's, it was this novel that brought Schneider his first widespread notoriety and earned for him nearly universal critical acclaim. Modeled on Georg Büchner's nineteenth century masterpiece of the same title, the story told of the growing political disillusionment and aimlessness of the young intellectual Lenz. Schneider wrote here primarily of his own experience, but he captured in his novel the confusion and frustration shared by others of his generation as well as the political malaise of the young German Left.

Schneider's fiction centers on the interplay between the personal and the political in the lives of his protagonists. Like Schneider himself, the figures in his books—often former student activists of the 1960's—attempt to find their way in contemporary West German society, a society with which they continue to be at odds. For example, his second novel, published in 1975, took up the controversial "radicals decree," a measure, adopted by the West German state governments in 1972, that had been used to exclude potential "enemies of the constitution" from state employment. The novel documents the repercussions of the decree on the personal life and career of the teacher Kleff, whose earlier student activism is used as grounds for his dismissal. Likewise, the stories in the collection *Die Wette* (1978, the wager) focused on the effects that the radical politics of the 1960's and early 1970's had had upon the personal, nonpolitical life of Schneider's generation, while his screenplay for Reinhard Hauff's celebrated film, *Messer im Kopf* (1979; *Knife in the Head*, 1981), dealt with the character Hoffmann's struggle to reestablish his personal and political identity after a bullet wound in the head robs him of his memory and thus of the experiences that had earlier defined his existence. While portrayed here in extreme terms, Hoffmann's loss of identity is in some ways typical of the central characters in Schneider's fiction. They too seem to be in search of an elusive former identity, of a sense of community and certainty that had once existed for them but which now has inexplicably vanished. They, like Hoffmann, are in a very real sense stranded and homeless in the midst of their own society.

Schneider returns to the question of personal and political identity in his most recent novel, *The Wall Jumper* (published in the Federal Republic of Germany in 1982 as *Der Mauerspringer*). Here, however, he moves beyond the confines of the political struggle in the West in order to explore his theme further within the broader context of the "German Question" and to examine the lasting effects of Germany's division on the national consciousness. Somewhat surprisingly, Schneider's book is the first serious German fiction to focus its attention on this question of national identity since Uwe Johnson's novel *Zwei Ansichten* in 1965 (*Two Views*, 1966). Although Germany's "national trauma" has been the subject of frequent debate and ideological posturing in the political arena, its long literary neglect is perhaps a better indicator of the depth of the psychological scars left by the partitioning of the country into East and West.

The reality of these scars is presented strikingly in the image drawn by Schneider in the opening passage of the book. The narrator describes how a plane, when approaching Berlin to land, must cross over the city and its infamous Wall three times. From the air, the Wall seems in its zigzag course to be "the figment of some anarchic imagination" and "more a civic monument than a border." To the stranger, the two parts of the city, each with its television tower, stadium, and other public landmarks, are indistinguishable in their sameness. Once on the ground, however, the traveler is forced to realize that only the plane's shadow is free to move back and forth between the two halves of this "Siamese city."

For the narrator—like Schneider, a writer who has lived in Berlin for twenty years—the Wall has become something that he, as is the case with most Berliners in East and West, no longer really sees. In both parts of the city, the Wall had lost soon after its construction a good portion of its reality for the city's residents. In the West, it degenerated quickly to a metaphor and became the "Wall of Shame" that marked the border between freedom and Communist tyranny, a "mirror that told [Germans in the West], day by day, who was the fairest one of all"; in the East, the Wall—officially proclaimed as the anti-Fascist "Bulwark of Peace"—was merely the state border, beyond which a "foreign" and hostile neighbor resided.

It is this perplexing indifference to the Wall that causes the narrator to reflect upon its effects on the mentality of Berlin's citizens. He explains his decision to collect stories about life in the divided city: "I'm not sure of my purpose in collecting these stories. It isn't the sense of an unbearable situation that has pushed me to the project; rather, my uneasiness at the absence of that sense." It is an uneasiness that grows, too, from the observation that the ideological antagonism of the two opposing systems "had permeated the behavior and reflexes of each individual" and from a disturbing awareness of "individual plasticity" that makes Germans on each side of this border "in a frightening way interchangeable." Thus, the narrator arrives at the question that he will repeat in various forms throughout the text: "What would I have become, how would I think, how would I look, *if?*"

While Schneider's fiction has always been drawn to some degree from his own experience, *The Wall Jumper* openly ignores the pretense of a conventional plot, adopting instead the pose of a direct autobiographical account. Indeed, the book, while maintaining the form of fiction in its loosely constructed narrative frame, is not a novel at all in the normal sense of the term. Rather, Schneider treats autobiographically the day-to-day existence of a writer in search of material for a story, documenting this search with his comings and goings, his meetings and relationships with various of his friends, and scenes from the everyday life of Berlin. The fictional "plot" concerns primarily the genesis of Schneider's own book, a book which describes itself. There are interspersed throughout the narrative numerous essaylike commentaries, individual portraits, personal observations, and reminiscences related to the narrator's search. Here, as well, are the several stories that he discovers in his own past or which are told to him by his two friends, Robert, an East German poet now living in the West, and Pommerer, a writer still residing in East Berlin. These are the fanciful stories of the "Wall jumpers," people who for various reasons cannot come to terms with the division symbolized by the Wall and who are compulsively drawn to overcome it.

There is, for example, the story of Gerhard Schalter, who initially travels each day to East Berlin in order to take advantage of the cheaper telephone rates when calling a woman friend in Africa and who gradually finds that he is more at home in the "foreign" half of his city and finally stays there. There is Mr. Kabe, an unemployed welfare recipient who, rather than availing himself of an official border-crossing point, quite literally jumps the Wall fifteen times from West to East, with the result that authorities on both sides of the city have no choice but to declare him crazy. Asked for his motives, he offers only the explanation that he had merely taken the most direct route east from his apartment in the western part of the city. In contrast to Kabe's apparently "pathological" unwillingness to recognize the Wall as a border, the three East Berlin teenagers, Lutz and the two Willys, simply exploit a weakness in the Wall's security. On twelve successive Friday afternoons, they "overcome" the Wall in order to see the latest American Westerns playing at a theater on West Berlin's Kurfürstendamm, always taking care to return home in time for supper. On the other hand, Walter Bolle and Michael Gartenschläger, both East German refugees, declare war on the Wall and its builders. Bolle becomes a double and triple agent, moving back and forth across the heavily fortified border between East and West, until in the end even he cannot say on whose orders he is acting; Gartenschläger, obsessed by the goal to "set someone or something free from the DDR [East Germany]," decides to disarm individually each of the twenty-two thousand self-triggering robot weapons mounted along the East German border with West Germany.

As bizarre as these stories may appear with their often humorous mixture of fantasy and reality, they are upon reflection no more bizarre than the everyday reality of life in the divided city. Indeed, the stories are meant as ironic reflections of the narrator's own back-and-forth movement across Berlin as he visits his friends on both sides of the Wall. In the course of these visits, he gradually is able to define the nature of the story that he is seeking. He realizes at one point that it should be the story of a man who loses his sense of identity as he crosses more and more often from one half of the city to the other, the story of a "boundary walker" who, having rejected the preformed identities each state would offer him, is only at home on the border between the two states. The story that the narrator is looking for is the very story that he himself is attempting to live. He is, or wishes to be, a "boundary walker" who is able to strip away his West German birthright and the identity which it imposes upon him. It is not the barrier of citizenship per se that he desires to overcome; rather, it is the division in the national consciousness itself, a division that seems irrevocably to separate him from his East German friends.

Because he is not bound ideologically to either system, the narrator can be a detached observer of the uniquely German absurdities of the life around him. Nevertheless, it is not long before he too must recognize that even he and his friends cannot speak to one another without their respective states speaking through them. Thus, he and Robert find that a minor difference of opinion too often escalates into a major argument in which each remains stubbornly true to "his" state and the "articles of faith" learned in childhood, even though both have long since rejected the notion that their states retain any influence whatsoever in the views they hold. Likewise, the narrator is gradually able to understand better—although he remains unable to accept—the barrier that separates him from Lena, the young East German woman with whom he had lived for several months. Reflecting upon his relationships with his East German counterparts, the narrator observes that he and they all eventually succumb to the "disease of comparison." Even though each has in some way declared his independence from the state of his birth, none can free himself from the "canned language, the state grammar, the lesson dutifully learned"—from all that has been "predetermined by a half-country that over thirty years has acquired an identity in opposition to its other half."

In the course of his story, the narrator pauses several times to ask the central question: "Where does a state end and a self begin?" His experiences force him to recognize that this distinction is not always readily made and that the "Wall in our heads" is a far more formidable obstacle than the concrete and mortar that divide his city. This wall, he concludes, will take longer to tear down than the time required in some distant future to dismantle the Wall that can be seen.

The implications of Schneider's discovery transcend the narrow German context in which they are presented. While Berlin and the German Question provide the specific point of reference here, Schneider's anecdotes and examples ultimately illustrate the shaping and forming power of all states in the lives and thinking of their citizens. In this respect, Schneider's conclusion reveals its darkest aspect, for in this view, the state's existence extends far beyond the external structure of government itself to reside within each of its citizens.

In the closing pages of the book, the narrator, who has gradually projected himself into the ideal role of the "boundary walker," is brought crashing back to Earth. At a routine crossing into East Berlin one evening, his car is subjected to a thorough search for contraband. Although nothing is found, he is, for no apparent reason, refused permission to enter the DDR, and his crossings over the Wall are brought to an abrupt end. Schneider's point is not without self-irony: The ideal of the "boundary walker" does not represent a real choice. In spite of his professed ideological detachment, the author Schneider, like his narrator, is forced to accept the sobering reality of his West German birthright and the ideological inheritance which he has in the course of his career as a writer so often sought to deny.

James R. Reece

Sources for Further Study

Booklist. LXXX, February 1, 1984, p. 805.
Contemporary Review. CCXLV, July, 1984, p. 45.
Harper's Magazine. CCLXVIII, February, 1984, p. 72.

Kirkus Reviews. LI, November 15, 1983, p. 1180.
Library Journal. CIX, April 1, 1984, p. 734.
Listener. CXI, May 31, 1984, p. 26.
Los Angeles Times Book Review. March 11, 1984, p. 4.
The Nation. CCXXXVIII, March 17, 1984, p. 328.
The New Republic. CXC, March 5, 1984, p. 36.
The New York Times Book Review. LXXXIX, January 22, 1984, p. 13.
The New Yorker. LX, April 9, 1984, p. 144.
Observer. May 13, 1984, p. 23.
Publishers Weekly. CCXXIV, November 18, 1983, p. 59.
Times Literary Supplement. July 30, 1982, p. 814.
Village Voice Literary Supplement. March, 1984, p. 7.
World Literature Today. LVII, Spring, 1983, p. 288.

WALT WHITMAN
The Making of the Poet

Author: Paul Zweig (1935-1984)
Publisher: Basic Books (New York). 372 pp. $18.95
Type of work: Biographical criticism
Time: Primarily 1848-1855
Locale: The United States

As Zweig examines "Song of Myself" and the other major poems in Leaves of
Grass, *he creates a high moment in biographical criticism and reminds the reader of
the limits of other critical approaches*

How does one unravel a miracle? That is the question Paul Zweig set
before himself when he undertook to explain the unexpected blossoming of
Walt Whitman's poetic genius. How does a conventional short-story writer
and minor-league journalist and editor turn into his nation's first poet of the
first rank? Zweig's answer is developed patiently, with the rich complexity
and inspired insights this subject demands. Zweig's uplifting book becomes
not only an exploration of Whitman's transition from journeyman to high
master but also a testimony to the power of human will and spirit—of Whitman and of anyone who turns a corner and finds himself transformed. It is
the story of self-making, a process that remains no less miraculous for being
so well explained.

Zweig opens his discussion with this bald fact: "In 1848, Walt Whitman
was twenty-nine years old and had not yet written a single text that we now
remember." Furthermore, there were no predictions of a talent-in-the-
making. Nevertheless, seven years later, a strange book called *Leaves of
Grass* appeared, largely unheralded. In due time, this book, an ongoing
compilation that went through a series of shape-shifting editions, would be
recognized as the product of genius. Zweig brings the reader as close as he
can ever be to the metamorphosis of Walter Whitman, Jr., a man of marginal accomplishment in a wide range of activities, into Walt Whitman, the
self-defined singer and prophet of America. The story, then, is about the
making of poems and about the making of a man-myth. By demonstrating
how the two stories are one, and how the one story has a double track,
Zweig approaches the psychology of the creative personality in a concrete,
sensitive way. He sets a high standard for a type of study that rarely finds
such a fruitful subject and rarely succeeds. What is startling is that Zweig
accomplishes so much without establishing any theoretical underpinning,
though one is readily available. If Zweig had read and made use of Otto
Rank's *Art and Artist* (1932), his investigation of Whitman might have been
even more revelatory and even more convincing. After all, it was Rank who
most forcefully established the thesis that an artist's fundamental "work" is
his own artistic personality.

The strands that Zweig lovingly weaves together are many and various, though some are more successfully developed than others. Early in the book, Zweig explores the father-son dynamics of Whitman's fiction. He reveals Whitman's obsession with the "rejected son who longs to come home; an angry son who longs for revenge; a guilty son who discovers, in a terrifying economy of mental symbols, that he can take revenge and punish himself in the same act." As he traces Whitman's role in his own family, Zweig finds provocative parallels—even to the point of Whitman's success-ful drive to replace his father as head of the household. This trail, however, ends up being a relatively blind alley. Zweig notes, as have other critics, the absence of fathers in Whitman's important work and the presence of only the stereotypical, idealized mother of nineteenth century popular fiction. The transformation of family dynamics is not viewed as a fundamental part in the making of *Leaves of Grass*, which leaves the reader wondering at Zweig's careful analyses of the stories and of the Whitman family. Obvi-ously, though, the business of rebelling and fathering is part of the persona of *Leaves of Grass*, and, as Zweig sees quite clearly, Whitman's "parenting" of wounded Civil War soldiers was a manifestation of tendencies revealed early in his life.

Zweig's examination of Whitman's love for theater, especially opera, is put to better use. Impersonation, music, and oratory seized the imagination of the young journalist in profound ways. Whitman's reviews and relevant notebook passages are used by Zweig to bring the reader close to the aes-thetic that blooms in "Song of Myself" and the other major poems. Whit-man was always excited by the sweeping public gesture, by the majestic scale of operatic staging and performance. He honored the spellbinder (though he remained an enemy of the learned allusion, of art that leaned on other art and did not stand independently, such as an Emersonian hero, on its own two feet). Zweig lets the reader understand that the programmatic passages in Whitman's notebooks leading up to *Leaves of Grass* are the plans of a man who has tested, both emotionally and rationally, the effects of popular entertainment and art: The reader beholds a man rooted in his time who is ready to leap out of it. In similar fashion, Zweig treats Whitman's interest in the visual arts, political thought, and miscellaneous intellectual fashions, the most intriguing of which is phrenology.

Whitman's concern with health and appearance is a vital thread in the making of the mythic figure of Walt Whitman and of the poems that verify him. Beginning in mid-1849, when he paid his first visit to the Fowler & Wells Phrenological Cabinet, Whitman maintained a growing interest in the relationship between soma and psyche. Zweig's treatment of this portion of the Whitman puzzle is engaging and convincing. The reader sees a man ready to find a bigger, fuller self in the image provided by a phrenological charting. The reader sees a man refashioning his appearance while working to project a new and distinctive personality. Fowler & Wells publications demonstrated that man was "morally and organically improvable" and that the two realms were linked. The firm's motto, "Self-made or never made," was, in Zweig's words, "a huckster's version of Emerson's chaste virtue of self-reliance." Here in the popular science of his day, Whitman found a resource for his ongoing program of self-making. Walt Whitman, the rough-and-tumble character who exuded a peculiarly American glow of well-being, is a living fabrication spun out of that unremarkable Walter Whitman, Jr., whose own family was marred by ill health. Zweig sees the Fowler & Wells influence (and other health-oriented matter in Whitman's aggressive reading) as a major strand in the braided persona. The worship of bodily well-being in "Song of Myself" is a stance developed over time and out of need. Health: expansiveness: democracy: As metaphors for one another, these terms capture much of the Whitman ideal. A fourth term would be "poetry," if Whitman had allowed himself or his art to be considered as merely or conventionally poetic.

For Whitman sought an expressive mode that would somehow capture the amazing variety of American life that he had encountered on his endless walks through New York City. His months spent in New Orleans (during 1848) as well as the trips there and back confirmed Whitman's vision of an endlessly vast and burgeoning America—one that deserved a new type of song and a new kind of singer. This singer would be a man of the people, a man in shirt-sleeves, who would know no boundaries of region or class or creed. His would be a health-giving spirit, a spirit of the nation's scope and promise—something beyond the restrictions of inherited forms. To be witness to the assembling of this singer, with Zweig as guide, is to be witness to a miracle.

Beginning in 1849, Whitman's occasional prose and his notebook jottings begin to suggest a man looking at himself anew. In the years that follow, he became a far more voluminous note-taker and a compulsive clipper and saver of all kinds of printed material. Placing the reader over Whitman's shoulder, Zweig conducts him through this frenzy of verbal and ideational stockpiling, giving him coherent glimpses of the grand inventory that will supply the inventory passages of many Whitman poems. It is as if Whitman were collecting a special memory bank for the special man who would emerge, almost as a fictional character, in the cornerstone poem of *Leaves of Grass*, "Song of Myself." In the notebooks, the reader can see Whitman talking to himself, establishing a poetic credo. The radical genius who seems to spill himself over the pages of his strange new book was the result of a long period of preparation; the art of the new poetry, or antipoetry, was a highly conscious art developed in the lecture and rehearsal hall of Whitman's notebooks. As Zweig guides the reader through these materials, the miracle of transformation is most astonishingly revealed.

While Zweig displays the myriad influences on Whitman's aroused sensibilities through the early 1850's, he keeps in view the ongoing, though sporadic, work of the cultural journalist that Whitman still was. Whitman's reactions to painting and photography are made part of the pattern, and the imprint of music on the embryonic poet personality is explored lucidly. A constant theme in Zweig's analysis is just how much Whitman the iconoclast was a man of his times. The most provocative correlative to the poetic that Whitman was about to release was the Crystal Palace exhibition of 1853, the largest industrial exhibition that the United States had yet staged. Zweig places Whitman as a frequent visitor to the colossal New York structure, and he speculates that its representation of the great young nation affected Whitman at a crucial time. The mounting notebook jottings soon to be spun into "Song of Myself" reflect the ambition to create a work that "would be a compendium of all knowledge, all experience, housed in a form as outsized, in its way, as the glass and cast-iron cross next to the reservoir: Whitman's capacious 'self.'" The detailed treatment of parallels between the poem and the Crystal Palace is tantalizing, as is Zweig's analysis of the poem itself.

For that is where the book has been heading. Zweig has taken the reader along the trails that lead from the reporter-editor-politico-housebuilder named Walter Whitman, Jr., to the rough, open-collared lounger, the vagabond bard of America named Walt Whitman. "Song of Myself" is that place in time when one figure releases the other. It is not only a great moment of radical art but also (and simultaneously) a great moment of self-creation. Zweig calls "Song of Myself" an "engine of self-making," and so he shows it to be. Its voice, its range, its patterns, its concerns, its seeming formlessness, its glorious bravado—all can be understood as the projection of an enormous will seeking to be realized and finally succeeding. As Zweig examines "Song of Myself" and the other major poems in *Leaves of Grass*, he creates a high moment in biographical criticism and reminds the reader of the limits of other critical approaches.

Zweig goes on to record the publication history of the first and later editions of *Leaves of Grass*, all the while seeing Whitman's art and self as dancing partners. He shows the reader, here and elsewhere, Whitman's "twoness": his paradoxical outspokenness and reserve, his spontaneity and crafty self-promotion, his mixed sense of fulfillment and despair. Zweig also provides an intelligent account of why Whitman's creative periods were so few, leading the reader to view the created personage as a partial displacement of possible literary works. Whitman's three years of hospital work following his discovery of America's wounded Civil War youth is one example of a transference of energies from one field of action to another in which equivalent psychic needs were met. Zweig shows the reader, too, the growing conservatism of Whitman's work after the middle 1850's as well as his partial enslavement by his self-made public role.

For all of his analyses and explanations, Zweig does nothing to diminish the miracle itself. His investigation serves, as it should, to bring added awe along with added understanding. Whitman remains the great original even after the reader has learned how much he was formed by his times, how his weaknesses fueled his ambition, and how he ransacked so much of his reading and his own earlier, mundane writing. This is a great human story, a great American story, and Zweig's version of it is so vibrant and inventive that it partakes of the power of its subject.

Philip K. Jason

Sources for Further Study

America. CLI, July 7, 1984, p. 17.
Booklist. LXXX, April 1, 1984, p. 1097.
Library Journal. CIX, March 15, 1984, p. 585.
Los Angeles Times. August 13, 1984, V, p. 8.
Macleans. XCVII, June 4, 1984, p. 49.
New Leader. LXVII, May 14, 1984, p. 13.
The Nation. CCXXXVIII, April 14, 1984, p. 457.
The New York Review of Books. XXXI, April 26, 1984, p. 3.
The New York Times Book Review. LXXXIX, May 6, 1984, p. 1.
Publishers Weekly. CCXXV, February 24, 1984, p. 132.

WALTER SCOTT
The Making of the Novelist

Author: Jane Millgate (1937-   )
Publisher: University of Toronto Press (Buffalo, New York). 223 pp. $24.95
Type of work: Literary criticism

A study of the early Waverley novels, focusing on the way in which Sir Walter Scott came to master the craft of fiction

When the noted scholar Edgar Johnson published his biography of Sir Walter Scott in 1970, he chose for his title *Sir Walter Scott: The Great Unknown*. Recognizing that the subtitle refers to an epithet Scott inherited in his own day, one might still think that Johnson was being unfair to modern readers, for Scott has not been "unknown" for some time. On the other hand, considering the educated public's familiarity with the bulk of Scott's works, Johnson might just as well have selected for his subtitle "The Great Unread." In the 1980's, only a modest number of people can claim to know many of Scott's works, though many have read (or skimmed through) at least one. High school students plod through *Ivanhoe* (1820). College undergraduates who enroll in novel courses take home from the bookstore copies of *Waverley* (1814) or *The Heart of Midlothian* (1818). An occasional enterprising graduate student makes his or her way through *Rob Roy* (1818), *The Bride of Lammermoor* (1819), or *Redgauntlet* (1824).

From crib sheets and critical surveys, students (and teachers, in many cases) learn that, in addition to being a competent poet whose verse narratives were popular until Lord Byron began writing in the genre, Scott wrote a series of works now known as the Waverley novels. The student may also learn from a secondary source that Scott was "prolific" and that he was the father of the historical novel.

A trip through the library shelves gives one a hint as to why, in today's fast-paced world, in which best-selling fiction often runs to less than three-hundred pages, Scott remains largely the property of the academic community. Forty-eight volumes, neatly arranged and often covered with a uniform coating of library dust, bear the Waverley imprint and the gold-lettered Scott on their spines.

It may be hard to imagine that, once upon a time, Sir Walter Scott was the most widely read novelist in the world, his works the standard against which others' novels were judged. Taste in fiction changes rapidly, however; only a scant thirty years after he died, Scott was dubbed "irresponsible" by the young Henry James, and as the art of fiction became more sophisticated, Scott became less a "must-be-read" figure.

The popularity of the form which Scott created did not diminish. Historical novels appeared in abundance throughout the nineteenth century; a turn-of-the-century scholarly study reviewed almost three thousand of them.

With academic interest in the form itself taking precedence over attention to individual works, Scott's novels became a touchstone for evaluative, or genre, criticism. In ways curiously (if somewhat perversely) reminiscent of Aristotle and the neoclassical critics, literary analysts turned to Scott's works to discover the "elements" of the "true" historical novel. How far removed from the present did the action of the novel have to be to merit the term "historical"? What proportion of real-life characters had to inhabit the pages? How closely must the events of the fiction parallel history? In Scott, the critics found answers, usually with little regard to the artistry of the Waverley novels themselves.

It is no surprise, then, that the modern scholar who chooses to write about Sir Walter Scott's works faces a task both easy and difficult. There is no lack of materials: In addition to the forty-eight volumes of the Waverley collection, there are about a dozen volumes of verse. (By contrast, James Joyce, one of the most intensely studied twentieth century figures, produced only four major works in his lifetime.) Certainly, someone who really wants to write about Scott's work can find an angle that has not been used before on one or more of the lesser-read novels or poems. That seems possible even in the face of a substantial body of criticism, which includes both individual monographs and shorter studies numbering in the hundreds, perhaps thousands. If one wishes to say something worthwhile about Scott, though, one is still faced with having to read a mountain of material, much of it requiring a considerable background in both history and literature to appreciate fully. Any scholar who does so deserves special attention. Jane Millgate is such a scholar, and her new investigation of the early Waverley novels merits a close look by both nineteenth century literary specialists and the academic community in general.

Millgate's thesis is that, if read correctly, the early Waverley novels can reveal something about Scott's theory of fiction. With remarkable skill and a deft ability to introduce other scholarship without making it appear obtrusive, she begins by showing how the poems Scott wrote immediately prior to publication of *Waverley*, the first novel in the series, anticipate what Scott will do in his fiction. The chapters on these poems do more than demonstrate Scott's interest in preserving the heritage of the Scots Highlands and the Border culture: Millgate shows that Scott's method of narration is a key to understanding his eventual need to shift to the form of the novel to explore topics that really interested him. In relating these fantastic tales, Scott was careful to maintain a firm base in the real world. He created a framework for presenting the minstrel's ballads so that the reader could accept the veracity of the fantastic by having a realistic point of reference. What had really begun to interest Scott, however, was the way in which changing human situations and the press of events affect the lives of individuals and make them change and grow. Having found the conventions of verse narrative too inflexible for dealing with the developmental process of a hero, Scott turned to the novel as a means of exploring this phenomenon. The novel provided a way of introducing the domestic as well as the heroic side of life; what Millgate finds in virtually all of the early Waverley novels is a constant balancing of heroic and domestic which allowed Scott to explore at length the changing characteristics of human nature.

Without harping on the point, Millgate quietly dispels the notion that frustration with losing his readership to Byron is what drove Scott to the novel. Having demonstrated the ideological basis for Scott's decision to experiment with the novel, she turns her attention to the first group of Waverley novels, those that tell the story of the Scots people. Set in the century immediately preceding Walter Scott's own generation, these novels demonstrate their author's concern with the problems of melding two ideological as well as literary traditions. The Highlanders represented for Scott all things Romantic; characters almost larger than life, they appeared to stand in sharp contrast to the more settled, pragmatic Lowlands society which represented the idea of progress in an Augustan age. The same contrast appeared in the two major literary forms of Scott's day: poetry, which was (according to popular critics) to deal with people and events elevated above the ordinary, and the novel, a vehicle for investigating domestic, social, mundane concerns of daily life.

Scott's methodology reflects his concern for winning over his readers by grounding his tales in the real world while simultaneously acknowledging the power of the realm of the romance. In fact, Millgate asserts, only when Scott worked within the apparently rigid limitations of the historical framework was he truly creative. Scott first had to overcome doubts (his own as well as the reader's) about the validity of the imaginative experience to give his creative powers free play; ironically, by limiting that free play within the bounds of historical circumstance, Scott was able to explore more fully the human situations at the heart of all of his historical fiction. Millgate's summaries of the novels clearly demonstrate the emphasis Scott placed on the fictional characters whose lives were shaped by historical events; their stories, not the historical events themselves, are the real subjects of Scott's fiction.

Millgate examines these novels from two perspectives simultaneously: first, as separate texts, each with its own story and its own moral dimension, and second, as parts of the series that Scott was consciously creating. Through the series, Scott created a dialogue between himself and his readers about the conventions of the novel and specifically about the kind of novel he was attempting to write. Hence, Millgate is as concerned about the persona who mediates between the reader and the story as she is with the stories themselves. The task she has undertaken is a formidable one, especially in the short space of barely two-hundred pages of text. That one comes away with a sense of understanding is a tribute to Millgate's skill both as a scholar and a prose stylist.

A good example of the way in which Millgate approaches her subject can be seen in her discussion of *Waverley*. The first novel in the series that bears its name, *Waverley* has in recent years risen in critical status. Most critics have seen it as an attempt by Scott to reject the ideological and literary tenets of Romanticism in favor of conventional, or conservative, notions of morality and literature.

Millgate takes a different view, seeing *Waverley* as Scott's attempt to explore "the problem of the maturation of the dreaming boy"—that is, the problem of the young Romantic. Millgate claims that by 1813, Scott saw maturation as a process involving not a rejection of romance, but a deeper immersion in its dangers, so that the special insight into human nature which one gains from romance can become a part of the mature experience of life. The "timeless picaresque" of Edward Waverley's journey into the Highlands, dramatized by numerous motifs taken from the romance tradition, stands in apparent contrast to the political nature of the events in which the hero becomes involved. Throughout the novel, the developing moral and social awareness of Edward Waverley is balanced by the fully developed and unchanging perspective of the narrator. The complex interplay of attitudes which the careful reader notices in these two characters (for the narrator is certainly a character in the novel) provides an essential tension that demands resolution. What one finally realizes is that, though Edward's idealistic view of the world is clearly in need of revision, the narrator's is not necessarily the correct one either. The elements of the romance, attractive in contrast to the staid Augustan pronouncements of the aloof narrator, have something of merit in them.

Millgate makes no case that the novel is radical in anything other than its particular use of history, and even on this point she is less strident than many earlier critics. Most of her discussion centers on the qualities of *Waverley* as a *Bildungsroman*, a subgenre already popular in Scott's day and in use by most Romantic novelists. *Waverley* operates within the Romantic tradition as well as acting as a commentary on that tradition. Millgate illustrates her points through a careful analysis of the structure of the novel and through an examination of the function of the many elements of the romance that Scott uses. In Millgate's view, the literary traditions of romance and realism operate not in contrast but in complementary fashion. The elements of romance illustrate the stages through which the power of youthful imagination passes on its way to maturity. Viewed as a literary device, the use of elements of the romance becomes a way of highlighting both the strong and the weak points of the realistic novel, demonstrating that romance and realism can both be means of illustrating truths of human nature.

Millgate's exploration of the literary, structural, psychological and moral dimensions of *Waverley* are typical of the sensitive and respectable scholarship that characterizes this study. Beneath the "oneness" of the Waverley series lies a considerable amount of variety, and Millgate highlights that variety consistently. No two novels are approached in exactly the same way; no two yield the same satisfaction to either critic or reader. Clearly, some are more valuable than others in helping Millgate focus on Scott's development as a novelist. For example, *The Antiquary* (1816) is a text in which Scott investigates a subject close to his own life and which contains a character (Sir Johnathan Oldbuck) much like Scott himself. In discussing this novel, Millgate helps the reader understand something about the value Scott placed on different forms of "knowing" and the value of literature itself. Not all of these early novels work so directly to reveal their author, though, and Millgate seldom forces her case to make them do so.

Occasionally, Millgate becomes so involved in explaining what happens and why that the reader is led astray from the central focus of this study. On the other hand, Millgate's readings are sensible, and one comes away understanding something about the novels she examines. Also, she is no single-minded devotee of Scott; when Scott fails, as he does in *The Black Dwarf* (1816), Millgate says so, unabashedly. That kind of candor is refreshing, and necessary, if scholarship is to do a service to the reading public at large.

A good part of Millgate's study is concerned with analysis of Scott's literary game-playing with the reading public. *Waverley* was published anonymously. Why that happened is easy enough to explain: Scott, a man of stature in the community and an accomplished poet and scholar, may have been concerned about the reception the novel would receive, and, not wanting to be associated with a failure, he prudently withheld his name from the title page. *Waverley* was an immediate success, however, and certainly Scott could have derived some benefit from announcing his authorship, yet the second novel in the series, *Guy Mannering* (1815), had on its title page, "By the Author of *Waverley*." Subsequent works continued the game, some being attributed to the pseudonymous Sir Jedediah Cleishbotham, others marked as the work of the Waverley novelist. Only a few of Scott's friends knew the truth.

Why the need for continued anonymity? Millgate offers several possibilities. First, the same reasons which caused Scott to refrain from announcing his authorship of the first novel were still valid; he had a certain reputation to protect. Second, he found it becoming increasingly difficult to write poetry, and to proclaim publicly that he had become a novelist would perhaps have been a tacit admission of defeat as a bard. Meanwhile, part of the enjoyment which the first readers of the Waverley novels had was in trying to guess whose fluent pen was turning out these thrillers.

Millgate, however, sees more to Scott's need for anonymity. In almost every discussion of individual works, she returns to the question of Scott's authorial stance. From the cloak of anonymity, Scott was able to explore both literary and personal issues, to work out for himself his proper role as a literary man and as an artist. Millgate hints that on occasion, the masks of the various narrators allowed Scott to admit things about himself and his world that he dared not say as the Lord of Abbotsford. For these investigations alone, Millgate's study is worth the attention of scholars interested in Scott's personality as well as his professional career. One comes away from *Walter Scott: The Making of the Novelist* with a sense of having become a little more familiar with "The Great Unknown." For that reason, also, the book is to be valued.

Laurence W. Mazzeno

Source for Further Study

Times Literary Supplement. March 1, 1985, p. 240.

THE WAR OF THE END OF THE WORLD

Author: Mario Vargas Llosa (1936-   )
Translated from the Spanish by Helen R. Lane
Publisher: Farrar, Straus and Giroux (New York). 568 pp. $18.95
Type of work: Historical novel
Time: 1896-1897
Locale: Primarily the backlands of Brazil

A tale of the famous rebellion in the Brazilian backlands, of its leader, the millenarian Counselor, the utopian state he created in Canudos, and the apocalyptic war that marked its end

Principal characters:
  THE COUNSELOR, an apocalyptic prophet and the lord of Canudos
  GALILEO GALL, a revolutionist and phrenologist
  EPAMINODAS GONÇALVES, head of the Progressivist Party
  THE BARON DE CANABRAVA, head of the Bahia Autonomist Party
  RUFINO, a tracker and guide
  JUREMA, Rufino's wife, Gall's victim, and the journalist's lover
  THE NEARSIGHTED JOURNALIST, the reporter whose mission it is to explain Canudos

In 1903, six years after the siege of Canudos (1897), the Brazilian engineer and journalist Euclides da Cunha, one of the two people to whom *The War of the End of the World* is dedicated, published *Os Sertões: Campanha de Canudos*, translated by Samuel Putnam as *Rebellion in the Backlands*, 1944. In Cunha's epoch-making work, called by some the Bible of Brazilian literature, are all of the facts from which Mario Vargas Llosa weaves his fiction: the charismatic leadership and revolutionary preaching of Antonio Conselheiro, the establishment of a bizarre millenarian community in the backlands (*os sertões*) of northern Brazil, the military campaigns to suppress the anti-Republican community of converted bandits and outlaws, and the opposition of Brazil's two major political forces (monarchist and republican) in a country that had recently become a republic. Vargas Llosa molds the scientific, geographical, and sociological elements of Cunha's classic text into a highly wrought narrative of revolution, religion, love, honor, and political expediency which has enduring implications not only for Brazil but also for his native Peru, of which he has written much in recent years concerning the Maoist revolutionary movement *el sendero luminoso* (the shining path). Vargas Llosa departs from the main outline of historical facts in few particulars, mostly in the introduction of new characters and in the fleshing out of several historical figures that Cunha mentions briefly; when he does so he is careful to preserve an authentic and precise background against which to set his impressive array of characters and their concerns.

At the novel's core is the journalist's attempt, and the author's attempt, to make sense of a surprising cultural and political revolution that pitted a band of fanatical true believers against the military strength of the Brazilian

Republic, which represented to them the coming of the Antichrist foretold in the Book of Revelation. Those who choose to join the elect at Canudos are subjected to an unusual scrutiny aimed at discovering their orthodoxy and purity of belief in several contexts. Candidates for political and spiritual refuge at Canudos are not necessarily bound to renounce Satan, his works, and his pomps; instead, they must renounce the Antichrist, the Republic, the expulsion of the Emperor, the newfangled separation of Church and State, civil marriage, the metric system, and the census questions. The revolutionaries' singleness of purpose goes far toward explaining their otherwise inexplicable success at rebuffing the forays of the well-organized Republican army against the revolutionaries' stronghold in Canudos. The strength of their singlemindedness and its danger to the young republic may also account for the severity of their eventual destruction, a devastation of apocalyptic proportions as final as the destruction of Carthage in Livy's chronicles: No one remains alive in the stronghold; few escape; and no brick is left upon another. So threatening is the community and its rebellion that one thing is clear about the journalist's attempts to record the history of Canudos: No one wants to hear the truth and the details about the uprising, and all would wish the incident forgotten.

The journalist does not care that the political establishment would wish Canudos consigned to oblivion. His own passion for the truth about the community, about the Counselor and his followers, carries him forward to explore the political motivations of the Republicans and Monarchists and their complicated machinations to use the Counselor and his community to their own advantage, in plots which include implicating such improbable allies as the British Empire and the Roman Catholic Church in aiding the rebels. The journalist's shuttling back and forth across Brazil and through time as he describes his own impressions—impressions that are blurred about the siege of Canudos, since he lost his glasses there—and collects the impressions of others unifies the majority of the work. As he exclaims at one point, Canudos is filled with stories: These stories form the basis of his and of Vargas Llosa's accounts.

The telling of these stories through highly individualized characters is one of the novel's great strengths. Vargas Llosa uses expert description and analysis, an accumulation of physical and psychological details, and direct, realistic dialogue to make his work a credible and forceful reflection of life in nineteenth century Brazil and of the lives of his highly wrought characters. The Counselor himself is, expectedly, the focus of considerable interest, and Vargas Llosa succeeds in giving him both a realistic and a mysterious existence from a more partisan perspective than Cunha's. Where Cunha spared no opportunity to characterize him as an unstable and dangerous fanatic, Vargas Llosa makes him an effective, mystical, charismatic leader who inspires his followers with a zeal and fervor that, though misguided, are complex in their implications and effects. The Counselor's mystique pervades the work and the lives of all the characters as he draws to himself the poor, the outcast, the physically deformed, and the fallen who join him in the building of a New Jerusalem in the desolate region of Canudos. His effect upon his followers and even upon some of his detractors and some of the skeptical, who are neither for him nor against him, is profoundly messianic as he assumes the biblical proportions of an Old Testament prophet, a new John the Baptist, and a reincarnated Jesus of Nazareth; his message and teachings proclaim good news for his followers, but the message is surely one of foolishness to the children of this world.

Vargas Llosa populates Canudos and other reaches of the backlands with superb military types, fierce bandits and outlaws, desperate adventurers, clerics who prefigure some of today's liberationist theologians, strange traveling circus performers, and a host of born-again souls. In the sheer complexity of his creations, their stories and their interconnectedness, Vargas Llosa becomes part of a tradition of writers, such as Henry Fielding, Honoré de Balzac, James Joyce, and William Faulkner, he calls God supplanters. In the richness of his characters, their internal consistencies, and their range of emotion and experience Vargas Llosa most closely approximates Charles Dickens. One of his most successful creations, after the Counselor and the journalist, is the truly Dickensian Galileo Gall. Gall is a wandering phrenologist, Marxist revolutionary, and great proclaimer of himself who drifts to Brazil after several brushes with European revolutions and establishments, volunteers to help the revolution at Canudos which he mistakenly thinks epitomizes the great international revolutionary movement, and thus plays into the hands of the Machiavellian Epaminodas Gonçalves. Gonçalves is the head of the Progressivist Republican Party and the publisher of the *Journal de Notícias* who dupes Gall into running guns to Canudos and plans to have Gall killed and exposed as a British agent provocateur in the pay of the Baron de Canabrava, head of the Bahia Autonomist Party, and all monarchists supported by Queen Victoria. Gall's exotic appearance and behavior, his rambling, doctrinaire diatribes, his unwilling complicity in the destruction of Canudos, his several narrow escapes from death, and his extreme oddity make him a picaresque figure who is among contemporary fiction's more interesting, if not admirable, characters.

Greater than Gall and the novel's true protagonist is its unexpected heroine, Jurema. In many respects, the novel is Jurema's story: She is the only one who can provide the journalist with the details of his own experience, her experience, Gall's adventures, and the information the journalist needs to connect the gun running to Gonçalves and, thus, to an arrangement between Gonçalves and the Baron de Canabrava. Jurema embodies the stereotypical lot of Latin American women and yet transcends that lot in surprising ways. Married to the guide Rufino and unwillingly caught up in

Gall's smuggling operation, she is Gall's victim and comforter. Caught up in the attempted assassination of Gall, she saves his life in a fierce struggle that, in turn, precipitates a fiercer struggle with Gall, who, for reasons he cannot understand, rapes her. Together, Gall and Jurema make their pilgrimage to Canudos, relentlessly pursued by Rufino and aided along the way by an assortment of characters, including a bearded lady and a dwarf, in their journey along an ironic Yellow Brick Road. For Gall, it is the pilgrimage of a true believer to a shrine of idealism; for Jurema, it is a journey into the unknown. Having been dishonored by Gall, she seems to have no alternative but to accompany him, heal the wounds he received in the ambush, and simply wait for Rufino to find and kill her. Her initial passivity, however, is gradually transformed as she is forced by circumstances and events to become increasingly more resourceful in saving her own life, Gall's, and, ultimately, the journalist's. Indeed, the journalist is the only character who appears to understand and comprehend her fully and who presents her as the heroine not only of his own life but also of his manifold tales of Canudos.

Vargas Llosa has rescued this important and troubled chapter of Brazilian history from relative obscurity outside of Brazil and of South America by breathing new life into the facts of the case and creating characters of depth and complexity. In some places, he replicates the aridity of the region and the matching aridity of Cunha's narrative in seemingly interminable descriptions of physical geography. In other places, the Spanish (and the fine English translation) contain lyric celebrations of the country and its people. Like the majority of his work, this novel contains both sublime and patently incongruous and absurd elements. At nearly every turn, for example, the high spiritual endeavors of such characters as the Abbot Joao and the Little Blessed One are played off against their invincible ignorance and their bizarre sense of their missions in life and the means whereby they can carry out their missions. These and other characters are not only the victims of their own ideologies; they are also victims of considerable authorial irony. The ironic handling of characters and their situations helps make this troubled era and its people more accessible and credible to the modern reader. This, in turn, is of great importance to a writer who aims at having fiction not only complement the ordinary experience of individuals but also compete with it. Further, the act of creating anew the conditions, actions, motives, and thoughts of the participants in an event which represented a turning point in the history of Brazil is not only an exercise in the reordering and interpretation of experience but also an opportunity to do as his fictional journalist does, to realize fully for oneself the possibility of meaning an event can have for those involved in it directly or tangentially.

The novel works best as a novel in the interaction of its characters. As in every historical novel, however, characters evolve and act only within the confines of their background and setting. One great virtue of the novel is the well-communicated sense that this is the work of an eyewitness; another is that it contains realistic depictions of actual participants from their own perspective, not from the perspectives of officialdom and of official historians. Vargas Llosa has succeeded extraordinarily well in this truly epic novel, clearly his most ambitious work to date, in providing modern readers with an intensely compelling popular history of the campaign of Canudos while never forgetting to tell the stories of those whose lives both give and receive meaning as a result of it.

John J. Conlon

Sources for Further Study

Book World. XIV, August 26, 1984, p. 1.
Choice. XXII, December, 1984, p. 564.
Commonweal. CXI, October 19, 1984, p. 566.
Kirkus Reviews. LII, July 1, 1984, p. 600.
Los Angeles Times Book Review. September 2, 1984, p. 1.
The New Republic. CXCI, October 8, 1984, p. 25.
The New York Times Book Review. LXXXIX, August 12, 1984, p. 1.
Publishers Weekly. CCXXV, June 29, 1984, p. 97.
Vogue. CLXXIV, September, 1984, p. 582.
The Wall Street Journal. CCIV, December 10, 1984, p. 24.

WATERLAND

Author: Graham Swift (1949-   )
Publisher: Poseidon Press (New York). 310 pp. $15.95
Type of work: Novel
Time: The 1940's and the 1980's
Locale: The East Anglia fens of England; London

A history teacher, recently relieved of his duties, looks back over his life growing up in the East Anglian fens, and the lives of his ancestors as well, with special concern about events in the summer of 1943 which led eventually to his wife's stealing another woman's baby from a supermarket cart

> *Principal characters:*
> Tom Crick, a middle-aged history teacher, and the narrator
> Mary Crick (née Metcalf), his wife
> Dick Crick, the incestuous product of Tom's mother and grandfather, and a retardate
> Price, Crick's bright, impolite student and thorn-in-the-side representative of the next generation

With its ambition to chronicle the history of the East Anglia region of England and its air of apologia for traditional rural ways, Graham Swift's *Waterland*, which sent the British literary press atwitter in 1983 and was nominated for the highly sought-after Booker McConnel Prize for Fiction, has put many American reviewers in mind of William Faulkner. Undoubtedly, there are similarities: The brewery-founding Atkinsons recall Faulkner's Snopes; the storytelling emphasis echoes *Absalom, Absalom!* (1936); and the gothically flawed past of both Crick and his family suggests inevitably that other House of Atreus, the Compsons. Curiously, however, in its largest themes, the novel may be most profitably compared not with Faulkner's works but with those of another American, F. Scott Fitzgerald.

Like Fitzgerald, Swift explores the inability of people to come to terms with the past's demands upon them, their failed attempts to alter it, and their own identities as it has shaped them to suit their present purposes. When the title character of Fitzgerald's *The Great Gatsby* (1925), on being told that one cannot repeat the past, replies, "Of course you can," he really means that one can somehow abolish the cause-and-effect sequence which has flowed from past decisions (in this case, Daisy Buchanan's decision not to marry him). Consciously or compulsively, the characters in *Waterland* all attempt to relive and so expunge their pasts; Tom Crick, above all, wishes to reclaim his past, as if, by possessing his past completely, he will cease being possessed by it. Crick, as the narrator who constantly addresses the reader as he would his history class, and who conflates world history with his own family history, presents this struggle with a past that resists complete assimilation to the present but refuses to relinquish its hold.

The attempt to deprive the past of its sting by finding reasons and excuses for its events is part of the larger project on which Swift meditates—that of containing the unfathomable and the irrational, reclaiming it for civilization and reason. The title evokes the continual agon between the watery fens and the human attempts to control them with sluice gates, as Tom's father, Henry, does in the course of earning his living. Land—or civilization—is ever at war with water—or chaos. It is part of the process of storytelling to reclaim this silty past, making it palpable, manageable, and tame. The fatal ambiguity here, though, and one to which Swift invariably points the reader, is that the way one reclaims the past can make its irrational hold on the present all the stronger, as when superstition proffers an explanation of a local flood: What seems to shore up land may, in the end, serve to weaken it. Crick's own efforts to recapitulate his past and so to understand it partake of this ambiguity. Hoping to shed light on his own past, he ends by becoming entangled in its obscurities, and his history is scarcely distinguishable at times from the fairy tales people tell one another to overcome their fear of the dark. As apocalypse may well be the ultimate darkness and fear, Crick aptly remarks at one point that "when the world is about to end there'll be no more reality, only stories."

Swift has already shown his dedication to story by publishing such works as *The Sweet Shop Owner* (1980), *Shuttlecock* (1981), and *Learning to Swim and Other Stories* (1982). He thus came to this task as no novice to fiction or stranger to its vicissitudes. The strategy of casting a history teacher in the role of narrator works to emphasize the precarious status of both fiction and fact, and it effectively undermines the tendency so common in this time to privilege the latter over the former. By including so much narrative from a seemingly public domain—lengthy recountings of the rise of the Atkinson brewers, of Ernest Atkinson's standing for Parliament on the Liberal ticket right before World War I and losing his deposit, and so on—Swift seems at times to cross the border from the watery realm of fairy tale to the *terra firma* of fact. This sense, however, is never a certainty; the reader remains landlocked and waterlogged in a fenlike nether region combining history and legend, blending public knowledge with darker, private intimation and belief. When Tom Crick says that history is "a yarn," this is meant positively; by the same token, Swift presents his yarn as a kind of history.

Along with a suspicion of history's claims of superiority over fiction, *Waterland* suggests a strong skepticism about that attempt to extend into the future history's supposed causal clarity that one calls belief in progress. The two emblems for such belief in progress regularly invoked throughout the book are the French Revolution (one of the major items on the syllabus that is ignored by old "Cricky," leading to his early forced retirement) and the British Empire, whose falsity has driven grandfather Atkinson into his home and perhaps out of his right mind. Swift, via Crick, makes much of the eagerness of the French to take up Napoleon's retrograde challenge: "Follow me, said the Corsican, and I will give you your Golden Age. And they followed him—these regicides, these tyrant-haters." As for the Empire, the last quarter of the nineteenth century was "a period of economic deterioration from which we have never recovered." Grand projects such as revolutions, empires, and wars—for example, World War II, which figures as backdrop for much of the novel's action—constitute nothing so much as narratives in which ordinary people like to see themselves as characters and their actions as endowed with dramatic meaning. (This, by the way, is another of the deliberate thematic links drawn between superstitious legend and modern history.) Crick's love of history amounts to a love of stories, both the large public ones and the small private ones, and part of history's allure for him is that it puts the events of the past into a causal sequence of some sort: "Explanation, explanation," runs the imperative, and it is implied that the explanations do not always have to be very good, either.

Repeatedly in the novel, however, whether the incident is the Atkinson brewery fire in 1911 or the death of Crick's childhood classmate Freddie Parr in July, 1943, the explanation that can be agreed upon as fact (in both cases, "accident") explains, in reality, very little. It is only misty conjecture and rumor that begin to provide a sense of context for these actions. History teacher Crick, with these parables, suggests that the narratives in which one indulges can be informative indeed about the past, so long as they are not expected to be more than narratives. Crick tells his children—and above all a clever, irreverent punk pupil named Price, who is clearly a surrogate son—never to stop asking the question why. This admonition stems less from the fact that one may find out the answer, which at any rate "never seems to come any nearer," than from the expectation that the kinds of answers one hazards, superstitious, anxious, and limited as they are, will reveal much about the one hazarding those answers, even if they do not "solve" the incidents one strives to understand.

For Tom Crick, these incidents are above all traumas from his own life, which, as the reader meets him in inglorious middle age, is quietly falling apart. His wife, the latest victim of the insanity that seems all too prevalent in this novel, has been institutionalized for snatching the baby of another woman at a supermarket. At roughly the same time, and perhaps owing to his marital travails, Crick has begun to abandon the standard history syllabus to tell his class stories about his East of England boyhood. The headmaster, a physicist named Lewis, gets wind of the heterodoxy of putting oneself into history, as he terms it, and decides to retire Crick, whom he has never liked, and simultaneously to begin "phasing out history," which he does not especially like either. Thus, ironically, Crick's attempt to account for the wreckage of his own life, to himself as well as to his history class, has the effect of worsening his situation. Another endeavor to shore up the land ends up weakening it.

The bulk of his narrative concerns a series of events that occurred in the 1940's in the Fenland, Crick's boyhood region. Crick and Mary Metcalf, a neighboring girl, begin adolescent exploration into "holes and things," which leads in its ineluctable way to pregnancy. As the cause-and-effect chain progresses, it emerges that Mary has also been exploring with Tom's half-witted brother, Dick. In order to protect Tom from Dick's jealous rage, Mary asserts that Freddie Parr is the father: a lie that results in Freddie's death at Dick's hand. (The death instrument, in a heavily symbolic touch, is a bottle of Ernest Atkinson's notorious 1911 Coronation Ale.) The other result of this pregnancy is a horrifically crude abortion that renders Mary, Crick's future wife, permanently sterile. At somewhat greater length, the incident leads to the Crick brothers' trip to their attic, wherein lies their grandfather's chest. A letter in the chest, which Tom patiently explicates for his brother, tells Dick what the reader has already known: that his retardation is the product of grandfather Ernest's incest with his daughter Helen: "There's been a mix-up somewhere and he's the result." Perhaps sensing this, Dick slips back into the river Ouse (pronounced as in "primal ooze") and swims out of the Cricks' world for good. Having consumed several bottles of Atkinson Coronation firewater before diving in, Dick returns to the sources of both the Atkinson and the Crick sides of the family: alcohol and water, respectively.

As he threads his way through the gothic welter of his past, Crick comes up against the persistence of history in what is called, by his students and by Lewis, the "here and now." As old Cricky tells his history class, "For most of the time the Here and Now is neither now nor here." Usually, it is an empty space inhabited by the ghost of history, the desire to give the raw material of one's life a narrative pattern, or the "bastard but pampered child [of history], Nostalgia." Rather than progressing, then, "we move in circles," compulsively repeating or atoning for past actions. The cliché, as one knows, concerns the way those who forget the past are condemned to repeat it, and Swift's narrative dramatizes this process in many ways, the starkest of which may well be abortion. In a desire to obliterate the past, stained now with the murder of Freddie Parr, Mary and Tom go to the abortionist, who in relieving them of the evidence of their past also disposes of "What the future's made of." The abortion is a quasi-scientific procedure rendered in prescientific, superstitious terms, as if to forecast that just as science never vanquishes superstition, so this intention to flee both the past and its future consequences will also fail. Indeed, this foreclosing of the future does not neuter the past; rather, this very willed amnesia makes Mary incapable of moving, either biologically or psychologically, into the future. Tom and Mary Crick, in their antiseptically furnished London Regency apartment, become prisoners of the past they thought to reject: The past and its superstition avenge themselves on those who would forswear them.

When the middle-aged Mrs. Crick steals another woman's baby, she believes that God has ordered her to do it.

Tom's brother, Dick, is a slightly different reminder of the sins of the fathers. In this case, the sin is that of Dick's grandfather, who sees the product of his incestuous union with his daughter as the hope of revivification, "the saviour of the world." (The parallel to Mary's "God-made-me-do-it" justification for stealing a child seems here strategic.) Disillusioned with empire and his fellow fenmen, Ernest Atkinson sees in his daughter's baby what Mary sees in her theft: an act of will that can reverse the deterioration of his world, can break the causal links to history and effect a revolution, as the original savior is said to have done. (There is also the suspicion that just as Mary sought to atone for the willed amnesia of her abortion, so Ernest may be atoning for attempting to burn his own bridges with the past and with his community: He is thought in many quarters to have been responsible for the brewery fire of 1911.) Just as with Mary's theft, Ernest's act of reclamation only makes matters worse: Helen gives birth to a "potato-head." Neither destroying the past nor willing the future into being has the desired effect in this novel: The characters who try either path only get saddled more firmly with the consequences of past actions. Ultimately, Dick Crick disappears—and mythically returns—into the Ouse, part of a past which ever threatens the present and which, in the apocalypse Price and his classmates dread, bids fair one day to engulf it.

Price's obsession with the here and now and his injunction to old Cricky to "stuff your past" provide a foil for the drift of the argument presented by Swift, which is that all the desires to be done with the past and break cleanly with history come down to willed amnesia, even—and here the fundamental conservatism of the novel arises—an offense against the natural order. There is a long section on eels, for example, followed by chapters on "natural history" and "artificial history"; motifs such as these, combined with an apparently retributive mythic structure where abortion and incest are punished, may lead the unwary to conclude that Swift's purpose is to assert the claims of nature against those of man, to show that human history, with its elaborate network of sluice gates, is puny and ineffectual against the flood tide of eternal nature, whose law all must obey.

It is true that as a teacher one might expect Crick to derive a pedagogical point of some sort, a moral of some kind from his story; the fact that he calls the readership "children" to boot hints that didacticism is in the air. The point, however, seems to be less that history never matters than that the "Grand Narrative" of history matters less than one is accustomed to think. Whether the great story concerns revolution or empire, this "filler of vacuums," this "dispeller of fears of the dark" may seduce its audience into darker voids than the ones it pretends to fill. This is not a call to give up, despite the pessimistic tone of the book's conclusion. To the contrary: this stoic novel cautions against despair as much as it guards against the frantic hopes that prepare despair's way. Chapter 49, "About Empire-building," sums up Crick's position—and since it is transmitted without irony, it is presumably the novel's as well: "My humble model for progress is the reclamation of land. Which is repeatedly, never-endingly retrieving what is lost." This retrieval process produces what little there is of something called civilization. "No one ever said it was real," says Crick. "It's built by the learning process; by trial and error. It breaks easily. No one ever said it couldn't fall to bits. And no one ever said it would last for ever." This trial-and-error process means that many things one may think will bring progress actually aid chaos and old night, and the explanations one turns to, to make sense of events, may confuse instead of clarify. Nevertheless, the imperative to try to understand is as much a part of one's natural legacy as the blind forces against which one's efforts and explanations are directed. Swift's narrator states this case for a modest affirmation of human effort by defining this retrieval process: "A hard, inglorious business. But you shouldn't go mistaking the reclamation of land for the building of empires."

This novel is at once, then, a chronicle of life in a regional backwater of England and a meditation on what it is to tell a story, to put the past into narrative—a dual function that accords with the dual setting of the Fenland past in all of its mistiness and the London present in all of its false clarity. The process by which Crick loses job and wife provides a dramatic context for his meditations on history and civilization, while the East Anglia plot is a more straightforward evocation of growing up among the lore of a specific region. In melding playfully self-reflexive technique with the epic depiction of a community's tangled history, *Waterland* may put one in mind of Gabriel García Márquez's *One Hundred Years of Solitude* (1967), but the two narrative lines, not to mention the two aspects of the novel they represent, are hard to juggle well, and this difficulty gives rise to two major difficulties with the narrative.

The first problem with the work is one of tone and rhetoric. Swift's prose is so self-conscious, so aware of its own artifice and eager to let the reader in on the secret, that even the scenes of greatest potential drama are undercut by postmodernist high jinks. For example, the abortion chapter introduces its title this way: "let me tell you ... 'About the Witch.'" The constant reminders of the reading situation (the addressing of "children," for example), the rambling parenthetical sentences, and the overly clever conceits all indicate a style too in love with its own craft to advance the story. This is not an argument against an elaborate style as such, only against one that seems too elaborately facetious to sustain its subject.

The second, more serious problem has to do with psychology and character. For a novel that purports to vindicate the claims of the smaller-scale histories against the grand narrative of official history, this book contents itself with developing the more public events of East Anglia rather than nuances of psychology on the whole. This holds even at the most urgent points of incident in Crick's own life. One possible consequence of this is that an inordinate number of characters lose their minds in order to advance the plot: Sarah Atkinson in the nineteenth century, Ernest in the early twentieth, Dick Crick, and Tom Crick's wife. Thematically, the importance of madness in Swift's text is valid; it is the chaos of spirit ever in danger of swamping the land of reason. What makes sense thematically, however, is not made to work on the ground of personal history—which, after all, Crick thinks to take as his province. In a similar vein, the many pages on the courses of the rivers Leem and Ouse, on brewery construction, on silt, on eels, and whatnot—these things have a thematic reason for being in the novel, but for this reader, that did not stop them from being boring.

One might conclude that, despite its ambition to craft a heartfelt epic of the fens, *Waterland* neither has the insight into nor the attachment to the people or region needed to make the story resonate. This owes in large measure to the kind of skepticism about the efficacy of stories and storytelling that the meditative passages reveal. For whatever cause, there is little doubt that while, as the London *Observer* says, this novel "appropriates the fens" very well, the reader is less likely to feel as if he or she has appropriated them after reading the novel. Because of its stoicism and its modishly contemporary insistence on its own fictionality, *Waterland* must rely on its gothic plot turns, improbable as they are, to sustain reader interest in the chronicle, while matters of tone, character, and description are oddly remote and schematically rendered.

These objections, however, make the novel sound unduly glum. In fact, *Waterland* consistently absorbs one by virtue of its intellectual play, its sophisticated way of revealing plot, and its witty style. It is simply that for a novel with such deeply wrenching events, the narrative betrays little passion about those events. That could be a defect of its singular virtue, though, for this is one of those rare novels whose fidelity to their conceptual design is so complete that their manifold details are all conscripted in the service of the pedagogical point.

That conceptual design, as remarked at the outset, involves the persistence of the past and how one accounts for it. The eerie final sequence, with brother Dick mysteriously merging with the watery ooze from which he mythically sprang, presents the triumph of chaos over civilized order. Still, the boundary between the irrational past and the putatively enlightened present, which is forever being eroded by the novel's rhetoric and theme, is fortified anew by the rigor with which it pursues its line of argument. A novel so insistent about the overwhelming force of the past should not be so facile in making that narrated past a servant of present design, perhaps, but the resultant flaws are probably only part of the trial-and-error appropriation of lost memory which makes storytelling and history alike part of civilization's holding action, that hard, inglorious business. The need for this reclamation, whether for one's own sanity or that of one's nation, and the long odds against it enduring success, are held in an unquiet equipoise in this novel of ideas from the twilight of empire. One comes away from the elegiac conclusion of Swift's novel reflecting again upon Nick Carraway's famous backward look at the hope that founded the New World, a look that concludes *The Great Gatsby*. The dream of progress there is the green light on Daisy's dock, shining across the bay, but just as the myth of the future becomes nostalgia for the empire in Swift, so the belief in manifest destiny becomes the subject of eulogy in Fitzgerald. As Swift's text ends, the water of the Ouse has crested to engulf a man who was once seen as the hoped-for "Saviour" who would sunder the past. In the same way, Nick's final sentence, which invokes not the dock across the bay but the turbulent waters of the bay itself, sees both the necessity of this hard, inglorious work of reclamation and the failure and disappointment that accompany it. His lament for the characters of Fitzgerald's work applies with equal force to those in Swift's as well: "So we beat on, boats against the current, borne back ceaselessly into the past."

Mark Conroy

Sources for Further Study

Christian Science Monitor. LXXVI, March 28, 1984, p. 30.
Kirkus Reviews. LII, January 1, 1984, p. 15.
Los Angeles Times Book Review. April 1, 1984, p. 1.
The Nation. CCXXXVIII, March 31, 1984, p. 392.
New Statesman. CVI, October 7, 1983, p. 26.
The New York Review of Books. XXXI, August 16, 1984, p. 47.
The New York Times Book Review. LXXXIX, March 25, 1984, p. 9.
Newsweek. CIII, April 30, 1984, p. 74.
Newsweek. CV, June 24, 1985, p. 74.
Publishers Weekly. CCXXV, January 13, 1984, p. 64.
The Wall Street Journal. CCIII, March 28, 1984, p. 30.

A WAVE

Author: John Ashbery (1927-   )
Publisher: The Viking Press (New York). 89 pp. $15.95
Type of work: Poetry

A collection of forty-four poems (many previously published) offering God's plenty of everything; its masterpiece is the title poem, a song of life, but more discriminating, more restrained than Walt Whitman's

John Ashbery is not a new voice in the poetry world: This is his tenth volume of poems. He is no stranger to honors: *Self-Portrait in a Convex Mirror* (1975) won for him the Pulitzer Prize, the National Book Award, and the National Book Critics Circle Award. *A Wave* can only enhance what is already an outstanding reputation. It has already won for him the Bollingen Prize for Poetry.

Most of the forty-four poems printed here, including the title poem, have appeared previously in various journals and anthologies. It is entirely possible, and perhaps useful, to evaluate this splendid collection without specific references to the school with which Ashbery is associated, the New York Poets, or to the influences usually remarked: the French Symbolists, the Surrealists, the Dadaists, the American abstract expressionist painters.

Ashbery's work of recent years (and the poems here are certainly an example) has become more accessible, but it seems likely that his complexity was overstated in the first place. His technique—syntactical balance, minimal imagery, alliteration, fairly heavy use of the iambic line, complex but scannable sentences varied with short sentences or phrases, for example—is less disjointed and abstruse than that of many of the early moderns. In a few poems, the pronoun with no antecedent is finally unreadable, and in other poems, "They Like," for example, there are no discernible stanzaic connections, no transitions. In other poems, however, such as "When the Sun Went Down," Ashbery is so painstakingly clear that he verges on triteness.

The opening of "Proust's Questionnaire" is somewhat atypical in technique for this collection; there are more short, staccato lines, more breath stops, as in:

> I am beginning to wonder
> Whether this alternative to
> Sitting back and doing something quiet
> Is the clever initiative it seemed.

In some of the more difficult poems, "A Fly," for example, one does get the feeling that Ashbery intends for the reader to read the poet's own mind, to know, when he says in the opening, "And still I automatically look to that place on the wall," exactly what *place* means and why he looks at it. It seems more likely, though, that he intends for the poem to create its own language, to explicate itself, for later in the poem he says: "The thing is that this is places in the world,/ Freedom from rent,/ Sundries, food, a dictionary to keep you company. . . ."

Like an Ernest Hemingway hero, Ashbery's speaker either finds his "patch of light" or at least knows what he is looking for, so here the speaker is perhaps defining the place he mentioned in the poem's opening line as the little joys to be salvaged, to be automatically looked for.

There are other examples of straining the sweet from the bittersweet of experience; in fact, this is a major theme of the collection. Other themes covered in the shorter poems and then elaborated on in the title poem are the nature of time, of love, of language and Ashbery's own work, himself, what the critics have made of his work. Nearly every poem that appears in the collection expresses a kind of joy in ambivalence, a thirst for the "variegatedness" of life.

Of the shorter poems, "Try Me! I'm Different!" may make the clearest statement about what Ashbery tries to do in his work—one comes to the point in reading this book where it seems ridiculous to call the speaker anything other than Ashbery. Here are the last five lines of the concluding seven-line stanza:

> No one criticizes us for lacking depth,
> But the scandal shimmers, around and elsewhere.
> If we could finally pry open the gate to the pastures of the times,
> No sickness would be evident. And the colors we adduced
> Would supply us, parables ourselves, told in our own words.

When Ashbery is good, he is very, very good—as in "A Wave" and many other poems in this collection—and when he is bad, he is merely silly. The prose poems, though not silly, do not match the power of "A Wave," and "The Songs We Know Best" is surely intended as a joke. It may be that Ashbery aims this poem at his critics because it reads like a trivialized version of his vision, so exquisitely stated elsewhere. The obvious meter and rhyme may be his way of reducing his technique to simplistic absurdity as a little jibe at those who have found him too difficult: "Too often when you thought you'd be showered with confetti/ What they flung at you was a plate of hot spaghetti." What other excuse for this nonsense could there possibly be? In "A Wave," he addresses his critics in a different tone when he speaks of people who "appear so brilliantly at ease/ In the atmosphere we made" and who find in his life/work "charms we weren't even conscious of," which is fine, he allows, except that "it fumbles the premise/ We put by, saving for a later phase of intelligence. . . ."

The collection offers God's plenty of everything, but its masterpiece is the title poem, "A Wave." This exquisitely controlled, wondrously coherent, twenty-two-page poem reminds one that no matter how much praise has been heaped on Ashbery's head, no matter how many awards have been granted, more are sure to come. A good poem is a poem that satisfies the reader's lust for lovely things done with the language, with ideas, with perceptions. A great poem satisfies expectations the reader did not know he had, placates hungers he was not aware of until reading the poem.

This is a poem, surely, about John Ashbery—who he is and was and is becoming—about his work, about what has been said about his work, about what he wants to say at this point in his life. His

> . . . landscape came to be as it is today:
> Partially out of focus, some of it too near, the middle distance
> A haven of serenity and unreachable, with all kinds of nice
> People and plants waking and stretching, calling
> Attention to themselves with every artifice of which the human
> Genre is capable. And they called it our home.

The central metaphor of the poem, of the entire collection, is expressed in stanza 6:

> As with rocks at low tide, a mixed surface is revealed,
> More detritus. Still, it is better this way
> Than to have to live through a sequence of events acknowledged
> In advance in order to get to a primitive statement. And the mind
> Is the beach on which the rocks pop up, just a neutral
> Support for them in their indignity. They explain
> The trials of our age, cleansing it of toxic
> Side-effects as it passes through their system.
> Reality. Explained. And for seconds
> We live in the same body, are a sibling again.

The poem is a song of life, but it is more discriminating, more restrained than Walt Whitman's:

> True, those things or moments of which one
> Finds oneself an enthusiast, a promoter, are few,
> But they last well,
> Yielding up their appearances for form
> Much later than the others.

It is extremely difficult to explain exactly how such a long, discursive, cerebral poem can retain its power throughout. There is little variety really in syntax—a few short sentences to break what might have been the monotony of too many complex or compound-complex sentences, very little imagery, except the ongoing metaphor, the wave. It may be that there is some kind of pleasure in reading something that seems fairly complex on the surface but which is really quite simple in meaning. All great ideas originate in a childlike candor, someone once said or should have: It is the little child who sees the emperor's nakedness; it is a falling apple that triggers Isaac Newton's mind. Ashbery is so honest, so free of affectation, so disarmingly eager to communicate. The occasional difficulty makes the reader feel guilty and hasten back to the previous stanza or earlier poem for the clarification that always occurs.

The poem is awesomely uncynical, generously fair to life (a rarity):

> ... So a reflected image of oneself
> Manages to stay alive through the darkest times, a period
> Of unprecedented frost, during which we get up each morning
> And go about our business as usual.

The speaker does not indict the Romantics, those "who leave regularly/ For the patchwork landscape of childhood, north of here. . . ." He simply prefers to stand and wait in the present because that best

> ... suits the space
> Of our intense, uncommunicated speculation, marries
> The still life of crushed, red fruit in the sky and tames it
> For observation purposes.

The "raw state" of earlier feelings, however, can be restored: He is not bereft of them, and what is restored

> Becomes stronger than the loss as it is remembered;
> Is a new, separate life of its own. A new color. Seriously blue.
> Unquestioning. Acidly sweet.

If one must "pick up the pieces," one can notice that the pieces are "separate puzzles themselves." "It takes only a minute revision, and see—the thing/ Is there in all its interested variegatedness. . . ."

"Interested variegatedness," "acidly sweet," the impossibility of knowing good without the bad, the slippery nature of all thought, all experience, and always, and most marvelous of all, there is the poem:

> ... growing up through the floor,
> Standing tall in tubers, invading and smashing the ritual
> Parlor, demands to be met on its own terms now,
> Now that the preliminary negotiations are at last over.

Ashbery writes of love that "came and went" and of "how it keeps coming and going"; he speculates that everything may be "attudinizing," nothing more than "images reflected off/ Some mirrored surface we cannot see. . . ."

Still, there is

> ... something else—call it a consistent eventfulness,
> A common appreciation of the way things have of enfolding
> When your attention is distracted for a moment,
> ... an appetite,
> For want of a better word. In darkness and silence.

The colors, the colors of first love, or first intense love, have not changed, though thirty-three years have passed: "You have done that,/ Not they. All that remains is to get to know them. . . ." Even as the speaker rejoices in being able to stand up to the definition assigned him, "Being tall and shy, you can still stand up more clearly/ To the definition of what you are," he realizes that all definitions will one day be dismantled, and he is aware of his own diversity: "Simultaneously in an area the size of West Virginia/ The opposing view is climbing toward heaven. . . ." He recognizes what has been truly lost—the literal home where his room has been kept intact can never again have that "hidden abundance." He recognizes the possibility that

> . . . it is going to be perpetually five o'clock
> With the colors of the bricks seeping more and more bloodlike through the tan
> Of trees, and then only to blacken.

Even with this ambiguity, one thing remains the same: "Yet the thirst remains identical, always to be entertained/ And marveled at."

There is so much to sustain the speaker, and best of all, his final words: "But all was strange."

This is a brilliant piece of work, far beyond the reach of most contemporary poets.

Mary Ellen Miller

Sources for Further Study

Book World. XIV, May 20, 1984, p. 6.
Christian Science Monitor. LXXVI, October 5, 1984, p. B4.
Georgia Review. XXXVIII, Fall, 1984, p. 628.
Los Angeles Times Book Review. October 21, 1984, p. 2.
The Nation. CCXXXIX, September 1, 1984, p. 146.
The New York Review of Books. XXXI, June 14, 1984, p. 32.
The New York Times Book Review. LXXXIX, June 17, 1984, p. 8.
Newsweek. CIV, July 16, 1984, p. 78.
Publishers Weekly. CCXXV, April 13, 1984, p. 57.
Quill and Quire. L, July, 1984, p. 77.

THE WEIGHT OF THE WORLD

Author: Peter Handke (1942-   )
Translated from the German by Ralph Manheim
Publisher: Farrar, Strauss and Giroux (New York). 243 pp. $16.95
Type of work: Journal
Time: November, 1975, to March, 1977
Locale: Paris

> *As a literary experiment, Handke sets down his immediate reactions to events in and around him during a seventeen-month period*

Peter Handke, the prolific Austrian writer whose works have been regularly translated into English since 1969, no longer needs an extended introduction to an American audience. It was in Princeton, New Jersey, in the mid-1960's that he caused a small scandal by his irreverent disruption of the annual meeting of the *Gruppe 47*, a loosely bound association of the postwar German literary establishment. Controversy still accompanies the publication of his works, although he is no longer accused of the sensationalism and self-promotion that some saw reflected in the incident in Princeton. Literary scholarship has not only assigned Handke an honorable position in an Austrian literary tradition that includes Ferdinand Raimund, Johann Nestroy, Ödön von Horváth, Adalbert Stifter, and Franz Kafka, but also ranks him as one of the most significant German-speaking representatives of postmodernism in world literature.

The Weight of the World (published in Germany in 1977 as *Das Gewicht der Welt*), a journal that records Handke's perceptions and reflections almost on a daily basis from November, 1975, to March, 1977, a period he spent almost entirely in Paris, is the first of three such diaries to be translated into English. In a short preface which is regrettably missing in the translation, Handke relates how he had originally begun his jottings with the intent to bring them into a coherent work of fiction. Experience and impressions were formulated in language and brought to paper only insofar as they seemed to fit a master design. As the project grew, however, Handke became increasingly aware of the events in consciousness which fell outside this frame and thus had to be discarded and forgotten. These experiential gleanings gradually shifted to the center of his attention until he finally dropped his original shaping intent altogether. Thus freed from an organization imposed by a given literary aim, Handke's journal entries became an account of the linguistic reflexes to apparently random perceptions and feelings, a sort of running commentary on consciousness. What was lost in coherence and unity was gained in immediacy. The weight of an *a priori* system yielded to the weight of the world.

Unlike the otherworldly ballast of the German cultural tradition whose roots Milan Kundera finds in Ludwig van Beethoven and Friedrich Nietzsche (*The Unbearable Lightness of Being*, 1984; reviewed in this volume), the heaviness of Handke's metaphor stems from this world, a perceptual rather than a metaphysical weight. He fantasizes about an escape from the mental systems and structures that absorb much of the world's force and that dull awareness. The goal of his escape is what he calls an "era of consciousness," in which the human perceptual apparatus would face a landscape of phenomena stripped of symbolic significance.

Taken as a whole, the unrelated single entries of Handke's journal, most of them no longer than a few lines, often resemble a recurring situation in Handke's writing. An observer is placed in a position in which he can see the reactions of a second person, yet the stimuli producing these reactions are blocked from the observer's view. The person's behavior can only remain a mystery to the observer, or at most take on a subjective significance for him, as long as he is unable to view it in the context that gives it its objective meaning. Handke's journal repeatedly places the reader in a position similar to that of the observer. His fragmented notes rarely allow a glimpse of concrete events and people touching his life during the span that the journal covers. Few traces of even the most personally significant events remain beyond those left by the death of a friend, several sessions with a psychoanalyst, and a hospital stay. Clearly more pressing as stimuli are literature, films, dreams, fantasies, emotional states, physical sensations and the automatic patterns of everyday speech, gestures and behavior that he observes in himself and others. Handke proves particularly astute in recalling to consciousness these automatisms, thus providing evidence—as trite and banal as it sometimes appears—of what he calls his "passion for perception."

The clearest human image to emerge is that of his daughter, whom Handke identifies like all others—only by an initial. Most of the notes sparked by human contact—those with his daughter are an exception—confirm Handke's reputation as a loner who prefers hypnotic fascination with the self to superficial contact with others. The profound skepticism toward language which informs his early works also underlies his irritability with casual conversation, its vacuousness and enslavement to cliché. He prefers to be alone and declares at one point that once he had reached a state of self-awareness as a child, he knew that he had discovered an activity which would fill his life. Handke's fictional works are as directly rooted in this self-exploration and expansion as his journal. They reflect a common desire for a protean self dislodged from a constant identity, a subject wandering through a multiplicity of predications. Handke's search is not that of the Existentialists for the "true" self, but for the self as seismograph, infinitely sensitive to the profusion of earthly stimuli and weights. As with Kafka and Max Frisch, whose diaries are an integral part of their total work, Handke's journal and his fiction are mutually illuminating. Keuschnig, the main character in the novel *Die Stunde der wahren Empfindung* (1975; *A Moment of*

True Feeling, 1977), who finds himself inexplicably torn from the tangle of systems that defined his life, moves haltingly toward an idealized existence in which he discovers the world anew from moment to moment. Most lives, however, such as that of Handke's mother in *Wunschloses Unglück* (1972; *A Sorrow Beyond Dreams*, 1974), become ensnared in familial and societal expectations and are brought to premature closures. In the preface to this book stands a line borrowed from Bob Dylan which expresses the tragedy of this arrested evolution: "He not busy being born is busy dying."

While all diaries and journals are generically tied to a preoccupation with the author's private musings, Handke's perspective differs by the radicality of its exclusion of a reality that is at any distance from his immediate surroundings. The reader will search these pages in vain for objective, considered judgments on any subject that was of widespread public concern to Handke's contemporaries. When the work originally appeared in 1977, the reviewer for *Der Spiegel* magazine criticized Handke for his neglect of almost everything that had moved and affected him during that same period of time. Beyond a single sentence condemning his native Austria, he exhibits few sentiments which might by any stretch of the definition be labeled political. Even this comment is a highly egocentric view metaphorically couched in terms of physical revulsion.

Reactions to literature, the thematic center of Handke's journal, are idiosyncratic responses to texts which he happens to hold in his hands at the moment. Personal encounters with other writers, literati or cultural luminaries, the stock in trade of countless diarists in the past, are here noticeable by their absence. With the exception of Friedrich Dürrenmatt, Handke's reading list during these months excluded contemporary writers, and scarcely a hint of literary animosity casts a shadow across these pages. Earlier sources of irritation and intimidation—concrete poetry, Andy Warhol, Karl Marx, Sigmund Freud, and structuralism—are abruptly dismissed as empty catchwords of intellectual fashion. Of the writers Handke cites with approval, there are passages by Novalis, Friedrich Schlegel, Friedrich Hebbel, Hermann Hesse, and Heimito von Doderer. Johann Wolfgang von Goethe towers above all the rest in importance, particularly his novel *Die Wahlverwandtschaften* (1809; *Elective Affinities*, 1872) and the autobiographical *Italienische Reise* (1816, 1817; *Travels in Italy*, 1883). Recuperating in the hospital, Handke turns to Kafka's diaries and later to those of Robert Musil. The sustaining fascination of these literary encounters is not with the text but rather with himself as a reader of texts. Fiction as well as autobiographical writing are sources of life-expanding possibilities, of novel predications for his own amorphous sense of selfhood.

Operating on the assumption of a fundamental and recognizable boundary between reality and art, critics have traditionally mined writers' diaries for the elements of truth that lie behind their fictional works. Even though

Handke casts himself primarily in a passive role in his journal, he, too, occasionally allows glimpses into the workshop of his own art. As in any modernist workshop, however, where reality has become a highly problematical concept, the stress is more on the tools than on the concrete phenomena of raw material and art. Handke's observations are more closely akin to those of a poet concerned with the processing of experience than to those of a prosaist at ease with everyday notions of reality. As he himself freely admits, however, theoretical reflection does not rank high on his own list of intellectual interests or skills. The observations on his own writing are less important as the skeletal frame of a theory on literary creativity than as an indicator of personal values. If the writing of others enhances the richness of his own existence, Handke at times equates his own activities as a writer with life itself.

Personal journals, even those of the most famous and established individuals, must inevitably justify their publication either extrinsically, as a source of information about the author, his writings, the people and events in whose proximity he lives, or intrinsically, on their own merits as works of artistic value. In the original preface to *The Weight of the World*, Handke foresees the potential criticism which his journal as a commentary on consciousness might provoke, yet he describes it as a unique literary experiment. For the author, then, the work must stand or fall on aesthetic grounds alone. Some readers will miss that very organizing scheme around which Handke had originally gathered his thoughts and may find little literary merit in material that appears too random and too often out of any objective context. With more invention and greater selectivity, such readers may reasonably argue, Handke might have created a sequel to *Die Aufzeichnungen des Malte Laurids Brigge* (1910; *The Notebooks of Malte Laurids Brigge*, 1930, 1958), Rainer Maria Rilke's autobiographical novel written in the form of a journal. Neither narrative completeness nor coherence, however, were part of Handke's method of spontaneously reacting to events of the moment. If his journal can be granted the literary status its author claims, then it must be able on its strength to affect the reader.

Despite the appearance of being a very private work, *The Weight of the World* is in a very real sense the work of its readers. Handke judiciously addresses it "to whom it may concern," and as it will certainly not concern some readers at all, it will concern others to varying degrees. For those in the latter group, passages with a latent personal significance will tap memories, experiences, emotions, and perceptions buried in a personal past and bring them to awareness in a moment of surprised recognition. The free associations of the author form the basis for the reader's own freely associated response. The true pleasure in reading the minutiae which Handke records about his life is the pleasure of rediscovering a detail of one's own life that larger matters have pushed from consciousness. Detached from the fictional thread as a source of textual coherence and intertextual significance, the fragments of Handke's experience find an enriched resonance and meaning in the response of the reader.

The several works of fiction and the two journals which have appeared since *The Weight of the World* reflect a writer impatient with the *status quo* of his life and art. Movement and change have always had a value in themselves for Handke, although they are becoming less radical as he inclines increasingly toward Goethe's classical and late works as models. In the later diaries, his emphasis has clearly shifted from the self as percipient to the self as literary creator. This finally represents not an essential change of focus, however, but merely a change of perspective, as Peter Handke continues to be his own most fascinating topic and richest resource.

Francis Michael Sharp

Sources for Further Study

Book World. XIV, August 26, 1984, p. 7.
Booklist. LXXX, June 1, 1984, p. 1373.
Choice. XXII, November, 1984, p. 429.
Kirkus Reviews. LII, May 1, 1984, p. 440.
Library Journal. CIX, July, 1984, p. 1327.
The New Republic. CXCI, September 3, 1984, p. 37.
New Statesman. CVIII, September 28, 1984, p. 29.
The New York Times Book Review. LXXXIX, July 22, 1984, p. 10.
Publishers Weekly. CCXXV, May 18, 1984, p. 138.

WHAT'S TO BECOME OF THE BOY?
Or, Something to Do with Books

Author: Heinrich Böll (1917-1985)
Translated from the German by Leila Vennewitz
Publisher: Alfred A. Knopf (New York). 82 pp. $11.95
Type of work: Memoir
Time: January 30, 1933-February 6, 1937
Locale: Cologne, Germany

The author recounts his life as a high school student during the first four years of the Hitler regime

Principal personage:
HEINRICH BÖLL, a noted German novelist

Heinrich Böll, who won the Nobel Prize for Literature in 1972, was the first German thus honored since Thomas Mann received the award in 1929. As Mann was then identified with the best that Germany's Weimar Republic had made possible, Böll is now widely considered the most representative figure of West Germany's postwar culture. In contrast to Mann, who liked to speak of himself as a born representative, Böll has always felt curiously ill at ease in the role of a semiofficial writer in residence, preferring to call himself at best an unrepresentative representative. Older than Günter Grass, Rolf Hochhuth, or Martin Walser by at least ten years, Böll occupies a unique position in the first generation of postwar writers. He, who was almost twenty-eight years old at the end of World War II, frankly admits that he was obviously old enough to know what had happened and in what he had, though unwillingly, participated. While clearly formulating his identity as a German writer within the continuity of his country's unsavory history, Böll has become one of the most outspoken critics not only of Germany's past but also of its specifically West German present.

When someone of Böll's literary and public stature sits down to write his first autobiographical work, readers tend to expect a representative assessment. Even if one keeps in mind that Böll has chosen to write about only four years of his adolescence, the years on which he focuses—his last four years of high school, Adolf Hitler's first four years in power—make the eighty-two small pages he offers in *What's to Become of the Boy?* (published in Germany in 1981 as *Was soll aus dem Jungen bloss werden?*) seem a strangely offhanded, ineffectual appraisal. If this brief memoir at first glance looks unrepresentative, however, containing little more than the inconsequential reminiscences of an elderly celebrity, the reader must be cautioned that Böll has always cherished the deviously understated perspective of the atypical in his search for the typical in Germany's past and present.

From the very beginning of the Nazi rule, the fifteen-year-old Böll and his family appear to have been equipped with an amazing political astuteness which resulted from a most atypical combination of heavyhearted fear and lighthearted irreverence. The political leadership of the Third Reich was judged with an instinctive horror as much as it was dismissed with an instinctive disrespect. Adolf Hitler, whom Böll's mother recognized as a crazed warmonger from the day he came to power, was also caricatured by her as a turnip head. The debauched Hermann Göring, with his operatic craving for outlandish uniforms, was hated for his unashamed brutality but was relegated to the realm of farce rather than that of tragedy. At Ernst Röhm, the ravingly homosexual leader of the brown-shirted SA, the Bölls thumbed their noses with a dirty joke, while Baldur von Schirach, the head of the Hitler Youth Böll so adamantly refused to join, they ridiculed as a comically sentimental poetaster. Though the reign of terror these men unleashed on Germany was only too real and did not leave the Bölls unaffected, they recognized its power as arising from the crushing presence of "a howling void," revealing a profound discrepancy between the magnitude of the deeds and the paltriness of the actors which alternately called for chilling silence or hysterical snickering from those watching the cruel spectacle.

With a similarly mocking nonchalance, Böll undercuts his recounting of events that are widely known for their political or symbolic significance. Hitler's coming to power on January 30, 1933, Böll remembers as having surprised most people in Cologne, himself included; on that day, he was in bed, under the numbing influence of alcoholic remedies generously dispensed against the effects of an annual flu epidemic. The notorious book burnings of a few weeks later he recollects not for their cultural barbarity but for his discovery that books really do not burn well on command. Recollection of Hitler's first open breach of international law, the occupation of the demilitarized Rhineland in 1936, brings to mind how Böll's father responded to the imminent threat of war by reenacting for the benefit of the whole family his simulated attack of appendicitis which had cost him his appendix but had saved the rest of his body from being sent into the death mill of Verdun in World War I. Even where Böll's recollections rise to the level of passionate indictment, he remains determined to wrest from them an unexpected perspective. The execution of seven young Communists in Cologne in the fall of 1934 reaches its most powerful evocation in the description of the young men's reemerging religiosity as they faced death. The constant street terror imposed on the city by roving bands of storm troopers and Hitler Youths, a terror that threw such a pall over Böll's temperament of the loafer, is seen in conjunction with the rigor with which such comparatively human institutions as black marketing and prostitution were eliminated in favor of an inhuman legality.

What is one to make of these disconcertingly idiosyncratic flashbacks into history? What do they tell about Böll, what about the continuity of German history with which he wants to identify? As Böll stressed in an interview with the French critic René Wintzen in 1975, growing up in Nazi Germany would not have been essentially different for him from growing up in a Germany in which the Nazis had not come to power. The Nazi temperament, Böll is convinced, has always existed and probably always will exist in Germany or, for that matter, in any other society. Much more important than any dramatic resurrection of the historical events, therefore, is for Böll to understand why he and his family proved so strangely immune to this temperament's attractions even before total power manifested its full savagery.

Böll, first of all, does not want to have his memoir misunderstood as the self-congratulatory account of a political wunderkind. Never did it occur to him to consider himself either better or more courageous than his classmates. Still, one thing was certain at all times: his unconquerable aversion for everything related to the Nazi mentality. The Third Reich had established itself when he was sick—Böll takes this coincidence quite seriously—and it continued to make him sick, physically sick, as long as it lasted. A chronic sinus infection, which Böll in retrospect feels justified to diagnose as politically induced, plagued him for years with bouts of nausea and disappeared rather miraculously only at the end of the war.

The reason for Böll's allergic reaction to everything smacking of Nazi style is probably best summarized by another coincidence which Böll refuses to acknowledge as such, an incident which he considers important enough to serve as an appropriate preface for all of his subsequent recollections. His high school diploma, in Germany officially known as a certificate of maturity, listed his date of birth incorrectly, giving Böll sufficient excuse to wonder about the validity of the whole document and the maturity it was supposed to witness. Böll, who proudly insists that he refused to do his German duty by suffering in school, cannot disguise the delight and comfort he still takes from the fact that he had the good fortune to belong to a family in which the much-praised middle-class maturity was almost totally lacking. More than the terror and tedium of the times, Böll ultimately intends to revive the seemingly un-German charm of his family as an effective antidote against all Fascist temptations, as the nucleus of a saner, if not always sensible, social alternative.

It is not easy to describe this family, because what made it special was precisely the indefinable social situation in which it found itself. The Bölls were simply too poor to live according to the middle-class values which they might otherwise have been tempted to espouse. At the same time, they were much too Catholic and too independent—Böll's father owned his own modest carpenter's shop—to feel at home in the arms of the proletariat. Thus firmly, though by no means comfortably, planted between the classes and their respective ideologies, the Bölls adopted "that explosive mixture of petty-bourgeois vestiges, Bohemian traits, and proletarian pride, not truly belonging to any class, yet arrogant rather than humble, in other words almost 'class conscious' again." This odd, almost anarchic position between the classes also kept the Bölls from experiencing Hitler's much-heralded economic recovery. Living on the edge of insolvency, if not poverty, certainly added to the gulf which they saw widening between themselves and the organized mania around them. Though desperate and depressed, they refused to buckle under, remaining reckless and often not a little hysterical in their demands on life, even if this meant inducing euphoria by popping Pervitin pills at six pfennig apiece. In the end, their economic difficulties did for them what the prosperity around them did not manage to achieve: "in some non-sensible way they made us sensible."

As much as Böll acknowledges his personal history to be unrepresentative of the prevailing mood, he nevertheless believes it to be representative of a larger, often neglected German tradition, the culture of the Catholic Rhineland. Cologne had always remained deeply suspicious of the typically Prussian devotion to order at all cost and shared the Bölls' Bohemian distrust of all secular or ecclesiastical authority. How formative the Rhenish tradition of anticlerical religiosity and antibourgeois humanism was for the young Böll is also emphasized by the fact that the most unsettling problems of these years did not arise from his stance toward the Nazis but from a conflict within his native culture, his antagonism toward the Catholic Church. In school, all of his rebelliousness was reserved for his teacher of religion, whose middle-class version of Christianity Böll found utterly offensive. It did not take him long to recognize that this bourgeois variety of the provincial Catholicism of Cologne had the least trouble accommodating itself to the unholy system it should have resisted. Nationally, this *modus vivendi* found its most preposterous slogan in a motto which suggested that one should join the Nazis in order to Christianize them from within; internationally it was sanctioned as early as 1933 by the Vatican's willingness to conclude a Reich Concordat with Hitler. What could have provided a better object lesson for Böll's suspicion of all organizations than the formation of such incongruous alignments? Böll, in the end, could be a Catholic only in the way in which he wanted to be a German: in a highly unorganized form which gave itself the right to fuse a spontaneous loyalty toward ideals with an equally spontaneous disloyalty toward all institutions claiming to be in their service.

What, then, did become of the boy? While Böll's memoir concludes with his choosing an apprenticeship in a bookstore, the reader knows better. Something to do with books soon led to Böll's writing them. What this memoir, however, tells, more directly and succinctly than anything Böll has written before, is why he became the writer he did and why, to his chagrin, his particular German identity still relegates him to the role of an unrepresentative representative in his own country and culture. The irony of history decided that other men from Cologne were to become postwar Germany's new political and spiritual leaders. Chancellor Konrad Adenauer, former mayor of Cologne, and Joseph Frings, Cardinal of Cologne and leader of Germany's Catholic Church, set about reshaping the new Germany in the image of its quickly recouping, feisty middle class. As the odd man out from Cologne, Böll cannot resist needling the bourgeois mind of the now so perfectly democratic society of West Germany with calls for a less orderly, less prosperous yet more perceptive, more flexible, and more liberated social environment. Surreptitiously linking past and present, work and life, this volume, on closer inspection, must be viewed as an important document, not only because it gives access to an autobiographical validation of Böll's social vision, but also because it witnesses his continuing insubordination to the representative Germany of his old age.

Joachim Scholz

Sources for Further Study

The Atlantic. CCLIV, November, 1984, p. 148.
Kirkus Reviews. LII, August 1, 1984, p. 722.
Library Journal. CIX, September 15, 1984, p. 1751.
Los Angeles Times Book Review. November 25, 1984, p. 6.
The New York Times Book Review. LXXXIX, October 7, 1984, p. 3.
Newsweek. CIV, October 15, 1984, p. 100.
Publishers Weekly. CCXXVI, August 17, 1984, p. 49.
Saturday Review. X, November, 1984, p. 81.
Washington Post. November 16, 1984, p. C3.

THE WHITE WAVE

Author: Kate Daniels (1953-   )
Publisher: University of Pittsburgh Press (Pittsburgh, Pennsylvania). 47 pp. paperback $6.95
Type of work: Poetry

A chronology of the gaps between the author and those around her

The white wave in the title of Kate Daniels' first book of poetry is a pun. She uses it in "Sometimes When I'm Singing" and in "On the River" to mean a wave of water and a wave of the hand—that is, death and goodbye, separation and beckoning. Of these, separation, or the space between people, is the main theme of the book, as the various things the hand does is its main image. The first section of the book, "Bodies of Kin," deals with those to whom the poet is bound without choice, while the second section, "The White Wave," concerns those to whom she has chosen to be bound. Both sections include people who have simply come to her attention. In each case, it is the gap between the poet and those whom she takes up that concerns her.

"Family Gathering" comes before both sections and sets their tone. The twelve-year-old narrator observes the people in her family from a corner where no one seems to pay any attention to her. Just as she is separated from the grown-ups, they are separated from one another: The women do the dishes and care for the babies and keep an eye on the older children; the men digest their meal on the front porch where they also smoke and generally loll about as though they had nothing better to do or were useless. The women's hands are for work, nourishment, and protection. The men's hands are for pleasing themselves, though the hand of one of them—the narrator's cousin Jonathan—once saved her from drowning. It seems that the men are good in emergencies, but they are not so good in the daily tasks of love. The narrator is mystified by this discontinuity—by how she was brought into being by creatures who are as abstract to her as the figures in her picture book, by the fact that one adult (her cousin) saved her life and another (her father) touched her in the wrong spot (on her head, not on her legs where her scars are), and by how the children playing outside touch one another all over and the women touch the babies, but the men keep their hands mostly to themselves.

These are the people that Daniels is connected to by blood, and it is the paradox of her being disconnected from them, and they from her (especially her father and mother), that interests her. In "My Father's Desk" and "Portrait with Money," she concentrates on her father's exhaustion. It has resulted from the time he has spent and the work he has had to do as a family man, and it has made him withdrawn and awkward with his daughter. There is a photograph of her hugging him when she is one year old, but it is only a picture, and when he pats her on the head, he does it differently, at a distance, as it were, without empathy or warmth, as though the contact might damage her.

Daniels' mother also strikes her as a distant figure. Though her mother worried over her as a baby, she is in love with winter, with withdrawal, as though the season when nothing grows and death comes made the most sense to her ("Why I Don't Write You Anymore"). In "The Playhouse," it is her mother's vanity and nostalgia that cut her off from her daughter. She may beckon her daughter from the window to come inside, but her major gesture is brushing her own hair in the mirror, while her child remains in the playhouse, a fake place full of fake babies—that is, as cut off from live human contact as possible. Not that her mother is without feeling; the example that Daniels gives readers of it, though, in "Small but Strong," features her mother gripping a candlestick, about to strike her husband in anger, while his own hand forbears the gesture that will make her do it. Both of them end up not touching each other at all, confirming Daniels' image of the distance between them.

"Self-Portrait with Politics" carries on this motif with the poet's brother. Though they were close when they were children, their lives have diverged. It is not simply that Daniels has chosen a life of the mind and done well with it, while her brother has become a forklift operator, but that her brother—who has been bright from the start—hates her for becoming what he has not. This is the real distance between them, and there is no way to rectify it: He remains envious and she becomes indifferent on the surface, left with the thin hope that her own children will make up for the separation by staying close to each other in later life, touching each other as they will have in childhood.

Finally, the poet's grandmother (who appears in the second section of the book as a kind of leftover from the first) frustrates her in "Grandmother, I'm Reading Tolstoy" because she has willed herself to die, adding the remoteness of her view to the separation of her death. Leo Tolstoy may have been able to get inside his characters, but Daniels cannot get inside her own grandmother; she can only touch the pages of the book that reminds her of the problem.

Daniels does not fare much better with those with whom she has chosen to be intimate. These include a friend who was murdered, a child who died, and her husband, all of whom appear in the second section of the book.

Actually, in "Epilogue: After a Murder," it is hard to tell who was murdered, except that the victim is male. In any event, the murder is an occasion for Daniels to consider how cruelty separates people and how death confirms this separation. The hand of the murderer not only separates its victim from the living but also signifies the distance that marks a lack of feeling. In order to keep alive their personal memories of the dead, the living withdraw from one another and close up into themselves. The dead, in fact, take the special feeling one had for them away with them. At the end of the poem, Daniels, having learned from her baby to treasure love, longs for the feeling she had when her friend was alive and close to her. It is, however, only longing; the impoverishment, the separation, remains.

"Elegy" adds a twist to this idea. Though she assumes contact with her dead child by addressing him, Daniels writes that she finds it hard to remember him because she is pregnant again. Thus the pressure of life itself makes death more of a separation than it might otherwise be.

Daniels applies the theme of separation, or distance, to her husband in a group of poems. In "Apologia," her hand becomes an image for how she hurts him. She notices the difference between them: He, it seems, behaves like a baby, immersed in the troubles he had as a child; she has trouble sharing anything. "Rushing Away" features her loss of love for him and how—though moving about in the morning while he is still asleep allows her to think for a moment that she still loves him—there is no bridging the gap this creates. Boredom and regret seal her in isolation. "Geese in Snow" shows how Daniels' and her husband's view of things separates them: She is like a magician evoking forms (poetry) with her hands, while he treats life at one remove, as though it were the book that he (a slow learner) turns the pages of "methodically." In "Why We Won't," Daniels resumes the difference that she brings up in "Apologia"; again the image of touching is used, this time to show her egotism as she embraces herself and her husband's childish absorption as he puts a seashell to his ear, puzzled by the sound in it. The self-centeredness of each is why they will not connect themselves to each other by having a child.

Throughout the book, Daniels inserts poems about people she observes from one distance or another. Sometimes she projects to overcome the distance. In "Sometimes When I'm Singing," she pretends that her song makes those who are suffering feel better. It is not clear whether she has made them up or not, and there is something forced in the response she attributes to them, but in any case she expresses the hope that the singer (or poet) can connect with these people to alleviate them in their isolation. She sees the parents of the dead child touching the "smile" her singing brought to the lips of the girl. "Winter Coats," too, shows Daniels wishing the people in the subway at rush hour to be open to one another, kindly, for they are forced to touch one another anyway and they all have the same desire—to get rid of the shields of their coats. Her wish moves her to the point of projecting what the commuters are really looking forward to at home.

This hopeful note is echoed in "The Smallest Movement." Though it starts out by showing Daniels withdrawing from those whose grossness upsets her, it ends with a vision of momentary human contact—"everyone joining hands."

Mostly, however, Daniels' poems along these lines are dark. As a mythological figure, Alcestis (in the poem by that name) is distant at first, and Daniels uses her as a symbol for the human urge to escape as well as the urge to join what it is a woman wishes to escape. Alcestis does not want to be touched by the living, but by the dead, for the dead cannot really hold her. Hercules' hand pulling her back to life is hot and drives her crazy, but it also arouses her sexual passion. The waves, which come to the shore from the wake of the boats that Daniels looks at through a window, beckon her like hands to join the people on the boats. That prospect, though, repulses Daniels because it makes her feel like "a servant being called to my master" ("On the River"). The prose piece "After the Operation" features the narrator cut off from the world by blindness and her hand groping to reestablish a contact with it that is tenuous at best. As with Alcestis, Daniels goes to the literary in "For Miklos Radnóti: 1909-1944" to discuss the gap between tormentor and victim (Radnóti died on a forced march near the end of World War II); the poet who writes about the suffering he goes through because of this gap allows Daniels to see in her mind the connection between the victims of the past and the victims of the present. Alas, the connection is literary, for the victims stay cut off from those who are not victims. At least Radnóti put his hands to good use in writing poetry about the horror he saw and underwent, and Daniels forces her own hand to touch another veteran of war's horror ("Christmas Party"). It was only chance, however, which exhumed the poetry written on scraps of paper from Radnóti's burial site, and Daniels, being at a party, is more or less stuck with the gap between the good time and idle hands of the party and Leonel's story about what he has seen war do. In "Not Singing" (which closes the book as a gloomy counterpoint to "Sometimes When I'm Singing" near the beginning), Daniels again highlights the separation between herself and those she observes. She may belong with the parents in the hospital since her own child is there as the result of a car accident; still, she feels apart from them, unable to understand how the victims of the tragedies from whom she feels remote continue to live. She is thinking of human suffering as a whole, and feels dwarfed by it, cut off from it. There may be a literary intimacy with it in that she writes about it, but that is not good enough. She cannot even succor the helpless parents in the hospital who are being pulled apart inside in the face of their children's pain.

A child's view of the world, however, is at the heart of the most appealing piece in the book. "Hundertwasser and the Six-Year-Olds" is prose. That it admits itself as such (unlike the poems, which, though filled with a kind of dramatic detail, are prosy) accounts for its authentic, unforced tone. It does not bother with the current fashion of family troubles and melodrama in chatty versification. It uses the primitive painting which is its subject simply to come out for the freedom children have in seeing the world, arranging it to their own liking. In their world, there is no such thing as the physically impossible: The living can overcrowd a boat and not sink it, and the dead can go to a place where they are happy. The separation which Daniels brings up in the piece is without the complexity, the mordant edge, and the vague selfishness that run through the poems; it is the separation between the way children and grown-ups see things—that is all. No beating it to death, no moaning about it.

One hopes that Kate Daniels' next book will have more of this kind of writing. It may have a hard time winning a prize and getting published, but it would certainly offer its readers a fresher, more delightful and memorable book than they are accustomed to getting from contemporary poets.

Mark McCloskey

Sources for Further Study

Library Journal. CIX, May 1, 1984, p. 902.
Publishers Weekly. CCXXV, May 11, 1984, p. 268.
The Village Voice. XXIX, September 18, 1984, p. 52.

WILLIAM GODWIN

Author: Peter H. Marshall (1946-   )
Publisher: Yale University Press (New Haven, Connecticut). Illustrated. 497 pp.
$30.00
Type of work: Historical and literary biography
Time: 1756-1836
Locale: England

A critical biography of William Godwin, philosopher and novelist, whose major
works are An Enquiry Concerning Political Justice *(1793) and* Caleb Williams *(1794)*

> *Principal personages:*
> WILLIAM GODWIN, a political philosopher and novelist, 1756-1836
> MARY WOLLSTONECRAFT, his first wife, an author and feminist
> MARY GODWIN SHELLEY, their daughter, an author who married
> Percy Bysshe Shelley
> PERCY BYSSHE SHELLEY, a major English poet who became
> Godwin's son-in-law
> MARY JANE CLAIREMONT GODWIN, Godwin's second wife

Peter H. Marshall's critical biography is a significant addition to the study
of William Godwin and his times. With access to a number of new sources,
Marshall has undertaken an in-depth analysis of Godwin's philosophy and
novels. The appearance of Don Locke's *A Fantasy of Reason: The Life and
Thought of William Godwin* (1980) and several scholarly articles here and
abroad have indicated a continued interest in Godwin in the 1980's. An
original political thinker, he formulated in his major work, *An Enquiry
Concerning Political Justice, and Its Influence on General Virtue and Happiness* (1793), basic concepts of philosophical anarchism that were to be
echoed by most of the subsequent adherents to this view of government.
Through Robert Owen, a Welsh industrialist and social reformer, Godwin's
ideas were disseminated among the working classes, and he thus became a
major influence on the rise of the labor movement in England, one of the
most significant developments in nineteenth and early twentieth century
Britain. The textbooks and children's books published by Godwin's Juvenile
Library and written under a variety of pseudonyms went into many editions.
Caleb Williams (1794) is still of interest to students of literature, as are
Godwin's relationships with and influence on other writers, most notably
Percy Bysshe Shelley.

Godwin's life spanned a period of change comparable in scope to that witnessed by a person living from 1904-1984. In 1756, France was under the
rule of Louis XV; the Revolution was thirty-three years in the future. In England, George II was still on the throne. The future United States was still a
group of colonies, over which France and England were at war. The Industrial Revolution had barely begun. Alexander Pope, Jonathan Swift, Henry
Fielding, Samuel Richardson, Joseph Addison, and Samuel Johnson were

among the more influential authors. Transportation was by horse and stagecoach or by sail and river barge. Georges Louis Leclerc de Buffon, Carolus Linnaeus, Isaac Newton, and John Locke dominated science and philosophy. By 1836, when Godwin died, the French and American Revolutions were history, and William IV had only one more year to reign before being succeeded by Victoria. The Reform Bill of 1832 had passed. The Industrial Revolution was in full flood. Romanticism was fading: Shelley, Lord Byron, John Keats, William Blake, Samuel Taylor Coleridge, and Robert Burns were dead; only William Wordsworth remained.

Godwin's life, devoted primarily to writing and scholarship, was outwardly rather uneventful. Born in 1876 into a family of Dissenting clergymen, Godwin himself was trained for the ministry at Hoxton Academy near London, the leading Dissenting institution of higher learning. Dissenters had been tolerated since 1689, but unless they conformed to the Anglican Church's Thirty-nine Articles, they could not officially register births and marriages, be buried in consecrated ground, nor enter the national universities or hold public office. Nevertheless, Godwin, upon entering Hoxton, was both a Tory and an adherent of Sandemanianism, an extreme form of Calvinism which accorded grace and salvation by neither good works nor faith but "only by the rational perception of divine truth." When he left Hoxton five years later, Godwin still adhered to these religious and political views, but the reading of Locke and Newton and, above all, the atmosphere of freedom of inquiry and the encouragement to examine rationally all beliefs had laid the foundations of his later atheism and philosophical anarchism.

After several attempts to establish himself as the minister of a Dissenting congregation, Godwin at age twenty-eight moved to London in 1783, determined to earn his living by writing. In the decade that followed, he wrote essays, political pamphlets, novels, and history, and, his first published work, *Life of Chatham* (1783), which was well received but not lucrative. During that decade he gradually became known in literary circles. Through publishers and friends he also met various political personages and foreign visitors, such as John Adams, the poet Joel Barlow, with whom he had several conversations, and Thomas Paine. With fellow writer Thomas Holcroft and reformer Thomas Brand Hollis, he found a publisher for *The Rights of Man* (1791) after the original publisher had refused to print Paine's work. In 1793, Godwin achieved instant fame with the publication in February of *An Enquiry Concerning Political Justice, and Its Influence on General Virtue and Happiness* (hereafter *Political Justice*). The immediate success and wide sales of *Political Justice* were all the more notable when one considers that it was not only a work by a relatively unknown author but also an abstruse philosophical treatise of almost nine hundred pages. It was, however, highly topical, written at such a pace that the beginning was being typeset while Godwin was still writing the latter sections. Dealing with most of the basic questions of the time, and differing with or repudiating several widely held notions, Godwin provided something to interest, or to offend, everyone.

Marshall summarizes the main points of Godwin's arguments in twenty-four tightly reasoned pages. It is unfortunate that he has chosen to quote Godwin so fragmentarily that one does not get an adequate sense of Godwin's clear and forceful style. With the utilitarians, Godwin believed that the goal of a just society is the promotion of virtue and happiness and that the moral individual will always prefer the action which will promote the most general good. He held to a Newtonian view of the universe, with its necessary and universal natural laws, though he included mind among the causative agents. Godwin accepted the existence of "Platonic . . . immutable truths," which were "discoverable by the unaided use of the reason," as well as Locke's sensationalist psychology, which rejected the concept of innate ideas. Believing implicitly in the efficacy of human reason, he found mankind capable of perfectibility, yet, realistic about the limitations of "things as they are" (as he was to title the original edition of *Caleb Williams*), he also accepted man's irrationality, his dreams, and the relationship of unconscious motives to action. Strongly individualistic, he believed that "every case is a rule unto itself" and that moral action can be determined only by examining the circumstances of each event. Further, he challenged the idea of inalienable rights, asserting that man has "only a duty to practice virtue and to tell the truth." Society has no right to judge the individual; society cannot enact statutes which "trample on reason." Therefore, speech must be free, and society has no right to punish offenders. A moral act is one which proceeds from reason, and offenders must simply be made to see the light by their more enlightened brethren.

Godwin's concept of political organization and the state is based squarely upon his concept of the moral universe. Rejecting the idea of social contract, he sees society as originating in voluntary association arrived at by common deliberation. He finds tyranny and aristocracy inimical to the right exercise of human reason and democracy the best solution to the problem of government while making the transition to the ideal state. Nevertheless, he strongly objects to representative government and, above all, the vote. In the one case, no man can truly—or morally—speak for another. A vote of the majority simply imposes the tyranny of the majority over the minority, even if the minority consists of one person. For the same reasons, Godwin was critical of the constitution established by the French revolutionary leaders, on the grounds that the institutionalization of revolution sets up new threats to human liberty. For Godwin, the only true revolution was a "revolution in opinion." With the Reign of Terror to begin a few months later (June, 1793), his analysis was not only perceptive but also prophetic and may suggest that his immediate and popular appeal was primarily to those who were looking for a liberal and philosophical solution to what increas-

ingly seemed like the uncontrolled and uncontrollable outcome of the translation of political theory into action. Godwin proposed to arrive at a state of
enlightened anarchy, a world of small, self-contained communities in which
all citizens would have a voice and all would have sufficient but not excess
property; there would be no marrying or giving in marriage, and there
would be no warfare. Food and goods would be plentiful and less time-
consuming to produce, providing everyone leisure to reflect and to live rationally and therefore morally; this beneficial use of technology would be in
marked contrast to the industrial slavery of his own day, which reduced
workers to the status of cogs in a machine producing luxuries for the few.
Ever aware of "things as they are," he reflected that the world has a long
way to go to achieve the perfectly just society: "we are not yet wise enough
to make the sword drop out of the hands of our oppressors by the mere
force of reason."

Godwin's ideal society is strongly suggestive of both the ideal primitive
Christian community and of the nostalgic view of English country life before
the enclosure of common lands and the rise of industrialization. He also had
in mind Swift's Houyhnhnms, evidently taken on their own terms without
Swiftean irony. Marshall particularly emphasizes the influence on Godwin's
political thinking of Sandemanianism, though it was but one of many influences. These include the Roman historians, several French *philosophes*, his
contemporaries on all sides of the current political debates, and a wide
acquaintance among the leading Dissenters in London. Godwin's concept of
the gradual phasing out of the state and government strongly foreshadowed
the Marxist thesis of the state's withering away, but Marshall does not press
the parallel, as Godwin posited not collectivism but an extreme form of in-
dividualism. Still, the links between the Commonwealth Puritans and Dissenters of the seventeenth century and the rise of philosophical anarchism,
the labor movement, and anticapitalist thought are worth considering.

While Godwin did not promote atheism as such, he considered religion an
"accommodation to the prejudices and weaknesses of mankind," and, of an
afterlife, he observed that "all that can be told me of a future world . . . is
so foreign to the system of things with which I am acquainted, that my mind
in vain endeavours to believe or to understand it." For the rest of his career,
he was to be identified as an atheist, with adverse effects on his literary and
personal reputation, and consequently on his finances. Equally notorious
was his example of a utilitarian moral decision: Given a choice between res-
cuing from a fire the philosopher Archibishop François de Salignac de la
Mothe Fénelon or his chambermaid, one should rescue the philosopher,
who contributes more to the general good, even though the chambermaid
might be one's wife or mother. Despite its content, *Political Justice* escaped
censorship, the government's reasoning being that the book was so expensive as to be beyond the means of those who might be corrupted by it.

Clubs of workingmen and others, however, pooled their resources to purchase the work and read it aloud to one another.

Godwin went on to revise *Political Justice*, issuing a second edition in 1796 and a third in 1798. Among his modifications were the deletion of references to Platonic idealism and an emphasis on the role of the family and other close relationships in nurturing a benevolent and moral attitude. Though he still insisted that marriage as defined by society and the state was "a monopoly, and the worst of monopolies," he did not condemn all monogamous unions. He also clarified his distinction between the voluntary and the communal sharing of property. Among notable readers of this work who were influenced by it in varying degrees were Wordsworth, Coleridge, William Hazlitt, and Robert Southey. Coleridge, in turn, eventually was instrumental in moderating Godwin's atheism into a rather Wordsworthian religious sense.

Political Justice is the ideal of the rational man in the rational world, or things as they should be. In 1794, *The Adventures of Caleb Williams; Or, Things as They Are* established Godwin's reputation not only as an original thinker but also as a novelist of scope and power. If *Political Justice* championed man's perfectibility and his reason, Godwin's title character and his nemesis Falkland typify the irrational, guilt-haunted world of "things as they are." Both men are driven by an obsession—a ruling passion, in eighteenth century terminology. Falkland, an aristocratic landowner, values his reputation to the extent of committing murder to protect it. Caleb Williams, in Falkland's service, is insatiably curious. When he discovers Falkland's secret, the latter pursues Caleb no matter where he tries to flee or in what disguise. In the course of the pursuit, Godwin shows the reader scenes of misery caused by landlords and prisons. In the end, both men confess and repent, Falkland dying of a broken heart and Caleb living on with the burden of his history. *Caleb Williams* was avowedly political in intent, the original preface being withdrawn from the first edition because of its possibly seditious tone. It was, however, the vivid and suspenseful narrative and the psychology of the characters which created the demand for three editions by 1797. The novel also appeared in the United States and in Ireland, in French and in German translation, and is still read today.

Though Godwin spoke of "men" to refer to humankind, he was an advocate of feminism. In 1797, he married Mary Wollstonecraft, the author of *A Vindication of the Rights of Women* (1792), a marriage reported with derision by *The Times* as the espousal of a philosopher who did not believe in marriage and the author of a book on women's rights. Godwin pointed out that this was definitely a case in itself: She was to bear his child. Their courtship and brief marriage was the happiest period of Godwin's life, one which ended with her death in childbirth in 1797. Godwin was left not only with their infant daughter, Mary, but also with a stepdaughter, Fanny Imlay,

Mary Wollstonecraft's daughter by an earlier liaison. Godwin consoled himself by writing *Memoirs of Mary Wollstonecraft* (1798), only to be vilified when this frank and honest account of his wife's life and her relationships with him and with others was published.

With his lifelong interest in education, it is not surprising that Godwin chose the Juvenile Library for his attempt to establish himself as a publisher. He had, in 1801, married Mary Jane Clairemont, a widow with two children, Charles and Jane (later Claire Clairemont), and in 1803 Godwin's son, William, was born. With a wife and five children to support, Godwin needed a regular source of income. Knowing that his reputation as "a seditious man and an atheist" would prevent schools from buying his books, he hired Thomas Hodgkins to manage the firm under his own name. Godwin then wrote a series of volumes under various pseudonyms, bringing out *Fables, Ancient and Modern* in 1805 under the name of Edward Baldwin. Written in a lively style and attractively illustrated, it was a good example of Godwin's conviction that learning should be made as appealing as possible to children. Though in *Political Justice*, he numbered schools among the institutions that should be dispensed with, he thought that in the interim children should be treated as rational beings, unequal to the teacher only in experience and in knowledge, and that education was most effective in small groups or with a tutor and one student. He educated his own children at home, despite his wife's objections to his encouraging the children to learn at their own pace, motivated by curiosity, and to develop their imaginations, which he considered an essential component of genuine moral thought. One has only to consider the nineteenth century school as it appears in the novels of Charles Dickens to realize how far ahead of his time Godwin was in educational theory or developments in twentieth century education to appreciate the soundness of his views. Later, with his usual acceptance of "things as they are," he sent Charles and William to public school when he realized its importance to their careers.

The Juvenile Library series eventually ran to more than twenty volumes, including histories, editions of Greek and Roman myths, poetry (contemporary poetry as well as classics), a dictionary and grammar that became a standard text and went through many editions, and works commissioned from others. The best known of the latter is *Tales from Shakespear* (1807) by his friend Charles Lamb and his sister Mary. Despite the success of the publications, the Juvenile Library failed financially. Godwin himself was improvident and seemed never to be able to manage his affairs; Marshall attempts not very successfully to extenuate this failing.

Early in 1812, an admiring letter from the nineteen-year-old Percy Bysshe Shelley began a relationship which was to be increasingly difficult. Godwin constantly importuned his young admirer for money, and though their subsequent breach was ultimately mended when Shelley eloped with Mary

Godwin in 1814, Shelley increasingly resisted Godwin's pleas for financial support, though he cumulatively contributed about six thousand pounds. Godwin's literary reputation suffered with the publication of his lengthy and not-very-well-constructed novel *Mandeville* (1817) and even more with his attempt in 1820 to rebut the *Essay on the Principle of Population* (1798) by Thomas Malthus. Godwin insisted that there was room in unexplored territory for future populations and argued somewhat more soundly for the increase in food that the application of technology to agriculture might bring. Though his *History of the Commonwealth of England* (1824-1828) was well received, as was his *Thoughts on Man* (1831), he was near destitution. Financial mismanagement and his abrasive wife had alienated many of his friends, but through the aid of those who remained, he was provided with a government post which gave him two hundred pounds a year and a residence, where he spent his few remaining years in obscurity. In his two major works he had summarized and made a major contribution to the thought of his time, but thereafter he drifted from the mainstream of ideas. Six years after his death, a fourth edition of *Political Justice* (1842) appeared, a printing of the third edition in one volume. Appearing earlier in eleven parts at sixpence each, the work thus reached many groups of workingmen, most notably the Chartists.

By including a considerable amount of information on the historical and literary background and on Godwin's many literary and political friends and acquaintances who influenced him and were influenced by him, Marshall manages to sustain interest in a man whose life was essentially spent in writing. Occasionally, however, he burdens the reader with irrelevant details. Marshall, who is a tutor in philosophy, Department of Extramural Studies, University College of North Wales, and author of *Journey Through Tanzania* (1984), is stronger in his discussions of Godwin's nonfiction than his fiction. Plot summaries of the slighter novels are perhaps too detailed, and in the earlier chapters some of Godwin's experiences are related to events in novels not yet discussed, possibly confusing the reader who is unfamiliar with Godwin's fiction. Marshall, however, does better by Godwin's ideas, in particular in his explications of the various editions of *Political Justice*. The extensive bibliography is usefully divided into categories, including a division between secondary works written before and after 1900. There are a number of well-chosen illustrations, but the typesetting is uneven, with some of the words run so closely together as to distract the reader.

A. E. Rodway, in the preface to his study, *Godwin and the Age of Transition* (1952), summed up Godwin thus: "Godwin is among the smaller giants; those rather of an age than for all time. For that reason he is peculiarly important for an understanding of the spirit of the age; and, contrariwise, some knowledge of the age is necessary for a just understanding of the spirit of Godwin." Though Rodway's assessment still has some validity, Marshall assembles a mass of evidence to qualify this judgment. Recent scholarship in social history has pointed out the significance of groups such as workers and schoolchildren, several generations of whom were influenced by Godwin's textbooks and by *Political Justice*. Though Marshall occasionally overstates the case for Godwin—some of his works may indeed continue to be of "real value" but not necessarily of "burning interest"—he has made a major contribution to the study of Godwin and his age.

Katharine M. Morsberger

Sources for Further Study

Library Journal. CIX, August, 1984, p. 1441.
Listener. CXII, July 12, 1984, p. 24.
The New Republic. CXCI, December 31, 1984, p. 25.
The New York Times Book Review. LXXXIX, October 21, 1984, p. 24.
The Observer. July 15, 1984, p. 21.
Spectator. CCLIII, August 25, 1984, p. 24.

WILLIE AND DWIKE
An American Profile

Author: William Zinsser (1922-   )
Publisher: Harper & Row, Publishers (New York). 170 pp. $13.95
Type of work: Biography
Time: 1930 to 1983
Locale: China, the United States, and Italy

A biographical account of the childhood, education, and professional experience of two black American jazz musicians

Principal personages:
WILLIE RUFF, a bassist and French-horn player
DWIKE MITCHELL, a jazz pianist
WILLIAM ZINSSER, the author

Although *Willie and Dwike* is most easily classified as a biography of two American jazz musicians, it is a book that explores a wide range of mid-twentieth century experiences. This is not a traditional biography, in which one would expect to find such things as a thorough treatment of the details of a person's life, the motivations of his actions, and the correlation between his life and the historical moment. Rather, Zinsser's book is a selective account of certain experiences of Willie Ruff and Dwike Mitchell developed within an effective but unusual narrative form. Zinsser chooses the experiences in such a way that the biography becomes a history of a set of circumstances that existed in the United States at a particular time. Certain characteristics of American society in the several decades preceding the civil-rights revolution determined much about the events that would intertwine the lives of these two outstanding jazz musicians. Zinsser also considers the relationship of jazz to a broad range of musical types, discusses the stages of its development as an authentic American music, and clarifies its importance to the social history of the United States in the twentieth century.

William Zinsser is the author of eleven books of nonfiction. In the world of writing and publishing, he has engaged in activities as diverse as writing for the New York *Herald Tribune*, *Life*, *The New York Times*, and *The New Yorker*, teaching writing at Yale University, and serving as executive editor of the Book-of-the-Month Club. Included among his other books are *On Writing Well* (1976) and *Writing with a Word Processor* (1983). The first of these is widely used as a text in writing courses; the second is an informative, delightfully humorous treatment of the complexities of confronting the technology that has revolutionized the transference of well-wrought language to paper.

It is evident that Zinsser knows how to follow his own advice, for his profile of Ruff and Mitchell is flawless in its style and in its form. Zinsser's work is reminiscent of the best journalistic writing of magazines such as *The New Yorker*, in which selections of the book first appeared. At no point in *Willie and Dwike* does the reader hesitate over a phrase, nor does he have any doubt that this writer has complete mastery of his language and of his material.

The form of the book contributes significantly to its effectiveness as an evocation of a specific period of the recent American past. Much of the material consists of directly quoted testimonies from the two musicians, as would be found in an interview or book of "conversations with . . . ." The other part of the interview, that of the interlocutor, is missing here, replaced by Zinsser's observations on the significance of what his subjects say and by historical and biographical information that places their words in the context of their experience. The author's observations form the narrative itself, the story of the lives of Ruff and Mitchell, lives which gradually came together through a very complicated series of events. Over the years, their partnership developed into one of the most significant forces in the revival of interest in jazz in the 1980's and the preservation of that music as an art form.

The titles of the chapters of *Willie and Dwike* indicate the curious range of this biography and the breadth of the experience and influence of its subjects. "Shanghai," "Dunedin," "Muscle Shoals," "Columbus," "Davenport," "New York," and "Venice" suggest two salient characteristics of the history that Zinsser tells. It is both cosmopolitan and rural. The international experiences of China, New York, and Italy are balanced by the confrontation with the middle-American, provincial life of Florida, Alabama, Ohio, and Iowa. This is a story not only of jazz and jazz musicians but also of the influence of art on the lives of people in places as diverse as the People's Republic of China and the Quad Cities of Davenport, Bettendorf, Moline, and Rock Island. As he considers the unlikely blend of the cultural influence of institutions as outrageously contradictory as the Shanghai Conservatory of Music and the John Deere farm-implement factory, Zinsser creates a chronicle that is delightfully humorous and entertaining. The juxtaposition of the facts of the story and the clarity of Zinsser's observations produces a sense of wonder at the marvelous, remarkable thing that the world can be.

Perhaps because Zinsser himself is an amateur musician, the book is directed toward an audience that has some knowledge of jazz. Although some of the names that appear frequently—Lionel Hampton, Jerome Kern, W. C. Handy, George Gershwin—would be recognized by most readers, regardless of their awareness of this kind of music, others would be familiar only to jazz buffs or serious jazz musicians. That the enormous contributions to the history of the American music of artists such as Art Tatum, Charlie Parker, Harold Arlen, and Billy Strayhorn should be unknown to the majority of educated American is lamentable, but it is nevertheless the case. Zinsser does not attempt to explain who most of these musicians are, but he does elucidate to some extent the way in which they were part of the important social experience that he is narrating as he tells the intricate story of the Mitchell-Ruff Duo.

A significant part of the story is the delineation of the sources of jazz music; Zinsser examines the ways in which those roots were also the sources of the interest and training of his two subjects. Both Ruff and Mitchell are black Americans, and in the chapters on Dwike Mitchell's childhood in Dunedin, Florida, and Willie Ruff's early experiences in Muscle Shoals, Alabama, there are fascinating stories of the influence of the gospel music of the black churches and the blues tradition of Southern black culture. As a child pianist in the local church, Mitchell learned to "work" the preacher with his background music just as a piano man in the silent cinema would adjust his music at every point to the intended effect of the film. As Mitchell says, it was high drama dependent on the unspoken and unplanned collaboration of the minister and the musician. Zinsser's clarification of the relationship between this gospel experience and the spontaneous communication that must exist between the members of a jazz ensemble is an example of the effectiveness of his presentation. He directs his exploration of the influences on the lives of Willie and Dwike toward an explanation of how those influences have contributed to their excellence and their understanding of the art of jazz.

Zinsser also deals extensively with a question often ignored by historians of jazz—the very firm classical foundation on which this music is based. Once again, he treats this aspect of the music through a narrative of the experience of the musicians. His discussions of the contact which Mitchell and Ruff had with jazz artists who were avid fans of Sergey Rachmaninoff, Frédéric Chopin, Dmitry Shostakovich, Edvard Grieg, and other classical composers, as well as his account of Ruff's training with Paul Hindemith at Yale University, place in perspective the contemporary experience of the revival of interest in jazz in unlikely places. The book opens with the Mitchell-Ruff concert in the Shanghai Conservatory, continues with reports of jazz concerts included in classical artists series, and ends with Willie Ruff's playing Gregorian chants and W. C. Handy's blues arrangements of spirituals in Saint Mark's Cathedral in Venice.

As Zinsser deals with the phenomenon of the newfound respectability of jazz, he analyzes the progression of the music from a popular idiom to an art form. According to the convincing argument of Zinsser, Mitchell, and Ruff, the decline of jazz as popular music can be attributed to three trends: the decline of nightclubs as a result of the growing popularity of television, the exclusion of black performers from television, and the rapid success of rock music. Thus, beginning in the 1950's, the American popular music scene largely excluded the jazz music of the first half of the twentieth century. A related phenomenon, also a significant factor in the history of jazz, is the limited contact that the present generation of young blacks has had with its own gospel tradition. The revival of interest in jazz has placed this once-popular form in the more serious context of a kind of artistic expression that benefits from analysis and scrutiny. One of the most authentic forms of American music has become something that must be explained and taught in order to survive. To a great extent, Zinsser's book deals with the ironic loss of tradition, both the oral tradition of black music and the improvisational tradition of jazz.

The examination of the revival of this music leads Zinsser to a consideration of the place of art in contemporary American society, always in terms of the involvement of Mitchell and Ruff in the artistic renaissance. The chapter on Davenport, Iowa, is fascinating for its narrative of what is happening in places which traditionally have been out of the mainstream of significant artistic activity. Zinsser deals not only with the advent of serious jazz in the heartland of America but also with the other evidences of cultural interest—the John Deere factory designed by Eero Saarinen as well as the work in the foundry with the Deere employees by the sculptor Beverly Pepper.

Much of the importance of *Willie and Dwike* derives from its clarification of the role of the intricate structure of American racial relations in the history of jazz music. The death of jazz was due in great part to the racial attitudes that prevented black jazz musicians from taking advantage of the extraordinary advent of television as the primary entertainment of the masses. The eventual collaboration of Mitchell and Ruff was determined by a series of coincidences which were almost entirely the result of the strictures placed on blacks by white Americans. The information provided by Zinsser about the existence of an elite air-force base for blacks in Columbus, Ohio, about the talent agencies that catered to black performers, and about the problems of black musicians traveling through white America evokes sympathy and respect for those who, like Willie and Dwike, survived and prospered.

Even though *Willie and Dwike: An American Portrait* centers on these two extraordinary musicians, it also reveals much about William Zinsser. To some extent, the book is a memoir, not so much of Mitchell and Ruff, but of the author himself and his fascination with the lives and careers of these men. Zinsser admits at one point that his experience as a musician has been influenced by his contact with Willie and Dwike, as theirs was by their early tutelage under the jazz artists of their childhood, artists whose names were never known beyond the boundaries of the small Southern towns in which they practiced their art. This excellent and fascinating book is, in fact, a recognition of the influence that creative, dedicated people can have on one another.

Gilbert Smith

Sources for Further Study

Booklist. LXXX, June 15, 1984, p. 1428.
Kirkus Reviews. LII, May 1, 1984, p. 449.
Library Journal. CIX, June 15, 1984, p. 1242.
Los Angeles Times Book Review. July 22, 1984, p. 2.
The New York Times Book Review. LXXXIX, July 15, 1984, p. 14.
The New Yorker. LX, September 3, 1984, p. 95.
Publishers Weekly. CCXXV, April 27, 1984, p. 77.
The Wall Street Journal. CCIV, August 17, 1984, p. 13.
Washington Post. June 20, 1984, p. B1.

THE WITCHES OF EASTWICK

Author: John Updike (1932-   )
Publisher: Alfred A. Knopf (New York). 305 pp. $16.95
Type of work: Novel
Time: The late 1960's
Locale: Rhode Island

Three divorced women, each possessing magical powers, befriend a stranger in town, who practices a modern form of alchemy; the group enjoys a brief heyday of self-indulgence, but murder, suicide, and a mysterious death for which they feel responsible destroy their coven and alter their lives

> *Principal characters:*
> ALEXANDRA SPOROFF, a sculptress
> SUZANNE "SUKIE" ROUGEMONT, a local news reporter
> JANE SMART, a cellist
> DARRYL VAN HORNE, a self-employed entrepreneur

An event becoming almost as regular as death and taxes is the yearly appearance of a new book by John Updike. The prolific Pennsylvanian-turned-New Englander has managed to produce a volume annually since 1957. In the process, he has shown himself a capable practitioner of a variety of literary genres: poetry, short stories, essays, reviews, and especially novels.

His 1982 and 1983 contributions to the literary scene were collections of previously published works: a novel woven out of seven short stories (*Bech Is Back*, 1982) and a massive gathering of book reviews, miscellaneous essays, and criticism (*Hugging the Shore*, 1983). In 1984, he returned to the genre for which he is most acclaimed by the American reading public, the novel, offering as his fare a subtly drawn local-color piece that doubles as a venture into the realm of the Gothic, *The Witches of Eastwick*.

Updike has woven into his story all the ingredients of a good television soap opera. Eastwick, Rhode Island, a small New England town where extramarital goings-on rival those of the now-familiar neomythical Peyton Place, is the locale for these adventures. The heroines—Alexandra Sporoff, Sukie Rougemont, and Jane Smart—are three middle-aged divorcées who have found themselves on more than one occasion involved in affairs with married men in town. Suddenly they find their lives disrupted by the arrival of Darryl Van Horne, an eligible and apparently wealthy bachelor who moves into a decaying mansion along the shore. This shadowy figure has strong sex appeal, no visible means of support, and a bizarre taste in parties, art, and decor. In his newly renovated home, complete with sauna done over in black, the women find a new meeting place for their traditional weekly gatherings. Sex, drugs, and alcohol become mainstays at their soirees. Initial concerns about who will eventually win Darryl's heart (and hand) give way to a curious camaraderie among the women when they discover that he wants them all, at least for a time.

Such behavior sits ill with more decorous neighbors; Felicia Gabriel, a crusading do-gooder, speaks vehemently against the goings-on at the mansion. Her husband, a lover of one of the divorcées, kills Felicia in a blind rage, then commits suicide. When the Gabriels' grown son and daughter return to Eastwick to settle the family estate, the group of divorcées introduces them to the environs of the Van Horne mansion. Quietly, Van Horne begins to show favor toward the daughter, Jenny; he finally marries her. In retaliation, the women plot to do away with Jenny, but she dies of cancer. The final ironic touch occurs when Van Horne leaves town with Jenny's brother, Chris, with whom he has always been in love. Disillusioned, the three divorcées adjust to the disappointment of being jilted; eventually each finds a new husband.

Such goings-on are hardly remarkable in an Updike novel. Extramarital affairs, small-town boorishness and prudishness, men and women trying to make meaningful lives for themselves in the modern world—such has long been the stuff of which Updike novels are made. Fans of Updike who have not read this book but who are familiar with the Rabbit novels (*Rabbit, Run*, 1960, *Rabbit Redux*, 1971, and *Rabbit Is Rich*, 1981) and with *Couples* (1968) will not be surprised by this description of the action in *The Witches of Eastwick*. Updike has long been recognized as one of the most important novelist in the realm of social realism. A surprise is in store, however, for those who read the work. Updike has produced a story with a Jamesian turn of the screw. The three central characters in this book are witches—not middle-aged women who act like witches nor ugly hags who remind one of witches—but real witches.

Updike's heroines possess magical powers and can use them for diabolical purposes. They can change inanimate objects into living creatures. The charms they concoct can affect people's lives. Adding to this rather bizarre notion is the fact that Darryl Van Horne is a kind of modern devil, a necromancer who experiments with a contemporary form of alchemy, trying to turn common substances into energy. He behaves in many ways like the satanic figures from medieval treatises on the king of the underworld, conducting mock Eucharists, emitting cold semen, becoming depressed at the arrival of the Easter season. Even his name is suggestive of the role he plays. Certainly the introduction of the innocent Gabriel children into the mysteries of the Lenox mansion group parallels scenes from earlier novels such as Matthew Gregory Lewis' *The Monk* (1796) and Charles Robert Maturin's *Melmoth the Wanderer* (1820). Social realism has been joined by elements of the Gothic to form a novel radically different from most others in the Updike canon—one which, like its predecessors in the Gothic tradition, uses the fantastic to lend credence to moral and social lessons about the real world.

What goes on at the home of Darryl Van Horne is a twentieth century version of traditional New England black magic and devil worship. Sometimes graphic in his descriptions of the lewd and blasphemous ceremonies, Updike gives the reader a sense of the world only hinted at by writers such as Nathaniel Hawthorne. Amazingly, he is almost convincing in his portrayal of these characters as real creatures in service to the devil. This he accomplishes through his matter-of-fact descriptions, using his mastery of the language to create, through understatement, a feeling that the events these women bring about actually occur because they will them. Hence, when the vituperative Felicia Gabriel begins ranting to her husband about the immorality of the three witches, Updike, without authorial comment, describes how a steady stream of bits and pieces of floor sweepings—feathers, eggshells, dead wasps—appear on her tongue and choke her speech. Tennis balls turned into birds fly away from the court where the witches engage in sport; no one seems to find the event unusual, only annoying. When the three women find themselves displaced in Van Horne's life by the lissome ingenue Jenny Gabriel, they assemble in coven to create a spell that will cause her to die. Working together to bring about the end which they desire, they are apparently successful: The girl dies of cancer.

Were the portrait totally convincing, one might be tempted to dismiss this novel as pure fantasy. Updike has been careful, however, to provide enough hints that there may be another explanation for the events which occur. For example, the Puritanical Felicia Gabriel, whose hypocrisy is apparent by her actions in supporting various "causes" while ignoring her family, is clearly a woman driven by hate. Jane Smart, one of the witches, offers a telling gloss on Felicia's character when she observes, "It was the hate coming out of her mouth that did her in, not a few harmless feathers and pins." Her husband has suffered years of being ignored and reviled; it takes no witchcraft to explain his impulsive decision to strike his wife with a poker and then, in remorse, to end his own life. Similarly, the illness that kills Jenny Gabriel, cancer, is one that needs no witches' spell to infect even the youngest in society. In fact, Updike prepares the reader for Jenny's death from the earliest pages of the novel; cancer is one of the central images in the book. Alexandra Sporoff, the oldest of the witches at thirty-eight, expresses a constant fear of it. That Jenny, and not Alexandra, should die from cancer simply adds to the irony that permeates this work. Perhaps Updike is suggesting through the novel that at the heart of this society lies a disease which will eventually destroy it from within.

Like the masters of the Gothic novel before him, Updike has used the conventions of the fantastic as a metaphor to point the way toward interpreting the world around him. In *The Witches of Eastwick*, "being a witch" is a kind of extended metaphor, a sign of the life-style of the middle-aged divorcée in American society, a mode of existence forced upon such women rather than sought out by them. Viewed by the men around them as eager and available for illicit sexual reveries, by their married contemporaries as threats, the divorced women are forced to turn to black magic to retain power and dignity in a world that denies them respectability because they are no longer married.

Darryl Van Horne offers the three witches temporary escape from the society that has branded them outcasts. Like Mephistopheles, he offers them something in exchange for their souls. Each woman is an artist of sorts, and Van Horne plays to their vanities in this realm by encouraging them to extend themselves in their chosen medium. He agrees to help Alexandra market her sculptures in New York if she will cease making handheld baubles and create larger figures. He practices with Jane, a cellist, so that she may one day join a professional group. He encourages journalist Sukie Rougemont to begin the novel she has been dreaming of writing. The reader is never deluded into thinking that Van Horne offers anything substantive. The art collection he flaunts is nothing more than an assemblage of bad pop-art junk (the discerning reader may recognize in the description of this collection parallels to that "beautiful" array of ornaments that Huck Finn finds in the Grangerfords' parlor). Van Horne's musical ability is no better; his "original" compositions are pastiches of radically different tunes that, wrenched together, produce only cacophony. The women, temporarily blinded to these deficiencies by their own delusions, willingly place themselves at Van Horne's command. When he is discovered to be a fraud, their hopes are dashed.

The ends to which these "witches" use their magic at the conclusion of the novel appear at first to be grossly anticlimactic. All three women, who at various times have cast spells which defy natural laws and cause great harm in the Eastwick community, end up concocting charms to snare new husbands for themselves. Despite their powers, none lands a prize catch: Alexandra's Prince Charming is merely another student in her design class, a "leathery limping man well into his forties." Jane's magic brings her "a perfectly suitable little man in a tuxedo and patent-leather pumps" who lives with his parents. Sukie's charm produces a chance meeting with a man who resembles all of her lovers since her divorce. All three women abandon Eastwick for new lives with these men who offer not riches or fame, only an opportunity to regain respectable anonymity in a world that prizes the façade, at least, of the mundane and usual. There is strong suggestion in these scenes that this "black magic" is no different from that performed by countless other women in similar situations.

The underlying commentary on modern society which Updike weaves through this neo-Gothic fantasy makes it difficult to agree with reviewers who have suggested that the novelist is simply acting in fun (*The New York Times*) or that nothing serious lingers from the work (*The Wall Street Jour-*

nal). Perhaps more than in any previous novel, Updike displays his satiric gifts in *The Witches of Eastwick*. Beneath the layer of the fantastic lies a very real story, and beneath that story lies a commentary which Updike himself voices in a rare authorial intrusion into the novel. Describing the town in winter, he notes how its inhabitants are "martyrs": the teenagers who have little to do, the town drunk, and finally, the respectable citizens:

> martyrs too of a sort were the men and women hastening to adulterous trysts, risking disgrace and divorce for their fix of motel love—all sacrificing the outer world to the inner, proclaiming with this priority that everything solid-seeming and substantial is in fact a dream, of less account than a merciful rush of feeling.

With glancing allusions to William Shakespeare's *Hamlet*, Updike reminds his readers that the inner world is often the most important part of people's lives, that how people appear is not always indicative of what they really are.

In *The Witches of Eastwick*, Updike reveals to the reader the world of witchcraft from the point of view of the witches, stretching the bounds of reality to demonstrate the desperation of middle-aged women who will risk whatever is necessary to make something of their lives. Readers may recognize that the "sins" which these women commit are wrong, and, as Jane Smart astutely observes, "You pay for every sin." Nevertheless, while the sin may be damnable, the sinners demand—and from the discerning reader receive—sympathy. Hate the sin, love the sinner: That is the message of Christianity. Once again, Updike has shown that beneath the veneer of sex and trivial concerns which characterize his novels, he is dealing with issues fundamental to all humanity. For that, *The Witches of Eastwick* deserves attention.

Laurence W. Mazzeno

Sources for Further Study

Christian Science Monitor. LXXVI, July 18, 1984, p. 21.
Library Journal. CIX, May 1, 1984, p. 917.
Los Angeles Times Book Review. May 13, 1984, p. 1.
The New York Review of Books. XXXI, June 14, 1984, p. 3.
The New York Times Book Review. LXXXIX, May 13, 1984, p. 1.
The New Yorker. LX, June 25, 1984, p. 107.
Newsweek. CIII, May 7, 1984, p. 92.
Publishers Weekly. CCXXV, March 23, 1984, p. 66.
Time. CXXIII, May 7, 1984, p. 113.
Times Literary Supplement. September 28, 1984, p. 1084.
The Wall Street Journal. CCIII, June 20, 1984, p. 28.

MAGILL'S
LITERARY ANNUAL

1985

CUMULATIVE AUTHOR INDEX
1977–1985

ABBEY, EDWARD
Down the River (83) 205

ABEL, LIONEL
Intellectual Follies: A Memoir of the Literary Venture in New York and Paris, The (85) 451

ABRAHAMS, WILLIAM, editor
Prize Stories, 1978: The O. Henry Awards (79) 556

ABRAMS, M.H.
Correspondent Breeze: Essays on English Romanticism, The (85) 142

ABSE, DANNIE
Collected Poems, 1948–1976 (78) 192

ACKROYD, PETER
T. S. Eliot: A Life (85) 932

ADAMS, ALICE
Superior Women (85) 879
To See You Again (83) 811

ADAMS, HENRY
Letters of Henry Adams, The (84) 441

ADAMS, HENRY H.
Harry Hopkins: A Biography (78) 375

ADAMS, RICHARD
Girl in a Swing, The (81) 377
Plague Dogs, The (79) 546

ADAMS, ROBERT M.
Bad Mouth: Fugitive Papers on the Dark Side (78) 81

ADLER, MORTIMER J.
Philosopher at Large: An Intellectual Autobiography (78) 654

ADLER, RENATA
Pitch Dark (84) 699
Speedboat (77) 776

AGAROSSI, ELENA, and BRADLEY F. SMITH
Operation Sunrise? The Secret Surrender (80) 631

AGEE, JOEL
Twelve Years: An American Boyhood in East Germany (82) 854

AIKEN, CONRAD
Selected Letters of Conrad Aiken (79) 652

AITMATOV, CHINGIZ
Day Lasts More than a Hundred Years, The (84) 219

AJAR, ÉMILE
Momo (79) 454

AKSYONOV, VASSILY
Burn, The (85) 68

AKSYONOV, VASILY, et al., editors
Metropol: Literary Almanac (84) 533

ALBEE, EDWARD
Lady from Dubuque, The (81) 475

ALEICHEM, SHOLOM
Best of Sholom Aleichem, The (80) 77

ALGREN, NELSON
Devil's Stocking, The (84) 230

ALLAIN, MARIE-FRANÇOISE, and
GRAHAM GREENE
Other Man: Conversations with Graham Greene, The (84) 651

ALLEN, GAY WILSON
Waldo Emerson (82) 902

ALLEN, LOUIS
End of the War in Asia, The (80) 285

ALTER, ROBERT
Lion for Love: A Critical Biography of Stendhal, A (80) 497

ALTHER, LISA
Kinflicks (77) 391

AMICHAI, YEHUDA
Amen (78) 42
Great Tranquillity: Questions and Answers (84) 334

AMMONS, A. R.
Coast of Trees: Poems, A (82) 92

ANDERSCH, ALFRED
Winterspelt (79) 883

ANDERSON, JERVIS
This Was Harlem: A Cultural Portrait, 1900–1950 (83) 800

ANDERSON, SHERWOOD
Sherwood Anderson: Selected Letters (85) 820

ANGELOU, MAYA
Singin' and Swingin' and Gettin' Merry Like Christmas (77) 738

ANTHONY, SUSAN B., and ELIZABETH CADY STANTON
Elizabeth Cady Stanton, Susan B. Anthony: Correspondence, Writings, Speeches (82) 214

ANTONOV-QVSEYENKO, ANTON
Time of Stalin: Portrait of a Tyranny, The (82) 845

APPELFELD, AHARON
Age of Wonders, The (82) 1
Retreat, The (85) 752
Tzili: The Story of a Life (84) 890

ARCHIBALD, DOUGLAS
Yeats (84) 988

ARDREY, ROBERT
Hunting Hypothesis, The (77) 367

ARENDT, HANNAH
Lift of the Mind: One/Thinking, Two/Willing, The (79) 393

ARLEN, MICHAEL J.
Camera Age: Essays on Television, The (82) 73
View from Highway 1, The (77) 884

ARMSTRONG, SCOTT, and BOB WOODWARD
Brethren: Inside the Supreme Court, The (80) 104

ARTAUD, ANTONIN
Antonin Artaud (77) 52

ASHBERY, JOHN
As We Know (80) 31
Houseboat Days (78) 408
Wave, A (85) 1008

ASHTON, ROBERT
English Civil War: Conservatism and Revolution, 1603–1649, The (80) 297

ASIMOV, ISAAC
In the Beginning... (82) 386
ATLAS, JAMES
Delmore Schwartz: The Life of an American
Poet (78) 249
ATWOOD, MARGARET
Bodily Harm (83) 65
Dancing Girls and Other Stories (83) 169
Lady Oracle (77) 400
Life Before Man (81) 512
Second Words (85) 785
Selected Poems (79) 661
AUCHINCLOSS, LOUIS
Book Class, The (85) 52
Dark Lady, The (78) 229
Narcissa and Other Fables (84) 603
Watchfires (83) 878
Winthrop Covenant, The (77) 923
AUDEN, W. H.
English Auden: Poems, Essays and Dramatic
Writings, 1927–1939, The (79) 193
AUERBACH, JEROLD S.
Unequal Justice (77) 866
AUERBACH, NINA
Woman and the Demon: The Life of a
Victorian Myth (83) 913
AYER, A. J.
Philosophy in the Twentieth Century (83) 592

BAILEY, ANTHONY
Rembrandt's House (79) 580
BAILEY, THOMAS A., and PAUL B. RYAN
Hitler vs. Roosevelt: The Undeclared Naval
War (80) 404
BAILYN, BERNARD, et al.
Great Republic: A History of the American
People, The (78) 360
BAINBRIDGE, BERYL
Winter Garden (82) 958
BAIR, DEIRDRE
Samuel Beckett (79) 636
BAKER, LEWIS
Percys of Mississippi: Politics and Literature in
the New South, The (84) 682
BAKER, LIVA
I'm Radcliffe! Fly Me! (77) 376
BAKER, RUSSELL
Growing Up (83) 317
BAKHTIN, MIKHAIL
Problems of Dostoevsky's Poetics (85) 706
BALDWIN, JAMES
Just Above My Head (80) 456
BALLANTYNE, SHEILA
Imaginary Crimes (83) 353
BALLARD, J. G.
Empire of the Sun (85) 218
BARICH, BILL
Traveling Light (85) 923
BARKER, PAT
Blow Your House Down (85) 47
Union Street (84) 895
BARKER, RALPH
Blockade Busters (78) 108
BARNARD, MARY
Assault on Mount Helicon: A Literary
Memoir (85) 27

BARNET, RICHARD J.
Giants: Russia and America, The (78) 345
BARRETT, WILLIAM
Illusion of Technique: A Search for Meaning in
a Technological Civilization, The (80) 409
Truants: Adventures Among the Intellectuals,
The (83) 833
BARTH, JOHN
Friday Book, The (85) 307
Letters (80) 466
Sabbatical: A Romance (83) 665
BARTHELME, DONALD
Amateurs (78) 37
Great Days (80) 385
Sixty Stories (82) 776
BARTHELME, FREDERICK
Moon Deluxe (84) 576
Second Marriage (85) 780
BARTHES, ROLAND
Barthes Reader, A (83) 44
Camera Lucida: Reflections on
Photography (82) 78
Eiffel Tower and Other Mythologies, The (80)
269
Empire of Signs, The (83) 230
Lover's Discourse: Fragments, A (79) 404
New Critical Essays (81) 609
Roland Barthes (78) 730
BARTLETT, IRVING H.
Daniel Webster (79) 143
BARTON, ANNE
Ben Jonson, Dramatist (85) 37
BARUK, HENRI
Patients Are People Like Us: The Experiences
of Half a Century in Neuropsychiatry (79)
532
BARZUN, JACQUES
Stroll with William James, A (84) 837
BASKIR, LAWRENCE M., and WILLIAM A.
STRAUSS
Chance and Circumstance: The Draft, the War
and the Vietnam Generation (79) 88
BASS, JACK, and WALTER DE VRIES
Transformation of Southern Politics, The (77)
832
BATCHELOR, JOHN CALVIN
Birth of the People's Republic of Antarctica,
The (84) 91
BATE, W. JACKSON
Samuel Johnson (78) 735
BATESON, GREGORY
Mind and Nature: A Necessary Unity (80) 536
BAUMER, FRANKLIN L.
Modern European Thought: Continuity and
Change in Ideas, 1660–1950 (78) 581
BAUMONT, MAURICE
Origins of the Second World War, The
(79) 516
BEATTIE, ANN
Burning House, The (83) 86
Chilly Scenes of Winter (77) 154
Falling in Place (81) 304
BECKETT, SAMUEL
Company (81) 184
BELITT, BEN
Double Witness, The (78) 276

CUMULATIVE AUTHOR INDEX

BELL, DANIEL
Cultural Contradictions of Capitalism,
The (77) 184

BELL, MILLICENT
Marquand: An American Life (80) 517

BELLOW, SAUL
Dean's December, The (83) 179
Him with His Foot in His Mouth and Other
Stories (85) 390
To Jerusalem and Back (77) 828

BENET, JUAN
Meditation, A (83) 464

BENJAMIN, WALTER
Reflections: Essays, Aphorisms,
Autobiographical Writings (79) 575

BENNETT, EDWARD W.
German Rearmament and the West, 1932–
1933 (80) 344

BENSON, JACKSON J.
True Adventures of John Steinbeck, Writer,
The (85) 927

BERG, A. SCOTT
Max Perkins: Editor of Genius (79) 428

BERGER, THOMAS
Feud, The (84) 295
Neighbors (81) 606
Reinhart's Women (82) 671
Who Is Teddy Villanova? (78) 899

BERGERON, LOUIS
France Under Napoleon (82) 296

BERGREEN, LAURENCE
James Agee: A Life (85) 473

BERKHOFER, ROBERT F., JR.
White Man's Indian: Images of the American
Indian from Columbus to the Present,
The (79) 847

BERLIN, ISAIAH
Against the Current: Essays in the History of
Ideas (81) 9
Personal Impressions (82) 632
Russian Thinkers (79) 627

BERMAN, MARSHALL
All That Is Solid Melts into Air (83) 15

BERNHARD, THOMAS
Concrete (85) 131

BERNSTEIN, JEREMY
Science Observed: Essays Out of My
Mind (83) 689

BERRY, FAITH
Langston Hughes: Before and Beyond
Harlem (84) 422

BERRY, WENDELL
Standing by Words (84) 813
Unsettling of America: Culture and
Agriculture, The (79) 795

BERRYMAN, JOHN
Freedom of the Poet, The (77) 299
Henry's Fate & Other Poems, 1967–1972 (78)
384

BESCHLOSS, MICHAEL R.
Kennedy and Roosevelt: The Uneasy
Alliance (81) 467

BETHEA, DAVID M.
Khodasevich: His Life and Art (84) 408

BETHELL, NICHOLAS
Palestine Triangle: The Struggle for the Holy
Land, 1935–48, The (80) 634

BETTELHEIM, BRUNO
Uses of Enchantment, The (77) 876

BEYERCHEN, ALAN D.
Scientists Under Hitler: Politics and the Physics
Community in the Third Reich (78) 743

BIDART, FRANK
Book of the Body, The (78) 136

BIENEK, HORST
First Polka, The (85) 286

BILLINGTON, JAMES H.
Fire in the Minds of Men: Origins of the
Revolutionary Faith (81) 340

BILLINGTON, RAY ALLEN
Land of Savagery/Land of Promise: The
European Image of the American Frontier in
the Nineteenth Century (82) 421

BINION, RUDOLPH
Hitler Among the Germans (77) 357

BIOY-CASARES, ADOLFO, and JORGE LUIS
BORGES
Six Problems for Don Isidro Parodi (82) 771

BISHOP, ELIZABETH
Collected Prose, The (85) 121
Geography III (77) 326

BITOV, ANDREI, et al., editors
Metropol: Literary Almanac (84) 533

BLANCHARD, PAULA
Margaret Fuller: From Transcendentalism to
Revolution (79) 422

BLANKFORT, MICHAEL
Take the A Train (79) 737

BLOOM, HAROLD
Agon: Toward a Theory of Revisionism (83) 1
Poetry and Repression (77) 627

BLUM, JEROME
End of the Old Order in Rural Europe,
The (79) 188

BLUM, JOHN MORTON
Progressive Presidents: Roosevelt, Wilson,
Roosevelt, Johnson, The (81) 665
V Was for Victory (77) 880

BLY, CAROL
Letters from the Country (82) 444

BLY, ROBERT
Man in the Black Coat Turns, The (83) 439

BODE, CARL, editor
New Mencken Letters, The (78) 603

BÖLL, HEINRICH
And Never Said a Word (79) 29
Bread of Those Early Years, The (77) 119
Missing Persons and Other Essays (78) 577
What's to Become of the Boy? Or, Something
to Do with Books (85) 1018

BOMBAL, MARÍA LUISA
New Islands and Other Stories (83) 523

BONKOVSKY, FREDERICK O.
International Norms and National Policy
(81) 445

BONNIFIELD, PAUL
Dust Bowl: Men, Dirt, and Depression,
The (80) 244

BONTEMPS, ARNA, and LANGSTON
HUGHES
Arna Bontemps-Langston Hughes Letters:
1925–1967 (81) 57

MAGILL'S LITERARY ANNUAL

BOOTH, PHILIP
Before Sleep (81) 71
BORGES, JORGE LUIS
Book of Sand, The (78) 131
Borges: A Reader (82) 63
BORGES, JORGE LUIS, and ADOLFO BIOY-
CASARES
Six Problems for Don Isidro Parodi (82) 771
BOSWELL, JAMES
Boswell: Laird of Auchinleck, 1778–1782 (78)
140
BOSWORTH, PATRICIA
Montgomery Clift: A Biography (79) 457
BOSWORTH, SHEILA
Almost Innocent (85) 7
BOURJAILY, VANCE
Game Men Play, A (81) 364
Now Playing at Canterbury (77) 575
BOWEN, ELIZABETH
Collected Stories of Elizabeth Bowen,
The (81) 173
BOWLES, PAUL
Collected Stories, 1939–1976 (80) 151
BOYD, WILLIAM
Ice-Cream War, An (84) 363
BOYLAN, CLARE
Holy Pictures (84) 347
BOYLE, KAY
Fifty Stories (81) 325
BRADBURY, MALCOLM
Rates of Exchange (84) 72
BRADBURY, RAY
Stories of Ray Bradbury, The (81) 769
BRADLEY, DAVID
Chaneysville Incident, The (82) 82
BRADLEY, MARION ZIMMER
Mists of Avalon, The (84) 561
BRADY, FRANK
James Boswell: The Later Years, 1769–
1795 (85) 479
BRADY, KRISTIN
Short Stories of Thomas Hardy, The (83) 747
BRALY, MALCOLM
False Starts (77) 269
BRANDYS, KAZIMIERZ
Warsaw Diary: 1978–1981, A (84) 926
BRAUTIGAN, RICHARD
Sombrero Fallout (78) 785
BRAZEAU, PETER
Parts of a World: Wallace Stevens
Remembered (84) 668
BRECHER, MICHAEL, and BENJAMIN GEIST
Decisions in Crisis: Israel, 1967 and 1973 (81)
228
BRECHT, BERTOLT
Bertolt Brecht Short Stories: 1921–1946
(84) 86
BREITMAN, RICHARD
German Socialism and Weimar
Democracy (82) 315
BRENT, PETER
Charles Darwin: A Man of Enlarged
Curiosity (82) 87

BRINK, ANDRÉ
Chain of Voices, A (83) 101
Writing in a State of Siege: Essays on Politics
and Religion (84) 983
BROCH, HERMANN
Hugo von Hofmannsthal and His Time: The
European Imagination, 1860–1920
(85) 410
BRODER, DAVID S.
Changing of the Guard: Power and Leadership
in America (81) 127
BROMBERT, VICTOR
Victor Hugo and the Visionary Novel
(85) 969
BROMWICH, DAVID
Hazlitt: The Mind of a Critic
(85) 363
BRONK, WILLIAM
Life Supports: New and Collected Poems (82)
466
Vectors and Smoothable Curves (84) 905
BROOKNER, ANITA
Look at Me (84) 476
Providence (85) 712
BROOKS, CLEANTH
William Faulkner: First Encounters (84) 950
William Faulkner: Toward Yoknapatawpha and
Beyond (79) 874
BROOKS, PETER
Reading for the Plot: Design and Intention in
Narrative (85) 723
BROOK-SHEPHERD, GORDON
Uncle of Europe (77) 861
BROUMAS, OLGA
Beginning with O (78) 91
BROWN, ROSELLEN
Autobiography of My Mother, The (77) 72
Civil Wars (85) 101
BROWN, STERLING A.
Collected Poems of Sterling A. Brown,
The (81) 168
BROWN, WILLIAM, HERMAN KAHN, and
LEON MARTEL
Next 200 Years, The (77) 559
BROZAT, MARTIN
Hitler State: The Foundation and Development
of the Internal Structure of the Third Reich,
The (82) 363
BRUCCOLI, MATTHEW J.
James Gould Cozzens: A Life Apart (84) 384
Ross Macdonald (85) 766
Some Sort of Epic Grandeur: The Life of
F. Scott Fitzgerald (82) 782
BRYAN, C. D. B.
Friendly Fire (77) 309
BUCKLEY, WILLIAM F., JR.
Atlantic High: A Celebration (83) 29
Marco Polo, If You Can (83) 447
Story of Henri Tod, The (85) 874
BUCKMAN, PETER
Lafayette: A Biography (78) 495
BUECHNER, FREDERICK
Godric (81) 382
Now and Then (84) 624
Sacred Journey, The (83) 670
BUNTING, BASIL
Collected Poems (79) 119

IV

CUMULATIVE AUTHOR INDEX

BURCH, PHILIP H., JR.
Elites in American History: The New Deal to the Carter Administration (81) 268

BURGESS, ANTHONY
Beard's Roman Women (77) 81
Earthly Powers (81) 260
End of the World News, The (84) 267
Ernest Hemingway and His World (79) 196
Napoleon Symphony (77) 525
1985 (79) 484

BURL, AUBREY
Prehistoric Avebury (80) 688

BURNER, DAVID
Herbert Hoover: A Public Life (80) 400

BUSH, CLIVE
Dream of Reason: American Consciousness and Cultural Achievement from Independence to the Civil War, The (79) 165

BUSH, RONALD
T. S. Eliot: A Study in Character and Style (85) 937

BUTSCHER, EDWARD, editor
Sylvia Plath: The Woman and the Work (78) 809

BUTTEL, ROBERT, and FRANK DOGGETT, editors
Wallace Stevens: A Celebration (81) 879

BUTTERFIELD, HERBERT
Origins of History, The (82) 604

BUZZATI, DINO
Siren: A Selection from Dino Buzzati, The (85) 825

BYRON, GEORGE GORDON, BARON
Byron's Letters and Journals, Vol. 10: 1822–1823, 'A Heart for Every Fate' (81) 108
Lord Byron: Selected Letters and Journals (83) 418

BYRON, WILLIAM
Cervantes: A Biography (79) 84

CALDER, ANGUS
Revolutionary Empire: The Rise of the English-Speaking Empires from the Fifteenth Century to the 1780's (82) 675

CALDER, JENNI
Robert Louis Stevenson: A Life Study (81) 694

CALISHER, HORTENSE
Mysteries of Motion (84) 593
On Keeping Women (78) 613

CALVINO, ITALO
Difficult Loves (85) 184
If on a Winter's Night a Traveler (82) 380
Italian Folktales (81) 450
Marcovaldo: Or, The Seasons in the City (84) 509

CAMPBELL, JEREMY
Grammatical Man: Information, Entropy, Language, and Life (83) 301

CANETTI, ELIAS
Torch in My Ear, The (83) 827

CANTOR, MILTON
Divided Left: American Radicalism, 1900–1975, The (79) 157

CARDOZO, NANCY
Lucky Eyes and a High Heart: The Biography of Maud Gonne (79) 409

CARLYLE, THOMAS, and JOHN RUSKIN
Correspondence of Thomas Carlyle and John Ruskin, The (83) 153

CAROTENUTO, ALDO
Secret Symmetry: Sabina Spielrein Between Jung and Freud, A (83) 709

CARPENTER, HUMPHREY
Tolkien: A Biography (78) 851
W. H. Auden: A Biography (82) 923

CARR, VIRGINIA SPENCER
Dos Passos: A Life (85) 194

CARROLL, JAMES
Mortal Friends (79) 462

CARROLL, LEWIS
Letters of Lewis Carroll, Vol. One: ca. 1837–1885, The (80) 474

CARTER, JARED
Work, for the Night Is Coming (82) 968

CARTER, JIMMY
Why Not the Best? (77) 906

CARVER, RAYMOND
Cathedral (84) 143
What We Talk About When We Talk About Love (82) 926
Will You Please Be Quiet, Please? (77) 914

CASE, JOHN
Understanding Inflation (82) 866

CASEY, JOHN
Testimony and Demeanor (80) 811

CASSILL, R. V.
Labors of Love (81) 471

CAUDILL, HARRY M.
Watches of the Night, The (77) 896

CAUTE, DAVID
Great Fear: The Anti-Communist Purge Under Truman and Eisenhower, The (79) 255

CAVALIERO, GLEN
Charles Williams: Poet of Theology (84) 158

CEDERING, SIV
Letters from the Floating World: Selected and New Poems (85) 544

CÉSAIRE, AIMÉ
Aimé Césaire: The Collected Poetry (84) 5

CHAISSON, ERIC
Cosmic Dawn: The Origins of Matter and Life (82) 130

CHAMBERS, JAMES
Devil's Horsemen: The Mongol Invasion of Europe, The (80) 220

CHANDERNAGOR, FRANÇOISE
King's Way, The (85) 515

CHANDLER, DAVID
Waterloo: The Hundred Days (82) 912

CHANDLER, RAYMOND
Selected Letters of Raymond Chandler (82) 757

CHAPPELL, FRED
Bloodfire (79) 60
Earthsleep (81) 264
Wind Mountain (80) 877

CHASE, JOAN
During the Reign of the Queen of Persia (84) 252

CHATWIN, BRUCE
On the Black Hill (84) 638

CHEEVER, JOHN
Falconer (78) 309
Oh What a Paradise It Seems (83) 558
Stories of John Cheever, The (79) 713
CHEEVER, SUSAN
Home Before Dark (85) 405
CHERRY, KELLY
Relativity: A Point of View (78) 700
CHIAROMONTE, NICOLA
Worm of Consciousness and Other Essays,
The (77) 956
CHOMSKY, NOAM
Reflections on Language (77) 668
CHRISTIE, AGATHA
Mousetrap and Other Plays, The (79) 470
CLAMPITT, AMY
Kingfisher, The (84) 413
CLARK, RONALD W.
Edison: The Man Who Made the Future (78)
284
Freud: The Man and the Cause (81) 357
Greatest Power on Earth: The International
Race for Nuclear Supremacy, The (82) 343
Life of Bertrand Russell, The (77) 423
CLARKE, ARTHUR C.
2010: Odyssey Two (83) 844
CLARKE, AUSTIN
Selected Poems (77) 715
CLIFTON, LUCILLE
Generations (77) 318
COCHRAN, THOMAS C.
Frontiers of Change: Early Industrialism in
America (82) 301
COETZEE, J. M.
Life & Times of Michael K (84) 455
COGGINS, JACK
Campaign for North Africa, The (81) 113
COLES, ROBERT
Flannery O'Connor's South (81) 350
COLETTE
Collected Stories of Colette, The (84) 194
COLINVAUX, PAUL
Why Big Fierce Animals Are Rare: An
Ecologist's Perspective (79) 857
COMBS, JAMES E., and DAN NIMMO
Subliminal Politics: Myths & Mythmakers in
America (81) 773
COMMAGER, HENRY STEELE
Empire of Reason: How Europe Imagined and
America Realized the Enlightenment,
The (78) 290
COMMINS, DOROTHY BERLINER
What Is an Editor? Saxe Commins at
Work (79) 839
COMMONER, BARRY
Politics of Energy, The (80) 671
CONGDON, LEE
The Young Lukács (84) 992
CONNELL, EVAN S., JR.
Double Honeymoon (77) 242
Saint Augustine's Pigeon: The Selected Stories
of Evan S. Connell (81) 703
White Lantern, The (81) 916
CONOT, ROBERT E.
Streak of Luck, A (80) 790

CONQUEST, ROBERT
Kolyma: The Arctic Death Camps (79) 354
CONRAD, JOSEPH
Collected Letters of Joseph Conrad, Vol. I:
1861-1897, The (84) 178
COOKE, HOPE
Time Change: An Autobiography (82) 839
COOPER, JOHN MILTON, JR.
Walter Hines Page: The Southerner as
American, 1855-1918 (78) 888
COOPER, MATTHEW
German Army, 1933-1945: Its Political and
Military Failure, The (79) 245
Nazi War Against Soviet Partisans, 1941-1944,
The (80) 577
CORNELISEN, ANN
Women of the Shadows (77) 937
CORNELL, JAMES
First Stargazers: An Introduction to the Origins
of Astronomy, The (82) 280
CORNWELL, DAVID. See LE CARRÉ, JOHN
CORTÁZAR, JULIO
Certain Lucas, A (85) 84
Change of Light: And Other Stories, A (81)
122
Manual for Manuel, A (79) 418
We Love Glenda So Much and Other
Tales (84) 931
COSER, LEWIS A.
Refugee Scholars in America: Their Impact and
Their Experiences (85) 738
COTT, JONATHAN
Forever Young (79) 23
COWARD, NOËL
Noël Coward Diaries, The (83) 549
COWART, DAVID
Arches & Light: The Fiction of John
Gardner (84) 40
COWLEY, MALCOLM
—And I Worked at the Writer's Trade:
Chapters of Literary History, 1918-
1978 (79) 24
Dream of the Golden Mountains:
Remembering the 1930s, The (81) 249
View from 80, The (81) 867
COZZENS, JAMES GOULD
Just Representations: A James Gould Cozzens
Reader (79) 343
CRAIG, GORDON A.
Germany 1866-1945 (79) 249
CRAMPTON, MARY. See PYM, BARBARA
CRANKSHAW, EDWARD
Bismarck (82) 50
Shadow of the Winter Palace, The (77) 730
CRAWFORD, ALAN
Thunder on the Right: The "New Right" and
the Politics of Resentment (81) 804
CREELEY, ROBERT
Collected Poems of Robert Creeley: 1945-1975,
The (84) 189
CRICK, FRANCIS
Life Itself: Its Origin and Nature (82) 462
CRISTOFER, MICHAEL
Shadow Box, The (78) 762
CRITCHFIELD, RICHARD
Villages (82) 879

CRONIN, VINCENT
Catherine, Empress of All the Russias (79) 80
CROSSMAN, RICHARD
Diaries of a Cabinet Minister, The (77) 211
CULLER, A. DWIGHT
Poetry of Tennyson, The (78) 665

DALE, ALZINA STONE
Outline of Sanity: A Biography of G. K.
Chesterton, The (83) 582
DALLEK, ROBERT
Franklin D. Roosevelt and American Foreign
Policy, 1932–1945 (80) 328
D'ALPUGET, BLANCHE
Turtle Beach (84) 886
DANGERFIELD, GEORGE
Damnable Question, The (77) 188
DANIELS, KATE
White Wave, The (85) 1023
DARR, ANN
Cleared for Landing (79) 113
DAVENPORT, GUY
Da Vinci's Bicycle (80) 195
Eclogues (82) 185
DAVENPORT, JOHN and DYLAN THOMAS
Death of the King's Canary, The (78) 238
DAVIDSON, EUGENE
Making of Adolf Hitler: The Birth and Rise of
Nazism, The (78) 552
DAVIE, DONALD
Collected Poems, 1970–1983 (84) 183
These the Companions: Recollections (83)
787
DAVIES, ROBERTSON
Rebel Angels, The (83) 641
World of Wonders (77) 952
DAVIS, JOHN H.
Guggenheims: An American Epic, The (79)
260
DAVIS, KENNETH C.
Two-Bit Culture: The Paperbacking of
America (85) 952
DAVIS, PETER
Hometown (83) 344
DAYAN, MOSHE
Moshe Dayan (77) 513
DEAN, JOHN W., III
Blind Ambition (77) 96
DE BEAUVOIR, SIMONE
Adieux: A Farewell to Sartre (85) 1
When Things of the Spirit Come First: Five
Early Tales (83) 890
DEBRECZENY, PAUL
Other Pushkin: A Study of Alexander Puskin's
Prose Fiction, The (84) 657
DE GALBA, MARTÍ JOAN, and JOANOT
MARTORELL
Tirant lo Blanc (85) 907
DEIGHTON, LEN
Blitzkrieg: From the Rise of Hitler to the Fall of
Dunkirk (81) 88
DE JONGE, ALEX
Fire and Water: A Life of Peter the Great (81)
335

DELANY, PAUL
D. H. Lawrence's Nightmare: The Writer and
His Circle in the Years of the Great
War (80) 223
DELANY, SAMUEL R.
Stars in My Pockets like Grains of Sand
(85) 860
DELBANCO, NICHOLAS
About My Table (84) 1
Group Portrait: Joseph Conrad, Stephen
Crane, Ford Madox Ford, Henry James, and
H. G. Wells (83) 312
DE LILLO, DON
Names, The (83) 515
Players (78) 661
Ratner's Star (77) 647
Running Dog (79) 617
DEL VECCHIO, JOHN M.
13th Valley, The (83) 791
DEMADARIAGA, ISABEL
Russia in the Age of Catherine the Great (82)
708
DESAI, ANITA
Clear Light of Day (81) 156
DESCHNER, GÜNTHER
Reinhard Heydrich: A Biography (82) 666
DES PRES, TERRENCE
Survivor, The (77) 797
DETZER, DAVID
Brink: Cuban Missile Crisis, 1962, The (80)
110
DE VRIES, PETER
Consenting Adults: Or, The Duchess Will Be
Furious (81) 198
I Hear America Swinging (77) 372
Madder Music (78) 546
Sauce for the Goose (82) 742
Slouching Towards Kalamazoo (84) 796
DE VRIES, WALTER, and JACK BASS
Transformation of Southern Politics, The (77)
832
DICKEY, JAMES
Strength of Fields, The (80) 794
DICKEY, WILLIAM
Rainbow Grocery, The (79) 570
DICKSTEIN, MORRIS
Gates of Eden: American Culture in the
Sixties (78) 328
DIDION, JOAN
Book of Common Prayer, A (78) 121
Democracy (85) 172
White Album, The (80) 862
DIEHL, JAMES M.
Paramilitary Politics in Weimar Germany (79)
526
DILLARD, ANNIE
Encounters with Chinese Writers (85) 223
Holy the Firm (78) 404
Living by Fiction (83) 413
Teaching a Stone to Talk: Expeditions and
Encounters (83) 773
DILLARD, R. H. W.
First Man on the Sun, The (84) 304
Greeting: New & Selected Poems, The (83)
309
DILLON, MILLICENT
Little Original Sin: The Life and Work of Jane
Bowles, A (82) 470

DINESEN, ISAK
Carnival: Entertainments and Posthumous
Tales (78) 150
Daguerreotypes and the Cold War (80) 180
DIVINE, ROBERT A.
Eisenhower and the Cold War (82) 195
DJILAS, MILOVAN
Wartime (78) 894
DOCTOROW, E. L.
Lives of the Poets (85) 574
Loon Lake (81) 524
DODGE, JIM
Fup (85) 318
DOERR, HARRIET
Stones for Ibarra (85) 869
DOGGETT, FRANK, and ROBERT BUTTEL,
editors
Wallace Stevens: A Celebration (81) 879
DOIG, IVAN
English Creek (85) 232
DONALDSON, FRANCES
P. G. Wodehouse: A Biography (83) 587
DONLEAVY, J. P.
Destinies of Darcy Dancer, Gentlemen,
The (78) 254
DONNER, FRANK J.
Age of Surveillance: The Aims and Methods of
America's Political Intelligence System,
The (81) 16
DONOGHUE, DENIS
Ferocious Alphabets (82) 271
DONOVAN, ROBERT J.
Conflict and Crisis: The Presidency of Harry S.
Truman, 1945–1948 (78) 210
DOOLITTLE, HILDA. See H. D.
DOSTOEVSKY, ANNA
Dostoevsky (77) 230
DOUGLAS, ELLEN
Rock Cried Out, The (80) 722
DRABBLE, MARGARET
Ice Age, The (78) 431
Middle Ground, The (81) 564
DRAKE, WILLIAM
Sara Teasdale: Woman & Poet (80) 741
DREYFUSS, JOEL, and CHARLES
LAWRENCE III
Bakke Case: The Politics of Inequality,
The (80) 45
DRUCKER, PETER F.
Unseen Revolution, The (77) 872
DRURY, ALLEN
God Against the Gods, A (77) 332
Return to Thebes (78) 708
DUBERMAN, MARTIN
Visions of Kerouac (78) 878
DUBIE, NORMAN
Selected and New Poems (84) 761
DUBOFSKY, MELVIN, and WARREN VAN
TINE
John L. Lewis: A Biography (78) 478
DUBUS, ANDRE
Times Are Never So Bad, The (84) 873
DUNCAN, ROBERT
Ground Work: Before the War (85) 329

DUNNE, GERALD T.
Hugo Black and the Judicial Revolution (78)
418
DUNNE, JOHN GREGORY
Dutch Shea, Jr. (83) 216
DUPUY, T. N.
Genius for War: The German Army and
General Staff, 1807–1945, A (78) 332
DURANT, WILL, and ARIEL DURANT
Age of Napoleon, The (77) 33
Dual Autobiography, A (78) 280
DURRELL, LAWRENCE
Sicilian Carousel (78) 771

EAGLETON, TERRY
Literary Theory: An Introduction (84) 464
EATON, CLEMENT
Jefferson Davis: The Sphinx of the
Confederacy (78) 464
EBAN, ABBA
Abba Eban: An Autobiography (78) 1
EBERHART, RICHARD
Of Poetry and Poets (80) 610
ECKHOLM, ERIK P.
Losing Ground (77) 450
ECO, UMBERTO
Name of the Rose, The (84) 598
Postscript to The Name of the Rose (85) 697
Semiotics and the Philosophy of
Language (85) 807
EDEL, LEON
Bloomsbury: A House of Lions (80) 88
Stuff of Sleep and Dreams: Experiments in
Literary Psychology (83) 765
EDEN, ANTHONY
Another World, 1897–1917 (78) 59
EDEY, MAITLAND A., and DONALD C.
JOHANSON
Lucy: The Beginnings of Humankind (82) 514
EDWARDS, G. B.
Book of Ebenezer Le Page, The (82) 59
EHRENPREIS, IRVIN
Swift, the Man, His Works, and the Age: Vol.
III, Dean Swift (84) 849
EIKENBAUM, BORIS
Tolstoi in the Sixties (83) 816
Tolstoi in the Seventies (83) 821
EINSTEIN, ALBERT
Albert Einstein: The Human Side, New
Glimpses from His Archives (80) 19
EISENHOWER, DWIGHT DAVID
Eisenhower Diaries, The (82) 199
ELEY, GEOFF
Reshaping the German Right: Radical
Nationalism and Political Change After
Bismarck (81) 682
ELIADE, MIRCEA
Ordeal by Labyrinth: Conversations with
Claude-Henri Rocquet (83) 572
ELKIN, STANLEY
George Mills (83) 273
ELLEDGE, SCOTT
E. B. White: A Biography (85) 209
EMERSON, RALPH WALDO
Emerson in His Journals (83) 224

CUMULATIVE AUTHOR INDEX

EMMERSON, JAMES THOMAS
  Rhineland Crisis, The   (78) 712
ENCHI, FUMIKO
  Masks   (84) 514
ENDO, SHUSAKU
  Samurai, The   (83) 674
  Wonderful Fool   (84) 967
ENGELS, FRIEDRICH, and KARL MARX
  Selected Letters: The Personal
    Correspondence, 1844–1877   (83) 722
ENGELS, JOHN
  Blood Mountain   (78) 117
EPSTEIN, JOSEPH
  Familiar Territory: Observations on American
    Life   (80) 310
  Middle of My Tether: Familiar Essays,
    The   (84) 539
EPSTEIN, LESLIE
  King of the Jews   (80) 458
  Regina   (83) 650
ERDRICH, LOUISE
  Love Medicine   (85) 584
ERICKSON, CAROLLY
  Bloody Mary   (79) 64
  Great Harry   (81) 391
ESSLIN, MARTIN
  Antonin Artaud   (78) 68
EVANS, SARA
  Personal Politics: The Roots of Women's
    Liberation in the Civil Rights Movement and
    the New Left   (80) 655
EWALD, WILLIAM BRAGG, JR.
  Eisenhower the President: Crucial Days, 1951–
    1960   (82) 205
EWEN, DAVID
  All the Years of American Popular Music: A
    Comprehensive History   (78) 33

FAIRFIELD, CICILY. See WEST, REBECCA
FARAGO, LADISLAS
  Last Days of Patton, The   (82) 428
FARRAR, L. L., JR.
  Arrogance and Anxiety: The Ambivalence of
    German Power, 1848–1914   (82) 22
FAST, HOWARD
  Second Generation   (79) 648
FAULKNER, WILLIAM
  Faulkner, a Comprehensive Guide to the
    Brodsky Collection: Vol. II, The
    Letters   (85) 266
  Uncollected Stories of William Faulkner
    (80) 838
FEIN, HELEN
  Accounting for Genocide: National Responses
    and Jewish Victimization During the
    Holocaust   (80) 10
FELDMAN, IRVING
  Leaping Clear   (77) 408
  New and Selected Poems   (80) 580
FENSCH, THOMAS
  Steinbeck and Covici: The Story of a
    Friendship   (80) 780
FENTON, JAMES
  Children in Exile: Poems, 1968–1984   (85) 96
FERLINGHETTI, LAWRENCE
  Endless Life: Selected Poems   (82) 229

FEUERLIGHT, ROBERTA STRAUSS
  Justice Crucified: The Story of Sacco and
    Vanzetti   (78) 487
FIEDLER, LESLIE
  Freaks: Myths and Images of the Secret
    Self   (79) 235
  What Was Literature: Class Culture and Mass
    Society   (83) 884
FIELD, ANDREW
  Djuna: The Life and Times of Djuna
    Barnes   (84) 234
  Nabokov: His Life in Part   (78) 590
FIELD, GEOFFREY G.
  Evangelist of Race: The Germanic Vision of
    Houston Stewart Chamberlain   (82) 256
FIGES, EVA
  Light   (84) 459
  Waking   (83) 869
FINLEY, M. I.
  Ancient Slavery and Modern Ideology   (81) 43
FINNEY, BRIAN
  Christopher Isherwood: A Critical
    Biography   (80) 145
FISHER, M. F. K.
  Sister Age   (84) 792
FITCH, NOEL RILEY
  Sylvia Beach and the Lost Generation: A
    History of Literary Paris in the Twenties
    and Thirties   (84) 854
FITZGERALD, F. SCOTT
  Price Was High: The Last Uncollected Stories
    of F. Scott Fitzgerald, The   (80) 693
FLANAGAN, THOMAS
  Year of the French, The   (80) 880
FLAUBERT, GUSTAVE
  Letters of Gustave Flaubert, 1830–1857,
    The   (81) 494
  Letters of Gustave Flaubert, 1857–1880,
    The   (83) 395
FLEMING, THOMAS
  Officers' Wives, The   (82) 570
FLEXNER, JAMES THOMAS
  Young Hamilton: A Biography, The   (79) 922
FLINT, RONALD
  Resuming Green: Selected Poems, 1965–
    1982   (84) 731
FONER, ERIC
  Politics and Ideology in the Age of the Civil
    War   (81) 661
FOOT, M. R. D.
  Resistance: European Resistance to Nazism,
    1940–1945   (78) 704
FORBATH, PETER
  River Congo, The   (78) 717
FORBIS, WILLIAM H.
  Fall of the Peacock Throne: The Story of
    Iran   (81) 297
FORCHÉ, CAROLYN
  Country Between Us, The   (83) 161
  Gathering the Tribes   (77) 314
FORD, ELAINE
  Missed Connections   (84) 552
FORD, FORD MADOX
  Presence of Ford Madox Ford: A Memorial
    Volume of Essays, Poems, and Memoirs,
    The   (82) 652

FORD, FORD MADOX, and EZRA POUND
Pound/Ford: The Story of a Literary
Friendship (83) 621
FORD, JESSE HILL
Raider, The (77) 642
FORREST, LEON
Two Wings to Veil My Face (85) 946
FORSTER, E. M.
Selected Letters of E. M. Forster, Vol. I: 1879–
1920 (84) 773
FOUCAULT, MICHEL
Language, Counter-Memory, Practice:
Selected Essays and Interviews (78) 504
FOWLER, WILLIAM M., JR.
Baron of Beacon Hill: A Biography of John
Hancock, The (81) 66
FOWLES, JOHN
Daniel Martin (78) 225
Mantissa (83) 443
FRAME, JANET
Living in the Maniototo (80) 502
FRANCIS, DICK
Banker (84) 76
Twice Shy (83) 841
FRANK, JOSEPH
Dostoevsky (77) 236
Dostoevsky: The Years of Ordeal, 1850–
1859 (84) 244
FRASER, ANTONIA
Royal Charles: Charles II and the
Restoration (80) 732
FRASER, NICHOLAS, and MARYSA
NAVARRO
Eva Perón (82) 249
FREDERICKSON, GEORGE M.
White Supremacy: A Comparative Study in
American and South African History (82)
937
FREIDENBERG, OLGA, and BORIS
PASTERNAK
Correspondence of Boris Pasternak and Olga
Freidenberg, 1910–1954, The (83) 147
FRENCH, MARILYN
Shakespeare's Division of Experience (82)
767
FRIEDAN, BETTY
Second Stage, The (82) 752
FRISCH, MAX
Bluebeard (84) 105
Man in the Holocene (81) 545
FRYE, NORTHROP
Great Code: The Bible and Literature,
The (83) 306
Northrop Frye on Culture and Literature
(79) 496
FRYE, ROLAND MUSHAT
Renaissance *Hamlet*: Issues and Responses in
1600, The (85) 742
FUCHS, DANIEL
Saul Bellow, Vision and Revision (85) 776
FUENTES, CARLOS
Burnt Water (81) 103
Distant Relations (83) 200
Terra Nostra (77) 807
FUGARD, ATHOL
Notebooks: 1960–1977 (85) 653

FULLER, CHARLES
Soldier's Play, A (83) 751
FULLER, JACK
Fragments (85) 301
FULLER, JOHN
Flying to Nowhere (85) 297
FULLER, MARGARET
Letters of Margaret Fuller, The (84) 449
Letters of Margaret Fuller, Vol. III: 1842–1844,
The (85) 559
FURBANK, P. N.
E. M. Forster: A Life (79) 183
FUSSELL, PAUL
Abroad (81) 5
Boy Scout Handbook and Other Observations,
The (83) 70

GAGLIARDO, JOHN G.
Reich and Nation: The Holy Roman Empire as
Idea and Reality, 1763–1806 (81) 678
GAILLARD, FRYE
Watermelon Wine: The Spirit of Country
Music (79) 835
GAINES, ERNEST J.
Gathering of Old Men, A (84) 323
In My Father's House (79) 311
GALBRAITH, JOHN KENNETH
Age of Uncertainty, The (78) 23
Life in Our Times: Memoirs, A (82) 458
GALL, SALLY M., and M.L. ROSENTHAL
Modern Poetic Sequence: The Genius of
Modern Poetry, The (84) 570
GALLOWAY, DAVID DARRYL
Family Album, A (79) 204
GARCÍA LORCA, FEDERICO
Selected Letters (84) 768
GARCÍA MARQUEZ, GABRIEL
Autumn of the Patriarch, The (77) 77
Chronicle of a Death Foretold (84) 163
In Evil Hour (80) 421
Innocent Eréndira and Other Stories (79) 318
GARDNER, JOHN
Art of Fiction: Notes on Craft for Young
Writers, The (85) 22
Mickelsson's Ghosts (83) 475
October Light (77) 580
On Becoming a Novelist (84) 633
On Moral Fiction (79) 511
GARNETT, DAVID
Great Friends: Portraits of Seventeen
Writers (81) 386
GARRETT, GEORGE
Collected Poems of George Garrett, The
(85) 116
James Jones (85) 484
Luck's Shining Child: A Miscellany of Poems &
Verses (82) 509
Succession: A Novel of Elizabeth and James,
The (84) 842
GARSIDE, ROGER
Coming Alive: China After Mao (82) 111
GASS, WILLIAM HOWARD
On Being Blue (77) 594
World Within the Word, The (79) 913
GATES, JOHN D.
du Pont Family, The (80) 240
GATZKE, HANS W.
Germany and the United States: A "Special
Relationship?" (81) 368

CUMULATIVE AUTHOR INDEX

GAY, PETER
Art and Act (77) 67

GEERAERTS, JEF
Black Ulysses (79) 55

GEIST, BENJAMIN, and MICHAEL BRECHER
Decisions in Crisis: Israel, 1967 and 1973 (81) 228

GHISELIN, BREWSTER
Windrose: Poems 1929–1979 (81) 935

GIBBONS, REGINALD, editor
Poet's Work: 29 Masters of 20th Century Poetry on the Origins and Practice of Their Art, The (80) 668

GILBERT, MARTIN, editor
Winston S. Churchill: The Prophet of Truth, Vol. V: 1922–1939 (78) 917

GILBERT, SANDRA M.,and SUSAN GUBAR
Madwoman in the Attic: The Woman Writer and the Nineteenth-Century Literary Imagination, The (80) 512

GILCHRIST, ELLEN
Victory Over Japan (85) 973

GILDNER, GARY
Runner, The (79) 613

GILMAN, RICHARD
Decadence: The Strange Life of an Epithet (80) 210

GINSBERG, ALLEN
Collected Poems, 1947–1980 (85) 110
Journals: Early Fifties Early Sixties (78) 483

GINZBURG, EUGENIA SEMENOVA
Within the Whirlwind (82) 963

GINZBURG, NATALIA
Family Sayings (85) 255

GIVNER, JOAN
Katherine Anne Porter: A Life (83) 376

GLENDINNING, VICTORIA
Edith Sitwell: A Unicorn Among Lions (82) 190
Elizabeth Bowen (79) 179
Vita: The Life of V. Sackville-West (84) 916

GODDEN, RUMER
Five for Sorrow, Ten for Joy (80) 325
Peacock Spring, The (77) 614

GODWIN, GAIL
Mr. Gedford and the Muses (84) 556
Mother and Two Daughters, A (83) 501

GOEBBELS, JOSEPH
Final Entries, 1945: The Diaries of Joseph Goebbels (79) 212

GOLAN, MATTI
Secret Conversations of Henry Kissinger, The (77) 709

GOLD, HERBERT
Family: A Novel in the Form of a Memoir (82) 267
He/She (81) 426

GOLDBERG, MICHEL
Namesake (83) 518

GOLDING, WILLIAM
Darkness Visible (80) 184
Moving Target, A (83) 506
Paper Men, The (85) 672
Rites of Passage (81) 690

GOLDSTEIN, THOMAS
Dawn of Modern Science: From the Arabs to Leonardo da Vinci (81) 690

GORDIMER, NADINE
Burgers Daughter (80) 123
July's People (82) 417
Selected Stories (77) 725
Soldier's Embrace, A (81) 745
Something Out There (85) 844

GORDON, CAROLINE
Collected Stories of Caroline Gordon, The (82) 106

GORDON, MARY
Company of Women, The (82) 115
Final Payments (79) 218

GORDON, SUZANNE
Lonely in America (77) 455

GORNICK, VIVIAN
Essays in Feminism (80) 302

GOSNELL, HAROLD F.
Truman's Crises: A Political Biography of Harry S Truman (81) 836

GOULD, STEPHEN JAY
Mismeasure of Man, The (82) 527
Panda's Thumb: Further Reflections in Natural History, The (81) 640

GRADE, CHAIM
Rabbis and Wives (83) 630

GRAHAM, JORIE
Erosion (84) 279

GRAHAM-CAMPBELL, JAMES
Viking World, The (81) 873

GRASS, GÜNTER
Flounder, The (79) 226
Headbirths: Or, The Germans Are Dying Out (83) 336
Meeting at Telgte, The (82) 523

GRAY, FRANCINE DU PLESSIX
Lovers and Tyrants (77) 455

GREEN, MARTIN
Children of the Sun (77) 144
Transatlantic Patterns: Cultural Comparisons of England with America (78) 860

GREENE, GRAHAM
Doctor Fischer of Geneva or the Bomb Party (81) 244
Human Factor, The (79) 286
Monsignor Quixote (83) 489
Ways of Escape (82) 918

GREENE, GRAHAM, and MARIE-FRANÇOISE ALLAIN
Other Man: Conversations with Graham Greene, The (84) 651

GREER, GERMAINE
Obstacle Race: The Fortunes of Women Painters and Their Work, The (80) 600

GRIFFITHS, TREVOR
Comedians (77) 174

GRIGG, JOHN
1943: The Victory That Never Was (81) 619

GROSSER, ALFRED
Western Alliance: European-American Relations Since 1945, The (81) 911

GROSSKURTH, PHYLLIS
Havelock Ellis: A Biography (81) 412

GUBAR, SUSAN, and SANDRA M. GILBERT
Madwoman in the Attic: The Woman Writer and the Nineteenth-Century Literary Imagination, The (80) 512

GUERARD, ALBERT J.
Triumph of the Novel, The (77) 847
GUEST, BARBARA
Herself Defined: The Poet H. D. and Her
World (85) 374
GUEST, JUDITH
Ordinary People (77) 597
GUILLERMAZ, JACQUES
Chinese Communist Party in Power, 1949–1976,
The (78) 174
GUNN, THOM
Selected Poems, 1950–1975 (80) 750
GUSTAFSSON, LARS
Tennis Players, The (84) 866
GUTMAN, HERBERT G.
Black Family in Slavery and Freedom, 1750–
1925, The (77) 87

HADFIELD, ALICE MARY
Charles Williams: An Exploration of His Life
and Work (84) 153
HAFFENDEN, JOHN
Life of John Berryman, The (83) 410
HAFFNER, SEBASTIAN
Meaning of Hitler, The (80) 528
HÄGG, TOMAS
Novel in Antiquity, The (84) 618
HAILE, H. G.
Luther: An Experiment in Biography (81) 535
HAINES, JOHN
News from the Glacier: Selected Poems, 1960–
1980 (83) 527
HALBERSTAM, DAVID
Powers That Be, The (80) 684
HALEY, ALEX
Roots (77) 690
HALL, DONALD
Remembering Poets: Reminiscences and
Opinions (79) 584
HALL, OAKLEY
Bad Lands, The (79) 47
HALLE, LOUIS J.
Out of Chaos (78) 626
HALPERIN, JOHN
Gissing: A Life in Books (83) 283
Life of Jane Austen, The (85) 564
HAMILTON, IAN
Robert Lowell: A Biography (83) 654
HAMILTON, NIGEL
Brothers Mann: The Lives of Heinrich and
Thomas Mann, 1871–1950 and 1875–1955,
The (80) 119
Monty: The Making of a General, 1887–
1942 (82) 531
HAMRICK, S. J. See TYLER, W. T.
HANDKE, PETER
Left-Handed Woman, The (79) 363
Moment of True Feeling, A (78) 585
Weight of the World, The (85) 1013
HANKLA, CATHRYN
Phenomena (84) 686
HANNAH, BARRY
Airships (79) 5
Ray (81) 674

HANSEN, RON
Assassination of Jesse James by the Coward
Robert Ford, The (84) 54
HARDWICK, ELIZABETH
Bartleby in Manhattan (84) 82
Sleepless Nights (80) 768
HARDY, BARBARA
Advantage of Lyric: Essays on Feeling in
Poetry, The (78) 11
HARRINGTON, MICHAEL
Twilight of Capitalism, The (77) 857
HARRIS, MACDONALD
Yukiko (78) 942
HARRIS, MARVIN
Cultural Materialism: The Struggle for a
Science of Culture (80) 170
HARRIS, RICHARD
Freedom Spent (77) 304
HARRISON, GILBERT A.
Enthusiast: A Life of Thornton Wilder,
The (84) 272
HARRISON, GORDON
Mosquitoes, Malaria and Man: A History of the
Hostilities Since 1880 (79) 466
HARRISON, JIM
Legends of the Fall (80) 462
Selected & New Poems: 1961–1981 (83) 718
HARTRICH, EDWIN
Fourth and Richest Reich, The (81) 353
HARVEY, NANCY LENZ
Thomas Cardinal Wolsey (81) 800
HARWIT, MARTIN
Cosmic Discovery: The Search, Scope, and
Heritage of Astronomy (82) 135
HASLIP, JOAN
Catherine the Great (78) 155
HASS, ROBERT
Twentieth Century Pleasures: Prose on
Poetry (85) 941
HASSLER, JON
Love Hunter, The (82) 499
HAVENS, THOMAS R. H.
Valley of Darkness: The Japanese People and
World War Two (79) 804
HAWKE, DAVID FREEMAN
John D.: The Founding Father of the
Rockefellers (81) 459
HAWKES, JOHN
Passion Artist, The (80) 644
Travesty (77) 837
HAYDEN, ROBERT
Angle of Ascent (77) 48
HAYMAN, RONALD
Brecht (84) 118
Kafka: A Biography (83) 372
HAYWARD, MAX
Writers in Russia: 1917–1978 (84) 977
HAZZARD, SHIRLEY
Transit of Venus, The (81) 822
H. D.
End to Torment: A Memoir of Ezra Pound by
H. D. (80) 290
Gift, The (83) 278
HERmione (82) 349

HEANEY, SEAMUS
Field Work (80) 315
Station Island (85) 865
HEAT-MOON, WILLIAM LEAST
Blue Highways: A Journey into America (84) 95
HÉBERT, ANNE
In the Shadow of the Wind (85) 436
HECHT, ANTHONY
Millions of Strange Shadows (78) 572
Venetian Vespers, The (80) 841
HECKMANN, WOLF
Rommel's War in Africa (82) 700
HEILBUT, ANTHONY
Exiled in Paradise: German Refugee Artists and Intellectuals in America, from the 1930's to the Present (84) 284
HELLER, ERICH
In the Age of Prose: Literary and Philosophical Essays (85) 431
HELLER, JOSEPH
Good as Gold (80) 372
HELLMAN, LILLIAN
Scoundrel Time (77) 702
HELPRIN, MARK
Ellis Island and Other Stories (82) 219
Winter's Tale (84) 954
HEMINGWAY, ERNEST
Ernest Hemingway: Selected Letters, 1917–1961 (82) 245
HEMINGWAY, MARY WELSH
How It Was (77) 362
HEMMINGS, F. W. J.
Baudelaire the Damned: A Biography (83) 49
HENDERSON, BILL, editor
Pushcart Prize, III: Best of the Small Presses, The (79) 565
HENDRICKSON, ROBERT A.
Rise and Fall of Alexander Hamilton, The (82) 687
HENLEY, BETH
Crimes of the Heart (83) 165
HENSON, ROBERT
Transports and Disgraces (81) 827
HERBERT, FRANK
Children of Dune (77) 139
God Emperor of Dune (82) 329
White Plague, The (83) 900
HERM, GERHARD
Celts: The People Who Came Out of the Darkness, The (78) 164
HERR, MICHAEL
Dispatches (78) 272
HERRIOT, JAMES
Lord God Made Them All, The (82) 480
HERSEY, JOHN
Walnut Door, The (78) 883
HERZSTEIN, ROBERT EDWIN
War That Hitler Won: The Most Infamous Propaganda Campaign in History, The (79) 823
HEYMANN, C. DAVID
Ezra Pound (77) 264
HIBBERT, CHRISTOPHER
Days of the French Revolution, The (81) 222
HIGHAM, CHARLES
Adventures of Conan Doyle, The (77) 22

HIGHWATER, JAMAKE
Anpao: An American Indian Odyssey (78) 63
Journey to the Sky (79) 335
HILDESHEIMER, WOLFGANG
Marbot (84) 498
HILL, CHRISTOPHER
Milton and the English Revolution (79) 444
HILL, GEOFFREY
Somewhere Is Such a Kingdom (77) 758
HILL, MELVYN A., editor
Hannah Arendt: The Recovery of the Public World (80) 395
HILLESUM, ETTY
Interrupted Life: The Diaries of Etty Hillesum, 1941–1943, An (85) 456
HILLGRUBER, ANDREAS
Germany and the Two World Wars (82) 321
HINGLEY, RONALD
New Life of Anton Chekhov, A (77) 543
Nightingale Fever: Russian Poets in Revolution (82) 555
Pasternak (84) 673
HOAGLAND, EDWARD
Edward Hoagland Reader, The (80) 260
Red Wolves and Black Bears (77) 658
Tugman's Passage, The (83) 836
HOBAN, RUSSELL
Turtle Diary (77) 852
HOFFMANN, PETER
History of the German Resistance, 1933–1945, The (78) 388
HOFFMANN, STANLEY
Primacy or World Order: American Foreign Policy Since the Cold War (79) 551
HOFLING, CHARLES K.
Custer and the Little Big Horn: A Psychobiographical Inquiry (82) 161
HOFSTADTER, DOUGLAS R.
Gödel, Escher, Bach: An Eternal Golden Braid (80) 367
HÖHNE, HEINZ
Canaris: Hitler's Master Spy (80) 124
HOLLANDER, JOHN
Blue Wine and Other Poems (80) 94
Spectral Emanations: New and Selected Poems (79) 699
HOLST, SPENCER
Spencer Holst Stories (77) 780
HONAN, PARK
Matthew Arnold: A Life (82) 518
HONOUR, HUGH
New Golden Land, The (77) 538
HORGAN, PAUL
Thin Mountain Air, The (78) 821
HOUGH, RICHARD
Mountbatten (82) 542
HOWARD, MAUREEN
Grace Abounding (83) 296
HOWARTH, DAVID
Voyage of the Armada: The Spanish Story, The (82) 891
HOWE, IRVING
Celebrations and Attacks: Thirty Years of Literary and Cultural Commentary (80) 136
Leon Trotsky (79) 368
Margin of Hope: An Intellectual Autobiography, A (83) 451
World of Our Fathers (77) 947

HOWELL, ROGER, JR.
Cromwell   (78) 219
HOYT, EDWIN P.
Improper Bostonian: Dr. Oliver Wendell
Holmes, The   (80) 414
To the Marianas: War in the Central Pacific,
1944   (81) 817
HUFF, ROBERT
Ventriloquist, The   (78) 873
HUGHES, H. STUART
Prisoners of Hope: The Silver Age of the Italian
Jews, 1924–1974   (84) 705
HUGHES, LANGSTON, and ARNA
BONTEMPS
Arna Bontemps-Langston Hughes Letters:
1925–1967   (81) 57
HUGHES, TED
Moortown   (81) 569
River   (85) 762
HUGO, RICHARD
Making Certain It Goes On: The Collected
Poems of Richard Hugo   (85) 603
HUMPHREYS, JOSEPHINE
Dreams of Sleep   (85) 199
HUNT, GEORGE W.
John Cheever: The Hobgoblin Company of
Love   (84) 389
HUNT, JOHN DIXON
Wider Sea: A Life of John Ruskin, The
(83) 908
HUXLEY, ALDOUS
Human Situation: Lectures at Santa Barbara,
1959, The   (78) 422
Moksha: Writings on Psychedelics and the
Visionary Experience (1931–1963)   (79) 451
HYDE, LEWIS
Gift: Imagination and the Erotic Life of
Property, The   (84) 330

IENAGA, SABURO
Pacific War: World War II and the Japanese,
1931–1945, The   (79) 520
IGNATOW, DAVID
Tread the Dark: New Poems   (79) 777
Whisper to the Earth: New Poems   (83) 894
ILLICH, IVAN D.
Medical Nemesis   (77) 489
INGRAO, CHARLES W.
In Quest and Crisis: Emperor Joseph I and the
Habsburg Monarchy   (80) 426
IRELAND, TIMOTHY P.
Creating the Entangling Alliance: The
Origins of the North Atlantic Treaty
Organization   (82) 145
IRVING, DAVID
Hitler's War   (78) 398
Trail of the Fox, The   (78) 856
War Path: Hitler's Germany in the Years 1933–
1939, The   (79) 819
IRVING, JOHN
Hotel New Hampshire, The   (82) 368
World According to Garp, The   (79) 908
ISHERWOOD, CHRISTOPHER
Christopher and His Kind   (77) 158
ISKANDER, FAZIL
Sandro of Chegem   (84) 756
ISKANDER, FAZIL, et al., editors
Metropol: Literary Almanac   (84) 533

ITAYA, KIKUO
Tengo Child   (84) 863

JABÈS, EDMOND
Book of Questions: Yaël, Elya, Aely, The
(84) 108
JACOBSEN, JOSEPHINE
Chinese Insomniacs: New Poems, The
(83) 110
JAMES, CLIVE
Unreliable Memoirs   (82) 870
JAMES, HENRY
Henry James Letters, Vol. III: 1883–1895
(81) 421
Henry James Letters, Vol. IV: 1895–1916
(85) 368
JAMES, ROBERT RHODES
British Revolution, 1880–1939, The   (78) 145
JHABVALA, RUTH PRAWER
Heat and Dust   (77) 352
JOHANSON, DONALD C., and MAITLAND A.
EDEY
Lucy: The Beginnings of Humankind   (82) 514
JOHNSON, DIANE
Dashiell Hammett: A Life   (84) 212
Terrorists and Novelists   (83) 783
JOHNSTONE, ROBERT M., JR.
Jefferson and the Presidency: Leadership in the
Young Republic   (79) 331
JONES, DOUGLAS C.
Arrest Sitting Bull   (78) 72
JONES, JAMES
Whistle   (79) 843
JONES, PRESTON
Texas Trilogy, A   (77) 812
JONES, R. V.
Wizard War: British Scientific Intelligence,
1939–1945, The   (79) 888
JONG, ERICA
Fanny: Being the True History of the
Adventures of Fanny Hackabout-
Jones   (81) 309
How to Save Your Own Life   (78) 413
JORDAN, JUNE
Things That I Do in the Dark: Selected
Poetry   (78) 826
JUDSON, HORACE FREELAND
Eighth Day of Creation: The Makers of the
Revolution in Biology, The   (80) 273

KAEL, PAULINE
Reeling   (77) 662
KAFKA, FRANZ
Letters to Friends, Family, and Editors   (78)
526
Letters to Ottla and the Family   (83) 401
KAHN, DAVID
Hitler's Spies: German Military Intelligence in
World War II   (79) 281
KAHN, HERMAN, WILLIAM BROWN, and
LEON MARTEL
Next 200 Years, The   (77) 559
KAPLAN, BARRY JAY, and NICHOLAS
MEYER
Black Orchid   (78) 100

KAPLAN, FRED
  Thomas Carlyle   (84) 869
KAPLAN, JUSTIN
  Walt Whitman: A Life   (81) 883
KARL, FREDERICK R.
  American Fictions, 1940–1980: A
    Comprehensive History and Critical
    Evaluation   (84) 21
  Joseph Conrad: The Three Lives   (80) 449
KATZ, JACOB
  From Prejudice to Destruction: Anti-Semitism,
    1700–1933   (81) 362
KAUFFMAN, JANET
  Places in the World a Woman Could Walk
    (85) 688
KAZIN, ALFRED
  American Procession, An   (85) 12
  New York Jews   (79) 475
KEARNS, DORIS
  Lyndon Johnson and the American
    Dream   (77) 465
KEEGAN, JOHN
  Face of Battle, The   (78) 305
KEELEY, EDMUND
  Modern Greek Poetry: Voice and Myth
    (85) 624
KEENE, DONALD
  Dawn to the West: Japanese Literature in the
    Modern Era   (85) 157
KEES, WELDON
  Ceremony and Other Stories, The   (85) 79
KEILLOR, GARRISON
  Happy to Be Here   (83) 326
KELLY, LAURENCE
  Lermontov: Tragedy in the Caucasus   (79) 373
KEMAL, YASHAR
  They Burn the Thistles   (78) 817
  Undying Grass, The   (79) 787
KENEALLY, THOMAS
  Gossip from the Forest   (77) 336
  Schindler's List   (83) 684
KENNAN, GEORGE F.
  Cloud of Danger: Current Realities of
    American Foreign Policy, The   (78) 183
  Decline of Bismarck's European Order:
    Franco-Russian Relations, 1875–1890,
    The   (80) 215
KENNEDY, EUGENE
  Himself! The Life and Times of Mayor Richard
    J. Daley   (79) 273
KENNEDY, WILLIAM
  Ironweed   (84) 379
KENNER, HUGH
  Colder Eye: The Modern Irish Writers,
    A   (84) 173
  Joyce's Voices   (79) 340
KENNEY, SUSAN
  In Another Country   (85) 427
KERMODE, FRANK
  Art of Telling: Essays on Fiction, The   (84) 49
KERT, BERNICE
  Hemingway Women, The   (84) 337
KIDDER, TRACY
  Soul of a New Machine, The   (82) 787
KIELY, BENEDICT
  State of Ireland, The   (81) 766

KIMBALL, PHILIP
  Harvesting Ballads   (85) 352
KINCAID, JAMAICA
  At the Bottom of the River   (84) 59
KING, RICHARD H.
  Southern Renaissance: The Cultural
    Awakening of the American South, 1930–
    1955, A   (81) 753
KING, STEPHEN
  Danse Macabre   (82) 171
  Dead Zone, The   (80) 205
  Different Seasons   (83) 189
KINGSTON, MAXINE HONG
  China Men   (81) 137
  Woman Warrior, The   (77) 932
KINNELL, GALWAY
  Mortal Acts, Mortal Words   (81) 582
  Selected Poems   (83) 726
KINSELLA, W. P.
  Shoeless Joe   (83) 742
KISSINGER, HENRY A.
  White House Years   (80) 866
KLUGER, RICHARD
  Simple Justice   (77) 735
KNOTT, BILL
  Selected and Collected Poems   (78) 748
KNOWLES, JOHN
  Peace Breaks Out   (82) 621
KOESTLER, ARTHUR
  Janus: A Summing Up   (79) 326
  Thirteenth Tribe, The   (77) 817
KOGAWA, JOY
  Obasan   (83) 554
KONRÁD, GEORGE
  Loser, The   (83) 423
KONWICKI, TADEUSZ
  Minor Apocalypse, A   (84) 547
  Polish Complex, The   (83) 611
KOOSER, TED
  Sure Signs: New and Selected Poems   (81) 782
KOPELEV, LEV
  Ease My Sorrows   (84) 263
KORDA, MICHAEL
  Charmed Lives: A Family Romance   (80) 141
KOSINSKI, JERZY
  Blind Date   (78) 104
  Passion Play   (80) 649
KOSKOFF, DAVID E.
  Mellons: The Chronicle of America's Richest
    Family, The   (79) 434
KOTT, JAN
  Theater of Essence, The   (85) 890
KOVIC, RON
  Born on the Fourth of July   (77) 115
KRAMER, KATHRYN
  Handbook for Visitors from Outer Space,
    A   (85) 344
KRAMMER, ARNOLD
  Nazi Prisoners of War in America   (80) 573
KRAMNICK, ISAAC
  Rage of Edmund Burke: Portrait of an
    Ambivalent Conservative, The   (78) 686
KREN, GEORGE M., and LEON RAPPOPORT
  Holocaust and the Crisis of Human Behavior,
    The   (81) 439

KREYLING, MICHAEL
Eudora Welty's Achievement of Order
(81) 288
KREIGER, LEONARD
Ranke: The Meaning of History (78) 690
KRISTEVA, JULIA
Desire in Language: A Semiotic Approach to
Literature and Art (81) 231
KUMIN, MAXINE
Our Ground Time Here Will Be Brief
(83) 577
Retrieval System, The (79) 593
Why Can't We Live Together Like Civilized
Human Beings? (83) 903
KUNDERA, MILAN
Book of Laughter and Forgetting, The (81) 99
Farewell Party, The (77) 283
Joke, The (83) 363
Unbearable Lightness of Being, The (85) 958
KUNITZ, STANLEY
Poems of Stanley Kunitz, 1928–1978, The
(80) 665
KURLAND, PHILIP B.
Watergate and the Constitution (79) 830

LACOUTURE, JEAN
André Malraux (77) 43
LADER, LAWRENCE
Power on the Left: American Radical
Movements Since 1946 (80) 680
LAGERCRANTZ, OLOF
August Strindberg (85) 32
LALL, ARTHUR
Emergence of Modern India, The (82) 223
LANE, HARLAN
Wild Boy of Aveyron, The (77) 910
LANE FOX, ROBIN
Search for Alexander, The (81) 712
LANG, JOCHEN VON
Secretary, Martin Bormann: The Man Who
Manipulated Hitler, The (80) 746
LANGER, ELINOR
Josephine Herbst: The Story She Could Never
Tell (85) 499
LANGGUTH, A. J.
Saki: A Life of Hector Hugh Munro (82) 726
LANGLAND, JOSEPH
Any Body's Song (81) 53
LANGLEY, LESTER D.
United States and the Caribbean, 1900–1970,
The (81) 853
LAQUEUR, WALTER
Terrible Secret: The Suppression of the Truth
About Hitler's "Final Solution," The (82)
834
LARDNER, RING, JR.
Lardners, The (77) 404
LARKIN, PHILIP
Required Writing: Miscellaneous Pieces, 1955–
1982 (85) 747
LASCH, CHRISTOPHER
Culture of Narcissism: American Life in an Age
of Diminishing Expectations, The (80) 175
LASH, JOSEPH P.
Roosevelt and Churchill, 1939–1941 (77) 685

LAWRENCE, CHARLES, III, and JOEL
DREYFUSS
Bakke Case: The Politics of Inequality,
The (80) 45
LAWRENCE, D. H.
Letters of D. H. Lawrence, Vol. I: September
1901–May 1913, The (80) 469
Mr Noon (85) 619
LAW-YONE, WENDY
Coffin Tree, The (84) 168
LAYE, CAMARA
Guardian of the Word: Kouma Lafôlô Kouma,
The (85) 334
LAYMAN, RICHARD
Shadow Man: The Life of Dashiell
Hammett (82) 761
LEAKEY, RICHARD E., and ROGER LEWIN
People of the Lake: Mankind and Its
Beginnings (79) 535
LEAVITT, DAVID
Family Dancing (85) 250
LEBEAUX, RICHARD
Thoreau's Seasons (85) 895
LE CARRÉ, JOHN
Little Drummer Girl, The (84) 468
LEDEEN, MICHAEL, and WILLIAM H. LEWIS
Debacle: The American Failure in Iran (82)
175
LEE, ANDREA
Russian Journal (82) 713
Sarah Phillips (85) 771
LEE, J. M.
Churchill Coalition: 1940–1945, The (81) 147
LE GUIN, URSULA K.
Eye of the Heron, The (84) 291
Orsinian Tales (77) 601
LEITHAUSER, BRAD
Hundreds of Fireflies (83) 348
LEM, STANISŁAW
His Master's Voice (84) 342
Imaginary Magnitude (85) 421
Memoirs of a Space Traveler: Further
Reminiscences of Ijon Tichy (83) 469
LEONARD, THOMAS C.
Above the Battle: War-Making in America
from Appomattox to Versailles (79) 1
LEOPARDI, GIACOMO
Operette Morali (84) 643
LEOPOLD, JOHN A.
Alfred Hugenberg: The Radical Nationalist
Campaign Against the Weimar
Republic (78) 28
LEPPMANN, WOLFGANG
Rilke: A Life (85) 757
LESSING, DORIS
Documents Relating to the Sentimental Agents
in the Volyen Empire (84) 239
Making of the Representative for Planet 8,
The (83) 432
Marriages Between Zones Three, Four, and
Five: (As Narrated by the Chroniclers of
Zone Three), The (81) 555
Shikasta (80) 753
Sirian Experiments: The Report by Ambien II,
of the Five, The (81) 737
Stories (79) 708

LEUTZE, JAMES R.
Bargaining for Supremacy: Anglo-American Naval Collaboration, 1937–1941 (78) 85
LEVERTOV, DENISE
Life in the Forest (79) 386
LEVI, PRIMO
Periodic Table, The (85) 682
LEVINE, GEORGE
Realistic Imagination: English Fiction from Frankenstein to Lady Chatterley, The (83) 635
LEVINE, PHILIP
Ashes: Poems New & Old (80) 35
LEVIS, LARRY
Afterlife, The (78) 17
LE VOT, ANDRÉ
F. Scott Fitzgerald (84) 318
LEWIN, ROGER, and RICHARD E. LEAKEY
People of the Lake: Mankind and Its Beginnings (79) 535
LEWIS, WILLIAM H., and MICHAEL LEDEEN
Debacle: The American Failure in Iran (82) 175
LEWIS, WYNDHAM
Snooty Baronet (85) 835
LEWY, GUENTER
America in Vietnam (79) 14
L'HEUREUX, JOHN
Desires (82) 181
LIDDY, G. GORDON
Will: The Autobiography of G. Gordon Liddy (81) 928
LINCOLN, W. BRUCE
Nicholas I: Emperor and Autocrat of All the Russias (79) 479
LINDBERGH, ANNE MORROW
Flower and the Nettle, The (77) 294
War Within and Without: Diaries and Letters of Anne Morrow Lindbergh, 1939–1944 (81) 890
LINDBERGH, CHARLES AUGUSTUS
Autobiography of Values (79) 43
LINDSAY, NICHOLAS VACHEL
Letters of Vachel Lindsay (80) 479
LITTLETON, TAYLOR, editor
Time to Hear and Answer: Essays for the Bicentennial Season, A (78) 841
LITWACK, LEON F.
Been in the Storm So Long: The Aftermath of Slavery (80) 65
LIU, WU-CHI, and IRVING YUCHENG LO
Sunflower Splendor (77) 792
LIVESAY, HAROLD C.
Samuel Gompers and Organized Labor in America (79) 641
LLERENA, MARIO
Unsuspected Revolution: The Birth and Rise of Castroism, The (79) 799
LLOSA, MARIO VARGAS. See VARGAS LLOSA, MARIO
LO, IRVING YUCHENG, and WU-CHI LIU
Sunflower Splendor (77) 792
LODGE, DAVID
Souls and Bodies (83) 761
LOEWINSOHN, RON
Magnetic Field(s) (84) 487

LOGAN, JOHN
Only the Dreamer Can Change the Dream: Selected Poems (82) 599
LOMASK, MILTON
Aaron Burr: The Years from Princeton to Vice President, 1756–1805 (80) 6
LOPATE, PHILLIP
Bachelorhood: Tales of the Metropolis (82) 40
LORD, BETTE BAO
Spring Moon: A Novel of China (82) 806
LORD, WALTER
Lonely Vigil: Coastwatchers of the Solomons (78) 534
LORDE, AUDRE
Chosen Poems, Old and New (83) 113
LOTTMAN, HERBERT R.
Albert Camus: A Biography (80) 15
Left Bank: Writers, Artists, and Politics from the Popular Front to the Cold War, The (83) 390
LOUIS, WM. ROGER
Imperialism at Bay: The United States and the Decolonization of the British Empire, 1941–1945 (79) 305
LOW, ALFRED D.
Jews in the Eyes of the Germans: From the Enlightenment to Imperial Germany (80) 439
LOWELL, ROBERT
Day by Day (78) 233
Selected Poems (77) 720
LUCIE-SMITH, EDWARD
Joan of Arc (78) 472
LUDINGTON, TOWNSEND
John Dos Passos: A Twentieth Century Odyssey (81) 464
LUKACS, JOHN
1945: Year Zero (79) 490
LUKAS, J. ANTHONY
Nightmare (77) 565
LUPTON, KENNETH
Mungo Park the African Traveler (80) 550
LURIE, ALISON
Foreign Affairs (85) 297
LYONS, F. S. L.
Charles Stewart Parnell (78) 169

MAASS, JOACHIM
Kleist (84) 418
MCALEER, JOHN
Ralph Waldo Emerson: Days of Encounter (85) 717
MCAULIFFE, MARY SPERLING
Crisis on the Left: Cold War Politics and American Liberals, 1947–1954 (79) 138
MCCAGG, WILLIAM O., JR.
Stalin Embattled, 1943–1948 (79) 702
MCCARTHY, ABIGAIL
Circles: A Washington Story (78) 179
MCCARTHY, MARY
Cannibals and Missionaries (80) 133
MCCARTHY, PATRICK
Camus (83) 96
Céline (77) 134
MCCLANAHAN, ED
Natural Man, The (84) 608

MCCORMMACH, RUSSELL
Night Thoughts of a Classical Physicist
(83) 532
MCCULLOUGH, COLLEEN
Thorn Birds, The (78) 831
MCCULLOUGH, DAVID
Mornings on Horseback (82) 537
Path Between the Seas: The Creation of the
Panama Canal, 1870–1914, The (78) 636
MCDONALD, FORREST
Alexander Hamilton: A Biography (80) 23
MACDONALD, ROSS
Blue Hammer, The (77) 105
MCDOWELL, EDWIN
To Keep Our Honor Clean (81) 813
MCEWAN, IAN
In Between the Sheets and Other Stories
(80) 417
MCFARLAND, PHILIP
Sojourners (80) 771
MCFEELY, WILLIAM S.
Grant: A Biography (82) 338
MCGUANE, THOMAS
Nobody's Angel (83) 544
Something to Be Desired (85) 849
MACK, JOHN E.
Prince of Our Disorder, A (77) 637
MACK SMITH, DENIS
Mussolini's Roman Empire (77) 520
MCKAY, NELLIE Y.
Jean Toomer, Artist: A Study of His Literary
Life and Work, 1894–1936 (85) 489
MACKENZIE, NORMAN, and JEANNE
MACKENZIE
Fabians, The (78) 300
MACLAVERTY, BERNARD
Cal (84) 132
Secrets and Other Stories (85) 790
MACLEISH, ARCHIBALD
Letters of Archibald MacLeish: 1907–
1982 (84) 436
New & Collected Poems, 1917–1976 (77) 534
Riders on the Earth (79) 601
MCLELLAN, DAVID S.
Dean Acheson (77) 197
MCMILLAN, CAROL
Women, Reason and Nature: Some
Philosophical Problems with Feminism
(84) 964
MCMILLAN, GEORGE
Making of an Assassin, The (77) 470
MACMILLAN, HAROLD
Past Masters, The (77) 610
MCMURRAY, LINDA O.
George Washington Carver: Scientist and
Symbol (82) 310
MCMURTRY, LARRY
Cadillac Jack (83) 90
Desert Rose, The (84) 225
Somebody's Darling (79) 689
MCNEILL, WILLIAM H.
Plagues and Peoples (77) 618
Metamorphosis of Greece Since World War II,
The (79) 438
MCPHEE, JOHN
Giving Good Weight (80) 358

MCPHERSON, WILLIAM
Testing the Current (85) 884
MACSHANE, FRANK
Life of Raymond Chandler, The (77) 427
MADDEN, DAVID
Pleasure-Dome (80) 659
Suicide's Wife, The (79) 727
MADDOW, BEN
Sunday Between Wars: The Course of
American Life from 1865 to 1917, A (80)
798
MADSEN, AXEL
Hearts and Minds (78) 379
MAILER, NORMAN
Ancient Evenings (84) 31
Executioner's Song, The (80) 306
Genius and Lust (77) 322
Pieces and Pontifications (83) 597
Tough Guys Don't Dance (85) 912
MALAMUD, BERNARD
Dubin's Lives (80) 231
God's Grace (83) 291
Stories of Bernard Malamud, The (84) 819
MALONE, DUMAS
Sage of Monticello: Jefferson and His Time,
Volume VI, The (82) 722
MALOUF, DAVID
Harland's Half Acre (85) 348
MALRAUX, ANDRÉ
Lazarus (78) 515
MAMET, DAVID
American Buffalo (78) 46
Water Engine and Mr. Happiness, The
(79) 828
MANCERON, CLAUDE
Twilight of the Old Order, 1774–1778 (78) 864
MANCHESTER, WILLIAM
American Caesar: Douglas MacArthur, 1880–
1964 (79) 20
MANFRED, FREDERICK
Manly-Hearted Woman, The (77) 480
MANSFIELD, KATHERINE
Collected Letters of Katherine Mansfield, Vol.
I: 1903–1917, The (85) 106
MARCUS, STEVEN
Representations (77) 673
MARIANI, PAUL
William Carlos Williams: A New World
Naked (82) 946
MARKUS, JULIA
Uncle (79) 783
MARSHALL, PETER H.
William Godwin (85) 1028
MARTEL, LEON, HERMAN KAHN, and
WILLIAM BROWN
Next 200 Years, The (77) 559
MARTIN, DAVID C.
Wilderness of Mirrors (81) 924
MARTIN, JOHN BARTLOW
Adlai Stevenson and the World (78) 6
Adlai Stevenson of Illinois (77) 12
MARTÍN GAITE, CARMEN
Back Room, The (84) 71
MARTORELL, JOANOT, and MARTÍ JOAN
DE GALBA
Tirant lo Blanc (85) 907

MARX, KARL, and FRIEDRICH ENGELS
Selected Letters: The Personal
Correspondence, 1844–1877   (83) 722
MASEFIELD, JOHN
Selected Poems   (79) 666
MASON, BOBBIE ANN
Shiloh and Other Stories   (83) 739
MASON, HAYDN
Voltaire   (82) 885
MASSIE, ROBERT K.
Peter the Great: His Life and World   (81) 651
MASTERS, HILARY
Last Stands: Notes from Memory   (83) 386
MATERER, TIMOTHY
Vortex: Pound, Eliot, and Lewis   (80) 855
MATTHEWS, JAMES
Voices: A Life of Frank O'Connor   (84) 921
MATTHEWS, WILLIAM
Flood: Poems   (83) 262
MATTHIESSEN, PETER
Sand Rivers   (82) 737
Snow Leopard, The   (79) 685
MAXWELL, WILLIAM
So Long, See You Tomorrow   (81) 741
MAYER, ARNO J.
Persistence of the Old Regime: Europe to the
Great War, The   (82) 626
MEAD, MARGARET, and RHODA
METRAUX
Aspects of the Present   (81) 62
MECKEL, CHRISTOPH
Figure on the Boundary Line: Selected Prose,
The   (85) 276
MEDVEDEV, ROY A.
Nikolai Bukharin: The Last Years   (81) 614
October Revolution, The   (80) 605
MEE, CHARLES L., JR.
End of Order: Versailles, 1919, The   (81) 277
Ohio Gang: The World of Warren G. Harding,
The   (82) 575
MEHTA, VED
Ledge Between the Streams, The   (85) 539
MEISNER, MAURICE
Mao's China: A History of the People's
Republic   (78) 557
MELLOW, JAMES R.
Nathaniel Hawthorne in His Times   (81) 593
MENCKEN, H. L.
Choice of Days: Essays from *Happy Days*,
Newspaper Days, and *Heathen Days*,
A   (81) 142
MEREDITH, WILLIAM
Cheer, The   (81) 133
MERK, FREDERICK
History of the Westward Movement   (79) 277
MERRILL, JAMES INGRAM
Changing Light at Sandover, The   (84) 148
Divine Comedies   (77) 222
From the First Nine: Poems, 1946–1976
(84) 314
Mirabell: Books of Number   (79) 448
MERWIN, W. S.
Compass Flower, The   (78) 205
METRAUX, RHODA, and MARGARET
MEAD
Aspects of the Present   (81) 62

MEYER, NICHOLAS, and BARRY JAY
KAPLAN
Black Orchid   (78) 100
MICHENER, JAMES A.
Chesapeake   (79) 99
Covenant, The   (81) 210
MILLER, ARTHUR
Theater Essays of Arthur Miller, The   (79) 742
MILLER, J. HILLIS
Fiction and Repetition: Seven English
Novels   (83) 253
MILLER, JOHN CHESTER
Wolf by the Ears: Thomas Jefferson and
Slavery, The   (78) 928
MILLER, MERLE
Lyndon: An Oral Biography   (81) 540
MILLER, NATHAN
Roosevelt Chronicles, The   (80) 726
MILLGATE, JANE
Walter Scott: The Making of the Novelist
(85) 989
MILLGATE, MICHAEL
Thomas Hardy: A Biography   (83) 806
MILLS, HILARY
Mailer: A Biography   (83) 428
MIŁOSZ, CZESŁAW
Bells in Winter   (79) 51
Issa Valley, The   (82) 403
Land of Ulro, The   (85) 520
Native Realm: A Search for Self-
Definition   (81) 597
Seizure of Power, The   (83) 713
Separate Notebooks, The   (85) 811
Visions from San Francisco Bay   (83) 860
Witness of Poetry, The   (84) 959
MILTON, DAVID, and NANCY DALL MILTON
Wind Will Not Subside, The   (77) 918
MINTER, DAVID
William Faulkner: His Life and Work   (81) 932
MOERS, ELLEN
Literary Women   (77) 439
MOHAMMAD REZA PAHLAVI
Answer to History   (81) 47
MOJTABAI, A. G.
Autumn   (83) 39
Stopping Place, A   (80) 785
MOMADAY, N. SCOTT
Names: A Memoir, The   (78) 594
MONEGAL, EMIR RODRIGUEZ
Jorge Luis Borges: A Literary Biography
(80) 444
MONTAGUE, JOHN
Dead Kingdom, The   (85) 167
MONTALE, EUGENIO
New Poems   (77) 553
Second Life of Art: Selected Essays, The
(83) 705
MOONEY, MICHAEL MACDONALD
Evelyn Nesbit and Stanford White   (77) 260
MOORE, BRIAN
Doctor's Wife, The   (77) 226
MOORE, MARIANNE
Complete Poems of Marianne Moore,
The   (82) 126
MORAVIA, ALBERTO
1934   (84) 613
Time of Desecration   (81) 809

MORGAN, JOHN S.
Robert Fulton   (78) 726
MORGAN, ROBERT
Groundwork   (80) 390
MORGAN, TED
Maugham   (81) 559
MORLEY, JOHN F.
Vatican Democracy and the Jews During the
Holocaust, 1939–1943   (81) 861
MORRIS, EDMUND
Rise of Theodore Roosevelt, The   (80) 717
MORRIS, ROGER
Uncertain Greatness: Henry Kissinger and
American Foreign Policy   (78) 869
MORRIS, WRIGHT
Earthly Delights, Unearthly Adornments:
American Writers as Image-Makers
(79) 175
Fork River Space Project, The   (78) 219
Plains Song: For Female Voices   (81) 655
Real Losses, Imaginary Gains   (77) 652
Solo: An American Dreamer in Europe,
1933–34   (84) 803
Will's Boy   (82) 950
MORRISON, TONI
Song of Solomon   (78) 789
Tar Baby   (82) 828
MORTIMER, JOHN
Clinging to the Wreckage: A Part of Life
(83) 127
MOSLEY, LEONARD
Blood Relations: The Rise & Fall of the du
Ponts of Delaware   (81) 93
Dulles: A Biography of Eleanor, Allen, and
John Foster Dulles and Their Family
Network   (79) 170
Lindbergh   (77) 433
MOSS, HOWARD
Notes from the Castle   (80) 597
MOSSE, GEORGE L.
Toward the Final Solution: A History of
European Racism   (79) 761
MOSSIKER, FRANCES
Madame de Sévigné: A Life and Letters
(85) 595
MOTT, MICHAEL
Seven Mountains of Thomas Merton,
The   (85) 815
MUELLER, LISEL
Need to Hold Still, The   (81) 603
MULDER, JOHN M.
Woodrow Wilson: The Years of
Preparation   (79) 892
MUNRO, ALICE
Moons of Jupiter, The   (84) 580
MURDOCH, IRIS
Nuns and Soldiers   (81) 628
Philosopher's Pupil, The   (84) 690
MURRAY, K. M. ELISABETH
Caught in the Web of Words   (78) 160
MYRER, ANTON
Last Convertible, The   (79) 359

NABOKOV, VLADIMIR
Details of a Sunset and Other Stories   (77) 206
Lectures on Don Quixote   (84) 427
Lectures on Literature   (81) 485
Lectures on Russian Literature   (82) 437
Strong Opinions   (77) 789
NABOKOV, VLADIMIR, and EDMUND
WILSON
Nabokov-Wilson Letters: Correspondence
Between Vladimir Nabokov and Edmund
Wilson, 1940–1971, The   (80) 564
NAIPAUL, V. S.
Among the Believers: An Islamic
Journey   (82) 6
Bend in the River, A   (80) 69
Finding the Center: Two Narratives   (85) 281
Return of Eva Perón: With the Killings in
Trinidad, The   (81) 686
NAJDER, ZDISŁAW
Joseph Conrad: A Chronicle   (84) 395
NARAYAN, R. K.
Malgudi Days   (83) 436
Painter of Signs, The   (77) 605
NAVARRO, MARYSA, and NICHOLAS
FRASER
Eva Perón   (82) 249
NAYLOR, GLORIA
Women of Brewster Place: A Novel in Seven
Stories, The   (83) 918
NELSON, RAYMOND
Van Wyck Brooks: A Writer's Life   (82) 874
NEMEROV, HOWARD
Collected Poems of Howard Nemerov,
The   (78) 200
Figures of Thought: Speculations on the
Meaning of Poetry & Other Essays   (79) 209
NEWBY, P. H.
Kith   (78) 491
NEWELL, NANCY PEABODY, and RICHARD
S. NEWELL
Struggle for Afghanistan, The   (82) 817
NICHOLL, CHARLES
Cup of News: The Life of Thomas Nashe,
A   (85) 147
NICOL, CHARLES, and J. E. RIVERS, editors
Nabokov's Fifth Arc: Nabokov and Others on
His Life's Work   (83) 511
NICOLSON, SIR HAROLD
Harold Nicolson: Diaries and Letters, 1930–
1964   (81) 406
NIMMO, DAN, and JAMES E. COMBS
Subliminal Politics: Myths & Mythmakers in
America   (81) 773
NIMS, JOHN FREDERICK
Selected Poems   (83) 730
NIN, ANAÏS
Diary of Anaïs Nin: 1955–1966, The   (77) 217
Diary of Anaïs Nin: 1966–1974, The   (81) 234
Early Diary of Anaïs Nin: Vol. II, 1920–1923,
The   (83) 220
Early Diary of Anaïs Nin: Vol. III, 1923–1927,
The   (84) 257
NISBET, ROBERT
History of the Idea of Progress   (81) 430
Sociology as an Art Form   (77) 753
NIXON, RICHARD M.
RN: The Memoirs of Richard Nixon   (79) 605
NORMAN, GEOFFREY
Midnight Water   (84) 543

CUMULATIVE AUTHOR INDEX

NOSSACK, HANS ERICH
Wait for November   (83) 864
NOZICK, ROBERT
Philosophical Explanations   (82) 638

OATES, JOYCE CAROL
Angel of Light   (82) 17
Bellefleur   (81) 78
Bloodsmoor Romance, A   (83) 61
Childwold   (77) 149
Last Days   (85) 524
Mysteries of Winterthurn   (85) 640
Night-Side   (78) 608
Profane Art, The   (84) 716
Son of the Morning   (79) 693
O'BRIEN, EDNA
Fanatic Heart: Selected Stories of Edna
O'Brien, A   (85) 260
O'CONNOR, FLANNERY
Habit of Being, The   (80) 391
O'CONNOR, FRANK
Collected Stories   (82) 100
O'FAOLAIN, SEAN
Collected Stories of Sean O'Faolain, The   (84)
198
O'HARA, JOHN
Selected Letters of John O'Hara   (79) 656
O'HEHIR, DIANA
I Wish This War Were Over   (85)
OLDS, SHARON
Dead and the Living, The   (85)
OLSON, CHARLES
Maximus Poems, The   (84) 519
O'NEILL, GERARD K.
2081: A Hopeful View of the Human
Future   (82) 860
ONG, WALTER J.
Orality and Literacy: The Technologizing of the
Word   (83) 568
ORIEUX, JEAN
Voltaire   (80) 850
OSBORNE, CHARLES
W. H. Auden: The Life of a Poet   (80) 860
OSBORNE, JOHN
Better Class of Person, A   (82) 45
OZICK, CYNTHIA
Art & Ardor   (84) 44
Bloodshed and Three Novellas   (77) 101
Cannibal Galaxy, The   (84) 137
Levitation: Five Fictions   (83) 405

PACKARD, VANCE
People Shapers, The   (78) 649
PADOVER, SAUL K.
Karl Marx: An Intimate Biography   (79) 349
PAGELS, ELAINE
Gnostic Gospels, The   (80) 363
PAGELS, HEINZ R.
Cosmic Code: Quantum Physics as the
Language of Nature, The   (83) 156
PAINTER, GEORGE D.
Chateaubriand: A Biography, Vol. I (1768–93):
The Longed-for Tempests   (79) 95
William Caxton: A Biography   (78) 909
PAKENHAM, THOMAS
Boer War, The   (80) 97

PALMER, DAVE RICHARD
Summons of the Trumpet: U. S.-Vietnam in
Perspective   (79) 732
PANCAKE, BREECE D'J
Stories of Breece D'J Pancake, The   (84) 824
PANCAKE, JOHN S.
1777: The Year of the Hangman   (78) 757
PARFIT, DEREK
Reasons and Persons   (85) 729
PARKINSON, ROGER
Tormented Warrior: Ludendorff and the
Supreme Command   (80) 827
PARMET, HERBERT S.
Jack: The Struggles of John F. Kennedy
(81) 454
PARTRIDGE, FRANCES
Love in Bloomsbury: Memories   (82) 504
PASTAN, LINDA
Five Stages of Grief, The   (79) 222
PM/AM: New and Selected Poems   (83) 603
Waiting for My Life   (82) 897
PASTERNAK, BORIS, and OLGA
FREIDENBERG
Correspondence of Boris Pasternak and Olga
Freidenberg, 1910–1954, The   (83) 147
PASTERNAK, LEONID
Memoirs of Leonid Pasternak, The   (84) 528
PATON, ALAN
Ah, But Your Land Is Beautiful   (83) 6
Knocking on the Door   (77) 396
PAULEY, BRUCE F.
Hitler and the Forgotten Nazis: A History of
Austrian National Socialism   (82) 360
PAWEL, ERNST
Nightmare of Reason: A Life of Franz Kafka,
The   (85) 645
PAYNE, STANLEY G.
Fascism: A Comparative Approach Toward a
Definition   (81) 314
PAZ, OCTAVIO
Selected Poems   (85) 802
PEARSON, JOHN
Sitwells: A Family Biography, The   (80) 763
PERCY, WALKER
Lancelot   (78) 501
Lost in the Cosmos: The Last Self-Help
Book   (84) 482
Second Coming, The   (81) 717
PERELMAN, S. J.
Last Laugh, The   (82) 433
PERL, JEFFREY M.
Tradition of Return: The Implicit History of
Modern Literature, The   (85) 917
PERRETT, GEOFFREY
Dream of Greatness: The American People,
1945–1963, A   (80) 226
PERRY, RICHARD
Montgomery's Children   (85) 629
PETESCH, NATALIE L. M.
Duncan's Colony   (83) 210
PHILLIPS, JAYNE ANNE
Machine Dreams   (85) 589
PHILLIPS, WILLIAM
Partisan View: Five Decades of the Literary
Life, A   (85) 677

XXI

PIAGET, JEAN
  Grasp of Consciousness, The   (77) 341
PIERCY, MARGE
  Braided Lives   (83) 75
  Circles on the Water: Selected Poems   (83) 119
PINCHERLE, ALBERTO. *See* MORAVIA,
  ALBERTO
PINSKY, ROBERT
  Explanation of America, An   (81) 293
  History of My Heart   (85) 399
PINTER, HAROLD
  Proust Screenplay, The   (78) 673
PLANTE, DAVID
  Country, The   (82) 140
  Woods, The   (83) 923
PLATH, SYLVIA
  Collected Poems, The   (82) 96
  Journals of Sylvia Plath, The   (83) 367
PLOWDEN, ALISON
  Elizabeth Regina: The Age of Triumph, 1588–
  1603   (81) 272
PLUMLY, STANLEY
  Summer Celestial   (84) 846
PODHORETZ, NORMAN
  Breaking Ranks: A Political Memoir   (80) 101
POIRIER, RICHARD
  Robert Frost: The Work of Knowing   (78) 722
POLLACK, JACK HARRISON
  Earl Warren: The Judge Who Changed
  America   (80) 255
POLLITT, KATHA
  Antarctic Traveller   (83) 20
POLLOCK, JOHN
  Wilberforce   (79) 862
POMERANCE, BERNARD
  Elephant Man, The   (80) 280
POPOV, YEVGENY, et al., editors
  Metropol: Literary Almanac   (84) 533
POTTS, WILLARD, editor
  Portraits of the Artist in Exile: Recollections of
  James Joyce by Europeans   (80) 675
POUND, EZRA, and FORD MADOX FORD
  Pound/Ford: The Story of a Literary
  Friendship   (83) 621
POUND, EZRA, and DOROTHY
  SHAKESPEAR
  Ezra Pound and Dorothy Shakespear: Their
  Letters, 1909–1914   (85)
POWELL, ANTHONY
  Hearing Secret Harmonies   (77) 397
  Infants of the Spring   (78) 447
  O, How the Wheel Becomes It!   (84) 628
  Strangers All Are Gone, The   (84) 833
POWELL, PADGETT
  Edisto   (85) 213
PRANGE, GORDON W.
  At Dawn We Slept: The Untold Story of Pearl
  Harbor   (82) 33
PRENSHAW, PEGGY WHITMAN, editor
  Conversations with Eudora Welty   (85) 137
  Eudora Welty: Critical Essays   (81) 283
PRICE, REYNOLDS
  Source of Light, The   (82) 790
PRICE, RICHARD
  Breaks, The   (84) 112

PRIESTLEY, J. B.
  Found, Lost, Found   (78) 325
PRITCHARD, WILLIAM H.
  Frost: A Literary Life Reconsidered   (85) 312
  Lives of Modern Poets   (81) 520
PRITCHETT, V. S.
  Collected Stories   (83) 131
  Gentle Barbarian: The Life and Work of
  Turgenev, The   (78) 340
  More Collected Stories   (84) 584
  Myth Makers: Literary Essays, The   (80) 560
  On the Edge of the Cliff   (80) 627
  Selected Stories   (79) 669
  Tale Bearers: Literary Essays, The   (81) 786
PROFFER, ELLENDEA
  Bulgakov: Life and Work   (85) 62
PROSE, FRANCINE
  Household Saints   (82) 373
PROUST, MARCEL
  Marcel Proust: Selected Letters, 1880–
  1903   (84) 504
PRYCE-JONES, DAVID
  Paris in the Third Reich: A History of the
  German Occupation, 1940–1944   (82) 615
PUIG, MANUEL
  Buenos Aires Affair, The   (77) 129
  Eternal Curse on the Reader of These
  Pages   (83) 235
PURDY, JAMES
  In a Shallow Grave   (77) 380
PYM, BARBARA
  No Fond Return of Love   (83) 536
  Some Tame Gazelle   (84) 809
  Unsuitable Attachment, An   (83) 855
  Very Private Eye: An Autobiography in Diaries
  and Letters, A   (85) 964
PYNCHON, THOMAS
  Slow Learner: Early Stories   (85) 830

QUANDT, WILLIAM B.
  Decade of Decisions: American Policy Toward
  the Arab-Israeli Conflict, 1967–1977   (78)
  243
QUENNELL, PETER
  Selected Essays of Cyril Connolly, The   (85) 793

RABAN, JONATHAN
  Old Glory: An American Voyage   (82) 580
RABINOWITCH, ALEXANDER
  Bolsheviks Come to Power, The   (77) 109
RABINOWITZ, DOROTHY
  New Lives   (77) 549
RANSOM, JOHN CROWE
  Selected Essays of John Crowe Ransom
  (85) 797
RANSOM, ROGER L., and RICHARD SUTCH
  One Kind of Freedom: The Economic
  Consequences of Emancipation   (78) 622
RAPPAPORT, LEON, and GEORGE M. KREN
  Holocaust and the Crisis of Human Behavior,
  The   (81) 439
READ, PIERS PAUL
  Married Man, A   (80)
  Polonaise   (77) 632
RECTOR, LIAM
  Sorrow of Architecture, The   (85) 855

CUMULATIVE AUTHOR INDEX

REED, ISHMAEL
Shrovetide in Old New Orleans   (79) 681
Terrible Twos, The   (83) 778
REILLY, ROBIN
William Pitt the Younger   (80) 873
REISCHAUER, EDWIN O.
Japanese, The   (78) 459
REMINI, ROBERT V.
Andrew Jackson and the Course of American
Empire, 1767–1821   (78) 50
Andrew Jackson and the Course of American
Freedom, 1822–1832   (82) 11
REUTHER, VICTOR G.
Brothers Reuther, The   (77) 124
RHYS, JEAN
Letters of Jean Rhys, The   (85) 554
RICE, ANNE
Interview with the Vampire   (77) 384
RICH, ADRIENNE
Dream of a Common Language: Poems
1974–1977, The   (79) 160
Of Woman Born   (77) 584
On Lies, Secrets, and Silence: Selected Prose
1966–1978   (80) 622
Wild Patience Has Taken Me This Far: Poems
1978–1981, A   (82) 942
RICHARDSON, H. EDWARD
Jesse: The Biography of an American Writer,
Jesse Hilton Stuart   (85) 494
RICHARDSON, JOANNA
Sarah Bernhardt and Her World   (78) 740
RICOEUR, PAUL
Time and Narrative: Vol. I   (85) 902
RIDLEY, JASPER
Napolean III and Eugénie   (81) 587
RIVERA, EDWARD
Family Installments: Memories of Growing Up
Hispanic   (83) 240
RIVERS, J. E., and CHARLES NICOL, editors
Nabokov's Fifth Arc: Nabokov and Others on
His Life's Work   (83) 511
ROBERTSON, JAMES OLIVER
American Myth, American Reality   (81) 39
ROBINSON, JANICE S.
H. D.: The Life and Work of an American
Poet   (83) 331
ROBINSON, PHYLLIS C.
Willa: The Life of Willa Cather   (84) 945
ROBISON, MARY
Amateur's Guide to the Night, An   (84) 16
RODGERS, DANIEL T.
Work Ethic in Industrial America, 1850–1920,
The   (79) 904
RODRIGUEZ, RICHARD
Hunger of Memory: The Education of Richard
Rodriguez   (82) 377
ROLLIN, BETTY
First, You Cry   (77) 291
ROOKE, LEON
Shakespeare's Dog   (84) 784
ROSE, PHYLLIS
Parallel Lives: Five Victorian Marriages
(84) 662
ROSENTHAL, M. L., and SALLY M. GALL
Modern Poetic Sequence: The Genius of
Modern Poetry, The   (84) 570
Sailing into the Unknown: Yeats, Pound, and
Eliot   (79) 632

ROSSNER, JUDITH
Attachments   (78) 77
ROTH, JACK J.
Cult of Violence: Sorel and the Sorelians,
The   (81) 215
ROTH, PHILIP
Anatomy Lesson, The   (84) 26
Ghost Writer, The   (80) 354
Professor of Desire, The   (78) 669
Zuckerman Unbound   (82) 981
ROTHENBERG, GUNTHER E.
Art of Warfare in the Age of Napoleon,
The   (79) 38
ROVERE, RICHARD H.
Arrivals and Departures   (77) 62
RUDDICK, SARA, and PAMELA DANIELS,
editors
Working It Out   (78) 937
RUÍZ, RAMÓN EDUARDO
Great Rebellion: Mexico, 1905–1924,
The   (81) 396
RUKEYSER, MURIEL
Collected Poems, The   (80) 148
RUSHDIE, SALMAN
Shame   (84) 788
RUSKIN, JOHN, and THOMAS CARLYLE
Correspondence of Thomas Carlyle and John
Ruskin, The   (83) 153
RUSS, JOANNA
How to Suppress Women's Writing   (84) 353
RYAN, PAUL B., and THOMAS A. BAILEY
Hitler vs. Roosevelt: The Undeclared Naval
War   (80) 404

SÁBATO, ERNESTO
On Heroes and Tombs   (82) 585
SAGAN, CARL
Broca's Brain: Reflections on the Romance of
Science   (80) 116
SAGAN, FRANÇOISE
Silken Eyes   (78) 776
Unmade Bed, The   (79) 791
SAID, EDWARD W.
World, the Text, and the Critic, The   (84) 971
ST. AUBYN, GILES
Edward VII: Prince and King   (80) 264
SALISBURY, HARRISON E.
Russia in Revolution, 1900–1930   (79) 622
SAMUELS, ERNEST
Bernard Berenson: The Making of a
Connoisseur   (80) 73
SANDERS, RONALD
Lost Tribes and Promised Lands: The Origins
of American Racism   (79) 398
SANER, REG
Climbing into the Roots   (77) 184
SAPERSTEIN, ALAN
Mom Kills Kids and Self   (80) 541
SARDE, MICHÈLE
Colette: Free and Fettered   (81) 161
SAROYAN, WILLIAM
Chance Meetings   (79) 92
My Name Is Saroyan   (84) 588
SARRAUTE, NATHALIE
Childhood   (85) 89

SARTON, MAY
World of Light, A   (77) 941
SARTRE, JEAN-PAUL
Life/Situations: Essays Written and
Spoken   (78) 529
SAVAGE, THOMAS
I Heard My Sister Speak My Name   (78) 427
SAYLES, JOHN
Anarchists' Convention, The   (80) 28
SCAMMELL, MICHAEL
Solzhenitsyn: A Biography   (85) 839
SCHAMA, SIMON
Patriots and Liberators: Revolution in the
Netherlands, 1780–1813   (78) 642
SCHAPIRO, LEONARD
Turgenev: His Life and Times   (80) 832
SCHEIN, SETH L.
Mortal Hero: An Introduction to Homer's
Iliad, The   (85) 635
SCHELL, JONATHAN
Fate of the Earth, The   (83) 244
Time of Illusion, The   (77) 822
SCHICKEL, RICHARD
Another I, Another You   (79) 34
SCHIFFRIN, HAROLD Z.
Sun Yat-sen: Reluctant Revolutionary
(81) 777
SCHINE, CATHLEEN
Alice in Bed   (84) 12
SCHNEIDER, NINA
Woman Who Lived in a Prologue, The
(81) 941
SCHNEIDER, PETER
Wall Jumper, The   (85) 978
SCHOENBRUN, DAVID
Soldiers of the Night: The Story of the French
Resistance   (81) 750
SCHORER, MARK
Pieces of Life   (78) 657
SCHORSKE, CARL E.
Fin-de-siècle Vienna: Politics and
Culture   (81) 330
SCHULZ, BRUNO
Sanatorium Under the Sign of the
Hourglass   (79) 645
Street of Crocodiles, The   (78) 804
SCHUMACHER, E. F.
Guide for the Perplexed, A   (78) 364
SCHUYLER, JAMES
Morning for the Poem, The   (81) 578
SCHWARTZ, DELMORE
Letters of Delmore Schwartz   (85) 548
SCHWARZ, JORDAN A.
Speculator: Bernard M. Baruch in Washington,
1917–1965, The   (82) 800
SCIASCIA, LEONARDO
Candido: Or, A Dream Dreamed in
Sicily   (80) 129
SCOTT, PAUL
Staying On   (78) 795
SEE, CAROLYN
Rhine Maidens   (82) 684
SEGAL, LORE
Lucinella   (77) 460
SELBY, HUBERT, JR.
Requiem for a Dream   (79) 589

SENN, FRITZ
Joyce's Dislocutions: Essays on Reading as
Translation   (85) 509
SETTLE, MARY LEE
Killing Ground, The   (83) 381
Scapegoat, The   (81) 707
SEWARD, DESMOND
Eleanor of Aquitaine   (80) 277
Hundred Years War: The English in France,
1337–1453, The   (79) 291
SEXTON, ANNE
Anne Sexton: A Self-Portrait in Letters   (78)
54
Complete Poems, The   (82) 120
Words for Dr. Y: Uncollected Poems with
Three Stories   (79) 897
SEYMOUR-SMITH, MARTIN
Robert Graves: His Life and Work   (84) 746
SHACHTMAN, TOM
Day America Crashed, The   (80) 200
SHAFFER, PETER
Amadeus   (81) 27
SHAKESPEAR, DOROTHY, and EZRA
POUND
Ezra Pound and Dorothy Shakespear: Their
Letters, 1909–1914   (85) 243
SHANKS, BOB
Cool Fire, The   (77) 180
SHANOR, DONALD R.
Soviet Triangle: Russia's Relations with China
and the West in the 1980s, The   (81) 759
SHAPIRO, KARL
Collected Poems 1940–1978   (79) 124
SHATTUCK, ROGER
Innocent Eye: On Modern Literature and the
Arts, The   (85) 445
SHATZ, MARSHALL S.
Soviet Dissent in Historical Perspective   (82)
795
SHAW, IRWIN
Bread upon the Waters   (82) 67
SHAW, STANFORD J., and EZEL KURAL
SHAW
History of the Ottoman Empire and Modern
Turkey: Vol. II, The   (78) 393
SHAWCROSS, WILLIAM
Sideshow: Kissinger, Nixon and the Destruction
of Cambodia   (80) 758
SHEED, WILFRID
Good Word & Other Words, The   (80) 375
Transatlantic Blues   (79) 772
SHEEHAN, EDWARD R. F.
Arabs, Israelis, and Kissinger, The   (77) 57
SHELLEY, MARY WOLLSTONECRAFT
Letters of Mary Wollstonecraft Shelley, Vol. I:
"A Part of the Elect," The   (81) 501
SHEPARD, SAM
Sam Shepard: Seven Plays   (82) 731
SHIPPEY, T. A.
Road to Middle-Earth, The   (84) 736
SHORRIS, EARL
Under the Fifth Sun: A Novel of Pancho
Villa   (81) 844
SHOSTAK, MARJORIE
Nisa: The Life and Words of a !Kung
Woman   (82) 559

CUMULATIVE AUTHOR INDEX

SHOSTAKOVICH, DMITRI
Testimony: The Memoirs of Dmitri
Shostakovich (80) 808
SHULMAN, ALIX KATES
On the Stroll (82) 590
SIEBURTH, RICHARD
Instigations: Ezra Pound and Remy de
Gourmont (80) 431
SIGMUND, PAUL E.
Overthrow of Allende and the Politics of Chile,
1964–1976, The (78) 630
SILK, LEONARD
Economists, The (77) 251
SILK, LEONARD, and MARK SILK
American Establishment, The (81) 36
SILKO, LESLIE MARMON
Storyteller (82) 812
SILLITOE, ALAN
Her Victory (83) 340
Lost Flying Boat, The (85) 579
Second Chance and Other Stories, The (82)
747
Widower's Son, The (78) 904
SIMMONS, CHARLES
Wrinkles (79) 918
SIMON, JOHN
Singularities (77) 742
SIMON, KATE
Bronx Primitive: Portraits in a Childhood (83)
80
SIMON, LINDA
Thornton Wilder: His World (80) 815
SIMPSON, EILEEN
Poets in Their Youth: A Memoir (83) 608
SIMPSON, LOUIS
Best Hour of the Night, The (85) 42
Revolution in Taste, A (80) 709
Searching for the Ox (77) 706
SINCLAIR, ANDREW
Jack: A Biography of Jack London (78) 454
SINCLAIR, CLIVE
Brothers Singer, The (84) 127
SINGAL, DANIEL JOSEPH
War Within: From Victorian to Modernist
Thought in the South, 1919–1945 (83) 873
SINGER, ISAAC BASHEVIS
Collected Stories of Isaac Bashevis Singer,
The (83) 135
Lost in America (82) 485
Old Love (80) 614
Penitent, The (84) 678
Shosha (79) 677
SÎN-LEQI-UNNINNÎ
Gilgamesh (85)
SINYAVSKY, ANDREI. See TERTZ,
ABRAHAM
SIRICA, JOHN J.
To Set the Record Straight: The Break-in,
the Tapes, the Conspirators, the Pardon
(80) 822
SISSMAN, L. E.
Hello, Darkness: The Collected Poems of L. E.
Sissman (79) 264
SISSON, C. H.
Avoidance of Literature: Collected Essays,
The (80) 40

SITKOFF, HARVARD
Struggle for Black Equality, 1954–1980,
The (82) 822
SKLAREW, MYRA
Science of Goodbyes, The (83) 694
ŠKVORECKÝ, JOSEF
Bass Saxophone, The (80) 54
Engineer of Human Souls: An Entertainment
on the Old Themes of Life, Women, Fate,
Dreams, the Working Class, Secret Agents,
Love and Death, The (85) 227
SLAVITT, DAVID R.
Rounding the Horn (79) 608
SLOAT, WARREN
1929: America Before the Crash (80) 591
SMITH, BRADLEY F.
Reaching Judgment at Nuremberg (78) 695
Road to Nuremberg, The (82) 695
SMITH, BRADLEY F., and ELENA AGAROSSI
Operation Sunrise: The Secret Surrender (80)
631
SMITH, DAVE
Goshawk, Antelope (80) 380
In the House of the Judge (84) 374
SMITH, DENIS MACK. See MACK SMITH,
DENIS
SMITH, HEDRICK
Russians, The (77) 694
SMITH, JOHN CHABOT
Alger Hiss (77) 38
SMITH, LEE
Oral History (84) 647
SMITH, LILLIAN
Winner Names the Age, The (79) 879
SMITH, MARK
Death of the Detective, The (77) 202
SMITH, MARTIN CRUZ
Gorky Park (82) 333
SMITH, PAGE
New Age Now Begins, A (77) 529
SMITH, STEVIE
Collected Poems of Stevie Smith, The (77)
168
Me Again: Uncollected Writings of Stevie
Smith (83) 458
SMITH, WALTER W. (RED)
Red Smith Reader, The (83) 645
SMITH, WILLIAM JAY
Traveler's Tree: New and Selected Poems,
The (81) 831
SNOW, DONALD M.
Nuclear Strategy in a Dynamic World:
American Policy in the 1980's (82) 565
SNYDER, GARY
Axe Handles (84) 65
SOLBERG, CARL
Oil Power (77) 588
SOLZHENITSYN, ALEXANDER I.
Gulag Archipelago: Three, Parts V–VII,
The (78) 370
SONG, CATHY
Picture Bride (84) 695
SONTAG, SUSAN
Illness as Metaphor (79) 295
On Photography (78) 618
Susan Sontag Reader, A (83) 769
Under the Sign of Saturn (81) 848

SORRENTINO, GILBERT
  Aberration of Starlight (81) 1
  Blue Pastoral (84) 99
  Mulligan Stew (80) 544
SOYINKA, WOLE
  Aké: The Years of Childhood (83) 10
SPALDING, FRANCES
  Roger Fry: Art and Life (81) 699
  Vanessa Bell (84) 900
SPARK, MURIEL
  Loitering with Intent (82) 475
  Only Problem, The (85) 668
  Takeover, The (77) 802
  Territorial Rights (80) 804
SPEER, ALBERT
  Infiltration (82) 398
  Spandau (77) 764
SPENCE, JONATHAN D.
  Gate of Heavenly Peace: The Chinese and
    Their Revolution, 1895–1980, The (82) 305
SPENCER, SCOTT
  Endless Love (80) 294
SPENDER, STEPHEN
  Thirties and After: Poetry, Politics, People,
    1933–1970, The (79) 745
SPIELMAN, JOHN P.
  Leopold I of Austria (78) 518
SPURLING, HILARY
  Ivy: The Life of I. Compton-Burnett (85) 461
STAFFORD, WILLIAM
  Glass Face in the Rain, A (83) 288
  Stories That Could Be True: New and Collected
    Poems (78) 799
STANFORD, ANN
  In Mediterranean Air (78) 439
STANNARD, DAVID E.
  Puritan Way of Death, The (78) 682
STANTON, ELIZABETH CADY, and SUSAN B.
  ANTHONY
  Elizabeth Cady Stanton, Susan B. Anthony:
    Correspondence, Writings, Speeches (82)
    214
STARBUCK, GEORGE
  Argot Merchant Disaster: Poems New and
    Selected, The (83) 25
STARK, GUY D.
  Entrepreneurs of Ideology: Neoconservative
    Publishers in Germany, 1890–1933 (82) 240
STARR, S. FREDERICK
  Red and Hot: The Fate of Jazz in the Soviet
    Union, 1917–1980 (84) 726
STEAD, CHRISTINA
  Miss Herbert (77) 509
STEEL, RONALD
  Walter Lippmann and the American
    Century (81) 886
STEGNER, WALLACE
  One Way to Spell Man (83) 563
  Recapitulation (80) 702
  Spectator Bird, The (77) 769
STEINBECK, JOHN
  Acts of King Arthur and His Noble Knights,
    The (77) 7
STEINER, GEORGE
  Antigones (85) 17
  Portage to San Cristóbal of A. H., The
    (83) 616

STERN, FRITZ
  Gold and Iron: Bismarck, Bliechröder and the
    Building of the German Empire (78) 354
STERN, GERALD
  Lucky Life (78) 540
  Red Coal, The (82) 661
STERN, RICHARD
  Packages (81) 636
STEVENSON, WILLIAM
  Man Called Intrepid, A (77) 475
STEWART, DESMOND
  T. E. Lawrence (78) 813
STINCHCOMBE, WILLIAM
  XYZ Affair, The (82) 972
STONE, NORMAN
  Hitler (81) 434
STONE, ROBERT
  Flag for Sunrise, A (82) 284
STOPPARD, TOM
  Dirty Linen and New-Found-Land (78) 268
  Night and Day (80) 586
STOREY, DAVID
  Prodigal Child, A (84) 711
STRAND, MARK
  Selected Poems (81) 723
STRATTON, JOANNA L.
  Pioneer Women: Voices from the Kansas
    Frontier (82) 642
STRAUB, PETER
  Ghost Story (80) 349
STRAUSS, WILLIAM A., and LAWRENCE M.
  BASKIR
  Chance and Circumstance: The Draft, the War
    and the Vietnam Generation (79) 88
STROUSE, JEAN
  Alice James: A Biography (81) 21
STUECK, WILLIAM WHITNEY, JR.
  Road to Confrontation: American Policy
    Toward China and Korea, 1947–1950,
    The (82) 690
STYRON, WILLIAM
  Sophie's Choice (80) 774
  This Quiet Dust and Other Writings (83) 796
SULLEROT, EVELYNE
  Women on Love: Eight Centuries of Feminine
    Writing (81) 947
SUTCH, RICHARD, and ROGER L. RANSOM
  One Kind of Freedom: The Economic
    Consequences of Emancipation (78) 622
SUTTER, ROBERT G.
  Chinese Foreign Policy After the Cultural
    Revolution, 1966–1977 (79) 108
SWANBERG, W. A.
  Norman Thomas (77) 570
  Whitney Father, Whitney Heiress (81) 921
SWEET, PAUL ROBINSON
  Wilhelm von Humbolt: A Biography, Vol. I:
    1767–1808 (79) 868
SWENSON, MAY
  New & Selected Things Taking Place (79) 472
SWIFT, GRAHAM
  Waterland (85) 1000
SYMONS, JULIAN
  Critical Observations (82) 156

CUMULATIVE AUTHOR INDEX

SZATMARY, DAVID P.
Shays' Rebellion: The Making of an Agrarian Insurrection (81) 732

SZULC, TAD
Illusion of Peace: Foreign Policy in the Nixon Years, The (79) 300

TAKAMURA, KOTARO
Chieko's Sky (79) 105

TALBOTT, JOHN E.
War Without a Name: France in Algeria, 1954–1962, The (81) 896

TATE, JAMES
Collected Poems, 1919–1976 (78) 188
Constant Defender (84) 202
Viper Jazz (77) 888

TAYLOR, TELFORD
Munich: The Price of Peace (80) 555

TENNANT, ROBERT
Joseph Conrad (82) 412

TERRAINE, JOHN
To Win a War: 1918, The Year of Victory (82) 850

TERRILL, ROSS
Future of China After Mao, The (79) 240
Mao: A Biography (81) 549

TERTZ, ABRAHAM
Voice from the Chorus, A (77) 892

THANT, U
View from the UN (79) 809

THEROUX, PAUL
Consul's File, The (78) 215
Family Arsenal, The (77) 274
Half Moon Street (85) 338
London Embassy, The (84) 472
Mosquito Coast, The (83) 496
Old Patagonian Express: By Train Through the Americas, The (80) 619

THOMAS, D. M.
Ararat (84) 36
White Hotel, The (82) 932

THOMAS, DONALD
Robert Browning: A Life Within Life (84) 741

THOMAS, DYLAN, and JOHN DAVENPORT
Death of the King's Canary, The (78) 238

THOMAS, EMORY M.
Confederate Nation: 1861–1865, The (80) 156

THOMAS, KEITH
Man and the Natural World: A History of the Modern Sensibility (84) 492

THOMAS, LEWIS
Medusa and the Snail: More Notes of a Biology Watcher, The (80) 533

THOMAS, MERLIN
Louis-Ferdinand Céline (81) 529

THOMPSON, E. P.
William Morris: Romantic to Revolutionary (78) 913

THOMPSON, JOHN M.
Revolutionary Russia, 1917 (82) 679

THOMSON, GEORGE MALCOLM
First Churchill: The Life of John, 1st Duke of Marlborough, The (81) 344

THORNE, CHRISTOPHER
Allies of a Kind: The United States, Britain and the War Against Japan, 1941–1945 (79) 9

THURMAN, JUDITH
Isak Dinesen: The Life of a Storyteller (83) 358

TIERNEY, KEVIN
Darrow: A Biography (80) 188

TILLOTSON, GEOFFREY
View of Victorian Literature, A (79) 814

TODOROV, TZVETAN
Mikhail Bakhtin: The Dialogical Principle (85) 614

TOLAND, JOHN
Adolf Hitler (77) 17
No Man's Land: 1918, The Last Year of the Great War (81) 624

TOLKIEN, J. R. R.
Letters of J. R. R. Tolkien, The (82) 448
Silmarillion, The (78) 780

TOLSTOY, LEV
Tolstoy's Letters, Vol. I and Vol. II (79) 754

TOMALIN, RUTH
W. H. Hudson (84) 935

TOOLE, JOHN KENNEDY
Confederacy of Dunces, A (81) 188

TOOMER, JEAN
Wayward and the Seeking, The (81) 904

TORREY, E. FULLER
Roots of Treason: Ezra Pound and the Secret of St. Elizabeths, The (84) 751

TOTH, SUSAN ALLEN
Blooming: A Small-Town Girlhood (82) 55
Ivy Days: Making My Way Out East (85) 466

TOTMAN, CONRAD
Japan Before Perry: A Short History (82) 408

TOURNIER, MICHEL
Fetishist, The (85) 272
Four Wise Men, The (83) 267

TRASK, DAVID F.
War with Spain in 1898, The (82) 908

TREVOR, WILLIAM
Beyond the Pale and Other Stories (83) 57
Stories of William Trevor, The (84) 829

TRILLIN, CALVIN
Uncivil Liberties (83) 849

TRILLING, LIONEL
Last Decade: Essays and Reviews, 1965–75, The (81) 480
Speaking of Literature and Society (81) 764

TRISTAN, FLORA
Flora Tristan's London Journal, 1840 (82) 288

TROYAT, HENRI
Catherine the Great (81) 117

TUCHMAN, BARBARA W.
Distant Mirror: The Calamitous 14th Century, A (79) 151
Practicing History: Selected Essays (82) 647

TUOHY, FRANK
Collected Stories, The (85) 126

TURGENEV, IVAN
Turgenev Letters (84) 879

TURNER, FREDERICK
Beyond Geography: The Western Spirit Against the Wilderness (81) 82

TYLER, ANNE
Dinner at the Homesick Restaurant (83) 194
Morgan's Passing (81) 573

TYLER, W. T.
  Rogue's March   (83) 659
TYLER-WHITTLE, MICHAEL
  Last Kaiser, The   (78) 509

UBALDO RIBEIRO, JOÃO
  Sergeant Getúlio   (79) 672
UEDA, MAKOTO
  Modern Japanese Poets and the Nature of
    Literature   (84) 566
ULAM, ADAM B.
  In the Name of the People   (78) 442
  Russia's Failed Revolutions: From the
    Decembrists to the Dissidents   (82) 717
ULLMAN, LESLIE
  Natural Histories   (80) 569
UNAMUNO, MIGUEL DE
  Private World: Selections from the Diario
    Íntimo and Selected Letters, 1890–1936,
    The   (85) 701
UNGAR, SANFORD J.
  FBI   (77) 287
UNGER, DOUGLAS
  Leaving the Land   (85) 535
UPDIKE, JOHN
  Bech Is Back   (83) 53
  Coup, The   (79) 133
  Hugging the Shore   (84) 358
  Marry Me   (77) 485
  Problems and Other Stories   (80) 697
  Rabbit Is Rich   (82) 656
  Witches of Eastwick, The   (85) 1041
URIS, LEON
  Trinity   (77) 842
UROFSKY, MELVIN I.
  Louis D. Brandeis and the Progressive
    Tradition   (82) 488

VANDIVER, FRANK E.
  Black Jack: The Life and Times of John J.
    Pershing, Vol. I and Vol. II   (78) 96
VAN TINE, WARREN, and MELVIN
  DUBOFSKY
  John L. Lewis: A Biography   (78) 478
VARGAS LLOSA, MARIO
  Aunt Julia and the Scriptwriter   (83) 34
  Captain Pantoja and the Special Service
    (79) 75
  Cubs and Other Stories, The   (80) 165
  War of the End of the World, The   (85) 995
VIDAL, GORE
  Creation   (82) 151
  1876   (77) 256
  Lincoln   (85) 570
  Second American Revolution and Other Essays
    (1976–1982), The   (83) 700
VIVANTE, ARTURO
  Run to the Waterfall   (80) 736
VOGELGESANG, SANDY
  American Dream Global Nightmare: The
    Dilemma of U.S. Human Rights Policy
    (81) 31
VON ABELE, RUDOLPH
  Cage for Loulou, A   (79) 70

VONNEGUT, KURT
  Deadeye Dick   (83) 174
  Jailbird   (80) 436
  Palm Sunday: An Autobiographical
    Collage   (82) 609
  Slapstick   (77) 749

WAGONER, DAVID
  Collected Poems 1956–1976   (78) 197
  First Light   (84) 299
  Who Shall Be the Sun? Poems Based on the
    Lore, Legends and Myths of Northwest
    Coast and Plateau Indians   (79) 852
WAIN, JOHN
  Pardoner's Tale, The   (80) 640
  Professing Poetry   (79) 561
WAITE, ROBERT G. L.
  Psychopathic God: Adolf Hitler, The   (78) 677
WAKOSKI, DIANE
  Man Who Shook Hands, The   (79) 414
WALCOTT, DEREK
  Fortunate Traveller, The   (82) 293
  Midsummer   (85)
  Star-Apple Kingdom, The   (80) 777
WALKER, ALICE
  Color Purple, The   (83) 139
  In Search of Our Mothers' Gardens: Womanist
    Prose   (84) 368
  Meridian   (77) 501
  You Can't Keep a Good Woman Down
    (82) 976
WALSER, ROBERT
  Selected Stories   (83) 734
WAMBAUGH, JOSEPH
  Glitter Dome, The   (82) 325
WARNER, SYLVIA TOWNSEND
  Letters   (84) 432
  One Thing Leading to Another   (85) 658
  Scenes of Childhood and Other Stories
    (83) 679
WARREN, EARL
  Memoirs of Earl Warren, The   (78) 567
WARREN, ROBERT PENN
  Being Here: Poetry 1977–1980   (81) 76
  Now and Then: Poems 1976–1978   (79) 501
  Rumor Verified: Poems 1979–1980   (82) 704
  Selected Poems, 1923–1975   (78) 753
WARREN, ROSANNA
  Each Leaf Shines Separate   (85) 204
WATT, IAN
  Conrad: In the Nineteenth Century   (81) 193
WAUGH, EVELYN
  Charles Ryder's Schooldays and Other
    Stories   (83) 105
  Diaries of Evelyn Waugh, The   (78) 258
  Essays, Articles and Reviews of Evelyn Waugh,
    The   (85) 238
  Letters of Evelyn Waugh, The   (81) 489
  Little Order: A Selection from His Journalism,
    A   (81) 517
WEBB, SIDNEY, and BEATRICE POTTER
  WEBB
  Letters of Sidney and Beatrice Webb, The
    (79) 378
WEBSTER, GRANT
  Republic of Letters: A History of Postwar
    American Literary Opinion, The   (80) 705

WEEKS, EDWARD
Writers and Friends   (83) 928
WEIGLEY, RUSSELL F.
Eisenhower's Lieutenants: The Campaign of
France and Germany, 1944–1945   (82) 210
WEINBERG, ARTHUR, and LILA WEINBERG
Clarence Darrow: A Sentimental Rebel
(81) 152
WEINGARTNER, JAMES J.
Crossroads of Death: The Story of the
Malmédy Massacre and Trial   (80) 162
WEINSTEIN, ALLEN
Perjury: The Hiss-Chambers Case   (79) 540
WEINSTEIN, FRED
Dynamics of Nazism: Leadership, Ideology,
and the Holocaust, The   (81) 254
WEINTRAUB, STANLEY
London Yankees: Portraits of American
Writers and Artists in England, 1894–1914,
The   (80) 508
WEISS, THEODORE
Views & Spectacles: New and Selected Shorter
Poems   (80) 846
WELCH, DENTON
Journals of Denton Welch, The   (85) 504
WELDON, FAY
Puffball   (81) 670
WELTY, EUDORA
Collected Stories of Eudora Welty, The
(81) 178
One Writer's Beginnings   (85) 663
Eye of the Story: Selected Essays and Reviews,
The   (79) 200
WEST, ANTHONY
H. G. Wells: Aspects of a Life   (85) 380
WEST, JESSAMYN
Life I Really Lived, The   (80) 491
Woman Said Yes, The   (77) 928
WEST, REBECCA
Young Rebecca: Writings of Rebecca West,
1911–1917, The   (83) 932
WHARTON, WILLIAM
Birdy   (80) 79
Dad   (82) 166
Midnight Clear, A   (83) 480
WHEELOCK, JOHN HALL
This Blessed Earth, New and Selected Poems,
1927–1977   (79) 749
WHELDON, DAVID
Viaduct, The   (84) 910
WHETTEN, LAWRENCE L.
Germany East and West: Conflicts,
Collaborations, and Confrontation   (81) 373
WHITE, E. B.
Essays of E. B. White   (78) 295
Letters of E. B. White   (77) 413
WHITE, PATRICK
Flaws in the Glass: A Self-Portrait   (83) 257
Twyborn Affair, The   (81) 840
WHITE, T. H.
Book of Merlyn: The Unpublished Conclusion
to The Once and Future King, The   (78) 126
WHITE, THEODORE H.
In Search of History: A Personal
Adventure   (79) 314

WHITTEMORE, REED
Feel of Rock: Poems of Three Decades,
The   (83) 250
Poet as Journalist, The   (77) 623
WICKWIRE, FRANKLIN, and MARY
WICKWIRE
Cornwallis: The Imperial Years   (81) 203
WIDEMAN, JOHN EDGAR
Brothers and Keepers   (85) 57
Sent for You Yesterday   (84) 779
WIDENOR, WILLIAM C.
Henry Cabot Lodge and the Search for an
American Foreign Policy   (81) 416
WIENER, MARTIN J.
English Culture and the Decline of the
Industrial Spirit, 1850–1980   (82) 234
WIER, ALLEN
Blanco   (80) 83
WIER, DARA
Blood, Hook & Eye   (78) 112
WIESEL, ELIE
Somewhere a Master: Further Hasidic Portraits
and Legends   (83) 756
WILBUR, RICHARD
Mind-Reader, The   (77) 505
Responses   (77) 679
WILKINSON, J. HARVIE, III
From Brown to Bakke, The Supreme Court and
School Integration: 1954–1978   (80) 334
WILLIAMS, C. K.
Tar   (84) 859
With Ignorance   (78) 923
WILLIAMS, JOHN A.
!Click Song   (83) 124
WILLIAMS, RAYMOND
Keywords   (77) 388
WILLIAMS, T. HARRY
History of American Wars: From 1745 to World
War I, The   (82) 354
WILLIAMS, TENNESSEE
Memoirs   (77) 494
WILLS, GARRY
Explaining America: The Federalist   (82) 26
Inventing America: Jefferson's Declaration of
Independence   (79) 322
WILSON, A. N.
Hilaire Belloc   (85) 385
WILSON, ANGUS
Diversity and Depth in Fiction: Selected
Critical Writings of Angus Wilson   (85) 190
Setting the World on Fire   (81) 727
Strange Ride of Rudyard Kipling: His Life and
Works, The   (79) 717
WILSON, DICK
People's Emperor: Mao, a Biography of Mao
Tse-tung, The   (81) 645
WILSON, EDMUND
Forties: From Notebooks and Diaries of the
Period, The   (84) 309
Letters on Literature and Politics, 1912–
1972   (78) 522
Thirties: From Notebooks and Diaries of the
Period, The   (81) 795
WILSON, EDMUND, and VLADIMIR
NABOKOV
Nabokov-Wilson Letters: Correspondence
Between Vladimir Nabokov and Edmund
Wilson, 1940–1971, The   (80) 564

WILSON, EDWARD O.
 On Human Nature   (79) 506
WILSON, HENRY S.
 Imperial Experience in Sub-Saharan Africa
 Since 1870, The   (78) 436
WILSON, LANFORD
 5th of July   (80) 320
 Talley's Folly   (81) 790
WILSON, SLOAN
 What Shall We Wear to This Party?   (77) 901
WIMSATT, W. K.
 Days of the Leopards   (77) 194
WISER, WILLIAM
 Crazy Years: Paris in the Twenties, The
 (84) 207
WITCOVER, JULES
 Marathon: The Pursuit of the Presidency, 1972–
 1976   (78) 562
WOFFORD, HARRIS
 Of Kennedys and Kings: Making Sense of the
 Sixties   (81) 633
WOHL, ROBERT
 Generation of 1914, The   (80) 337
WOJTYLA, KAROL
 Love and Responsibility   (82) 494
WOLF, CHRISTA
 Cassandra: A Novel and Four Essays   (85) 74
 No Place on Earth   (83) 540
WOLF, JOHN B.
 Barbary Coast: Algiers Under the Turks, 1500–
 1830, The   (80) 49
WOLFE, TOM
 Purple Decades: A Reader, The   (83) 626
 Right Stuff, The   (80) 713
WOLFF, CYNTHIA GRIFFIN
 Feast of Words: The Triumph of Edith
 Wharton, A   (78) 314
WOLFF, GEOFFREY
 Black Sun   (77) 91
 Duke of Deception: Memories of My Father,
 The   (80) 236
WOLFF, TOBIAS
 In the Garden of the North American
 Martyrs   (82) 392
WOLPERT, STANLEY
 New History of India, A   (78) 598
WONGAR, B.
 Track to Bralgu, The   (79) 768
WOODS, DONALD
 Asking for Trouble: Autobiography of a
 Banned Journalist   (82) 28
WOODS, JOHN
 Striking the Earth   (77) 784
WOODWARD, BOB, and SCOTT
 ARMSTRONG
 Brethren: Inside the Supreme Court,
 The   (80) 104
WOOLF, VIRGINIA
 Diary of Virginia Woolf, Vol. I: 1915–1919,
 The   (78) 264
 Diary of Virginia Woolf, Vol. II: 1920–1924,
 The   (79) 147
 Diary of Virginia Woolf, Vol. III: 1925–1930,
 The   (81) 240
 Diary of Virginia Woolf, Vol. IV: 1931–1935,
 The   (83) 185
 Diary of Virginia Woolf, Vol. V: 1936–1941,
 The   (85) 178

 Letters of Virginia Woolf, Vol. II: 1912–1922,
 The   (77) 418
 Letters of Virginia Woolf, Vol. III: 1923–1928,
 The   (79) 382
 Letters of Virginia Woolf, Vol. IV: 1929–1931,
 The   (80) 483
 Letters of Virginia Woolf, Vol. V: 1932–1935,
 The   (80) 487
 Letters of Virginia Woolf, Vol. VI: 1936–1941,
 The   (81) 506
WOOLLEY, BRYAN
 Time and Place   (78) 836
WORMSER, BARON
 White Words, The   (84) 940
WORSTER, DONALD
 Dust Bowl: The Southern Plains in the
 1930s   (80) 248
WRIGHT, JAMES
 To a Blossoming Pear Tree   (78) 847
WRIGHT, J. KEITCH, JR.
 Only Land They Knew: The Tragic Story of the
 American Indians in the Old South,
 The   (82) 594
WRIGHT, RICHARD
 Richard Wright Reader   (79) 597
WRIGHT, STEPHEN
 Meditations in Green   (84) 523
WU CH'ÊNG-ÊN
 Journey to the West: Vol. IV, The   (84) 401
WYDEN, PETER
 Bay of Pigs: The Untold Story   (80) 59
WYND, OSWALD
 Ginger Tree, The   (78) 349

YANKELOVICH, DANIEL
 New Rules: Searching for Self-Fulfillment in a
 World Turned Upside Down   (82) 548
YATES, RICHARD
 Easter Parade, The   (77) 247
 Liars in Love   (82) 453
YEATS, WILLIAM BUTLER
 Poems: A New Edition, The   (85) 692
YEHOSHUA, A. B.
 Late Divorce, A   (85) 530
YERGIN, DANIEL H.
 Shattered Peace   (78) 766
YEROFEYEV, VIKTOR, et al., editors
 Metropol: Literary Almanac   (84) 533
YGLESIAS, HELEN
 Family Feeling   (77) 277
YORK, HERBERT F.
 Advisors, The   (77) 27
YOUNG, PHILIP
 Hawthorne's Secret: An Un-told Tale
 (85) 358
YOUNG-BRUEHL, ELIZABETH
 Hannah Arendt: For Love of the World
 (83) 322
YOURCENAR, MARGUERITE
 Abyss, The   (77) 1
 Dark Brain of Piranesi and Other Essays,
 The   (85) 152
 Fires   (82) 275

CUMULATIVE AUTHOR INDEX

ZINSSER, WILLIAM
   Willie and Dwike: An American Profile
   (85) 1036

ZUKOFSKY, LOUIS
   "A" (80) 1